FLORENCE HARDING

FLORENCE HARDING

HARDING

The First Lady, the Jazz Age,
and the Death of America's Most
Scandalous President

**CARL SFERRAZZA
ANTHONY**

William Morrow and Company, Inc.
New York

Library of Congress Cataloging-in-Publication Data
Anthony, Carl Sferrazza.
Florence Harding : the first lady, the Jazz Age, and the death of
America's most scandalous president / Carl Sferrazza Anthony.—1st ed.
p.   cm.
ISBN 0-688-07794-3
1. Harding, Florence Kling, 1860–1924.   2. Presidents' spouses—
United States—Biography.   3. Harding, Warren G. (Warren Gamaliel),
1865–1923.   I. Title.
E786.2.A58   1998
973.91'4'092—dc21
[B]   97-49955
                                                                             CIP

Printed in the United States of America
First Edition
2   3   4   5   6   7   8   9   10
BOOK DESIGN BY BERNARD KLEIN
www.williammorrow.com

For
Byron, Meredith, Craig, Ellen, and Edward

Contents

Part Three: The Senate, *1916—1920*

Part Four: Campaign and Transition, *1920—1921*

Part Five: First Lady, *1921—1923*

Prologue: Talking to the Dead

The moon hung vaguely in the August sky, like a silver dab on a black canvas while thunderbolts flashed silently across it like a flickering newsreel. An ethereal "dull mist" blanketed Washington. The capital had emptied some two months before. Now the principals suddenly returned to the marble Union Station and its cavernous ceiling of mythological mosaics.

Without any assistance a small figure, draped entirely in black, carefully descended the high steps of the funeral train bearing the flag-draped coffin of her husband, President Warren G. Harding. They had just traversed the plains and cities of America, back from San Francisco, where he died, after a strenuous trip to Alaska and the West. With a dash of morbid whimsy, the widow was swathed in a sheath of black chiffon that went from the crown of her roller-brimmed hat to just inches from the ground. She strode briskly along the platform, like some Jazz Age sorceress, the march of her step reverberating on the concrete. She was neither weeping nor broken. One witness said she was "granite." The press was calling her "the woman who did not break down." Noted a reporter: "Only the extension of her black-gloved hand to intimates showed she was animate."

She had every right to hold herself high. The nation had never known such a First Lady, whose words were quoted in newspapers and magazines and whose image was instantly familiar to them in newsreels. At this point in August 1923, except for young Frances Cleveland who had been a bride, and legendary hostess and war heroine Dolley Madison, Florence Harding was the most popular woman to have lived in the White House. Many of her predecessors drew the public's respect, admiration or pity, but Mrs. Harding was extraordinarily popular.

If somehow First Ladies could be judged on their accomplishments independent of the men to whom they attached their fortunes, Florence Harding would even rank as one of the greatest achievers among them. Instead she was doomed to be known as wife of the greatest failure in the presidency. In years to come Eleanor Roosevelt would be held high as the ideal modern woman, but it was Florence who had first begun holding informal press conferences for women reporters, who had flown in an airplane, who had expressed herself as a feminist, arguing for the political, social, and economic equality of women in emphatic letters published in national newspapers. None before her had so vigorously supported suffrage and even advocated militant violence to retaliate against extreme cases of injustice. She didn't wear a wedding ring and further shocked traditionalists by encouraging women to exercise, play sports, and be as physically fit and competitive as men. She foresaw an America where a wife could be the chief breadwinner and the husband would merge his career into hers. She had been the first woman able to vote for her husband for President of the United States.

Few First Ladies had such an acute sensitivity to the nation's pulse. She had introduced to the White House everything from jazz music to mah-jongg to the radio. With a brilliant sense of public relations, she had reopened the gates of the "people's house" for use as a public park, given tours of the rooms herself, encouraged groups to come meet with her, and cultivated the national press—especially the newsreel camera-men—to cover all of her public events and appearances, perfecting the modern photo opportunity. She had invited Hollywood stars to the White House for the first time, using them to political advantage as she had during her husband's presidential campaign. If this woman with the marcelled gray hair turned her pet dog into a national celebrity, it would be not only to make her husband seem benevolent but to promote animal rights—a radical notion—calling for public education on humane animal care and an end to vivisection. Balancing her public activism with po-litical caution, she managed to intercede on behalf of immigrant children who got lost in the bureaucracy, helped make Zion National Park a reality, and fostered the first federal reformatory prison exclusively for women. All of this was apart from her central role as the President's partner and colleague to Cabinet members.

Leaving the railroad yard, Florence, whom intimates called the Duchess, ascended a marble staircase, lined by rows of uniformed men standing at present arms, as if she were reviewing the troops. Her veil was now lifted, revealing a locked jaw and tightly pressed lips of "an almost deathlike pallor," said a reporter. Her luminous blue eyes, mag-nified by her pince-nez spectacles steamy with the night's dew, darted about the scene.

The sight of Evalyn McLean must have stunned the Duchess. Mil-lionairess, morphine addict, and Florence's best friend, she had sped by special train down from her summer home in Maine to be there for the First Lady. Alice Roosevelt Longworth had first introduced them, ex-pecting that her cohort Evalyn would join her in deriding the parvenu senator's wife from Ohio. With a malice as deadly as the stiletto she kept in her oversize purse, the daughter of the late President Theodore Roosevelt—the spoiled, beautiful "Princess Alice"—had socially sliced Florence when she first arrived in the capital in 1915. Instead Evalyn had dropped Alice and taken up Florence as her companion. Just months before, however, the First Lady had learned from Alice that Evalyn had permitted the President to use her estate, aptly named Friendship, for an assignation with one of his mistresses. Florence had been betrayed again.

There had always been another woman during the Hardings' marriage. Three years after their wedding Warren had gotten pregnant Florence's best childhood friend, Susie Hodder. Next was his relationship with Florence's closest adult friend, the tempestuous Carrie Phillips, the only known mistress in U.S. history who successfully blackmailed a presidential candidate. She managed to get a lump sum of some twenty thousand dollars from loyal Harding friends, as arranged by the National Republican Committee. Other Presidents were accused of affairs, but with Harding there was tangible documentation: a cache of his love letters to Carrie covering their fifteen-year relationship—discovered years later—including his acquiescence to the blackmail. Accused of being a German spy during the First World War, she was also Warren's favorite mistress. They made love everywhere from kitchen tables to the deck of an ocean liner, often with Florence just a wall away. Florence had kept the devastation of this to herself, confiding only to her private diary. It would not be in her private papers but rather turned up in a central Ohio barn in 1997.

Impatient Grace Cross, on Harding's Senate staff, had been unsuccessful in her blackmail effort. Once, when she and Senator Harding fought, she cut his head, and the police were called in; another time, asking Grace for forgiveness following a spat, he pathetically crawled about in his pajamas in front of some of her friends. Woodrow Wilson's attorney general ran her out of town—later to have a prosecution against him dropped by Harding's attorney general.

The only man Florence had ever loved had juggled affairs with many other women: Augusta Cole, said to have had her pregnancy by Harding terminated in an abortion when he sent her to Battle Creek Sanitarium; Rosa Cecilia Hoyle, who claimed to have given birth to Harding's only illegitimate son; an unnamed upstate New York woman who was so distraught when Warren didn't leave Florence for her that she committed suicide. There was also the story of the prostitute who was accidentally killed in President Harding's presence when she was hit with a glass bottle during a raucous party at the Love Nest, the hideaway party house owned by Evalyn McLean's husband. Nan Britton, the most famous of his mistresses, claimed that Harding had impregnated her at age twenty-two in his Senate cloakroom and that her daughter was also his. She said she made frequent visits to the Oval Office for their trysts in an adjoining room, facilitated by two of Harding's Secret Service agents. Once they were nearly caught in the act by the First Lady herself. The first presidential mistress to write her memoirs, Nan was one of the few Harding girlfriends Florence did not know about, for according to reporter Bertha Martin, the First Lady hired Gaston Means, a Justice Department agent who moonlighted as a private eye, to spy on the President's extramarital activities.

None of that could be discussed with Evalyn now, nor could Florence finally ask her why she had permitted Warren to use her home for his pathological adultery. But the mere fact of Evalyn's presence in that station, and her promise to come alone to the Duchess later that night, were the strongest sign that the breached friendship would heal.

As she made her way into a limousine, Florence was escorted by Charles E. Sawyer, whom everyone called Doc. A mere sparrow of a man, this brigadier general of the Army Medical Corps with pronouncedly thick spectacles and a pointy white goatee was suspicious of anyone—particularly medical experts—whom he perceived as threatening his status as close friend and homeopathic physician to the Hardings. The Duchess said Doc was the only person who could keep her alive. He was, Alice Longworth later said, the First Lady's own Rasputin.

As the limousine pulled away from the station, there was a view ahead of the nearby Capitol dome, a bluish sarcophogus without its usual high-beam lumination. The Duchess and Doc passed thick rows of citizens clustering the streets, kept behind iron cables, but hanging on trees, massing on staircases, standing on rooftops. Among the tens of thousands of these dusty-faced mourners were many already whispering their theories on the *real* reason for the beloved President's sudden and mysterious death.

During this last trip Doc had announced that the President had suffered food poisoning in Alaska but would fully recover with no fear of death. It was a lie. Joel Boone, the naval physician and second-in-command, had taken an electrocardiogram and was alarmed by Harding's heart condition. On the trip Boone diagnosed that Harding had a heart attack, but Doc cut off Boone's access, refusing to let him care for the President or talk to the First Lady. Doc began plying the President with some homeopathic concoction that he said would cure Harding of the poison; in everything he did and said, he had the tacit approval of the First Lady, and at every turn, he had the final say over not only Boone but the former American Medical Association's president, and the heart specialist whom Boone arranged to be brought into the case.

At the moment of Harding's collapse, Doc said, Florence was in the room, then said he was there too. One press report had him giving a hypodermic needle to the President. Another report had the regular nurse absent and a night nurse giving the President his medicine. Yet another story had both nurses there. The nation's newspapers had numerous conflicting accounts. When New York *Times* reporter Richard Oulahan tried to get the real story—who was in the room, how Harding died, what did he die of and exactly at what time—he was stymied. Instead there was an "official" statement crafted to say that the President died of a sudden cerebral hemorrhage—despite the fact that consulting doctors did not agree.

The Duchess had refused to permit an autopsy or a death mask. There was, in truth, a cover-up. Was it a case of premeditated murder by the Duchess, in retaliation for Warren's adultery or to protect him from breaking scandals? Or was she merely an accomplice in negligent homicide? Not until the 1990s—following the unsealing of Boone's private diary—would the full truth be revealed.

When she arrived at the White House, the Duchess stepped up onto the North Portico without assistance. The instant that she reached the top step, a shooting star dropped from the sky, casting a flashing but discernible trail of light. Everyone noticed it. No doubt it would be seen as an omen for a woman like the Duchess. As the schedule of the funeral train had become delayed, Florence had become disturbed. Superstitiously believing that the corpse must rest in the White House before the next morning's sun rose, she wanted to get to Washington.

The shining, artificial light of the porte cochere's great chandeliers glared down hard on her heavily rouged face, her neck ornamented by her trademark black velvet collarband and large diamond sunburst that Evalyn had picked out for Warren to give the Duchess as a Christmas present. Evalyn had her own large blue diamond, the cursed Hope Diamond, which legend claimed would bring tragedy to all who came in contact with it.

Ever since she was a girl and saw the hex signs on the barns of old German families, Florence had believed in the power of the supernatural. She studied the star formations and had even once gone to a spiritualist camp in Indiana. To take control of her and Warren's lives, Florence relied on clairvoyance, the tarot cards, a crystal ball, and especially the zodiac. She sought to guide the President's appointments by astrology. Her notebooks were filled with astrological scribblings and clippings. She amused the White House staff with her various superstitions, but not all of her fears of assassination attempts were mere paranoia.

The capital's society soothsayer, Madame Marcia, had told Florence Harding that Warren would die a "peculiar, violent and sudden death" after he was elected President. During Marcia's last secret reading in the White House, Florence had sensed the end coming. The night of August 2, when Harding's astrological chart showed him passing through the House of Death, Marcia had been asked by a gathering of her clients, including a respected journalist, about the newspaper reports that the President was recovering from his food poisoning. Marcia had her hand on Harding's chart. She turned to look at the ticking clock. It was just after seven-thirty in San Francisco. Marcia calmly spoke. "The President is dead." And he was.

Once inside the mansion, Florence would neither rest nor reminisce. She headed to her bedroom. From her view in the darkened bedroom, the shaft of the Washington Monument was dark gray against the black sky, its floodlights turned off, "almost grim in its majestic bulk as if in sadness for the dead," a reporter noted. Meanwhile, at the North Portico, six bay horses drew up, carrying the caisson bearing the flag-draped coffin of Warren. The coffin was placed in the East Room, the corpse's head facing east, under a massive chandelier. The new President, Calvin Coolidge, Cabinet members, Supreme Court justices, congressional and military leaders arrived with bowed heads and paid their respects. The Duchess stayed upstairs, waiting, her window opened, to what another reporter described as the "sweet, misty August gloom" hanging in the phosphorescent night.

As a teenager Florence had frequently sneaked through her bedroom window late at night after her flirtatious nights out at the roller-skating rink. Thus she avoided a confrontation with her tyrannical father, Amos Kling. He had socialized her as his first male child, teaching her business and finance; even her musical education at the Cincinnati Conservatory of Music was intended to provide her with a potential means of supporting herself as a piano teacher. She had grown up the daughter of the wealthiest man in Marion, Ohio, but in the small, largely Protestant town she contended with the intolerant rumor that she had Jewish blood.

As she blossomed, the whippings with the cherry switch from her father hurt more as humiliation than physical pain. She found her escape

in getting pregnant at nineteen years old by, she claimed, her neighborhood chum Henry De Wolfe, already an alcoholic. They were said
to have eloped six months before baby Marshall was born, but it was a
sham. They were never married. Henry abandoned her and the baby,
and when she was refused refuge in her father's home, she was left
temporarily homeless. She won a divorce, based on a common-law marital arrangement. Her father refused to forgive her: she became a single
working mother teaching piano. Finally he made a cruel offer: He would
take from her the baby she could barely afford to keep.

When she began dating Warren Harding, the handsome and
younger editor of the Marion *Star,* her father grew furious. He didn't
want her marrying a man rumored to have a strain of African blood.
Her father threatened to cut her off from any inheritance if she did so.
She defied his threat, and he did not acknowledge her until seven years
after she had wed Harding. It was another seven years before he permitted her in his home. During that time she became the business manager of the *Star* and helped make it a financial success. She continued
to manage Warren through the state senate, the lieutenant governorship,
the U.S. Senate, and the presidency. Her son, meanwhile, had died of
alcoholism. No such woman—pregnant bride, abandoned, homeless, divorced, a single working mother, her husband's business partner—had
ever served as First Lady.

Finally the officials left. The household staff retired. The lights were
dimmed. The heavy East Room doors were closed, and the military
sentinels began their motionless vigil protecting the dead President. The
glow from the lit candelabra caused the soldiers' shadows to dance. They
surrounded the coffin, which was closed. Now utterly alone, Florence
Harding contemplated not only the loss of her husband but the power
she had enjoyed overtly exercising.

She had bragged openly that she had made her husband President.
She had successfully insisted that her friend Charlie Forbes be named
head of the newly created Veterans Bureau, that Doc be given a military
appointment, that women be placed in federal positions. She blocked the
appointment of a southern racist. She reported the proceedings of the
international naval disarmament conference to the President, but her
strong anti–League of Nations view bore down on his more conciliatory
view. She chose which criminals in federal penitentiaries would be pa-
roled, insisted that the State Department locate and help a Russian Jew
trapped in Eastern Europe to emigrate to America, and blocked passage
of funding for a vice presidential mansion. She edited the President's

State of the Union addresses and corresponded on any range of political issues with the Cabinet. She was not offended by the jokes or the cartoon dubbing her the "Chief Executive," and on the fatal western tour she had served at any number of events as the "Acting President," even making whistle-stop speeches to the crowds. She had had her own network of women spies within the government to keep her informed of what she perceived correctly to be growing scandals.

In just a few short hours daylight would come and bring a day of services at the Capitol and the train trip back to Ohio for the burial, all of it requiring more public appearances for the Duchess. So now, for a brief while, she could complete any last task she wished to do privately, without notice. Within the hour a limousine with drawn shades was waved through the White House gates. At the North Portico a woman in black emerged. She entered the mansion, padded up the stairwell and down a long, dark hall, and then gently rapped on Florence's door. Evalyn McLean had arrived. Washington society had gossiped that it was her obscene show of new wealth that bought her shameless access to the new power of this First Lady twenty-six years her senior. Indeed Evalyn knew the White House and its shadows and secrets.

Evalyn McLean and her husband, Ned, had helped protect the Hardings even at the risk of breaking the law. The only book published in peacetime to be suppressed by the United States government—a work that focused on Warren's alleged black blood and Florence's Jewish blood, his adultery, and her premarital pregnancy—was burned by the boxful at the McLean estate. Evalyn held on to the original manuscript with notes, later to be tucked into her papers at the Library of Congress. As a dollar-a-year Bureau of Investigation agent, through his friendship with one Jess Smith, Ned had received a flow of confiscated and otherwise illegally obtained whiskey during Prohibition to quench the rampant McLean alcoholism.

If Ned had ripped Nan Britton's dress to retrieve the Harding love letters she had tucked into her blouse, and if he had contributed to the Carrie Phillips blackmail fund, Jess had set up the intimidation of Grace Cross. When Jess was found with a bullet through his skull, Evalyn did not believe the official report of suicide. If Jess was murdered, many wondered, was it at the order of the man he loved, his live-in companion, the attorney general, Harry Daugherty? In Jess's name Harry had set up a secret bank account, allegedly the blackmail fund for Harding's mistress. It was clear that Jess knew too much, including allegations of Harry's criminal misconduct.

Evalyn had spurred Florence's dogged devotion to her "boys" by bringing her into the wards of wounded, shellshocked, and blinded veterans of the Great War. The First Lady interceded in dozens of their cases. She had depended on her loyal friend and Veterans Bureau director Charlie Forbes for help. Instead, she soon discovered, he took millions of dollars in kickbacks from building contracts and the resale of new medical supplies and prompted the first major scandal of the Harding administration. It provoked an enraged President to choke him in the Red Room. Forbes's legal adviser then shot himself in the very house where Florence and Warren had lived during their Senate years, which he had bought from them when they entered the White House.

As she and Evalyn spoke, Florence avoided any embarrassing conversation, talking instead of the Alaska trip. At one-thirty in the morning she had a sudden, macabre impulse. "Mrs. Harding decided that she was lonesome for want of her husband's companionship," Evalyn recalled. "I held her arm, soft and dropsical as we descended the curving white marble staircase. . . . He was downstairs in the East Room of the White House, in his coffin." The coffin was opened. Florence began talking to Warren.

What she said to him has been lost to history, but in all likelihood she spoke to him in death as lovingly—and stringently and complicitously—as she had in life.

She had done her best to protect Warren's public image, but his appetites could not always be controlled. She herself had mixed the alcoholic drinks in the private quarters of the White House during his poker games with his cronies, ignoring the Prohibition laws. She had not, however, been in the Oval Office the day he met with union leaders and was allegedly drunk, as FBI records declassified in 1995 stated. He had been an easy mark for wild rumors. This same man whispered to have black blood was also said to have knelt in the Green Room just months before and repeated the secret vows of the Ku Klux Klan. Although he played the stock market recklessly, she knew for a fact that he had not profited from it; in fact, he had lost heavily. Despite more tales soon to be forthcoming, the Duchess also knew that none of the hundred thousand dollars delivered in a little black bag for former Interior Secretary Albert Fall, or the bonds put into an account for Fall, had ended up in Warren's pocket. Fall had profited mightily from his secret leasing of naval oil reserves to oilmen Edward Doheny and Harry Sinclair, but it was Warren Harding who was permanently tarnished for the dirty deals. Despite Harding's instituting the government's Bureau of the Budget and sponsoring America's first international disarmament conference, his progressive views on racial equity and fighting religious intolerance, his support of government programs for better women's health, his promotion of new American technology industries like moving-picture shows, air travel, radio, and the automobile, his successful demand to industry that they institute a fair, eight-hour work day, Warren G. Harding's name would always be recalled by those oil leases—in California at Elk Hills and in Wyoming at Teapot Dome.

Florence Harding spoke for nearly two hours with her dead husband. Then the coffin was closed. She picked wildflowers from the floral arrangements and placed them on top. "No one can hurt you now," she said matter-of-factly to Warren's remains as she ended her vigil.

She would certainly see to that—this time with Evalyn's help.

Through the early-morning ramblings of the Duchess, Evalyn had stood by, silently listening to it all. Despite her love of intrigue and gossip, she never betrayed Florence again. Except for recording the widow's parting remark, Evalyn never related the details of the monologue she heard that night in the East Room. But that was a small respect compared with what she was to next do in the name of friendship.

For days after Warren Harding's burial, black curls of smoke rose from beyond the protective walls of Friendship. The public knew only that the President's widow was resting there. What remained hidden from sight was the bonfire roaring behind the mansion house, fueled by the Duchess and, for the first few days, Evalyn. They were burning the President's private papers, some public documents, a packed suitcase, boxes of books, the contents of a wall safe—anything Florence Kling Harding thought history could "misconstrue."

Despite all this, she would be forever remembered as the First Lady who poisoned the President.

Before the burning could begin, however, the Duchess would have to take Warren in his coffin to Union Station and head west to the small Ohio town both Hardings had called home for most of their lives. There she would endure the rituals of mourning with family and old colleagues and neighbors. Finally she would arrange for his proper burial, and when she would step out of Warren's temporary crypt, she could not help but see the tallest monument in the cemetery, the one her father had built on the highest spot. A reporter would notice that she was not crying but had an unearthly iridescence to her eyes.

"Now that it is all over," she told Evalyn during their bonfire, "I am beginning to think it was all for the best."

It had been quite a trip from Marion to Friendship.

FLORENCE HARDING

Part One

EARLY
LIFE
1860-1891

I was taught while yet learning to walk that to be in the middle of the road was not all there was to a journey, but that I must look to the right and to the left and observe and look and listen if I would count myself alive. And so I began life with my senses alert, which afterward served me well.

1

A Proud Family, a Shrouded Family

She was born above the store, on Main Street. But even before her life began, the odds were stacked against her.

Amos Kling always got what he wanted. He wanted a son. So confident was Kling that as soon as he learned that his wife, Louisa, was pregnant, he bragged to everyone in their town of Marion, Ohio, that his firstborn would be a boy.

From the moment Florence Mabel Kling entered the world, she began a battle of wills with Amos Kling. As an intimate explained, this child "did not take life as she found it. She grasped it fearlessly and firmly and forced it to yield to her demands." Such an attitude distinguished her for the sixty-four years of her existence.

The birth of his first child might have been a distraction for the penurious twenty-seven-year-old Amos, but he was probably at Louisa's bedside with her parents and a midwife in their small flat, just one flight of steps above his hardware store at 127 South Main. However much he "bitterly resented" the sex of the child born on August 15, 1860, recalled neighbor Jane Dixon, Amos devised a practical solution and "consoled himself by bringing her up more as a boy than a girl."

Just then, however, he had business at hand. Amos always had business at hand. By the time eight-month-old Flossie was crawling, the Civil War had begun. Although Kling never had any moral objections to slavery, Marion was a central link in the Underground Railroad, and Ohio was a bastion of support for President Lincoln, elected from the newly dominant political party, the Republicans. Kling became avidly Republican. It was good for business.

It's doubtful that Amos's parents ever even thought about politics. Michael Kling and his wife, usually referred to as Elizabeth, were farmers in Lancaster County, Pennsylvania, the parents of four daughters and five sons; Amos was the third child, born on June 15, 1833. Although he had been raised to be a farmer, Amos had broader ambitions. After primary school he apprenticed as a tailor, continuing after his family migrated in 1850 to Richland County, Ohio, and then to Lucas County, where they settled in Mansfield. He began what he called his "battle in the business channel of life" by attending W. W. Granger's commercial college in Mansfield; he graduated in 1854.[1]

In 1855 Amos Kling made for the nearby town of Marion, his motivation uncertain, but he found immediate work as an accountant and a salesman for hardware store owner John W. Bain, earning a salary of twenty-nine dollars a week. Amos kept the books for three years and learned all he needed to about making money in hardware. At twenty-four, he had saved enough money to buy out Bain and begin his own hardware business.

Colonel George Christian, the grandson of a Marion pioneer, a cousin-in-law to the prominent De Wolfe family, which was fatefully to intertwine with the Klings, was gentry compared with the scrappy migrant, but Kling made an immediate impression on him. He later wrote:

> In many respects he was the most remarkable personality that had come to try his fortune. He worked early and late and gained not only the confidence of his employer but of the business community as well ... amassing a large fortune within a very short period. He made no risky and doubtful investments. His judgement in all business matters seemed to be absolutely unerring. He became a very popular merchant with the trade, buying carefully and always discounting his bills, paying in cash. When the civil war began this popularity resulted in his getting many tips from the great jobbers of building and shop hardware which resulted in heavy purchases of materials that advanced so rapidly in price that the financial returns gave him an independent cash capital of his own to carry on his rapidly growing business.[2]

War was Kling's fortune, for his most rapid profits were in bulk sales of nails, with a large part of his business being with the Union army, in desperate need of building supplies. The war took its toll, however, on his family. His brothers followed Amos to Marion but lacked his enterprise. The eldest, Jacob, wounded in the war, died a bachelor after working for Amos, while George was taken into several joint ventures with him. Henry was a Union captain killed in November 1863 at the Battle of Mission Ridge, and Michael, a private, had died six months earlier at Milliken's Bend. "When the war began, three of five Kling brothers entered the army by agreement," Amos later snapped when asked why he hadn't enlisted. "When this record has been met by other well known families, I will expect our family to be called upon for further sacrifice."

At the time of Florence Kling's birth Marion had 1,844 residents. Within ten years its population grew by over 30 percent. Although the old Kerr House, a four-story hotel with storefronts, still stood as a symbol of early days, the frontier quality of Marion was rapidly fading with a building boom. Every Sunday the Klings sat through the sermons of L. C. Webster at Epworth Methodist Church, with Flossie attending Sunday school at the Wesley Chapel at Center and State streets, wearing her trademark red ribbons and calico dress from A. D. Matthews, fancy goods dealer. During the week she took piano lessons from "professors" W. D. Benner and C. E. Vardon. Marion was the sort of mid-nineteenth-century midwestern town that became eulogized in decades to come, a place where hard work, prayer, and neighborliness could earn a man and his family all the success and respectability anyone could hope for in his life. Even the town eccentrics were tolerated off on Gospel Hill.

Being quintessentially American, Marion housed a natural hierarchy, based not only on wealth and virtue but on lineage, race, and religion. By the 1860s Marion already had, as a later resident put it, "the order," and though subtle, it was not imagined or ignored but rather "controlled a social structure more complicated than a central Ohio town might initially seem to have." When, for example, Ed Huber, Marion's most important industrialist, wanted to create and fund a mechanics' library, he encountered resistance from the older, wealthier men who sensed a threat in the potential advancement of the working classes. As a councilman Amos Kling was to help pass legislation to create the late-night library.[3]

Despite the money and power Kling amassed, he was always considered a "made" man, not one of gentry like the Christians, De Wolfes, Bartrams, and other families descended from English-American pioneers who had founded Marion and prospered by it. While established families did not yet dismiss newcomers simply by background, there was a subtle struggle of "the Germans versus the English," said later resident Carroll Neidhart, descendant of German farmers in the region. Unlike the English, who had money to go west via river transport, the Germans had walked across Pennsylvania into central Ohio. German was not an unfamiliar language at the Marion markets. There was a German Society and newspaper, songfests, beer gardens, and the "Sageneichts" or political parties. And Amos Kling was German.

In later attempts to burnish the Kling background, one romantic version described Amos's parents as settling Ohio in "pioneer days." Given the conditions of anti-Teutonic sentiment during an American war with Germany, it was understandable that, as an adult, Florence eagerly abetted the prevarication that the Klings were "a strain of Holland Dutch blood." The claim that her "sturdy Pennsylvania Dutchman" grandfather had founded "the Kling fortunes," however, was untrue. Amos himself would make the first concerted effort to shroud the Kling origins.

Although he prospered in Marion, his parents never moved there from Lucas County. Perhaps the presence of illiterate farmer parents to one who became Marion's most successful adopted son in commerce, banking, education, real estate, and civic endeavors was too embarrassing and not encouraged by him. Perhaps Amos wanted to suggest that he had sprung from the earth himself. Nor did he wish to return to the earth in their presence. Although Amos bought a vast family cemetery plot, in which his brothers lay, his parents were not to be buried there. His father lived seventeen years and his mother for at least twenty after Flossie's birth. Florence never spoke of them in later life.[4]

If his parents—save for their names—are oddly absent from the record, their lineage is obscured in even more mystery. One Margaret Kling, in her precise genealogy of a prominent Kling family, that of John Ludwig, who emigrated in 1755 to Philadelphia from Württemberg, tried unsuccessfully to connect Amos to them. She concluded that "it is impossible for us to state the Christian name of the ancestor of Amos Kling." When sociology professor William Chancellor later interviewed old residents, he finally uncovered the legend that seemed to explain the years of shrouding the family. "The Klings were Rhinelanders," he wrote. "[S]ome believe that they were originally Jews."

While records indicate that there were Jewish families in the region where the Klings were said to originate, they do not list family names. The claim was no more than a legend, but it was a sensitive issue for the family and may have undermined young Flossie's sense of self in a nearly exclusively Protestant culture, as she always sought to blur the truth about her Kling ancestry. Bigotry against German descendants in 1860s America was far rarer than anti-Semitism. The mere mention of the *legend* that the Klings were originally Jewish could understandably provoke fear of rejection in them. Besides claiming that the Klings were Dutch, for example, Florence said that they were Mennonite when in fact they were Lutheran. Such attempts to conceal even mere rumor of course often fueled its credibility.[5]

The origins of Amos Kling's mother are also shrouded, except for two brief remarks by Florence to a confidante: She stated that her paternal grandmother's maiden name was Vetallis, and that she was "born in southern France." With purposeful evasiveness, under the heading "parentage" in the 1870 census, Amos Kling omitted any reference to the "foreign birth" of his mother, yet there exists no record for any native-born Vetallis or similarly named family in Lancaster from 1810 to 1830—the period during which she would have lived there. Amos unwittingly revealed the truth when, in 1867, he traveled to France and referred to it as his "old country."

Florence later bragged in an abstract manner of her beloved "French grandmother," who taught her proper posture and movement and whose elegance affected her fashion sense and grooming style. Yet it was her *mother's* mother, a descendant of English Puritans married to a man who had a French Protestant or "Huguenot" surname from one of his ancestors two centuries earlier, who lived in Marion. When Florence bragged that she had "the best blood of France," it was said as a "descendant of a French Huguenot," a sharp differentiation from an immigrant "French grandmother." Why did she distort the facts?

In seeking to avoid any obstacle to his rise in Marion's social order, Amos thought he also had to obscure his Vetallis lineage, perhaps because of religious affiliation. French attacks on its Protestant population in the previous two centuries had led most of them to resettle near the German border, particularly in Alsace. The religion of *southern* French immigrants, however, was almost exclusively Roman Catholic, and so was perhaps the mysterious "Elizabeth" Vetallis Kling. Anti-Catholic sentiment flourished in 1850s America, especially toward immigrants; the Know-Nothing movement in fact organized in fear of a papist plot to infiltrate the government.[6]

With her Kling and Vetallis lineage suppressed by her father, Flossie's Bouton and Hanford ancestry had a profound influence. With her father focused on work and her mother pregnant just months after her own birth, the black-haired toddler with large deep blue eyes became the center of attention for her maternal grandparents, Harvey and Emily Bouton, and Flossie was to take all her clan pride in their families. From early childhood, Flossie studied the glass-framed Bouton coat of arms—a ferocious animal with the motto, "De Gules a la Fasce d'Or," or in loose translation, "a force as of a leopard when it attacks with its red mouth open."

The first Bouton in America, twenty-year-old John Bouton, son of Count Nicolas Bouton, was a French Huguenot who fled to England, then left Gravesend for Boston in July 1635 on the *Assurance*. The legend of the "Boughton race," as a genealogy called it, dated back to the fifth century and, as ancient family histories inevitably do, traced itself if not quite to royalty, then in its presence, allegedly fighting with the Gaul chieftain Clovis in defeating the Romans and establishing France. One Bouton distinguished himself as the Marquis de Chamilly; after he was appointed marshal of all France, his life-size portrait hung at Versailles. In America the family was equally noteworthy, helping to found New Canaan, Connecticut, and fighting in the Revolution. The sixth-generation Harvey Bouton, born in 1803, married Emily Hanford, a mariner's daughter, in 1826. Emily's family had an ancestral castle in Pershore, England, Wallas Hall, built during Elizabeth I's reign by Sir Charles Hanford, with the motto "Memorare Norissima" carved in the stone entrance. In 1642 Thomas Hanford, "an eminent divine," settled in Norwalk and married a woman of the surname Miles, "of position and property in the new land."[7]

Inculcated with tales of armored knights and Puritan maidens, Flossie had a presumption to imperiousness bred into her early, counterbalancing the insecurity of kept secrets on her father's side. If she was the daughter of an enigmatic businessman of questionable lineage, then by some ancient divine right, she was also a minor royal. If nothing else, her heritage gave her deep self-confidence, for at times she later retreated into ancestor worship to shore up her sense of great destiny. Yet there was never any claim of pretense by her own mother, Louisa.

Of Harvey and Emily's three daughters, only the last, born on September 2, 1835, and named Louisa Mabel, survived. The family was active in the New Canaan Methodist Church, which Harvey's parents had helped found across the street from their home, and Louisa's cultivated voice was a feature of the choir. She attended a "little red schoolhouse" near the fork on Town Farm road, just down from the old Canoe Hill graveyard, where generations of Boutons lay. "She was one of the finest girls ever born," recalled schoolmate Junius Benedict. "The most popular girl in New Canaan, Louisa Bouton was. And she deserved to be. She had the best disposition of any girl I ever knew and was mighty good looking. There wasn't a boy in town who wouldn't have been glad to have her." After meeting her during an 1859 visit to his friend L. M. Monroe, Amos "wooed and won" Louisa. Benedict recalled, "When this young man Kling came on from the West and married her and took her away he left some sad hearts behind." She wrote out invitations to their wedding of September 27, 1859, one of which Flossie later found and cherished. At the same time Harvey relocated his shoe manufacturing business to Painesville, Ohio, so all three Huguenot Yankees became Buckeyes.[8]

Colonel Christian recalled that when Louisa first arrived in Marion, she was a "young lady remarkable for refinement, education and beauty." Several accounts claim that she quickly became an "invalid," yet there exists no evidence she ever had any disease. She was physically sturdy enough to travel far and wide for long periods without male escort, to swim in the Atlantic, to attend Methodist missionary meetings, and to list her "occupation" in the 1870 census as "Keeping House." As was the case with tens of thousands of other such female "invalids" of the era, Louisa probably suffered from depression, almost certainly a result of Amos's terrifying dominance of the home. Family friend Jane Dixon recollected that Louisa was "a kindly mother creature, with a devotion to her family, brooking no worldly interference. Hers was the sweetness that tempered the more austere attitude of the father toward the children." Louisa was expected simply to obey and be quiet. It seems she did.[9]

Ruthlessly harsh in his view of the world and life in general, Kling was driven only by work and money. Other ambitious men his age might sometimes attempt to relax with their families, but there exist no such recollections about Kling until later in life. Even commitments to civic and altruistic endeavors were calibrated as a means to one end: money. He refused to provide financial backing for any local effort, for example, in which he had no controlling voice. The discipline to earn, save, and invest forged "old man Kling," a name Marionites often called him.

As Louisa coped alone with her subsequent children, Amos invested his profits in cash—never on credit—into more of the building, painting, mechanic, shoemaking, blacksmithing, and farming implements and supplies always in demand in Marion. He never offered any bargains at the vast and rapidly expanding A. H. Kling & Bro., explaining in an ad that "it is money that forms the basis of all business transactions, it charms the world, it is what we want for our goods." Indeed Kling's money quips soon became legendary, his most famous being "There is no pursuit or calling that seems to give more pleasure than that of spending other people's money." Despite such abrasive shrewdness, Kling, said Christian, "was not a man to deal unjustly with any one. While exacting in his dealings, believing the law protected the diligent creditor, he was honest and upright."[10]

From behind his counter, Kling offered the latest and the best in his new departments. He also now had his own apprentice, kept at his side for training. On any given day a figure with short hair in red ribbons, barely visible above the counter, took in every transaction, every movement, every conversation. Later recalling how she was "always around with him," Amos made the child increasingly "familiar with all the details of his hardware business." As soon as Flossie could walk, Amos took her to the store. There, amid the commotion, she learned the smells, sounds, and textures of hardware: steel tools, copper wiring, freshly shaved and milled wood planks, and those silver Kling nails available for sale in all sizes. The child had the tactile sense of men and men's business, the sandpapered voices of sales, the pungency of cow dung on boots, hide pouches of sweet tobacco, stultifying cigar curls. It was the man's world where Flossie comfortably grew up.

"I was taught while yet learning to walk," she said of her earliest memory, "that to be in the middle of the road was not all there was to a journey, but that I must look to the right and to the left and observe and look and listen if I would count myself alive. And so I began life with my senses alert which afterward served me well."[11]

The Girl on the Horse

Flossie's ferocity, stamina, and competitive assertiveness caught the notice of all her friends. Despite the trademark red hair ribbons, she seemed like a boy.

As one resident said of the earliest recorded incident of Florence's life, she "tomboyed her way valiantly through the games of childhood and demonstrated her gift for leadership by being the only person in town to guide a bobsled down Gospel Hill without dumping her precious load of human freight in the snowdrifts along Cucaw Creek in the hollow." Flossie said her favorite "boy and girl game" was to outrun the pack into a yard and club nuts until they fell from trees, then gather and eat them until she was chased out by the owner.

One story later mistakenly claimed that Florence was an only child for twelve years, but it certainly seemed that way. Amos treated her as his only child. Her younger brothers, Clifford Bouton, born on October 13, 1861, and Vetallis Hanford, born on November 7, 1866, were always "shy, unobtrusive lads" dominated by tyrannical Amos and tough Flossie. In recalling her father's "stubbornness and a will that must always be obeyed," she said, "I lived my life so completely with my father that when my brothers came into the family he forgot his early disappointment in my being a baby girl."

Marionite Jack Warwick concurred that her role was "that of a favorite child" but, further, that "she more than they seemed to have inherited the strong will and restless energies of the father." Seeing how his obstinance commanded respect, Flossie began to mimic Amos. Robert Small recalled that even as a young child she "always possessed his aggressiveness, ambition, forcefulness, and dependable judgment." Amos, said another friend, "ruled his daughter and his entire household with a hand of iron," but while his wife and sons would "tamely submit," the growing Flossie now occasionally "chafed under and resented bitterly the restraint placed upon her." Posed for her first photograph during a visit to New Canaan, she was no sweet-faced imp. Her hand in a fist, her arm pressed across her chest, she sternly scowls for the camera like a capable, hard miniature adult, as if resenting that she has been ordered to remain still.[1]

Although her school records are not extant, Amos put "a high estimate on the value of an education," and she was thoroughly taught by male and female teachers in math, science, English, writing, surveying, rhetoric, logic, philosophy, history, geography, Latin, Greek, even German, cartology, and astronomy. Beginning in 1866, she attended primary school at the eight-year-old public Union School, a large, square brick building with long white-framed panes of glass and a shuttered bell tower. She attended high school there for a three-year course of study in the classics. It was not her teachers who engraved a permanent memory in her mind from this period, however; it was the solemn faces of Union soldiers now meandering northward home. The war was over, and the boys in blue needed jobs.[2]

In the postwar economy Kling sensed that big money was no longer in hardware. Banking gave him the roost to rule Marion. "He was a natural banker," said Christian, "and with a large capital cash on hand, decided to retire from the hardware business and become indirectly a banker. He was constantly loaning money, always requiring ample security and getting for the same the rather high rates which were the rule." As the Farmers' and Mechanics' Bank president Kling bragged of his "careful, conservative head so essential to the success of such an institution," and as the founder-president of the Marion Building, Savings and Loan Company, he said he "rendered invaluable service to the community." Organized with one million dollars' capital, it yielded Marion's highest dividends. "Its original scope," ran one account, "has been greatly enlarged through his energy and enterprise and its officers are numbered with the leading capitalists of Marion." Once he became Marion County Bank's president, Kling refitted rooms above it to headquarter his own mortgage and loan office; he would not waste space.

Amos had already begun buying acres of farm property. Occasionally he still farmed. Once he put aside his own plow horse, he rented the land to tenants, superintended planting and harvesting, and financed other farmers. With each generation of Marion property maps, the name Kling multiplied lot to lot. With Tom Wallace and J. J. Hane, he owned nearly four hundred acres. By the fairgrounds, where new housing for the labor class was rising, as well as in other outlying areas broken into subplots, Amos owned about twenty acres, and with his brother George he shared a string of plots in an area that linked the fairgrounds area and the center of town. By 1870 Amos possessed $53,800 in real estate and $43,000 in cash, the accumulation of which, one local publication announced, was due to his "perseverance, industry and business ability." A friend more bluntly credited his "knack of squeezing every possible dollar from the soil he tilled."

In the early seventies Amos dickered successfully with some quarrymen, and within days, recalled Jane Dixon, "heavy loads of white limestone were carted to a lot on East Center Street, a brief two blocks from [his] bank and loan office. In due time, there sprang up one of those large, square substantial, top towered edifices known in the parlance of a small town as a mansion." The Klings moved into the corner site, across Center Street from the Methodist Episcopal parsonage, and right next door to dry goods salesman David McWilliams, whose daughter Susie Pearl became Florence's childhood companion.

Meanwhile Amos expanded into municipal services that would stimulate local industry: He was an original stockholder and a director of the Columbus & Toledo Railroad, Agricultural Society president, school board member, building committee member of the new courthouse, builder and founder of the Marion Opera House auditorium, underwriter of rooms at the old ladies home, trustee of the Marion Cemetery Association, and donor of the land for the new YMCA headquarters—on the condition that fifteen thousand dollars be raised for the building within thirty days. Of all his endeavors, however, Amos took his most personal pride in his livestock, forming a cattle partnership in Wyoming with a Marionite, as well as a Marion County Importing Company with two other businessmen.

When Flossie was seven, Amos made his first overseas trip to purchase Normandy horses at the Paris Exposition. He returned to France in 1868 and again in 1870, making himself "the medium of introducing some of the finest horses into this section that Marion County has ever seen," one journal reported. The horses were sold throughout the Midwest and increased the value of Marion horses since they were bred with those from Normandy.[3]

There were also straw-packed crates arriving at 326 East Center Street from Europe, and neighbors peeking through the plate glass windows got a sense of just how far up "the order" Amos was pushing. Inside the crates were white marble statuary, sets of monogrammed silver table services, a tea service, pink-flowered china, gold-encrusted blue china, and porcelain candy dishes. Humble chairs from the days above the store were replaced by ornate Gilded Age sofas, ottomans, and chaises in eye-boggling blue and green stripes, tassels, and dots. A heavily carved Chickering piano dominated the main parlor, and in the bathroom were hand-painted sinks. Despite the sturdy impressiveness of the Kling mansion, it always seemed gloomy to locals: the stone front porch and columns painted gray and shadowed by the awnings, the shuttered cupola always closed, all within a black gate. There was also tension within. Still depressed, Mrs. Kling now turned all housekeeping over to an Irish Catholic immigrant, Margaret Younkins. Marionite Jack Warwick said Amos was "accustomed to having pretty much his own way, because most people let him have it," but "Aunt Mag" did not. In her, said her nephew, Kling met his "match in temperament."

Throughout her life Flossie expressed no sentimental attachment to anything about this house: not the silver French vanity set in her large bedroom suite and certainly not the complicated front-door lock system. Her obsession was in the stables in the backyard. Flossie Kling loved horses.[4]

Warwick recalled that Miss Kling "above all else was a daring horsewoman. She probably knew more about horses than four-fifths of the men in the town." Besides her beloved saddle horse Billy, Flossie drove "a spirited pair" with a McMurray Sulky Company buggy. When

Amos refused to enlarge his stables, Flossie lodged her horses at "Captain" Drake's livery stables around the corner, where as an adolescent she could frequently be found. Drake rented horses and carriages for dating sweethearts, weddings, funerals, hauling groceries, mail delivery, and cab service from the train. Here she learned the art of riding.

George Christian remembered how Flossie "delighted in handling the reins over a good horse and was always ready for a canter or a race across the country[side]." Riding sidesaddle by the time she was ten years old, she was described as the best woman equestrienne in the county, and her skill began to develop a genuine self-confidence in her. The happiest moments of her life, she later recalled, were "when I used to ride up on my own white horse to the judges' stand . . . to receive the blue ribbon." Equally telling was Mag Younkins's memory that even before she was a teenager, Flossie was "the best horsewoman I have ever seen"; she "rode and drove more like a man than a girl," always "dashing swiftly up the street on Billy . . . [rather] than walking with the other girls of her social circle." Delicate girls would "pile into Florence's phaeton and ride with perfect confidence behind her speedy Billy."

Her attachment to horses soon extended into a concern for all animals, an interest far beyond what most people felt for their pets. "It has always been a source of pleasure to me, that I have been from childhood very fond of animals; but it has been still more of a satisfaction," she later wrote, "that animals were seemingly prejudiced in my favor. Men and women assumed a great responsibility when they made the animals their servants or their friends; they assume the responsibility for the comfort and happiness of the dumb creatures that have given up so much of their capacity for happiness through a natural life, in order to serve their human masters. So I always think of our duty to the animals, as in kind, though of course not in degree, similar to our obligation to children."

While benevolent toward "dumb" creatures, Florence Kling was also learning to protect herself with unusual physical strength and vigilant control. When Flossie was about fifteen, Warwick recounted, Billy "was trying to show his rider that he was a little of the best circus performer in town and capable of doing about as he pleased. In his wild caperings, with the girl in the saddle, he attracted a crowd of business men who stood around in helpless fear that the girl would be killed. But it didn't happen. The horse overdid the performance, the climax coming when he reared too straight, overbalanced and fell. As he went over backwards the rider slipped to the ground and, when the animal was prostrate, caught him by the bridle, pinned his head to the ground and sat on it until the fiery steed had time to give his better instincts a chance to work."[5]

Flossie's agility with horses also served a purpose for Amos. By her early teens, she had become so expert at the business skills she had learned in hardware that Amos, who, according to her, was "obsessed with disgust over the ignorance of the majority of women in business matters brought to his attention daily in his banking affairs," trained her in not only banking but real estate and farm tenant management. Flossie later claimed that her mother's "long invalidism" was a reason for Kling's adapting her into his "constant companion" and "chief director and friend," as if she were a surrogate wife. It was, Flossie said, as she "rode horseback with dad, [and] traveled about with him," that she "made up to him in every way the loss of mother's companionship." But the relationship also served to draw her into a darker world. As they "used to drive over miles of farm country," beyond Marion's border, into the isolated landscape where the blackness of night dropped rapidly, Flossie had her first exposure to elements of the occult.

Kling leased his farmlands to many German families who lived in fear of Satan and cast spells to ward off evil. On New Year's Day they always served sauerkraut and ham, a meal that promised good luck. In kitchen windows opening onto the endless land, housewives would put a sprig of dog fennel into a suspended glass "Witch's Ball," and if the sprig turned gray, an evil spirit had been successfully captured. The most visually arresting demonstrations were the hex signs nailed on barns to keep demons at bay, and it was these colorful shields against the devil that first caught Flossie's fascination as she waited for Amos to collect the rent. That kernel of consciousness grew into a belief in metaphysical signs, symbols, and messages and then enlarged into an overwhelming faith in astrology and clairvoyance as a way of calming fears and controlling fate.

Such beliefs abounded in Marion, and Flossie carried them with her far beyond its borders. "Spirit pictures," photographs of the ghostly apparitions of the deceased, fed by the postwar cult of mourning, were popular during Flossie's youth. At any given time mediums were tucked about the shady side of Marion, ready to answer questions for cash, via tarot cards, zodiac charts, and crystal balls. Flossie undoubtedly heard the local legend of "Old Black Henry," who cast a spell on two women, who manifested symptoms of demonic madness the next day. How deeply she studied the occult while still under her father's roof can't be fully ascertained, but her niece claimed that Flossie did already feel that some sort of mark on her forehead—never visible in photographs—was a sign of magic destiny.[6]

Besides seeing to it that Flossie learned French, dabbled in oil painting, attended Epworth Methodist each Sunday dressed in appropriately restrained clothing, and participated in church activities, Mrs. Kling had enough wherewithal to prompt her to learn to play the piano, and Amos insisted that she do it superbly. "I've always worked," Florence later stated proudly about her meeting her early challenges. "Between them I was kept busy and found I liked it. I may wear out, but I shall never rust out." It was apparent to anyone who heard her classical pieces that superseding parental expectation, Flossie had a genuine talent, soon "cultivated by the instruction of capable professors," as she put it.[7]

Her artistic talents were now matched with mental agility and a gift for sharp, witty, and intelligent conversation, especially political conversation. Spending hours in her father's office, Flossie eagerly looked forward to speaking with his business associates. "She had a charming frankness and ideas of her own," Joe Chapple, a later associate, learned. "Even in her youthful days she was keenly interested in public affairs and public men, and was known as one young woman who read the newspapers thoroughly and was posted on political affairs and current events. She loved the zest of meeting all sorts of people in her own natural way." Kling's power having grown, many of these men were from far outside the county and state, most of them Republican. According to Robert Small, a friend of Flossie's and a later reporter, "His political influence was also extensive." Among those Amos had met and supported were former governor Rutherford Hayes—elected President in 1876—and the rising congressman from Canton, William McKinley.[8]

Though he lived in an era in which neither his daughter nor any other American woman could vote, Amos Kling was entirely progressive in his conviction that women were as capable as men. Florence said Amos believed that "every girl should have a knowledge of business methods with some profession or trade by which they could earn a living if necessity called. He insisted that I be trained in the business world." One of his maxims that she seemed to have already learned was: "Do it honestly and don't ever lose." As Christian observed, "She inherited from her father to a most remarkable degree the business acumen and forcefulness for which Mr. Kling was noted." Yet as Flossie grew into womanhood, it became stingingly apparent that her business skills would be outweighed by the reality of her society. No matter how "masculine" her professionalism might seem, or how seriously her father treated her, she would always be treated as a woman and thus dismissed from powerful positions and independent prosperity. Florence knew this. "I love business and believe if I had been born a boy, as my father hoped, I would have made a fortune for myself. . . . I would have become a business man."

Still, Miss Kling was also learning there were advantages to being a woman in society. Described by friends as "animated" and "independent," Flossie manifested a peculiar sensitivity to human nature, studying the body language of people, becoming a "shrewd observor of facial expression," and using them to assess a person. Amos had taught her that if she went about her activities with her head "in the air, looking neither to the right nor to the left," she "would miss the interesting realities of life—the people." Such intuition was considered a feminine trait. It was certainly something that Amos Kling never possessed but that his daughter did. "My father counted success only by the usual standards. He didn't look forward; he didn't see the hidden qualities," she remarked smugly. "In other words, he was a man, not a woman." Finally the daughter had something over her father.

If Amos Kling was the best booster for Marion, he was also the best booster for Amos Kling.

Nobody crossed him—except his daughter.[9]

3

Whipped with a Cherry Switch

"From earliest youth," a friend revealed, "Florence evinced a determination to do things." That most of her teenage girlfriends did not entertain the idea of having a career, was irrelevant to Flossie Kling. She announced that she would "become a musical celebrity and to that end left no stone unturned." She evidenced no thoughts of marriage, motherhood, or housekeeping. Instead she would gain recognition in the concert halls of the East and Europe. Those who heard her play were encouraging. As a neighbor later stated, "Had it been a question of livelihood, there is no doubt but that she would have won recognition as a musician."

After graduating from high school in 1876, Florence focused even more intensely on her music, recalling, "I spent seven hours a day at the piano for over three years." She was as driven by Amos as much as by her own ambition. One day, according to family lore, as angry proof of her determination to meet his demands, she practiced until her fingers bled. "When my family learned that I possessed some ability as a musician I was given a thorough training in music," she said. Aspiring to study in New York, she kept to herself her first faint desires to slip from the clutches of old man Kling. Making beautiful music was not practical enough for Amos. He would let her study at the Cincinnati Conservatory of Music to develop a skill "for earning her own living in case she were ever thrown upon her own resources" as a piano teacher.[1]

Cincinnati was to the Midwest as Boston was to the East, a city already renowned for its appreciation of fine music, partly because of its cultivated German and Jewish families. Concert halls, orchestra associations, recital programs, musical instrument sales, and music schools thrived there. The year before Florence arrived, a New York newspaper admitted: "The nine muses appear to be going West, and Clio and Euterpe are hovering over Cincinnati, if not already settled on it." It was also a city of wealthy families like the Tafts, Longworths, and McLeans, who underwrote cultural endeavors, such as the annual May Festival of Music. In this atmosphere Clara Baur, a small red-haired immigrant from Stuttgart, Germany, whose studies included excellent music and voice training, had founded the conservatory in 1868. Initially "ridiculed" by Cincinnati's Clara Nourse, who ran the city's most exclusive girls' school, Baur rapidly went from teaching Nourse's students to starting her own school. Flossie Kling began at the conservatory in the autumn of 1877, boarding in one of the thirty rooms of the top two floors of a four-story brick building at downtown Eighth and Vine streets. Her course of study was primarily piano, but she continued her French and other courses for the "finishing school" touch. At conservatory events and recitals there was always formal receiving, with Miss Baur leading the line of young girls dressed in white while beautiful flowers accented the rooms. Renowned scholars and musicians came to lecture and perform; they included *New York Tribune* music critic Henry Edward Krehbiel and Boston Symphony Orchestra conductor Arthur

Nikisch. Baur's mission was as stated, "to fit young people for professional career or social position as circumstances dictate, by utilizing the highest culture of the art of music, that they may wield a more potent influence for the good."

Free from parental constraints, Cincinnati opened her to an entirely new world of cultural events and great architecture, sophisticated transportation and technology, newer fashions from Europe and the East. When Flossie sank into the velvet-cushioned chairs of the Cincinnati Music Hall, she was mesmerized. "I remember distinctly the first opera that I attended," she recalled. "While in school in Cincinnati, I was taken to hear Lohengrin. It is still my favorite opera." When Edison's phonograph disk machine became available, operas formed a large part of Florence's vast collection. Finally, with her "entrepreneurial acumen," the single Miss Bauer seems to have had as much of an impact on Flossie as the training did. Advocating a "professional career" and "potent influence" for young women of the 1870s was radical, but it was a formula that appealed to Florence Kling. Perhaps Amos sensed her strengthening independence. By the spring he had ordered her back to Marion.[2]

Before leaving for Cincinnati, Flossie had smiled softly for a picture, her silky chestnut hair piled geisha style atop her head, her large eyes set behind the pince-nez spectacles that she now always wore; she was described as a lithe, bright woman who laughed easily and spoke in a deep but sweet voice. A picture taken after her return to Marion illustrated a striking transformation: her hair tightened into bangs and a topknot and pulled back from a stern face rigid in a throat clasp and stiff collar. Five feet six inches tall, with a prominent nose, she had the mannish look of the stereotypical American bluestocking. She seemed markedly unhappy. Soon after her father had her return to Marion, Flossie began plotting her way out.

Louisa Kling's "illness," worsened by the death in June 1878 of her father, was the ostensible reason Amos wanted Flossie back, "to assume feminine responsibilities in the home of an invalid mother," according to a later chronicler. But if Amos thought that having his blooming daughter under his control again would be easy, he was mistaken. Hysterical tirades, screaming fights, and confrontations between Amos and Flossie sometimes lasted until dawn and were loud enough to be heard beyond the windows streaked with yellow gaslight on East Center Street. As one Marionite delicately recalled, Miss Kling " 'livened things up' at the limestone mansion." Florence even conceded, "I can never remember a time in our old home when father's will did not move the household[.] [A]utocratically his opinion ruled even in the minor affairs of the house management."

If, as a friend said, the "impetuous" Florence "had no restraint" when she returned to Marion, her behavior was in direct reaction to Amos. From those who described their relationship, Amos was of "unbending convictions, unyielding temperament, unflinching determination. . . . He had his own ideas of what a young girl should and should not do. Most of the things he believed she ought not to do and which he forbade, Florence Kling desired of all else to do. It was inevitable that this father and daughter should clash. . . ."

Resenting her call home, Florence determined to retain the independence she had in Cincinnati. As a contemporary told Samuel Hopkins Adams, "Chafing in the stiff, stodgy, sect-conscious society of her circle, she went a little beyond the strait limitations of being a perfect lady. In the contemporary phrase, she was 'a mite wild.' This must not be construed in terms of moral turpitude. It meant no more than that she frequented the skating rink, sometimes went out with boys who would not have been welcomed in the Kling household. . . ." Indeed her betting on horses seemed to anger Amos less than her staying out late at the skating rink. Teenagers of all classes came together at Marion's new Merry-Roll-Round skating rink. It was a chance not only for girls to skate to sprightly waltzes, provided by a band located in the rink's center, but to mix unchaperoned with the opposite sex—who often stole a glance under the petticoats when a girl fell. A cornet player, originally from nearby Blooming Grove, often played at the rink and recalled, "Quite frequently young ladies show more of themselves than is meant for general observation, but the boys, all the boys look the other (?) way."[3]

After her return to Marion, defiance became ingrained in Florence's personality, the most thorough description of it coming in later years from Kathleen Lawler, an aide who worked beside her often for twelve hours a day. Lawler used the words "shrewd," "alert," "quick-tempered," "ambitious," "opinionated," and "impulsive" to describe her, conceding that others found her "steely, arrogant, domineering, overbearing, self-willed." She thought that Florence's "large, strong, powerful, crushing" hands not only indicated her "capacity to overcome all obstacles" but was "illustrative of a further disparity." Lawler believed it was obvious Florence "had the dominant, driving brain of a strong man." A later generation was to view such qualities as signs that Florence had been socialized as a firstborn male, and she herself admitted she was "something like a man." If such unfeminine characteristics made life as a teenage girl difficult, it seemed to help in her combating Amos.

Lawler's most indelible impression of Florence was her reaction to domineering men, recalling that she "never permitted her own individuality to become merged" and "resented, with all the strength of her forceful nature, any encroachment upon which she conceived to be her own, or the rights of others." Florence's "keen sense of right and wrong" and "abiding sense of justice" further seemed a visceral reaction to the humiliation of continuing to have personal boundaries violated. In the German custom of *Ohrenfeige*, physical discipline administered by a father to his children, Amos did not hesitate to whip Florence with the dreaded "switch from the cherry tree," a neighbor recalled, despite the fact that she had matured into a woman. He never violently abused Florence, but the shame affected her. After a fight with him, she often ran to the stable, got on Billy, and rode hard out of town, slowing only when she could calm herself in the bucolic countryside.[4]

At no time in her life did she ever express an interest in being a wife like her mother or wed to a man like her father. It was from the marriage of writer George Eliot and her husband that Florence drew her concept of the "ideal family relationship," based on an equality that extended into the professional. "Miss Eliot was the great genius of that combination," she later wrote, "but I think . . . that her genius would never have bloomed and borne its wonderful fruit had it not been for the inspiration which she derived from her husband's companionship." Perhaps because of Kling's wealth and power, some young men expressed interest in marrying Florence, and Amos wanted her to marry well. Though she scouted no partner akin to George Eliot's, she was, said a friend, "always being a prime favorite with men" and had what another mysteriously termed "a persuasive way" with them. A more salacious suggestion by an anonymous local was the gossip that Florence "always had a gift for getting on with men. Where others wasted what they got in this fashion, she saved her money."

To what degree Flossie Kling explored her sexuality is unknown. It was true that many nights she did not get home by the Kling curfew of eleven, at which time Amos angrily bolted the locks of the double-front door, closing her out, but confronting her in the morning. As a result, she often had to slip secretly into the bedroom window of her friend Carrie Wallace and sleep in her room. Other nights she went elsewhere.

The Kling yard faced the rail tracks and a freight depot building that was owned by a kindly widower, the same man whose large red-brick home on Mill Street also faced the Kling yard. He was Simon Eugene De Wolfe. Florence knew his daughter, Belle, several years her junior, but she more enjoyed the company of Belle's brother, Henry.

Gossip was already rife about Flossie's defiance of Marion's richest man. "You just ask anybody in Marion what they think of so-and-so," said Betty Bartram generations later when referring to the power of town gossip, "but don't ask if you don't want to know." Long years after, Marionites could still recall stories of "how something suddenly went wrong" with Florence in 1879.

If Amos pinned some last hope on taming Florence through the reticent example of her mother, it was too late. He had kept his daughter removed from Louisa's direct influence for so long that Florence bristled at the suggestion. "Mother had ill health for so many years that she was glad to defer to father's opinion," Florence recalled. "Besides that, she was a refined and conservative Eastern woman; a stickler for form and convention that had I to follow closely in her traditional social regulations, it would take much of joy out of life."

If there was a remote chance of Florence confiding any troubles to her mother, it was dashed four days after Christmas, 1879. The death that day of Emily Bouton left Louisa more broken than her father's passing had. It is hard to imagine her being capable of providing support to anyone at that time. Florence had no intimate to whom she could turn. And she was in trouble, real trouble. After one of her most recent "sharp encounters" with Amos, that she reacted impulsively in "an evil moment of rebellious impetuosity." Suddenly she found herself in what a friend called "one of the most unfortunate occurrences of her life." Flossie Kling knew she wanted out. Getting married was a way out. And there was one way to make sure she got married.

Florence was pregnant.

"To sanction the inequity of man, but demand purity of woman, has become an attitude of society," she later wrote resentfully in her diary. She more cryptically explained the situation she found herself in as 1880 began, "Vice often comes in at the door of necessity, *not at the door of inclination.*"[5]

4

Living in Sin

Even her loyal assistant Kathleen Lawler admitted that Florence got pregnant "to gain her freedom" from Amos. The closest Florence herself came to acknowledging this was that she had followed her own "rule," which was that she "was entitled to live her own life."

To his best pals, Henry Atherton De Wolfe was always Pete or Petey. Roguishly handsome with sandy hair, he brimmed with bravado, wisecracking and laughing as he played "chicken dare" on the tracks that faced the back of his and Flossie's houses as the night wail of trains approached. He would "hoot and holler" his way home down East Center until all the neighborhood dogs barked. He was friendly and idle, and despite the efforts of the Marion Woman's Christian Temperance Union to convince locals to "refuse to touch, taste or handle the deceitful serpent," Petey drank often and copiously. As Gilcrest Allen, a nephew, remembered, "Henry was a drunk, the black sheep of the De Wolfe tribe, and to that extent it was hush-hush." Pure trouble, he appealed to Flossie.

Henry was born on March 4, 1859, into a distinguished Huguenot family. Simon De Wolfe, a native of New York's Oneida County, served with valor in the Civil War and as a coal company official eventually moved to Marion, where he diversified into grain and bought warehouses. Henry's easy warmth came from his father. After Sunday services at the Presbyterian Church, Simon passed out candy to the children and invited visitors to his home for Sunday dinner. He sent the family nursemaid, Emma, out with food baskets to the poor and sick in town. The sudden death of his wife, Susan Busby, however, left Simon devastated; teenage Henry consequently had little parental direction.

Simon was also, as Colonel Christian recollected, "outspoken and unafraid, as he termed it, of either the money or the muscle of any man." As it turned out, that meant Amos Kling. Christian continued: "Amos and Simon had several clashes and disagreements . . . as to cause a coolness that was not likely to produce any feelings of neighborliness between the two families." The animosity between the two men may in fact have spurred Petey and Flossie into what Christian termed "their rather intimate friendship," and when neighbors "whispered about that young De Wolfe was paying serious attention to Florence Kling, society in Marion threw up its hands in holy horror realizing the explosion that would follow if such a union were contemplated." Flossie and Petey seemed to share mostly a desire to spite their fathers, a modest mutual attraction, and an interest in skating. Henry, however, was too immature to be genuinely in love. "Henry did not love Florence," said his niece Miriam Stowe. "They just lived across the street from each other. It was happenstance."[1]

At some point in the fall of 1879 Flossie Kling lost her virginity to Petey De Wolfe or—according to people sympathetic to him—some other boy. When, some four decades after the fact, Professor Chancellor interviewed old residents, he was told that Petey "at times disputed [the child's] paternity, which he attributed to another man," but that when Florence "asserted" he was the father, "he agreed to call the boy his son." Edna De Wolfe, for one, always insisted that her half brother, Henry, was "definitely not the father," and she retained a "sore spot" toward Florence because of it. The most darkly malicious whisper suggested to Chancellor was that Amos himself fathered the child, evidently by force. With perhaps the physical violence he inflicted upon his teen-age daughter as the only possible root for such a claim, a man as successful as Kling undoubtedly had enough jealous enemies eager to stain his name with this vilest of accusations.[2]

Florence Kling never did marry Henry De Wolfe. Their child was technically born out of wedlock. Their elopement sometime in March 1880 was legend, not fact. In the De Wolfe version of the relationship, Simon, upon being told by Henry that he had probably gotten Florence pregnant, admonished him to "get her out of there and run up to Columbus and get married as soon as possible." According to his niece, "Henry put a ladder at her window at the appointed hour, she climbed down and into a buggy and they went off into the night."

They may have *gone* to Columbus, but despite the claim of De Wolfe genealogical charts, they never married there. In all the records of Franklin County—for a period of ten years preceding and following the alleged wedding date—after what the deputy clerk of the probate court called a "diligent search of the marriage records," "no records can be found" of any kind of certificate or abstract for Henry and Florence.

If, contrary to legend, the couple did not go to Columbus but remained in Marion, they did not marry there either. There is no record of a marriage between Florence Kling and Henry De Wolfe in all of Marion County in its Index of Marriages, and not only is there no record in Marion, but there's none in Prospect, where the child was born. Nor is there a probate court record listing of any Kling marrying any De Wolfe in the town of Galion, in nearby Crawford County, where they soon set up house. Only under common law could Flossie and Petey be considered "married," though Marionites assumed they had taken vows before a justice of the peace.[3]

Whether Flossie refused to appear before a justice of the peace with Pete because of uncertainty about his paternity or for another reason is unclear. She might have wanted to *claim* that she was now "Mrs. De Wolfe" to prevent her father from legally insisting that she terminate the pregnancy and come home. Whether Amos discovered that she hadn't actually wed is also uncertain, but his reaction to "Mrs. De Wolfe" was swift. One townswoman said he simply "opposed the idea" because Florence was "too young," but his reaction was more vehement: He cut all contact with her.

According to Colonel Christian, "If the young people expected parental forgiveness and a return to father's house, they were certainly disappointed. Neither family approved, and so they were left to their own resources. The groom had nothing but health and youth and no certain occupation." Eventually the benevolent Simon did give his son a job at the De Wolfe warehouse in Prospect, eight miles from Marion.

On September 22, 1880, when Amos Kling became a grandfather less than six months after Flossie's "elopement," he was undoubtedly humiliated. In one of the only two legal documents attesting to the existence of the De Wolfe "marriage"—the handwritten Record of Births in the Probate Court for Marion County—the name De Wolfe, Eugene Jr., was registered in Prospect. Oddly, the names of his parents were left unrecorded, but their residence was listed as Marion. If it was obvious that Florence was the mother, the paternal identity is obscured by the entry listed under the court record's column "By Whom Reported." Again, without listing a name, the single word written was "Father." Also peculiar is that the presumed father's name was Henry Atherton De Wolfe, not Eugene De Wolfe, Sr., and while the presumed paternal grandfather's middle name was Eugene, his *first name* was Simon. Curious too is the name Marshall, by which the child was formally called but which is not on his birth record. Who was Marshall? Eugene De Wolfe, Jr.'s birth raised more questions about his status in the world than it answered.[4]

The fact that Marshall was born "a little too soon" became common knowledge in Marion, as did, to a lesser degree, the fact that Petey and Flossie were "living in sin." Amos was unforgiving. That was now, however, of little concern to Florence. It had been an extremely difficult birth for her, and as a young mother she was forced to take care of the infant by trying to establish a home as best she could.

Mother and child could not have survived if Pete weren't working at the warehouse and other odd jobs for which Simon paid him. The new father, however, did not give up the saloon. "Marriage did not reform the rounder," a contemporary told reporter Samuel Hopkins Adams. "He continued to be a festive wastrel." Some locals defended Florence, one of them claiming that before playing house with Henry De Wolfe, she "knew nothing" of his "personal habits [that] made life with him intolerable." Others thought him the victim. "I understood that she treated Henry like the dickens," recalled his niece. "She drove him to drink." A relative by marriage to the Klings, Ada Denman, recalled to historian Francis Russell, "Far from settling Pete, marriage to the dominating Flossie broke whatever small spirit he had and turned him to drink, a turning to which he had already shown himself inclined. Incapable even of making the effort to earn a living, resentful of his wife and indifferent to his child, he idled away his days and roistered his nights. Sometimes he would be gone from his home for weeks at a time."

There is no record of Flossie's life with Henry, but according to local lore, she did not leave, and he always returned. Sometime in December 1882 several of his friends financed the construction and opening of a skating rink in Galion, the Ice Palace, and offered Pete the job of manager. Excited, he moved Flossie and Marshall from Prospect to a small furnished room in Galion. The rink was scheduled to open on Christmas Eve. Flossie and Marshall settled in while Pete worked all month, organizing a "gala program" for the big holiday premiere of the Ice Palace. For the first time it appeared that the marriage might work.

Then, on December 22, 1882, Florence Kling De Wolfe's life shattered. Pete vanished from town without any warning, explanation, or lead as to what happened to him. This time he left no money, food, or coal for his wife and child. He had found work that apparently appealed to him and still he had left.[5]

Perhaps with the holiday season exacerbating her emotional desperation, Flossie faced reality and felt she had come to a turning point. She later told her version of the abandonment to Kathleen Lawler, who noted that after "she had demonstrated beyond all doubt, that it was entirely useless, that she was merely wasting her life and herself on a wholly unworthy object, that she was battling against a helpless proposition which was utterly impossible for her to make better or correct, she took her boy, to whom she was always passionately devoted, and with characteristic independence made her own way."

For a day and a half, perhaps as long as the food held out, Flossie considered her options. She didn't know anyone well in Galion, but even if she had, she was not the sort to beg. Then, in the snowy dark of Christmas Eve, the twenty-two-year-old mother bundled herself and Marshall against the cold, walked to the Galion train station, and listened for the clanking of the approaching train. She introduced herself to the conductor as Amos Kling's daughter and for the only time in her life she begged. He let her and the child ride for free. It was after midnight when Florence arrived back in Marion, a night she described as "rough and cold," but fear of Amos Kling's inevitable reaction told her that even in the early hours of Christmas she should not head for her father's home. She knew of an empty house owned by a friend's family near the station. She broke into it. Finding a corner, and wrapping Marshall in her woolen dress to keep him warm, she finally slept. "Not exactly a Christmas idyll," Samuel Hopkins Adams later remarked, "but it shows the stuff of which Florence Kling was made."

Pete's abandonment left her more wounded than anything Amos had done to her. For her, that Christmas marked the end of her youth. Years later she remarked only once, with cryptic bitterness, about the "marriage" to De Wolfe, "That short unhappy period in my life is dead and buried. It was a great mistake. It was my own private affair and my mistake. I did all that was possible to correct it and obliterate it."[6]

After dawn on that Christmas, Florence went to the home of her friend Carrie Wallace, whose father permitted Florence to live in a spare room, apparently without mention of rent. She, however, needed money for food. Colonel Christian said that after her "struggle with constant failure . . . Mrs. De Wolfe felt that she could go no further in her rather helpless situation." Thus friends made overtures to Amos for assistance on her behalf. Almost with delight, Kling refused. Although friends continued their entreaties to Kling, so rejected, Florence stubbornly refused to solicit her father directly. As Marion native Norman Thomas remembered, Amos "made life a misery for her when she came home after her first unfortunate marriage."

The crisis did provoke Louisa Kling to act in secret defiance of Amos, for as she heard from time to time about her daughter and grandson, she gave Florence a small but steady stream of cash and her old clothes and those of her sons through intermediary friends. Yet it was Amos who unwittingly aided his daughter most, for he had not only taught her the discipline of survival but instilled in her a strong entrepreneurial spirit. During the first weeks of 1883, with Carrie Wallace watching Marshall, Florence arranged to borrow a piano and began giving lessons at fifty cents an hour. "Even the most reluctant of the neighborhood children were sent to her to learn their scales," a later historian learned from Ada Denman. Impressed by such tenacity, and probably embarrassed by his son's behavior, Simon De Wolfe soon ensured Florence's grocery bills. Eventually she was able to rent a room for herself and her son.

Through 1883 and 1884 the piano teacher toiled grimly as a single working mother, leaving unexplained to students the obvious presence of the toddler. She seemed to will away her De Wolfe debacle. "As far as that marriage is concerned, I never heard it mentioned," recalled John Bartram. Kling eventually grew rankled by stories concerning the struggling daughter and grandson of the wealthiest man in town who were being denied even small monetary aid. Some four years after the child's birth Amos asked Florence to move with Marshall back into her old room. He also suggested that she assume her maiden name and that the baby go by Kling as well. Florence refused his offer.

In the two years after abandoning Florence and Marshall, Henry De Wolfe occasionally drifted back to Marion, never with the intention of reuniting with Florence, despite what Samuel Hopkins Adams termed his father's "feeble efforts to patch things up." By September 1884 she filed for separation from Pete. Ironically, in the processing for separation, the marriage was legally recognized. Even legal separation, however, could not liberate Florence from motherhood. Marshall was a wailing reminder of her poor judgment.

Florence never discussed her feelings for Marshall. Ada Denman later told historian Francis Russell that "once he was past his babyhood she felt no overpowering affection for him." However, she continued to fulfill her material, if not maternal, obligations to Marshall, perhaps to prove herself responsible. "She was determined she was going to earn her own money to raise her son, who did stay with her while she was single," recalled Betty Bartram.

Having learned of his daughter's separation, Amos Kling sent word to Florence of a new offer. It was cruel but practical. Amos would not provide money for Florence to raise Marshall. Instead he would take the child as his own, thereby permanently relieving Florence of all financial burden. In all outward manners except legally, Marshall would become Amos's "adopted son," even using the Kling name instead of De Wolfe.

Florence gave up her son.

Although there would be holidays, vacation trips, and overnight visits with her in a new life, when she let go of Marshall in 1884, she essentially ended her obligations of motherhood. She abandoned Marshall for the same reasons Henry had abandoned her: a fundamental inability to cope financially and emotionally with the premature obligations to another human being. Her relinquishment of her son was to exact a heavy toll on him.

From the trauma Florence came to develop a lifelong empathy for those struggling against societal expectations, and she refused to judge the choices of those attempting to survive in dire and compromising circumstances, for she had been "over the same road." Because she had endured severe rejection of both her father and husband, her character became elementally altered. Deepened insecurity and suspicion—but also a proven self-reliance now fused with her youthful independence. Others professing devotion could abandon her, but she knew that she never need depend on them. In fact, she often distrusted the abilities of others. "In her nervous, highly-tensioned state," recalled Lawler, "she felt she must do everything herself." Having been a homeless mother on Christmas Eve, and bereft of family solidarity, she also learned to function by burying emotional problems, as she said later, with saddening pride, to "shut it away in my mind's secret cupboard and lock the door upon it."[7]

If she hid her wounds, they remained deep. Once, years later, when she saw a photo of a young nephew posed with his sweetheart, she summoned him in alarm. "Aunt Florence wanted to know who the girl was—what did I know about her—were her family, background, ability such that she could go up in the world with me?" he recollected. "She used to give [other young men] . . . the same business-like yet motherly advice. Perhaps her own early marriage and disappointment made her aware of the importance of early attachments."[8]

A seed of feminism had also been planted in Florence Kling. The suffrage movement calling for voting rights for women and eventually other political, economic, and social issues of equality was, at the time of her separation, rising into the mainstream American consciousness. With her own daily survival concerns, Florence did not have the luxury of becoming involved in the movement, but she now had developed iron beliefs regarding the rights and abilities of women to determine their own course without male interference. She came to repeat a maxim of sorts, a familiar signature line when she was discussing the subject of equality, a line that was a direct result of her emergence from the control of Amos Kling and Henry De Wolfe. "No man, father, brother, lover or husband, can ruin my life," said Florence. "I claim the right to live the life the good Lord gave me, myself."

The Marion that Florence De Wolfe had found upon her return in 1882 was at full tilt, forged by the railroads running to Indianapolis, Chicago, Columbus, and Toledo. The Huber Manufacturing Company, the factory that had perfected a steel hay binder, continued to draw a permanent population of workers. That year the wood courthouse dating to Jackson's presidency was replaced with a gleaming, domed marble edifice. On Florence's twenty-third birthday, Amos had celebrated the opening day of his Marion Hotel, the grandest in Ohio. Local insurance rates were lowered because Marion faced a lesser threat of fire—the waterworks had been voted in—and those new rates sparked a building boom as new houses and stores rose on empty lots. A sewage system, paved streets, a new rail depot, and a city hall were moving from blueprint to reality. More than ever Marion offered opportunities. For better or worse Florence cast her fortunes here.

Others were drawn to the town. On July 1, 1882, just five months before Florence De Wolfe had returned home to Marion, a tall and strikingly handsome sixteen-year-old with black hair and blue eyes meandered in on a tired mule. "As I neared the town," he later remembered, "the evening bells were ringing for the mid-week prayer. I do not know that I have ever heard a concert of bells that sounded so sweet."[9]

5

Divorce

"I never lived," Florence later recalled of her early life. "I never had any real life or pleasure until after I was thirty years old, and all that other chapter was over and dead and buried long before that time."

The prospects for a divorced woman in a small town were limited at best, but Florence was successful enough at teaching to survive on her own without help from her rich father. She had a number of regular, paying music students who remained personally loyal to her for many years. It may have been a difficult way to make a living, but it never discouraged her. As one friend reflected of Florence at the time, "She rose, over and above all the obstacles and handicaps . . . through her own efforts, will power and force of character, as well as her grim determination. . . ." Despite the continued gossip about her and the fact that she made no attempt to live up to the status quo of daughter of the richest man in town, Marionites begrudgingly respected her drive. "She continued to be active socially, and was accepted," recalled John Bartram.

Even with her failed marriage, Florence never resigned herself to being alone. "I have no desire to sit before a desolate fireplace," she would write in her diary, "gazing at the dead embers of an unfortunate past." A "stalwart physique" even stopped her while she was shopping one day with Carrie Wallace. "Who is that handsome young fellow?" Mrs. De Wolfe asked. "Do you know him? I'd like to meet him." He was the new owner and editor of the *Marion Star* newspaper.

Florence also drew closer to her mother and better appreciated what she had endured in the name of marriage. After Louisa had helped found a branch of the Women's Home Methodist Missionary Society, Florence joined. "Some people go through life looking as if they were sorry they had ever started," she wrote in her diary, also obliquely referring to her mother's depression, which she realized she too was prone toward by circumstance and fate. "My life has been a series of tragedies and while I have never allowed myself to bend to the heart-breaking sorrows that have fallen me, I feel that much of my unhappiness was in the blood and I have never been able to lay down this birthright."

Florence began taking short trips with her mother, with the *Marion Star* reporting on May 13, 1885, and December 15, 1887, of their visits to Cincinnati. It also noted that "Florence Kling" went to Cincinnati with her brother Vetallis on October 5, 1887, and again, with their mother, the next year. Similarly, the paper reported that she and a friend had gone to Yellowstone Park. The young newspaper editor had apparently noticed Florence too.

The livelier "black sheep" of her brothers, Vetallis, known as Tal, did accounting for his father, but he also showed signs of rebelliousness toward Amos, by taking contract accounts with other merchants, attending Friday night drills of a militia group, the Henry Rifles, and maintaining a secret romance with their housekeeper's widowed daughter, Nona. Her more passive brother Cliff managed some Kling properties but occupied himself most with heraldic organizations; he went on to wed a wealthy woman eight years his senior, Susan B. Wallace, in 1889 and fathered two daughters, Hazel and, a decade later, Louise.

Florence went home for dinners and holidays to see Marshall without any pretense of participatory motherhood. She remained conflicted about him, feeling deeply guilty about his circumstances, yet still viewing him as a living repudiation. "Under the lashing of remorse I have suffered," she wrote, "at sometime or another, the sins of our youth come back to plague us." That Amos Kling now had Marshall upset even his father, who still made appearances in Marion. "Henry was a broken man because she gave the son away," his niece said. The De Wolfes blamed Florence for dumping the boy on her father simply because, they believed, "Marshall was in her way." Yet Florence forever kept two coats he had worn as a child, some treasured reminders of Marshall long after he was gone.

At some point Florence even tried living at home again. Amos easily could support her and the entire extended family. The taxpayers' list in the June 15, 1887, *Star* showed that his Marion property alone was valued at $119,350, while the Huber Manufacturing Company was only $58,912 and the newer Steam Shovel Company $14,300. After interviewing locals, journalist Samuel Hopkins Adams recorded, "By what mutual concessions she and her father drew together again may only be surmised . . . they made up and she went back to her home to become again the richest-man-in-town's daughter. Marriage had not greatly changed Florence. Her liking for the bright lights was not lessened. She began to 'play around' again to an extent which her father considered unseemly . . . a married daughter, living under his roof, was entitled to no more license than a maiden. Florence differed. The old quarrel was resumed." Florence soon left, renting rooms not far from the Kling mansion on East Center Street.[1]

Florence had again begun to frequent the Merry-Roll-Round in the evenings. Jack Warwick, who now worked at the *Marion Star* recalled that after putting the newspaper to bed, he and the paper's editor, who played the cornet in the band at the large rink, went there on free passes because "it lightened the work of running the *Star* during the long winter of 1884–5." He further noted, "The rink was a splendid source of small local news, with now and then a sensational elopement. After a young man had carried a girl around the rink a million times he began to feel that it would be a bright idea to carry her off to the matrimonial altar." Apparently the local piano teacher thought so too.

If Florence enjoyed teaching by day and skating by night, her ersatz husband was floundering. In 1885 a drunken De Wolfe tried to rob a train, then left for Nebraska. Simon posted a notice in the *Star* stating: "My son, H. A. De Wolfe, has no authority to collect money for me." The next year two bartenders were arrested "for selling intoxicating liquors to a person in the habit of getting drunk—Henry De Wolfe." While he was drunk working as a railroad brakeman in Chicago, Henry fell under a freight car wheel and lost an arm. Back in Marion the next year, he was selling cigars, "choice oranges, bananas and fine candies," according to an advertisement. Six weeks later he vanished again, and Simon had to "carry on the business until he [could] disperse of the stock," the *Star* announced. In the spring of 1886 Florence filed for divorce, on the grounds of "gross neglect of duty."

The De Wolfe family believed that her impetus for divorce was as suspect as the incidents leading to her "marriage" to Henry. Not only did Florence never discuss her divorce, but she eventually obfuscated the truth by circulating the tale that De Wolfe had died and left her a "widow" before she considered remarriage. "She brought on the divorce herself. She was an engineer," noted Pete De Wolfe's niece. "An expeditor. And pretty much all for Florence."

One of Florence's students was a girl named Charity Harding, the daughter of homeopathic doctors. The family lived only a few houses from Florence's rented rooms, and she went to the Harding home to teach Charity. The Hardings had their own piano and a black-haired, blue-eyed son, who was the owner and editor of the *Marion Star* and the cornet player at the Merry-Roll-Round. His name was Warren Gamaliel Harding. He was five years younger than Florence.

Romanticized tales later had Florence meeting Warren at a sedate dance "late in the eighties," upon which "a romance began." The De Wolfes knew otherwise. "Harding liked roses. And she had a rose garden at the place she rented on East Center. They talked over the fence. And my uncle Henry was a railroader and away," said Henry's niece. "I think that he was probably intrigued by her. They had, you know, sort of *visited* over that back fence for quite a while—she was still married to Henry. And it's a small town. *Very* small town, so people knew what was going on. You bet they did."[2]

On May 5, 1886, Florence filed her petition for divorce, and a summons was issued to De Wolfe. Later that day Sheriff F. L. Beckley served Henry. On June 1 he filed his answer—and ripped into Florence with damaging malice. Henry claimed that for some time before her filing, Warren Harding "became acquainted with Florence, as did many other men," but because she had thriftily saved money, she was especially attractive to Warren, who hoped to put down a payment for his own home. De Wolfe said Florence "made it a habit to spend hours every day at the printing [the *Star* publishing] shop." He portrayed Flossie as not regarding her married state as "very serious, frequenting the skating rink of the little city and neglecting" him and their child. "So flagrant was her style of living that her father would have nothing to do with her." De Wolfe admitted that he had tuberculosis as a result of drinking but that "the conduct of his first mate drove him to drink." He had wanted "an annulment of the mating" and filed a wedding date "that showed that the boy was born soon after the union; while Florence set up a much earlier date." De Wolfe "at times disputed its paternity, which he attributed to another man, however, [other] than Warren. . . ." When a marriage certificate was requested for court processing of the divorce, it became clear to county officials "that there had never been any wedding."

How she responded to these accusations is not known, but some years later Florence suggested that Henry was not entirely wrong. "The truth about most divorces is that both parties are to blame," she wrote in her diary. "One party is never all good and the other never all bad. Both are to blame and that makes philosophizing and generalities difficult." On June 12, 1886, the court took final action on the civil suit, granting her divorce on the "gross neglect of duty" charge and declaring that the "marriage contract" previously existing was dissolved, both parties being "released from the obligations of the same." She was permitted to resume her maiden name and given "custody, care, education and control" of Marshall, which she had, of course, already turned unofficially over to Amos. Henry was allowed visitation for a half day the first Tuesday of each month, "at his home at suitable times." Finally Florence was told she could recover court costs from Henry. He never reimbursed her the $7.76. Nor did he ever visit Marshall.[3]

If Henry De Wolfe could never be relied upon for financial support, Warren Harding didn't offer much hope either. His early attempts at house painting, farming, and the study of law failed to hold him. The $150 commission he made in selling Amos Kling fire insurance for the Hotel Marion he promptly spent on a cornet. Warren may have owned the *Star*, but it was "loaded down with mortgages and still had to make a place for itself in the community," said a friend later. Although Florence would not judge Warren's worth on the basis of his wealth, there remained another impediment to her increasingly obvious intentions: He had a steady girlfriend, Nettie Hecker, and also liked what were called "unmarriable" women. Still, he was a worthy challenge for Florence. She, like dozens of Marion girls, found something extraordinarily appealing in the genial, virile newcomer to this small Ohio town.

Born in rural Blooming Grove, raised in nearby Caledonia, Warren had grown up in a stable, healthy, and unusually loving family, including brother George, sisters Charity, Daisy, and Carolyn, who was fourteen years his junior; their mother, Phoebe, was a Seventh-Day Adventist midwife, and his sentimental father was a man as thrilled by a simple walk in the woods as by gambling. His friend Jack Warwick's remark that they "lived in a splendid state of harmony" was no hyperbole. "Warren's respect and love for his mother, brother and sisters and myself was beautiful," recalled his father, "a mutual admiration society. Whatever one did, the other applauded." A born talker, the boy was encouraged to enter his first oratorical contest at age four. A year later, when he heard bells toll, he had piped up, "They're ringing for [George] Washington. Some day they will ring for me." Phoebe repeatedly predicted that he would become President.

Dr. Harding, beloved by children for his sugar pills, enjoyed telling how, as a Union soldier, he had shaken Lincoln's hand in the White House. Phoebe had what others called a "magical" effect on people around her. Placing cool cloths on the eyes of Warren's friends who slept overnight at the Harding family's "cheerful comforting place," she had a "spirit that spoke in a quiet voice ... humming some sweet familiar song, unconventional in her unconsciousness of the world around her . . . [and she] tranquilized the whole household," recalled Warwick. This nurturing environment was "the kind of place where young people liked to congregate . . . a refreshing refuge." In stark contrast to the Klings, Warren's parents balanced their lessons of thrift and hard work with indulgent praise, with Phoebe assuring Warwick, "You and Warren will make a success of the *Star*." Every Sunday Warren brought flowers to his mother, even arranging for their delivery while he was away.

The year that Marshall De Wolfe was born, Harding entered Iberia College with an interest in "debating, writing and making friends," according to a roommate. He started the school's newspaper, the *Iberia Spectator*, filled with local advertisements, jokes, college news, and editorials. After losing his nine-dollar weekly salary as a Marion *Democratic Mirror* reporter because he supported Republican James Blaine for President in 1884, Warren with two friends bought the Marion *Daily Pebble*, a little four-page newspaper, renamed it the *Marion Star*, and soon bought out his partners.

There were better Marion reporters than Harding, and he was no "newspaper genius," said Warwick, but none was "more human. Warren rejoiced in reporting the news of births and marriages. He was not at home in writing the little stories of tragedy that come into the life of a town. He could not handle horrifying accidents with reportial composure," Warwick continued. "I wish we could cut out all the police court news," Warren confessed. He had, said Warwick, a "compassion for the men whose weaknesses got them into trouble. . . ." This characteristic reverberated throughout his life, often with damaging consequences. He was of course far from perfect. Lax with money, he was addicted to poker and gambling. Although he was never a drunk like Henry De Wolfe, Colonel Christian recalled that Warren enjoyed drinking, and he frequently caroused at one of Marion's fifty-four saloons. He also kept hidden his bouts of high anxiety. In addition, Harding, a chronic insomniac, suffered from peptic upsets and severe heartburn. Moreover, at all costs, Warren avoided confrontation. Perhaps the greatest deficiency that might keep most women at a distance was his ravenous appetite for sexual adventure. Even his father found this disturbing. "Warren, it's a good thing you wasn't born a gal . . . you'd be in the family way all the time. You can't say No."

Florence Kling, however, was not like most women. Avidly she pursued him. At a large summer picnic she spotted him across a field lying in the hay with another woman, and trotted over to interrupt their love whispers, chatting enthusiastically about the weather until Warren's friend got the hint and left. Warren politely remained, and Florence consumed his attention that afternoon. On another occasion she waited for him at the train station, where he was returning from a visit to his girlfriend Nettie Hecker. Spying her from the window, he attempted to slip out on the other side of the train. "You needn't try to run away, Warren Harding," she yelled out. "I see your big feet!" She drove him away in her buggy.[4]

6

"The Thirst for Love"

It wasn't long before word of Florence Kling's courting of Warren Harding went around town. When she slipped into the *Star* office for clandestine meetings with its editor, none of the male staff was fooled. George Christian noted the "little ripple of gossip" about Florence and Warren "strolling arm in arm" in the dark woods. After a business enemy of Harding's heard of it, he told Amos Kling, but when Amos confronted Florence at dinner about it, she silently took her streamered hat and walked out to meet Warren.

Indeed, Christian continued, the pairing was "puzzling," and he could "only conjecture" what brought them together. Many Marionites found theirs a peculiar coupling, especially given Warren's reputation as "an amiable rake." The gossip at the Presbyterian Church, which the family of Norman Thomas attended, was that Florence "strenuously courted" Warren, "whose efforts to escape . . . had weakened both because of her determination and his thoughts of the Kling money and prestige." It was not long, however, before they were publicly "inseparable," on horseback in the countryside or playing duets. Warren recalled: "I used to take the horn over to her house. She played the piano very well too."

When the courtship was confirmed to him, Kling unleashed all his fury, raging to Florence that "Harding would never amount to anything" and that she was throwing herself "away a second time." If she married Warren, he threatened to cut her off entirely from any potential financial support or inheritance. Again, this backfired. As Florence declared later, "The very lessons my father had drilled into me of careful thought, self-reliance, determination, gave me strength to use my own judgment despite objections." Amos was more direct when encountering Warren at the courthouse: If Harding had any notion of marrying Florence, Kling would murder him by gunshot.

The fierceness of his enmity was attributed to various causes: a hatred for Harding's father because of a bad real estate investment, a desire for Florence to marry an enormously wealthy man he had in mind. Florence's version was that "he wanted me to finish my education in music and thus establish a career for myself. He was so bitter in his opposition. . . ."[1] The root of Kling's disapproval, however, was his belief in a story that by then had permeated Marion. Since childhood Warren had been called "that nigger Harding." And in his attempt to humiliate Florence into halting her courting of Warren, her father, and some of his business allies, began to circulate the tale that the Hardings had African blood.

Initially Harding was enraged. "I shall tell him that he must go no further with *this lie*—that if he does I will clean up the street with him the next time I meet him!" Kling's response was: "I shall be prepared." The fight never took place.

The Harding family had long lived with the story, as did other white abolitionist families of the same region and era who happened to have dark coloring. There were four such cases in Marion's early history. Kling heard the story of Harding's supposed black ancestry on May 20, 1887, when George Crawford, editor of the Marion *Independent,* the town's main Republican newspaper and now a rival to the *Star,* called its editor a "kink-haired youth." Knowing it was a tactic to destroy the competition, Warren's paper called Crawford "a lying dog . . . retailer of Harding's genealogy." The young Hardings had no particular interest in ancestry. Charity had said, "I had always heard the folks say that . . . Scotch or English [is] in our blood. I couldn't say for sure, but have always thought so." Dr. Harding's uncle traced the story's origin to the resentment of proslavery Ohioans for his efforts as a young guide for runaway slaves to the Underground Railroad route. Still, many of Harding's black associates and friends assumed the story was true. Bernice Napper recalled that her mixed-blood father, a descendant of Norwich, Connecticut, founders, "just accepted Harding as a black man who chose to pass white, it was his decision." A descendant of generations of mixed-blood blacks of central Ohio, Mary Elizabeth Moore, recalled, "My family knew Harding's grandmother and said she had the hair and complexion of mixed blood. She was married to a white, and was buried in the white part of the cemetery." Moore's mother, a friend of Florence's, said: "It didn't make a difference to her [Florence] whether or not" Warren had partial African ancestry.

It *did* matter to Amos, and the more he repeated the rumor, the more he gave it credence in Marion, fueling what Colonel Christian called a "social earthquake," forcing many business leaders to take sides. Wealthier, older businessmen with more capital at risk still feared Kling's revenge if they supported the young editor, but with years of quiet resentment toward Kling's financial control of Marion, many younger professional men sided with Harding. With quiet confidence, he felt wholly unthreatened. "I have about decided that I would rather have Kling's enmity than his friendship. As it is, he now lets me alone. If he were friendly, he would want to tell me how to run my business."

"Mr. Kling was on the war path," Christian continued, "and uniting at this time several local politicians of some strength, a fresh attack carefully organized, was directed against the equally determined followers of the fortunes of Mr. Harding." Underlining the personal feud, however, was the reality of Marion's shifting business fortunes. With the *Star* avidly supporting Marion's booming industry and population, Harding was building a solid force of friends, supporters, and advertisers. He had begun the movement to keep the terminal facility of the Chicago & Atlantic Railroad in Marion and stop the potential loss of local income when the Erie Railroad bought it with the intention of moving it to Galion. As Citizens Board of Trade chairman, however, Kling was slow to aid the effort. Harding fired a shot in the October 20, 1890, *Star:* "The board of trade is to look after our industrial progress . . . who is to look after the board of trade?"

A month later Harding was more pointed: "The new board of trade was inspired by the newspapers, but how many give them credit for it?" On January 3 his attack contained a thinly veiled warning about himself and his supporters: "Last summer a public meeting was hurriedly called to consider means to secure the Erie division and shops for Marion . . . men of moderate means, but much enthusiasm and interest, responded to the call . . . moneyed men elevated their noses in a sneering way and ridiculed the idea. . . . It doesn't always do to sneer at the fellows who are not yet wealthy. They haven't been financial barbers long enough to attain fortunes, but they get there just the same." Further outraged by such disrespect, Kling spoke openly of his plan to destroy the *Star*. Harding publicly retorted about the "quiet fizzle" of the trade board, writing on March 26 of the "belly-aching whines of a few members because the *Star* doesn't stop publication."[2]

If Kling could not manipulate Florence emotionally or Warren professionally, he would try to destabilize the Harding family by buying Dr. Harding's pathetically small land speculation debts and initiating petty lawsuits against him. The strategy backfired colossally. Seemingly in retaliation, in early 1891, Harding, Colonel Christian remembered, "threw aside all secrecy and declared his intention to marry Florence, the daughter of Mr. Kling, with the consent of his fiancée." She immediately accepted.

Why, the local gossips asked, would Warren ask a divorced single mother five years his senior to marry him? Ignoring the fact that he had arrived in Marion some thirty months *after* the child's conception, some suspected he was Marshall's secret father. He could not have married her for money, for it would be years before she would inherit anything and only if Amos ever forgave her, as seemed less than likely. Nor would the match open the more select social set to Harding, for Florence was largely removed from her old peers who did not have to earn their living. However, Florence's painful past drew his sympathy. He had a "love" of "anything neglected," recalled his sister Carolyn," 'down and outers' he called them." One bond that forever cemented the couple was their vast capacity to love animals. Warren was tenderly affectionate with his Newfoundland, Senator, and later his mastiff, Jumbo. Once encountering a man with a crate of doves, Warren bought the box, rushed to the *Star*'s roof, and released them into the air.

Harding's decision to marry Florence De Wolfe was carefully thought out, and coolly considered. According to Jack Warwick, "Harding's lovemaking was normal; . . . his methods were painstaking; thorough and practical. This means that he was sane." It was likely that Warren found something appealing in one-upping Kling in the most demonstrative way possible, or simply determined to make himself an inevitability in Kling's life. He may have considered that Kling's influence in the Ohio Republican party might eventually play to his advantage. As a later Marion mayor commented, "Harding was interested in politics and getting involved in the state party before he married. He had a hard time being a Republican in Marion, because it was controlled by Democrats. I'm sure that was an attraction for her. She knew power and recognized the potential for it in him." But Warren's greatest attraction to Florence ultimately came from her intelligence, drive, and ability. Some men choose women to marry because of sexual passion, others for social prestige, still others for money, but Warren recognized that with Florence he could create a superb partnership. He could count on her. She had already put a short-term plan into action to reduce the *Star*'s lingering debts, enough so that Warren could now complete the building of a house, which she helped design.

Turning up wherever he seemed to be, exciting him in conversation, and presenting no potential obstacle to his career, Florence seemed to coax Warren into marriage. She knew exactly what kind of marriage she was agreeing to—or thought she did. In practically analyzing Warren, she recognized his potential at the same time she was cautioned by his inertia; later she wrote of him as "a stationary man" and of herself as a "progressive woman"; and also confided a series of thoughts to her diary about the union. She believed that among a human's basic desires were financial security and a healthy life, but that "Greatest of all is the thirst for love." Aware of the pains of her parents' marriage, and her own disastrous one, she observed: "Unhappiness is the root of all evil . . . meanness, vice, bitterness, injustice. Happiness is the sacred spirit, the mother of virtues. . . . Look at the bright side, and if there is *no* bright side, burnish up the dark side." Along with her commitment to herself and her work, Florence confessed her belief that "the life of a woman is completed by her love for her husband." She apparently ignored any unanswered questions she may have had about his wandering eye.

For Florence, there was something in Warren beyond charm, handsomeness, and raw material to develop her own ambitions around. Though historians claimed otherwise, Harding was a stimulating conversationalist, curious to explore with her the worlds outside their own. "I knew thirty-five years ago that Warren Harding was an exceptional man," she later said. "He first attracted me by the way he talked. He was *interesting*." Although she had focused on the works of Eliot, Emerson, and Shakespeare, Warren exposed her to American and world history, his favorite authors Dickens, Carlyle, and Pope, as well as literary criticism and journals of quality fiction, Zane Grey and detective novels. They read and discussed newspaper stock reports and overseas bulletins, and he even enjoyed the funnies, from which he said he "got a great lesson."

If his attractions to her were uncertain, there was no questioning hers for him. Florence's genuine love for Warren had been not only persistent but consistent. Perhaps the single most beautiful picture of her was taken in May 1891, some eight weeks before her wedding. Her eyes bright and wide, a smile creeping across her face, she seemed to be in some kind of dream. Warren Harding was the greatest love of her life.[3]

Welcomed by the Hardings without judgment of her divorce, Florence found in them a universe apart from the Klings. She was among a family that enjoyed laughter, which explained Warren's deadpan wit, sarcasm, and practical jokes. What she saw as Phoebe's "splendid executive ability" made her mother-in-law an easy mentor. After Phoebe's death and the unmarried Daisy's leaving home to take a teaching job, Florence willingly looked after her father-in-law, even washing the breakfast dishes. The Hardings did find peculiar Florence's growing fascination with the occult, Warren's nephew admitting that they were sensitive to discussions of her "superstitious outlook" that made her "look abnormal," emphasizing instead that she was "business like and to the point." Warren "put up with her interest," but his sister Carolyn shared Florence's belief in astrology.

When Amos asked to see Florence and she arrived with Warren, Kling refused to permit him past the porch. This provoked an acrimonious argument, and she stormed out and marched with her fiancé over to the house they were building. She did so, said a neighbor, "knowing him well enough to realize that it [Amos's house] would thereafter be closed against her." As far as father and daughter were concerned, it was the last time they would speak.[4]

By the spring of 1891 the couple was focused intently on the completion of their house, based on the design of the home of his sister Charity and her husband, Elton Remsberg, in Springfield, Illinois. At a cost of thirty-five hundred dollars, the house eventually had hot-air and hot-water radial systems, stained glass windows imported from Germany, pale green and blue fireplace tiles, parquet floors, and a party line telephone—a convenient vehicle for gossip. The kitchen had ample cupboards, enough space to hold a hundred pounds of ice, and even an ice-cream churn. Eventually Florence had an herb garden, a cherry tree, a rose garden, a grape arbor, mint beds, apple and pear trees, and a horseshoe pit in the alley. Starting with brown print wallpaper and green velvet curtains, Florence chose the furnishings, including a master bedroom set of bird's-eye maple. There were two separate high headboard beds.

Florence had managed to make some of the more expensive purchases with secret gifts of money. Slipping over to watch the house's progress was a woman not only curious but worried about the couple about to live there. Louisa Kling, "regardless of the objections" of

Amos, recalled Jack Warwick, wanted to see her daughter happy. It was she who finally gave the Klings' marital blessing. Considering her submissiveness, Louisa's secret "aiding and abetting" of the union were extraordinary, but she "thoroughly approved" of her future son-in-law and did what she could to see that their home was furnished.

Amos did all he could to wreck havoc on the wedding ceremony, preventing it from taking place at Epworth Methodist, where he was a trustee. The simple invitation reflected a woman independent not only of her father but of her recent past and first husband: "Warren Gamaliel Harding and Florence Mabel Kling request the pleasure of your company on the evening of their marriage. . . ." She was also a bride conscious of her age: She lied on her marriage license, making herself two years younger.[5]

On July 8, 1891, in their new Mount Vernon Avenue house, Florence and Warren were married on the stair landing. In his knickers, the son and namesake of the neighbor next door—Colonel George Christian—opened the door for the three hundred guests. As children raced up and down the stairs, the guests watched the door to see who else had the courage to attend and willingly incur the wrath of old man Kling. As each cautious person came in, laughing cheers went up. Warren jokingly called out, "Standing room only!" Someone suggested that instead of a wedding march, a band should play "See the Conquering Hero Comes." Some guests did, however, suffer serious repercussions. After Kling's oldest friend, Bartholomeo Tristram, attended, Amos cursed him and refused ever to speak with him again. Another attendee was informed that he was now to be "shut out from all loans" from Kling's banks.

Florence wore an ivory dress of crepe de chine with a satin scroll design and ivory satin pumps. She had no attendants. A Dayton harpist played the wedding march and other music. The ceremony, by Florence's order, was to begin precisely at eight and end before eight-thirty. Among her new superstitions was that no decision or participation in an important act should occur when the minute hand was on the rise between six and twelve. If the ceremony was not concluded before eight-thirty, she wanted it halted and begun again promptly at nine. As the Reverend Richard Wallace rushed through the vows, Florence nervously glanced over her shoulder toward the wall at the Waterbury cherry clock. The clock hit eight-thirty just as Warren kissed her. Florence was married just in the nick of time.

If some guests raised their eyebrows at the presence of Henry De Wolfe's sister Belle, it was the quiet presence of another guest that was truly shocking. At the last minute a woman slipped into the house from the kitchen door. Everyone had been corralled to the staircase by the nervous Florence so the ceremony could take place on time. Thus only those at the back of the crowd turned to witness the single greatest act of defiance ever committed by Louisa Kling. She left before Florence saw her.[6]

The next day the *Star* ran the story, "The Editor Gets Married," and announced a honeymoon tour of Chicago, St. Paul, Yellowstone Park, and the Great Lakes. Upon their return on August 1, when word reached her that some of the town's wealthier set thought she would never find the material comfort as a wife that she had as a daughter, Florence, said a later historian, "simply made up her mind all the more firmly that she was right and that she would one day show them all what sort of man she had married."

Actually she had given a hint of what she had in mind just moments after taking her wedding vows. As the refreshments and wedding cake were being served in the dining room, Florence Harding joked—or so it seemed—that she now "would make him President."

While pleased to be referred to as "Mrs. Warren G. Harding" in polite society, the new bride was proud of her first unconventional decision as a wife. "I never wore a wedding ring. I don't like badges. And perhaps it's just a crotchet of a woman who knows women's province but insists on having a personality."[7]

Part Two

THE MARION STAR AND COLUMBUS
1891–1915

... neither the man nor the woman alone can embody all the elements that should go to a properly proportioned career.... [T]he man and the woman, properly mated—and they should not be mated at all unless properly—are complements of each other, mutually helping, supporting and sustaining.... But I'd rather go hungry than broil a steak or boil potatoes. I love business.

7

Business and an Illegitimate Baby

Florence, said a friend, "nurtured and worshipped Warren Harding from the beginning." But she had no respect for his business.

The *Star* was now situated at its permanent headquarters, 195 East Center Street, beside a red-brick church. Dr. Harding shared a small office with his wife as headquarters of their haphazard homeopathic practice on the second floor. Papered with images of Ohio Republicans, such as Presidents Ulysses Grant and James Garfield, Senators Joe Foraker and Theodore Burton, and political boss Mark Hanna—and his hero Napoleon—Warren's office was also here. City editor and editorial manager Jack Warwick's office, the reporters' desks, the composing area, the public service counter, and presses and machinery were on the ground level, which stank of undumped cuspidors. Warren's own tobacco addiction had begun in the newsroom. At any given time there were also "tramp printers" actually living in the work space, and Warren also encouraged local businessmen, minor political figures, and town loafers to drop by and "bloviate" with him about state and local news.

Among the staff were the florid reporter George Hinds, long-winded editor Henry Sheets, cartoonist Arthur Porter, humorist Kelly Mount, and foreman Billy Bull. With all these men of varying talents and egos, Warren had infinite patience, insisting that they worked with, not for, him, as he still did printing and solicited ads. Hoping to have the paper go daily, he began seeking circulation in the outlying farm districts and a cut of official county announcements, "making use of his personality in advancing the good-will of the paper." Yet, falling for every sob story, excusing staff slouching and subscriber debt, Warwick emphasized that Harding was "never the boss."[1]

Still teaching piano during their courtship, Florence had familiarized herself with the *Star* operation when she stopped there for lunch with Warren. She had made observations but kept her distance. After the wedding, however, she relinquished any idea of making a profession out of music. Instead she would make a profession out of Harding. "Once that they were married, Warren became her hobby," wrote sociologist Chancellor after interviewing former *Star* staff; "she poured out her life for him and for the newspaper on which she worked like a slave."

Florence saw something in Harding that no others had. As a *Star* writer put it, "Destiny alone never reached out for Warren. . . . Destiny in his case had an ally in a woman—his wife. She had faith in his future. She believed he had the making in him of a great man. She urged him on and on." She knew what needed to be done. One morning in the autumn of 1891 she simply walked to work with him and pulled out the account records. She cast her "shrewd, accustomed eyes . . . up and down the columns of the books." Harding recalled with understatement, "When I took hold of the paper the circulation was managed by contract. She thought we were not getting enough revenue, so I canceled the contract and put her in charge. The first month showed an increase of $200 in the circulation revenues." He called her "a good business-woman," but Florence's transition from reviewing circulation to the position of business manager occurred simply because she made it happen, in response to an emergency. After only eighteen months of married life, Warren suffered his second nervous breakdown in four years.[2]

Just weeks into their marriage, when Warren humored his wife, who insisted that he bring order to the *Star*'s business, she became incessant in her demands for change. He began developing sudden night attacks of indigestion and had to have his father roused to treat him so frequently that his parents made the newlyweds move in with them temporarily. For nearly their first six months together, Warren and Florence lived in cramped quarters, which only exacerbated his edgy state of mind and uncertain health. In reaction, Warren began indulging in what his friends termed a propensity for traveling and what his enemies called an escape from an overbearing wife. Using the free railroad passes he received as editor, Harding attended Ohio Republican meetings and caucuses, where he spoke and introduced others. He enjoyed the attention his beautiful voice and handsome face attracted, and he loved roaming alone. At the 1893 Chicago World's Columbian Exposition he marveled at the spiderweb of strung electric lights and the exotic dancer known as Little Egypt. Florence stayed in Marion. He also made his first trip to Washington, in 1892, alone.

Despite these pleasure excursions, Warren showed signs of depression. On January 7, 1894, he checked into Dr. J. H. Kellogg's famous Battle Creek Sanitarium, the Seventh-Day Adventist institution in

Michigan, where reverent attention was given to stool samples, vege-tarian concoctions, electric baths, and laughing as therapy. He had gone there once before, in the fall of 1889. During this second episode he was there on and off for nearly a year, not returning full-time to the *Star* until the next winter. Although his treatment at Kellogg's was understandable, given his mother's Adventist faith and his belief in ho-meopathic methods, the seriousness of Warren's mental and physical illness and Florence's reaction to it are unknown.

As Warren was being massaged at Battle Creek, the *Star*'s business manager quit. Someone alerted Mrs. Harding. She saw her opportunity. The next morning she got on Warren's bicycle, rode to the *Star*, took over, and never left. As she recalled, "I had always told Warren that he wasn't getting the money out of his circulation that he should get. The papers were just sold over the counter in the business office. There was no delivery. I went down there intending to help out for a few days, and I stayed fourteen years."

When she began, about seven hundred subscribers were paying ten cents a week. Florence's first order of business, she said, was to "build a circulation department." She hired and trained a newspaper carrier service with a child labor force. According to Charity Harding, "She didn't just sit at a mahogany desk and give orders. She had to carry out most of her ideas!" Through ads and word of mouth, Florence assembled several dozen boys, most under ten, from working-class fam-ilies that would welcome the boys' wages in the home. Some were pranksters and truants who had existed without social structure and needed constant supervision and guidance. Florence's task was to create a small army, with herself as general. With "dynamic energy," said an employee, she "galvanized the whole force into a strong team. One of her strongest assets is her gift for organizing and the driving force of a strong will."

Drawing from the lists of customers who were obliged to come down and pick up their papers at the counter, Florence mapped out several routes on a grid and thereby devised Marion's first door-to-door delivery service, her fleet of "newsies" serving private homes and busi-nesses. To increase circulation, she also decided to use the RFD postal system and have the *Star* available by delivery to the most isolated parts of the county. Her decision enlarged the newspaper's fortunes and thus the Hardings'.[3]

In Marion the children were known as "Mrs. Harding's boys." As reporter Jane Dixon recalled, "Every newsie was to her a potential son, and she treated him as such. She was their confidante, their big sister and their boss. When they fell ill, she sent them bulging baskets of goodies and a first class doctor. When they were well, she made them 'bustle like all get out.'" She also boosted their self-esteem, organizing a social club, establishing a value system from which she gave out awards for achievement and demerits for bad work. The boys were paid weekly in silver, but a customer complaint meant pay in cumbersome pennies. "Next week, if you do a better job," she told her miscreants, "you get a silver dollar again." Her annual Christmas gifts served a practical purpose; one year she gave pocketknives to cut bindings, and another year whistles, to anounce the arrival of the paper as they came up to houses. The boys were held responsible for their actions. When some whittled a fence, she docked their pay to cover repair costs. "Here is one of my boys," she often said while patting one of them; "he will be famous some day."

Generally she had a gentle touch. Henry De Wolfe's brother-in-law Ted Cunningham watched her organize the boys in an adjacent lot before they went off on their routes, "washing their faces and packing their papers." If, while they were waiting for the papers, however, one boy got rowdy, Florence would angrily emerge and begin hitting *all* of them, a technique to encourage them to monitor each other. An often hard and unyielding discipline proved to be the only way she could break down many of the boys' behavioral problems, and most often that meant spanking, slapping, shaking, and striking them. Having been hit by her own father, Florence never had any reservation in doing so even with other people's children. A reporter later carefully described the newsboys as being "under her hands" because "their shoulders and ears and even the posterior portion of their haberdashery were often used as contact points in emphasizing orders and inducing speed."

Florence later admitted, "I certainly did bustle them around," but hastened to add that "those chaps thank me for it and admit that the *Star* office awoke them to their own possibilities and started them towards success." Still, some of the boys resented the hitting and sought revenge. One boy rigged up the press so that when her hand touched it, she got a shock. She lined up all the boys, kept them there until the culprit confessed, then spanked him in front of the others. When another set up a thin wire to trip her, she saw it, grabbed him, put him over her knee, then spanked him with her shoe. When she then delivered his papers in the rain, he feared losing his job and reformed. One newsboy, Smith Witter, took her seriously. "If she told you to do something, you knew she really meant it." While she was "quite pleasant," Witter said she could also be "austere."

Pug Wilson long remembered her as harsh and unkind—perhaps because as an "independent," he bought papers for a penny, then sold them for two cents. "She could be the meanest of any woman I ever heard talking to those newsboys. She was brilliant and determined. She was the power behind the throne, no question about it. She would talk to those newsboys in such a way that if I were a newsboy, I would have quit right there. I would just stand there and laugh, because I was buying and selling. There was no question about it, she was a very determined woman, the way she would abuse those boys."

Even outside the *Star* offices Florence hit her boys. "One of the paperboys was creeping through her back fence to get some apples," a neighborhood boy later said. "She caught him and frightened him with her large mastiff dog. She shook him like hell by the collar. Smacked him up, pulled him by the ear into her house. She told him that whenever he wanted an apple he should come to the door and ask. Then she gave him a big heap of pie." Other Marion children became wary of Florence. Ruth Guthery confessed, "She frightened me. She paddled those newsboys right out on the street." Mike Stafford concluded that the "kids in the neighborhood did not like Mrs. Harding any too well." Later to become a renowned Socialist leader, Norman Thomas, who proved to be the most successful of her newsboys, recalled her with qualified warmth, despite their political differences as adults. "Mrs. Harding, in those days, ran the show. She was a woman of very narrow mentality and range of interest or understanding, but of strong will and within a certain area, of genuine kindliness. She got along well with newsboys . . . in whom she took a kind of maternal interest. It was her energy and business sense which made the *Star*. . . . Her husband was the front."

Ultimately Florence's discipline seemed to benefit the newsies; a majority grew up to become successful businessmen and journalists. For her, the relationship was an outlet for her mothering instincts and displaced affection for Marshall. One boy became the first of a series of young men who entered her life as a kind of "adopted son." The fatherless son of Swiss immigrants, Ora "Reddy" Baldinger had to work to support himself and his mother, and Florence admired his drive. The "red-headed youngster that we took an especial fancy to" became a fast companion to her for the rest of her life.[4]

Florence's next task was to streamline and organize all business accounts. The new printing equipment that was put in place just before the Harding wedding had been bought entirely on credit, and the interest on the debt was greater than the actual debt itself had been five years earlier. Cost-efficiency details bored and befuddled Warren. At the end of the day, if the bell of the battered old money drawer didn't ring to indicate a proper balance, he joked, "All paid in—all paid out—books square." He did enjoy payday, when he could dole out fresh bills to the gathered staff, cracking, "Here's your insult." Livid at the high interest rates that Warren never questioned, Florence dickered some short-term loans at lower rates from bank loan officers she knew through her father. In her bold, thick handwriting, she personally kept the business ledgers, cutting customer accounts if they went three weeks unpaid, and she watched every single penny, packing them into jars.

"No pennies escaped her," Warwick noted. "They may have disappeared before her advent, but none got away. . . . She took them home from day to day, and after the accumulation reached bankable size it was carried downtown and banked. I have seen W.G. marching down to the bank with a gallon of pennies in either hand."

Beyond being circulation and business manager, she sat at the "registration bureau" and handled complaints, "responded to the calls over the counter and the telephone orders which were received." As a friend later recalled, she also "soon was in charge of advertising . . . buying the print paper and other supplies, and even standing by the presses. . . ." One account said that she "worked in practically every department of the paper to help put it on a paying basis. . . ." She even had what one employee termed a "practical knowledge of the mechanics of a newspaper plant" and learned how complicated machinery ran and how to fix it herself, saving all repair costs. She long glowed with pride in recalling the day she had the new presses installed, from which the first profits were expected, as well as her decision to subscribe to a large news service.

Florence often talked of how much of the important world news came over the service by two o'clock in the afternoon, which meant stories could be printed in the *Star,* an afternoon newspaper. When the Spanish-American War broke out, she seized the moment. Reporter Robert Small recalled: "It was Mrs. Harding who had most to do with obtaining a complete direct wire press report, the first ever received in Marion. That was the turning point. Success came in waves. The business was larger than the Hardings had ever dared to dream of. Through all those years Florence Harding spent her days at the office, counted out the papers for the newsboys, directed the deliveries and street sales, saw to the purchases and saw that collections were made on time."

One report claimed that she "sometimes in his [Harding's] absence acted as editor." While it was true, according to Warwick, that Florence "did not at any time edit the paper or dictate its policy . . . did no reporting; neither did she write editorials," she did make some editorial decisions. New reporter G. W. Freeman remembered that his first news assignment came from the "all-business kind of woman [who] walked in without knocking . . . laid something on my desk and left." Florence often suggested stories based on leads that she had or that she'd picked up from other papers. Her "instinct," said a reporter, gave her "an eye for news," and she frequently looked for "items of human interest," particularly stories "that a woman sees and that she knows will interest other women." Along those lines Florence made a radical move on behalf of gender equality, hiring the first woman reporter in perhaps all Ohio, local writer Jane Dixon. "She helped and sponsored Jane, when the townspeople frowned on her for being unwomanly enough to write pieces for the paper," said Dixon's later colleague Edna Colman. "A girl reporter was something new in Marion."[5]

Whatever the male staff first thought of this woman manager, they came to accept her as an "office worker," said Warwick, and she "became one of them in the spirit of splendid good fellowship. . . ." While she may not have embraced the principles of feminism during her *Star* years, in practice she lived them. Later Florence Harding reflected proudly on how well she and her male coworkers had managed: "I believe the womanly way to get what we want or what we know belongs to us is by gentility and firmness minus militancy. When I want a particular thing I invite the person in whom is vested the power for gratifying my desire to dinner and we talk it over reasonably. I was in business with my husband years and years before suffrage was even mentioned, except in a jocular way. No one attempted to interfere with my work because I was a woman. I was allowed to progress in the business world as fast and as far as I could. And remember we were small town folks, too, and small towns' conventions are more hidebound."

The one person at the *Star* who seemed ambivalent about such untraditional women's roles was Warren himself, who enjoyed writing corny editorial commentary about "new" women but often with a bitter edge. As for women rallying publicly for temperance, he belittled their cause by suggesting that these were the sort of women to wear pants—

and look ugly in them. "Now a woman has a perfect right to talk temperance and the good her sex has done is undisputed, but her right to wear pants and make the night hideous on the streets is questioned," he noted on September 15, 1895. Conceding that an emerging social discussion of women's health and exercise was fine, he added, "[W]e're willing to bet that none of 'em will make the cheeks of girlhood rosier than helping mothers with the wash."

If Warren never evaluated Florence with such physical criteria as he did other women, upon his full-time return to the *Star* in early winter 1894, he was not only stunned at her success but awed. Seeking to protect him from relapse into nervous exhaustion, Florence furthermore served as his nursemaid at home, while continuing to go to work every day at the paper. "Sparing his strength, shielding him from anxiety, she took active charge," recounted a reporter who discussed the situation with her; "through her eternal watchfulness, her persistent care of him, her busy spirit . . . he was restored to health." Harding not only realized just how much he needed Florence at both home and office but, grateful for her devotion, developed a strong affection for and attachment to her. They were genuinely a team, and whatever else might later be said for his deficiencies as a husband, his respect for her opinion and independence was part of his commitment to this unusual and capable woman. The downside of this was that she often pushed him to meet her high expectations of himself, exacerbating his nervousness only then to coddle him. To some degree, she was the tonic for the nervousness she could prompt.

In marriage to him, Florence's aspirations flourished, and her brightness blossomed as it never had under the previous men in her life, Amos Kling and Henry De Wolfe. Harding's optimism was the catalyst for her developing sense of humor and conversational skills. Both Hardings loved to talk. As Jane Dixon remembered, "Her wit, given proper play, showed signs of the rapierlike quality which . . . made her a distinguished and a welcome guest. . . ." If in later years he did things that brought out the worst in her, in their early marriage he drew out her best qualities.

Outsiders often assumed that she just nagged him, but Warren encouraged her. "She was very frank. She wasn't a yes-lady in any sense of the word," remarked John Bartram. "He respected her judgment and felt that she helped his judgment enormously in both business and personal matters." Florence could only push Warren so far, however. When she prodded too vigorously, she admitted, he "set his jaws and [said] NO." She backed off when she realized she had provoked him. "This talk about being the boss is fine conversation," said Florence, "but I can tell you I know when to retreat."[6]

Florence made no apologies for defying societal expectations of a woman's domesticity. "I do not like to cook. I hate fussing with food. I can clean out the garret or even the cellar if I must and I like to decorate and care for rooms. But I'd rather go hungry than broil steak and boil potatoes," she breezily confessed. "I love business."

Nevertheless, she believed that maintaining an efficient home was as important as being business manager. The duality between the feminine traditional and the feminist progressive became the two poles of her life. Her ideal of the modern woman was forged nightly when, an hour before Warren went home, she bicycled there on an Eclipse—with new coaster brakes—put food out, and then returned to work. "Every wife owes such service to her husband and to her home," she explained. "When she has discharged this duty she should be free to pursue her own work, her art, her business, but this much at least . . . is her part of the marriage bargain. She need not . . . perform the household labors herself, but she should see they are properly performed."

Florence Harding later elaborated on her remarkably progressive view of spousal equality: "I confess that the family, rather than either the man or the woman, has always seemed to me to be the true social unit. In saying this I mean that I have felt that neither the man nor the woman alone can embody all the elements that should go to a properly proportioned career. . . . [T]he man and the woman, properly mated— and they should not be mated at all unless properly—are complements of each other, mutually helping, supporting and sustaining." If the woman had self-respect and esteem, Florence thought a "wife may very well be content to merge her own career in that of the husband. . . ."

Although Florence did learn to cook and bake certain foods, like chili sauce, cherry pie, hickory nut cake, lemon almond cookies, and Warren's favorite Sunday waffles, and even took up china painting at the Marion Arts Club, her entertaining, according to neighbor Mildred Christian, was intended to "provide a social background for his political career." Except for indulging her increasing love of theater and vaudeville—with free Music Hall tickets given to the *Star* editor—she "gave little attention to the social diversions of the town." It was Warren who played the local old-boy game, buying stock even in unpromising local efforts, joining civic organizations, performing in the Elks' "Grand Circus Carnival" as "the Contortionist, in His World Daring Human Serpent Act." If Florence boosted Warren and the *Star,* he and the paper, said Warwick, boosted "Marion and Marion men against all outsiders

... [A]s the paper grew in size and circulation. . . . [i]f a Marion man wanted a State office or a congressional nomination . . . his cause was the *Star*'s cause against all comers." The *Star* increased only *Warren's* popularity, however. "People said Florence was 'quite a woman,' but never 'I just love Florence,'" recalled Glen Elsasser. Sister-in-law Charity believed the bias was sexist, explaining, "She went to work at a time when it was still against tradition for a married woman to work—even in her husband's office. It shocked a lot of her old friends." Indeed, Miriam Stowe confirmed that women were often offended by Florence for being "abrasive, very abrupt. She had no time to chat, never the kind to pay a call or return a visit. Strictly a working business lady." Even after she did don a floral dress to entertain some "ladies of leisure," they expressed shock at having glimpsed her earlier that day in a business suit at the *Star*. Her thrift was also not appreciated. "I mowed Mrs. Harding's yard, and must admit very candidly that I never liked her very well. She was very cold—and tightfisted. She only paid me 75 cents to mow her yard. Too ambitious and driving woman," Gilcrest Allen recalled. Her grating, nasal Ohio diction didn't help; Colonel Christian admitted that "once heard [it] was never forgotten."

"Florence Harding?" piped up one Marionite. "Runs her house; runs the paper . . . runs Warren; runs everything but the car, and could run that if she wanted to."

County and state journalists thought differently, judging her not as a wife but as a professional. "She was considered one of Ohio's best known newspaper women," noted the Cincinnati *Enquirer*'s editor's wife. Through her work, rather than social contact with wives, Florence also came to know Ohio business and political leaders. As neighbor Margaret Norris remembered, "she met the gentlemen on a business rather than on a social basis." With them, she was "direct, made eye-to-eye contact and firmly shook hands."

It seems, in fact, that both Florence's and Warren's personas were partially calculated. As journalist Mark Sullivan wrote, the general image to the mere "passer-by" was of an "active and aggressive and talkative woman" who "bustled about" on the first floor while Warren relaxed his outstretched feet out of his second-story office window. Harding was not so uncomplicated. His genuine need to be liked and thus avoid hurting others also served his friendly business relations, which had a purpose in his growing ambition to enter state politics. Thus, Florence's image as the aggressive counterbalance served him well. With his tough wife on the premises Harding could avoid responsibility for unraised wages, unpaid bills, refused favors, or unanswered promises. He could just shrug and blame it on "the boss"—and never antagonize potential supporters.[7]

Florence's obsession to make the *Star* not just succeed but flourish was also motivated by her unspoken ambition. As Norman Thomas discerned, "a great deal that Mrs. Harding did was done to make that crabbed character . . . Amos Kling, recognize that in her second marriage she had chosen a good man. . . . She [would] at least [have] the satisfaction of seeing him capitulate before he died." Kling remained the town's leading citizen. His anger at their marriage had solidified into a resolute refusal to acknowledge them, even when on the same sidewalk. The Hardings retaliated not just by ignoring him but by making sure that they walked to work arm in arm, loudly laughing, right past the Kling mansion, with Amos often stalking them under the maples and fuming.

Harold Alderfer, who interviewed Harding's friends, learned that "with every resource within his power" Kling, still feeling "very bitterly" toward Florence, sought to embarrass and destroy Warren financially, politically, and socially. He bought up twenty thousand dollars of his debt notes and pressed for immediate payment. Harding was saved only by borrowing money from his growing circle of friends. Kling was even financing the *Republican Transcript* to put the *Star* out of business as party oracle. He bullied other businessmen against investing in any civic endeavor Harding supported. At the courthouse or on the streets, when Warren was within sight, Amos muttered "nigger." When he did this to Dr. Harding, the old man beat up on his son's father-in-law and knocked the fat man to the ground.

Harding refused to fight Kling. When Kling ran for a minor council post, Warren only gently criticized the "the old gent," now worth close to half a million dollars, because Kling "knew how to spend money effectively" and had a "barrel" of it that he "would open up" to buy votes. Even when the Hardings were in Kling's presence with mutual friends from Marion in Daytona Beach, Florida, for a winter respite in 1893, Amos looked through them as if they had not existed. "My father's estrangement from us after my marriage," Florence said, "was due entirely to a pride of having his own way . . . he could not yield for seven years in his stiff-necked pride to the extent that he wished to exchange visits. I knew he was struggling with himself—that he felt in fact that we could live without him better than he could live without us, but it took that many years to move him to the first advance of asking us to visit him."

It was different with Louisa Kling. After she was overcome by a wave at Daytona, and Warren appeared to help her to safety, she became openly friendly to him. It was, however, a short-lived affection. Just months after her return from Florida, Louisa Kling died at age fifty-eight on June 23, of peritonitis. At the funeral and burial Amos again looked through Florence. Her reaction to the loss is unrecorded.[8]

After a few years of marriage Florence dropped her maternal nick-name for Warren, Sonny, for the more entrepreneurial and remote "Warren Harding" or "That Man Harding." He had called her Boss, but that nickname for her was soon replaced with the imperious one that she was called for years to come by close friends and strangers alike: the Duchess. Some later assumed that Warren had derisively chosen the nickname after the ugly drawing of the mean Duchess in the famous illustrated version of Lewis Carroll's *Alice in Wonderland*. That was not true, but he was inspired from a fictional character. In 1895 the satirical character Chimmie Fadden, created by Edward Townsend Brady, first began appearing in the New York *Sun* as a se-rial story in roughneck dialect. Warren became an avid fan. Chimmie, a "Bowery boy," is footman to Miss Fannie and confounded but im-pressed by her fussy, overworked maid, whom he marries and calls the Duchess.

Warren's view of Florence as the Duchess is clear. Her character was "cool an' smooth," had "curves in der brains," and "runs de money end." Temperamental, she orders Chimmie and others about, knowing full well when he was trying to sneak away to gamble at the races or drink at the bar, taking on responsibility for everything that needed to be done efficiently, keeping him from spending his "boodle." All that was true of Warren's own Duchess. Another parallel was her jealousy over Chimmie's giving "de jolly" to Maggie, a married character. "Dat's de funny ting 'bout women. Dey is never jealous of you 'bout anodder woman what has a steady, but when de odder woman marries de steady den she's jealous of her again, even if you just jollies her a bit. I'd like t' know what t'ell . . . if a steady makes a woman safe, den a husband ought to make her safer. Dat's right, ain't it? Sure."

Indeed, at about that very time, Warren's coded kinship with Chimmie as he gave "de jolly" to a married woman was crushingly painful for his real-life Duchess. It was his first extramarital affair, and it was with one of his wife's childhood friends.[9]

In the brief period that Warren was back in Marion from the sanitarium, sometime before April 12, 1894, he unintentionally got the wife of a local merchant pregnant. The realization of this by Warren and then by Florence may perhaps have even provoked his sudden return to and lengthy stay in Battle Creek so soon after his release.

Warren had long been an enthusiastic sower of wild oats. He was to sow them all his life. At college he had lived in the only mixed-sex dormitory—separated by sealed-off floors—but during that time, according to Marion lore, Warren had his first sexual experience, visiting a whorehouse with two friends. Just beneath the shine of booming Marion were the seamier realities of small-town life, including those shadowed shacks of raucous laughter and women. "It was also a town where ministers tried to steal members and argued theology, where wearing an open shirt on Sunday, you might be yelled at, where Henry Ford was not allowed to build because it would raise worker wages, and where an entire male world existed near the railroad at night: pool halls, bars, whorehouses," recalled native Hugh Cleland. In every way Marion was indeed America.

The most popular spot to find girls was John and Lizzie Lazalere's Red Bird Saloon, near the railroad tracks. That Warren knew it well was indicated in an early edition of the *Star* when after luring a newspaper rival there, he staged a fake raid and the next day made barnyard allusions to it in his paper. In a later private letter Warren confessed that he had earlier suffered from gonorrhea perhaps contracted from one of Lizzie's girls, perhaps not. His dalliances were not confined to the ladies of the evening. There were the young and single, mature and widowed, even the respectably married. While thousands of husbands had such episodes, for Warren it at times almost seemed to become a pathological compulsion. "If ever there was a he-harlot," noted his friend, journalist William Allen White, "it was this same Warren G. Harding."

Several Marionites later gossiped to William Chancellor about the downside of a wife's working at the *Star:* that Warren "saw so much of his wife at the printing shop that he did not bother to spend his evenings with her," that "His health was often in sour condition from heavy drinking and night excesses. Several attacks are known to have occurred of delirium tremens. . . ." Ted Cunningham added: "Anyone that lives with Florence Harding *deserves* extra-curricular activities." Yet when Florence was away from home, too often Warren was also. "One day plumbers came into a home of a local widow to fix a sink. And who comes out of the master bedroom but Harding in shirt sleeves. He had obviously just bedded down the woman of the house. He guffawed and then asked plumbers to give him a ride downtown," said Glen Elsasser, having heard the story through Florence's sister-in-law.[10]

Beyond the satisfaction Florence got from her work, her striving on Warren's behalf seemed to be rooted not only in improving his civic standing but perhaps in an eagerness to have him reciprocate her love to a degree where he could never remove her from his life. For her, emotional fidelity and sexual fidelity were one, but she knowingly wrote in her diary, "A man's heart is like a filing cabinet, each section is complete in itself." Still, if a dark hour with one of Lizzie Lazalere's "floozie mackenzies" could be silently tolerated, fathering a child by a respectable woman married to another man was utterly unspeakable.

There exist various theories about why she had no child by Warren: that they weren't intimate, that Marshall's difficult delivery had left her unable to bear more children. It was not due to her poor health; she had no such debilitating illness until after some fourteen years of marriage. Warren later stated that having already had a child, Florence consciously chose to have none by him and that she used "Dr. Humphrey's number 6 pills" to prevent pregnancy. The most prevalent gossip, but the least believable reason, was that Florence "admitted that fear of her father made them avoid parentage," suggesting that she believed Kling's rantings about Harding's ancestry. "Even if someone of colored blood passed white, many mixed couples didn't have children since they might have a child who turned out blacker than the parent," observed Mary Moore.

Certainly the couple had some sexual relationship, however brief or rare it might have been. While Florence may in fact have no longer or ever had sexual interest in men, she was sensitive to her own sensuality; her bureaus were crammed with private garments that showed no prudish embarrassment about the graces nature bestowed upon her. Warren must have been at least fleetingly allured. He was a man who took conscious note of the beauty of women's skin and pallor, their perfumes and hairstyles, their buttons, bows, hats, and other accessories; he was aware of their vanity and attempts to appeal to males, often peppering the *Star* with remarks such as "Why is February like a woman? Because it never reaches thirty."

In his autobiographical entry in the *History of Marion County*, Warren said that he was "united in marriage with a lady of many social graces and of charming personality." He genuinely praised her loyal devotion, acumen, drive, intelligence, and wisdom and acknowledged his reliance on her, but never in private letters or remarks did he describe or allude to her in any way as physically attractive to him. The closest he came was in mock response to the question "At what age is a woman most beautiful?" He sarcastically quipped, "At the age of my wife."

Florence surely sensed the wall to physical intimacy that Warren created, and she certainly did call him on his wandering eye, some cynics claiming that her attempt to keep him from other women was the only reason that she was at the *Star* every day. "A man has one conscience, one code, before marriage," she wrote, "another after." A woman observant and shrewd about human motivation, she knew how other women responded to him. Clara Wallace, a conservative member of the Trinity Baptist Church choir, where Warren was a member, said that "regardless of the fact that Mr. Harding was married, when he walked by or was in the presence of many of the church matrons they could feel their heart skip a beat or two."[11]

During their courtship and first years of marriage, with his sensitivity to her early traumas, Florence idealized Warren's gentle inability to hurt anyone vulnerable. He continued to strive to protect her feelings, even if it meant withholding the truth. Harding illustrated this philosophy in an 1896 editorial: "Most of us would hate to destroy the Santa Claus tradition. Some of us revel in legendary lore, delight in poetry and treasure the fairy tales of our youth." Those zealously loyal to the Hardings long claimed that their "one keen regret was that they never had any children" and were unable to because Warren was sterile from childhood mumps. Like Santa Claus, the "mumps" perhaps gave Florence a sense of security for as long as the story could be safely propounded—not long, given the pregnancy he caused in April 1894. "Perhaps the proverb that the end justifies the means," she soon wrote to herself, "is the only thing that can be said in favor of white lies."

Only three years into his marriage, Warren Harding commenced a sexual liaison with none other than Susan Pearl McWilliams Hodder, Florence's next-door neighbor and childhood friend. Susan's father was David McWilliams, at 322 East Center Street, now retired from his dry goods store business. Sometime in the mid-1880s Susie, as she was often called, had married Thomas Harry Hodder, but their union proved unhappy, and they had no children. Although they did not divorce, they were estranged. Susan was living right next to Amos Kling, in her father's home, at the time she began her relationship with Warren. Some months into the relationship the visible impetus to finally dissolve the Hodder marriage grew embarrassingly apparent. Susan had to leave Marion to have Harding's child. Their daughter, born in Grand Island, Nebraska, in 1895, was named after her hometown, Marion Louise. Throughout her youth the little girl was supported in part by Harding. She married Arthur R. Fling, had a daughter by him, and moved to

New York City, but died of tuberculosis when she was twenty-two years old.

According to Susie Hodder's granddaughter, it was more the unmanageable lust of a brief physical tryst rather than conscious malice that led Warren Harding to bed his wife's childhood friend and neighbor. That didn't make the emotional toll on Florence less devastating. He may have resented his own passive reluctance to say no when Florence pressed for marriage. Now he seemed to release his deep-seated resentment of her. It was all the more unconscionable on Warren's part considering the betrayals Florence had already endured. How and when she discovered the affair and Warren's bastard daughter are unknown, but her reactions are recorded. There was no outlet, no special friend, for Florence to express her devastation to, but even if she'd had one, admitting vulnerabilities regarding such an unspeakably scandalous act was not done in the proper society of the 1890s. Her internalized emotions, however, managed to emerge in a diary. Into an old 1891 calendar book she now furiously wrote painful realizations about herself, Warren, adultery, the social judgment of women, and the fickleness of human nature. Written between household notions and reminders was the most revealing document Florence left about herself.

Sometimes cryptic, her thoughts nevertheless make clear the varying degrees of hurt, rage, and acceptance she experienced in coping with Warren's serial adultery. "There is no devotion like a husband's provided he is far enough out of his wife's sight to do as he pleases," she noted with seemingly begrudging acceptance of Warren's inclinations, adding, "The happy wife is not the woman who has married the best man on earth, but one who is philosophical enough to make the best of what she has got." Yet, with unvarnished bitterness, she believed that, "The 'misunderstood husband' is he who makes his wife's frailties his excuse for the full dialogue of sins against her—and every other woman he meets." She seemed as hurt by the disrespect as by the betrayal. "A man should be as patient and tactful with his wife as with his business associates." In the end she made herself come to some peace with the Hodder affair, not blaming herself but feeling she'd come to understand better the man she had married, concluding that "I have been a better wife for all the difficulties I have passed through."

Although her girlhood friend had also betrayed her, Mrs. Harding still would search for genuine friendship. Harding's only extant record of the Hodder affair was in a letter he wrote some two decades later to another married wife of a local merchant, the great love of his life— and the new best friend of the Duchess.[12]

8

Friends, Neighbors, and the Mental Institution

During the Hardings' winter sojourn south in 1897 Harding, his nerves broken, again became seriously ill. While visiting friends in Mississippi, he was felled by influenza and bedridden. After he was able to travel again, he and his Duchess went to Indianola House on Merritt Island in Florida, then to the Marion colony at Daytona Beach, where they stayed with their friends the MacMurrays and used the facilities of the Daytona Yacht Club. He tried to relax by playing golf. While he developed a lifelong addiction to the links, by the time he returned to Marion Warren was exhausted with "nervous disease" and yet again, in May, had to be hospitalized at Battle Creek. Except for a few days there some six years later, however, Warren no longer needed to travel for treatment. Soon it was available to him just around the corner.

About seven weeks after Warren returned from Battle Creek, a tragic emergency arose that rocked Marion and nearly destroyed the Harding family. On July 18, 1897, from the office she shared with her husband in the *Star* building, Phoebe Harding was beckoned by local meat dealer Tom Osborne to treat his vomiting and diarrhetic ten-year-old son. A graduate of Cleveland's Homeopathic Medical College, like her husband, she used the homeopathic powders and dried concoctions he did and gave the child a mixture of "lactic-pepsin and carbo vegetables." Shortly after the child fell asleep. The next day an alarmed Osborne called Phoebe again; the boy had not awakened. She thought he was under an opiate influence. She called her husband. Panicked, Dr. George Harding turned for help to a young homeopathic colleague, new to Marion. Meanwhile the boy began spasming and died the next day. A grieving, suspicious Tom Osborne took some of the pepsin mix for examination by a local druggist, who said it contained morphine, and then declared that Warren Harding's mother had poisoned his son.

Phoebe said there was not any morphine in the powder and that other children had used it with no ill effect. The scandal threatened to ruin not only George and Phoebe but Warren and Florence. The *Star* boldly printed that the accusation of poisoning was "rank idiocy or dangerous lunacy." Warren suggested that the boy's grandmother might have poisoned the child purposely. Then the burgeoning scandal came to an abrupt halt. Dr. Harding's young colleague had slealthily been at work, carefully devising a statement more legal than medical. The baby had died of a brain fever, he cryptically stated, not from morphine. He did not declare that there had been no morphine in the mysterious powder. He simply did not mention it. And nobody pressed him on it. If he was not lying, he certainly was not being entirely forthcoming.

Dr. Charles Edward Sawyer saved the Hardings. "This statement," the usually Harding-hostile *Transcript* calmly reported, "from a man of Doctor Sawyer's ability and standing in the community relieves Mrs. Harding from all responsibility in the affair."

Now, with his abdominal pains, mental duress, insomnia, exhaustion, palpitations, fears, and anxieties, Warren Harding—and Florence—came under the professional care of Dr. Sawyer and began a lifelong association that was to have historic repercussions.[1]

Like millions of Americans, Harding believed in homeopathy. The practice was founded in the late eighteenth century by German Dr. Samuel Hahnemann, who experimented with dozens of plant powders and mineral derivatives from which he concocted his list of "medicines." His basic tenet was that if some substance created illness in the healthy human, then an infinitesimal amount diluted in liquid would cure a sick person by spurring the production of antibodies. By the end of the nineteenth century, America had twenty-two institutions teaching and graduating homeopathic students and about fifteen thousand practitioners, nearly 20 percent of the American medical profession, Doc Sawyer among them.

Precise and expedient, Sawyer helped not only the Hardings but himself. The *Star* editor seemed to know everyone: advertisers, building suppliers, insurance dealers, political leaders. Harding was going places, and Sawyer was determined to go along with him. Such calculation served him well. In just the two years since his arrival in Marion he had managed to build up a thriving practice "for the treatment of Nervous and Mental Diseases" at his Sawyer Sanitarium, which many people called "the mental institution."

Scion of a Connecticut family and, like Florence, born in 1860, Sawyer was the first of six children and among his siblings the only survivor. Born in Wyandot, raised in Nevada, Ohio, he graduated in

1881 from the Cleveland Homeopathic Hospital College and practiced first in Larue, then in Indianapolis, Indiana. Realizing the time and cost of constantly having to retrieve and return many rural patients by buggy to and from his home, where he and his wife treated them, Sawyer built an addition onto his house and charged for room and board. He came to Marion in 1895, he said, with "testimonials of the highest character as to professional skill," and established his Dr. C. E. Sawyer Sanitarium for nervous dysfunctions. It was part of his larger Ohio Sanitarium Company, which included a Columbus hospital. The South Main Street sanitarium grew rapidly, wings and verandas being added to the four-story structure, electric elevators, telephones, call bells, and electropathic baths being among the growing list of features. By the new century it was so successful that the company was organized with a capital stock of $450,000.

With equal rapidity, Sawyer insinuated his way into directorship of the Marion National Bank and the City National Bank of Marion and presidency of the Marion Masonic Temple Company. Not long after their acquaintance began, Warren and Doc—as Harding dubbed him— became founding directors of the Marion Commercial Club, which developed "a movement towards bigger and better things and has induced men with capital and sold institutions to select Marion for the future homes."

On religion, however, Doc and Warren diverged. With no illusions about human nature, let alone God's heaven, Sawyer said that once the body was dead, there was no spirit. Harding was highly spiritual, with proper and received faith in all the wonder of angelic afterlife and the natural goodness of mankind, although his attendance with Florence at either his Trinity Baptist or her Epworth Methodist was largely to meet social expectation. Florence's belief in astrology only increased. In her diary she even scribbled her own guide: "Jupiter, good on money matters, generous; Leo, always governed by the sun . . . Mercury, not reliable, quarrelsome. . . ." In her attempts to develop a "sixth sense," the Duchess visited Camp Chesterfield in Anderson, Indiana, a spiritualist center begun in 1886. Many nights, in lonely insomnia, she slipped out to lie on the grass, and study the star formations. She told her niece, "You can count on the stars. They never lie."

Sawyer tactfully withheld ridicule of such leaps into metaphysical phenomena; instead he lavished his charms on Florence, who was suspicious of this tiny, spectacled man with the pointed prematurely white goatee beard. Yet Doc bore down in his self-proclaimed status as the Hardings' best friend, insisting that he was so indispensable that he and his wife, Mandy, must even travel with them and provide gratis care for Warren. When the Hardings were going to the St. Louis fair on free railroad passes, for example, Sawyer considered it a wise investment to pay full fare for his and Mandy's tickets. In his pursuit of the prominent, he studied their fears and became expert on their personalities, further enabling his flattery. If he was incapable of genuine compassion, Doc's word was good, his promises were unconditional, his efficiency was guaranteed, and his loyalty unqualified. "Nobody could be as close," Doc's grandson later proudly insisted. "My grandfather learned what made them tick better than anyone ever."

Doc's hefty wife, May Elizabeth "Mandy" Barron, did the sanitarium's bookkeeping, oversaw its medicinal vegetable gardens, managed the bottling and canning, and served as treasurer. For all the time she spent with Florence as a traveling companion, however, the secretive, unanimated Mandy never became her confidante. The Sawyers' only child, Carl, born in 1881, was not so much as officious as his father as he was pompous. Encouraged to befriend Florence's son, he was singularly condescending to him.[2]

Despite his deeply troubled nature, Marshall De Wolfe, now occasionally sporting the name Pete Kling, had become a bright and intelligent teenager, studying Latin together with his stepaunt Carolyn Harding at Marion High and diligently developing his gift for writing. With his mother's large eyes and none of his father's rakish handsomeness, Marshall parted his dark hair in the center and combed it behind his ears, like his dowdy Kling uncles. Seemingly trapped between a nervous mother and an overbearing grandfather, he could brim with energetic enthusiasm, then withdraw into deep melancholy. After Louisa Kling's death Amos sent Marshall away to boarding school for two years and was relieved to have him spend part of his summer with Florence when he returned. If his presence still made Florence uncomfortable, Warren instantly took to the boy, "ever more than a good father," she recalled, inviting him to come work beside him at the *Star,* insisting Marshall call him Jerry, the nickname he sported with Doc, Tal, and Cliff Kling. Desperate for such attention, the boy soon clung to Warren, announcing that he would be a reporter and writing about news scoops for his graduation essay, with sad irony, in light of how grim a future lay before him: "To scoop conveys the idea to beat to be first, to triumph, if you please to excel in all professional endeavors. . . . The attainments of all great men have been acquired by most diligent and careful application and not by mere chance. Energy, diligence, penetration and alertness are qualities sure to bring success, whether in the journalistic ranks or in any other."

Harding helped Marshall with his homework, encouraged his writing, and eventually helped establish him in a business. He set aside a room for Marshall and gave him a guitar at Christmas, leading their next-door neighbor Colonel Christian to observe that it seemed Marshall had truly become part of Harding's "family." Warren, however, could only get so close. Marshall was still possessed by Amos, if not in spirit, then certainly by the leash of financial dependence. His primary home remained the Kling mansion. At such a crucial time in the young man's development, Warren may have very well been Marshall's last hope. He was already extraordinarily confused about his own identity; he was even listed in his graduation program as Kling in one place and De Wolfe in another. His rootlessness was grounded only in a fervent devotion to animals, equal to his mother's. His proudest moment was giving his "stepfather" the gift of a bull terrier, Hub.

Had Florence insisted on bringing Marshall completely into her household, Amos would probably have relented at this point, but she did not. Since she was never able to love her son openly, her fanatical affection for the dog he brought into the household was telling. She made Hub her constant companion. Louise Kling recalled that her aunt would even lovingly "wash his feet every night before he could sleep on the foot of her bed."

Ironically, while Marshall was never to receive a full measure of parental love, he unwittingly began to heal a breach in the family. June 1898 found a nervous Florence at high school graduation day, but not only as the mother of a graduate. In the commencement program was the familiar praiseful description of the Board of Education's president as "a practical business man . . . who applies to his work on the board the same business methods which have brought to him substantial results in the business marts." Amos Kling was passing out the diplomas this day.

If it was still true that Kling's "progressive citizenship and public spirit" were "fully realized by the people of Marion," so too was Harding's civic activism. Kling's bitter grudge against Florence had reached the point that it began to reflect poorly on the old man's judgment. If her marriage was no romance, it still thrived, and Florence could hardly be considered immoral or foolhardy any longer—especially not by the widening circle of younger, influential Harding friends who resented Kling. The "seven years" of which Florence later spoke frequently were finally over. After the ceremony Amos Kling publicly came up to his daughter to congratulate her on Marshall's graduation. Appropriately, that day the band played "Don't Forget the Old Folks."

In the fall Marshall enrolled at the Michigan College of Liberal Arts. While Florence later claimed that he was "a frail boy," the only illness he seemed to suffer from was alcoholism. "Every time Michigan came to play Chicago," Carl Sawyer's son said, "Marshall came to visit my father. And he stayed for about two weeks, and didn't go back until he sobered up." When Amos refused to send money to pay his gambling debts, Marshall began begging the Hardings, and Warren sent small sums. On school breaks Marshall stayed at his room in the Harding house, where he hung a Michigan pennant and his painting of Hub. After two years at Michigan, he drifted back to Marion and never went back to graduate.

Marshall sometimes visited his De Wolfe cousin Bobby Burns in Cincinnati and vacationed with his younger aunts Edna and Lucille, but he never sought out his father. Marshall seemed just as embarrassed about Henry as Florence was. She would always insist that Henry had died soon after their divorce, somehow trying to make it seem that she was a "widow" when she married Warren, but De Wolfe lived in Marion well into her second marriage. Missing an arm, alcoholic, and finally suffering from tuberculosis, he was unable to care for himself, and his father's second wife insisted that he reside in the De Wolfe home. He died there on March 8, 1894, and was buried in his family plot. Neither Florence nor Marshall visited him or attended his funeral.[3]

There was a tacit understanding among Marionites that the past should remain buried and the name Henry De Wolfe should never be raised with Florence or Warren. This was particularly true for anyone who sought the blessing of the man now recognized as the leading town voice of Republicanism, not only through the *Star* but as a frequent speaker at rallies, caucuses, conventions, and other state gatherings. Defeated in 1892 in a race for county auditor, Harding still served as a member of the Republican County Committee, having first been appointed in 1886. Although he supported Joe Foraker as Ohio's United States senator, he refused to criticize Foraker's rival political boss, Mark Hanna, who had helped place McKinley in the White House. Warren's strategy was to be conciliatory; he would rather arrange deals than fight. It was a philosophy best illustrated by both Hardings' hospitality to guests of extreme political persuasions.

The Harding house, repainted from red to green, was fast becoming a social center. To entertain crowds in style, there were now Wedgwood and Meissen's Blue Onion china and a 333-piece gold-encrusted monogrammed crystal set from the Central Glass Works of Wheeling, West Virginia. After Sunday church, dozens of people might drop in as Florence worked her waffle iron, turning out waffles for them. Christmas was celebrated with seasonal flowers, greens, and pine ropes, each window featuring a wreath, the buffet table of food baskets "continually set," recalled a neighbor, and the rooms upstairs filled with gifts, which Florence had meticulously wrapped. At their annual Christmas Eve party the thirteen-inch pink Limoges china bowl was always filled with a heavily liquored eggnog, and again at their annual New Year's Day open house. In a January 1 *Star,* Warren asked, "Did you get on the water wagon this morning? Even if you can't stick it out for the year, it will do no harm to make the effort."[4]

Despite their Democratic loyalties, the Christian family next door were at the core of Harding set, picnicking and playing croquet with them in the summer, always celebrating Thanksgiving in their company, and spending many winter nights in their fireplace-lit library playing Parcheesi. On her horse, Florence, in "side-saddle, dressed in the height of fashion," recalled the Christians' daughter, Mildred, always yelled for her at a side door before cantering off, and her brother, George, Jr., became loyally attached to Warren. Another Democrat, Dr. Samuel Britton, had a warm friendship with Harding, dating back to when the doctor had begun sending the editor stories of country life in nearby Claridon, where he practiced, which Warren printed in the *Star.* The family of Britton's wife, Mary, were old Marionites, and his sister, Dell, was a close friend of Carolyn Harding's. After the birth of his daughters, Elizabeth in 1893 and Nan in 1897, Sam relocated to Marion. A medical graduate of Western Reserve University, a member of the American Medical Association and the Ohio Medical Society, Sam was named to the United States Pension Examining Board for Marion County and elected coroner. Along with Harding, Britton was an Elk.

At the Commercial Club Warren befriended another successful Marion transplant, James E. Phillips from Marseilles, Ohio, a Marion Savings Bank board member devoted to city improvement: building the Carnegie Library, installing various utilities, street paving and sandstone sidewalking and extending sewage disposal. Rising over the years from a clerkship, he moved to Marion in 1885 with Frash's dry goods, then became a partner in what became Marion's leading store, Uhler & Phillips. He was especially proud of his witty, young, and stunning bride, whom he married in 1896. A Bucyrus schoolteacher, the former Carrie Fulton was, thought Doc Sawyer's grandson, "one of the most beautiful women in the country." A foot taller than Jim, she resembled the idealized Gibson Girl, with a full face, classic features, strawberry blond hair, and clear pale blue eyes. Descended from Robert Fulton, and the Swiss reformer Ulrich Zwingli, Carrie was drawn to the Teutonic character, studying European history and landmarks, speaking a passable German. Her passions were mercurial, and as the only girl among six brothers, she enjoyed being indulged in her every whim by men. In fact, she expected it. For Carrie and their daughter, Isabelle, born a year after their marriage, Jim bought a house on Gospel Hill. Although it was five years before her second child was born, the big-bosomed Carrie was still quite young—fourteen years younger than the Duchess. And Warren took notice.[5]

If, by the end of the century, it was obvious that the Duchess was redirecting her energies to cultivating friendships and sprucing up her home, she could well afford it. By 1898 the *Star* was eight pages—twelve on Saturdays—and had a daily circulation of more than 3,350, extraordinary for a town with a population of just over 10,000. International stories and photographs graced the front page. Daily management was now assumed by George Van Fleet, the husband of her old friend Carrie Wallace, hired as managing editor, "through Mrs. Harding's favor," said an employee. Florence's personal transformation from working woman into lady of the house was made dramatically apparent after she began visiting the new beauty shop on South State Street run by the twin sisters Ethel and Esther Gardner. When Ethel returned from Paris with the style of the French roll twisted at the nape, Florence insisted on adapting this to her own long, salt-and-pepper hair and had the crown waved into a tight marcel. She was equally excited about using the new nail polish from Paris.

The Duchess could also be difficult, as Ethel's daughter, Mary Elizabeth Moore, recalled. "She always wanted *everybody* to wait on her when she came in. My mother and my aunt would curl her hair, one on each side, and two manicurists, one for each hand, and a shoeshine doing her shoes, all at once! When it got busy, they couldn't give her all that attention, so my mother—knowing how superstitious she was—said, 'You know, Mrs. Harding, it's bad luck to have more than one person working on you at one time.' That backfired, because when she was too demanding and they wanted to get her out quickly, more than one person would begin working on her and she'd say, 'Oh, no, it's very bad luck to have two or more people working on you at one time!' My father would try to flatter her by saying she had nice legs—she just ate it up. In fact, she was self-conscious about her piano legs. My mother held her breath in fear that as a child I would say something about those legs."

As Florence approached her fortieth birthday, her envy over younger, more attractive women began to emerge. "Mrs. Phillips was stunning, absolutely beautiful with naturally red cheeks," recalled Mary Elizabeth Moore. "And after Mrs. Harding had her treatments, she sat there, smacking her own face, to lift the natural red into her cheeks and to try to look like Mrs. Phillips. And when my mother and aunt caught her doing that, they would all laugh with her about it. She could be a very good sport."

For anyone else, the change in image might simply have been a matter of a woman who had worked her whole life, found herself approaching middle age, and wanted to reflect the prosperity of her labor. Florence Harding, however, was still Amos Kling's daughter. She was never to lose her practicality. "She developed a pride about her appearance, a haughtiness," reflected a Kling relative by marriage, Glen Elsasser. "But then, she didn't take to fixing herself up until she and Warren seriously decided to finally pursue public life."[6]

Political Wife

Contrary to legend, the Duchess did not simply order an unwilling Warren into politics. Colleagues and associates of the time, however, do recall her convincing an *uncertain* Warren finally to make the plunge. Some years later, while discussing his first successful campaign, she confessed to having had a June 1899 "conference" with him. After their meeting he announced his candidacy for the state senate.

Warren had long wanted to move from the *Star* into elected office, but with the Democratic party entrenched in the county, and Marion City Hall Republicans a tight circle excluding him, his only opportunity was to get himself nominated as the Republican candidate for the state senate seat of the Thirteenth District, which covered Marion, Hardin, Logan, and Union counties. This district was Republican, and by tradition each county chose the candidate in rotation, 1899 being Marion County's chance. It was Florence who strenuously urged Warren to make the run, however much of a long shot it might be. "She got interested because of him," observed Marionite John Bartram, "but after she got interested in it, why, she was very capable in getting him to run." A *Marion Star* reporter later concurred that "unquestionably [she] was a force in spurring him to enter political life." De Wolfe niece Miriam Stowe was more direct: "She had her ideas and went for it. She was the engineer. Nobody in Marion was surprised."

The 1899 race was not the last time she took on the job of bucking up his confidence. Reporter Charles Michelson stated that "she goaded him into running for political offices with varying success." This became an emerging pattern. Even when Warren was doing what he most enjoyed, "bloviating" Republicanism around the state, he could still be stricken with insecurity about the reaction he might get. When a lodge group unexpectedly asked him to address it because its scheduled speaker had become ill, he instead suggested one of two local lawyers. The Duchess interrupted. "Help the boys out, Warren. You can do it alright." He acquiesced, and according to a listener, it was "one of the best such addresses ever delivered before or since in our lodge room." Jane Dixon recalled the Duchess's first campaigning experience, which included managing the finances, as she "entered into the fight with all the enthusiasm and ardor of her intense nature. She campaigned with and for him. She managed the practical part of the campaign, leaving her chosen candidate free to expound his principles and his ideals."[1]

There was also a personal motivation spurring Florence's ambition. Predictably enough, Harding's most immediate opposition came from Amos Kling.

According to a later friend, Kling made his first, indirect approach to Harding through others, declaring he had his best interests at heart. He let it be known that he believed Harding should not risk his business for an unreliable chance at politics. The Duchess smelled a rat. "Again and again," writes Professor Willis Johnson, "[Kling] urged him to let politics alone. Had it not been for his wife, who urged him to keep to his political course, Mr. Harding might possibly have heeded his father-in-law."

Realizing what his daughter had done, Amos fought dirty. "Kling became a power in the affairs not only of Marion," said reporter Robert Small, "but of all that part of Ohio. His political influence was also extensive." When Kling's influence with his friend boss Mark Hanna did no good in preventing Harding's nomination, however, the covert motive for Kling's opposition emerged predictably enough: racism. Kling stumped the Thirteenth District, "opposing his son-in-law's candidacy for the senate on the grounds that Harding was a colored man." The rumor, now infused into the political machinery beyond Marion by his very own father-in-law, publicly plagued Harding forever as a campaign issue.[2]

If the campaign underlined the continuing schism with Kling, it illustrated Harding solidarity. Dr. George enthusiastically put his son's photograph everywhere he could despite Warren's modest attempts to stop him. And when despite Marion and Hardin counties' going Democratic, Harding won the election with the Republican majority of Logan and Union counties, his mother blurted, "Warren Harding, this settles it. You are going to be President some day." On election night a radiant Duchess stood with her senator-elect in their door as they were serenaded with song and horns. Victory surely was sweet revenge, though she withheld comment. Jane Dixon noted, "If there was a drop of bitterness in her cup of success by reason of the continued ill will and opposition of Amos Kling she gave no sign. She had abundantly justified her defiance of parental objection."

Although Florence's "pride in and joy over his first election," Dixon continued, were long "remembered in the home town," it was also recalled for reasons besides the victory. So many well-wishers jammed the wood porch that it collapsed. In its place the Hardings built a larger, wider heavy stone porch held by white pillars, its white columned balustrades wrapping fully around the house; it looked like a bandstand. Here Florence brought out her Victrola on summer nights for informal dances. Though she was able to tick off the names of Boston, Chicago, and Cincinnati symphony directors, she had taken to the era's ragtime music, along with turkey trots, waltzes, and the popular light operas of Victor Herbert and Gilbert and Sullivan; she listened to her favorite work, Saint-Saëns's *Carnival of the Animals,* in solitude.[3]

A week before Florence and Warren's victory, fate had already paid its call in the yard of the Globe Hotel in Richwood, Union County, where Warren spoke at a rally. That morning at the water pump a chunky, red-faced, double-talking master Machiavellian of Ohio Republicanism's Byzantine system was chewing on tobacco and nursing a hangover. Swiping a glance at the handsome Marionite and hearing his silver voice, he instantly thought, "Gee, what a great-looking President he'd make!" He introduced himself as "Doker-de." After a few drinks at the hotel bar, this man with one blue eye and one brown buttonholed local officials and told them to make Harding the rally's *lead* speaker. Although the repercussions of the brief introduction were not felt for some years, it proved to be the best deal ever cut by Harry Micajah Daugherty.

A former Republican State Committee chairman, and two-term representative, a failed gubernatorial candidate, and a prominent lawyer in his hometown, Washington Court House, Harry now lobbied lucratively for wealthy tobacco, gas and electric, telephone, and meat-packing interests. If he lacked ethics, he knew the right judges. Harry knew everybody. Even the cousin of his invalid wife, Lucie, was married to Boss—*Senator*—Foraker. Through his brother Mal's efficiency in shady banking and business endeavors, Harry's financial base was always secure. With his wife ill, and his son, Draper, and daughter, Emily, both alcoholic, however, he had a grim private life. It was in a tall and fat mama's boy named Jess Smith, who inherited a lucrative family department store and a full city block of businesses in Washington Court House, that Harry found his companion–man Friday–henchman–secretary–spy extraordinaire. Jess later was aptly described by Harding chronicler Samuel Hopkins Adams: "He had a passion for texture and color; he loved fabrics and the sheen of silk. Women consulted him on the cut of a skirt or the choice of a shade . . . the snappiest dresser in town. . . . He was a keen businessman . . . [with] returns from his operations in the broader field of political graft . . . timorous as a rabbit, afraid to be in a room or apartment alone after nightfall . . . he could blubber like a child over a slight . . . especially when he had been drinking. He never went in for athletics, being flabby and indolent of physique. . . . He was mortally afraid of firearms. It was his fond pride to be known as Harry Daugherty's confidant and pal. People liked him with a sort of amused tolerance. One flaw of character is to be noted. Jess had no moral sense."

Constantly traveling and dining with Jess, Harry insisted that the door between their bedrooms always be kept open. When they were separated, Harry forlornly beckoned Jess to return promptly. Jess always wired back, signing "Your little friend." Although homosexuality was not then discussed as openly as it was in later generations, many of that era's euphemisms for it were used to describe Jess. When his divorce was granted from tall, red-haired teenage Roxy Stinson on the ground of mental cruelty, there was "joke and libel," according to their friend Aileen Hess Harper. The "queerer aftermath" was how Roxy became his pal, a recipient of his ceaseless flow of stocks and bonds, a confidante who knew of his illegal dealings and where the bodies were buried. "She knows enough," said an Ohio pol, "to hang us all." Roxy and Harry fought over Jess, though friends insisted that both men were—as Harper put it to Samuel Hopkins Adams—"thoroughly masculine" and weren't in any "abnormal phase" together. Indeed, at their Deer Creek Park cottage, the Shack, local resident Louise Sayre recalled wild parties, attested to by a stack of women's hats in a closet—presumably not used by the men.

Florence was at first suspicious of the overfriendly Daugherty—but not yet because of unclaimed millinery. In him she saw a possible rival in managing Warren's career. In time the slick fixer managed to charm even her. With the guidance of dandy Jess, she also began to indulge in a rather lavish wardrobe, customized by dressmakers and appropriate for capital life. When the Ohio Assembly gathered for its first day on January 1, 1901 (assuming duty took place more than a year after the election), Warren diplomatically said, he "took her with me," but after his affair with Susie Hodder, Florence Harding had put into practice the maxim of her political career: "Never let a husband travel alone."

Promptly upon their arrival in Columbus, Florence took Warren to the store of the prestigious Paul Gettum, where she purchased him appropriately tailored suits, arranging his public appearance. They lived in a parlor-bedroom suite at the Great Southern Hotel across the street from the statehouse. Along with them came their "surrogate son," Reddy Baldinger, to serve first as Warren's senate page and later as general legislature page. The Duchess made certain that he sent his five-dollar-a-week earnings back to his poor mother at home, who saved for his eventual education at Staunton Military Academy in Virginia.

Florence attempted never to let Warren out of her sight—even if it meant watching legislative proceedings from the gallery. When he took day excursions, she went with him, and they often dropped in on other newspaper offices, where Florence took notes on management and reported them back to editor Van Fleet. On occasion she returned to Marion and the *Star* office, and when she learned that Warren had left an order never to boast in print of his work as senator, she overrode it. "Well, just now I am boss. Forget that old order. I'll take the responsibility." Otherwise Florence found herself with more free time than she had ever had, enough to let her imagination wander—along with her fears. It was in Columbus that she began her habit of consulting an astrologer regularly.[4]

Since the seventy-fourth session of the Ohio Assembly was to meet only until April 16, 1901, and not again until after the November election, few legislative wives moved to Columbus with their husbands, and many of Ohio's leading political figures thus had the chance to take a first and unobstructed notice of Florence. Democrat Alfred M. Cohen recollected, "Mrs. Harding was the companion of her husband during his term as State Senator, and was with him during the entire session. Mrs. Cohen likewise accompanied me, and the friendship of Senator Harding and myself was extended similarly between Mrs. Harding and Mrs. Cohen. They were constantly together." Both Hardings also formed a lifelong friendship with the assembly clerk Frank Edgar "Ed" Scobey and his wife, Mary, as well as with Malcolm Jennings, the clever assistant clerk, and his wife, Ethel. It was not these people but rather the glib glad-handers who came to drink, smoke cigars, and play poker in their suite, and were always eager to please Warren whom Florence mistrusted. She had learned her suspicions from Amos on his climb to power. Journalist and Harding friend Mark Sullivan left an unflattering but undoubtedly honest recollection of the new political wife: "As a wife, she had that particular kind of eagerness to make good which, in a personality that is at once superficial and unsure of itself, sometimes manifests itself in a too strenuous activity, a too steady staying on the job. Daytimes she bustled, sparrow-like, in and out of Harding's office with pert chatter to him and his friends. Evenings at home she sat in at the games of bridge and poker, or, if she were unneeded as a player, kept the glasses filled, always brightly jabbering. In appearance she was a little too mechanically marcelled, too shinily rouged and lipsticked, too trimly tailored. Towards her, Harding was always gravely deferential, and his men friends learned to be the same. They, and he, always addressed her as 'Duchess' and gave her a deference and eminence appropriate to the fantastic title."

It was not only the *men* of Columbus, however, who worried Florence. "She was at all times jealous and at most time suspicious of Harding," a friend—probably Van Fleet—told Sullivan, who witnessed and further observed: "The too-hecticly active-minded Mrs. Harding . . . [had] a busying quality . . . coupled with a desire to be always where her husband was, always showing to the public, and to herself, her possession of her handsome mate. It had, too, the motive of safeguarding her possession; her presence near him was a 'No Trespassing' sign, not unneeded. . . . Harding's habitual manner of grave respect toward her may have been the atonement a husband sometimes unconsciously pays for having let his inner heart admit to itself that his marriage entails living up to a bargain that might have been better. A good many exercises of quiet patience must have entered into the induration that enabled him to endure the harsh, catarrhal r's of her half-commanding, half-archly playful, 'Now Warren—' From other women, bemused by his vital maleness and handsome figure, he had heard tones more seductive."

Her fears were not unfounded. As Marionite John Schroeter delicatly put it, Harding was "popular . . . in certain pleasantly unmentionable places." He heard about Harding in Columbus: "There was all kinds of entertainment being thrown their way by the lobbyists—for railroads, the gas companies—all seeking their influence. This was not real life. By nature he was slightly amoral. It's easy to see how Harding and women had an affinity in Columbus." Even Doc Sawyer's grandson knew about "an office girl" in Columbus whom "Harding often went into 'the dark' with."[5]

Because he did not stir the rancor that arises from political zealotry—although he was initally progressive on some issues—Harding was extraordinarily popular, personally and politically. His most winning quality was his ability to bridge any intraparty chasm, or at least appear to, with his artfully phrased words and genuine friendliness. Though he was a direct disciple of Boss Foraker, he managed never to alienate himself from Boss Hanna. He was reelected in 1901, an unprecedented occurrence for that seat. Despite his private contention that his best was "not quite good enough for the Duchess," she encouraged such tactical middle ground rather than his taking a larger gamble as some fervid leader of a cause. It reflected her own pragmatism. "The more we are opinionated," she stated with lofty abstraction, "the less able we are to plump the depths of truth."

Nevertheless, except for her social cultivation of Governor George Nash, the next move up the political ladder was due entirely to Warren. On January 16, 1903, just days after beginning his second term as senator, Harding announced his bid for the governorship. Boss Hanna having other plans, the nomination and victory went to Cleveland banker Myron Herrick, but after willful and unrelenting pressure at the June convention in Columbus, Warren was nominated for the lieutenant governorship, a post he won that fall. When the Hardings returned to Marion from a lavish victory dinner in Columbus, the large staff of *Star* employees gathered to welcome them at the train station. Anticipating their assumptions about the new Harding prosperity, Florence—who had again managed campaign financing—dashed any notion of the traditional fifty cents' pay hike that came annually. "You needn't look for a raise this time. That little show cost us $1,300!"[6]

After being sworn in on January 11, 1904, Harding continued to live with Florence in their hotel suite; as their social and political contacts quickly expanded beyond Ohio, she was always there, "unostensibly but unshrinkingly." They were overnight guests at the mansion of the newly elected governor Herrick. There would soon be trips to New Hampshire, Nova Scotia, and Bermuda, the last with Marionites including Jim and Carrie Phillips. After assembly clerk Ed Scobey moved to Mercedes, Texas, the Hardings made frequent sojourns to his ranch there, and after Mary's death they attended his wedding to his second wife, Evalinda. Congressman Nicholas Longworth, of the prestigious old Cincinnati family, invited them to visit; he took to Warren instantly. Harding was now often in Washington, and according to Assistant Treasury Secretary Charles Hilles, "On all of these trips he was accompanied by Mrs. Harding." On her first trip to the national capital, she marveled at the gleaming white marble Beaux-Arts Union Station, just opened in 1903.

The Ohio lieutenant governor began earning national attention as one of the most popular speakers touring the Chautauqua circuit, the traveling summer festival of lectures, speeches, and performances by prominent political, social, and entertainment figures that went from town to town throughout the heartlands. Nebraska, Iowa, Missouri, Michigan—from brown duckcloth tents to sweaty auditoriums of clacking wood folding chairs, both Hardings were seemingly everywhere. Irritated by the blistering heat of the plains and bumpy, dusty rides, however, Florence nagged an equally discomforted Warren. After once enduring her squawks about his cigar, posture, and suit, he finally burst out with "Goddammit, shut up!" Others were tested by her rigid accounting for reimbursements. Chautauqua manager Harry P. Harrison recollected, "Chautauqua people did not like Harding's wife. She was demanding and most talent had heard her say—or at least had heard from somebody else who heard her say—that 'the way to keep a husband is never to let him travel alone.' Taking her own advice she spent weeks each summer on the road with him."

Florence now saw more of the recently reconstructed Marion Union Station than she did the *Star* offices. The only negative aspect to politics for both Hardings was that it kept them from exploring the world on lengthy expeditions beyond a winter trip to the islands. After hearing about friend Ed Stowe's adventures of the Yukon gold rush, Warren's desire to see Alaska was superseded only by the near obsession of Florence to go there. They began sending for travel schedules and brochures of every faraway place their imaginations brought them.

Whenever foreign visitors came to town, they were often encouraged to call on the lieutenant governor–editor. Marion's Harding pride grew in proportion to his prestige. One Ohio paper even mentioned how Marionites believed he would someday run for President.

If Marion's fading leading citizen had relented enough to speak to Florence after Marshall's graduation, he now realized it was bad business to bad-mouth the lieutenant governor. After Warren's election was certain, Amos Kling let it be known the Hardings could pay a call. "Hand in hand," Jane Dixon remembered, "Florence and Warren Harding went back to the big limestone mansion to eat of the fatted calf, to rejoice in the roles of favorite children." While Kling had relented for practical purposes, he now came to know and like Harding as a person. He also did not entirely relent. At a men's dinner he commented, "My daughter married a nigger, but he's a smart nigger."[7]

When in Marion, the Hardings were apt listeners in the Chautauqua tent. Warren served as Marion Chautauqua president, and Jim Phillips was on the executive committee. Not to be left out, Doc Sawyer had Warren nominate him as vice-president. The obsequious Doc, in his overreaching manner, tended to overlook Florence's more irksome qualities and defended her more effusively against critics than Warren himself did. Even his son Carl and even later Carl's son long denied the "cold, taciturn autocrat" impression of her, claiming it was created by "bitter" journalists "who had known her biting wrath." Whatever else could be said about Doc, his devotion to Florence proved itself absolute. Whether it was her Columbus or Chautauqua critics, the hectic travel schedule, or other unspoken anxieties, early in 1905 there was ample stress on Florence Harding to provoke the first major illness of her life.

Occurring in the midst of Warren's dicey maneuverings to somehow capture the next gubernatorial nomination, Florence's illness was catastrophic enough for him not only to cancel their planned Caribbean trip but to stay home with her. When he next went to Columbus, it was to bring his dying wife there for emergency surgery on February 24.

Florence's kidneys had stopped functioning. The illness, nephritis, resulted from a "floating" kidney, an apparent birth defect, which meant that because it was slightly smaller, the organ was not stationary. Turned just slightly, it blocked the tubular passage that permits the proper dispelling of toxins. These poisonous toxins then seeped into the general system. If enough of it circulated into the blood, it meant death. Stress could provoke a recurrence. In an era without antibiotics, surgery was risky, but Doc Sawyer saw no alternative to removal of the bad kidney. She was rushed to Grant Hospital.

With Dr. James Fairchild Baldwin, Florence was in the best hands. Having pioneered the use of nitrous oxide as a local anesthetic, he was a renowned modern surgeon and women's health specialist, who perfected the hysterectomy, developed postop gynecological plastic surgical techniques, and performed Columbus's first successful cesarean. He founded the Columbus *Medical Journal* and made the city a national center for the study of surgery. Baldwin had opened Grant Hospital in 1900; by the time of Florence's admission it was the world's largest private hospital. With private rooms and marble baths, it was the utmost in sanitary and modern surgery and postsurgery care.

Ultimately, because of the heart damage Florence had suffered, Baldwin decided not to remove the kidney, contrary to later belief, but to "wire" it into place. For Florence, the illness was a first, terrifying confrontation with death. "By the hints of mortality and by the infirmaties [*sic*] of a life of sorrow and fatigue, I have reason to think I am not a great way off from, if not very near to, the great occasion of eternity," she wrote in her diary. "The time may not be long before I embark on the last voyage." She was confined to her hospital bed for weeks and then restricted to her room there for just over five months. Her open wound was cleaned and dressed twice daily. She later credited the experience with giving her a palpable empathy for any human confined to a hospital. It also revived old insecurities. Her hands and ankles swollen, her hair now gray, she developed a fanatical meticulousness about her appearance and an aversion to being photographed. She had to master her general nervousness or else be threatened with recurrences.

Jane Dixon later suggested that it had been at Warren's urging that Florence accepted Amos Kling's invitation to call at his home and reconcile. Perhaps also at Warren's prompting, a telegram arrived at Grant Hospital for Florence from a lonely widower in Florida: "Be calm cheerful and full of hope for you will surely be well again." Unwittingly Amos Kling had again challenged his daughter. Her most serious complication from her illness was not medical. Convalescing, she could no longer keep Warren company, and he took advantage of the opportunity. As she lay in her Columbus hospital bed, she could now only guess where Warren lay in Marion.[8]

10

Adultery Again

Like many other parents who had lost a young child, Jim and Carrie Phillips had been having marital difficulties following the 1904 death of their two-year-old Little Jim. Many, including the Duchess, had called with their sympathies, but not even Jim's constant attentiveness could pull Carrie out of the house and her depression. The death had left him numb too. After a year of this stress he was teetering on nervous collapse. That was why Warren Harding sent him away from his wife.

Harding insisted that Jim rest at the reliable Battle Creek Sanitarium, not the nearby Sawyer Sanitarium, from which he might have run his store, seen his family, but ignored his health. With Florence in the Columbus hospital, Warren said he could look after Jim's daughter and wife. Indeed, Warren called on Carrie, alone in her home.

With their spouses away, Warren and Carrie quickly discovered that they not only were lonely and liked each other's company but were immediately, overwhelmingly attracted sexually to each other. Their desire was consummated simply one afternoon. They went to her bedroom. They kissed, groped, and disrobed. "Fate timed that marvelous coincidence," he later recalled to her of their physical union. "It was impossible for us to have planned, and I count it to be the best-remembered moment of my existence."

They were neighbors. They were married. They gave way to all carnal passion. Warren began furtively to court Carrie, the unsuspecting Marion mailman his accomplice. In his first love letter to his "Dearie," Warren confessed not only sexual compatibility with Carrie but his lack of it with Florence. "I want to weld bodies, unite souls, I want the divine embrace, the transcending union, the blissful affinity, and with them all the excruciating joy and unspeakable sweetness that I never did know," he wrote her, "and can only know when fastened by you."

Stuck in the Columbus hospital, Florence could suspect one of Lizzie's floozies as filling Warren's desires back home. But it would be unfathomable to her that a year after she had comforted her friend Carrie, the bereaved mother would find solace in the arms of Warren Harding.[1]

In June, when a recuperated Florence returned home, Warren took her to Jamaica for ten days. Afterward, however, she was unable to resume the hard travel of the Chautauqua summer circuit with Warren, and he went out on the road alone. At least that was what he told her. It was not long before Carrie began slipping away to safely distant Ohio towns to meet him in hotel rooms. If Florence asked about his leisure time, he protectively pulled out a small white lie. "[W]ith his placid disposition and reluctance to face unpleasant situations," Harding friend and journalist Mark Sullivan noted, "he let her have her own way, or appear to have it, oftener than most men would have. . . ."

When Jim was away, Warren met Carrie in her bedroom, but more often it was at night in her garden; they were so careful that no neighbor yet suspected his "detours from the primrose path," as one later put it. When Jim returned, Warren's passions were limited to letters—a risk considering that Jim could have easily found them—yet Warren could glance at Carrie while the two couples took motor trips in the country-side.

Warren had become one of the first in Marion to buy an auto-mobile, a green six-passenger Stevens-Duryea motorcar, and he learned not only to change tires but to drive at top speed. Often he drove himself to his speaking engagements, once even to Gettysburg, Pennsylvania, on the anniversary of the Civil War battle. Given honorary membership in a chauffeurs' association, he wrote solemnly in the *Star:* "Every day there is a grist of fatal automobile accidents in the daily press. There will continue to be until people concerned about their safety refuse to ride with fool drivers . . . the fevered lunatics that drive in madness scat-ter death traps all over the land." Yet his driver, Frank Blacksten, re-ported, "Don't let anybody tell you the boss is slow. Say, one night we were coming back from Columbus and a fellow was hogging the road in front of us. I kept blowing the horn. . . . Finally the boss says, 'Here gimme that wheel,' and he gave a blast of the horn and stepped on the gas and we went by that fellow and took one of his fenders with us."

Both Frank and his wife, Berenice, hired as housekeeper, were full-time live-in servants for the Hardings, along with African-American cook Inez McWhorter. They could easily afford the help and the car, having reorganized internal finances at the *Star,* creating the Harding Publishing Company with capital stock set at a par value of eighty thousand dollars, of which they kept 75 percent, with the rest offered to employees, now unionized. In a September letter to his sister Carolyn, now married to a Seventh-Day Adventist missionary, Heber Votaw, and in India, Harding wrote that he had been preoccupied with Florence, who had been home from the hospital for only two months. Harding had managed their home on his own until the servants were finally hired, and he took Florence on Sunday drives through the country. Railroad trips didn't discomfort Florence as much, and by fall she was often off on her own, as a board member of a work training center for under-privileged young women. Her health prevented her from riding, but she sentimentally kept her childhood horse, Billy, and when a fire burned the stable, Warren remarked, "If we had lost Billy I think Florence would have had nervous fits."

With all of Harding's sisters now out of Marion, and her brother Cliff's wife Suzie Kling never being close to her, Florence had no intimates. Although she was a member of the Twigs women's club, one of them said Florence was "different from the other ladies" and had no particular friend. During her recovery, if there was any woman whom Florence Harding seemed to begin to trust, it was the mutual friend of hers and Warren's—Carrie Phillips. They began to travel and shop together, apart from their husbands. "Loyalty to friends," thought Jane Dixon, was "the dominant force in Florence Harding's character."

Another Marion woman earned Florence's respect for her work ethic. The first reader of the local Christian Scientist Church and wife of the local coroner, Warren's friend Sam, Mary Williams Britton was trying to help build her husband's medical practice, not unlike the way Florence had helped build the *Star*'s circulation. "Mrs. Harding was very close to the Brittons," noted a later Marion mayor. Mary tried to imbue her children with her own modest practicality. She succeeded with all but her middle girl. As local children walked to school, Philamen Gregg remembered Howard Britton fondly and Jeanette as a "nice kid," but "that Nan—she was a very nervy person . . . Helen Grigsby was in Nan's class. Helen said that when the girls all got together, Nan barged in, took over, made herself the queen bee. She was not particularly popular in her own circle."[2]

Despite the era's romanticization of the Gibson Girl, nervy girls weren't limited to Marion. Following the January 8, 1906, swearing in ceremony of his successor as lieutenant governor, having been thwarted early in his attempts to gain the governorship, Harding took Florence to winter in Cuba. There they first met the world's most famous nervy girl, newlywed "Princess" Alice Roosevelt, President Theodore Roosevelt's daughter and the new wife of Warren's friend Congressman

Nick Longworth. Witty but desperate for attention, Alice Roosevelt Longworth smoked on rooftops and swam in evening gowns. No details of their first meeting survive except for Florence's memory of the "vivid sunshine" around them. Then, in Florida, Amos Kling let the Hardings use his Daytona house. "Florence got down here safely, stood the trip well, and is improving," Warren wrote a cousin in early 1906. "We are living in her father's house here, keeping house as at home." While the Hardings were in Florida, however, Florence's father remained in Marion. The seventy-three-year-old Kling took this opportunity to marry a widow thirty-eight years his junior, Caroline Beatty Denman.

As Warren wrote to Carolyn, Amos's marriage did "fuss" Florence quite a bit, "but it is no matter. She didn't marry to please her father, and must not expect him to remain a widower to please her." Florence had no need to worry about her inheritance, however. On June 12, 1906, Amos drew up a prenuptial contract stating that upon his death Mrs. Denman was to receive none of his fortune. She signed it a month later. Others attributed Kling's softening to his new wife, one local person claiming Carolyn Denman believed that Amos still had too much rage against the Hardings and, fearing that the stress was "shortening his life[,] . . . persuaded him to allow his daughter to come to see him occasionally." There were other signs that Kling was human. He had formed a friendship with a bright, little neighbor boy Teddy De Wolfe, the grandson of Simon De Wolfe. Unaware of family feuds, Teddy always dropped by to see old Amos, and when the nine-year-old died of spinal meningitis, Kling broke down and called on his onetime adversary, Simon.

Amos went further yet, naming Florence his primary heir and beneficiary. It spoke volumes about his now-overt respect for her acumen and his acceptance of Warren. Even unctuous Doc tried to weave himself into the breach healing, asking Warren to tell Kling that the Sawyers wouldn't be making it to Daytona. By 1907 Kling formally wrote to Warren apologizing for his past malice, ending his letter: "This is a duty as well as a pleasure on which I ought to have realized long ago." Eventually he signed letters to Warren as "Daddy." He went even further, offering to take Florence and Warren to Europe with him and his new wife—and *pay for all of it.*[3]

On July 30, 1907, the Klings and Hardings left Marion for the Old World, via New York, where Florence took a brief detour to see the metropolis's famous elevated train before catching a hack to the West Side piers, where she joined Warren and the Klings and boarded the SS *Arabic*. Their six-week itinerary had them all over England, then Berlin, Dresden, Munich, Nuremberg, and on to Vienna and Switzerland, with ten days in Paris and its environs. Warren kept busy scribbling letters, including a rather coded one to Carrie Phillips, but wrote his sister Carolyn that although Florence had promised to write to her as well, "she is the laziest mortal on this trip that I have ever met, and I won't believe she has written until the thing is done." Indeed she did not, but in a rambling letter to Coonie Christian, Colonel Christian's wife, Warren painted the scenes of their crossing and revealed his wandering eye:

> . . . Glorious days, beautiful nights . . . the women dreaming of things they are going to buy. There is no prospect of unhappiness until they wake up. . . . Kling is kicking because they have no general, public drinking tanks. . . . Florence and I are writing in the library and lounging room, as large as the Sawyer Sanitarium dining room. Her father is sleeping just by, and Florence had to awaken him because a group of passengers were gambling whether it was a fog horn or a man snoring which they heard. . . . We are to return on the fastest vessel afloat, the *Kaiser Wilhelm II* . . . but the excess fare we had to pay made two women wanting new dresses faint to think about. . . . White, the chewing-gum millionaire, with the dizzy blonde who succeeded his divorced wife, is along with his valet and her maid, but I would rather sleep with Hub than his blonde. . . . Tell the Colonel . . . I'll think of him when I see the English bar maids and recall his Presbyterian advice when the girls kick their highest in Paris.

In Europe the Duchess bought new house furnishings and table services, Robert Burns poetry, biographies of great composers, Parisian parasols, music and jewelry boxes, even a pink ceramic electric lamp in the shape of a gowned woman. On the Seine she posed with Warren for silhouettes, and at Versailles she undoubtedly hunted down the grand life-size portrait of her ancient ancestor Le Marshal Boughton. If she and Amos made no ancestral search in Germany, Florence never forgot that she was half Bouton.[4]

While his mother was away, Marshall had made a valiant attempt to straighten out his life, learning about state politics and handling Warren's correspondence. George Christian, Jr., wrote Harding that Marshall had been "quite a man," and all had noticed his admirable conduct and attention. When Marshall first insisted on working at the *Star* in an alcoholic stupor, Warren had angrily written Carrie about "my good-for-nothing drunken stepson." Now his drinking seemed to be under control. Shortly after the Hardings and Klings returned on September 19, even Florence felt proud enough of the twenty-seven-year-old to travel with him to Madison, New Jersey, where he was serving as best man to Carl Sawyer, who was marrying Grace Curtis. Soon after, Florence learned that Marshall was also marrying, to eighteen-year-old Esther Neely, the daughter of Marion's Democratic mayor. The Duchess proudly held court at the reception—even among De Wolfes—and gave her new daughter-in-law one of the many pieces of Dresden porcelains that she had acquired by the crate in Germany.[5]

That Christmas everyone seemed to get a piece of Dresden as a gift, and Florence set the buffet with her own gold china set of it, which she had dickered with a German shopkeeper to monogram. In a yuletide note to the Christians Florence dictated through Warren—he signed himself "Secretary to Mrs. Harding,"—both evidenced humor about her nagging: "The Duchess has been bossing Santa Claus, because he stands for it and she likes to boss. She has ordered the Dresden candlestick allotted to Coonie—a personally imported bit of old Dresden, tariff paid. Seems to me I have seen stacks of them in the ten cent stores—nothing over ten cents—but her ladyship says I am wrong. The pink socks are for Mildred. A pink sock is a mighty pretty thing when—but let that pass. We are hoping to get a glimpse of these at the next ball. The proof of the wearing is not so important to the Duchess but I'm from Missouri."[6]

Christmas always found Warren sentimental, but this year he found that his passions could no longer be held down. At the same time the Duchess was dusting off the punch bowl for her Christmas party, right beneath her nose Warren was coming to realize that he had truly fallen in love with Carrie, and she with him. They always remembered the day of this realization: Christmas, 1907. It would always be, as Warren wrote, their secret "anniversary."[7]

In the spring of 1908 Florence suffered a minor relapse of her kidney ailment and was again under Doc's thumb. As the summer wore on, she grew increasingly dependent upon his homeopathic concoctions for all her physical problems, real and imagined, believing Doc was the one man who could keep her alive. Yet when she was well, his hovering presence was often an unwanted reminder of her potentially mortal illness. It was the beginning of her own complex emotional yet unromantic entanglement with him.

Meanwhile, Carrie began gently pestering Warren about going to Europe with her and their spouses. That Easter, as Florence dressed for church, he had burst forth with joy to "Carrie Darling, Sweetheart Adorable" in a love letter:

> I am extremely in love with you this morning. I want you. I wanted to call and find you so, in all your freshness and elegance and sweetness and charms. . . . I wanted to kiss you out of your reserve—a thousand of them, wistful, wild, wet and wandering and I wanted you to kiss as only you can. . . . And I wanted to feast my eyes, to intoxicate them in glorious breasts and matchless curves and exquisitive shapeliness. And I wanted to fondle and feel of beauty and superbness. . . . I'd caress and fondle while I worshippingly admired until you caught the spell and answered kiss with kiss and caress with caress. God! I do love that I am wild about it. Heavens! How I would revel in your matchless charms. I'd pet and coddle and kiss and fondle and admire and adore, utterly impatient until I made you the sweetest and purest and darlingest wanton. . . . There is one engulfing, enthralling rule of love, the song of your whole being which is a bit sweeter—the 'Oh Warren! oh Warren!' when your body quivers with divine paroxysm and your soul hovers for flight with mine. . . .

With Jim and Carrie Phillips, Warren planned a tour of Madeira, Egypt, Spain, Italy, Germany, and Switzerland. Florence prepared for the tour through the summer, fall, and winter of 1908, poring through travel books and pamphlets, studying the governments of countries they would see, and mapping out an itinerary of concerts and operas, while Warren anticipated his forthcoming appropriated moments with Carrie. "My health was not good and it seemed restful to be able to enjoy revving about without responsibility," Florence later said, believing that this was the trip's impetus. "We were both passionately fond of music, loved grand opera and reveled in the art life of the old world." Departing New York on the SS *Deutschland,* the Hardings and Phillipses left on February 4, 1909, for two months. Warren again wrote Coonie Christian—not without a slip of jealousy over Carrie, who caught the captain's eye: "The Duchess and Mrs. Phillips wanted to leave enough money in the shops there so they could do business until we got back and scatter more. . . . Captain Kaknepf has been very attentive to our party, inviting us to coffee and cigars in his cabin . . . when he entertained us very agreeably. The Captain is a bachelor and I think he looks after our party because of our good looking women . . . [S]topped at Madeira, drank of the wine, bought of the embroideries and sent a wave of prosperity over the island. . . . All the time that I have been trying to write I have been confused by a culminating chatter by the Phillips, the Duchess. I couldn't fire them, so I let them go on. . . ."

The highlight of the trip for Florence was the cruise down the Nile, her "imagination stirred by the tales" of the ancient land. Renting their own boat, the Hardings stopped in many small towns and cities along the river, all the spots in Luxor, walking through the ruins of the lower regions. Italy, however, was the country of choice for the Duchess. When, searching for a tarot reader, she saw a Gypsy who gave her a lava bracelet to keep away the Angel of Death, Florence skirted black magic. Veiled, she also made a visit to the Vatican. She went to La Scala, and she bought the statuary she had been intent on getting in Naples and Pisa. Besides a copy of "The Three Graces," there was also a bust of Prussia's Queen Louisa from Germany. It was not only the same name as Florence's mother, but she thought it looked like her. To counterpoint Warren's choice of a statue of the naked and beautiful Roman goddess Diana—Warren told Carrie it looked like her—Florence also bought Priscilla, the Puritan Girl. From Naples they went north. She had walked through ancient ruins and heard new languages; now she was eager for home.

Carrie felt differently. As the trip neared its end she realized that her heart was in Germany and decided that she must live here, somehow, with or without Jim. Or Warren. Whether she discussed her feelings with Florence on the return trip is unknown. The Duchess certainly did not know of Carrie's escapades in the wee hours with Warren on the ship's deck. He had written Coonie: "The weather has permitted living on deck, day and night, but we have needed our heavy wraps and our blankets." He was mostly warmed by Carrie. There, as the silver moonlight spilled over the black ocean, the two lovers met just steps from their sleeping spouses. Carrie was troubled by the adultery, but not he— as long as Florence wasn't hurt.[8]

After nine days at sea the party docked in New York on April 30. "It was a glorious vacation," Florence said later, "and when we returned we found our political friends insistent that my husband enter the arena." Indeed Ohio papers were talking up Harding for governor in 1910. Warren found "all the signs favorable" and declared, "I am willing, but I am sure I do not wish to rush my friends into the thing. . . ." Rather quickly, however, his wife and his friends wanted to rush him into it. By January there were already printed postcards in Columbus featuring Harding and declaring his candidacy.

Despite her resentment of Warren's return to politics, Carrie decided to continue the affair upon their return from Europe. It set a pattern. When, at the cost of time and attention to her, politics absorbed him, she fired histrionic threats to break off with him. Through the uncertain territory of his political fortunes, his hectic speaking and traveling schedules, she never did make good on her threats. Emotionally empty apart from her, Harding sought to relive their joy by composing erotic verse, a portion of one poem reading:

I love your back, I love your breasts,
Darling to feel, where my face rests,
I love your skin, so soft and white,
so dear to feel and sweet to bite,
I love your knees, their dimples kiss,
I love your ways of giving bliss,
I love your poise of perfect thighs,
when they hold me in paradise. . . .

Warren remained steadfast in his Victorian mores when it came to his choice of words; he was never pornographic. He used the same nickname that Marshall, the Klings, Doc, and the Christians knew him by. But with Carrie, his name Jerry was anatomically intimate in references. "Jerry is standing up beside me while I write you," he informed her. Warren lovingly called her vagina Seashell. Soon they developed an entire code between them, keeping their liaison a safe secret, or so they thought.

Everyone noticed Warren's instinct to tip his hat to any pretty women his intense blue eyes fixed upon, nor could Carrie help attracting other male eyes. Even young George Christian wrote of her that "learning that Jim Phillips might go to the farm, I tendered the prospective grass widow much affectionate interest." Stories of suspicions later abounded around Marion in what some called oral history, and others simply gossip. Neighbors of the Phillipses' wondered why Harding visited there so often when Jim was at the store, and several curious children once laughed at what they glimpsed in the Phillipses' window. One morning Carrie had been seen in bright-colored shoes at the market by the Harding cook, Inez McWhorter. Later that day, with the Duchess away in Columbus, Inez was about to enter the kitchen from the back entrance. She rapidly retreated when she glimpsed Warren, "trousers at his ankles," and Carrie "on the kitchen table—still in those shoes!"[9]

One fourteen-year-old paid close attention to the whispers, particularly since she was a friend of Carrie's daughter, Isabelle. She recalled: "There was in Marion a very attractive and very extravagant woman.

... Gossip had it that Mrs. [Phillips] and Warren Harding were very friendly, and gossip-mongers wondered how Mrs. Harding could be so blind to such a mutual infatuation. These things reached my ears from the girls at school whose parents kept in close touch with anything smacking of scandal. ... But this knowledge ... did not move me to condemnation of either Mr. Harding or Mrs. [Phillips]. ... The only thing I regretted was that I was not her age, and that I had not travelled in Europe, and that I was not 'in society' or in any kind of position to attract his notice."

This particular teenager was Sam Britton's daughter, often spotted in hiding across the street from the *Star* so she could see Warren emerge and then follow him home. "I knew that I was in love with Warren Harding," she declared. Taking her sister along, Nan brazenly stopped on the Harding porch and actually spoke with Warren—and Florence. "Mr. Harding's oft-interposed opinions invariably met with vigorous protests from his wife who seemed to me to be very sure that her information about so-and-so was the last word in authority upon the subjects and whose remark to her husband, I remember distinctly, usually was either, 'Now, Warren, you don't know anything about it!' or, 'Well, Warren, *I* know *better*!' The topics did not concern me, but I did question any piece of information which could inspire such disputatious quality in the tone of Mrs. Harding's voice." Finally, Nan's sister blurted out, "You know, Mr. Harding, Nan talks of nothing but you! She has little campaign poster pictures of you all over the walls of her room!" Terrified, Nan looked at Florence and recalled soberly, "She did not smile."

Schoolmates were the first to learn of Nan's crush, as she scribbled, "Warren Harding—he's a darling," in her notebook, then wrote on the chalkboard, "I love Warren Harding," when the teacher's back was turned. Marion lawyer Grant Mouser recalled how Nan was "wildly infatuated and carried away with one whom she denominated her Adonis" and how this "strange obsession" became "common town gossip."

It disturbed the teenager that the Twigs "thought it quite scandalous that I should be so freely declaring my adoration for a married man." To "appear more 'in form,'" Nan decided to act as if it were the Duchess whom she liked. "She was not my 'type' of heroine at all, but I used to pretend I was a great admirer of her anyway. I remember how I used to telephone the Harding residence when I thought Mr. Harding might be there. ... I would ask for Mrs. Harding. Sometimes she herself would answer. Once, I remember, mother came in while I was calling . . . she took the receiver and talked with her herself. It may have been that very time when Mrs. Harding informed mother that she could tell Nan that so far as 'Warren' was concerned, 'distance lends enchantment.' " Florence's distrust was shared by Hub. When Nan went to pet Florence's dog, he "snapped at me so fiercely that I backed off with all possible speed." Because she liked Nan's mother and her friend Isabelle Phillips, however, Florence saw the young girl as a curious nuisance. Besides, at the time she was coping with another family dilemma and a political campaign.[10]

Throughout 1909 Marshall had been having difficulty breathing. Doc examined him, and the news was bad: Tuberculosis had consumed half his right lung, and to survive, he would have to relocate to a dry climate. By the end of the year he had left for Denver's Agnes Memorial Sanitarium. After his release he and Esther rented a farm in Kersey, Colorado, but their attempts to raise sugar beets and potatoes in a drought failed terribly. Panicked, Marshall became a querulous echo of his father, badgering the Hardings for money to pay mounting debts. A testy Harding, coping with his own mother's recent death, finally set Marshall up in a printing business in Colorado. Although she did not know it at the time, Florence was never to see her son again.

Harding at the time was fighting to win his party's gubernatorial nomination. Although he had received only a vague nod of support in a White House meeting with President William Howard Taft, Harding doggedly pursued uncommitted delegates, who would be the first to be nominated by the voters themselves and whose support might counter the power of the bosses, who were not rallying to his cause. He did get support from Amos Kling, although ancient prejudices held fast. Kling jokingly wondered if now Ohio would get "a nigger Guv."

With their old friend from the state legislature Mac Jennings acting as the campaign's ostensible manager, the Duchess ventured to Columbus for the July convention with high expectations. As the balloting began, there was a surge for Longworth, but in a reserved box overlooking the floor, his wife, wearing a brown cartwheel hat, angrily shook her head no: "Princess Alice" wouldn't trade Washington for Columbus. Alice then noticed that down at a desk with the press corps was a nervous woman who was adding numbers on a scrap of paper with each ballot, as if keeping score of a ballgame's innings. "Mrs. Harding was near me in the gallery, very much excited, cheering and waving," noted a furiously fanning Alice Longworth. As the third ballot call nominated

Harding, Alice disgustedly watched the thrilled Florence burst into tears—even as she tallied her numbers. The Princess shuddered and left.

Despite a tree-ripping, telegraph pole–knocking thunderstorm, Marion dished up a triumphant victory welcome for the Hardings, with locals gathering at their home and a brass band blaring, "Hail, Hail, the Gang's All Here!" Before the fall campaign got under way, the Hardings and the Phillipses took a break, motoring some three thousand miles, to Boston, where they dropped in on Florence's aunt and cousin, to the Isles of Shoals, New Hampshire, where they stayed at the Oceanic Hotel, to Maine, down through Massachusetts, New York, Baltimore, Washington, through West Virginia, and back to Marion. In preparation for Harding's campaign, Charles Hilles, secretary to President Taft, arranged for them to make a "drop-by" to see the Tafts at the summer White House in Beverly, Massachusetts. Privately Harding found humor in being able to introduce his mistress to the President. In September Florence pulled a bit of her own blue smoke and mirrors in her first press interview, with the New York *Daily Tribune*'s G. E. McCormick. An unflattering picture had her on the front porch with Hub, but she rosily posed herself as a leisurely "leader in society" and described her "lovely, homelike home," never mentioning her business work.

The autumn campaign reached its apex in Marion the night before the election, when it seemed as if all eighteen thousand town residents had rallied for Harding. There was a torchlight parade, led by a martial band, followed by men carrying "Boost a Booster" banners past hundreds of Harding pictures and posters in all the bunting-trimmed store windows and on the telephone poles. The parade climaxed with a roaring fireworks display in the crisp black sky, above the rustling orange oak leaves. Everyone then packed in the Opera House, filling its six hundred seats. Warren roused the audience with what was more a talk to the home folk than one of his endless orations. "I was nominated in spite of the bosses, and said that in Cincinnati, too. I owe allegiance to only one boss—and she sits right over there in that box," he said, pointing to a beaming Florence. "She's a mighty good one too." Among those shrieking cheers in the rafters was Nan Britton.[11]

Conspicuously absent was Carrie Phillips. When Warren lost the election the next day to Judson Harmon, she found cause for celebration. Carrie had begun to fantasize about divorce and remarriage. She knew Warren would never divorce Florence if he were elected governor. But if he were out of politics, she stood a greater chance of becoming his wife. Indeed Warren had encouraged this notion with some vague suggestion of what he might do after the election. "I could be content to give up the years and their offerings for a few months with you," he wrote her, "then pay the fullest penalty." There could be no higher penalty than the results of instigating a divorce to run off with a mistress. The scandal would end his political future. Seven weeks after he lost the election, on their "third anniversary," he sent her his picture with a note on the back: "I love you more than all the world, and have no hope of reward on earth or hereafter, so precious as that in your dear arms, in your thrilling lips, in your matchless breasts, in your incomparable embrace. . . ."

As 1911 began, however, Carrie seemed to realize that she was being deceived as much as Florence was. While Warren never suggested that his love for her was waning, neither did he suggest that his love of politics had abated either. Carrie began making firm suggestions that they both begin by divorcing their respective spouses. Warren hedged. As much as he loved Carrie, Warren could not just up and divorce the Duchess. He depended upon her; he could never so abrasively betray her. Though he might resent her as the impediment that kept him from his Carrie, only his wife's death would spring him free. Moreover, Florence was central to his business and political management. If Florence could show him that his political career was not finished, Carrie could salve his emotional insecurities about losing. Carrie, however, would not be manipulated. She again pointedly asked if he was ready to divorce Florence. If he was not, she was moving to Germany. Thinking it a bluff, Warren did not directly respond, distracting her instead with what he was sure would be a delightful surprise, another voyage for the Hardings and Phillipses, an "economy trip" to Bermuda departing on March 1, 1911.

The island retreat was tonic for all; Warren and Jim fished at the Devil's Hole, and Florence and Carrie shopped in Hamilton. Despite the distractions, Carrie, however, remained adamant with Warren: divorce or Germany. However passively, Warren made his own adamant statement: Bermuda would be the last trip the couples could make together. On her return to Marion later in the month, Carrie made good on her threats by sending a check to Berlin's Willard School, covering two terms there for Isabelle, starting in September. Promising to return by the summer of 1912, she convinced Jim to book her voyage. Faced with losing her, Warren grew upset and pleaded that she stay: "I stand more than willing. If, after trying and seeking, or pondering and measuring, you think I can give you my love to nearest heaven and you want me then I'm yours now, any time—for all time." She would not.[12]

Blissfully unaware of the real reason for Warren's depression, the Duchess focused intently on regrouping her efforts to keep Warren's political star aloft. As Jane Dixon noted, "Defeat only sharpened her determination." Samuel Hopkins Adams reported: "Her ambitions were not to be chilled by a setback which her resolute spirit regarded as no more than temporary. While the editor was back at his desk, she was keeping a watchful eye on developments." Asked about the failed election, the Duchess simply laughed, saying, "Warren Harding can and will go higher."

A half century before, Flossie Kling had been born above a hardware store on Main Street, but she truly arrived in the world the day a thick cream-colored invitation, stamped in gold with the seal of the President of the United States, was delivered to Mount Vernon Avenue. For the first time Florence, with Warren, was invited to the White House, to attend the President and Mrs. Taft's silver wedding anniversary party.

Florence left no record of the June 1911 lawn party, but she must have been struck by the connections between her and First Lady Nellie Taft. Graduate of the Nourse School (longtime competitor to the Cincinnati Conservatory of Music), trained in economics as well as music, Nellie had supported herself as a teacher. Her marriage was an overt political partnership, Nellie being passive Will's most aggressive advocate for the presidency. She had even publicly supported women's higher education and suffrage. If the First Lady's story inspired the Duchess, she never said, but the parallels were obvious.

Only one woman rivaled grand Nellie in her diamond tiara that night. She would be compared to a "slinky, black panther racing about"; openly smoking from her long holder was Princess Alice herself, also said to have the highest political ambitions for her husband. Though Nick was casual about his extramarital affairs, Alice masked her reactions through wit and a shrug, but behind her charming smile a biting jealousy often flashed. This night at the White House, however, there was an equally bright, if bourgeois, Duchess, comfortable in a political conversation on Britain's changing economy or Germany's kaiser. She had grown worldly, capable of slipping easily into this sort of crowd. Indeed Florence had grown to love politics: the glad-handing, the boosting, the backroom maneuverings, the parades, rallies, conventions, caucuses, the attention from crowds, and, perhaps most of all, her husband's public pledge of "allegiance" to her. She was not the intellectualizing maker of policy but rather the instinctual political manager. The *Star,* the state senate, and the gubernatorial campaigns had proved that.

Perhaps purposefully, the frenzied rush and constant distractions of politics had left Florence little time to muse on the dramatic changes of the last few years of her personal life: the rapprochement with Amos Kling, Marshall's marriage and terminal condition, Phoebe Harding's death, her own brush with death and her months in the hospital. In the spring Florence had earned the dubious title of grandmother, when Esther gave birth to a girl named Eugenia, called Jean. And what was she to make of her relationship with Warren in the decade and a half since the Hodder affair?

If she had deeper suspicions about what occurred during the times she was *not* with him, she apparently did not want to explore them. That her boon companion Carrie Phillips was suddenly uprooting herself out of America to another country for no apparent reason and that Warren was sullen about something, certainly must have registered at some level with her. Florence, however, was less interested in Carrie's peculiar rantings about German efficiency than she was in the frequency of letters with a Columbus postmark coming to Warren. Harry Daugherty was persistent in pursuing a friendship with Warren, and considering her husband's state of mind, she found herself curiously grateful for dogged Harry's flattery of Harding's talents. She probably began to recognize a comrade. Florence also noticed another letter that came for Warren one day during that summer of 1911. It was a local letter, with recognizable writing. It was from Carrie Phillips.

The Duchess ripped the envelope open and read the letter.[13]

11

Betrayal and Confrontation

The discovery that her best friend and her husband were having an affair did not send the Duchess into a weeping spell. She was stung, devastated. She was also enraged.

Her immediate reaction was to seek to divorce Warren Harding.

She confronted him. Stunned, he reported Florence's discovery and reaction in yet another letter to Carrie. Francis Russell, who read Warren's
missives, said that it made clear that Florence had "intercepted a letter
from Carrie to Harding, and a confrontation followed in a lawyer's
office," that of Harding's attorney, Hoke Donithen. When Warren informed Carrie of what had happened, she assumed that the situation
would resolve itself happily: She and Jim would divorce, Warren and
Florence would divorce, and she and Warren would marry, although
the cuckolded Jim still did not know about the adultery.

Archivist Ken Duckett, who also later read the letters, said that
while they revealed that "Florence Harding knew of her husband's relationship with Mrs. Phillips," the Duchess had suspected it, "probably
as early as 1909," long before she had proof in hand. Carrie's sending
the letter was all the more malicious because she had purposely intended
for Florence to find out. For Warren to send Carrie letters from out of
town was indiscreet, but he could be fairly certain she would get them
at home before Jim arrived to see them. The only point in Carrie's
sending her letter to Warren at his home was to rupture the Harding
marriage. For too long, said Russell, she had "lived in hope that Harding
would divorce his wife and marry her."

In fact, before this dramatic, final effort, Carrie had once similarly
"tried to precipitate a divorce" between the Hardings, according to Russell. To prove that she could find happiness without him, she had sent
Warren a packet of "letters from another of her lovers." Carrie Phillips,
it soon was revealed, was as promiscuous as Warren. Harding became
jealous over one of her other lovers, a Mr. Robinson; one Marion resident informed Chancellor that the "very showy and vain" Carrie had
"a passion for men. . . . This woman has made herself useful to men of
a kind. She got in with Warren, who as usual, paid no attention to his
wife who [became] passé [to him] through the years."

As Florence forced a discussion of divorce, both Hardings kept up
appearances, continuing to live under the same roof. Once again, because of her secretive nature and the social stigma of adultery, the Duchess had no person to whom she could turn for counseling or express
herself. Once again she returned to the same small 1891 calendar book
in which she had revealed her inner self during the Susan Hodder adultery episode. She had kept it among her possessions for some fifteen
years. Now her rage against the male-female double standard was more
pointed. "Most of the pain in this world is located in the hearts of
women," she wrote. "Many women are forced into mute acceptance of
disloyalty, faithlessness and humiliation because this is, after all, a 'man's

world,' and up to very recent years woman has had no redress since she must depend upon the man for support." With bitter humor Florence even mused on a technique betrayed wives could use: "To test a man, set a dog on him—and set a woman on him. That is to say test his courage—and self-control. Show the man off his guard." More personally, she seemed to see herself not only as unloved but as unlovable. "Passion is a very transient thing. To me, love seems to have been a thing of tragedy." She addressed herself in the second person, burying even deeper from herself some other wound: "Some of your hurts you have aired. And the strangest, you have still survived. But what torment of grief you endured from the evils which never aired."

She clipped a newspaper article written by a husband, "George," who belatedly regretted his brutal neglect of his wife, "Jane," and her suspicions about his relationship with "Miss Reese," their maid. The man wrote:

> I had eliminated all expressions of my love, the consequences being that I had driven Jane, who I believed had loved me, to a condition of apathy as far as I was concerned. . . . If I had my life to live over again . . . I would give to my wife, to my home, more of myself. . . . We had started so happily! Could I ever forget our delightful honeymoon? But when was it? Years ago! And instead of our happiness increasing with the years, there was, to all appearances, no trace of our mutual love left. Coldness, indifference had taken its place. I recall once when I attempted a caress—after returning from the hospital with Miss Reese—that Jane said: 'It's too late for sentiment George. Especially if it doesn't mean anything. Our marriage seems to me to have been pretty much of a failure.' "

Warren was faced with his freedom. He could divorce Florence—surrendering as well honor, respectability, and the public acclaim he so relished—and marry his lusty mistress. In weighing the options, he may finally have realized that as much of a domineering nag as Florence could be, her demands were to protect, improve, and promote *his* business, political aspirations, and personal well-being and were done so entirely without the selfish absorption of Carrie Phillips. Carrie's interest in Warren was for adoration of herself. It is doubtful that she cared enough to understand, accept, or even love Warren as his wife of twenty years did. Carrie provided sexual fulfillment and emotional passion, but the Duchess was the engine of his livelihood. Without Carrie, he could not *enjoy* the life he had, but without Florence, he would not even *have* the life he had. Warren wanted both physical intimacy and practical support. He did not want to choose. He remained passive.

Florence's options were also limited. She might have returned home to seventy-seven-year-old Amos Kling's home and become a spinster caretaker to her father, but he had remarried, and there was no role for her there. She had poured her resources into more than just the living, breathing facet of Warren; she had invested everything she had into the very idea of "Harding" as her career. Perhaps she acknowledged that she could not satisfy his sexual desires and would have to ask no questions about what he did on his trips without her, despite every indication that, as Mary Elizabeth Moore observed, "she was still madly in love with him. Even despite his indiscretions." Were they inextricable partners? In her diary Florence alludes to just such a conclusion: "Why stick stubbornly to decisions made in the heat of anger? It is only big souls who can see there must be a change of their minds in cooler moments."

Ultimately, then, as Russell recorded, "Harding's wife refused to let him go, however erring, and Harding could not bring himself to leave." Some years later Florence made clear the forgiveness necessary to continuing her partnership, with only the vaguest of references to her husband's adultery: "The broad point of view is to understand each other's weaknesses, to be tolerant and to understand that there are other *demands* upon your husband. There are things outside of yourself. You know I am speaking of a woman." They made some sort of agreement, one that might even have involved a financial remuneration to Florence some years later. In every way except through sexual fidelity, and his honesty about that, however Warren displayed increased respect for Florence. The instances when he lashed out at her became rare. If she could never entirely control him, she continued to boss him with a confidence exhibited only by the sort of wife who knows her husband will never leave her. Perhaps out of guilt, he permitted this. It was a trade-off: He knew that *she* knew, and this was his way of letting her "have him." His trust and faith in her never wavered, but now the relationship, forever changed, settled into a different pattern: He would honor, cherish, and obey if she asked no questions. Her jealousy never actually abated, but her attempts to keep him from other women became more a matter of protecting his career and *their* work on the career's behalf. There was what one friend gently termed "the perfect understanding which existed between them."

The Phillips affair did, however, leave Florence with a permanent mistrust of Warren. "Love makes all men liars," she noted. "Some liars are so interesting that we are sorry when we cannot believe them. New promises can never take the place of broken ones." In so accepting this as a reality with Warren, she also seemed to accept the fact that when he was away from her, he would be sexually unfaithful to her. "No wife ever knows all about her husband," she wrote. "He insulates his experiences instinctively. Love, to a man, is a sensation only. Never a complete giving of himself to one forever." Ultimately, after listing a variety of possible relationships between men and women—"friendship, flirtation, near-love, love" among them—Florence Harding began to accept two that seemed workable for her and Warren: "platonic affection, good fellowship."

What Florence did lose was the person who had come closest to being her first genuinely close woman friend. It seemed to devastate her almost as much as the adultery. "True happiness consists not in the multitude of friends, but in their worth and choice," she wrote in her diary. "Friendship supplies the place of everything to those who know how to make the right use of it; it makes your prosperity more happy and it makes your adversity more easy." Her betrayal by such a valuable companion as Carrie Phillips inevitably caused her to build even more walls around herself. "It is always safe to learn," she noted, "even from our enemies." She could never fully trust Warren, but she also had not one confidante. Outwardly the situation made Florence more rigid, more stern, more the Duchess. She never again spoke to Carrie. She acknowledged her only occasionally in rageful, public attacks. "There is no enemy so bitter," she told her diary, "as the friend who's been trifled with." Florence now viewed herself as being at the lowest point since being abandoned by Henry De Wolfe: "It seems to me that to be friendless is the worst condition next to being in want, that a woman could be reduced to."

Whether or not Warren had promised Florence that he would stop seeing Carrie, the blowup provided the mistress with further incentive to go to Europe. Warren's refusal to divorce Florence for her enraged Carrie, yet perversely it drew him closer. On the heels of such an emotional tumult in his marriage, Warren just as quickly fell in lust again with his Carrie, unable to imagine her being physically unavailable. As Russell wrote, "Carrie in her anger upbraided him, calling him names, yet a few weeks later was again arranging a rendezvous."[1]

Before leaving with Florence in early August on an earlier arranged voyage to meet Ed and Evalinda Scobey in Switzerland, then to tour Austria, Germany, Italy and the British Isles, "Guv" worked out a secret code to be used in transatlantic love letters between him and "Sis." The code was largely practical ("Reverse—Answer at once to Berlin by cable"; "Revise—I will come sailing to you on—"; "Redoubt—White Star Line steamer"; "Defy—I will meet you at—"; "Immediate—mail your next letter to—"; "Gam—send me money to—"; "Decide—Answer by cable direct to me at Marion"; "Melanger—All mail received, don't worry"), romantic ("Gate—I want paradise in your embrace"; "Mellow—I want to come to you in your dreams, tonight, oh, so close"); referential to Jim and the Duchess ("Dolphin—Things have gone wrong here"; "Demure—Everything is All Severe here"); but hardly pornographic ("Deaver—I'd like to bring you the sceptre tonight and make you my queen"; "Gov Hard—Hungering me").

In September 1911, with Jim still compliant and unaware of his wife's adultery, Carrie left with Isabelle for Germany, where she took a suite in Berlin's Pension Polchow, determined to become a real German. She took German lessons, ate German pastries, and admired the rows of blue-uniformed soldiers and officers of the kaiser's army. She wrote about all of it to Warren—and sent all her letters to him at the *Star*. Although he would be on the Continent in the fall, Warren made no covert plan to see her.[2]

Florence's point of focus for this trip was unlike that of previous excursions. She still loved opera and concert music and attended performances of both in Europe, (although her favorite song, to become her trademark, was the 1910 "End of a Perfect Day," by American Carrie Jacobs Bond). Now, however, she was interested in learning for herself about the surges of political unrest she had been reading about. Her neighbor Eleanor Freeman later recalled that this third European trip made Florence take "a keen interest in the political and civil conditions of the people in whose lands she visited." She went this time, Florence said, because she was "deeply interested in the study of labor questions of England, France, Italy and Germany." No longer was she simply an Ohio matron with an interest in business and a bourgeois urge to soak up Old World culture. Now she was a woman who professed interest in public policy.

In England a latent feminism stirred in Florence. Though she had supported the idea of women being given the vote, she had never been an ardent suffragist. Now, in Great Britain, with women on hunger strikes, engaged in bloody protests, marching by the thousands for equal rights, she sympathized with their "militancy," as she called it. She later explained in one of her more remarkably frank public statements: "There are certain times and places, wherein women must be militant to attain their proper degree of justice and right. In England, for example, where women were not allowed equality of opportunity in any endeavor, where men refused them partnerships and erected before them the stone wall of petty convention, I understand why women smashed windows and hacked doors." Her quiet fury at the circumscribed role she had to play—especially one in an untrusting marriage that nonetheless was the source of her identity and position—might have stirred her sympathy for women who were more openly angry than she could afford to be.

Sometime after the Hardings had returned from Europe, when Ethel Jennings ran into a parade of suffragists in Columbus, she was surprised to glimpse the Duchess across the street, on the opposite side-walk, also watching. When Ethel caught up with her, Florence explained that she had been in the city for business earlier in the day, but hearing about the parade, she delayed her return so she could satisfy her curiosity to see women fighting for "our right to vote." When Ethel later joked about their mutual "waywardness," the Duchess quipped, "Nonsense. It is a liberty necessary for all women, homemaker and office girl alike, though I am not a marcher." While certainly her own experience had influenced her personal support of suffrage, political expediency influenced her public muteness on the hotly debated issue. It was an issue she increasingly heard discussed in Marion—as it was in the rest of America—during the presidential election year of 1912, particularly during the summer Chautauqua speeches.[3]

Marion had changed considerably since Warren had begun the *Star* relying on little more than hope. The look of the small city—the 1912 census claimed a population of 18,252—had drastically been altered. The city offices had grown so that they were dispersed from the 1857 city hall to larger buildings around town; the police and fire departments, created in the 1870s, expanded into new headquarters in the new century's second decade. By 1912, when the nine-day Chautauqua festival first came to Marion, it was held in canvas tents at Garfield Park, but within three years a permanent pavilion was completed to host it, drawing crowds from hundreds of miles. Shortly after Warren's 1910 election eve rally at the old Opera House, it burned and was promptly replaced by the Marion Photo-Plays Theater, "home of the Pipe Organ." Although there was still a stage for touring vaudeville troupes, the main attraction was the silver screen, where silent films flickered to the sounds of the organ. Hollywood had come to Marion, and both Hardings were movie devotees.

Marion's industry was no longer defined only by the revolving hay rake or steam shovel. Now there was a limestone quarry, the Gebhart Piano Company, and the Kowalke Chair Company. The city was a

crossroad of travel, with some eight rail lines converging there, as well
as two interurban lines. With progress came loss. The wildlife of deer,
beaver, grouse, gray squirrel, and some waterfowl plentiful in Flossie
Kling's youth had long been diminished from the town's outlying
regions. Nothing in Marion, however, changed its face or brought it
greater national attention than Doc Sawyer's new sanitarium. Doc's operation had become so prosperous that he had relocated it to the bucolic
130-acre White Oaks Farm, with its own dairy and hen farms, fruit
orchards, and vegetable gardens. As the nation's first private mental
hospital, and with Dr. Carl as one of the nation's first unlicensed but
practicing psychiatrists, Doc had widely marketed his services to wealthy
victims of "nervous diseases and mental disorders." In the pleasing Arts
and Crafts architecture, fifteen bungalows were connected by heated,
ventilated, and lit walkways, all facing a courtyard. Each building held
ten patients in private rooms with electric heat, fans, and buzzers for
nurses and with hot and cold running water. There were common dining, reading, and game parlors. The large nursing staff carried out Doc's
homeopathic remedies, but he promised "no fads, fancies or pet theories
to foist" on those suffering from "over-work, worry, business cares,
social demands and the like." Doc was progressive in his attitude toward
mental illness: "There is a general disposition on the part of the people
to consider mental affliction a disgrace and to relegate those so unfortunate as to be suffering from disorders of the mind to custodial care,
denying them the benefits which modern, scientific medicine has to
offer. . . . [T]hey need treatment just as any other diseased individual
needs it. . . ." Thus Sawyer developed a "Psychopathic Department"
under Carl's direction for posttrauma disorders, severe or manic depression, senility, dementia, paranoia, delirium, and phobias. The Sawyers did not accept "drug or liquor cases."

The typical regimen included rigorous outdoor exercise, light
therapy, hydrotherapy, massage, and "electrotherapy"; even X rays were
used to examine the skull for any "bony protuberances causing pressure
and pain." In the occupational therapy room, patients were encouraged
to make baskets, pillows, Campbell Soup kid dolls, hangers, tablecloths,
lace doilies, doll hats, clay animals, lamps, ashtrays, and pottery. But on
a large sign hung in the room, Doc warned, YOU ARE WORKING HERE
TO CREATE NEW IDEAS, NOT SIMPLY TO BE BUSY. THINK NEW
THOUGHTS. On Sunday Doc opened the grounds for band concerts,
encouraging visitors to stroll among the patients being pushed about in
wicker wheelchairs. He even got a railroad pit stop put in at White
Oaks, but he placed a large sign at the entrance: DON'T STARE AT THE

PATIENTS. The whole place was comforting yet weird, at once scientific and sympathetic as it was faddish and paternalistic—not unlike Doc himself.[4]

Through the spring of 1912 Florence often found herself seeking refuge at the sanitarium for the comfort Sawyer provided, as much out of a psychological need as any physical one. Lacking a confidante, fractured still by the adultery, Florence Harding was grasping for some security, some foundation. If ever she had an inner crisis, it was in the wake of the Phillips affair. Removed now for almost a decade from proximity to the political offices that she had relished for five years, her business skills at the *Star* welcome but no longer necessary, and the love she had poured into her marriage now tempered to an affectionate partnership, she was more uncertain about the direction of her life than she'd been since her days as a divorced single mother.

All her questionings were compounded by the shadow of her precarious health. Knowing that her kidney ailment could flare at any time of sustained stress, she fought to keep herself calmed. She often checked with Doc to ascertain her condition. As Dr. Carl became familiar with her health, he also learned to identify her natural hypochondria. Although Florence was never openly treated for "nervous disease" by the Sawyers, their knowledge of such problems and treatments undoubtedly came into play as they reassured and continually sought to strengthen her. Her visits to White Oaks may have ostensibly been for "social chats" or checkups in Doc's own home, but they were treatments nonetheless.

Never fervently pious, the Duchess also delved more deeply into her curiosity about astrology and enlarged her scientific study of it, based on astronomy. She learned to "read the sky" and identify the position of the various and changing zodiac signs, knowing which houses were rising and falling, fearing the full moons, basing her important decisions on the positionings of Leo, her birth sign. On many clear nights the Duchess found solace in her sky, sitting out on the front porch or walking through the neighboring woods, her head tilted upward. One night she took her niece for a walk and pointed out her destiny in the pattern of the points of light above. The girl was startled by how fervently the Duchess relied on astrology. "You cannot count on anything in this world, but you can always count on the stars," she repeated more doggedly than ever. "The stars never fail you."[5]

It was obvious that by 1912 Florence was casting about for a larger purpose to fill a void in her life. Her life had always been directed to boosting Warren for the sake of Warren, and even if her endeavors were not entirely selfless—for she was always trying to disprove old man Kling's dour predictions—they were never directly for her own good. Nevertheless, the years in Columbus and the campaigns had given her public notice, support, and personal satisfaction and reward for her managerial sensibilities. Thus she would consciously turn her energies again toward politics, encouraging, organizing, even prodding Warren back into the elective arena, less emotionally as the adoring helpmeet Florence and more calculatingly as Duchess, the campaign manager. She restored to herself the defiant energy she had exhibited after the 1910 election defeat but had lost in the Phillips debacle. Interestingly, in late March 1912 Harding considered an offer to have him run again for the governorship. It was several weeks before he made a decision, during which time he consulted Florence on their fortunes. He finally decided against doing so.

At about the same time, on the loop for political inside stories, the Duchess heard rumors—probably from Daugherty himself—that Senator Theodore Burton was tired of his work and would probably not seek reelection in 1914. One day at the *Star* she coyly discussed it with Van Fleet, the editor. "What's the matter with W.G. pointing for the Senate?" he asked.

"Do you think he can get it?"

"Why not. The Republicans are getting together. He's got a lot of friends."

"It costs such a lot of money to live in Washington."

"Oh, it isn't so expensive. And the paper isn't doing badly."

"If he was only a corporation lawyer and could pick up a lot of business on the side, I'd say yes. But he couldn't do anything there. No. I don't know as we can afford it *yet*."

If Florence transparently wanted him to forgo Columbus and instead go to Washington, the stars certainly seemed to be working in her favor, for he was soon granted the highest national visibility he had yet received. Since the spring Harding had an understanding with the White House that he would place President Taft's name in renomination at the Republican National Convention in Chicago. Following Harding's election as an Ohio delegate at large, Taft assured Harding the task was his. While Harding said he was "more honored by that request" than any other in his political career, the party was fraught with discontent when former President Roosevelt announced his candidacy against his onetime protégé, the more conservative Taft.

After a swooning version of "Moonlight Bay," as Warren placed Taft's name in nomination, there were jeers from Roosevelt supporters.

Nick Longworth, a longtime Taft friend but Roosevelt's son-in-law, was in a quandary, but the venom of his wife, Alice was now clearly directed to both Harding and the Duchess. Angry at Harding's seeming abandonment of her father for political opportunity with Taft, Alice angrily interrupted Harding when he came over to the box and offered his support of Nick for Governor, telling Warren, "[O]ne could not accept favors from crooks." She later recalled, "I must say it was a little obtuse and raw of Harding to make that offer to Nick in my presence. Insight and taste, however, were not his strong points. At intervals, for the next twenty-four hours, Nick . . . pleaded with me to see Harding, to say that I was sorry, that I had not meant to say that he was a crook. But that was what I had meant to say, so I did not see him. That, I think, was the beginning of my active distaste for Harding."[6]

A more glib figure was winding his way through the Ohio seats in the brick Chicago Coliseum, built to resemble a castle. This Ohio delegate had already written off the impact of Roosevelt and his followers, who bolted to form the Progressive party (also known as the Bull Moose party), and was already focusing on future races. The wiley politico Harry Daugherty was slipping back into Harding's life.

So too was another absent but not forgotten friend. As Democrat Woodrow Wilson defeated Taft and Roosevelt in the November election, Warren's thoughts turned again from politics and America to love and Germany. Carrie was still on his mind. He wrote her that he was hers "any time and for all time." Distance not only made the heart grow fonder but, he scribbled, made his "Jerry" long for her "Seashell." He sent her a subscription to *Vogue,* popular novels, and money. After he had seen a Broadway musical, *The Wedding Trip,* he retreated to his Hotel Manhattan suite and wrote her a poem of some twenty lascivious verses, fueled not just by fantasy but now by frustration.

In fact, so strongly did their coded love flow across the sea that at the time of their 1912 "anniversary" Carrie boarded a ship just to rendezvous with him for several days in Montreal. Florence, believing there was no longer a Carrie Phillips in her husband's life, did not ask to accompany Warren to Canada. Just weeks before, she had let him make a yachting trip to the Gulf of Mexico without her. When Carrie returned to Germany, there was more purple verse:

> I love your mouth, I love your fire
> I love the way you stir desire.
> I love your size and daintiness
> Love every thread in which you dress.

I love you garb'd, but naked MORE!
Love your beauty to thus adore.

Warren's and Carrie's longing for each other persisted to such a degree that she again crossed the Atlantic just for a clandestine reunion, however brief, in 1913. This time Warren told the Duchess that he was going on a hunting trip to Texas with Ed Scobey. Actually, he headed to New York, where he met Carrie's ship and spent a romantic weekend with her in a large hotel suite. Still, there could be no resolution. Morbidly anticipating Florence's imminent passing before his own, Warren insisted that he could be joined with Carrie as a husband only upon Florence's death, but he was now more firm in his decision never to divorce her. Carrie angrily went back to Germany, declaring it her true home, that she would not return to America the next year or ever—as long as he stayed with Florence. "Whenever the mood took her she was merciless to him," said Francis Russell, "and he grovelled." Again he backpedaled: "*I want you that way,* just all my *very own* . . . hurting to love and be loved. . . . Think of me stopping in a perfect avalanche of work to scratch you a line . . . I could be tolerably patient if I knew that the next time we met it was to be for keeps. Maybe! Who can tell?"[7]

12

Marion Exodus

If Carrie Phillips wrote Warren of her German lovers to provoke his jealousy, the equally persistent calls for attention he received from a high school junior were far gentler. With the sudden death of Sam Britton in June, Harding got his widow Mary a local teaching stint to help support her children, now including an infant. His personal inquiry and promise to Mrs. Britton that "maybe I can do something for Nan" excitedly fueled Nan Britton's obsession with Harding. "Nan was a pretty girl, blonde and slender," recalled her best friend, Ellen Metzger. "In those days, we girls were movie crazy and we couldn't wait until school was out to go to a movie or to read movie magazines. But Nan wasn't interested in the movie stars; all she could talk about was Harding. . . . I don't believe Mr. Harding encouraged her in any way. He didn't have to. Nan ran after him. He was so good looking, women chased him."

Nan was not among the juniors of 1913's "Brightest Ones" who maintained a ninety average in high school, but she did have the incalculable ability to be distinct. "We all know 'Nawn,' " said her yearbook entry, "Talking she knew not why, And she cared not what." A three-year Dramatic Society member, Nan wanted to be *in* the moving pictures, even staying in greasepaint and costume for the cast lunch after playing Claire, a "star-struck girl," in *Hicks at College*. On April 3, 1914, she showed her gumption in her senior oratorial. Other girls' addresses took on "Things Money Will Not Buy," "Children of the Slums," "Value of Domestic Science," and "The Large Field of Church Work." Nan shocked everyone with "What Woman Wants."[1]

Warren's frequent absences from Marion and Miss Britton's insistent silliness were the least of Florence's concerns in the winter of 1913. Suffering a serious kidney attack, this time provoked by her heart, she went to live at White Oaks under Doc's care. He feared that she wouldn't live out the year, but once again she rallied, though unfortunately in response to bad news. Marshall was struggling to survive physically and financially. After accumulating debts in his various endeavors, he had managed to lease the *Enterprise*, a weekly paper in Kersey, but he was so badly in arrears that he was unable to get proper advertising. With good intentions Jim Phillips, on a trip west, encouraged Marshall to keep trying. He bore news of her son's ill fortune back to Florence. Again she sent money. It was clear that her son, his wife, and now her grandchild were dependent upon her.

If Florence felt she held the responsibility for two younger generations, she now assumed it for the older as well. Upon his return from Daytona in the spring, Amos Kling rapidly declined with kidney disease and became bedridden. When Warren completed his August Chautauqua tour, he visited Kling, who seemed optimistic for recovery. At the same time, Florence again fell ill. On October 20, 1913, Amos died. To his sister, Warren reported with genuine concern for his wife: "Florence has been in bed for nine weeks with a bad heart and nervous breakdown. She is in bad shape. Deacon [Warren's brother George's nickname] thinks she will recover, but there is no chance of her getting out before

Christmas. Added to Florence's woes, her father passed through a long serious illness and died early last week. You can imagine the effect of all that on a daughter nervously broken down, and with a wobbly heart."

After directing that his just debts and funeral expenses be paid out, Amos had listed Florence first in his will, leaving her valuable real estate and thirty-five thousand dollars and directing her to manage a trust fund for the less responsible Tal. His three grandchildren got twenty-five thousand dollars each, his brothers, George and Donald, five thousand each, housekeeper Mag Younkins was given two thousand, and even his washwoman, Josie Yeager, got a thousand. Ten thousand dollars went to an endowment fund for the Waddells' Ladies' Home Association. For no apparent reason he left nothing to his church or any of the civic groups he had helped found. Cliff was left the estate's residual and the Kling mansion. As promised, Amos's widow got one hundred shares of rail stock but no cash. Despite such posthumous generosity, his iron hand still manipulated the proceedings from the grave: "Should any legatee herein named seek to contest or set aside this will or any Item thereof, his or her legacy shall thereupon become void and of no effect." His death, however, liberated all Klings. Marshall got immediate financial relief, and he badgered his mother, the executor, for an advance to clear his debts, leave Kersey, and take time to relax before deciding what to do next. Cliff and his family got the mansion, and he inherited enough cash to buy a grand winter home in Rockledge, Florida. The less responsible Tal was now also free to pursue his love, the Catholic Nona Younkins.[2]

For Florence, in a purely expedient manner, Kling's death may have been the great linchpin to finally breaking Warren's seeming indifference to making a fight again for political office. Samuel Hopkins Adams learned that Kling had been unrelenting in his case to Warren to put "an end to political activity." Said Adams, "I have talked with contemporaries who believe that Kling's persuasions were a decisive factor in Harding's temporary eclipse; with one old resident who, through no first-hand evidence, insists that the father-in-law made this a condition of the treaty of family peace."

If the path was now cleared in every way for Warren to run for the Senate seat, the Duchess had an eagerly unsolicited backer. Often sending ingratiating letters, Daugherty had continued to affix himself to the Hardings in hopes of helping to heft Warren's political star again. Despite President Taft's loss of the election to Woodrow Wilson, Harry remained persistently optimistic as he plied Warren with flattery. "One great thing resulting from this war we have had," he wrote after the election, "and that is that we are better friends than ever and understand each other thoroughly and will hang together through thick and thin."

Now Harry invited himself down to Marion and into Warren's office to make a pitch that he run for the Senate seat. At home Florence hit the same key. "Warren Harding, you can do it—you can win," she insisted. That they were working toward the same goal, though not yet consciously together, was illustrated early in the election year. When a percolating Warren coyly said he wouldn't openly seek the nomination but would never decline "to honor any draft made upon me by my party," Daugherty had his wedge. He trekked to Daytona. "I found him like a turtle sunning himself on a log," Harry fancifully wrote of Harding in the winter of 1914, "and I pushed him into the water." At the same time, he had what appears to be his first secret convocation with the Duchess, who was again in bad shape, having had another winter kidney attack. She helped push the turtle too. As Samuel Hopkins Adams recorded, "Some of their fellow-citizens believe that Mrs. Harding now allied herself with the state leader, that she was gazing longingly from afar upon fabled glories of Washington."

Florence put a different spin on her "longing," claiming like a properly deferential politician's wife that unlike some selfish women who would not want public life, she would not *prevent* Warren's candidacy: "I have always known my husband's great gifts. I have always been ambitious for him. I have rejoiced in his increasing influence in State and national affairs. Well, then the leaders came to him again. I thought of many women whom I have known who have allowed their desire for one sort of life or another, sometimes their mere whim, to stand in the way of their husbands' careers. I could not be like them. In spite of our intentions to retire and enjoy the fruits of our busy years, in spite of my ill health, I could not but urge him to go into the campaign for the Senate. I made up my mind to be well enough to participate in the campaign. I was."

Her ability to will herself metaphysically to excellent health now recurred as if a religious tenet for Florence. Her health, however, may have been a factor in Warren's hesitation to return to politics. If she died, he would truly be free for Carrie. Yet, as Florence grew stronger, so did his commitment to a political career. It may have seemed to him that with her knack for fighting back death, Warren would always remain married to her, thus never be free for Carrie. For Warren the consolation was still exciting: his future in politics. If he at least had his career and Florence at least had her "Harding" work, the loser in the arrangement seemed to be Carrie Phillips. Perhaps realizing this—and recalling her vengeful attempt to precipitate a divorce between the Hardings—Warren delicately wrote Carrie regarding his love letters to her: "Won't you please destroy? You are not always careful with letters, and if you destroy, you won't need to be careful."[3]

The Seventeenth Amendment went into effect in 1914, for the first time in American history allowing direct election to the U.S. Senate; senators had previously been chosen by state legislatures. Despite the opposition of his earlier supporter Boss Foraker and a last-minute re-entry by the incumbent Senator Burton, Warren was nominated in the August 11 Republican primaries.

There was soon enough greater motivation for the Duchess to get Warren out of Marion. It came in a shapely ball of fury straight from Bremerhaven. Carrie Phillips *was* coming home. The assassination of Archduke Franz Ferdinand at the end of July set off a domino effect across the Continent. In Germany nationalism was running high, and aliens were becoming intimidated. On August 24, 1914, just ten days after war broke out, Carrie sailed for America and into Warren Harding's arms before the fall campaign could even begin. Infused with the German spirit, she seethed with hatred of all things American. Warren, uncertain of his true feelings toward her but weak for her flesh, delighted in their physical reunion but hesitated on any commitment. By throwing his energy into campaigning, he had a more reliable, albeit platonic, companion in the Duchess.

Once the campaign was under way, Florence limited her work to advisory management, based on her practical sensibilities. An overwhelming pressure was put on Harding to make anti-Catholic remarks against his Democratic opponent, Timothy Hogan. He was flooded with bigoted letters urging him to use religion as an issue. According to Doc's grandson and Harding's namesake, it was Florence who viscerally responded in disgust to such an idea, imploring Warren to ignore it, not only because of its bigotry but because it would only provoke a virulent retaliation regarding the rumor that the Republican candidate had African blood. Whether he followed her lead or concurred, Harding refrained from using the tactics of bigotry; consequently the rumor of his racial ancestry had no perceivable impact. She helped in other small but tactical ways. When Florence received some correspondence from supporters who pressed Harding on issues he wanted to avoid, she responded with a disarming guile, acknowlegding the writer's question and simply promising to bring it to Warren's attention. Although he took pride in his electric speechmaking, she also gave him unsolicited advice to keep his orating short. Harding won the Senate seat by more than 102,000 votes.[4]

With victory came one purposeful congratulation. Along with good wishes, Marshall demanded more of his inheritance, "as soon as you folks can," so he could buy a Denver newspaper and make it "state-wide in scope," emulating his stepfather. As a justice of the peace, doing printing for political candidates, he was ever the optimistic failure. He assured Harding, "I am not blowing my money as you have concluded. May have spent more than you would desire but not blowing it. I must have some money this week or give up further attempt until some does come." He now had another child, Esther having given birth on September 30 to George Warren, whose name partly honored Harding.

If the return of Carrie Phillips to Marion was threatening to Florence, at least she saw the last of that tiresome teenager Nan Britton, who stopped by the Harding home to offer congratulations before leaving for Cleveland, where she was going to work as a salesgirl in a china shop. From there she would eventually settle in Chicago with her sister. By now the Duchess eyed this obviously blossomed young woman suspiciously. Nan sensed this. She began to seek Harding more surreptitiously, using any ruse to speak with him—without annoying Florence—such as being dared by her former teacher Daisy Harding, just to ring the bell: "Mrs. Harding came to the door in a pink linen dress. I braved her all right and asked if I might be permitted to speak to her husband. It was late afternoon and he was playing cards with his regular bunch. He came out, and I shall never forget his smile . . . and I was thrilled unspeakably under the touch of his hand. Mrs. Harding stood pat; it even seemed to me she curtailed any lengthy remarks Mr. Harding might have been tempted to make just to please me by drawing his attention to the gentlemen in the other room who were waiting for him. But she could have nothing to do with the pressure of a hand-shake which was Mr. Harding's seal of sincere cordiality to me."

Unknown to Florence, during the past summer Warren had begun his own polite dialogue with Nan, while she took a teaching course at Kent State College with her mother. Their correspondence was unknown to Mary Britton too, for the practical Nan sent her chums down to fetch Warren's missives in thick blue envelopes from the local post office. She tightly grasped her raincheck on his vague promise to "do something" for her.

Nan provided a flattering and refreshing relief for Warren, especially in the midst of the campaign when he had to face the incessantly demanding Carrie. After the election, as their "anniversary" approached, Carrie asked for a new car as a gift. He refused with mortification, seeming to close up and away from her, but at Christmas he sent her another poem, written to mark "The Seventh Anniversary":

> I love you more than all the world,
> Possession wholly imploring
> Mid passion I am oftimes whirled,
> oftimes admire—adoring.
> Oh, God! If fate would only give us privilege to love and live!

Carrie still wanted a car. Warren finally bought her a Cadillac. Although Jim Phillips must have thought it odd, he didn't question the gift. Jim had no reasons to be suspicious. When he had decided a year earlier to visit Carrie in Germany, it had been his own friend Warren who came over to help him pack. Harding stood near the same bed where he and Carrie had first begun their sexual relationship, a memory about which he then wrote her. Certainly Warren was careful about paying for the generous gift out of a discreet personal account. It can be assumed Florence never learned about the car or his continuing drama with Carrie.[5]

On New Year's Day, with his wife and children at his side, Marshall DeWolfe died. His death certificate read, "Advanced tuberculosis of the right lung aggravated by over-alcoholism." Whatever private grief Florence had over the end of this chapter of her life, she again refused to give words to it, yet her feelings were evident. Unknown to anyone except Warren and the Sawyers, later in the year she ventured out to Colorado, to clear her son's debts and name and was befriended by several people who had become close to Marshall and were kind to her. She kept in touch with them for years to come. Esther returned to Marion with the children, and although being a "Goggy," as the tots called her, made her feel old, Florence tried valiantly to grow close to them, but she became more of a practical aunt figure to them than a smothering grandmother. She would have limited time to spend with them, however, since the Hardings were to move to Washington in the fall for the start of the Senate session and return only during recess and holidays, distance lending a degree of remoteness to her devotion. Still, it seemed easier for her to cope emotionally with grandchildren than it had been for her with a child of her own. As a working woman she had avoided the traditional chores of motherhood. As a grandmother she enjoyed picking out Easter outfits and marveling at Christmas gifts without any further responsibility, then turning the toddlers back to their mother's care. Later her best friend admitted that Florence "never showed any interest in children."

The children did draw particularly close to Warren, and he showered them with affection. He said he was "never merrier" than when "our two kiddies" romped through his house. "They thought of Mr. Harding as their grandfather," recalled Betty Bartram, a friend of Florence's granddaughter. "They were very fond of him. They saw them as grandma and grandpa. No animosity among family members that I knew of. Long after Marshall died, his wife remained friends with Mrs. Harding. She was very kind to her daughter-in-law and two grandchildren. When Esther remarried to Roscoe Metzger, Florence always still signed herself as 'Mother' and Esther signed 'Your daughter' to her. She didn't interfere or demand that the grandchildren be raised in any particular way." Esther turned over Marshall's urn of ashes to her, and the Duchess kept them within her sight at home, refusing to do anything with them until later forced to. Somehow, after years of neglect, she could not now give up her son.[6]

In the months following Marshall's death, Florence was again Warren's travel companion. Originally he had promised her a world trip with India as the primary destination, to visit his sister Carolyn and her husband, Heber, but when the Votaws returned to America earlier than expected, the Hardings decided on a lengthy domestic junket. Although he was elected in November 1914, the Senate session would not begin until December 1915. In the interim the senator-elect made numerous and extensive pleasure and fact-finding missions around the country. By rail and ship, joined by the ubiquitous Sawyers and George Christian, Jr., hired as Warren's personal Senate aide, the Hardings made their first trip to California and Hawaii.

The first leg of the voyage in January 1915 was a series of speaking engagements through Texas and long days of poker and golf at the Scobeys' Rio Grande Valley ranch. Then they went on to San Francisco, from which they sailed on the *Matsonia* for ten days in the Hawaiian Islands. As they made their way down the gangplank, their fate was altered in the eager, fleshy handshake of one flabby, bespectacled "Charlie,"—Charles R. Forbes, the Wilson administration's director of construction at the new Pearl Harbor Naval Base. His equally unctuous wife, Kate Marcia, a freelance writer, gleefully threw leis of tropical flowers around the Duchess's neck.

Nobody played a better poker hand than Charlie, or cracked jokes, or arranged for creature comforts in such detail. The daily morning rap on the Hardings' Beach Hotel suite door was the welcome sound of the enthusiastic man, lavishing all his attention not only on the senator-elect but on the Duchess. This melted her. It had taken her some time to warm up to Harry Daugherty and his companion, Jess Smith, but she found herself instantly drawn to the charismatic Charlie. The Forbeses escorted the Hardings to scheduled programs—Warren's speeches as guest of honor at an Ad Club lunch, a bar association dinner, a Chamber of Commerce banquet, another dinner at the Buckeye Club, a review of troops at Fort Shafter—and arranged special events: a sail to Oahu, a tour of the Kahuku Marconi wireless plant, a submarine ride, a cruise to Hilo and Kauai, and a visit to Mauna Loa. Florence always remembered Hawaii because of the "generous, old-fashioned friendship and excellent citizenship" embodied by Charlie and Kate Marcia. She quickly counted them as her new favorites. "Forbes's genial nature, so typically savoring of the Old West of the big black hats and unrestricted hospitality, immediately won the heart of the Ohioan," noted reporter Carl Dickey. "It was not long before they were addressing each other as 'Warren' and 'Charlie.' When the visit at Honolulu was over, 'Charlie' had an invitation to visit the Hardings at Marion or at Washington."

It was to be expected that the gullible Warren would find Charlie's sychophantic chuckles natural and flattering. To seduce the more suspicious Florence, Forbes left nothing to chance. He rehearsed his repartee and rehashed and enameled his life story, always covering his tracks. It was nearly a decade before Florence learned that fifteen years earlier he had abandoned his first wife—and the United States Army.

Forbes was a naturalized citizen, born in British Columbia. Little is known of his earliest years until the record of his desertion from his wife and the Signal Corps of the Army, while he had been stationed across the river from Washington, D.C., in Fort Myer in 1900. Apprehended four years later in Massachusetts, he had been reinstated at Fort Strong. Given a second chance, Forbes went on to earn the rank of sergeant and was honorably discharged. He then became a Seattle railroad contractor and began to enjoy a modicum of political power, finagling a Wilson administration appointment as Honolulu's commissioner of public works. Assigned to escort political figures around the island, pointing out the new buildings, he shone as the perfect glad-handing host.

Not everybody was fooled by Forbes. Doc Sawyer, whom he ignored as politely as possible, was distinctly unimpressed. Still jealous of his self-appointed role as Harding Best Friend, Doc developed a distaste for Forbes as immediate as the Hardings' affection for him. "He wasn't very nice to my grandfather," said Warren Sawyer. "He treated him terribly, but [Forbes] just buttered up the Hardings. My grandfather always wanted to protect the best interests of the Hardings, but with Forbes, from the get go, my grandfather smelled a rat."

On Valentine's Day 1915 the Hardings and Sawyers sailed on the SS *Sierra* back to San Francisco. On their return the foursome stopped off in Santa Ana to see Warren's sister Charity Remsberg, her husband, Elton, and their daughters, and the city gave a luncheon honoring the senator-elect and Mrs. Harding. Florence took to California, and the trip there rivaled the excitement of her first trip to Europe, with the dry air superior to Florida's. She and Warren were especially fascinated by the burgeoning colony of motion-picture studios in Hollywood. The Hardings took time out to visit Universal City, where they witnessed the technological wonder of filming a moving picture, *The Stool Pigeon.* The Duchess's only disappointment was that she never did catch a glimpse of Charlie Chaplin, her favorite movie star.[7]

Upon their return from California, the Duchess left Marion again to make some living arrangements in Washington for her and Warren. She decided to rent a small house in the tony Kalorama section for a while before buying one. Back home she arranged for James C. Woods to become the *Star*'s business manager. After her final Marion exodus in the fall, she often directed "Jimmy" long distance, giving advice on management.

If she had become wrapped up in the minutia of moving, Florence's activities, like the rest of the world's, were called to attention in May, when the *Lusitania,* carrying some American passengers, had been sunk by the Germans, now at war with Britain. Though Warren was not to take his Senate seat until December 6, he spoke in favor of American preparedness for war. His words provoked unexpected rancor in Carrie. During their occasional trysts that year she fiercely reprimanded Warren for his statement, trumpeting her violent opposition to any American intervention. Stuck in her loveless marriage in Marion, jealous that Florence was going with Warren to Washington, Carrie raged against his "mad pursuit of honors."

Just weeks before their scheduled departure for Washington, Florence suffered a recurrence of her kidney ailment and had to be treated by Doc. Seeing that her illness was distracting Warren, who would not begin his new adventure without her, Florence again, peculiarly, remarkably, willed herself to recuperate. Jane Dixon folksily recalled the strange incident, saying Florence "put her foot on the accelerator and before the shocked medical experts could realize what she was about, declared herself 'fit as a fiddle, back on deck, with her hat in the ring.' " Nothing could keep the Duchess in Marion now.

It had been many months since Esther had turned over to Florence the urn with Marshall's ashes. Now, with luggage, moving crates, and storage boxes cluttering the house, time was forcing the issue. She had to leave, to move on. On November 23, the day before she and Warren were to begin their trip to Washington, the Duchess went into Lett's to have her hair marcelled. Instead of her usual upbeat self, she wore a "long face" and was visibly shaken, in a rare mournful state. Mrs. Lett asked what happened. She replied, "We just buried Marshall's ashes." He was to rest with his wife's family, seemingly displaced out of his own clans.[8]

The next day, as the train pulled into Washington's Union Station, Florence Harding disembarked into a new world. She carried her past with her.

Part Three

THE SENATE
1916-1920

I wonder if anyone ever anticipated the coldness, the aloofness that one meets here. . . .

13

Fish out of Water

For the first time since Amos Kling dominated her youth, Florence was defined solely through a man. At least then, however, she had been the daughter of the town's richest man. Now she merited no notice since, as merely another new senator, Warren did not command a high rating on the Washington society pecking order. If Marion's biggest fish was now in a bigger pond, one of Ohio's most successful businesswomen was completely a fish out of water. Florence Harding received scant attention in the capital, and it depressed her. "I wonder if anyone ever anticipated the coldness, the aloofness that one meets here at first, [more than] in any other city of the world," she said of her initial treatment. "It is indescribable. My home town was small and our neighbors were of the progressive and democratic citizenship type who cared little for form and more for achievement."

Within days of their arrival in Washington, Florence had the distraction of entertaining her first two guests, who wasted no time in hooking themselves on to the Hardings: Charlie Forbes and Harry Daugherty. "We had a very pleasant visit with the pair of them," Warren wrote to Doc, "and were treated to some very interesting views of Hawaiian life on the one hand and political conspiracy on the other." Once they departed, however, Florence's sense of displacement was exacerbated by having to live in rented quarters. In consideration of the full six-year Senate term, she shortly after bought a house at 2314 Wyoming Avenue near Embassy Row, but before she could move in, she fell ill again, all the more panicked for being in a strange town.

In the second week of January she suffered from heart palpitations, acute indigestion, and severe flu. She was under the care of one of the city's better physicians, a Dr. Ruffin, but, as Warren wrote Doc, she kept "saying each morning that if she is not better on the morrow that I must send for you to come down here. . . . [Ruffin] seems to be a very capable fellow, but does not command Mrs. Harding's confidence as you do, and for that reason, if no other, is much less effective in treating her." Florence, through dictation to Berenice Blacksten, now serving as the Harding housekeeper in Washington, informed Doc that "not since the days of my wound have I suffered so" and that she feared it must be her "sick kidney." Unprompted, Doc came from Ohio to her side, as always with services provided gratis, and shortly thereafter Warren reported to him, "Your unexpected visit did her an estimable amount of good, because you set at rest her very much perturbed mental condition brought on by reports from her local physician."

Frustration and depression had set in, with Florence depending on Doc to lift her emotionally. After being assured by Ruffin that her kidneys showed no dysfunction, she nevertheless reported to Doc, "[H]e is far more pleased with my condition than I am. Perhaps I am down in the dumps today. . . . I am really awfully weak. . . . When I have walked the length of the hall from my room to the front room and back three times it seems quite a distance. To tell you the truth I am considerably worried about this swelling in my abdomen. Seems I am conscious of it every moment while I never noticed it before the night I was taken with those terrible pains. Do you suppose there could be anything else growing there? . . . Possibly as soon as I can get out of doors and get my mind on other matters I may forget about my 'lump.' . . . Think I have now told you all my troubles."

The next night she wrote: "Have had a fairly good day today and am in a much happier frame of mind than when I wrote yesterday. My bowels feel very much more comfortable and that swollen place has either gone back to its old position or the swelling is reduced. It still gives me many anxious hours, but I try not to allow myself to brood over it. . . . I am inclined to make these letters gossipy rather than strictly professional . . . you must get dreadfully tired of hearing about my troubles all the time. But when I have the blues I must unload to some one. Why not you?" Over the next few days, Florence still reported herself being "dreadfully nervous," even signing one letter, "I am yours (nearly always in distress)."

Responding to such dark letters, often questioning the results of her various lab tests, Doc alternately frightened and calmed her, warning her once "not to put things off, because with your judgment and your experience you know how serious conditions are," yet reassuring her in another, "[G]et in the machine and get about a little. . . . All you need to do as you well know is to be careful and not overdo. You know the consequences of fatigue."

As she healed, Florence seemed embarrassed by her dependency on Doc yet affirmed his power over her: "I certainly was all wrong and you pointed the way. I want you to know that I am sticking to the course too. Really wanted you to come back this way, but feel I had been such a nuisance. I did not have the nerve to ask it of you . . . thanking you for all the trouble I have caused. . . . This Washington doctor . . . I never want to see him." Dosing herself with Doc's homeopathic "dark pellet," "green medicine," "flat white tablets," and "yellow pellets" to ward off all ills, real and imagined, once she felt secure, the Duchess was out full throttle. She soon took up the Washington ritual of paying calls, in strict ranking order, on political, diplomatic, and judicial wives. Florence avidly made the rounds of the largely European and eastern seaboard society class, but it resulted in no friendship. As acquaintance Ray Baker Harris reflected, "In such groups she was never at ease, and often on the defensive, but for the sake of her husband's position she was eager to be liked and anxious to make a good impression. In these circumstances, and considering the state of her health, when only personal courage prevented her from succumbing to invalidism, many of the trivial criticisms of Mrs. Harding, mostly by other women, seem . . . to have been unjust and even shabby." Protecting her vulnerability, she furthermore sought to mask the premature aging of her precarious health by heavily rouging her cheeks to look rosy, veiling her face, and making a black velvet band worn around her neck her trademark. Her kidney condition, said Warren Sawyer, "was not common knowledge."[1]

She found some distraction in furnishing her new house. Bought with fifty thousand dollars from her inheritance, the large neo-Georgian style building with terrace and side entry, had a spare look, the large drawing room featuring fine glass vases, a Sèvres china clock, a portrait of Warren, some current fiction and nonfiction books, framed personal photographs, and antique chairs. Her upstairs sitting room had "Sleepy Hollow chairs," bookcases, Warren's desk, and tan window draperies. There was a guest room with twin beds, where, for example, Harding's young nephews George and Warren stayed during their visits. The elegantly simply dining room displayed her exquisite china, silver, and crystal sets. The kitchen, overseen by Berenice, had a well-stocked supply of modern cookware on long rows of shelves. Occasionally the Duchess baked cream caramel cake there, but she often hired staff as she needed them, such as private secretary Genevieve McDonald or washwoman Lucy Benton. She also rated hired help in her notebook, warning herself about decorator J. Hevie, "have to watch him," and noting that window cleaner John Anderson was "just fair."

Florence's Senate notebook provides a glimpse into her thoughts and activities of this period of her life, reflecting both official business and cryptically personal thoughts. In between dress measurements, the brand names of various face and body creams she had bought in Paris, and a "wash for trees" recipe was a curious assortment of names, new and old, of those she kept in touch with. Not only did she keep tabs on Charlie and Kate Forbes, now living at Wakerton, Indiana, Myra Nye, a Los Angeles *Times* "newspaper girl," Edith Gattis, the "Supreme Queen" of the Daughters of the Nile, and the distantly related author Horace Harding, but also on Marion Hodder, Warren's illegitimate daughter, living at West 101st Street in New York. She had a roster of astrologers and clairvoyants: Mrs. Joseph in Cleveland, Marie Juliette Pontin, and Madame Sorel ("like her," Florence noted) in New York and the famous Evangeline Adams, who came down to Washington for special readings. Near her own home, she had Miss Madeira at 1330 Nineteenth Street and "David-Astrologer" at 1622 Q Street. Next to his name, she noted cryptically: "year 1911 is what I wish." Perhaps it was a wistful longing for that seemingly happy but blissfully unaware period of her life just prior to her discovery of Warren's adultery with Carrie Phillips.

Using astrological advice gave Florence a sense of control over her life during this time when she seemed extraordinarily nervous. Warren was often the recipient of her edicts. After the expense of outfitting a senator's home, for example, she irrationally feared debt. At the end of the year Warren sarcastically told Doc that "the dominating head of the family" had ordered that "there were to be no Christmas exchanges this year" and he had to send some secretly.[2]

By catapulting herself into busy mindless activity on behalf of constituents, Florence seemed to distract herself from her anxiety, as illustrated in her letters to her cousin Ada Denman:

My life these days seems to be one great rush. People coming and going all the time. Here's a sample this past ten days. [In town were a] Mrs. Thompkins from Columbus whose daughter is in school here, Mrs. Mc-Murray of Marion, a son in school, Mrs. Quigley from Cincinnati, Mrs. Mack [from] Sandusky, attending the D.A.R.'s. & Mrs. Laylin, DAR, Mrs. Donavin, Marion, Dr. Sawyer from home, and by the time I spend a day or two driving them about there is very little time for me. Mrs. Donavin was a house guest and when she left Friday at 11 A.M. I rushed off to have my hair and nails tended to and was at a luncheon at one o'clock given in honor of Mrs. Marshall, wife of the Vice President. At four my clothes were changed and by six o'clock I had made eight calls. Yet I enjoy seeing each and every one of them. Try to see Carrie [Votaw] at least once a week, but can't always do it. She and Heber are going to Ohio. . . . [I] was in Ohio two weeks ago for two days, also down to New York. W.G. was in N.Y. last night for a big dinner. You and Harry come and see us when you can.

Touring constituents through the city—frequently to the Smithsonian exhibit of First Lady gowns—she long recalled an incident at the White House gates, where she had taken some Ohioans. "A policeman was herding sheep which were grazing on the lawn. Spying us, he promptly ordered us to 'move on' and to step lively. It was slushy and in my haste to obey orders, I slipped and fell in the mud. My dignity was wounded more than I was physically hurt, but right then and there I resolved that if ever I had any authority about the White House, and were given permission to issue any orders, the policemen at the Executive Mansion would have some duties to perform other than herding sheep. . . ." She may also have been insulted that despite her status as a Senate wife, she was unrecognized.

The Duchess relished any public attention she received. She was eager even to provide an advertisement testimonial, for example, for Royce's flavor extracts. Trading in on her own experience and now access to inside information through Warren, she finally began to make headway with Washington's male political reporters and women society writers. Listed at NOrth 8658, she was always ready to talk to the press. "She will come to the telephone anytime she possibly can," said a reporter, "and chat as freely and as unconcernedly if she knows you at all . . . and then when you're hugging yourself at the perfectly wonderful interview you're getting, she says casually and sweetly, 'Of course you understand that you are not to quote me.'" These relationships served her well.[3]

Trying to recapture the working partnership of the *Star* days with Warren, Florence was a frequent presence in his Senate office, though she soon realized that his professional staff left her little to do. Although he had served as assistant secretary of the 1912 Democratic National Convention, George Christian put his friendship with the Hardings above all else, and Warren asked him to manage the office. He and his wife, Doris "Stella" Farrar, had even named the first of their two sons after him. Equally familiar to Florence was her brother-in-law Heber Votaw, now returned with Carolyn from India and working as the senator's primary clerk. Carolyn worked long hours in Washington's police welfare department, charged with the newly formed women's police bureau under the Public Health Service, where she established a voluntary probation department and helped "wrong girls" in a city where there were more illegitimate children per capita than anywhere in America. Although Heber commuted to their home in Takoma Park, Maryland, where he taught at the Seventh-Day Adventist College and worked part-time managing a sanitarium, Carolyn's work kept her in a downtown boardinghouse during the week. Disturbed by the separation, Heber unfortunately unloaded about her and Harding to an acquaintance curiously eager to befriend him, local education official William Chancellor. "She takes marriage lightly for herself—though strictly virtuous—and lightly for these unfortunate girls," Chancellor wrote, "most of the time she has not lived with her husband, though not actively hostile to him. . . ." Chancellor came to haunt the Hardings for years by rattling their skeletons.

The fifty-one-year-old widower of Henry Ward Beecher's niece, father of five, Dayton native William Estabrook Chancellor had graduated Phi Beta Kappa with bachelor's and master's degrees from Amherst College. He founded Johns Hopkins's educational department and George Washington University's teachers' college. He counted the sons of Presidents Roosevelt and Garfield as personal friends and wrote thirty-eight books, including *Our Presidents and Their Office*, published by reputable houses like Harper's and Houghton Mifflin. A contributor to *The New York Times*, Chancellor, who was tall with a crest of gray hair parted in the center, cut a commanding figure. An ardent Democrat who defended Wilson on Jim Crow laws in a Cleveland *Plain Dealer* editorial, he was also a racist fanatic, declaring that black Americans should have rights taken away from them, that segregation was critical to America's survival, and that the czar would fall to bolshevism because Jews had seized power in religious retaliation for hundreds of years of Russian repression.

As school superintendent he received a letter of introduction sometime before 1915 from Ohio Senator Foraker for Carolyn Votaw, who wanted to become a teacher. For some reason Chancellor thought she was a "quadroon," a person of partial African ancestry, and turned down the request. When he later learned that Warren had secured Carolyn her position in the District police department, some racist foghorn sounded in Chancellor, and he began not only obsessively scribbling down what he heard about the Hardings but asking people for information on them, using it all to prove his theory that those of African ancestry—reputed or otherwise—formed an inferior race that was a menace to American society. As a native Ohioan he had undoubtedly heard the rumors of Harding's African ancestry during his various campaigns, and with this man now representing the Buckeye State in the United States Senate, Chancellor became obsessed with destroying his career. He began assembling not only a dubious Harding genealogy but a roster of the senator's indiscretions. With the credibility of a later sociology professorial post at Wooster College in Ohio, he got people to talk. Curiously, the material he most sought—genuine evidence of Harding's ancestry—never materialized as reliable information, but in the process of his search over the years, he opened a Pandora's box of truths about both Warren and Florence: facts such as the Carrie Phillips affair, Warren's precarious heart condition, Florence's De Wolfe relationship and treatment of Marshall that were known by only those closest to the Hardings in Marion, facts that were not known in Washington.

Thankful for his seat in the world's most exclusive men's club, Harding relied on Florence's advice. As he dictated political correspondence, for example, she listened and often threw in a line, as when he wrote to Mac Jennings, "The Duchess is sitting by and listening and censors all that I say." Most notably on suffrage, however, there were limits to her influence. If by 1916 Florence Harding was an avowed suffragist, she could not budge the senator out of his indecision. He told a suffrage delegation in his office, "I have been up to this time utterly indifferent to the question—neither hostile towards it, nor for the suffrage cause. Believing as I do in political parties and government through political parties, I had much rather that the party . . . make a declaration, than to assume a leadership or take an individual position. . . ." Such genial reluctance to take a stand perversely thrust him into leadership in the years ahead. Because of his ambivalence, other people could assign to Harding their own agendas and desires.[4]

Mrs. Harding could frequently be found in the reserved seating of the Senate gallery. Suffrage, the European war, immigration—the debate on a variety of issues wafted up to her; there began Florence Harding's tutelage in national politics and the men who shaped it. It also served to fill her loneliness, as she later admitted. In finding "goodfellowship so remote" in Washington, she said, "I was not happy except when listening to the debates on the floor of the Senate."

The Duchess could not help noticing, as everyone else did, the youngish woman who came daily to watch the Senate, leaning forward intently over the railing, occasionally even scandalizing legislators by appearing there in pants. She was more than a congressional wife; she was a national celebrity, pointed out to tourists by the Capitol guides. Despite the fact that her husband was in the House, she knew the prestige and action were in the Senate, and so engrossed was she in its debates that once while hosting a luncheon at home, she received a call about an upcoming vote, grabbed her trademark black cartwheel hat, and abruptly left her guests to themselves. With Nick Longworth's 1914 reelection to Congress, after his humiliating defeat in 1912, Princess Alice was back, doing her best to ignore the Hardings except when Nick and Warren resumed their poker-playing and hard-drinking friendship.

If the Princess seemed indifferent to the Duchess, others started to observe Mrs. Harding. One Senate wife later anonymously recorded her blistering impression:

Florence Harding . . . [was] the classic example of the woman who leads a contingent life. . . . Therein lies her tragedy. It was her misfortune to have been born in a day when women could realize her ambitions only through a husband. . . . [H]ampered by the husband's limitations. . . . Florence had gifts of her own . . . an urge to achieve, to go on and on, to occupy first place . . . an urge that recognizes no limitations and sweeps every obstacle ruthlessly. The first time I saw Florence was after she arrived in the public eye. Once there, her possession of this ambition to be first was manifest to all beholders. Her political mind was a matter of common knowledge . . . it was Florence whom his friends and henchmen back home came to consult. Whereas most Senators interview such men in their offices, Warren saw them at his residence and Florence was usually present . . . making Warren do what she wanted . . . ready to study ways and means, discover the useful contacts. . . . Barring bad luck any one can play the game who is courageous, ruthless and shrewd. And Florence was all three . . . he took so seriously what Florence said. . . . He felt her opinion and the opinions of other men were more important than his own . . . pleasure-loving[,] he was the envy of his confreres because his wife did not seem to mind . . . it was always so easy to vote right. Florence was clever. If it was she who drew the conversation around to the bills and elicited advice that was helpful, he did not know it . . . the middle-aged, dowdy wife of an everyday senator did not interest Washington . . . she was more than a little bitter . . . already her ambition was soaring towards a position where she would have to be reckoned with socially as well as politically. Her hands were full. There was much political work to do. A state takes much looking after. There were constituents to be served, patronage to be distributed. . . .[5]

"Mrs. Harding was what my grandmother used to call 'a strainer.' Strained to get up there! Social ambition," said Lillian Parks, whose mother later worked for Florence. "She pushed her way up to be recognized. She wanted to be prominent among the Senators' ladies."

If the social Senate wives had little use for Florence, she became a "prime favorite" with one particular senator. With a black Stetson hat crowning a round face marked by a shoestring white mustache, and skin tanned to leather, drawling a broken Spanish in his native Kentucky twang between his spits of tobacco, he even carried his gun in Washington. When Warren Harding first took his seat on the Senate floor, the first hand to extend itself belonged to this senator from New Mexico who seemed more like Buffalo Bill than a legislator. His name was Albert Bacon Fall.

Elected in 1912, when New Mexico became a state, Fall described himself as an old Mexico prospector who had a "self-education, procured at night in a lonely camp by the light of a lantern or candle." He had announced that he admired "Chinamen" because they "drove the Apache, the Sioux, and other Indians out of the mountain country and finally back to their reservations, and made the country habitable, and prepared the way for the cattle and sheep men. . . ." Married in 1882 to native Tennessean Emma Morgan, the daughter of a Confederate congressman, who had been raised as an orphan in Arkansas, he made a vast profit in selling her inherited Texas properties along the Mexican border, where they relocated and raised a family of three daughters and a son. Because of Emma's poor health, they moved to New Mexico in 1887, and there, as a lawyer, Fall defended adultery cases for married Mexican Catholics who had crossed the border into America and taken second spouses. He also handled fifty first-degree murder cases. While serving in the territorial legislature, Fall stepped across the aisle to slap a colleague who disagreed with him. At the New Mexico Constitutional Convention he punched out a fellow delegate.

Fall built a large desert ranch for himself near Tularosa, New Mexico, called Three Rivers, and had his hand in dozens of land speculation ventures. He unapologetically exploited open land; he was openly contemptuous of conservationists like Theodore Roosevelt. When challenged by the National Park Service about the sad legacy the destruction of public lands would leave, Fall fired back: "Every generation from Adam and Eve down has lived better than the generation before. I don't know how . . . [the next generation will] do it—maybe they'll use the energy of the sun or the sea waves—but [they] will live better than we do. I stand for opening up every resource."

Fall's secretary recalled that he "was a real favorite of Mrs. Harding's," and she frequently invited him for political dinners at her home. At these conferences around her dinner table the Duchess was, according to Fall's aide, "the moving spirit, the center of things among them." Among Warren's other colleagues whom she grew close to were his frequent golf partners: New Jersey's Joseph Freylinghuysen, New York's James Wadsworth, Maine's Frederick Hale, and Congressman Fred Gillett, who became House Speaker. When the popular Warren was invited to the homes of senators for dinners and even vacations, the Duchess came along, meeting distinguished individuals prominent in their fields, such as engineer Herbert Hoover, who later organized the Food Conservation Division of the Food Administration. Those few wives with whom Florence could connect tended to be equally political: Emma Fall; Catherine "Bill" New, the wife of Indiana's Harry New; and Mary Hale, with whom the Duchess held many political "talk-outs." Alice Longworth remained steadfastly cold to her.[6]

Although Alice obligingly, "continuously" invited the Hardings to her home for Nick's poker games, she said, "I had never happened to go to theirs. It is odd to have seen so much of people whom I never liked as I saw of the Hardings. . . . Though Mrs. Harding did not play, she always came too, and the job of the Duchess . . . was to 'tend bar.' Harding and Nick and the others would say when they wished another drink, 'Duchess, you are lying down on your job.' And Mrs. Harding, who was watching the play of the hands, would obediently get up and mix a whiskey and soda for them." Alice quickly learned to mimic the Duchess and her flat accent, complete with grating yells for "Wurr'n!" She also imitated Nellie Taft; her cousin Eleanor Roosevelt, the wife of Franklin; and even her stepmother, Edith. Perhaps with paranoia, Alice later claimed that Florence kept a list of women who had snubbed her in Washington in the little red book the Duchess spoke about keeping. It was, in fact, a list of numerous people who had been kind to her. On the other hand, a reporter close to her, Boyden Sparkes, recalled her snub from an ink heiress and how Florence determined to revenge it. Sparkes observed, "She could be vindictive."[7]

Social ambition for Florence at best provided her with an uncertain status, only one way she might prove herself master of her fate. Since the Senate had been achieved and no other great goal now loomed, Florence seemed to turn in circles, ambitious just for the sake of being ambitious, growing more confused about her role in the management of Warren's career. There seemed nowhere else to climb. There *was* one other position up for grabs in 1916. But if Florence was consciously thinking of the presidency for Warren as early as 1916, she didn't express it. Warren, on the other hand, did, dismissing to Mac Jennings any talk of being run as a dark horse candidate: "I think you know me quite as well as anybody in Ohio, and you know that I am unsuited to the higher position if it were possible for me to attain it, and you know that I am truthful when I say that I do not desire it and most sincerely wish to escape the responsibilities that a candidacy alone would bring and the greater anxieties that would attend an election in times like these. Honestly, I would not have the place if I could reach out and grasp it, and I really do not want any of my friends to promote it in any way. On the contrary, I should prefer that every suggestion should be promptly punctured. . . . Wilson was quite right when he said to the Gridiron Club that anyone would be an audacious fool to wish the Presidency on his own account. Of course I am human to enjoy having friends who think well enough to suggest me for that position."

While Warren had no false modesty about his limitations, he nonetheless enjoyed the attention such speculation brought. When the chance arose for Harding to take center stage as temporary Republican National Convention chairman in Chicago from June 7 to 10, he relished the opportunity. Florence shared the spotlight with him. As he was introduced and came to the podium to deliver his speech, the Duchess, according to a Republican party worker, was "a conspicuous figure standing proudly beside her distinguished husband." Charles Evan Hughes was nominated to run against President Wilson, but the convention turned the freshmen Ohio senator into a "big Republican," worthy of national party interest for 1920.[8]

Despite Warren's prominence and her rounds of ancillary Senate activities, by summer it was clear that without an ambition greater than social calls or mixing drinks, without some self-imposed challenge to meet, Florence lacked meaning in her life. By 1916 Florence Harding considered pursuing her own career. In sketching her autobiography, she not only exhibited her stubbornly genteel small town pride but revealed her own "ambition for authority" as director of a social service organization:

> Mrs. Warren G. (Florence Kling) Harding, wife of the Senator from Ohio, was married to Mr. Harding in 1891. They have no children. Mrs. Harding was the only daughter of Mr. and Mrs. Kling, a foremost family at Marion, Ohio and was especially schooled in music, but gave of her energies and influence to help her young husband achieve the newspaper success with which he is accredited. A notable social grace and poise has

always been hers, and the leadership accorded her at home was without ostentation. She is fond of fiction and biography, but prefers travel above all else. Her fad is a fine horse, with special enthusiasm for good saddlehorses. In her youth, she was an excellent rider of the side saddle. She also confesses a fondness for dogs, but possesses none nowadays, because of her distress over the unavoidable sorrow in losing pets to which she was affectionately attached. Her one expressed ambition for authority is to direct a society for the prevention of cruelty to children and animals. She has been known many a time in Washington to stop her automobile and protest against a brutal teamster's abuse of his horses, or to advise an ignorant one in his pitiless ignorance to make horses understand. Every cruelty she could not correct she promptly reported to the police department. Mrs. Harding has a ready appreciation of people worthwhile, but is ever normally democratic because of her life in harmony with that of a small city and her association with a self-wrought career.

Florence's loneliness was exacerbated without the companionship of a dog. Three years earlier, however, following the traumatic discovery that Hub had been anonymously poisoned to death, she decided never to so attach herself again, feeling she couldn't bear another such possible loss. Her lavish love of animals had remained constant, but of all her pets, none had grown closer to her than Hub, all the more an object of affection because in a moment of clarity, Marshall had given him to her. Hub's poisoning had also turned the Duchess into an advocate of the growing movement against cruelty to animals. She joined the Animal Rescue League, the Humane Society, and the Society for the Prevention of Cruelty to Animals; she pressed the groups' literature on friends and was regularly a heavy contributor to the cause. She began to speak out against animal abuse and challenge it when she saw it. One night, for example, when Florence heard the commotion of a drunken man whipping his horse after the animal had fallen in front of the wagon, she ran into the street, tended to the horse, then pulled the whip away from the man and gave it to his wife. "If you have to," Florence told her, "use the whip—but not on the horse.'"

She continued to lament the use of motorcars because of the inevitable and widespread neglect of horses and mules, but Warren cracked that his car was the only thing he "ever owned that she did not have a desire to run." With brief but frequent returns to Marion, however—where they stayed with the Sawyers since their home was rented—she gave in to the car. In veiled hat and duster coat, with a shoe box full of sandwiches and cigars for Warren, Florence enjoyed speeding with the top down, in the open air.[9]

On trips back to Ohio, Florence always tried to accompany Warren, but with his promise to keep her informed during his stumping the country for Hughes in the summer and fall of 1916, she remained at home. His letters to her focused on reaction to his speeches. Despite the fact that Heywood Broun said of his convention speech that "sometimes one could hardly see Harding for the words about him," Democrat William Jennings Bryan said his timbre was "excellent" and delivery "splendid." Harding campaigned through New England, Pennsylvania, the Rockies, and the central West. "I seem to have a better and vastly greater reputation than at home," he told her. "My speeches seem to be well received."

While Florence only encouraged Warren in his political endeavors, Carrie, in their continuing correspondence, only derided him. He half agreed with her assessment that he didn't belong in politics but defended himself by praising Florence's support: "I am finally awakened to my utter incapacity and incompetence, but I can struggle to be partially fitted, and will. *Somebody* believes in me or I would not be here." Carrie delighted in torturing Warren's emotions, pressing him into admitting that had they been married, he would not have been separated from her by politics. "True," he had written her a month after becoming senator, "I went into politics for diversion and distraction at a time when you seemed lost to me (and you evidently were, in part at least)."[10]

Perhaps lingering doubts that Warren and Carrie had truly ended their love affair prompted Florence's chaperoning whenever he returned to Marion—although she insisted that their trips home be as short as possible. If, as she neared the end of her first year as a Senate wife, the Duchess still felt lost in the capital, she now also seemed uncomfortable in her hometown. There was no way for her to know that as she mixed drinks at yet another Longworth poker game that fall, she would find someone like a Carrie Phillips for herself finally, someone who focused energy on her, who asked questions about her life and thoughts, who could be a confidante for her insecurities, fears, and ambitions.

14

The Morphine Addict and the Hope Diamond

The din of laughter spilled from the glowing yellow windows on the second floor of Nick and Alice Longworth's M Street brownstone. Besides the Hardings, that night's guests included Ohio's Portsmouth *Daily Blade* publisher Charles Hard, and the owner of the Cincinnati *Enquirer* and Washington *Post*, and his wife, who was Alice's best friend. This woman recalled:

> That evening I decided that the junior senator from Ohio was a stunning man with a powerfully masculine quality to charm a woman. He did not pretend to be a ladies man although he never—unless she was around—tried to hide the fact that he liked ladies. . . . That night his white-haired kidney-troubled wife, whose chin was lifted haughtily each time she scented challenge, served all our drinks and did not play. Woman-like, I noticed that her neck was withering and her ankles thickly swollen almost before I realized that she was rich in spirits; a determined and a jealous wife. . . . By the calendar year she was five years older than her husband, but by all that matters in a marital partnership, she was far, far older than her easy-going, play-loving partner. Ill-health and a tendency to worry over what might happen, plus her nagging temperament had helped to wear her body; with Harding tomorrow was, at that time, just another day. Hers was the ambition; what he had was charm, an ability to get along with assorted persons; friendliness and a love of jovial companions . . . a small-town Elk by which I mean no disrespect to Elks or Harding.

As the evening wore on, the Duchess tired of making drinks and wandered into the drawing room alone. Only later, during a break between games, did everyone notice the sad sounds of a piano wafting through the room. The publisher's wife called herself out of the next game and wandered away, but before long, her comical, shrill singing voice—in what Alice later termed a bad emulation of Jeanette Mac-Donald—warbled along to a livelier Tin Pan Alley accompaniment by Florence, a version of the 1911 "Egyptia." Long years later Alice was still confounded by what these two—a young multimillionairess and an older "harridan"—could find in common and how they seemed to be having "their own grand time" at the piano. "Vinegar and water, vinegar and water," Alice sniped about the unlikely duo. Perhaps she had realized that in those few short moments she had lost her best friend.[1]

Her name was Evalyn Walsh McLean, and despite her great wealth, her background was humbler than that of either Alice or Florence. She was born on August 1, 1886, in Leadville, Colorado, the daughter of Tom Walsh, an engaging Irish immigrant miner who was Amos Kling's antithesis. Evalyn grew up in Rocky Mountain shacks and fleabag hotels: "The sheets were not always clean, but the guests were not particular." As a girl she admired "homicidal maniacs, nice women and prostitutes, Chinese and some Indians." She was compassionate, blunt, and highly spiritual, though hardly religious. "Well, if I was not a good Catholic," she said of her father's faith, "at least I was never a very good Protestant."

When she was twelve, her father discovered a gold mine, and the family went from rags to riches. They moved to Washington, their home a mammoth white marble mansion designed by Stanford White at 2020 Massachusetts Avenue. It was there, as a teenager, that she developed her daily taste for alcohol, beginning with sips from the crème de menthe in the cabinet. "Drink," she admitted, "has been an evil influence in my life." At fourteen, when Evalyn announced that she wanted to be an actress, she was sent to Paris for singing lessons and given a huge apartment. Instead of singing, she ran wild. She was so intrigued with the look of prostitutes ("they did not seem to lead such a bad life") that she began licking the red dye off books for rouge for her cheeks and rolled her eyes to lure men, horrifying her Scottish maid. Her father wired her to return. Instead she began coloring her hair, first blond, eventually red, then pink. In Washington Evalyn had been most fascinated by Alice, then the President's scandalous daughter, two years her senior, first glimpsing her while the Princess dressed for a dance in her honor at 2020. Not yet out to society, Evalyn was not allowed to attend, but behind her mother's closet she watched Alice powder her nose and smoke a cigarette. For "many years," Evalyn later recalled, "we have been about together . . . [but] that night I was just another Carmen willing to pull her hair or fight with other weapons." The battle line was drawn around bumbling dimwit and newspaper heir Edward B. McLean, known as Ned to his friends, genuine ones of whom he had few. "One of her favorite beaus," Evalyn said of Alice, "had been Ned. . . ." So Evalyn determined to get Ned.

Son of prominent Cincinnatians, Ned had been pathetically pampered as a child; his parents bribed other boys to let him win at Parcheesi and baseball. When Ned finally proposed to Evalyn, she said she wanted to "control him completely" because "Hell! The cards are stacked against us women in any other field we tackle." To some degree she was successful. "I was the only living human who ever exercised control over Ned McLean," she said. "I made myself believe I had the power to mold him into everything I wanted for the race of men." Their honeymoon was legendary for its recklessness. "Dosed with laudanum and whiskey, I did not care about the risk so long as we were not riding in the other fellow's dust," she said of their speeding about the Continent. "Dresden, Leipzig, Cologne, Düsseldorf—each one to me stands for a shopping spree." With a case or two of whiskey at hand—"for emergencies"—the bride bought a yellow velvet gown with diamond stars to match her yellow Fiat. She picked up the Star of the East green emerald for $120,000.

The most outrageous of her compulsive purchases came to haunt her. In Paris she checked in with Monsieur Cartier and, her warped love of danger overcoming her comparatively practical superstitions, purchased from him the legendary cursed Hope Diamond.

Said to have been part of a larger necklace owned by Marie Antoinette and carried away and broken into sections after her beheading, the large blue diamond necklace was surrounded by a satellite of white diamonds. The curse held that all those who were dear to its owner would perish by sudden and horrific demise. Her mother-in-law and one of her friends both warned Evalyn to sell it—Cartier refused to buy it back—and both died within a year. Her father died a painful death from lung cancer. Soon Evalyn became terrified about the fate of her sons, Jock, born in 1916, and Vinson, born in 1910. "I must confess I know better," Evalyn reflected on the curse, "and yet, knowing better, I believe. . . . I never let my friends or children touch it. . . ." As for herself, she was certain that "I have developed a sort of immunity to its evil." The diamond became so much of her own identity, however, that she could never part with it.

Despite her outrageous eccentricities, Evalyn became a star in the capital, ignoring the older—and poorer—society's remarks about her garish entertaining. At one dinner for forty-eight guests in 1912, Evalyn spent forty thousand dollars, but she quickly explained that it wasn't the food or liquor that cost so much; it was the four thousand yellow lilies imported from London for the night, which cost her two dollars each. With the death of both her own parents and Ned's, Evalyn reveled in an inherited world of unfathomable wealth, luxury, and high life. The late John McLean's downtown house was an urban palace, sharing an entire city block with only the old Shoreham Hotel, and Evalyn and John inherited the "gold-plated" mansion at 1600 I Street, near the White House. Adjacent to it was "the little house on H Street," which Ned's father had used as an office and hideaway. Then there was 2020, which Evalyn maintained. Clare Holland, the wife of a Keystone news service photographer who was often with Harding, remembered a New Year's Eve party there when Evalyn briefly appeared like a Maxfield Parrish sprite on the distant top step to peek at arrived guests, then darted away like a deer, wearing the Hope Diamond. And nothing else.

There were other homes as well. In the horse country of Leesburg, Virginia, the McLeans owned the twelve-hundred-acre Belmont Farm, and in Bar Harbor, Maine, they summered at Briarcliffe Manor, a "cottage" in the grand tradition. There were also family respites in Newport, Saratoga, and Palm Beach. For Evalyn, however, their real home was the McLeans' vast estate Friendship, in the countryside on a hill above Georgetown, where the Longworths had spent their first honeymoon night. To get from place to place, the McLeans took their own private railroad car, outfitted with triple-plated comfort.

Despite all that glittered, Evalyn was almost belligerently proud of being the gold miner's daughter. "Money is lovely to have, but it does not really bring the big things in life—friends, health, respect—" she said, "and it is apt to make one soft and selfish." For Evalyn, Alice had already done her condescending mimicry of Senator Harding's wife and laughed her off as "the parvenue of parvenues." That quip undoubtedly cut close for Evalyn. While Evalyn enjoyed flirting with Harding, she was instantly, sympathetically drawn to his wife, despite Alice. "She had been lovely in her youth," Evalyn wrote of her first vision of Florence, "anyone could tell that. Her eyes were blue, her profile finely chiseled, but her mouth was a revelation of her discontent. She was ambitious for herself and Warren." If it was music that initially drew them together, their mutual discovery—later uproariously ridiculed by Alice—that each of them believed in astrology and shared August births under the zodiac sign of Leo made them draw closer. To such like-thinking women, destiny brought people together for mystical reasons.[2]

Two weeks after their initial meeting, Evalyn had urged Alice to restage the poker game with the same guests, "designed to repeat the enjoyment of that splendid evening." Alice icily quipped that Florence was so "desperately sick" that it was "a question of whether she will live." Evalyn was stunned and told Alice "I would go to call on her the next day." She made her way to the Harding home and told Berenice at the door, "Tell Mrs. Harding I want to see her." She was let in. "Mrs. Harding was lying flat in bed and her complexion was blue," recalled Evalyn. "My roving eyes saw and appraised many things while we sat and chatted."

"I am very sick. I have sent to Marion for my physician," Florence explained, detailing her kidney ailment. In that instant, however, lying alone, again facing death, Florence Harding was moved beyond all her usual defenses. Why would this young, wealthy social celebrity come to visit her? Why would she care? Evalyn's visit so emotionally affected the Duchess at her most vulnerable that all the floodgates opened, and every detail of her hard life tumbled forth, as if it were the last time she would review them. In the only known instance of such a confidence to anyone, Florence recounted her marriage to Henry De Wolfe in detail, then went on to tell of her father's bitter opposition to her marrying Warren, how she had helped make the *Star* a "solvent enterprise" as she "scrubbed the office . . . would go around asking for circulation and . . . always, had to keep Warren Harding up to the minute because he was absolutely lacking in ambition. He wanted to have a good time and give other people a good time," Evalyn remembered. "There was the pattern of the fixed idea in what she said to me that day. . . . But I thought then and I think now that she was telling me not with pride as much as with resentment. I sensed this as soon as she started in to talk about 'Warren.' "

"You know, this town, Washington is an awful place, the most awful town I have ever lived in," Florence continued.

"Why, Mrs. Harding, I love Washington. Why don't you like it?"

"I'll tell you," Florence confided, now sitting up in bed. "Every woman in this town is after Warren. . . . It's so. I'll keep him close to home, until I am up again."

"An attractive man like that? I do hope he can go out after dinner. I certainly want to see more of him." Florence glared at Evalyn "up and down," then realized Evalyn was pulling her leg. Then and there, said Evalyn, "I was to be trusted."

"It will be a rare occasion when he is free to play around this town," Florence said. "He'll do what I say. I have *something* on him. He does not dare do other than as I say."

When she said good-bye, Evalyn promised to keep visiting Florence until she was well. To her delight, the Duchess discovered that Evalyn cherished animals, though the llama she kept on her lawn, the monkey in her bathroom, and the cursing parrot in her hallway were decidedly different pets from the dogs Florence had treasured. As soon as she returned home, Evalyn sent around to Florence a stunning get-well gift, leaving no question about her feelings toward her new best friend. In a two-and-a-half-foot-tall Steuben glass vase were stuffed a dozen long-stem roses, red for love. It was as if the younger woman were courting the older woman, avidly pursuing a companionship.

Evalyn was fascinated by the scrappy woman: "I love people who with determination succeed against overwhelming odds." Most of all, she was intrigued with what that "*something*" was that Florence had on Warren. "That was astonishing to me," said Evalyn, "and as I left their house I was completely puzzled." Early in 1917, after Florence's recovery, Evalyn took her by the hand to social events and sped her down to Belmont Farm for day trips. After being in the presence of Evalyn's "smart set," Florence retreated into her insecurities and "unfailingly each time" whispered, "What did they say of me?"[3]

Before she had arrived in Washington, Florence had begun the process of erasing away the blemishes of her early life for public presentation. In a Washington newspaper social note preceding her arrival in town, for example, she made no mention of the name De Wolfe—husband, son, or grandchildren—and submitted her flattering 1891 wedding photograph. With Evalyn, however, the real person who was Florence did not escape examination so glibly. Evalyn realized that Florence had for years "covered her almost continual suffering." As they grew close, Evalyn found her "very interesting and sweet," but as she came to know Florence's character, she uncovered deficiencies with the attributes, later revealing them privately to Boyden Sparkes: "Did not know as much about politics as she thought she did. She liked to think she did. Mrs. Harding was a superstitious woman. She always made me think of these robot men . . . mechanical man, going on and having a terrific force— is the nearest I can explain that woman. A driving power, a disregard for any except what was right in her path. She was a woman, she was emotional, and then in another way she was not. She had a hard streak in her, and a ruthless streak. She didn't care at all about children. Little incidentals didn't appeal to her at all. Yet in clothes they did. She was very vain. We spent about ten days in New York fitting her out with clothes . . . always wanted youthful things. She was very proud of her clothes and appearance."[4]

Florence had never before been the focus of such attention. Her model of a woman friend was someone with whom she played bridge or, worse, shared a trip to Europe; nor had she been this forthright with anyone except Warren. She was flattered enough to enjoy the attention. In the process she came to recognize that despite their superficial, obvious differences, Evalyn was as much a nonconformist as she was. Evalyn, though young enough to be her daughter, became a kind of junior sister to the Duchess, but the companionship well served the young woman too. Only Florence had ever grown close enough to understand Evalyn's own darkness.

Zaniness had been offset with cruel and sudden tragedy early in Evalyn's life. In 1905, while she was speeding in her red Mercedes from Newport with her brother, the car overturned, and he was instantly killed. Evalyn's leg was shattered, and she was put on powerful painkillers. So began her lifelong bouts with drug addiction. Before she was twenty, she was taking up to ten grams of morphine a day, often stashing it in a hole beneath a square she cut into an overstuffed chair cushion. Heavy alcohol use followed. She admitted candidly some years later:

I never read about those poor devils who get into trouble through robberies or other violences designed to gain for them the drug they crave without a throb of pity. I know that aching hunger. I know how cunningly it magnifies the slightest twitching of a nerve into a pounding, crushing all-pervading sense of pain. . . . Hell, I drink the whole bottle. I can drink a bottle and you could never tell it. I could drink you under the table so quick. Hah! . . . Always had. But I really started drinking hard after the accident. When Vinson was coming along I didn't take a drop. In those days, I was taking morphine and drinking too. I was drinking that black liquid stuff—laudanum. I never took it in injections. . . . At drug stores, I would copy prescriptions and I would always ask them to give me the prescription back and I would go to different drug stores. Then, if they wouldn't give it back to me I would have one on hand at home that I would copy. . . . Never went to an illicit dealer. I used to have to go myself and I'd go behind the counter. . . . I worry about everything. I hate to owe money and I fret an awful lot. . . . With morphine I never worried and I got a completely different outlook on life. It's the fight I had. It is my life.

Other habits marked her polar opposition to Florence. In New York Evalyn haunted nightclubs, burlesque theaters, and Harlem until dawn. "We live but once," she quipped, "and of all things in this world I hate boredom most." In brief attempts to alleviate her restlessness and addictions, Evalyn even consulted psychologists—to no avail. "I do them while they are doing me and they are much nuttier than I am. I put down each question they asked."[5]

Florence learned all this from Evalyn herself. "My habit," said Evalyn, "is to tell things first in preference to letting the gossips make exciting discoveries. . . . As a Washington hostess . . . I learned it is next to impossible to cover up anything, no matter how much you might like to keep a few secrets." To her detriment, as time proved, it was a quality Florence never adopted. It was still months before she confided everything to Evalyn and discovered—only after the story was spread by rumor—that they also both endured adultery.

One amusement for which they shared a passion was also sweeping the nation. As avid moving-picture fans, the Duchess was often fetched by Evalyn in her Duesenberg limousine for matinees. Florence had taken to Chaplin comedies and Hal Roach shorts like the Keystone Kops, but Evalyn was so devoted to film that she bought expensive studio equipment, "studied" with her friend the director D. W. Griffith, and became a camerawoman. "I had lots of fun and for about five years, I worked like a dog, delighted because I had discovered an entertaining, an absorbing means of self-expression." Setting up klieg lights in her Friendship drawing room, Evalyn used her friends as actors, coaxing the Hardings into film shorts and getting the double-jointed Alice to perform "all her parlor antics," such as putting her legs around her neck and scratching fast like a monkey—"the drollest thing!" thought Evalyn.

Mrs. Longworth was less than droll, however, about capital society's new social duo. The feelings were soon mutual. When Florence and Evalyn began holding bridge games in their homes for friends, Alice was not invited. When it became clear that the Duchess had usurped her best friend, Alice snapped with hostility and behaved badly toward Evalyn. At one event Evalyn noticed that Alice's underwear was slipping and asked if she knew it. "[S]he said, no, she didn't know it and what's more she didn't give a damn. 'I don't care if they do come off in front of everyone!' and with that she jerked 'em off," said Evalyn. "Another time somebody came to me and said she was missing. She used to drink terribly. Finally, I thought to look in the dining room and she was under the table. We pulled her out and had her sent home." Once she cooled down enough to consider more spiteful venues for her jealosy, however, Alice often sought revenge. Having long been compared with her virtuous cousin Eleanor Roosevelt, for example, Alice encouraged the love affair between Franklin Roosevelt and Eleanor's social secretary Lucy Mercer, then tried to tell Eleanor about it. Having nothing like the stable marriage of her brother Ted, Alice "made every effort to have her brother meet all kinds of women," in hopes that she could spark an extramarital affair for him, recalled Evalyn. The stiletto that the Princess kept in her oversize handbag was an apt metaphor. It should have served as fair warning for the Duchess.[6]

That Florence was enjoying herself and her new friendship—and better health than she had for years—was also jealously observed by others from afar. "Mrs. Harding is well and looking better than she has for three or four years," Warren wrote innocently enough on April 20, 1917, to Doc Sawyer in Marion. Doc's jealousy over Evalyn's new role in Florence's life had emerged several weeks earlier. "Mandy and me have begun to think that Florence has forgotten that she has any friends at White Oaks Farm. We have had but just one little card from her since visiting you the last time," Doc wrote Warren, keeping track of every slight. "I shall not attempt to answer for Mrs. Harding's neglect in writing," Warren responded sheepishly. "I know that she appreciates very much hearing from her friends, but have long since discovered that she is very negligent at times in her own correspondence."[7]

From White Oaks Farm, the Hardings were plied by Doc with hams, jams, eggs, and butter, his need to assure his status with the Hardings based on personal ambition as much as on jealousy. "You know a lot of people think because we are close friends that I can do many things that I would not think of attempting to do even with my best friends," Doc wrote Warren at the same time he was pressuring the senator to get him appointed to the Ohio Board of Medical Examiners. Harding connections even funneled patients to the sanitarium. "I called at his [Harry Daugherty's] office," Sawyer told Warren, "and renewed my acquaintance with him. He continuously is an enthusiastic politician." A year later Daugherty's chronically alcoholic daughter Emily became a long-term and recurring "guest" at the "farm."

Under the guise of concern for Warren's health now, as well as Florence's, Sawyer eagerly encouraged regular reports from the senator. Whether it was high blood pressure at 160 or "a little ptomaine poisoning," the unexamined Warren's self-diagnosis was all that Doc required before dispensing some of his homemade pills, powders, and tablets—no questions asked—such as the senator's request for "that golden brown dope for the nose that I used from your kit in the Hawaiian trip." And as in March 1917, when Warren reported being "extremely jaded and worn out" and needed to "take a complete respite from the toil and strain that characterizes public service at this time of anxiety and responsibility," Doc immediately arranged for the Hardings to share the Sawyers' rented Daytona house and meals—gratis.[8]

Still, as Christmas, 1917, was approaching, Doc sensed the Hardings had newer friends. "You will be at perfect liberty to make our house your home to come and go as you please," he then assured them, prematurely assuming they would be together in Marion. "We have two machines and lots of sausage." The Hardings had spent the previous Christmas away from Marion and had traveled extensively in New England, the West, and the Southwest that summer and autumn. Apologizing for their holiday absence, Warren told Doc that in Washington, "Though friends are plenty, it is not like home," yet added oddly, "If they are not the best, they certainly are the dearest." Indeed, unlike Doc, the McLeans applied no pressures and expressed no expectations. As Warren wrote Ned earlier that year, "Mrs. Harding and myself are very grateful for the good lives enjoyed through the courtesy of Mrs. McLean and yourself."[9]

Public association with the McLeans, however, was inevitably to earn the Hardings new enemies beyond those jealous of social friendship—political enemies in the White House. In late 1916 and early 1917, as rumblings of war—and accusations of treason—became more frequent, the McLeans were persona non grata to the Wilson administration. It was largely because of a *Washington Post* column under the nom de plume by-line of Riley Grandin but written by a Wilson staffer who had access to leaked information. There were many instances in which the Grandin column broke some news and beat the White House's official release of the information by twenty-four hours. Once America entered the war in April 1917, Wilson threatened to shut the *Post* down because national security was being violated. Evalyn wrote the President to go ahead and try. Wilson banned the *Post* from White House delivery but kept reading the copy that came through the servants' entrance. Knowing the true identity of Riley Grandin to be a Cabinet member, Evalyn later suggested that it was Wilson's son-in-law and treasury secretary, William McAdoo.

The rage of Wilson and his new wife, Edith Bolling Galt, toward the McLeans, however, had a personal basis. The popular joke of the day—"What did Mrs. Galt do when President Wilson proposed to her? She fell out of bed"—was gleefully spread about by Alice from Evalyn's sitting room to a British Embassy attaché—and Edith heard all about it. While the Wilsons had been courting, the *Post* had noted in its social column: "President Wilson was seen last night at the theater *entering* [emphasis added] Mrs. Galt in the box." That the proper word—"entertaining"—was dropped from the printed sentence was no mistake, provoking gales of laughter for Evalyn and company. More damaging, however, had been the cache of Wilson's love letters to one Mary Hulbert Peck, written while his first wife was still alive. The letters found their way into Evalyn's hands, meaning their spicier contents reached much of Washington by word of mouth.[10]

If the McLeans, Longworths, and Hardings found speculating about President Wilson's sex life an amusing distraction, it was with nervous laughter, for their kettles were the same color. Nick, Ned, and Warren all had committed adultery, and each wife had reacted differently. Ned was the most discreet; he was genuinely devoted to his family life, and Evalyn was pregnant again by the end of 1917. Still, he squandered outrageous sums of money on his mistress, Rose Davies, the sister of fellow publisher William Randolph Hearst's mistress Marian. With what a relative called "a wonderful pornographic sense of humor," Nick was the most flagrant, even once lying in the grass holding a girl's hand at a picnic in Alice's presence. His mistress was one Alice Dows, a New York music patron. She was the most special among "Nick's girls," as two reporters put it in print. Claiming to be "never terribly in love" with Nick, Alice reacted by having her own affair, with Idaho's senator William E. Borah, which resulted eventually in the birth of her only child, Paulina. Evalyn, on the other hand, philosophically accepted male philandering, pouring her energy into mothering her children, into her companionship with Florence, and maintaining a manic social life.

Florence's method of coping was the most stressful. The Duchess vainly tried to control the situation. Evalyn said, "[T]here can be no doubt about it: Mrs. Harding watched her husband as if he had been a youthful Turkish maiden and herself a bearded Turk. I cannot remember ever seeing him in Washington during those years he was senator unless she was along. At parties she was bound to grow alert each time he vanished from her sight. 'Where's Warren?' she would ask and then more shrilly pipe, 'Warren!' Once I heard him say to her in a tone half kindly, half impatient, 'For God's sake, Duchess, play the game.' "[11]

15

Lust and War

If Evalyn soothed Florence, Ned brought out the worst in Warren, and Nick was no better. As Alice's biographer later stated, Nick shared with Warren "a taste for liquor, gambling, and sex whenever and wherever the opportunity arose." A blasé Evalyn concurred, putting the men's behavior in the context of the Prohibition movement: "I knew that Warren Harding was counted as a dry senator, but that in his moments of relaxation he was ready to drink with Ned and Nicholas Longworth. Indeed I had often heard him boast that he could make a champagne cocktail just like the Waldorf bartender." Encouraged even by Doc to take freely of "spiritis frumenti" as a holiday "prescription," Warren drank more than usual around Nick and Ned. Ned often experienced blackouts, and after his 1912 congressional defeat Nick slid into alcoholism. He and what Alice called his "middle-aged drunkards," she said, "disgusted and angered me," though she held her own and made a "passable gin." Nick was no hypocrite, but Warren ultimately voted in favor of the Volstead Act, the prohibition of making and selling alcohol by the Constitution's Eighteenth Amendment. He continued to drink alcohol in his own and others' homes and offered it to guests in his own house.[1]

Harding was passive in his vote for the women's suffrage amendment—only at the last moment when it was a foregone conclusion did he do so—but courageously voted for Wilson's cutting of diplomatic ties with Germany in 1916 following its naval blockade of the British Isles, France, and the Mediterranean. As the war clouds had gathered, Carrie Phillips had belligerently defended the German cause back in Marion, and Warren had pleaded with the increasingly irrational woman to stop. He wrote her with the knowledge that she was under suspicion by the Secret Service as a potential German spy and that his letter might be intercepted. In one letter, first, he regretted being unable to attend a party she was hosting, flattering her. Then he praised Jim's fund-raising efforts for a YMCA drive. At last he eased into the hortatory point of the letter: "I suppose you are not a little perturbed over the diplomatic break with Germany. . . . I fear it means war, and pray that it does not. I know you are in rebellion. . . . If it does come, you will be American first of all. Even if you were to say Nay, I would know what is in your heart. In spite of your reverence and sympathy and love for Germany (much of which is justified) you are after all an American and ever must be, and you will wish that the anxieties—and great trials, perhaps, will exalt the American soul and spirit. It is a difficult time for a public servant, it is trying for individuals, but there can never be but one answer in the end, 'My Country—May it ever be right! But right or wrong, MY COUNTRY!' "

Carrie felt cornered. She turned on Warren, threatening that if he voted for war, she would reveal his love letters to not only her husband but also the press. Harding was terrified of the hell she could unleash yet simultaneously longed for her intimacy, and told her so. When he did vote for war in April 1917, however, she apparently still cared enough about him. She bluffed on her threat to make his letters public, though she did not offer to return them to him as she once had.[2]

If Carrie Phillips had become an irritant, Nan Britton's letter to Warren from New York received the first week of May, was unexpectedly welcome. She was looking for work. Did the senator remember her? Could he help? The senator responded that there was "every probability" he'd be in New York the next week and if he could "becomingly look you up," he'd "take pleasure in doing so. . . . You see I do remember you." When Nan responded on May 11, Warren wrote back: ". . . an ambitious girl of your character must succeed. . . . You write a fine letter, your intelligence is of the high Britton standard. . . . I will have no doubt you will make good from the very start. I like your spirit and determination. It is like I have always imagined you to be. . . . It will be a pleasure to look you up." In New York they met and talked in the lobby of the Manhattan Hotel, where he had often rendezvoused with Carrie. He then suggested they continue talking in his room—the bridal suite—the only lodging available that week because of a convention. They got in the room, barely closed the door, and began passionately kissing. He was fifty-one years old. She was twenty.

"Oh, dearie, tell me it isn't hateful to you to have me kiss you!" he exclaimed. They did not that day consummate their relationship. After they had kissed furiously, he told her it was best for her to remain working in New York rather than come to wartime Washington. He then tucked thirty dollars in her silk stockings. As they returned to her

YMCA typing class, he told her, "I love you more than all the world, and I want you to belong to me. Could you belong to me, dearie? I want you and I need you so." Nan introduced him to her teacher, and an odd conversation ensued, Harding oddly stating that the "Germans were actually attempting to create children by injecting male serum, taken at the proper temperature, into the female without the usual medium of sexual contact." He pronounced it "German madness" and declared that "children should come only through mutual love-desire." One classmate, Louise Beiderhause, vividly recalled and unwittingly corroborated Nan's account of the visit when she wrote him and reminded him that they had met through Nan.[3]

Some weeks later Warren again rendezvoused with Nan, and this time he arranged for her to be hired as the secretary to the chairman of the U.S. Steel Corporation. By so recklessly exposing his association with Britton, Harding took a great chance with his reputation. That he was never frozen by fear of accidental exposure of his various infidelities was all the more curious, since intelligence agents kept Carrie under suspicion. Amazing as it seemed, after thirteen years of his wife's affair with his friend, Jim Phillips still did not suspect her, though he did know that she was now being monitored. Given to erratic outbursts, Carrie began raising German shepherd dogs out of some bizarre sense of loyalty to the kaiser—and was outspoken too in noting the *dogs'* sexual habits. When some young men brought a dog to breed with one of hers, the dogs took the canine mating position as the boys watched. "I don't know why it embarrasses you," she told one of them. "It's the kind of thing I do all the time."

Although she still kept her adultery with Warren secret, Carrie vehemently became not only antiwar but anti-Harding. "She talked against him. She hated him," recalled Warren Sawyer, revealing that it was even whispered in Marion that Carrie—although it was never proven that she had any contacts with the German government—might have tried to get some form of intelligence out of her friend the senator to the Germans in some ill-conceived act of loyalty to her beloved *Deutschland*. Finally, at both Warren's and Jim's insistence, Carrie volunteered with the Red Cross and began sewing skullcaps and seeing the boys off to war at the Marion station. It was too little too late. "[B]ecause of her pro-German talk," William Chancellor reported, "the women of Marion looked askance upon her attempted Red Cross activities. They even suspected her as a spy in our ranks."[4]

The Duchess was active in all forms of war work. With limited housing available in Washington, she made an effort to find shelter for

Ohio women who were part of the influx of needed wartime government workers. She worked with Herbert Hoover's wife, Lou, in her efforts to provide dining and recreational hall spaces for the thousands of "lonely and almost friendless" women workers. For mothers who worked while their husbands were at the front, there was a sudden need for adequate child care, and Florence was a "frequent visitor at day nurseries and other child welfare centers," according to *Baltimore-American* reporter Edna Colman. She pored through national newspapers to keep herself abreast of the minutiae of the war's progress and taught herself foreign pronunciations to identify towns on the western and eastern fronts. Alongside Eleanor Roosevelt, occasionally Edith Wilson, and other political wives, Florence worked in the canteens set up in Union Station sheds, passing out tin cups of coffee and sandwiches to the hundreds of soldiers leaving by train for ships and eventually across the Atlantic to the war. Alice did only a brief tour, saying she had "canteen elbow."

"Adopting" a wing of Walter Reed Naval Hospital not far from the city, Evalyn McLean's largess extended beyond her underwriting of the day trips and amusements for the growing ward of wounded soldiers returned from the front, some gassed, some blinded, several shell-shocked. Evalyn visited the men weekly, taking Florence with her, and they spent time speaking with each man, taking dictation for those who could not use pens but wanted to write home, bringing candy, cigarettes, and flowers. Seeing the healthy young men off to war but returning stunned and disabled struck an emotional chord in Florence. She found a displaced motherly love for them, as she had with the *Star* newsies twenty years before. She plunged "body, soul and brain into war work," noted one reporter. The "boys" became her work and purpose, and alongside Evalyn, she found a sense of personal satisfaction that had long been sorely lacking in her life. When constituents came to town, Florence now took them to a more sobering site, the increasing rows of soldiers' white tombstones at Arlington National Cemetery.

Her sense of purpose converged with a new camaraderie initiated by Lois Marshall, the Vice President's wife, of weekly gatherings of Senate wives on Tuesdays. Establishing a Red Cross unit in a Capitol caucus room, the wives dressed in white uniforms and nunlike caps and manned whirring sewing machines, turning out sweaters, caps, socks, head caps, pajamas, undergarments, gloves, and scarves for the soldiers. The Duchess had never used a sewing machine, but after some short lessons she worked seven days a week. "[T]he war made women take count of stock and settle upon what they could do for themselves and their country," Florence said proudly, "should a long-drawn conflict require service of every one." She was particularly impressed with the hundreds of women who went to the front as war and navy nurses and the more than thirty thousand women who enlisted, some taking jobs as telephone operators, known as "hello girls."

Among the Senate wives Florence respected was Mary Borah, who looked after dozens of shell-shocked veterans, many claiming her as next of kin and depending on her for bail when they were brought into the police station for drinking or disorderly conduct. With her "letters home" to Spokane published in local newspapers, Mrs. Miles Poindexter also befriended the Duchess, who admired her forthrightness and followed her admonishment. "DON'T allow your husband to come to Washington alone," Mrs. Poindexter wrote in one of her published "letters home" to a Seattle newspaper. "There are flappers and buds, wily widows, grass and sod; matrons and grandmothers and strange, alluring spinsters. If you love him, hold his hand, lest he perish in this whirlpool—this social Washington."[5]

It was by *leaving* Washington, however, that Warren was able to cultivate his budding affair with Nan. He came to see her again in New York. When they rendezvoused in Indianapolis, she recalled that he joked about their romance, "What would Florence Harding say, I want to know!" Still, Nan refrained from giving up what she called "love's sweetest intimacy," despite his plea, "[W]hat do you expect? I'm a man, you know." They went to Chicago and shared a sleeping bunk. In hotels there they registered as husband and wife. Warren confessed his "early amours" with Susan Hodder and Carrie Phillips and told Nan that it had been "many years" since his "home situation had been satisfying." He also said he'd never been with a virgin.

They met again on July 30, at New York's Imperial Hotel, a less reputable one suggested to him by friends for more "unconventional circumstances." He registered as "Mr. Harwick." Nan felt uncomfortable in her pink linen dress, which, she later said, "was rather short and enhanced the little-girl look which was often my despair." That afternoon they finally made love as they never had before, Nan putting it delicately: "I became Mr. Harding's bride—as he called me—on that day." To make the occasion even more memorable, two house detectives broke into the room and caught the pair. They demanded to know Nan's name and age. "I remember he told them I was twenty-one years old, and I, not realizing that he wanted to make me as old as he safely could, interrupted him and stated truthfully that I was only twenty." Warren feared his entire career was ruined. Instead, when one of the detectives picked up Harding's hat and saw his name in the band, they immediately became apologetic and deferential and even helped sneak him out a side entrance. The senator thankfully gave them a twenty-dollar bill. "I thought I wouldn't get out of that [for] under $1000!" he said to Nan as they left in a taxi.

Warren visited Nan almost weekly in New York for overnight trips, risking their trysts in what she remembered as "hotels of that character [where] there was always the fear of being raided." He continued to take Florence with him on long trips, including one to Texas in the fall of 1917, but he billed the New York trips as frantic business forays that he assured the Duchess would be tiring for her to share. From what Nan suggested of what Warren said—and all of their affair was by her account alone—he viewed her näiveté as adorable, rather than a warning sign to danger. "I had never had," she averred, "a single talk with or from my mother on sex. As a matter of fact, I did not know how babies came into the world, and I frankly told Mr. Harding so." Nor did he heed how emotionally involved she was becoming. That August he gave her a wristwatch. But Nan was already asking for a ring.

Fornication with Nan was relatively easier to manage than adultery with Carrie. As he maintained a love correspondence with both women and even sent each a box of Martha Washington candy at Christmas, the senator remained concerned about his relationship with the more unpredictable Mrs. Phillips being discovered by federal agents, particularly after passage of the Espionage Act in June 1917. When he learned that Carrie was entertaining Swiss and German visitors at home in Marion, Warren's terror was renewed, and he implored her to come with Jim to Washington, so he could directly convey to her the gravity of the situation. She angrily refused. There were, said Senator Harding publicly, "miserable spies among us." Indeed Alice Longworth eagerly volunteered for military intelligence, hiding listening devices in the home of her German friend May Landeburg, the mistress of War Industries Board chairman Bernard Baruch, and listening along with agents to the couple's lovemaking. Evalyn later confirmed that Ned had also become a government informer, using any gossip that came across his desk at the Washington *Post*, without regard for journalistic ethics.

In this atmosphere anything remotely German became suspect. Sauerkraut became "Liberty cabbage," dachshunds were killed, and teaching the language was banned in some states. In Ohio many families of German ancestry who still celebrated their heritage, such as Cincinnati's wealthy Wurlitzer family, were suspect. Asked about her maiden name, the former Florence Kling first said that her father was "Pennsylvania Dutch"—a people who were of German ancestry, in fact from Germany—then amended it to just "Dutch," to suggest that the Klings had come from Holland. Distracting attention from this branch, however, Florence emphasized her French ancestry—in line with the Allies. When later a reporter interviewed her on July 14—Bastille Day—the Duchess went into mock drama over the fact that there was no French flag and, "in the spirit of a descendant of a French Huguenot," sewed together red, blue, and white strips to make one and be photographed doing so, then raised her handiwork on a flagpole.[6]

Mrs. Harding's bloodlines—and Warren's—along with every other questionable, unseemly, and private facet of their lives remained an indignant fascination for William Chancellor. If Harding seemed oversensitive about spying, his concern would have been amply justified if he could have known that Chancellor was now recording Harding's extramarital affairs—and during the Senate years there were more to uncover.

Early in 1918 publisher and Harding friend Charles Hard had written Warren about helping to find a federal job for Ohioan James E. Cross. "I shall be glad to make interested inquiry in behalf of Mr. Cross, but frankly I have not found very many desirable positions which are handed out upon any request of mine," the senator replied. He did find a job—not for James but rather for his wife, Grace Miller Cross, right in his office. Her friend the reporter Bertha Martin described Grace as tall, blond, and beautiful. She was also apparently quite bold. Although his government-paid staff positions were filled, the senator hired Grace immediately and paid her salary out of his own pocket, a practice followed by many legislators who wanted more staff. Evalyn later referred to "that Cross woman" as "just . . . another Harding girl," but with the twenty-eight-year-old Finley, Ohio, native living in Washington, Warren entered into this adulterous relationship more rapidly than he had others. In some ways Grace seemed to play the same emotional games that Carrie had: She was apparently somewhat cruel to the genial Warren, and there were arguments between them. When Bertha Martin and some other friends "had been to parties" at Grace Cross's apartment, they were shocked to see the senator "crawling around on the floor in his pajamas begging Grace Cross to forgive him" after some unspecified tiff. As with Carrie and Nan, Warren wrote Grace passionate love letters. Unlike his other affairs, however, this one seemed to possess a measure of violence.

"Some of Warren's affairs with the ladies were almost disastrous,"

Chancellor recorded several years later, speaking apparently of Grace
Cross, who lived in the capital, "as, for instance, in the case where the
police of the city of Washington were called to the house of his regular
lady friend to sober him up and stitch the cuts in his back which resulted,
according to her, from a dispute over finances. Those interested may
find and read it in the police records of 1918. This woman, who is about
thirty-five years old, was never even rebuked for this almost fatal attack
upon a member of the greatest deliberative body of the world. This
matter was given to the Democratic National Committee by the Department of Justice and the Washington police; but the Democrats were
too decent to use it [as an exposé against Harding in future cam-
paigns]. . . ."

Besides the simultaneous affairs with Grace, Nan, and Carrie, Harding compulsively involved himself with others. There was the oddly
enigmatic case of a woman identified only as Augusta Cole, of partial
Cuban ancestry. It was in Mrs. Cole's home that Carolyn Votaw temporarily boarded downtown during the week. Little is known of the
affair, except that apparently Augusta got pregnant. She evidently named
Harding as the father. This, according to Chancellor, "forced Warren
to disavow the act and send her to Battle Creek Sanitarium." The pregnancy was terminated. Cole's husband filed for divorce, and during the
trial Carolyn Votaw testified against Augusta. As with much of his inside
information, Chancellor evidently learned of the Augusta Cole affair
from his friend Heber Votar, Warren's brother-in-law and Carolyn's
husband. One Marion woman recalled hearing how the senator "had a
lot of great times in New York with girls." Besides Nan, there was one
young New York matron from a prominent family to whom Harding
had written some graphic letters, recalling their times together. It was
perhaps a different New York woman whom Warren helped to purchase
a small cabin at Big Moose in the Adirondacks, promising that he would
eventually divorce Florence and marry her. When it became clear this
would never happen, the woman committed suicide. Arrangements for
these trysts were not managed by Warren alone; he had various loyal
friends make hotel reservations. For example, political figure Maurice
Maschke set up a six-hour rendezvous for Warren at Cleveland's Statler
Hotel.

Warren's lust did not, however, escape as much notice as he
thought it did. In considering many "confidential" details about his affairs, Senate wife Clara Kellogg concluded to Cabinet wife Martha Lane
that Florence was "much the bigger person of the two. She had standards and strength of character." Warren himself could not help con-

victing himself even to Florence. "The Ziegfeld [Follies] Company is registered here, that is the stars [of it]," he wrote the Duchess from Boston, "and the hotel is full of chickens. I will miss them for I leave for Lynn at 6:30."

Harding's attraction to often very young women was no secret in Marion. Young George Thayer long remembered the summer Sunday in the Ohio countryside when the senator and some male friends were visiting, later telling all about it to his friend John Schroeter, who recalled: "He was on a farm owned by an Evans family, just outside of Marion. There was some squealing. George was inside, and then went back out of the house to see what the excitement was. Somebody had a water hose and was squirting the girls. These were young girls, teenagers. And the girls were naked. A bunch of older men were staring and laughing. And who was enjoying the sight most—Harding!" As one Senate wife drolly understated, "He took rash chances with his reputation."[7]

Despite such antics, Warren was still dangerously drawn to Carrie. After reviewing his numerous mistresses, liaisons, and one-night stands, Evalyn McLean flatly stated two decades later that despite the damage and threats she always presented, "Mrs. Phillips was his love." On April 18 Harding wrote Jim Phillips that the situation regarding Carrie's German allegiance was serious. America had been at war for more than a year, and the Sedition Act was soon to be passed; Carrie could well be arrested for her statements. Jim responded by suggesting Warren convince her to sell Liberty bonds, to prove her loyalty. Harding responded: "I wrote to her again yesterday very seriously and earnestly, warning her of impending dangers. She is under the eye of government agents, and it is highly urgent that she exercise great prudence and caution. I know, of course, that she is not deserving of surveillance, but feeling grows intenser . . . as the casualty list grows. . . . She forgets we are in war—hellish war—and she forgets how Germany treats those who are against the government. It is time to *think*. If she is loyal and prudent the cloud may pass. She must be. If she isn't there is certain humiliation and distress and annoyance and embarrassment in store. I dislike to write this, but I feel I must."

Carrie would have none of it. Warren, who could help her no more without compromising himself, wrote again to Jim on May 1: "I know she is no German informer—she couldn't be. Yet these things have been reported. . . . Hence the need of extreme prudence, caution, wisdom and tact. She and Isabelle ought not to come to Washington *now*. Nor ought they go to New York. I had some inquiry made about things said, and the Washington trip last year led to suspicion about [her] acting as an informer . . . and the suspicion was confirmed by the long stay at the naval base at Port Jefferson. Any call I made, any calls they made, would be watched. . . . This War Problem has distressed me infinitely more than you can guess. I believe I know Carrie is loyal and helpful. But Passions and prejudices are not at my command. The greater peril is some unheeding, impassioned, self-appointed sponsor of justice and patriotism who might humiliate or harm her."[8]

Florence's rage at Carrie Phillips remained as fresh as it had been a half decade before. She certainly knew that Warren had kept up some form of contact with her. In 1916, for example, he wrote Florence honestly during a trip out West that he had paid a visit to Carrie's parents and visiting aunt, at their Great Falls, Montana, home. Now Florence made her feelings about Carrie known in the most public way possible. Perhaps because of Carrie's surveillance, there was more talk than usual about the exact nature of her relationship with Harding. Either Florence may have suspected trouble brewing with Carrie and searched for some of the reports on her that Warren had access to, or she may have simply stumbled upon them. It is also quite possible that in his fear of what Carrie would reveal if imprisoned as a spy, Warren may have even told Florence of the dilemma.

Although she could apparently curse like a trooper when provoked (Warren gave up swearing but wrote her, "You can do it for the family . . .") the Duchess was not given to public displays of rage or inclined to fight, particularly with women. But if Carrie Phillips no longer had the power to destroy the Harding marriage, her indirect threat to the career that the Hardings had built together and for each other could not be tolerated. The bombshell exploded in the summer of 1918 at the Marion train station. The Hardings had joined townspeople to see off local boys to the war front at the station when they saw Mrs. Phillips off to the side complaining about the futility of fighting the Germans. Warren apparently did his best to ignore her, but not the Duchess. In clear view of hundreds of Marionites, Florence walked up to Carrie and unleashed a verbal lashing that might have seemed deranged to those who didn't know her underlying motive. Jane Dixon recorded the episode: "The home folks will relate to you with glee an incident of the departure of the Marion boys for far battle fields. All the town was on hand to cheer and 'tear' their farewell. Prominent in the crowd were the Hardings—Florence and Warren. At the crux of the excitement a local matron who had spent some time in Berlin educating her daughter and who had managed to be bitten by the dog of

Kaiserism, made some slighting remarks anent the sendoff. Florence Harding heard. Her temper, which rises to blinding white heat under provocation, flared like a flash. In a manner all the crowd might heed she publicly rebuked the foolish matron, leaving her to nurse her spleen against Uncle Sam in solitude, a move the entire town has since followed."[9]

As far as Florence was concerned, that was the last, the end of Carrie Phillips. Unfortunately the public humiliation only fueled Carrie's intent to strike back at the right moment, not only at Warren but now at the Duchess.

Despite the incident, Warren, *still* recklessly infatuated with Carrie, unable to make a clean break, managed to steal time after giving a speech and declare his love for her yet *again* in a letter while he was spending a furtive weekend with *Nan* at the Witherill Hotel in Plattsburgh. Just as astounding was the persistence of Carrie's recurring fantasy that he would divorce Florence, even though he gently pointed out that in his "present position" he "could not break up." His mention of incidents in Plattsburgh in his letter, which Carrie long kept, confirmed that Nan's account of her love affair with Warren might be romanticized but was generally accurate, for in her memoirs she recalled similar incidents. The forty-plus-page hand-scribbled letters to Carrie on scratch paper or blue Senate stationery, in large writing, further confirmed Nan's seemingly ludicrous claims that she also received love missives of such length in pencil. Grace Cross received them as well when he was away from Washington.

Warren's recklessness in writing love letters seems at times almost pathological, as if he were secretly hoping to be destroyed by them. Carrie Phillips, in a passing fury to end the relationship, had even once sent him back all of his several dozen love letters, and he not only refused to destroy them himself but returned them to her. He later reviewed this seemingly self-destructive decision with her: "[Y]ou cautioned me to write briefly and explicitly—that letters are dangerous things. I know that. If you and I were corresponding for the first time and I was so warned, I would surely heed. But it so happens that I have written you ten times enough already to damn me every hour I have to live, if you choose to betray. I knew that when I possessed your personal collection of them and might have destroyed [them] I had ample excuse. But I thought maybe that you treasured them . . . I knew at the time that I gave you a weapon to destroy me. . . . I have sowed, I must reap when so commanded. . . . We knowingly violated convention in yielding to our hearts. . . ."

That November, when Warren returned to vote in Marion, he had a lovers' reunion with Carrie, and upon returning to Washington, the senator wrote one of his torrid multiverse poems for her. He remained blind to her unstable and ultimately dangerous personality. Now, however, he was understandably distracted by the signals he was getting from his own body. His heart was beginning to fail him. In an August 17 letter to Carrie from Plattsburgh, Warren recounted how dizzy and winded he had become during a speech, how he "nearly keeled over." Three months earlier he frankly revealed that he had a serious heart condition. Even though he had a "high stomach," weighed over two hundred pounds, and relentlessly played his poker games into the wee hours—usually meaning a steady stream of scotch and cigars and cigarettes—Warren was given no direction or warning or scolding by Doc Sawyer. Yet with frequent shortness of breath, he knew something was wrong. "I had a serious spell of it," he wrote Ed Scobey of his heart troubles in May 1918, "covering a period of two or three years. As a matter of fact, I have never gotten wholly free of it."[10]

Doc Sawyer was more preoccupied with Florence's hydronephrosis. Just days after the war ended on November 11, her kidney had swollen to ten times its normal size, "far more painful than you can imagine," Warren wrote. Although she had suffered numerous attacks in the last few years, this appeared to be the most serious one since the time of her 1905 surgery. Doc's son Carl, stationed at Maryland's Fort Meade, treated her. By November 25 Warren was reporting to Doc that Carl "thinks she is doing everything possible to get out of the difficult rut which she is in . . . one of the kidneys is evidently clogged in its outlet and it is in a tremendous swollen condition because of accumulating contents. . . ." Since Carl was unable to see her daily, however, a Dr. Hardin was called in and Florence was placed under his care. "It is rather an unusual situation," noted Warren. "Mrs. Harding feels very great confidence in him and seems to like him very much. Notwithstanding he is in professional authority, she has never taken a dose of medicine that has not come from your office in Marion." Making their precarious health conditions the responsibility of the tried-and true Doc was easier for both of the middle-aged Hardings than honestly facing their own mortality."[11]

Despite his outrageous sexual needs, Warren Harding remained devoted to Florence as his great companion. Although he had numerous meetings scheduled in Ohio throughout the winter, he refused to leave her side until he was certain that she was mending, in the company of a trained nurse, and then only for an overnight visit to Nan. In a curious way it was a sign of the increasingly strong bond between them in the unique compact they had hammered out. Still, if her health left him unwilling to leave her alone, he was not about to give up his other women. With Florence confined to the Wyoming Avenue house, the senator took even greater risks. He began inviting Nan to come down to Washington.

Harding usually registered Nan at Washington's New Ebbitt or Raleigh Hotel as Miss Elizabeth N. Christian, the surname of his secretary, George Christian, and her most frequent alias, and she was often identified as a niece. That they dined together and walked around town posed no danger in Warren's mind. They walked through the Capitol grounds and went to see Al Jolson in *Sinbad the Sailor* and Fred Stone in *Jack o'Lantern*. As Samuel Hopkins Adams wrote, "Harding's fellow sports in Washington knew of the liaison." In the Biltmore Hotel lobby a woman, whom Warren identified only as "a friend with whom he sometimes played billards," shouted, "There goes Harding!" and spotted Nan with him. Warren's loyal but silent secretary, George Christian, later indicated his knowledge of the Nan Britton affair. Earlier in the summer of 1918 at Senator John Weeks's White Mountains home, when Warren overindulged in lobster, he became violently ill from ptomaine poisoning. Fearing that he would die that evening, he despairingly confessed to someone—probably Weeks, who also had a mistress—all about Nan Britton, so that some kind of financial assistance could be made for her.

Optimistic Nan was refreshing to Harding despite her insistent, if humble, requests: a coat, a train ticket, kisses, and hugs. She seemed happily satisfied with whatever little time he could give her, and in contrast with Carrie, she never expressed jealousy, hatred, or any ill will toward Florence, not even the hope or suggestion that they divorce.

Warren claimed to her that he had wanted to adopt a child but that "Florence would not hear of it." Nan recalled the remark "in connection with his recital of his domestic unhappiness, and his usual final exclaim [*sic*] was, 'She makes life hell for me, Nan!' And I, knowing this did all in my power to make up to the man I loved all his legal wife failed to do. . . . I felt sorry for Mrs. Harding, but I must confess I doubted very much Mr. Harding's love for his wife at any time in his life. . . . [H]e spoke very freely to me about what he would do if Mrs. Harding were to pass on—he wanted to buy a place for us and live in the country. . . . 'Gee, Nan, you'd make a lovely bride!' " Awed by this, she idolized Warren, predicting that he would someday become President. She never called him Warren, always sweetie, dearie, sweetheart, or Mr. Harding.

Late one evening at the end of January 1919, "somehow not particularly concerned about possible consequences," he had Nan come to his Senate office. They disrobed and stayed in the office quite late, longer, Warren said, "than was wise," but he wanted to watch her there, so he could "visualize" her during the day while he worked. Nan grew concerned that they lacked any of the "usual paraphernalia which we always took to the hotels." Warren, however, was "more or less careless of consequences" and told her that he was sterile from childhood mumps. "But," Nan said with outrageous understatement, "he was mistaken."

It was there, in the Senate Office Building suite of Harding from Ohio, Nan recorded with decorum, "we both decided afterward, that our baby girl was conceived . . . and of course, the Senate Offices do not provide preventive facilities for use in such emergencies."[12]

16

"I Do Not Permit Him to Run"

"[I]t would be a mistake for Warren, and I know it would be one for me," Florence declared at a winter Sunday brunch in her home to a group of senators who were suggesting her husband as a potential presidential candidate. "I am decidedly opposed to it."

A few weeks later Al Fall bravely laid aside his six-shooter long enough to raise the subject. With perhaps a little practiced humility, Warren gently turned the idea away, but Florence snapped at Fall, "Please let us alone. Warren Harding is happy in the Senate. We are delighted with our present place in life. Mr. Harding is contented and is doing good work in the Senate. We both want him to remain there.

This talk simply disturbs him, and it disturbs me for him. Just let it drop." Out of town, however, Florence's views could have no impact. February 1919 saw the first Harding for President club organized in Toledo by a handful of loyal Buckeye Republicans who liked their senator and believed that despite the almost certain chance that he'd lose, he should be honored as Ohio's favorite son candidate.[1]

By March the Hardings had plenty of pleasure to preoccupy them, centered on events at Friendship, the McLean estate, which Evalyn insisted they consider their home away from home. It was also, as Harry Daugherty's companion, Jess Smith, said, "a damn swell layout." Warren made good use of the eighteen-hole golf course. Florence read and laughed with Evalyn on the high second-floor enclosed back porch, hummingbird nests woven into the screen, overlooking a verdant fairyland of shallow, lengthy rectangular pools, duck and water lily ponds, endless lines of privet and clipped topiaries. Late into the warm spring night poker games, illuminated by strings of tiny white bulbs, the popular songs of Tin Pan Alley and racing pieces in the new jazz sound wafted as far out as Evalyn's new greenhouses as she cranked the Victrola.

During the latter years of the war Evalyn had permitted the overflow of convalescent soldiers to be cared for on the roaming old estate, but when they were moved out to Walter Reed on April 1, 1919, Friendship became the full-time home of the McLeans, whose family now included a third son, Ned, Jr., born the past July. The buff-colored mansion had been visited by George Washington and Dolley Madison before it became a Georgetown seminary for priests. Ned's father had bought it and an adjoining tract of dozens of acres. Evalyn had the place renovated and relandscaped, transforming it from a meandering country seat into an estate as dazzling as any on Long Island's Gold Coast. A high stone wall with black wrought-iron entrance gate protected the property from the curious. Giant cedars lined the main roadway to the house, with a manicured thick greensward flanking it as far as the eye could see. The crescent drive right before the house was lined with boxwood. For the children there were donkeys, goats, geese, ponies, horses, cows; for Evalyn, her llama, monkey, and cursing parrot. She most enjoyed dancing in the fountains imported from Europe—after a few cocktails.

In the main salon, crowded with comfortable, overstuffed chintz chairs and sofas, Evalyn had a movie screen built in for regular screenings, her favorite way of entertaining herself and guests. Friendship was a complete escape from the realities of downtown Washington, just minutes away by motor, as much a concept as a place. Florence said it was her idea of heaven.

Shortly after they moved in, Evalyn made plans to attend the Kentucky Derby but found herself disturbed by premonitions of death. "My depression was complete, and as I interpreted my feelings I was being warned that I was going to die. Something dreadful, of that I was sure, was going to happen to me." She made a will, hired extra guards around her children, and went with Ned to the Derby, where, fearing her own death, she sat up into daybreak writing pages of a letter to her son Vinson. At the race parties she "moved as if in a daze." When a call came that Vinson had a mild flu, Ned reassured her that everything was fine but, that they could leave immediately for Friendship if she wished. "I quite well knew my son was dead," she said. In fact, the "Million Dollar Baby," Vinson, had actually chased a ball into a road, been gently struck, played some more, then died in his sleep. It was Florence who now comforted Evalyn.

Evalyn's presentiment permanently affirmed her belief in the metaphysical. "The persons closest to me say that I am fey," she wrote. "I am aware of, in myself, some peculiar sensitivity that I cannot define; it simply happens to me from time to time that, without being able to say how, I feel I know that death impends for some life that touches mine." Ned locked himself away on a drinking binge, but instead of returning to her morphine and whiskey, Evalyn found strength in Florence. Both women wondered about the curse of the Hope Diamond. Evalyn admitted, "I did believe that blue diamond was a talisman for evil." She did what seemed rational to her: She took it to a Catholic church to have it exorcised. "Lightning flashed," she recalled. "Thunder shook the church."[2]

In August, the McLeans left for Briarcliffe, but Evalyn left Maine after a month, then spent October alone in her lingering grief at White Sulphur Springs, Virginia. In July, Florence returned to Marion for a happy event that nonetheless shocked the social set. Making the most independent decision of his fifty years, Florence's brother Vetallis Kling finally married his love, the Kling housekeeper's daughter, Nona Younkins. Tal married in St. Mary's Roman Catholic Church and bought a house "on the wrong side of the tracks," in the Irish Catholic section. Florence did not shun him. "Well, I know you're a Catholic now," she told Tal, "and that's just fine with me."

*   *   *

That summer both Hardings faced the issue that was to consume the nation and shape the 1920 presidential campaign, the League of Nations. President Wilson had returned from Europe on February 24 from the Paris Peace Conference with the Allied leaders: France's Georges Clemenceau, Italy's Vittorio Orlando, and Great Britian's David Lloyd George. Only after yielding large concessions to them had Wilson won their support for his dream of an international "league" that would require each participating nation to support and protect one another. When Wilson met with the Senate and House foreign relations committees, he got no support, and thirty-seven Republican senators signed an anti-League petition. Wilson returned to Europe to sign the Versailles Treaty, then submitted his League with the treaty for U.S. Senate ratification on July 19. On September 4 he was to begin a vigorous speaking campaign all the way to the West Coast, propounding his League.

Florence was in the Senate Chamber on July 10, when Wilson proposed America's entry into the League, and she and Alice saw eye to eye. Alice pathologically despised Wilson, partially blaming him for her beloved father's political and spiritual demise and his death in January 1919. She even made and pricked a voodoo doll of Wilson that she flung onto the White House lawn. For the Duchess, further international entanglements simply meant more American boys being killed in other nations' disputes. Warren seemed less rigid. As usual he tried to elude contentiousness and make no avowed enemies. Although he had voted for Prohibition, to go into effect on January 16, 1920, because of what he called "popular will," he mitigated his vote by saying, "I do not claim to be a temperance man. I do not approach this question from a moral viewpoint. . . ." On June 4, when women's suffrage was finally submitted to each state for ratification, Harding assured Harriet Taylor Upton that he had "a strong conviction" it would be "promptly ratified." When she and fellow Republican suffragists sought to defeat antisuffrage New York Senator James Wadsworth at the polls, however, Warren told Upton it was wrong for Wadsworth to be "persistently opposed because of his lack of accord on this one particular issue." Such "harmonizing," as Warren called it—which many saw not as spinelessness but as skill in balancing between conservativism and progressivism, offending none and trying to please all—only raised Harding's stock that summer as the perfect party man and a prospective compromise candidate for that next year's presidential election.

Warren did not put himself forth as a candidate because he didn't want it or feel worthy but because he didn't want to face the risk of losing. He wrote "My dear Forbes," now back in Tacoma, "I really am not concerned in any way about president politics. I have long since made up my mind that I would not seek the nomination. I am infinitely more happy where I am and I have a reasonable assurance of staying in the Senate another term if I so desire. To involve my friends all over the country in a presidential contest would be a task that I could not ask of them. It has been mighty good of you to personally boost my name but I really would not want you to waste any endeavors in an organized effort." Warren did admit that he didn't think there would be a "crystallization of sentiment" about candidates until the 1920 spring primaries. He concluded with chilling prescience, "A man is fortunate to have so enthusiastic a friend as you have ever proven yourself to be, and you may be sure I am always grateful."

Florence's resistance to the idea was also practical. As Ray Baker Harris stated, "She felt first of all that her husband had not been in the Senate long enough to be well known as a national figure, and feared that the effort to win the presidency might cost him his place in the Senate . . . [and] feared the life the presidency would involve." That autumn, after lunching in Columbus with longtime Harding friend Charles Hard, she refused to drop him off from her car. "She wanted to talk to me. She did. A plenty," he recalled. "Charley Hard, I'm on the warpath. You wait a minute. I have been wanting for some time to see you," the Duchess fired at him. "You think you are doing Warren Harding a good turn. I do not. You are not. I want you to stop your activity. I want you to promise me right here and now that you will stop talking about him becoming a candidate for president. . . ." Hard held fast against Warren's "never silent partner" and told her, "We have been counting on you to help us put him over. . . . I am unable to give you the promise you ask."[3]

A year before the election the prospects for a Republican sweep of both Congress and the White House looked good. The Democratic-supported League was dealt a dramatic blow when Wilson had a "nervous collapse" while touring the country and was rushed back to the White House. At Edith Wilson's insistence, Wilson's doctor and press secretary announced that the President was merely fatigued, and she acted as "steward" of the presidency, deciding which government issues to keep from her stricken husband. When Wilson did not resume his public life, the public became suspicious. On the Senate floor Al Fall publicly rebuked Edith for seizing control of the presidency: "We have petticoat government!"

Doc Sawyer wrote Warren, asking for inside information on the rumors that Wilson had suffered a stroke. He foreshadowed his own role in history by remarking, "I wonder if the facts given to the public press are the real facts in his case? We are inclined to suspect they are not." Warren responded, "I saw a snapshot photograph of him the night he landed in Washington . . . it was about the most pathetic picture I have ever seen. He really looked like a perfectly helpless imbecile. . . . The most dependable story which we get is that the right side of his face is paralyzed, that his speech is very much impaired, and that there has been some leakage of the small arteries of the brain. It is positively known that he has had periods of extreme loss of mental control." Harding's story was not wrong.

Meanwhile the Hardings joined the bitter fight against the League, led by Senator Henry Cabot Lodge, Foreign Relations Committee chairman. All of them met to plan strategy at Alice's house. The kind of Americanism that the Duchess had begun talking up during the war became a rallying flag for anti-Leaguers; as the wife of a Senate Foreign Relations Committee member she began to illustrate her principles by action. When she met the visiting Belgian Queen Elizabeth, the Duchess decided not to curtsy, as other Washington wives did. Instead she met the queen with a "level eye" and extended "an outstretched hand." She explained, "She was in our country. If I were being received by royalty in its own country, I should try to conform to the customs of the country. But this was in America."

Florence and Alice agreed with the so-called irreconcilables who opposed the League outrightly, regardless of how many reservations and safeguards to American autonomy were included. It was Article X, which allowed the League the right to order American troops to fight without congressional approval, that Lodge, Warren, and other "reservationists" resisted; with its removal they could have otherwise supported the League. Wilson's Democratic allies, however, refused to vote for a League with reservations. Thus, on November 18, 1919, the League was defeated in a final congressional vote. A midnight supper was organized at Alice's with ten senators. "Mrs. Harding cooked the eggs," recalled Alice. "We were jubilant—too elated to mind the reservationists—now that it was over, they seemed quite as happy as we were."[4]

Although journalist Thomas Russell said Florence, "like the wives of all members of Congress," exerted a "strong influence" over her husband's vote, in light of the criticism of Edith Wilson's power, Florence publicly backpedaled. She had done nothing to lobby her husband, she said publicly. Though she acknowledged she often expressed her opinions to her husband, she "vigorously opposed the employment of this influence where a vote in the Senate was involved . . . operating on the theory that Mr. Harding was Senator . . . [she] never once sought to influence his judgment in any measure of national importance." Senate observers thought otherwise. Kathleen Lawler, manager of her own political support staffing agency, had heard stories from her friend Al Fall of the Duchess's active participation in the Sunday political brunch gatherings. Late in 1919, when a Senate elevator operator told a gentleman that it was Florence Harding who had just gotten off on another floor, he retorted, "I wish I had known that was Mrs. Harding. I am for Senator Harding for president largely because of what I have heard about Mrs. Harding right here. I'm for her. Don't you know, young man? Senator and Mrs. Harding will make the best President we have ever had."[5]

Certainly Harry Daugherty continued to think so. He and the Duchess had already forged a working political relationship. As he wrote her, he promised always to tell her "just what I think about anything in the most inoffensive, conscientious, God-fearing and man-loving way I know of." When Harry finally confronted Warren in his Senate office to say that he "would have to take his chance on the Presidential candidacy and forego [*sic*] the Senatorial one," Harding, in one of his "rare bursts of anger . . . profanely . . . swore he would do no such thing." Harry knew his only ace was with the Duchess, despite her earlier crack to him: "Get on your way and stop trying to sell me this box of soap." Harry knew that getting Harding to run depended on her:

> I had a vague fear that Mrs. Harding would give me trouble. She and I had always been the best of friends. She trusted my judgment as a rule, against Harding's on political issues. She knew that he was a man easily fooled by his enemies. I would have to cultivate her to carry out my plans for the advancement of her husband. I went to Washington to see the Senator and took pains to sound out Mrs. Harding. At the breakfast table she said to me: "I want to talk to you" . . . I knew that I was in for a struggle and I must handle her with tact. Harding was very fond of her and held the profoundest respect for her judgment, which had been sharpened by five years of contact with public life in Washington. . . . I was afraid of his wife's keen eyes and brilliant mind if he should falter in ambition to make the race. If she backed our candidate he would make the fight. If she opposed it, the issue would be doubtful. She looked at me steadily for a moment: "You are going to ask Warren to run for the Presidency—"

"The people of Ohio will demand it—" I broke in.

"You're the people of Ohio now. The others will call for him if you say so."

"And you don't wish your husband to aspire to the highest office. . . ."

"No. . . . He likes the Senate. I like being a Senator's wife. There is no strain. No pressure. No nerve-racking anxieties. We have charming friends. . . ."

"And you have no desire to become first lady of the land?"

"None. I've seen the inside of the White House. I have a vivid picture of President Wilson harried and beaten by the cares of office. The office is killing him as surely as if he had been stabbed at his desk." She paused again and looked at me. "I've a presentiment against this thing. Don't ask him to run."[6]

She reacted similarly to Kansas City reporter and friend Mont Reily, making clear her power over her husband: "I am going to take you to your train at two o'clock and see that you get away! And I do not want you to come back here and talk Warren into running for President, for *I do not intend to permit him to run.* Because of the condition of his health it would bring a tragedy to us both. I know that a Presidential campaign means strenuous activity. . . ."

The remark to Reily was Florence's first admission of Warren's health problems, especially notable in light of the fact that Doc not only ignored the issue but also pushed Warren to run. To Harding he wrote that being ". . . so well acquainted with capable men . . . you would be able to surround yourself with a personnel that would help to carry us through this critical period . . . it is just as well for you now as ever to announce yourself as a candidate . . . so that your friends might know exactly where you are and that they can back you as necessary to make you a winner. . . . [O]pportunities to individuals is largely advantage taken of conditions and circumstances presenting. I have learned that there are few people in this world who have gotten very far along excepting that they have spoken for themselves and asked for what they wanted and taken part in the scouting of it. You are no exception to this general rule. Why hesitate?"[7]

Besides the wisdom of risking the Senate seat and the potential danger to Warren's health, the other factor that overwhelmed Florence was having to raise enough money to mount a presidential campaign through the primaries, though as she was learning, any mention of a bid for the White House brought second cousins out of obscurity and made them into strange bedfellows. In the midst of the Harding boom the Duchess got a desperate phone call from a distant cousin, Georgia Hamon. Georgia needed help keeping her marriage together. In return she could help the Hardings. With lots of money.

Georgia Perkins Hamon was married to the millionaire oilman Jake Hamon, of Ardmore, Oklahoma, where he had made a fortune in oil through extensive oil leases and royalties. When he met blue-eyed, red-haired nineteen-year-old Clara Smith, he persuaded her to become his "secretary." They took a suite at the Randol Hotel, and Hamon arranged for her to marry his nephew Frank, who was paid off and sent to San Francisco, leaving his bride behind. Humiliated, Georgia left for Chicago but did not forget or forgive. Jake lived with his new "niece," while raking in three million dollars a year in oil money. In New York he buttonholed circus king John Ringling and persuaded him to build thirty-one miles of railroad from Ardmore to the oilfields, using Clara as bait. Jake called her "my sweet little brains." Georgia Hamon knew what was going on. When she made an unannounced visit to Ardmore and went into Jake's room, Clara suddenly appeared, then ran out. Georgia took Clara's gun, which she had left in the room. Adultery in Ardmore was handled with considerably more drama than in places like Marion.

Hearing about the Harding boom, Georgia Hamon saw her opportunity. Although finer details of the arrangement are lost, it is known that she told Florence about Hamon's adultery. Georgia asked for the promise of getting Jake a Cabinet or ambassadorial position in exchange for his hefty campaign contributions and collections, as well as appointment as an Oklahoma national Republican committeeman; she hoped to reclaim his marital fidelity by having him offered a high-profile position on the condition that he break off with Clara. Thus, according to Ardmore lore, the deal was struck between the two women. A Harding campaign would get funding, and Georgia Hamon would get the promise of saving her marriage and making it respectable.[8]

Florence was ignorant of the results of her own husband's most recent extramarital affair. On October 22, in a small Asbury Park, New Jersey, house, was born the second illegitimate child fathered by Warren Harding. Realizing she was pregnant, Nan had written Warren in February at his Senate address, as always mailing it with a postmark from a post office different from her own and sealing it within multiple envelopes, the final one with "Mr. Renwick" on it to throw off anyone who happened across it. Warren kept Nan's letters in a locked drawer; he had instructed Christian to burn them if anything happened to him. She assured Warren that she was burning his letters, which he signed

as "Jerose," a slight variation on the "Jerry" nickname for his sexual
anatomy he had used in his letters to Carrie.

Warren told her "we must go at this thing in a sane way." He
gave her a bottle of Dr. Humphrey's No. 11 tablets, which the Duchess
had used to avoid pregnancy—obviously a useless remedy now. Nan
was already into her thirteenth week. Then he gently assured her he
had "ample funds" for an "operation" and that between "medicine" and
"the knife," he advised the latter. Nan recoiled, determined to have the
child because, as she told him, she dreamed of living "on a farm and
rais[ing] children with Warren Gameliel Harding!" She told her sister
Elizabeth Willits about everything; Elizabeth concurred with Harding
and nearly coaxed Nan into taking a "bitter apple" concoction. Nan
said she "could not bring myself to destroy the precious treasure within
me." The unnerved senator finally gave the girl the ring she had wanted,
and they "performed a sweet little ceremony." He concluded that
"worry kills," so he tried not to worry.

When her pregnancy became noticeable, he set her up out in Asbury Park, where she told a story that her "husband" was a "Lieutenant
Christian" stationed overseas. When she came unannounced to Washington and called him, he gave her a wad of money and put her back
on the train, although they laughed about what Carolyn Votaw in her
work with "fallen girls" would make of her brother's situation. Only
once did Nan's resentment surface, when Warren traveled to Asbury
Park, made a speech, and didn't call her. "After all, I had not got into
my condition by myself," she wrote him. Warren continued to provide
her with thick envelopes of cash, large sums of money he certainly didn't
spend on the Duchess.

The baby was named Elizabeth Ann "Christian." Warren wrote
directly to Nan after getting the news, a dangerous chance. "He tried
to protect me and himself and everybody," she later wrote, "but sometimes he surely did stupid things." Just weeks after the birth Nan was
confused, depressed, and nearly hysterical. Warren suggested potential
adoptive parents like the Scobeys or his sister Charity in California. Nan
refused to give up her child. She relocated to Chicago and hired a
woman to care the baby. Harding was vague about his sudden fatherhood, offering only faint hope of marriage, what Nan later referred
to as "the probability of Mrs. Harding's death far in advance of his
own."[9]

Later many Marionites disputed the child's paternity, but even
those who believed it was Warren's offspring still blamed Nan. "If
anything happened, it was *her* fault," said Miriam Stowe. "She had a

case of hero-worship, a little cuckoo for older men," said Gilcrest Allen. "Yet the child looked so damn much like Harding, it is really impossible to reject it." For now only Nan's patient sister Elizabeth and her husband, Scott Willits, knew about Harding's involvement with Nan, but they were safely away from Marion. And a month after the baby's birth, when the Hardings returned to Marion for Thanksgiving, it was not Nan but Carrie who was being whispered about.

The Hardings had been conspicuously absent from the September wedding of Isabelle Phillips to Army Air Service Private William H. Mathee, Jr., who had been born in Germany. Now Carrie's wartime bluff to reveal her affair with Harding paled beside the illegitimate child by Nan. Any public discovery of the child *would* ruin him. By late 1919 Carrie had become so entirely self-absorbed she could not offer comfort. Warren finally, belatedly, realized that their relationship had been "fractured." There were no more letters asking Warren to divorce Florence. Instead a bitter Carrie just wrote "ridiculing" his "ambitions."[10]

If the women in his life seemed less than supportive of his running for president, each of his male friends pushed for it: Fall, Forbes, Daugherty, Smith, Sawyer, Scobey, Hard, Jennings, Reily. Although the senator was angered at how Harry Daugherty had moved behind his back to drum up support, expressing his distrust of such techniques, Harding was flattered by the attention. With his past catching up with him in the form of a new baby and with his lust for license and women unquenched, however, he had reservations about his own quality of life. To Scobey he wrote, "I should never have any more fun or any real enjoyment in life if I should be so politically fortunate to win a nomination and election . . . it is very possible that I would make as good a President as a great many men who are talked of [but] . . . I have such a sure understanding of my own inefficiency that I should really be ashamed to presume myself fitted to reach out for a place of such responsibility." Yet it was fallacy that Harding only passively became a candidate. His correspondence with his extensive national network of encouraging friends shows a man coyly welcoming but not overtly seeking the presidency, at once passive and aggressive. Whatever misgivings he had about making the run, he encouraged others to convince him.

Ultimately Harry pushed the ambivalent Harding to make him run. In a rambling conversation Daugherty argued that Colonel Leonard Wood, Theodore Roosevelt's protégé and the favored man of the moment, wouldn't be nominated because he was too militaristic for the times, nor would Illinois Governor Frank Lowden because he was too wealthy. "Am I a big enough man for the race?" Warren asked. "Don't make me laugh," Harry responded. "The days of giants in the Presidential Chair is passed. Our so-called Great Presidents were all made by the conditions of war under which they administered the office. Greatness in the presidential chair is largely an illusion of the people."

"We had it out," Harry told Charles Hard. "I say to you and you can rely on it—he will be a candidate." Harry now began seeking declarations of Harding support—the first came from Roosevelt's Vice President Charles Fairbanks—emphasizing how Ohio was needed for a Republican win since it had gone Democratic in the last two elections and how Harding was another McKinley. His strategy was to convince committee members, delegates, and potential supporters to consider Harding as a later ballot choice if there were a deadlocked convention.

Florence also sent a mixed message about her ambitions. "I do not see myself in the White House," she declared convincingly. Evalyn thought she "meant it." Others were less convinced. Norman Thomas said she was driven to reach the highest possible pinnacle—far beyond anything Amos Kling could have possibly conceived for her or for himself. Alice Longworth believed that Florence wanted to be First Lady to repay the slights she first received in Washington, including those from her. "These people," Alice editorialized later, "were to realize that she was aware of their behavior." After interviewing Florence's friends about her true feelings on Warren's running in the primaries, Samuel Hopkins Adams concluded: "At times she had her doubts of him, distrusted his capacity, feared that he would not measure up to the requirements and responsibilities that increased with his amazing rise. But these misgivings she stifled. Of herself, I think she never had any doubts. She implicitly believed the professional seers and crystal-gazers who assured her that she carried the Star of Destiny on her brow."

By the end of 1919 she had discussed the issue from all angles with most of Harding's closest political advisers. She may have had some specific reasons for hesitancy—perhaps the skeletons in her closet and Warren's, such as his affairs and the circumstances of her first marriage, or her concerns about his health or her own. Warren would not definitively announce his candidacy unless Florence truly agreed with the decision. The Duchess wanted to wait until 1920 began, to wait until "the stars shone with promise." Fate at least bought her some time. As luck would have it, by a new law, Harding did not have to file for Senate renomination until the day that the balloting began at the Republican presidential convention in June.[11]

There was but one more adviser left with whom the Duchess must discuss the issue—her astrologer.

Part Four

CAMPAIGN AND TRANSITION
1920–1921

The reason why people do not achieve more in life is because they are too skeptical of opportunities offered them.

17

The Zodiac of Jupiter

Laughter and whispers flew above the shifting bridge cards splayed in the white-gloved hands of the Duchess, fellow Senate wives Mrs. Poindexter and Mrs. Sutherland, and congressional wife Mrs. Woodyard. It was the dead of January, but the November election was already all the talk. When the women began to discuss the vagaries of fate, Mrs. Woodyard suggested they make a sport of it. All the capital elite—from First Lady Edith Wilson to Supreme Court justices—were now consulting Madame Marcia. Woodyard had herself been there, appearing under the name Brown Pheasant because of the stuffed bird on her hat; Marcia never asked her clients' identities. Woodyard booked another appointment, and on a dark afternoon in the first week of February the four women drove up Sixteenth Street, eleven blocks from the White House, and to the three-story cream-colored green-trimmed town house at 1509 R Street.

Few vocations could have better suited the histrionic Marcia Champney, with her indiscernible "foreign" accent, than astrologer to the swells. It was a long way from Coney Island. Daughter of a French Canadian and Englishman who, according to Marcia, had "real Gypsy blood in his veins," she was born in Brooklyn in 1867, her earliest memory being her mother yelling her name from the window of their "cheap tenement house." Abandoned by her father, little Marcia ran errands for pennies from the "dirty old woman who looked liked a witch" in the basement and was fascinated by the goblins and knights on a pack of tarot cards she was asked to deliver to her. "Long, furtive hours I sat in the corner of her dirty parlor," Marcia recalled, as she watched the witch tell fortunes. Ever since she had predicted President Garfield's 1881 assassination, Marcia knew she had "clairvoyant powers" and a gift for "true occultism." She stole some of the witch's clients, and between stints as a peroxide blonde in tights performing for the sophisticated-sounding vaudevillian "Frank Deshon Opera Company," when she was the roommate of comic actress Marie Dressler, Marcia kept at her craft.

In 1890 Marcia married Horace Marion Champney, of "exclusive people" with no money. In less than a year she had a son, and then, just as quickly, a daughter, and the entire family moved in with her mother, subsisting on the weekly ten dollars Horace's family sent them. When Horace abandoned them, Marcia went to work in a millinery sweatshop, reading palms at lunchtime. A fellow sweatshop girl took her to Gypsy Olive on the Coney Island boardwalk. The next day, in black wig, bandanna, and fake gold earrings, Marcia was "Little Olive" living at the "Gypsy Camp," leaving wigs off her blond children to suggest they had been kidnapped from more proper American households.

Marcia's tarot, palm, and tea readings were so popular that by 1897 she had her own business. After reading *Dr. Janes' Vermifuge Almanac,* she "mastered the great science" propounded by the "Great Man of the Zodiac" and dropped palms for "something higher and finer." Along with astrology, she found "clairvoyance" particularly cost-efficient. This effort she performed by "throwing my mind into an infinity where there is neither time nor space. I close my eyes and turn all my thoughts within. I become oblivious of externals. I see things as they really are. . . . Pictures begin to unfold before my inner vision . . . at first, foggy and obscure. . . ." Business boomed after she predicted the correct outcomes of two sensational criminal cases: that killer Roland Molineaux would not get the electric chair and that accused murderer Nan Patterson would be acquitted. For good measure she paid her three dollars to become an ordained minister of the Spiritualist Church and made a steady income performing weddings, christenings, and burials.

Marcia relocated to Washington in 1909, settling in the fashionable Dupont Circle area. In her candlelit back parlor, which visitors entered by passing through a fringed veil of dyed black chiffon, Madame Marcia held her readings for the capital's superstitious notables. One of her first customers was Mrs. Norman Galt, the widow of a jewelry store owner. In her clairvoyant vision Marcia beheld the White House and predicted Mrs. Galt would be First Lady. Galt was amused—particularly since President Taft was married—but kept the prediction in mind. When six months after Ellen Wilson died suddenly, in August 1914, and President Wilson began sending passionate love letters to Edith Galt, she began bragging about Marcia's powers. By the time Edith became First Lady, Marcia was doing readings in the White House, arriving via the service entrance. Word spread through the Supreme Court, the Senate, press circles, and the bridge circuit. And so, even on this icy and unkind February day, the four political wives, who did not reveal their identities, were lucky to get an appointment.

"We want our horoscopes read," said Mrs. Poindexter. "We want to know which of us is to be the next first lady of the land." Sutherland and Woodyard laughed, but a silent Duchess stared Marcia in the eyes. Each woman was given a reading based on information she herself provided, but Florence had prepared hers cryptically, writing it down instead of speaking. Halfway through the group conference, Marcia pointed at her and asked how many homes she had. Florence said two, one in Washington and one in—at which point Marcia held up her hand to stop her from revealing her hometown and went on, "You will have three homes later. Within a year you will make a great change. Your whole life will be altered. A vista of power opens before you." Pointing again at Florence, she stated, "If any of you ladies are to be first lady, this is the one."

She then made her specific predictions for a person born on August 15, 1860. Florence provided her birth date but had not stated that it was hers. According to what Marcia remembered saying, she declared, "This is the map of a strong person. A dominant, willful, tenacious person of tremendous powers of concentration. A great desire to rule is indicated. She would be acquisitive and self-centered. The influence of Saturn points to melancholy and possible unhappiness over domestic affairs. With Mars in Capricorn, it is indicated that tragedy would wreck or ruin the career. Danger is indicated from secret enemies. Her own dominating and aggressive attitude is offered as a cause for failure and sorrow. Death would come suddenly, perhaps as a result of an ailment of long standing. It would follow her widowhood." With the melodrama— and later the pulp magazine fees—that hindsight provides, Marcia recollected that "I lifted my handkerchief to my face to conceal any emotions" and predicted for the Duchess a "dark and yet a glorious future." Although she was certain that Florence knew that her "path led to doom," Marcia said the Duchess "did not flinch." Marcia added that the person born in August 1860 would "die in honor." If somehow he or she escaped death from the long-standing ailment after the predicted two years in power, shortly thereafter the "Furies would swoop down" on the individual.

The women laughed. The spell broken, Marcia joked that she hoped that she would not have to continue coming through the White House service entrance for the next First Lady. Florence promised Marcia that she would come through the front door and that "Our next meeting will be at bridge in the White House." In fact, it was much sooner. Florence still would not identify herself except to give the initials FKH to have the charts marked in a folder. "Jupiter is dominant with you," Marcia told her. "Hereafter I shall call you Jupiter." Florence nodded firmly but silently. And she paid Marcia's fee.

Marcia may have genuinely used the rather scientific techniques in interpreting astrological charts, but she hedged her bets with a knowledge of who was who in the power structure of Washington. She had a copy of the *Congressional Directory*, which gave the birth dates of various legislators and other vital information. Wise to the ways of astrologers, however, the Duchess had craftily provided *her* birth date, not Warren's to further mask her identity. The Duchess wanted Marcia checked out. Indulging her love of intrigue, Evalyn took charge. "She wasn't a crook at all," Evalyn decided. Coaxing Marcia by phone to give a reading at Friendship, Evalyn dressed in a nursemaid's uniform to mask her identity, welcomed her at the door, and brought her to "Mrs. McLean," a nursemaid dressed in jewels and one of Evalyn's gowns. Evalyn asked Marcia for a reading, and the astrologer looked at her hands, then remarked, "You think you are pretty smart, don't you? Why on earth didn't you roughen your nails or something, then you might have fooled me!" Apparently that was all the test Evalyn needed. "We got her good and drunk and she had to be carried home. She weighed 250 pounds," she noted. "Then, I used to go down and see her all the time." Evalyn placed greater stock in the ability to read the thoughts of the dead. "The billions of people that have died—I think they have all left something. When you get right down to it, everything is vibrations you know. You tap ether waves from them. They are right behind you. You leave some part of yourself."

Encouraged by Evalyn, "Jupiter" returned alone to Marcia, taking a streetcar to avoid being identified by the license plates of the Harding car. Marcia was impressed with the occult knowledge possessed by this woman who still would not identify herself, commenting, "Not only did she have a smattering of the technical facts of astrology, but apparently a real appreciation of its application." Still using her initials, this time Florence gave Warren's birth date. "I hope this person is a man," Marcia said after studying the chart. "No woman could be strong enough." This offended the Duchess. "Don't say that, Marcia. A woman might be found who is strong enough to play that part. But you are right. This is the chart of a man prominent in public life."

Marcia saw the Sun in conjunction with Mars, Mercury, and Saturn, under Scorpio in the eighth house, that of Death, while Uranus was in the fifth house, of Karma. From this she saw suggestions of "earthly love and gambling for royal stakes" with "threatening and dangerous" influences. According to Marcia's reports of her reading several years later, the person's "fate would depend largely upon the action of his friends and on the influence exerted by marriage—or love. . . . Given to making promises and to extending complete confidence to his friends. Apt to be enthusiastic and impulsive. Money would be gained through the employment of many people or in public service . . . much perplexity over financial affairs . . . many love affairs of a clandestine nature . . . acute recurrent pessimism and melancholy. . . ."

Frightening away a new client was not Marcia's purpose, but when she backtracked a bit, Jupiter resisted, exclaiming, "I wish to know it all. I am not afraid."

"If this man runs for the presidency, no power on earth can defeat him," Marcia said.

"He is in the running," Jupiter declared.

"But you must know . . . he will die a sudden death, perhaps of poison. The stars say that he will give his life for a cause. Or that he will sacrifice himself for his friends. . . . This person will be the next president of the United States, but he will not live out his term. He will die in a sudden if not violent death. The end, when it comes will be sudden, after an illness of short duration. . . . Poison or its effects is indicated. . . . It is written in the stars. . . . Following the splendid climax in the House of Preferment, I see the Sun and Mars in conjunction in the eighth house of the zodiac. And this is the House of Death—sudden, violent or peculiar death. Tragedy. . . . The stars, Jupiter, never lie."

At this last remark, if Marcia really made it, Florence may have been particularly startled, for it was a line she herself had often repeated through the years. It may have prompted her to reveal further that the man in question was her husband. When Marcia asked if he believed in astrology, Florence confessed that he simply laughed at it but added, "I believe, Marcia, and I must guide him. You must tell me how." Marcia simply gave a vague direction that he "be strong, take a firm stand and hold to it" but dubbed Jupiter to be a "Child of Destiny."

How much of what Marcia repeated verbatim was in fact stated is difficult to know. She began making public these conversations with Florence months after Mrs. Harding's death, when many friends and staff could have—but never did—discount them. There were also various corroborative sources during Florence's life: newspaper stories, reprinted copies of letters from Florence to Marcia, statements and diary entries by staff, even a letter of former President Taft. That Florence unequivocally believed the predictions was clear from her own public statements, her various astrological scribblings in her record books, and Evalyn's recollections. With the zodiac laid out before her, how Florence could integrate her faith in astrology into the pragmatic political realities of February 1920 was another matter. She could certainly not bring her fears to Warren, nor did she quite have the wherewithal to challenge fate and Marcia's predictions. Florence had "feared [that] the time had not come for the presidency," that waiting until 1924 was wiser, and she had half hoped Marcia would affirm that belief. Instead she learned that Harding could win—but at a price. She began to speak obliquely of "tragedy." But she stopped talking about keeping Warren from running.[1]

Coincidence or not, less than a week after Florence's initial consultation with Marcia, at Toledo's Lincoln Day Address, Harding announced his candidacy, claiming that he did so to honor the urging and requests of Ohio Republicans. The Duchess "was greatly worried and still skeptical," wrote Kathleen Lawler, yet curiously, once "the formal announcement was made," Florence "never by word, or look, or act faltered." Her inner fears were promptly and regularly assuaged by Harry Daugherty. In fact, in the first weeks of the primaries campaign, Harry, said Evalyn, "nagged and coaxed" both Hardings to make a full-throttle effort. Charles Hard concurred that something still frightened Florence: "Mrs. Harding may have persuaded herself that she was sympathetic to his candidacy . . . but she did not wish him to run for President."

Harry became Harding's campaign manager and began soliciting funds. Among the first were a six-thousand-dollar donation by oilman James Darden and, oddly, a loan, not a donation, for seventy-five hundred dollars from a supporter of Leonard Wood's, another oilman by the name of Harry Sinclair, who came to be linked with Harding in scandal. In everything Daugherty did for Harding, the path was shadowed by Jess Smith. Despite the fact that Jess was, in the euphemism of the day, a "dandy," he was accepted as he was by the Hardings. Through Harry, Jess was privy to every backstage political promise for a large contribution, and thus so was Roxy.

Despite her misgivings, once Harry began keeping in touch with her, the Duchess began giving directions to him, such as how to capture Warren's way of speaking in staff-written speeches. "The plan you suggest will go," he responded to one of her letters. "You are the boss and as you know I never insist on having my way. That is a joke but I will do as you desire and with pleasure. I am trying to write an appropriate speech." In the meanwhile longtime Harding friend Mont Reily—the "queer duck" Harry called him—became Harding's western manager. Harding, Florence, and Harry opened the campaign in Texas the first week of March, then went to Kansas, Oklahoma, Colorado, and Nebraska. Shortly after, when Florence headlined a suffragists for Harding lunch, Charles Hard reported to Warren, "I saw Mrs. Harding two or three times yesterday. She was very enthusiastic about your western trip. The ladies had quite a time here yesterday and the effort was well worth while."[2]

Harry was laying the groundwork for proposing Harding as the compromise candidate in a convention that might not agree on a leader on the first several ballots. Charlie Forbes began soliciting support for Harding as a second-choice candidate if the convention deadlocked, and Jake Hamon agreed to throw his bloc of Oklahoma delegates to Harding in the same scenario. Florence's fears lingered, with Pennsylvania Senator George Pepper noting that she was "seldom carefree." Yet the more committed she became, the more she loved the attention. "Our escort consisted of the Chief of Police in his car, and twenty-four of Cleveland's 'finest' mounted police on splendid Ky. horses—ten plain clothes secret-service men and Heaven knows what else," Florence wrote the Scobeys during a swing through Ohio. "At each stop they all lined up to salute, etc. W.G. 'G-d D----d'it, and I, well I was quite thrilled and enjoyed the 'Show.'"

If she believed that she carried the star of destiny, Florence also began to talk of how Warren was predestined for the presidency, the first sign being that Lincoln had once touched the forehead of Warren's father, as if some mystical anointment had occurred, the Great Emancipator sparing Dr. Harding's life as he went off to war and making it possible for him to sire a future President. She did not openly disclose the real root of her faith in Warren's inevitable victory: Marcia's prediction. As the primaries in twenty states began in March, she focused on politics. She undoubtedly reviewed the most important speech of the primary campaign, for it reflected her concept of Americansim.

In all but declaring his candidacy on January 6 before New York's Ohio Society, Harding had outlined his America First theme. After a lumbering prologue—"The topic of the evening makes it befitting to allude to the contemporaneousness of the birth of Ohio and the beginning of Americanism"—he tied the founding of Ohio to the year of the framing of the Constitution, when "Americanism began, robed in nationality." He went on to elaborate a nationalist program: Alien nonresidents must no longer be allowed to immigrate, work, and earn money to take back to their native lands, never having committed themselves to citizenship. The League of Nations was the "plea of the patent-medicine fakir" and risked national security; besides, the world economy was already moving without the League. A better way of life for Americans would come only as a result of thrift, enterprise, and sacrifice. He concluded: "Call it the selfishness of nationality if you will, I think it an inspiration to patriotic devotion—To safeguard America first. To stabilize America first. To prosper America first. To think of America first. To exalt America first. To live for and revere America first. . . . Let the internationalist dream and Bolshevist destroy . . . we proclaim Americanism and acclaim America."

Rhetoric was one thing, reality another. When Harding won Ohio by only 15,000 votes, and lost Indiana with 20,819 to Wood's 85,776, Hiram Johnson's 79,829, and Illinois Governor Lowden's 31,118, he planned to withdraw so he could still file for candidacy for—and fairly certain reelection to—the Senate. In the Indianapolis home of Senator New, Warren telephoned headquarters and asked for Harry. Florence jumped into action, yanking the phone from him, yelling, "Warren Harding! What are you doing? Give up? Not until the Convention is over. Think of your friends in Ohio!" Then into the phone she yelled, "Hello! This is Mrs. Harding. Yes, Mrs. Harding. You tell Harry Daugherty we're in this fight 'til hell freezes over!"

During a brief return to Marion following the debacle of the Indiana primary, the Duchess confided to Colonel Christian, "You don't know anything about politics or how to run campaigns until you get an insight into the Indiana methods," referring to vote buying. If she was rudely awakened to voter manipulation and heard suggestions that Harding could never win after a third bad showing in the Michigan primary, the Duchess remained rigidly in the fight. As Evalyn said, Florence "was not one who believed in giving up once a fight had begun, and some of the men who knew most of the inside story of those trying weeks give to her the credit for keeping Mr. Harding in the race. . . ."[3]

How Warren was coping with the threat to his charmed life was harder to know. If she was obvious, he was inscrutable. The man whose anxieties had led him to Dr. Kellogg's clinic with a nervous breakdown some thirty years before was not one who now exhibited his passions or demons. As Mark Sullivan observed, "He seemed to have an inner life, which he did not permit to extrude upon his Marion surface. It was as if his daily touch with his neighbors had planed and smoothed his exterior to slide smoothy . . . while within himself, and to himself, he kept judgments and standards and points-of-view . . . a considerable intensity of emotional life might go on."

Nan Britton was learning this. While she was dining in Chicago with Warren, the name Carrie Phillips came up "naturally" in conversations as Nan told of her recent Marion trip. "I had never mentioned Mrs. [Phillips's] name to him in connection with the oldtime gossip I used to hear, but something I asked him brought forth this spontaneous ejaculation . . . 'Mrs. [Phillips] is a damned fool—a brilliant conversationalist but a damned fool—if she had *half* the sense of her daughter—' " In afterthought, Nan remarked, "I do not know a thing about the truth of things that were said concerning Mr. Harding's one-time relations with Mrs. [Phillips]."[4]

With a terrifying capacity for revenge, Mrs. Phillips was nobody's fool. In early April Warren received a letter in familiar handwriting, postmarked from Marion. A more devastating threat to Harding's candidacy than primary losses had arisen, complete with a personal vendetta against the Duchess. Hell hath no fury like the scorned mistress of a presidential candidate.

18

Blackmail

After fifteen years of frustrated fantasies of marrying Warren Harding, Carrie Phillips finally took decisive action. She told her husband all about it, everything.

Jim Phillips was not so stunned numb that he didn't manage to keep some kind of cool head. There had been many signs over the years that he should have heeded: the long midnight walks that Carrie took on ship deck during their 1909 overseas voyage with the Hardings; the rage she flew into when she heard that Harding was running for the Senate; the abrupt end of her friendship with Florence Harding; the frenzy of Senator

Harding about what Jim regarded as her annoying but harmless German flag-waving during the war. Somehow Jim seemed not only to forgive his wife but still to like his old pal Harding.

Throughout the winter of 1920 Warren wrote to Carrie from all over the country as he campaigned, just as he had for the last decade and a half. Now she responded with scorn, declaring that she knew he was "having affairs with other women," though she didn't name names, and that it was forever, truly over between them. He promised to "make amends," however vague he left the notion. They had a brief "interview" in his Senate office, discussing everything from his true motivations in running for President to her deep-seated hatred of Florence. She left even more angry, as she recognized how the Senate was the one thing that bonded Warren and her nemesis, his wife. It was something she immediately recognized that could destroy. Carrie threatened not only to derail Warren's presidential candidacy but simultaneously to wreck his backup plan, his near-certain Senate reelection. Carrie Phillips had all his love letters.

Warren would have to pay up in cash to her—dearly—or suffer the consequences. Her demand for compensation was no idle threat. If she were not paid, Carrie Phillips would go public with the story of their love affair, using the letters as proof. The sum she wanted amounted to an annual income. According to Francis Russell, who was familiar with the full context of the Harding-Phillips affair, the only alternative Carrie offered was familiar: Drop out of politics completely and divorce Florence. Never before had Carrie mentioned money in her threats. It so fearfully possessed Warren Harding that the man who might be President of the United States even thought of a final escape. He would never actually commit suicide, but he briefly wished passively to die.

Warren knew he had to respond to the blackmail. The mere act of writing about the affair in cold black-and-white was precisely the kind of confrontation this gentle man had spent a lifetime avoiding. In an extraordinary elliptical but brutal letter to Carrie—reprinted below—he began on a typically friendly note, with reference to legislation about German reparations, but then he addressed the great love of his life in coded but certain terms. He suggested that he was running as Ohio's favorite son to bolster the state power of those supporting him and make certain his Senate reelection was secure. He regretted her "revealment" to Jim and suggested that if she held off and he won the presidential nomination, his "power" would buy her a greater payoff. If he could win the presidency, it would serve her purposes even better. Otherwise he would find a way to pay her blackmail—not the unreasonable sum she presumably suggested but a more modest five thousand dollars a year while he remained in public office.

His response makes it clear that Carrie's blackmail was largely motivated by her jealousy of Florence; he mentions that his "tribute" to his wife had been too "often shown" and suggests that Carrie's blackmail was futile if she hoped to destroy Florence, for his wife was capable of emotional and financial independence. He furthermore scolded Carrie that the "one wrong impression which I must now correct" was that it was Florence who had influenced him to distance himself from Carrie: "Mrs. H. has not mentioned your name in years. She has no part in seeking to annoy you." Evidently the scene at the Marion train station between Florence and Carrie still humiliated her, but Warren said it had occurred solely because of Florence's wartime patriotism, stirring "a hostility that no personal quarrel could engender." He alluded to an arranged deal between himself and the Duchess, a "compact" they had struck about Carrie, adultery, their marriage, and political ambitions. That a presidential candidate would put in writing a reference to such a "compact" was unprecedented:

Your note and clipping rec'd. When I talked to you I believed the legislation referred to in the clipping had been dropt. I knew it had passed the Senate, and I had asked that it be dropt, and understood it was to be. It was my intent to tell you correctly. The passage was far more embarrassing than you can guess. One can't always control.

I have been thinking very intently, very solemnly about our interview and all you said. It is difficult to write, but I will, because a continuous suspense is intolerable.

I told you perfectly truly that I did not intend to be an aspirant in the big way. I had no such preference from personal inclination and I had had intimations of your hostility. I could not make myself believe that you would threaten me—real earnest, but I felt it best to retire and become lost in the multitude rather than invite embarrassment.

If you will recall, both my public and private utterances revealed my disinclination, and I certainly *wasn't cheating*. But one can't always decide for himself except in desperation. I yielded to the pressure I was being undermined in my own state, and good friends urged it to be a desertion of them to deny them such influence and cooperation as I could command. It is a great thing to have a few people think well of one (or even pretend to) in so important a matter. I drifted in unwillingly, then found myself pleased to be well esteemed. I have some good qualities.

I never betrayed a public trust. I try to be considerate and fair, and to
retain an even poise. But no matter about that. Thinking of you and
yours (as I did, and always do) it seems to me maybe greater influence
and power would enable me to make amends, and to do some of the
things wished for, and *frankly* I was heart-broken over your revealment
of last Wednesday night.

We have been in M[arion] so little—designedly so. It has been
avoided as often as can be. I have been indecently discourteous to lifelong friends at home because I could not be fully considerate of you.
No use to the public or my friends. If I must quit to pay the penalty,
let me start at once on the plans which make it the least difficult. I can't
just quit and be a yellow quitter but I can plan and work it out in a
fairly seemly way so that no one knows but ourselves. Can't you send
me a night letter at 143 Senate offices? No fast telegram. In a night letter
you can say, "We are writing. Go ahead with program with our best
wishes. Think it will be fine." I'll construe that to mean go ahead, and
do the best I can. If I must retire to save us both say in night letter,
"Don't bother about passports—think we will give up trip. Will write."
I'll construe this to mean cancellation of all plans. And by all means
write. The anxiety is killing.

We both understood. We were married. No lies were told. We felt
the same sense of family obligations. Happily there have been no irrep-
arable damages. There have been disappointments, irritations, the one
break, and all the regrets you utter and no incurable revealment. It is
my philosophy of life that mistakes can not be wholly cured but their
injuries can be minimized. I would make every reparation I can. It is all
we can do.

I have oftened [*sic*] wishes [*sic*] the final out for myself. In remorse,
worry and distress I would welcome the great sleep. But normal beings
cannot command it. We must live to make the best amends we can. Self
destruction will not add to the injuries done.

We have obligations, we owe to ourselves and those we have injured to meet these obligations. Your proposal to destroy me, and yourself in doing so, will only add to the ill we have already done. It doesn't
seem like you to think of such a fatal course. I can't believe your purpose
is to destroy me for paying the tribute so uttered and so often shown.
You don't effectively reach the object of your dislike [Florence]. But [do]
not [worry about] my side. You must think of yourself and yours.

I know you are saying I ought to have said that twelve years ago.
True! But I have confessed the blunder. Aren't we big enough to make
all the reparations we can, and do the best possible? But all these things
have occurred to you, and you know that the situation can still be saved.

I am not sure but it can be made a fairly happy one, in patience, poise and all around.

Now to specific things—I can't secure you the larger competence you have frequently mentioned. No use to talk about it. I can pay with life or reputation but I can't command such a sum! To avoid disgrace in the public eye to escape ruin in the eyes of those who have trusted me in public life—whom I have never betrayed—I will if you demand it as the PRICE—retire at the end of my term, and never come back to M[arion] to reside. I will also avoid any elevation but retire completely to obscurity. You must let me choose the process, but I will be retired fully, utterly, finally after next March 1. I can't instantly get out of the present entanglement, I can't get out until June, but I write you the solemn pledge to retire wholly and finally next March. I'll pay this price to save my own disgrace and your own self destruction to destroy me. That is one proposal, complete, final and covers all.

Here is another. If you think I can be more helpful by having a public position and influence, probably a situation to do some things, worthwhile for myself and you and yours, I will pay you $5000 per year, in March each year, so long as I am in that public service. It is not big, it is not what you have asked, but it will add to your comfort and make you independent to a reasonable degree. It is the most within my capacity. I wish it might be more, but one can only do that which is in his power. Destroy me and I have no capacity, while the object of your dislike is capable of going on on her own account.

I write these in good faith. I will, I must abide your decision. I am helpless to hinder. I beg of you to ponder it all and I beg of you to chose [*sic*] the way that will admit us to do the most and best we can to make it [*sic*] reparation to those we injured, and still make the most of life which is only a possibility if we make it so.

So much depends on your decision. I an nearly ill with the worry involved, but still hope, and still believe in your deliberate good sense [words obscured].

Please write me at once. So much impends, so much depends on your decision. I may have to alter a score of plans. Don't make me the fool [to] recite it all—you know it. But you have one wrong impression which I must now correct so that you may think more clearly. Mrs. H. has not mentioned your name in years. She has no part in seeking to annoy you. *I know.* It is a part of a compact, and it is kept. I dislike to write it, but crisis require truth for sane settlement. I do not mean to scold, to criticize. But I do know. You forget that we have gone through war, when tension was high and opinions prejudiced. You would speak as you felt. You offended and estranged and stirred a hostility that no personal quarrel could engender. Jim was close to serious embarrassment. *I know*. I will not dilate upon it, but this feeling, developed in war (needlessly and imprudently) is wholly to blame. It could be cured now, only you will not help, and only you can help effectively. Enough of this. It is only fair to all concerned that I write it.

Now to move to more intimate matters. We have blundered. We will not talk about the blame. I accept my full share of it. We did blunder. I give you the most tribute that a man can.

There was no cheating. [signed] Gov.

Inevitably, as he did in every great crisis, Warren turned to Florence for advice on the blackmail. She had long lived with the threat that Carrie would inevitably talk about Harding's adultery but now faced the prospect of his capitulation to blackmail: Even if Warren were somehow to be elected President, the dark secret of a payoff would haunt Florence, for that very fact could also be exposed by Carrie somewhere down the line. It became all the more intense because she would never share the details of it—even with Evalyn. If there was political pressure for Harding to withdraw, the worst possible personal crisis also now challenged him to do so.[1]

On May 20 the Duchess returned to Madame Marcia's salon. She looked quite different from her past two trips, stylishly turned out in blue silk, black hat, and white gloves, and according to Marcia's later recollections, this is when Florence finally revealed who she was and to whom she was married. "I have come to you for advice. Mr. Harding is under tremendous pressure from the highest party leaders to withdraw as a candidate. What should he do?"

"He must stick," Marcia claimed to have told Florence. "He will not be nominated until after noon on Saturday of the convention. But he will be nominated."

Florence said that she would see to it that Warren followed those orders. But something else was pressing her. Giving in to a rather dangerous impulse, Florence vaguely sought to suggest to Marcia the challenge of the blackmail attempt, "in that peculiarly terse and epigrammatic way," wrote Marcia, "that I learned to associate with Mrs. Harding" and that was evident as well in the diary entries Florence had made in reference to Warren's adultery.

Marcia never betrayed the Duchess by revealing the details of what she learned of her personal life, but the astrologer later alluded to the blackmail threat by writing that besides the "pressure from the highest party leaders," there was a "direct pressure being . . . made upon her husband to withdraw. . . . Neither he nor she were [*sic*] disposed to accede to it, and I think I strengthened her determination to resist. When she appeared a few days later she showed signs of the increasing strain. The pressure for Harding to abandon his candidacy was becoming acute. He himself was questioning the wisdom of continuing the fight. When she left me there was a renewed sparkle in her eyes, and from what she told me later I have reason to believe that he would have withdrawn during the next forty-eight hours had it not been for her insistence. . . . And, having explained something of her intimate problems to me, she never seemed to hesitate nor to show any desire to draw back from further confidences."

Just as they were to leave for the convention, in the first days of June, the Duchess again called on Marcia: "I want Warren to go to the convention. Our bags are packed and we have the last train reservations, but at the last moment Warren is reluctant to go to Chicago. He says it isn't dignified for a candidate to go to a convention city, although the others are there." Marcia told her, "If you are the wife of Warren G. Harding as you say you are—then GO. Go to that convention by the first train. And when you get there STICK. Do not be discouraged. Do not let your husband be discouraged. You will have a long, hard fight but you will win." On what ballot? Florence asked. "How can I tell that? But I will tell you this. He will not be nominated until after twelve o'clock noon. Then no power can keep him from the place the stars have pointed out for him." Independently corroborating the outcome of this session with Marcia was the statement of a staff member who had no knowledge of Marcia or her advice, but who observed that when Florence "threw the weight of her judgment," Harding "consented to go to Chicago."[2]

Between the blackmail threat, the astrologer's chart, and the deadline for filing for reelection to the Senate, the Duchess was faced with a minefield of complex choices: Even if Warren withdrew from the presidential race and made the Senate race, Carrie's blackmail price would remain in place, and without the kind of financial backing a presidential candidate could command, that price could not be met. By Marcia's estimate, if Warren were to win the nomination and then won the election, the price would be his life. If he won the nomination but lost the election, he would have also forgone his Senate reelection, and the Hardings would find themselves returning to Marion—and Carrie Phillips. Yet if he ignored Carrie's blackmail, she could destroy any chance at either the presidency or Senate reelection. But if Warren didn't win the nomination, he could not possibly comply with her financial demand, and she could still talk. Not paying Carrie risked both the presidential and Senate races. By blackmail Florence could possibly lose her life in Washington, be forced to return to Marion, and have Warren potentially beholden again to Carrie Phillips. By the stars, however, Florence could rise to the highest peak yet lose her husband to that "peculiar" death. No matter what her choice, fate and politics told her she was eventually bound to lose Warren.

Florence was perhaps assured by Daugherty that if Warren won the nomination, money could be found to pay for anything she felt necessary for the campaign—even for some unspecified purpose. Warren had made it clear in his letter to Carrie that her blackmail costs could best be met if he was nominated, and she seemed willing to wait until just after the convention, for she did not follow through with her threats before it. As for Marcia's dire prediction, Florence took a greater but still calculated risk. Since Warren did not believe in all her fears generated by the zodiac, there was simply no need to tell him. Warning him of some death prediction would have made him laugh. And he certainly had a history of withholding information that would affect her. Holding within her the fears of blackmail and the foretellings of astrology, an uncertain Duchess went to Chicago. Something else, however unconscious, also drove her, something strong enough that she seemed willing to risk the life of the man whose career she had made her life. Whether or not it was her now-ingrained need to exceed the expectations of Amos Kling's ghost, in her ambitions for her "career" of "Warren Harding," she had developed ambitions for herself.

Colonel Christian recalled an incident before the convention when both Hardings "reiterated their objections to seeking the presidency and their hope that yet there might be a chance to avoid it. Florence was particularly outspoken and became so excited over the matter that she proceeded to express her views in language that could not be misunderstood by those who had assisted in placing her husband in this undesirable situation. She became so warm in her statements and her language was so strong that I induced Mr. Harding to another part of the house to look over some imaginary papers I had." Christian told him, "[D]on't permit Florence to talk after this fashion. She is a woman of such strong character, so influential among her countless friends that I fear that she herself might damage your campaign."

A knowing smile crept across Harding's face. "Don't pay any attention to that," he said. "No woman ever lived who objected to becoming, if possible, the first lady of the land."[3]

19

Chicago

Florence Harding was a bundle of nervous contradictions in Chicago, optimistic with the press, pessimistic with advisers, certain Harding would win despite the fact that Wood, Lowden, and Johnson all led in committed delegates, and then privately fretting that Harding could never be nominated and must immediately file for Senate reelection. She managed to ignore Marcia's dark prediction of Harding's death but could become so fearful of it that she talked to the press about it. "I am contented to trail in my husband's limelight. But I can't see why anyone should want to be president in the next four years. I can see but one word written over the head of my husband, if he is elected, and that word is 'Tragedy,' " she told the Chicago *Tribune*. "Of course, now that he is in the race and wants to win I must want him to, but down in my heart—I am sorry. . . ."

Florence Harding played a more active role at the party convention than any candidate's wife had before. Despite her fears, she never advised Warren's withdrawing from the race. She apparently decided to cope with the dire prediction only if the other prediction—that Warren would be nominated after noon on Saturday—proved true and doubted that enough to cover her bases and make sure he filed for his Senate reelection.[1]

Harry had set up posh campaign headquarters, with Jess and lobbyist Howard Mannington, at the Congress Hotel. The suite included the large Florentine reception room, where her secretary recalled that the Duchess was "the life and central figure," coaxing delegates to listen to the Columbus Glee Club's hourly rendition of "A Great Big Man from a Great Big State and We'll Nominate Harding in the Morning" and directing friends like Charlie Forbes, Jake Hamon, George Christian, even oilman Harry Sinclair. Al Fall decided not to come, but his aide Kathleen Lawler was volunteering for Harding.

There was a substantial degree of press covering Florence because of her visibility and unusually colorful remarks. Nobody cultivated reporters as assiduously as did the former *Star* business manager. "Mrs. Harding is the only candidate's wife who came more than half way to meet newspaper reporters," *The New York Times* reported from the convention; "she was not afraid of them." She curried their favor: "I love the newspaper fraternity. I'd tell them where to get a story and they'd get it and never mention me. I trusted them often and they never betrayed me." She also tried to manipulate them with sentimental self-effacement: "We haven't any children. I wish we had. The Senator plays with every child he meets. . . . I'm of no importance. Don't say anything about me, but tell everyone what a wonderful man my husband is." She puffed some tales beyond recognition, telling reporter William Crawford that because they were still being "sweethearts," Warren often read aloud to her in the evenings, while she did needlework—not quite the Harding picture of marital reality.[2]

That Florence spoke for attribution to the press was startling enough, but her speaking frankly on convention machinations was unprecedented for political wives. She didn't hesitate to criticize Hiram Johnson's threat to bolt the convention if he lost: ". . . he is only telling that to scare them [delegates] into giving him the nomination, so he won't bolt. . . . [H]e does make a great noise at times. His bark is much worse than his bite." She also made it clear that she got that view from her own analysis, not "from a man."

Congressman Simeon Fess of Ohio remembered, "In the days preceding and during the convention, she was by his [Harding's] side to counsel and advise him. . . . At Chicago, Mrs. Harding might be said to have been his manager. No step was taken without consulting her, and her advice was rarely, if ever, ignored." Daily the Duchess took in the sessions of the convention, viewing it from a guest box of Harding supporter Fred Upham. She pontificated on this too: "From the box in which I sat I was able to study the delegates' faces, and watching them, thoughtful and impassive, I was not made apprehensive by the 'demonstrations' and the abortive 'stampedes.' I remembered that those sensible, shrewd men upon whom the choice rested knew the people whom they represented and knew Warren Harding's record; that at least half of them had been delegates to the Republican Convention in 1916, of which he was chairman. I knew that they recollected him as a man resolute, forceful and fair, a presiding officer able to hold a great assembly in order, and to satisfy all of its diverse elements. I had no doubts, no misgivings, whatever."[3]

Except for her affirmative remark "Yes, I'm a suffragist," Florence didn't opine on the National Woman's party picket march of the convention, although her friend Mary Batelle, the Women's Republican Club of Ohio treasurer and the wife of the Republican Finance Committee chair, joined the march. One more state was needed for the ratification of the suffrage amendment to the Constitution, but Connecticut's and Vermont's Republican governors both refused to call special legislature meetings to do so. Florence seemed to toe the defensive party line: More state legislatures with Republican majorities had ratified the Nineteenth Amendment; more Republicans in the U.S. Senate supported it, and the greatest opposition to it came from Democrats; it had been a Republican Senate and House that had submitted it to the state legislatures after the Democratic Senate had refused. But if she did not speak in favor of what most people considered the radical act of picketing a convention, she certainly did not speak against it.[4]

On Tuesday party chairman Will Hays opened the convention, but Senator Lodge was appointed permanent chair the next day, and platform business began then. On Thursday a vaguely worded plank for the "agreement among nations . . . to preserve the peace of the world," was accepted, appeasing both League reservationists and irreconcilables. Another resolution supported "equal pay for equal service" for all women employees of the federal government. The endless nominating speeches of candidates began on Friday. Wood was portrayed as a war hero, Johnson as the true Roosevelt heir, having served as the 1912 Bull Moose vice presidential candidate; Lowden was praised for cutting Illinois taxes and improving state services. Favorite sons had their moment with Massachusetts Governor Calvin Coolidge, who was praised for breaking the Boston police strike of 1919, Californian Herbert Hoover, for his success as U.S. food administrator during the war.

When Ohio's former governor Frank B. Willis ended his nominating speech of Harding with a reference to the new women voters—"Say, boys—*and girls too*—why not name . . . Warren G. Harding?"—one particular girl joined in the ensuing ten minutes of foot stomping and cheering. Nan Britton had been given a ticket to the convention by Harding himself. On Monday he had visited the apartment she shared with her sister and brother-in-law. Located at 6103 Woodlawn, three blocks from that new public curiosity the Robie house, designed by Frank Lloyd Wright, and from the bustling University of Chicago, her home was hardly in an inconspicuous neighborhood, but Nan had insisted Warren come, and he complied. When he waved good-bye to her from a local train platform, she thought the visit would be their "last unguarded tryst." If he was nominated, he warned that she would be "shadowed" by spies and agents. During the day she walked her baby alone, whispering to her, *"Your daddy is going to be President of the United States!"* Nan later said she "tried to persuade Mr. Harding to meet me some morning in the park so he could see her, but, though he pondered it all lovingly and said he was 'crazy to do it' as I was to have him, he never did." By not seeing the child, Harding never had to confront the absolute fact of his paternity.[5]

Working from the outside in, as the suffragists did, was never Florence's style. Her focus remained intent inside the arena. Despite Wood's lead, no candidate had enough committed delegates from those states that had held primaries or promises from those state delegates who were uncommitted, to win the required majority of 493. Wood had 124, Johnson 112, Lowden 72, and Harding 39. As the days of the convention went by without any candidate seeming to emerge a winner, as each ballot dragged on in the stuffy, steamy hall, the flutter of palm fans seeming to fuel the nervous boredom, Harry Daugherty's grin grew broader; he'd been counting on this.

At his prodding the Duchess spent most of the week cultivating individual delegates, urging even those unsupportive of Harding to consider him if the convention became hopelessly deadlocked. In this way Florence Harding played a more direct role in nominating her husband than any other woman before her, and she was the only woman among a crew of about five hundred men doing the same thing. Kathleen Lawler recalled Florence, in a blue silk dress with yellow flowers, intently lobbying "three delegates in tow whom she had captured upstairs," as she guided them into the Florentine Room for a free lunch. All of them "stuck thereafter" for Harding.

Harry explained, "We put loyal Harding lookouts in every hotel in town and got one or more of our representatives into the headquarters of every rival. . . . They met every train, shook hands with the incoming delegates and made engagements to see them. We ordered a roll made of every delegate from every state, got their addresses and the number of each room they occupied."

He gave Florence "a free hand in talking to anybody she pleased. I could trust absolutely her keen intuitions and her straightforward, honest thinking. She was a trained newspaper woman. She made friends with every reporter. . . . She disarmed criticism by her frank declaration that she only wished Harding's success because he wanted it. . . . We knew she would say this and she did. . . . She could talk indefinitely and never say a sharp or offensive word about a human being."

Circulating stealthily among the delegates was a man scribbling notes on everything he heard or saw of Harry, the Duchess, and their operatives. The stacks of coarsely printed pink flyers he surreptitiously left on hotel tables holding other campaign literature were mostly ignored and cleared into the garbage. Now a professor of history at Wooster College, William Chancellor had come to Chicago to propagate the story that Harding had mixed racial blood. Chancellor tailed the approximately 175 African-American delegates—constituting a bloc of one third of the number necessary to nominate a candidate. Grossly assuming they were paid for their votes and feeling that they were "anxious to get home and spend their money," he asked several how much they were paid and was told that travel, hotel, food, and incidentals were paid, along with "wages." He recorded: "None came away emptyhanded . . . handled by [Senator] Frank H. Hitchcock who makes a specialty every four years of fixing the Southern delegates in the Republican Convention. . . . He trades in negroes for political slaves to use in Republican Conventions. It was with very great pleasure that the negroes did vote for Harding, because they were told first, that he had negro blood. Second, that he would appoint negroes to many more offices than any other President has ever done."

Buying the black vote was a small part of the larger conspiracy Chancellor claimed to have discovered. According to him, Harry arranged for other delegates to be paid to abandon Lowden for Harding after several ballots for a total outlay of about three hundred thousand dollars—spending fifty thousand alone on getting the Oklahoma delegation with Jake Hamon's money, compared with, for example, seventy-eight thousand dollars for the total cost of renting the Harding headquarters.

If delegates were starting to think Harding, whether it was because the Duchess was whispering it in their ears or Daugherty was stuffing their pockets, they were not alone. Those cigar-smoking Republican senators who met daily in a Blackstone Hotel suite rented by publisher George Harvey and Will Hays, had long been alarmed by Leonard Wood's early lead. As the protégé of Theodore Roosevelt, whom he had served under in the Spanish-American War, the fifty-nine-year-old general embodied a nationalistic militarism that put off progressive and many moderate delegates, especially hardheaded senators. Wood could not be predicted; he was unwilling to compromise with the party establishment.[6]

In Friday night's seventh ballot Wood still led, followed closely by Lowden, Johnson a more distant third, and Harding a faraway sixth. Harry remained so optimistic that he rented a larger suite for the Hardings at the LaSalle, but the Duchess panicked. "I don't know why we're keeping the headquarters. It's simply a needless expense," she told a friend of Wood's, although it was none of her modest double-talk. "It's utter nonsense. Warren hasn't a chance to get the presidential nomination and he knows it as well as I do," she said more frankly to her brother-in-law Deacon. "It's a waste of time and money for him to be here as a presidential candidate." Her primary nervousness, however, was the looming last chance to file for Senate reelection. This was also on Warren's mind when he insisted on immediately consulting her on Friday night, sending an aide to fetch her from the convention hall. Losing his Senate seat, blackmailed by Carrie: Warren's buoyant facade was cracking. "The senator was stiff," convention chronicler R. Craig Sautter bluntly wrote. "Disheveled and nervous, he stalked the halls of the Blackstone, stopping any politician he could find. Many were shocked to detect more than just a whiff of whiskey on his unshaven face."

The deadline for filing a declaration and petition for renomination to the Senate was midnight on Friday. On Thursday night Warren had sent a friend, George Harris, to Columbus to wait for instructions to file for him before the midnight deadline. Yet if Harding did so and word leaked to the press, it was as good as announcing his withdrawal from the presidential race, destroying any chance at the nomination. Harry had scolded him on Thursday, "I don't want to have anything more to say about this matter. I have not changed my mind and I don't intend to. But I don't want to be arbitrary about it and if you want to file do so a minute or two before the filing time closes and have no publicity given it. I don't even want you to tell me about it."

Unwilling to affirm a decision on such a consequential matter alone, Warren turned to Florence, and she prevailed. On Friday night, word to file was sent a few minutes before eight, said Harry, because "Mrs. Harding coaxed him into it. . . . Mrs. Harding never discussed the matter of filing for the senate with me; knowing my position she was probably afraid it might bring on a quarrel and she never wanted to quarrel with me." Once the call was made, she relaxed enough to renew her bravado. "I talked with her in the headquarters late in the night," Congressman Fess recalled. "Her absolute confidence in the ultimate triumph was a tonic to all the 'boosters. . . .' "[7]

Meanwhile, with the convention broken for the night, a group of senators gathered to analyze the situation over dinner. It was not true that they controlled the nomination, but they certainly had varying degrees of manipulative power over some blocs of delegates. Until two in the morning about a dozen senators informally gathered for drinks and cigars in the Hays-Harvey suite and in the process casually debated just what the perfect candidate would need to break the deadlock, someone popular from a key state who would "go along" with them in Congress as a President.

The myth of the "smoke-filled room" sprang from a reporter's imagination of sinister party leaders secretly choosing Harding so he could be manipulated by them. New York Senator Wadsworth recalled the actual scene: "The atmosphere in that room was one of utter confusion and frustration. Men came in and out bringing reports and rumors from various delegations. The talk went on and on for hours and it is a fact that no decision whatsoever was reached." As the evening wore on, however, there was a growing consensus that Harding could prove to be a good compromise. As Senator Frank B. Brandegee said, there were no "first-raters" among the candidates, but Harding was the "best of the second-raters." All this was out of Harry's control—especially the late-night call to Harding himself, prompted after "some one brought up the gossip about Harding's love life," recalled reporter Raymond Clapper.

Indeed word was circulating about "women" and a "child," but with no specific names. It was possible that Harding had been trailed during his visits earlier in the week with Nan. He had told at least Senator Weeks about her and the child. Word of Carrie Phillips certainly had seeped out of Marion. In fact, Wood and Johnson supporters sought to exploit the rumors of Senator Harding's adultery. Samuel Hopkins Adams wrote: "To combat the rising threat of the dark horse, the opposition went to extreme lengths. Rumors of Harding's involvement with the Britton girl swelled from a whispering campaign to written 'testimony.' What purported to be signed statements about the illegitimate child were circulated. . . . An older scandal connecting Harding with the wife of a department store owner in Marion was raked up. All this was known to the newspapermen; none of it could be printed."

Rather than any one senator's questioning his colleague with such an impertinent violation of privacy, however, it was publisher George Harvey who confronted Harding alone, in the large bedroom of the suite. "We think you may be nominated tomorrow. Before acting finally, we think you should tell us, on your conscience and before God, whether there is anything that might be brought up against you that would embarrass the party, any impediment that might disqualify you or make you inexpedient, either as a candidate or as President." Harding was given ten minutes alone to think. Stunned and wavering, he withdrew into the room alone.

Never did Harding discuss his ruminations in that room, but certainly Nan and her child, his tempestuous affair with his Senate staffer Grace Cross, the child by Susan Hodder, the pregnancy of Augusta Cole, his more obscure relationships with a Cecilia Hoyle and Ruby Randall all had to weigh on his mind. Admitting to any of it would ruin his chance of nomination. It may be speculated, however, that Carrie's blackmail threat weighed heaviest and promised the greatest danger. At the least, if he hoped to raise the funds she demanded, he could do so only with the leverage of being a presidential candidate. Shortly after two in the morning he emerged from the room. He saw "no obstacle" to his nomination.

If Warren told Florence about this, it is unknown. He probably disclosed at least *some* of the little ritual to her. Certainly she feared that a presidential nomination could still provoke a scandal about Carrie Phillips; even if Carrie didn't talk, others might. Assurance that the blackmail fee could be met would have been some comfort. If any rumor about an illegitimate child reached her ears during the convention, Warren would never have said anything to raise her suspicions other than that the rumor referred to his child Marion Louise Hodder, now dead of tuberculosis. By the next morning the Duchess still remained less confident than Warren. "He's happy in the Senate. He can stay there as long as he wishes to remain," she told Deacon Harding. "If he hadn't filed for the Senate last night, he'd have lost that, too."[8]

At breakfast on Saturday the Hardings were joined by Deacon's sons, George and Warren, and the former remembered that his aunt "took a very strong position criticizing my uncle for even considering giving up his seat in the Senate which he enjoyed so much and which gave them all that they wanted in the way of a social position, public life and honor. . . . [S]he mentioned that they would have to return to Marion and a limited life, etc. . . . Perhaps the strong feeling of my aunt was the result of a close decision the night before as to whether to file it or not but of this I am sure, she was very positive that he had no business being a candidate for the nomination on that particular morning . . . she would have been much happier *at that particular time* to be out of the whole mess."

Yet unknown to Deacon and his sons, even to Warren, this "particular time" being Saturday *before* noon, enough of the superstitious remained in the otherwise pragmatic Duchess of the convention that she did not want Hardingng to withdraw from the race for the nomination just yet. Despite what to her was courting fate, she still clung to Marcia's prediction that something would turn the convention around *after* noon and she would find Warren the nominee. Though by her system of belief this would also ensure fatal consequences for him, she may have felt no choice but to accede to the stars. At one point before noon, frustrated with her weird ambivalence, Warren sent an angry note to her in a convention box, where she sat with Mrs. Woodyard, the congressional wife who had first brought her to Marcia.

"Florence, Why do you not want me to withdraw when you do not want me to have it?" The Duchess scribbled back quickly: "Stay until after 12 o'clock and I'll tell you."

The convention opened at 10:23 A.M., and the fifth ballot began. There was some shifting, Harding gaining 16 votes, but now with Lowden at 303, leading Wood by 4. On the sixth ballot Harding gained another 11 delegates. Strangely—by zodiac or not—after twelve, actually closer to one in the afternoon Harding gained in the New York delegation, and Kansas went entirely for him, placing him in third place, forging ahead of Johnson. "The delegates, perspiring in the heat, were tired and eager to reach a decision," recalled Senator Wadsworth. "[Harding] seemed to them to be the 'answer,' especially, as he had shown a substantial gain. . . . The result was, as the roll was called, announcements began coming from the floor switching votes from other candidates to Harding. In a comparatively short period the movement swept the convention. The delegates did it themselves." Whether Wadsworth was entirely correct, or Daugherty had bought delegate votes, or some of the "smoke-filled room" senators were pulling strings, the eighth ballot confirmed the trend: Wood and Lowden down to 290 and 307 respectively; Harding up to 133.[9]

From their "society row" boxes near Florence, contingents of wealthy families like the Medill McCormicks, Gifford Pinchots, Thomas Glovers, and Myron Herricks, loyal to Wood and the memory of Theodore Roosevelt, watched the Harding steamroller with disgust. Parmalee Herrick stomped away indignantly, gasping, "I cannot stay here and see *him* nominated." Ruth McCormick glared at the Duchess and began sweating, turning away the offer of a fan: "It would do no good. The heat is all inside me. Think of that woman going into the White House!" Although Nick Longworth believed Harding could never be nominated, he had supported Ohio's favorite son, but Alice admitted that her memory of Harding's 1912 support of Taft over her father tempered her enthusiasm.

Theodore Roosevelt's sister Corinne Robinson had been openly condescending during the nominating speech. "Who is this Harding?" she had asked when she was seated right beside Florence. Now, as each state seemed to swing for him, she stalked out, but not before murmuring something "disparaging" that stung Florence. Still, she kept her focus on the ninth ballot, penciling her own balance sheet of shifting trends of each state, Harry having foretold her of the various holds on delegates who *might* go for Harding and those who definitely *would*.

Connecticut went for Harding. Florida gave him six of its seven votes. Illinois remained locked. But Kansas was the state vote that Florence had been anticipating: "[I] never paid any attention to what the galleries were doing or shouting, that was propaganda, and did not impress me, but I did concentrate on the delegates. . . . I had my first experience with two or three delegates from Missouri. They were wavering but they did not want to break away from Missouri. I begged them not to do so unless they meant to stick with us. But my eye was on Kansas. I knew of the plots ahead and that Kansas was the pivotal key to the situation, so when some one later asked if I felt a sense of victory when my husband's name was announced as the successful nominee, I said, 'No, I felt that thrill very much earlier—I felt victorious when Kansas came over to us.'"

With Pennsylvania still holding out its votes for favorite son Governor William Sproul, the ninth ballot ended with Harding at 374 votes, still short the 119 more needed for nomination. Harry sent an immediate note to the manager of the Pennsylvania delegation. He then looked up to see the Duchess and made his way up the stairwell to her. "She had removed her hat in the sweltering heat and sat humped forward in her chair, her arms tightly folded," he later wrote. "In her right hand she gripped two enormous hat pins. . . . A deep frown shadowed her face. 'It's terrible, isn't it? All this wild excitement. This yelling and bawling and cat-calling. I can't follow it—' " Then Harry whispered that something was about to shock her, so she must remain calm, but she cut him off. "It's a hundred and ten in this place and you advise me to keep cool!" When Harry told her Harding had the votes to be nominated on the next ballot, she leaped from her chair and accidentally stuck him with her pins.

After the tenth ballot had begun and Pennsylvania had announced its entire delegate vote—and thus the nomination—for Harding, Florence spotted Mont Reily, "kissed him in the presence of many delegates," and joyously yelled, "You are the most wonderful man I ever saw!"

In that split second the Duchess also had a frightening realization:

Marcia's prediction of the time of the nomination had proved true. Mrs. Woodyard beside her sensed the change in Florence. As reporter Harry Hunt recorded in a news story three years later—which Florence did not challenge—just as soon as she realized what had occurred, a resolute, unshakable faith in the "secret world" of the metaphysical became an even more "mighty serious matter" to Florence Harding. Kathleen Lawler noticed this in Florence's dramatically peculiar reaction as she was whisked away to a car. "She was more excited and exhibited more emotion then than I ever saw her show upon any other occasion. She was almost hysterical." Even Florence obliquely referred to it: "I did not wait for the formal announcement of the vote, but started at once for headquarters. At the exit from the Coliseum I was surrounded; people grasped my hands, my arms, enthusiastically saying: 'What was your reaction? What was your thrill? What changes will you make in the White House?' I told them there was an election between me and the White House and that *it was not of it that I was thinking* [emphasis added]."

As she made her way out, the relieved delegates went wild, standing and screaming on chairs, banging their feet, tossing up hundreds of Harding postcards. Taking it in from the overheated rafters was a proud Nan Britton. Meanwhile Warren was in a room off the convention floor when he heard the pandemonium. As he was bundled away into a car back to headquarters, he repeatedly called out, "Where is the Duchess?"[10]

She was already on her way to the Congress Hotel. Her mood shifted now to joy. "As for that one great thrill that one can only feel, not explain," she explained shortly after, "it came while we were driving back to the hotel after Warren had been nominated in Chicago. Hearing the cheers of people in that great city whose citizens appear ordinarily to have no time to think of outsiders, I realized they were cheering for—my husband!" She added some sentimental exaggeration for the press in her account of the postnomination celebration: "I went to headquarters and found my husband. We have always faced facts squarely, we have never deceived ourselves or fed ourselves on illusions or delusions. We know the fickleness of political fortune. I said to him: 'Whatever happens, let us resolve that no disappointment, no bitterness of political contest, shall ever be allowed to disturb the serenity and happiness of our life.'"

At the headquarters suite, along with Harry and Jess, Forbes, and other Harding cohorts were many loyal Marion supporters, including Nan Britton. "I was entirely at ease with [Mrs. Harding] when she finally made her appearance," Nan said; "there was in her manner toward me almost an affection." A beaming Warren opened his arms to and kissed Florence warmly in front of the crowd, then gave what was perhaps the first such public recognition by a candidate of his wife's political management, "Whatever of honor has come to me this day, I owe to Florence."

"Nonsense, Warren," she responded, again with oblique reference to Marcia's zodiac reading, "It was all a preparation for this moment. Destiny has marked you for the man and so you are chosen." Then, in the only record of her doing so publicly, Florence Harding burst into tears of joy and fear—and memory. She later recalled that as she cried, she wished only that her father could have seen this day. When she later remarked that Warren had only gotten what he deserved, a friend interrupted, "What you *both* deserve."

With genuine, gentle concern, Warren embraced and calmed Florence, trying to cheer her as they prepared to meet the press. "If you want to make Mrs. Harding look pleased," he told the photographers, "tell her something about the price of millinery coming down." Florence broke into a smile, and pictures were taken.[11]

A fellow Senate wife observed it all with cynicism. "She had become a consummate politician. . . . I watched her there, tireless, indefatigable, meeting every one, at Warren's elbow every moment. When the decision of the convention was made, the Senator's astonishment was expressed in the words: 'Now what do you think of that? I've been nominated for president. I can't believe it. I've been nominated for president!' But if Florence was surprised, she did not let it be evident. She was probably already thinking of the campaign."

Indeed Florence immediately asked Kathleen Lawler to continue work on the campaign as administrative manager and her personal secretary. As soon as she heard that Governor Coolidge had been chosen later in the day as the vice presidential candidate, the Duchess instructed Harry to carry red roses to Coolidge's wife when he went to confer with them in Boston. Upon the Hardings' return to Washington, she gave press interviews for attribution. As Harding's biographical pamphlet was rushed to print, she even finally relented to pose for a picture to be included—but only after Harry had threatened to use one of her on a bicycle from the 1890s.[12]

Yet as the great days in Chicago passed, the Duchess could not shake her recurring fears, not of Warren's *losing* to the Democratic ticket—James Cox, Ohio's governor, and Franklin Roosevelt, the assistant navy secretary—but of *winning*. She stayed obsessed with

Marcia's prediction; many documents refer to her fear of "tragedy." As they drew that much closer to the White House, Warren's demise seemed all the more possible since to her mind, everything had proceeded as Marcia had said. She told a reporter, "I had a conviction that Mr. Harding would be named and he was"; she wrote Ethel Jennings, "I see only tragedy ahead"; and she told her aunt that besides congratulations from her she would "need your sympathy as well. Bright sunshine makes shadows—however, I shall hope to ignore the shadows and make the most of the sun."

Florence often felt she had to hide the reasons for her fears—except from Evalyn. As Ray Baker Harris noted, "Mrs. Harding's friends all knew her to be highly superstitious and she was much teased on this score. She allowed herself to be disturbed by all manner of household signs and omens. It was in strange contrast to the practical and business-like side of her nature." Still, so overwrought was the nominee's wife that she couldn't help herself from expressing her fear of Marcia's predictions to others outside her circle of personal friends. Norman Thomas received "an astonishing reply" to his congratulatory note, in which according to him, she said that now that she had "reached the summit of ambition, she was very much afraid." Thomas added an afterthought of understatement: "She had reason to be."[13]

Twenty days after the convention Jim Phillips came to the United States Senate office of the nominee for President of the United States to begin negotiating blackmail payments for the senator's *former* mistress.

20

Women

Contrary to popular legend, it was Warren Harding himself who conceived the strategy of his Front Porch campaign to be conducted directly from his house in Marion, nostalgically fashioned to hark back to, as one wag put it, "the way things never were" before the Great War in

Europe; the effort would be modeled on past campaigns of midwestern Republicans McKinley's 1896 campaign in Canton, Ohio, Harrison's in Indianapolis in 1888, and Garfield's in Mentor, Ohio, in 1880. If Pennsylvania Senator Boies Penrose stole the credit for the campaign idea from Harding, however, Harding may have stolen it as well, since the Boston *Post* reported, "Mrs. Harding is believed to be behind the idea of porch conferences."[1]

Durng the incessant hammering of wood plank seating and nailing of bunting through June at the Marion Chautauqua fairgrounds in preparation for Harding's official acceptance speech on Notification Day— the day of ceremony when candidates were officially given notice of their nomination—the Duchess remained terrified of, as Evalyn said, a "vile act, a threat that was real and not a phantom." Although she never revealed to Evalyn the "something" she "had" on Warren, Florence fearfully explained that Ohio politics was "more dirty than a feud in Kentucky. They fight like animals."

Finally, through "several reporters who worked for the newspapers under Ned's control," Evalyn was "informed of things that the Hardings were not apt to speak about; these incidents were rather fewer . . . than would be found in most men's lives if all their acts were sifted by small town gossips, as were Harding's." She may have given Harding the benefit of more doubt than he deserved, and "most men" less. In any case Evalyn finally found out about that "certain matron," though she noted that "by that statement I do not mean to say there were not others."

Meanwhile Marion began to swell with Republican party workers, campaign volunteers, reporters, visitors, and vendors, eventually totaling one-half million people. Delegations were met at the station by the Harding Welcome Wagon, volunteer Marionites, and marched in parade to the Harding house, distinguished by its famous front porch, bulging like a bandstand, wrapped with a white balustrade railing. Mount Vernon Avenue was renamed Victory Way and studded all along with white wood columns topped with gold eagles. The lawn was quickly torn up by the crowds—some days as many as twenty-five thousand—and replaced with crushed gravel.

For hundreds of international and national newspaper, magazine, and newsreel reporters and photographers, Marion was trimmed and bunted to cast the best light on its hometown editor. Like a theatrical set idealizing a wholesome town of Main Street, the bijou, and volunteer fire department, the image of Marion was of a magic land worlds away from the muddy trenches of foreign countries where American fathers, sons, brothers, and sweethearts had been killed or disfigured by the Huns. One writer called Marion "An American Idyl," evoking "ample, affluent farmsteads," "white-steepled churches," and "neighbors chatting across hedgeless yards in Summer twilights while the watering-hose plays upon the lawns." Recalled Kathleen Lawler: "All roads led to Marion that summer, and it seemed that the whole population of the United States went a-motoring that season. Billboards and sign posts pointed the way. Multitudes came by every possible means of transportation, and no hour was too early to see people arriving."

Underneath the streamers of course lurked the same sorts of skeletons that existed everywhere. In her later memoirs Lawler avoided recording the Harding house's derisive nickname, Uncle Tom's Cabin, but there was someone else who did. Among the thousands streaming into town came one man intent on skulduggery. Two days after Harding's nomination William Chancellor arrived in Marion. He hastily fanned through courthouse records and pried tales of the Klings and Hardings out of old-timers, even getting some to put their signatures on affidavit statements. Chancellor concluded that the rosy stories that the National Republican Committee publicists churned out later that summer on the Hardings' lives "began the most deliberate lying of a continued and systematic kind that America ever saw in any Presidential campaign."[2]

More objective journalists poked around as well. Kansas editor William Allen White observed on Notification Day that "every store front in Marion was a giant bloom of red, white and blue; every store front but one. And when the reporters asked about it, they heard one of those stories about a primrose detour from Main Street. . . ." If the Phillips-Uhler store was left unadorned by the cuckolded Jim Phillips, it was not long before he forgave his old friend Harding—and became Carrie's banker. Phillips came to Washington on July 1, for a private meeting with the senator. Carrie not only pushed Jim for her blackmail fee but now wanted a signed apology from Florence Harding for her remarks several years earlier at the train station confrontation. To his credit, Warren tried to protect his wife from such further humiliation. Carrie was trying the patience of both Jim and Warren. Harding gingerly addressed her on Senate stationery the day after the meeting:

> James and I have spent several hours together, discussing the wisest course to pursue. He is reluctant to return to Marion without the signed papers for which he came, so I am writing this to assume the responsibility, and to state to you the exact facts, which you are asked to consider

and then decide. Whatever your decision, shall be the decision for James and for me. This signed paper can be had. It will be signed and forwarded *at once*, on receipt of a telegram from James saying it is desired. The order shall have immediate attention. I have urged deferring the matter to your reflective judgment for selfish reasons, in part at least. This signature cannot be forced. The paper itself does not set forth a libelous or slanderous statement. The retraction itself covers an alleged statement which would not condemn any person living or to live hereafter. But if it satisfies your offended sense of things, I can get it signed, and will—and at once—but to do so I necessarily close all doors to any other plan. I must say that it will be the end of friendly relations with the Phillipses, and I can make that surrender if you insist but I do not think this damnant [damn thing] worth it, and on account of everybody concerned I am reluctant to close all doors to other possible plans which might be much preferred in the long run, especially if we are patient. James can tell you of conversations and plans and my hopes and wishes, though I will promise nothing certainly except to have this paper signed and signed soon if you still insist. All this is written to take from James' shoulders the failure of his mission. I have made it, but it shall be as you wish within 48 hours if you direct him to wire. I have said to him, and now write to you, that I am impelled by thoughts of self and by concern for everybody interested. I am seeking the most and the most lasting good, not a temporary triumph which shall be a bar to realizing future hopes. In any event, all blame is mine, and I write again, the signed paper shall be yours almost instanter if you direct James to wire me to that effect. P.S. If these suggestions and the reports James makes do not appeal to you as satisfactory I will be glad to meet you and discuss matters in person, at such time and place as is both convenient to you and nice for both. I can meet you in New York or Baltimore or Atlantic City, which James will undertake to arrange. Count me as ready at any time.

Their attorney, Hoke Donithen, was the only person with whom the Hardings had ever discussed the Carrie Phillips affair—when they were considering divorce. It was to Donithen that Harding ultimately unburdened himself about the blackmail demands that had to be immediately met. Donithen told Harry, who must have reeled at it since his career hinged on Harding's success. It was apparently only then that Warren confessed the dilemma to Harry. Daugherty must have been stunned—and certainly livid—as almost certainly was Will Hays.

Daugherty forever evaded any in-depth discussion of the Phillips blackmail. Some two decades later, when historian Ray Baker Harris encountered letters from Warren to Carrie and then asked Harry about them, he delicately chose the words of his response, revealing, in the context of what was later known, his unwillingness to give any detail: "I do not think [they] would be of interest to you. Jim was a business man . . . Carrie was his wife. They were friends of the President of long standing." Harry claimed that he didn't "think" he had met Jim, but "I know I never met her," he said with certainty, adding that "Harding never talked to me about her *but once* [emphasis added]," yet he refused to discuss what that "once" was all about, cryptically adding, "There is nothing about that I could tell you." He stated with finality that Carrie's relationship with Warren would not "be of interest to you," nor was it material Harris would "want to use."

Nimble-minded Harry was accustomed to working out such problems from his years of lobbying and politicking. According to Marion lore, it was he who then met urgently with Will Hays. Hays could not very well write a check on the account of the National Republican Committee requisitioned for blackmail, but he discussed the crisis with his clever vice chairman, advertising kingpin Albert Lasker, who had recently been appointed Harding-Coolidge campaign director of publicity. Lasker was said to have personally visited Carrie in Marion with a cash offer in hand. Although the best estimate of the actual lump amount was reputed to be twenty-five thousand dollars, with the promise of a monthly stipend of two thousand dollars as long as Harding was in public office, it was still an outrageous sum. Mrs. Phillips took it. She promised in return never to confirm or discuss her fifteen-year relationship with the man who would be President. The money, personally solicited by Harry, was evidently gathered from a handful of Harding's wealthiest friends and supporters, probably including Jake Hamon, certainly including Ned McLean. As Evalyn later told her biographer, "Ned put money in that, too." While he was at it, Lasker saw to it that another Harding amour was paid off. The unidentified New York woman held her cache of love letters from Warren tightly until she was paid handsomely for them, and they were apparently destroyed.

There is even a suggestion that Florence Harding herself was given money from the blackmail fund, perhaps in exchange for her signing some form of apology or affidavit claiming never to have accused Carrie Phillips of an adulterous affair with Harding. James Sloan, a Secret Service agent assigned to guard Harding in Marion that summer, later suggested that he had helped ferret out other potential women who might pose problems and claimed he told Nan Britton that "the money was going those days to far less worthy causes" than her own, "and they gave Mrs. Harding plenty of money, too!" As whispers of the blackmail fund slowly seeped out in Senator Harding's office, Grace Cross began to let it be known to friends like Bertha Martin that she had love letters from Warren but would hold them as blackmail evidence until the inauguration of the man she seemed certain would be President Harding.[3]

Harding chronicler Samuel Hopkins Adams claimed that although the Carrie Phillips affair "was the occasion of anxiety and eventually of action on the part of Harding's political supporters," it "never attained the publicity of an open scandal." Average citizens outside various Marion, Harding, and Republican circles, however, began to hear intimations of Carrie. As one Franklin Williams of Cambridge, Ohio, wrote Harding, the story was rampant that "you are chasing around with another woman."

Lasker met with Carrie Phillips on July 27—just in time. Five days before, at Notification Day, she certainly did not make herself scarce. Ohio Wesleyan professor Arthur Hirsch remembered how during the ceremony she "sat quietly in the crowd, while Mrs. Harding was on the platform. . . . While he was speaking, [Florence] would get up and shake her fist at, I suppose, Mrs. Phillips, get all excited, and sit down again." Those Marionites in the audience that day, particularly those who knew of the affair, must have certainly taken note of the Duchess's inability to withhold her rage at Carrie. In one speech at the start of the campaign Warren himself even drew unwitting attention to his past affair with Carrie when he introduced Florence to the crowds as "a good scout who knows all my faults and yet has stuck with me all the way."

Still, Mrs. Phillips could not ruin Mrs. Harding's pride on Notification Day. She had even helped craft the speech. As W. S. Hedges noted, "She sat on the edge of her seat and her lips quietly formed the words that were pronounced by the senator, for she knew his address by heart. . . . [The words] . . . told of the patience she had exercised in aiding him." Florence leaned forward with anticipation as Warren began talking about suffrage: "By party edict, by my recorded vote, by personal conviction I am committed to this measure of justice." When Hedges asked, "A mark of your influence, Mrs. Harding?" he reported that she "smiled and nodded an affirmative."[4]

As the campaign began, the electorate rapidly came to realize just how involved this woman was in her husband's career. After the ceremony, an article titled "Candidate for Position of First Lady" noted that she was "well versed politically and she can talk business with national committeemen, venerable senators, governors and other lesser lights." Indeed it was something that the Republican National Committee learned fast. At first, Hays and Lasker resisted consulting her. According to a Senate wife, "[T]hings were taken out of her hands by the National Committee, who naturally regarded her as merely the wife of a nominee, with a role to act . . . but of no importance to national leaders and not to be consulted about tactics. Perhaps it was because she felt so ignored that her ambitions leaped to a new role." When, along with Hays, Lasker seriously conferred with her, however, he was "completely captivated and won," and they began formulating the first "selling of the First Lady" in this first national election in which women were to vote. The Kansas City *Star*'s Philip Kingsley reported that soon she was "often in touch with Chairman Hays, and Chicago and New York headquarters."

Hays and Lasker, based in the main Chicago headquarters, sent publicist Judson Welliver to Marion. "Jud" got on instantly with Florence and found in her an eager partner in shaping and promoting her public persona. In response to inquiries about her, Jud churned out domestic data on her favorite color, flower, hat, shoe, outdoor activities (blue, delphinium, veiled tricorned, flat heels, horseshoes, swimming, bicycling, Ping-Pong). "There is going to be a need for this sort of thing right away," he noted, "in the selling [of] the Harding family to the country. . . ." A continuing effort of Jud's that constantly highlighted Florence was a newspaper series called "The Girl Next Door," written by Marion housewife Eleanor Freeland. With a "pantry window" view of the doings, she gossiped in a neighborly fashion to readers. "Oh I am sure you would like to hear about the inside of Mrs. Harding's house . . . nice little cretonne curtains . . . wait until she gets to the White House and she won't do a thing to those fussy glass chandeliers . . . those terrible old-fashioned looking pictures that clutter up the walls, and all the rest of the queer looking junk."[5]

The Front Porch campaign marked the first time photography was manipulated as a political tool: Numerous posed shots were taken as proofs for the one perfect "activity" shot to be distributed weekly by national headquarters to newspapers and magazines. The strategy was to "picturize" the Hardings, whether "hauling Old Glory to the masthead" of McKinley's flagpole, now transplanted to the Harding lawn, or sitting on the porch—a picture used in the *National Property Owners Magazine*. It was the work of Jud and Florence, who admitted, "I wanted the American people to see these pictures . . . to know that we were 'just folks.' "

Previous candidates' wives posed as wan props, but the Duchess gesticulated and smiled in pictures, and around her and Warren on the front porch's stone steps she often arranged for photos of visiting groups carrying slogans and banners, including one emblazoned, "We Are Boosters of Mrs. Harding." Florence's instinct for the "photo opportunity" was keen. She gathered former newsboys—dubbed the Florence Harding Campaign Club—around her and Warren and loudly asked, "How many of you boys have I ever spanked? Put your hands up." About six of the men did as told, and the corps of photographers snapped into a frenzy. When a band visited, she fetched Warren's cornet for him to hold in a picture. During a train tour, as Warren trotted to ride with the engineer, shouting, "Come on, Duchess!" she followed—with photographers and newsreel cameramen—and pictures were taken for the twenty-mile trek. With her glaring pince-nez and swollen ankles, she knew she took "ugly pictures," so she tried to work the camera her way, covering her wrinkles with her neckband or humor. To a photographer's yell that she was beautiful, she yelled back, "You need spectacles." For the campaign's good, however, she also posed. "Come on, boys. I always take a frightful picture and I hate this. But I know you've got to do it."

Whenever Evalyn visited, she noticed how determined Florence was when they were "out of doors, or any place where others might observe us. . . . I stood beside her one day as photographers prepared to take our picture . . . I was smoking a cigarette. Suddenly, aware of its smoke, she whirled on me and snatched the cigarette from my lips. She was as much concerned as if its tip had been hovering over a powder barrel. 'Evalyn, you've got to help us by being circumspect. The Lord knows *I* don't mind your cigarettes . . . but you must give a thought to what we are now doing.'" When Evalyn reminded her that Warren smoked cigarettes, Florence retorted, "Not when he is having his picture taken. Just let me catch him light a cigarette where any hostile eye might see him! He can't play cards until the campaign is over, too. A pipe, cigars, yes; but a cigarette is something that seems to infuriate swarms of voters who have a prejudice against cigarettes."[6]

Using the Harding house as the campaign's vortex enabled Florence to maintain simultaneous political and domestic personas. The porch was the common ground, the spot of convergence for private and public life, where the line between Florence's being a helpful wife and a tactical adviser was blurred to her advantage. She had approval over which meetings with which persons would be held within the more prestigious domestic kingdom, rather than just at the staff offices housed next door at the Christian house. "Often Mrs. Harding would rush through headquarters convoying important personages, and take them straight through to Senator Harding regardless of what he might be doing at the moment," remembered Kathleen Lawler.

In her home, Florence cleared the main floor's furniture into storage and set up wicker chairs and grass rugs in anticipation of the visitor traffic, but she then created a homey image by scattering small items inside—most of them pilfered as souvenirs—and meticulously keeping the yellow rambler roses growing outside, all to manufacture a semblance of domestic life. Even when Warren was in the press bungalow built twenty feet from the kitchen, the Duchess called over for him "to come to his meals," and the press of course reported it. If some of the reporters seemed fooled, one of their wives was not. Olive Clapper, wife of journalist Ray Clapper, was amused that although the Harding household help was in evidence, Florence would "run across the back yard carrying a bucket of paint or something," seeming to "do a lot of work herself."[7]

Precise with scheduling, she did not let even Warren escape her wrath when he was late for a front porch appearance. "That Man Harding has exactly ten minutes to shift and he is not even on his way over here yet," she yelled to an aide, then phoned headquarters to learn he was on his line. "This is Mrs. Harding. Please break in on Mr. Harding's wire. This is important." Then she chided him, "You have less than ten minutes in which to get over here to the house and get dressed." When he leisurely sauntered in, she continued: "Warren, what in the world are you thinking about? . . . How can you be so careless." Warren slowly replied, "Now, Duchess, never you mind. Don't get in a sweat. We will be there on time, and if we're not they will wait a few seconds for us. You are worth waiting for, even if I am not. They know that. So do I." She huffed back, "Warren Harding, you're the limit."

Ever aware that "a nomination is not an election," Florence let her managerial efficiency prevail. Between appearances and interviews, she made sleeping and dining arrangements for VIPs in her home, met with Harry and Warren to give her opinion on a speech, and even punched out a complaint letter and return for replacement of her Hoover carpet sweeper. Under such pressures her idiosyncrasies flared. She was superstitious if anything was hung on a doorknob or the back of a chair, incensed when incoming packaging string and wrapping paper were not reused. She frugally focused on even the smallest charges, scribbling to Charles Hard, now a volunteer in Marion, to "Please pay this bill now. It was sent back for correction" or to Warren, asking him to write out nine- or twenty-dollar checks for personal items, signing with the businesslike "F.K.H." She even kept gifts of food from strangers stored in the basement, then served them to guests.[8]

Thousands of groups, associations, and clubs badgered their Republican representatives, Harding headquarters, or other insiders for a chance to see and hear the candidate on the front porch. Hays and Lasker finally devised a series of special "days," each devoted to a general platform issue, broken into hourly appointments for specific groups. On "Foreign Voters Day," for example, groups of naturalized Swedish, Greek, Welsh, Scottish, Cornish, Italian, German, Hungarian, Norwegian, and Irish citizens were welcomed. Although the NAACP's request that Harding call for an end to restaurant and hotel segregation was ignored, African-Americans were given a "Colored People's Day." The delegation numbers were huge—the Chicago Business Men's Association of seventy-five thousand billed as the largest—but often inflated. When a scheduled delegation failed to arrive, the efficient publicity office still reported its appearance by rote, complete with Harding's released speech to it and, reported Chancellor, "the applause of the great crowd."

Like theater, before Harding's main act, various celebrities—General Black Jack Pershing, Lillian Russell, the elderly former House Speaker Uncle Joe Cannon—were trotted out to "open" the show. Groups were encouraged to bring their own brass bands and glee clubs, and when one delegation needed a piano to perform, the Duchess ordered George Christian to "Get one. And have it placed as I direct, at once." Christian headed the staff of about twenty, which included lobbyist Howard Mannington, Hard, and Welliver. Florence helped place the twelve-woman staff—the largest number to work in a presidential campaign headquarters—in respectable rented rooms. When she first met the staff members and they rose in deferential unison, she snapped, "Let me say to you, one and all, girls and boys . . . this is going to be a pretty busy workshop. Every minute is going to count. I am going to work right along with you, coming and going in and out constantly, probably dozens of times every day. . . . [T]his is a practical business which we have in hand here, and for you to lay aside your work and interrupt your train of thought every time I enter the headquarters will be distracting. It is a waste of good time."[9]

Harding's genial relationship with the press began with his building a Sears, Roebuck prefabricated bungalow on the lawn as a news service center and shelter. The eighteen national reporters covering the whole campaign, including Charles Michelson, Marion native Robert Small,

Ray Clapper, and Boyden Sparkes, were political journalists representing newspaper chains or wire services. On occasion Florence took them on drives in the countryside, pointing out Harding's boyhood sites and dominating the conversation. "Her frank, good-natured raillery sets any group at ease," remembered Clapper, surprised at her openness in admitting to superstitions, as when a black cat appeared in the road. Another recalled, "Mrs. Harding impressed it on all the newspaper folk that flocked around that she didn't talk for publication. But she talked right on, and much of what she said was just indiscreet enough to be interesting. But no one seems to have been inclined to make capital out of it."

Many of the press profiles on Florence showed her as an iconoclast. Zoe Beckley was immediately struck by her "colorfulness and dynamic qualities," coming upon her as she was "directing some workmen who were shoveling gravel," trailing her as she rushed around to the kitchen back door to check on a scheduled meal, then to staff headquarters, finally to the porch for the on-the-record interview. Florence not only waved her hand to show proudly that she refused to wear a wedding ring but bluntly admitted that she had no interest in cooking and cleaning and took pride in her business work. She again announced her great regret that Amos Kling had died before he could see his daughter and son-in-law make good. "How I wish he were alive now to see how fully my belief has been justified." The Duchess's initial attempts to act with traditional femininity rapidly failed. As a reporter for the Universal Services syndicate wrote in his lead story—lengthily quoting her frank talk about her childhood and her respect for her own political savvy— "she was affable and modest at first with a cautious restraint. Faster came the reminiscences until they tumbled forth a confused heap of ambitions, dreams and political aspirations. . . ."[10]

Nor did it take long for reporters to learn about her marital troubles. Olive Clapper recollected: "The newspaper corps had uncovered a few stories about this handsome man's lady friends. Three newsmen, for instance, invited to dine at the home of one of Harding's widow neighbors, were, during the evening, taken upstairs by an innocent eight-year-old member of the woman's family and proudly shown Harding's toothbrush. Said the child, 'He always stays here when Mrs. Harding goes away.' " The worst propagator of Harding's adultery, however, was not a child or old gossip but Carrie Phillips herself. Violating her agreement with Lasker, she couldn't help herself from basking in her notoriety amid Marion's international scrutiny. The single most audacious act on her part was to host a large lawn party and invite many reporters. Recalled Boyden Sparkes of the swirling rumors about War-ren's affair with Carrie: "Mrs. Phillips wanted everyone to know it too."

Florence was once again filled with frustrated rage toward this woman who continued to threaten her. Arthur Hirsch witnessed a nearly violent confrontation between them: "I stood some distance back one forenoon when Mrs. Phillips was standing only a few feet away on the Harding front lawn, talking to Mr. Harding. . . . With one eye on him and the other on the front door of the residence, she would take one cautious step, then another, toward the porch. Suddenly, Mrs. Harding appeared. A feather duster came sailing out at Mrs. Phillips, then a wastebasket. Mrs. Phillips did not retreat. Next came a piano stool. . . . Not until then was there a retreat. She tossed him a kiss and left quietly."

Off the record to Boyden Sparkes, Daugherty confirmed that he and the Republican National Committee would quickly send both Jim and Carrie Phillips out of Marion to another *continent*. Evalyn and Ned were also told by Daugherty "that a certain matron was traveling in other countries, with all expenses paid, until the campaign was ended. That trip was necessary in Daugherty's judgment, so we were told, because the matron loved to talk about the time when she was 'making eyes' at Harding when he was lieutenant governor of Ohio." Chancellor learned that it was Lasker who "had to enable Mrs. Phillips, the ena-morata [*sic*] of Harding, to make her getaway." The Phillipses were sent to Asia under the pretense that Jim would study the "raw silk trade" as potential merchandise for Uhler-Phillips as the midwestern distributor. Hastily arranged, lavishly underwritten, the tour included China, Japan, and Korea, and by fall the couple was gone, not to return until 1921. This second stage of the Phillips blackmail *did* reach the press bungalow, though revealing it was equated by the reporters with inhospitability. "We did hear about the Marion lady who had been sent off to China with her obliging husband, so that during the campaign no tongues could wag," said Ray Clapper later, "but we knew nothing of Nan Brit-ton. . . ."

Indeed Nan Britton was the real untold story that summer. Work-ing at Harding headquarters in Chicago, she steered clear of Marion through the campaign. In fact, the Phillips affair worked in her favor. As she later wrote, "it secretly amused him [Harding] to realize . . . that the scandal . . . in which Mrs. [Phillips's] name and his were linked very frequently, was for us the greatest source of protection, for while the Democrats who were 'slinging mud' played with Mrs. [Phillips's] name they were not looking for mine or any other." Warren kept in touch with Nan through the discretion of Secret Service agent Jimmy Sloan, although another agent, Walter G. Ferguson, also came to learn of her and the child.

Warren was surprisingly frank to an Indiana man who wrote about his smoking ("In this world we can only strive for perfection and never quite hope to attain it") and to a religious Marionite who asked about his drinking ("you have every opportunity of investigation among the people who have known me all these years . . . seek Divine Guidance in prayer"). He was never known to have responded directly to the infidelity charges. Although he apparently kept himself from any adulterous activity during the campaign, he hardly restrained his attention to women. One reporter wrote of his being "busily intent" on two southern women with details of their flirtation not "for publication." When aides sought to separate Harding from the women, "it was with great difficulty he was persuaded to include himself in the returning party"; Warren sighed to the ladies: "It is a devilish business—this being a candidate. There is no time for a bit of fun." Just such items— that could be related to reporters unknown to her—were what the Duchess feared. "Have all the boys be careful what they say or do," she admonished Mont Reily about the staff. "This is a warning to all of you as you report in this campaign." It was in fact too late. Those advisers loyal to Harding who knew about Carrie Phillips may have just talked about the adultery, but William Chancellor *recorded* its details:

> The Phillips case illustrates his sex instincts. Mrs. Phillips is the wife of a dry goods man in Marion, very showy and vain, with a passion for men. Jim Phillips is a poor little fellow who is part owner of a store there. . . . On frequent occasions, even after the nomination, he and Mrs. Phillips visited together at Upper Sandusky. It is said that [Lasker],* who knew about this, went to Jim Phillips and offered to send both himself and the woman to Japan, with an income guaranteed monthly so long as Warren was President. It was reported in every stage of the affair just what was paid. The stake was $25,000 down and $2,000 a month. The Phillipses went to Japan early in October, but not until Mrs. Phillips, who is a very talkative woman, had told all her friends just what she was to receive. All that Warren said even privately was that he could get another woman.[11]

Clearly the central woman figure of the candidate's public life— Florence Harding—was to be, according to reporter Bess Furman, "an actual vote-getter," in this first presidential campaign in which millions

*Chancellor here confused Lasker for Herrick.

of women were to vote. Except for occasional campaign paraphernalia (like the red paper parachutes printed with the message "Richland County Wants America to Make Mrs. Warren G. Harding First Lady of the Land" and dropped with little sandbags by famed war pilot Eddie Rickenbacker from his plane) there were no formal agendas or professional staff carrying out maneuvers to use her as a symbol, no substantive correspondence between her and Republican National Committee women members to target specific demographics. Instead the Duchess acted on instinct, directly appealing to the press and public, in letters and interviews and at appearances, becoming the most visible candidate's wife in history to that time. By simply drawing on the paradoxical elements of her real life—devoted middle-aged middle-American wife yet progressive feminist working businesswoman—Florence genuinely reflected a wider spectrum of potential women voters.[12]

If her frequently being in public print was novel, the public emphasis on her political influence was even more unprecedented—especially at a time when the press criticized Edith Wilson for acting as President in her sick husband's place. Florence bragged that while Warren was "the statesman," she was "the politician," and she often sounded as if she were running for office: "If my husband is elected, he will take the Congress with him when he decides the country's welfare and that he will choose a cabinet that will have a voice in presidential decisions. . . . [His] standards are high and he has never betrayed his friends. . . ." Neighbor Margaret Freeland wrote of the "deep and intelligent interest Mrs. Harding takes in things political and the readiness with which she enters into discussion relative to the important issues involved." The Chattanooga *Times* said women should "tell it to the men" that Florence was "a greater politician" than Warren, the *Delineator* magazine echoing that Ohio political figures stated this as well. The Washington *Post* revealed that "none kept better informed of what was done to further his candidacy than Mrs. Harding. She had opinions, and she was outspoken in expressing them to the men entrusted with management of the campaign . . . visited headquarters almost daily and talked political policies with his advisors. . . ."[13]

Beyond her being politically intelligent, however, reporters also revealed her influence on Warren, some even hinting at a copresidency. "If Warren G. Harding is elected there will be two p—" wrote Zoe Beckley, "well, *personalities* in the White House. For Mrs. Harding is no mere gentle shadow flitting in the background of her husband's greatness. No clinging vine. No echo. No self-effacing, silent worshipper at the feet of power." Even in a traditional women's magazine, the Duchess was called "an active element . . . what he may achieve will be the result of both their efforts, of an active partnership." Jane Dixon noticed that Warren "place[d] implicit confidence in his wife's judgment" and told male political figures: "I'll consult Mrs. Harding about that and let you know," "Better ask the Duchess," or "Talk with my wife. She will understand."

For an America unused to a potential First Lady who admitted to such overt influence, the press felt a need to cast her in masculine terms. One editorial said she "impresses the masculine mind with the strength of her individuality." *The New York Times* introduced her by saying, "She likes to participate in activities until recently regarded as men's spheres. She heartily believes in woman suffrage." The Baltimore *American* correspondent said Florence gave visitors "a man's handshake." Even Beckley noted that what made Florence a "peculiar complemental 'running mate' for an aspirant to public office" was that she had the "mental vigor and executive ability we are so fond of believing are the peculiar gifts of men."

Yet with the popularity of the suffragist as a news topic that summer, fed by the imminent passage of the Nineteenth Amendment, Florence's "masculine" strength was pegged as a "feminine" asset. "I seemed to thoroughly understand women," she said in an obvious appeal. "I never antagonized them." Indeed, while a New York *Herald* editorial promised voters that she was "loyal to her womanhood" and that "women may rest assured that . . . within the gift of their vote a courageous, unceasing champion for the cause of women" would be First Lady, it reassured them that she was not an "Amazonian creature putting wisdom into the mouth of her lord."[14]

By all accounts, Florence did not dominate Warren or the campaign advisers but was a welcome and equal participant. Each morning they went to her sitting room for an assessment of the impact of the previous day's speeches, press, and appearances. With these men she had no false modesty, once slapping campaign financier and friend Fred Upham on the shoulder and cracking, "If it had not been for you and me they would have given up the headquarters and quit the fight."

Florence drafted some campaign literature, followed various congressional races closely, and was particularly focused on the issue of the League of Nations. As Harry Price wrote after interviewing her, "Women write to her about the league of nations. It is a favorite topic, apparently, and most of the women who write denounce the project. It was that tendency of the sex, by the way, which convinced Mrs. Harding early in the campaign that the senator would get a large majority of the new women of the country. She could see it coming[,] this astute lady who has the faculty of perceiving many things not always plain to others." While Harding rejected the League as Wilson had presented it, he often suggested that he favored some sort of international alliance, a tendency Harry and Florence perceived as threatening; she once convinced Warren to scrap a reference to it in a speech. There is proof too of her consulting on other foreign affairs issue, with the intention of influencing Harding. After a meeting with Washington *Post* editor Ira Bennett, he wrote her with hope "that you will apply your judgment to the suggestions I made . . . they are *important* . . . and it is important that they be touched upon sooner than later. The Mexican subject affects the Senator's future freedom of action as President; therefore it seems that he should give notice that he proposes to keep a free hand and not be bound by what the present Administration may do towards setting up a government in Mexico. I expect to get proof that the U.S. is interfering in the Mexican presidential election. Now, if that is the case the Senator must not go into the White House and find himself obliged to acquiesce in such a thing. . . . I hope he will not take it amiss that I have outlined it to you."

On the porch Florence's political aid was obvious. Edna Blair reported: "She follows his every speech as though she were hearing him for the first time. . . . Not only does Mrs. Harding follow the Senator in his speeches but she has her eye on the crowd. She always knows where stands the man or woman who may have come to scoff and stays to pray." Constance Drexel said Florence watched Warren as if she were a "soldier ready to fire a gun in his defense . . . listened intently to every word . . . glancing from time to time over the crowd," and "made mental notes of what occurred and talked it over with the senator afterwards, answering questions and offering suggestions" to the speeches he made.[15]

There was no evidence any adviser had to pressure Florence to emphasize her own domesticity to counterbalance the public perception of her character. She did it herself. When the wives of men's groups, as opposed to professional women's groups, came to Marion, said Philamen Gregg, "she'd be sitting on the Front Porch in a housedress, knitting or darning socks, talk and talk . . . to get the housewives' votes." She did nervously blurt out to one reporter: "I can cook and have cooked many meals for my husband, and am proud of it, and just let me say to you that he likes my cooking. He admits it. In the Harding family, Warren does the talking and I do the cooking," directly contradicting her remark to Zoe Beckley that she hated cooking. Warren's complicity in this was almost sarcastic to those who knew better: "Mrs.

Harding usually joins me at breakfast, another old-fashioned custom, but I like the pleasant look of her across the table. She seems to keep cheerful when she sees me. Occasionally, not as often, between you and me, as I might like, Mrs. Harding herself makes the waffles, and if her husband does say it, they are the finest waffles in any man's world. . . . Mrs. Harding shines at coffee making."

Florence's most famous nod to domesticity was her almost tongue-in-cheek "waffle" campaign, begun when *New York Times* reporter Frank Stockbridge left a vivid account of eating her waffle iron handiwork on the front porch in the early morning with Harding. As the "queen of all waffle-makers" she had a "special and secret recipe" that was "the apotheosis of waffledom." Thus nondomestic Florence set off a waffle craze, with recipe requests pouring in and distinguished guests asking to be served waffles on their visits.

She didn't mind occasionally gilding the lily about her domestic virtues, but she could not abide being portrayed as utterly subordinate. Sycophantic Joe Mitchell Chapple became one of her least favorite journalists when in his cloying Harding campaign biography he compared her with the disengaged Edith Roosevelt. According to Chapple, Florence "believes that her husband belongs to the public, and in order to help him in his work maintains that her duty is first to the home. . . . Her ambition is that of a helpmate and home-maker. Maintaining the wholesome spirit and atmosphere of American home life . . . is the one life purpose of Florence Kling Harding." Furthermore, she told Kathleen Lawler she had little respect for Edith Roosevelt after learning how she had timidly turned over an admirer's request for her photo to Teddy, who sent his instead; she laughed at the consequences if Warren Harding even tried to do that for her.

The Duchess made her own decisions on press interview requests, as a rule not being quoted on political issues but otherwise speaking for attribution. "I have wondered if she did not sometimes smile a little grimly when she found herself answering questions about her housekeeping . . . as if these were important to her who had become a president-maker," mused a Senate wife. Had she been "asked her opinion on patronage, on wire-pulling, she might have amazed them. It was rather difficult at her age to be asked suddenly to appear as a clinging vine." Reporters themselves, however, were not discouraged from discussing her nontraditionalism. When women union members complained that Harding would be more supportive of organized labor if Florence had been like them, neighbor and columnist Eleanor Freeland pointed out Mrs. Harding's record as a working woman.[16]

If Florence mitigated her open discussion of issues, there was no attempt to dissuade from coming to the front porch even political women's groups perceived as radical, such as the National American Woman Suffrage Association and National Woman's party delegations, both welcomed by Florence as well as by Warren. "Harding had never been a noisy supporter of suffrage and some of their leaders were not friendly to him," Harry Daugherty admitted. "In a quiet efficient way, Mrs. Harding worked wonders, with the women of the west." Reporter Edna Colman recalled that she informally "made countless addresses" to women; these probably reflected her advocating that women register with a party as soon as possible, in preparation for their first vote, and her pride, expressed that summer in "the splendid women of America everywhere, who have risen so nobly to meet in the right manner, the new responsibility which has recently come to them. . . ." In a letter she permitted to be published, the Duchess stated emphatically, "I believe in the women of America. . . ."[17]

By the time of Harding's nomination, only one more state was needed to ratify the Nineteenth Amendment, but he resisted attempts to make that last state passage his personal goal, believing it not only would violate states' rights but was not worth his taking a zealous stand on. Yet he gave a deft speech providing tacit support without irritating the last foes, and when Tennessee went for ratification on August 18, even National Woman's party president Alice Paul wired Harding appreciation for his "cooperation." Harding was more comfortable with the majority of nonactivist, progressive women, and the campaign focused their efforts on these new voters, creating a "Women's Day" event, which its conceiver, Albert Lasker, thought was "possibly the most important day" of the campaign. Prominent women in business, education, publishing, and other fields were treated like royalty, marching in a parade that included floats of famous women in history and escorted by volunteers from the DAR to the Steam Shovel Girls.

While Charlie and Kate Forbes and Al and Emma Fall watched from inside the Harding home, those who had snubbed the Duchess at the convention—Mrs. Pinchot, Corinne Robinson, Ruth McCormick, and Alice Roosevelt Longworth—were left outside the house staring in. Alice, dying for a cigarette, whispered to author Mary Rinehart, who announced that she suddenly felt faint and was allowed inside with Alice. Mary managed the stairs, then shouted, "Come on, Alice," who got to smoke in private in an upstairs room.

Since the convention Alice had swallowed hard and tried to be nice. When she and Nick first visited Marion, they even stayed over as the Hardings' guests, belying her later comment that she had never stepped across their threshold. Lawler noted that Florence was "ever the genial hostess, likewise the clever politician" when she arranged to have publicity pictures of the couples together. Alice made it clear that she "would not engage in speaking" because the "effort would be too strenuous," yet after Women's Day, she made a third appearance in Marion for Harding and even attended Cincinnati's traditional massive Republican barbecue with the Duchess and Warren. "Soon after he was nominated," Alice admitted, "we talked of what he had said and done then, and agreed that we should both try to forget the details of that bitter year." She drove a bargain: In exchange for Roosevelt support, Harding had to appoint her brother Ted assistant navy secretary, the position his father had used as a political stepping-stone.

What Alice truly thought of the Duchess that day in her home she never said, but her friend Mary Rinehart did, noting how Florence looked "old in that cruel sun" and how even her powder room was that of "a busy practical woman who had had no time for the trimmings of life." Rinehart thought Warren believed "the past was past, and that the future was safe," as long as his "able woman who had made him" was "eternally watchful and vigilant. Suspicious and jealous, of him and for him; knowing his softness as well as his strength, and not too sure about either."

That day Harding did look ahead, speaking of equal pay for equal work, the end of child labor, and the "right of wholesome maternity" without government paternalism. His hope for a department of public welfare was not that day's only promise, however. The first candidate's wife to declare her own campaign pledge, Florence Harding said if she became First Lady, "I shall order the gates of the White House grounds thrown wide open," making accessible to the common citizen again both the lawn and the mansion's rooms, closed by Wilson during the war. She also said she'd refuse federal funds for decorating and cut excessive utility costs. Though these calculated declarations fell within the wife's domain of the household, she still sent a significant political message not only of her own public duty but in her coded promise to return the nation's house "back to the substantial simple American life," implying that the Wilsons had not lived that way, too interested in the well-being of Europeans.[18]

Behind the scenes Florence was wearing thin, willing herself to endure the grueling demands of the daily campaign in which she lived at the center exhibit. One blistering morning she was caught in a crowd of the Pittsburgh Women's Republican Marching Band, first-time college voters, and the Bicyclists Association; for three hours she was "pulled and hauled on every side," while snapping at Christian, who tried to help, "[Y]ou go back into the house and attend to your own business." She became a difficult boss. According to Kathleen Lawler, "In her nervous, highly-tensioned state, with her desire to see things go, she felt she must do everything herself. Had Mrs. Harding been commander-in-chief of the army she would have insisted upon firing every private's gun in every military engagement." When she tensed up like this, Doc Sawyer rushed over to hold her arm and repeat, "A little less strenuous this morning, if you can." She admitted to Lawler, "I must calm down. I owe my life many, many times to Dr. Sawyer. I could not live . . . without the Doctor." Those words would come to haunt her.

Warren Harding's health became a secret surreptitiously circulating among the campaign staff. The candidate had not only traces of blood in his urine and a blood pressure reading at 185 but serious heart problems. Daugherty later revealed, "It was a heart that was doubtful to begin with, which I never knew about until after he was nominated." Charles Hard confirmed this, learning of it from Christian: "While in the Harding Headquarters in Marion, I was told that Senator Harding had had heart trouble. That may have influenced [Florence] in not wishing him to take on presidential burdens. I am good about minding my own business and I never inquired about the heart trouble. But George Christian, Harding's old friend[,] would know."[19]

Harding, Florence, and Doc never seemed to respond to the candidate's health condition with anything but denial. Perhaps for Florence, there was no true escape from the "tragedy" foretold in the zodiac. Unwilling to cope with any more such predictions, she ignored Marcia's congratulatory letter for two months. But while the campaign press never learned of Florence's fear of Marcia's predictions, they did learn of Marcia. It was perhaps no accident that newspapers on August 13 carried a news wire story with the headline HIGH PRIESTESS OF CULT WHICH HAS DISPLACED OUIJA BOARD HAS PREDICTED THAT MRS. HARDING WILL BE FIRST LADY OF U.S. Nine days later Marcia finally received an acknowledgment from Florence, who signed herself as both "FKH" and "Jupiter." Whether she had been discovered by reporters or had leaked her predictions herself, Marcia became a minor celebrity, revealing in the news of her accurate prediction of Harding's nomination, but never suggesting her predictions of "tragedy." She had lived long enough around politics and ensure her own prosperity and prominence.

Confronted with the national story, the Duchess stated for the record: "It is true, we did make this visit in a spirit of curiosity and unbelief. Madame had not seen me before and in order that I should not give a clue I even remained silent when she gave me the initials of my husband's name." Florence made public reference to Marcia's predictions but emphasized the positive: "His destiny is the highest place a man can reach. I have always felt it and feel it today more strongly than ever. I believe there is some directing energy that mark certain people for certain ends." In the most unusual public statement ever made by a presidential candidate's wife, Florence Harding admitted, "I will tell you frankly that I believe in astrology and the indication of the planets as to a man or woman's fate." The only reaction even approaching ridicule was in a newspaper profile of her that quipped that "if the stars incline on November 2 . . ." she'd be the wife of a President.

Warren was now eager to get out on the road, beginning on Labor Day weekend, writing privately that "these front porch stunts for months and months and bands and processions and moving picture guns and camera batteries" were a "distraction and engrossment and attending weariness." For Florence, however, greeting tens of thousands of admirers at her doorstep was inspirational. People sought her out to take her picture and hear what she had to say. She told Evalyn that the Front Porch campaign was "the greatest . . . experience of my whole life."[20]

21

Racism, Scandal, and Movie Stars

If all America had been coming to Marion, Hollywood conquered Main Street one late summer day during the 1920 campaign. Through Evalyn, Florence had fallen under the magic of show business: musical theater, comedy, vaudeville, revues, and especially the movies. Acting on a suggestion that campaign publicity "may be accomplished with the movies," concurrent with Lasker's thinking of using "moving picture theatrical stars," Florence helped forge the first partisan use of the entertainment industry for a presidential campaign. On August 24, led by Al Jolson, the "Harding-Coolidge Theatrical League," including Pearl (*Perils of Pauline*) White, Ethel Barrymore, Mary Pickford, Doug Fairbanks, Eugene O'Brien, Eddie Foy, Lillian Gish, Mae Marsh, Anita Stewart, Blanche Ring, De Wolfe Hopper, Leo Carrillo, Ruby DeRemer, Zeena Keefe, Lew Cody, Irene Castle, Pauline Frederick, Henry Dixie, Ring Lardner, and the infamous, lawbreaking Texas Guinan, hostess of a New York speakeasy soon frequented by Evalyn, all arrived at the Marion train station on Pullman cars, to the cheers from tens of thousands of Harding supporters, visitors, Marionites, and starstruck movie fans. The cavalcade proceeded down Victory Way to the front porch, where the Duchess stood waiting with Warren to the strains of "Hail, Hail, the Gang's All Here," "Alexander's Ragtime Band," and "St. Louis Blues," played by the famous John Hand Jazz Band of Chicago.

On the porch Jolson introduced the stars, and they sang "Mr. Harding You're the Man for Us," the campaign song Jolson had written. Warren gave a speech with dramatic allusions, photographs and movies were taken, and the most prominent actors lunched in the Harding house, with the rest going to White Oaks Farm, where Doc Sawyer became smitten with Texas Guinan. There followed a singalong, poster autographing, and a park reception. Photos had Warren ogling a young starlet, while Pickford and Fairbanks distracted the starstruck Duchess, dressed in a cloak given her by Evalyn. The publicized conviviality did not include mention of flashing silver flasks quickly sipped and stashed away. Several times the Duchess had to straighten Jolson's tie. "He got drunk as a skunk and sang 'Avalon' from the train depot platform. He just gave it all it was worth," Louise Guthery recalled. "They had to pour him into the train when he left."

Hays was so dazzled by the expert use of silver screen glamour that the next morning he wired his thanks to the Duchess, who had made a positive impression on many of the stars. "It was simply great," he wrote, "Every one of them is a thousand percent for you."[1]

The Duchess seemed perpetually visible on the porch, yet the press did not know of the many late mornings she slipped away to the north side of town, near the railroad tracks. There, in a small house, she could truly relax by visiting Tal and Nona. A "strict line" was drawn between political appearances and the Kling brothers, but "whenever the relatives were needed," said Lawler, they "were always on hand." Cliff, for example, made himself available to his sister for any small errand or item that she needed. There was, however, a covert political reason for keeping Tal and Nona in the background: They were Catholic.

In the postwar era a virulent nativism in reaction to the millions of Catholic and Jewish immigrants pouring into industrial northern cities fed a bigotry that in turn led to a dramatic rise of the Ku Klux Klan, which had previously targeted only blacks with their hateful violence. It naturally found its way into the 1920 campaign. Personally neither Warren nor Florence had ever expressed the slightest bigotry. When B'nai B'rith opened a lodge in Marion just four days before the campaign began, for example, Harding had seized the chance to make his stand against prejudice known, saying he hoped "America would catch the spirit of the B'nai B'rith in the campaign against ignorance, intolerance, defamation and everything else aimed to rend the concord of citizenship."

Florence took action on her feelings. Kathleen Lawler had been refused rooms to rent in Marion because she was Catholic, and the Duchess helped place her, along with two other Catholic stenographers, in the home of friend Ella O'Hara. After Harding friend and supporter Senator John Weeks unsuccessfully tried to have Lawler fired so he could place his mistress in her position, he encountered "Mrs. Harding's objection . . . based on her knowledge of this type of woman . . . whom she had observed about Washington." Angry at Lawler, Weeks then tried to prevent her from working early or late at headquarters, claiming that he had "uncovered a deep-laid plot on the part of the Catholics of this country to turn it over lock, stock and barrel to the Pope at Rome" and that Lawler was on the papist payroll, assembling confidential material, which she then sent to the Knights of Columbus, thence to Rome. He failed, however, "to reckon with Mrs. Harding who did not share his enthusiasm." When Weeks blocked Lawler from entering the office, the Duchess flew down and handed two keys to Lawler: "This is a key to headquarters. Here is a key to our house, and you come and go as you see fit, at all times. . . . You are what this campaign needs." Then she turned on Weeks, snapping, "[W]ith that off my chest . . . that little matter [is] settled for all time. . . ." The majority of Americans, however, thus the vast proportion of Harding supporters, were Protestant, and the campaign had to make a careful effort not to alienate them. Many Masons insisted that Warren take an anti-Catholic stand. When a Democratic supporter wrote asking the Baptist Harding to promise not to hire Catholics, Christian carefully avoided feeding the bigotry but cordially replied that "we are getting much help from Democrats . . . you are quite right in your information that the Senator is a member of the Baptist Church."[2]

In such an atmosphere it was obvious why Tal Kling was kept under cover. Whether to throw reporters off the track from discovering her Catholic relatives, to contain potential anti-German sentiment, or to suppress local rumors that the Klings were originally Jewish, the Duchess propounded an illusory collection of ancestors. She still went on about her stylish "French grandmother," emphasizing her putative maternal French *Protestant* ancestry. She fanned the factual error that she was Dutch rather than German to the point where the Society of the Daughters of Holland Dames Descendants of the Families of New Netherland wrote Harding, "We are also glad that Mrs. Harding is of the Holland Dutch blood," and he responded, "We both rejoice to boast a strain," mentioning his Dutch family names but not the name Kling. A copy of his letter was even forwarded to Holland's Queen Wilhelmina. When a reporter posed specific questions about her ancestry, however, the Duchess snapped, "I am 100 percent American. Always remember that."

It was the muckraking William Chancellor who uncovered the local legend that the Klings were originally a Jewish family from Württemburg. Writing out of fierce anti-Semitism and questioning her French blood, he attributed Florence's character traits to a Hebrew heritage in a letter to the southern wife of a Ohio Supreme Court justice who was also the mother of a congressman:

> You say that you have seen Mrs. Harding but cannot understand her. You describe her as wearing a heavy coat of enamel upon her face and as being overdressed for her age. It will not be possible for me to tell any lady what is the inside explanation. But I can clear up some matters, and keep within bounds of polite correspondence.
>
> I ask you to think of Madam Sarah Bernhart [*sic*], who has three gifts, viz., personal beauty, dramatic genius, and executive ability, including no small talent for business. As you know, great changes have taken place in the character of Madam Bernhart in the course of her life. Early instincts have been suppressed, and the best in her has come out splendidly. By race, she is a French Jewess. How much of her blood is really Hebrew and how much Gallic, no one knows. The Klings were Rhinelanders; some believe that they were originally Jews.

Chancellor ruthlessly went on to slur the Duchess with questions about her early life and her personal thirst for power, spinning any truth about her in the most possible negative interpretation:

> Florence developed at an early age an inability to go to school; she became a horsewoman, a race-track and skating rink frequenter. In an-

other social environment, she might have gone upon the stage. She always had a gift for getting on with men. Where others wasted what they got in this fashion, she saved her money. Her father was a banker, but she early on left home. . . . She saw in Warren Harding what no one else saw—great possibilities. . . . Like her father, she could read character. . . . Whatever her race, she has had one power, that of persistence; she has stood for every fault of her husband, who in turn has surrendered to calling her The Duchess—surrendered everything except certain habits, such as midnight revels, cards, women and drink. She has run his business, paid his bills, advertised him, praised him as the greatest man living, run his political correspondence, written his speeches even. Being older than he and far more able, she has had him in tutelage. Often she has been ill, often discouraged but never baffled.

. . . You have probably seen the interview in which she described herself, not naively as her husband has so often described himself . . . but shrewdly. She says that she is naturally a business woman, without any interest in philanthropy, loves beautiful things, likes action, delights in getting things done, does not prefer much domesticity and is something like a man. She is a woman of the world, and more than a match for her husband. . . . Mary Todd "made" Abraham Lincoln, and [what] often . . . we ascribe to the man is to be credited to the wife. Warren Harding . . . was born to order for her management.

You speak of the moral character of her husband; it is as good as her own; and his sex-character is as good as that of Benjamin Franklin [who fathered several bastard children] and many another man of fame and power in business and politics. As to "the social taboo" [interracial marriage], it is wholly for the women to decide that. Northern women will probably swallow the situation. We must number Florence Kling among the prophets. She has won.

Finally Chancellor uncovered what was probably Florence's deepest held secret, that she had lived by common law as Henry De Wolfe's wife only after discovering she was pregnant: "Her only child was born when she was about twenty. She asserted that De Wolfe was its father, and he agreed to call the boy his son. But she tired of [him] . . . and they were separated by the Court, though no marriage was proven. . . . Her neglected son died."[3]

Chancellor, however, was not the only investigator in Marion that summer who discovered that Warren was not Florence's first husband. As politically savvy as she had always proved when it came to decisions affecting Warren's public life, she became so unraveled by revelations of her own life that her judgment became clouded and the campaign's attempt to control the damage only fueled the issue of divorce in a presidential campaign.

For the press, campaign publicity spun sugar halos around the Harding marriage and dusted it with fabrication. In the early part of the campain the Columbus *Algeresque Week* magazine sweetly noted that Florence had "never" lost her "implicit faith" in Warren, and even *The New York Times* fancied them bound in love by a mutual interest in music and sculpture. The longer the prettified tales went unchallenged, the more dangerously loose Florence herself was with her facts. Amos Kling's decision to raise her as a boy was now attributed to a *fourteen*-year gap between her and Cliff—"nothing to interrupt her father's direction of her upbringing." She averred that after her music training in Cincinnati she had "studies abroad." The most outrageous lie was Amos's immediate *approval* of her marriage. "And so when I gave up my musical career for a husband," she told the Washington *Post*, "he gave me my trousseau and his blessing. . . ."

Even when the issue of motherhood was raised in interviews, Florence massaged well. When *Outlook* magazine pictured Margaretta Cox, the wife of the Democratic candidate with her baby on her lap, Florence Harding posed with "a neighbor's child," romantically captioned that "neighbors like to drop in and bring their babies." In a *Modern Priscilla* magazine story on presidential and vice presidential candidates' families, Eleanor Roosevelt said, "I am happy and contented with my husband and children," while Florence admitted to no children, but "laments this fact openly. . . . I wish we did though. Senator Harding plays with every child he meets."

That she *did* have grandchildren was *never* mentioned to the press by Florence. "Jean and George were kept in the background," said John Bartram of the campaign. "In fact, I never saw them at any gathering." Their existence raised obvious questions about their parentage, which raised questions about Florence's first marriage, but it was not long before reporters did begin inquiring about some "Harding grandchildren" that they casually heard about in town.[4]

Florence's initial reaction, as always in such a potential crisis caused by unpleasant facts, was to "shut it away in my mind's secret cupboard and lock the door upon it." Without any coordination from her on the issue, the campaign staff did the best it could to "send up a very dense smoke screen," said Chancellor, often circulating explanations that were "mutually contradictory and exclusive." There was a claim that the Hardings were "loving grandparents" to many children, suggesting that were beloved elders to local youngesters who called them Grandpa and Grandma. Another version claimed that when a local woman in financial straits was suddenly widowed, the Hardings adopted her two children merely to help her financially. It was also explained as an error stemming from a wrongly captioned picture of the Hardings with two small children at the Front Porch as their "grandchildren." There were some outright lies: that a Harding son had died at twelve years old and it was too painful to discuss and another fib that Florence had simply never borne any child.

Although she did not know there had been no legal marriage, Kathleen Lawler, among others, thought that both Hardings made a "really serious political error, a tactical mistake" in their refusal to acknowledge publicly the De Wolfe debacle, believing it would have blown over with a press release from Florence stating her "keen regret" at having had no children with Warren but declaring that "to my son by a former marriage, he was more than a real father." Harding would not push Florence to do so, saying he "resented for her sake all that she had suffered and endured through this disastrous and short-lived alliance" and "could not bear any mention of it any more than she could."

As pictures of the De Wolfe grandchildren began circulating in newspapers, however, "gossip became rife," and the question did not simply fade away. Christian, Welliver, and Hard "begged and importuned" Florence to permit a bare factual statement to be issued before it began to plague the campaign. When a staffer pointed out that presidential candidates have no "private lives," the Duchess reacted with anger and conclusiveness, saying more than she ever had or would again on the issue of her first marriage: "That is my own private affair. It never had anything to do with Warren Harding. He knew nothing about it. He had nothing whatever to do with it and it has nothing to do whatever with this campaign. It has no bearing upon his ability to be President. . . . That short, unhappy period in my life is dead and buried. It was a great mistake. It was my own mistake. I did all that was possible to correct it and obliterate it. No man, father, brother, lover or husband can ruin my life. I claim the right to live the life the Lord gave me, myself. I never lived . . . until after I was thirty . . . that other chapter was over and dead and buried long before that time."

The more the Hardings refused to discuss the issue, the better it played as a "great mystery" begging investigation. As Lawler noted, "Lurid tales were readily concocted and went the rounds." Indeed some Ohio Democrats created a whispering campaign around the fact that Florence had married Harding as a Kling but had De Wolfe grandchildren. The truth that the court had restored her maiden name upon divorcing Henry was harmless enough, but by never confronting the real story, Florence willingly took a larger risk that one of the national news correspondents in Marion that summer could easily check the birth registry, compare it with the date given for the De Wolfe marriage in the divorce records, and discover that she had been a pregnant bride.

By August the divorce of Florence Kling De Wolfe Harding "played into the hands of the opposition": National Democratic Committee operatives. However, their candidate, James Cox, had also been divorced, a fact not widely known. Wisely the Harding campaign sought not to exploit this. The Democrats held Florence's divorce story as insurance in case the Republicans put out the details of Cox's first marriage, a strategy privately confirmed by vice presidential candidate Franklin D. Roosevelt. To former Harvard president Charles Eliot, FDR wrote confidentially: "Mrs. Harding was divorced by her first husband, and almost immediately afterwards married Mr. Harding. I hate, of course, to have this sort of thing enter into the campaign at all, but if the Cox divorce is made a factor . . . you may be sure that the Harding divorce will be brought out. . . ." Ultimately the issue remained a standoff, although the Harding campaign did respond to stray inquiries, one letter ignoring the De Wolfe issue entirely by stating, "Those of us who know the family best are inclined to be envious of the real domestic happiness that prevails."

The story of her first marriage that Florence finally agreed to be published implied that she was a widow when she married Harding. The candidate's official biography, Joe Mitchell Chapple's *Harding—The Man*, simply and misleadingly stated: "She married Henry de Wolfe, who later died, leaving her with one son. . . ." The more whitewashed version was Willis Fletcher Johnson's later account that "Then suddenly, when only eighteen, came marriage, a little son, widowhood and a return to her father's home" and that Kling wanted her to "become a musical celebrity" and this was why he didn't want her to marry Warren. Neither biography mentioned that Henry De Wolfe died in 1894, three years after the Harding marriage.

While Republicans held back on mentioning Cox's first marriage, there were other retaliatory stories aimed at the Democrats. Reporters in Marion were told off the record by Harding supporters that President Wilson's first wife died in neglect while he had an affair with Edith Galt and married her for her inherited wealth. Both tales transparently had seeds of the rumors about Florence: that De Wolfe died in despair because she was having an affair with Harding and that he married her for her eventual inheritance. The tale that Wilson "frequented vile places of Paris" was almost a duplicate of whispers that Harding went to Columbus bordellos. Surely in angry frustration at what had been said about her, Florence herself gossiped about the "unpleasant stories." Standing on a sidewalk, talking to two women in a car, the Duchess said she was "afraid that those dreadful stories about Mr. and Mrs. Wilson are true." Unfortunately for her, standing about fifteen feet away and hearing it all was William Chancellor himself, recording this for his list of sins. Chancellor had gathered enough damaging material on the Hardings that he was able to return to Wooster College for the fall term by Labor Day, but his dirty work had just begun.[5]

On September 7, the campaign moved from the Front Porch to a whistle-stop train tour, during which Warren spoke to crowds from the rear platform in depots and at various civic auditoriums for massive audiences. The Hardings were accompanied on different legs of the trips by the Sawyers, McLeans, Christians, Harry and Jess, Fall, Welliver, Hays, Lasker, and Forbes. They went first to the Minnesota State Fair, to St. Paul, Minneapolis, and Chicago, and then to West Virginia, Pennsylvania, and Maryland. They left on October 6 for Nebraska, Kansas, Oklahoma, Iowa, and Missouri. A southern trip begun on October 12 brought them through Tennessee and Kentucky. A fifth trip headed through New York State.

From the train's back platform, Harding always introduced the Duchess first, and the ovations she received from the crowds warmed them up for his formal addresses and impromptu remarks. As he spoke, she stood by his side, focused on the reaction of the crowds. "Mrs. Harding was the shrewdest observer at all these meetings. She paid strict attention to every feature," recalled Lawler. She was "his keenest critic. After every meeting and upon their return from every trip, before entering upon the next day's work, he sought out the Duchess for report, suggestions and counsel, just as he went to her for inspiration in the beginning."

On the road Florence enjoyed a popularity all her own. In Nebraska Senator Albert Cummins took the stage and gave the most prominent introduction any woman had yet received in a presidential campaign: "If the Senatorial crowd in the Chicago convention had been as potential as a certain misguided Governor [Cox] . . . imagined, we would have nominated a woman for President. . . . The Senatorial crowd, which habitually gathers about the hospitable fireside of one of the most charming and dignified women of the country, would have preferred . . . her, who not only has a keen and comprehensive knowledge of public affairs, but I want to tell you from personal experience, can cook as good a meal as ever satisfied the appetite of a hungry man. I . . . present to you my friend, the next lady of the White House." Thousands roared as she finally came onstage waving her bouquet, but as shouts from the first few rows caught her attention, she gave an impromptu and quick speech in response. "Nebraska and Iowa citizens are in love with Mrs. Warren G. Harding," wrote a reporter, because of her "rapid fire repartee."

In Oklahoma City, Jake Hamon gave the Hardings their most tumultuous reception, complete with a motorcar cavalcade, a banquet, a torchlight parade, and a fairgrounds speech and reception. A local reporter recalled that while Warren rested in his train car between speeches, Florence "sat at the window in the end of the observation car, ready to rise at a moment's notice to wave" to gathered crowds at depots and road crossings. In Chattanooga, at the Signal Mountains' Chickamauga Park, the Duchess kept the receiving line moving with her trademark brisk shake, and startled southern women were stunned by her "very deep and intelligent interest . . . in things political and the readiness in which she enters into discussion relative to the important issues involved."[6]

Evalyn joined her on the mid-Atlantic, southern, and midwestern whistle-stops, with the McLean private car *Inquirer*, attached to the Hardings' *Superb*. Evalyn hoped that Ned's devotion to Warren and his campaign might finally save her husband from "a disastrous end in dissipation." She herself was a star attraction. In an Indiana train station she absentmindedly leaned her arm against the window wearing a bracelet with an emerald "as big around as a silver dollar," and the crowd ran from the speech to the window. "Mrs. Harding almost had a fit," Evalyn recalled. "She ordered me to take it off and, obligated by my status as her guest, I did." Olive Clapper wrote that "we used to watch Mrs. McLean with fascination as she paced a station platform, attended always by a private detective, the Hope Diamond around her neck . . . and a half dozen priceless bracelets on her arm. In her plain blue print dresses, Mrs. Harding seemed quite a contrast to Mrs. McLean . . . [in her] smart fur coat and a large feathered hat held on with two huge glittering diamond hatpins."

The whistle-stop tours solidified both Florence's and Evalyn's friendship with Jess Smith, who played the court jester. "I supposed that Jess Smith was a guileless sort of fellow. He was most obliging, always," Evalyn said, "constantly trying to make himself useful. Sometimes he was a mite too forward in his efforts. . . . He loved the role of go-between. After a lifetime in Washington Court House, Ohio, as a smalltown merchant, what he was doing was all exciting." When the rear cars jumped the track on one trip, Jess ran back into the *Superb*, which was tilted over a high trestle, flung open the door to the powder room, and found Florence "seated there in such a situation," Evalyn said, as to "put her in a speechless rage." "Are you all right Duchess?" he asked. "I'll be all right, you Jess Smith, if you will close my door."

On that trip Albert Fall joined the whistle-stop in Baltimore. There was a strange—some thought suspicious—parting of the rails seconds after the train passed. This, along with an earlier minor train derailment, put fear into both Fall and the Duchess. Though Warren was shadowed by Secret Service agent Jimmy Sloan from a casual distance, Fall insisted that another agent, Boston's Walter Ferguson, be put at Harding's side. Yet threats that Harding would not live to see election day rapidly paled in Florence's list of fears by mid-September as yellow flyers mimeographed in purple and headed GENEALOGY OF WARREN G. HARDING began lining the gutters of Marion. Chancellor's work had been unleashed, courtesy of the racial rumors spread decades before by Amos Kling.[7]

Chancellor's claim that Harding was partially black fanned out through his network of white supremacist groups like prairie fire, spreading through farm townships and along the phone lines of big-city editors. When midwestern and plains women answered their doorbells late at night, they were quickly told by what one later historian termed "paid emissaries" things about the Hardings that "dare not be printed in the open." As others checked the morning mail, they found flyers with the caption "KEEP WHITE [picture of a house inserted] WHITE: VOTE FOR [picture of a rooster, meaning Cox]." In Ohio a circular, "To the Men and Women of America: An Open Letter," said Harding's father had "never been accepted by the people of Crawford, Morrow and Marion Counties as a white man." The notice carried excerpts from affidavits from old friends of Amos Kling's. Another flyer—signed by Chancellor—carried a darkened picture of Dr. Harding, describing him of "chocolate skin." And although Harding's ancestry was his obsession, Chancellor also printed blue flyers attacking Florence: over her alleged Jewish ancestry, her pregnancy, her nonmarriage to De Wolfe, and her acceptance of Warren's adultery.

In early October Chancellor's final "proof" in the form of detailed affidavits was ready. If it was impossible to substantiate backwoods vendettas besmirching families that stretched back a century, it was possible for George Cook, Montgomery Lindsay, Calvin Keifer—Marionites "of some appearance of responsibility"—to repeat what they had heard over the years, that "none of the Harding family has ever to his knowledge denied the report and the statement that there is negro bood in the Harding family." For all of his ninety-three years, Lindsay had always known them as the " 'nigger' Hardings" because his teacher, Rosalindy Harding, first cousin of Dr. Harding's, was black. Marionite Homer Johnson notarized the statements.

The late Amos Kling emerged as a witness against his son-in-law, as George Cook recollected in detail how he had "personally heard Mr. Kling publicly make the statement addressed to Bartholomeo Tristram, that he, Kling, wanted nothing further to do with Tristram after Tristram witnessed the marriage of his daughter to a negro." In another, Kling's ranting during Harding's 1899 state senatorial candidacy that a black man should not be elected was also recalled.

There was never evidence that the Democratic National Committee condoned the bigoted attacks on Harding. When Wilson's Irish Catholic press secretary was approached by a "shady-looking character" with the material, he expressed indignation with a racist rationale: "Suppose Senator Harding is elected. What a terrible thing it would be for the country if it came out that we had a President alleged to be part Negro! I'll have nothing to do with it." Still, someone in the Democratic party was the covert funding source for the dissemination of the rumors; there were tens of thousands of these flyers and pamphlets, and they were handed out on trains across the country, in depots, in city parks. In California, 250,000 were confiscated by the Post Office Department at Wilson's direction. It was all sparked by Chancellor, but the flames were now fueled by greater powers, who were never revealed.

Cox's reputed love affairs were even paired with Harding rumors in offensive ditties: "While Cox was on the front porch talking to ladies, Harding was on the back porch, Washing Nigger Babies." The Duchess always suspected that Cox might be behind the charges. "Mrs. Harding used to shake her head from side to side and cluck just like a hen as she sought to convince me," said Evalyn, "that Jimmy Cox was apt to do almost anything to win." West Virginia Senator Howard Sutherland informed Hays that Cox himself had told a game warden that a "great-grandmother of Senator Harding was a Negress." What the Republicans didn't know was that Cox had tried to seduce a young Marion girl, touching her knee, saying, "Let me tell you, young lady, I'd trust you anywhere in the world." Or so Nan Britton declared, mentioning that she had turned him down. She told Warren about it, together with Cox's remark "I understand Mr. Harding is a great one with the ladies."

Harding became even more infuriated: "I never did have any use for that man."

Chancellor went too far when he printed his name and Wooster College title at the bottom of the flyers smearing Dr. Harding. When Ohio Republicans cornered Chancellor, he lied, saying that the rumor about Harding might be true but that he didn't circulate it widely; he blamed the Democratic party. Regardless, the damage was done. Republican campaign official George Clark was frantic. "You have no conception of how the thing is flying over the state," he told Charles Hard. "It is everywhere. It is affecting the woman vote. We cannot get Hays and the National Committee fixed on any questions of policy with respect to the matter. . . . We have fought this thing through before, and we must fight it out again."

If national headquarters didn't take action, Harding's friends did. George Christian took it upon himself to deny the rumor in his official correspondence. The Marion postman was coerced into "losing" a package containing the original negatives of darkened pictures of Dr. Harding that the local Democratic anti-Harding newspaper had been waiting to print. If the negatives were "found" and Harding was elected, the postman was threatened with the loss of his job. Chancellor's original affidavits were mysteriously purloined from Wooster, almost certainly at Daugherty's orders, for along with other materials incriminating to Harding and stolen to protect him, they later turned up in Ned McLean's hand.

Evalyn McLean was a covert agent for the Duchess. Learning that Carolyn Votaw was scheduled to speak before a black Washington group, Evalyn called Florence and heard "a harsh and grating sound; Mrs. Harding was gritting her teeth." Then Florence yelled, "Get that sister of Warren Harding to come out to Friendship, if you love us. Keep her there! Do not let her make that speech if you have to lock her in your cellar!" Carolyn was invited for a sudden dinner at Friendship. "We kept her with us until we learned . . . that the meeting had been held and that the audience had dispersed," said Evalyn. Carolyn was placed on a train to Marion and sent to stay there until election day. Florence wrote Evalyn to "keep me thoroughly posted on everything that is doing. . . . I shall depend upon you for further information," adding that "I look upon you as one of my very tried and true friends." Evalyn, using Cincinnati *Enquirer* reporters as spies, kept informed of the smear campaign's movement. Robert Potter wrote her of the "thousands of circulars . . . very broad and very bold [with] no signature" making their way through Ohio, the South, and the East. H. R.

Mengert provided Evalyn with background on Chancellor, whom he knew "only casually."

Florence was enraged when she heard of Chancellor's swipes at her, again with subtle anti-Semitism, and his claims—later printed—about the "real" reason she and Harding never had children: "Though she is of European ancestry, she is as dark as her husband. [His] color has meant nothing to her. She knows nothing of the Southern views of the negro. . . . She has never seen in the mass the genuine blacks. At the same time, she has admitted that fear of her father made them avoid parentage." Chancellor added fuel to the fire when he mentioned that miscegenation was illegal in Ohio. Even Warren reacted angrily. "If you will just let me see this fellow Chancellor, I'll make him a subject for 'niggers' to look at," he yelled sarcastically, paraphrasing a Chancellor leaflet. According to Hard, "One morning Harding wanted to go over to Wooster and beat Chancellor up. It took some little time to get him to cool off." Still, when asked point-blank by Cincinnati *Enquirer* political reporter James Miller Faulkner if he in fact had African ancestry, Harding honestly reflected, then answered, "How do I know, Jim? One of my ancestors may have jumped the fence."

As election day neared and the rumor refused to die, Harding supporters became alarmed. With some mutual friends, Colonel Christian attempted to convince the Hardings that there must be a denial or Harding would fare even worse in the South than Republicans ordinarily did. Henry Cabot Lodge wired the Duchess: "Three words—'It's a lie'—will stop this. Why does not Harding speak them?" Hays and Lasker belatedly decided to release Dr. Harding's own genealogical tree, which could not be counted on for accuracy since Warren's father had traced an imaginary relation to Jefferson Davis and claimed family dating back to 1300. Lasker then asked a Chicago genealogist for a "perfect record" to "present to the public." In his only written comment on the issue, Warren thanked the Chicago man, "It was fortunate that you were able to furnish the data requested, although I do not as yet know what use will be made of it. I have always been averse to dignifying this talk with attention or denial, but if finally deemed necessary we will stamp it as the unmitigated lie it is." By October, however, there were so many "true" genealogies—proving that there was African blood, proving there wasn't, proving nothing—that coordinating them all would have meant one great-grandmother gave birth twice in 120 days. One even claimed Hardings in the Domesday Book of 1086.

By the campaign's last week the rumors threatened to break into print as a national, legitimate news story, spurring frantic attempts to stop this from happening. Harding phoned Robert Scripps of the powerful Scripps-McRae newspaper chain, who reassured him that "we were not interested in the story, and whether true or false, we had no intention of touching it. . . ." Ned held off on publishing front-page denials in his papers. Nevertheless, stories began appearing in respected publications. *The New York Times* made reference to the "odious propaganda" without mentioning it, but the New York *Herald* attacked the "dastardly conspiracy" of "cowardly circulars . . . sent out through the mails, passed from hand to hand and slipped under doormats at night by an army of cowards of a well-organized conspiracy bent on throwing the election." The Dayton *Journal* screamed it all: "The Vile Slanderers . . . The Most Damnable Conspiracy in History . . . In His Veins Only the Pure Blood of the White Man . . . Thousands of . . . statements . . . distributed . . . boldly by men low down in the democratic party . . . Even innocent children have them."

To counteract the deluge of flyers in Ohio, an intensive whistle-stop tour was hastily arranged to begin on October 27—Dayton, Cleveland, Akron, Cincinnati, Urbana, Columbus, Springfield—so that many Ohioans could physically see Warren for themselves, with attendant news stories that would spread nationwide. Still, no final decision had yet been made on how to handle what had become a consuming issue for the campaign. No one person, not even Harry Daugherty, would take the responsibility of making a decision that could potentially destroy the candidate by raising more questions. Finally a resigned Harding gave Harry permission officially to acknowledge the stories and declare that he would issue a statement of denial. As the train was crossing Ohio, Harry called the news correspondents into his parlor car. Reporter Charles Michelson recalled: "He told us that the candidate was writing a statement on the tale that he had colored blood in his veins. We were discussing where the train should stop long enough for us to file the matter, etc. when the door was suddenly flung open and Mrs. Harding strode in. She glared at Daugherty and exclaimed, 'I'm telling all you people that Warren Harding is not going to make any statement.' Then she went out. If Pullman doors were slamable, that one would have closed it with a crash. Daugherty rubbed his chin and followed her into the candidate's car. Of course, no statement was forthcoming."[8]

Determined to overcome the setback in the final stretch, the Duchess was fired up as she had never been before. Writing almost daily to Evalyn, she assured her: "Do not have any anxiety about the wild rumors floating around; it is last ditch, desperate propaganda . . . from the enthusiasm and the interested throngs, it would seem that the democrats are nearly extinct. We would not dignify these evil rumors by any recognition whatsoever."

Florence was not intent on just winning the presidency but on crushing Cox and getting a mandate for anti-League Americanism as national policy. More rigid than the candidate himself on this, the Duchess openly termed it a "battle" to be fought—not just for the presidency but for congressional seats. To House Speaker Joe Cannon, she observed that "the way in which the people flock to hear good Republican doctrine, it does not seem possible that there can be a Democrat left in the country . . . the better the information the harder I insist upon working." Writing Evalyn in a similar vein, she added, "I want to pitch in harder than ever. We must win—Big." She even dropped her defense that she was ambitious only for Warren, explaining to a reporter the drive that had always defined her personality when challenged: "[M]y own way always is to win as great a victory as possible, whether it be in the election of a Republican President, which is the most important thing in the whole world today—and not from a purely personal viewpoint— please believe me—or the most insignificant matter that comes my way." Routinely she now spoke of the presidential election in the plural: "We are going to win, and win just as big as we can. We want every single vote that we can get, and I know the opportunity ahead."

On October 30, at the last rally, in Columbus Memorial Hall, Daugherty publicly recognized Florence's crucial role to the campaign before a crowd of ten thousand. In response to rumors that he had tried to control the Ohio delegation at the convention so he could nominate his *second* choice, over Harding, Daugherty led the Duchess to the front of the platform. "Ladies and gentlemen, permit me to present to you tonight my only second choice for the Presidency, Mrs. Warren G. Harding!" The crowd broke into a wild ovation, while she muttered to him, "Harry, I could murder you for this. You never tell me what you are going to do." Warren felt the same way. On the way back to Marion, he confided to Frederic William Wile of the Washington *Star,* "I never could have put this thing across except for the Duchess."[9]

Florence, clutching a broom bearing the slogan "Clean Sweep for Harding," arrived home with an exhausted Warren at dawn, the day before the election. As they entered the house, the sun now risen, Warren went to sleep. The Duchess got right to work on correspondence, confidently writing Senator Joseph Frelinghuysen that she was "ready for the verdict of the American people, calm, confident and perfectly secure. We have fought a good fight. I know we have won." More combatively she assured Senate wife Catherine New that she was no longer "in the least disturbed" by the "miserable attacks" and that such "wild tales have been circulated before, but never so bad as in this campaign, probably because they have never been quite so desperate. We are unafraid, undismayed, and undisturbed. . . . We are going to win—and BIG!" To Evalyn, she reflected more personally that "I shall always regard this summer as one of the greatest epochs of all my life," yet admitted, "I shall not be sorry when the campaign is done and I am back in Washington . . . it is good to be missed."[10]

Election day dawned with leaden skies, the air filled with the aroma of fallen foliage and morning coffee, as the Hardings were driven to the voting booths set up in the garage of J. A. Schroeter. The night before, she had been nervously tending to errands until four. Through a steady rain and high winds lashing into a fury, for the only time since July, she stayed in bed until seven. Three hours later Florence Harding was before the cameras, waiting in line with Warren, sitting down to register, slipping behind a curtain to enter a booth and fill out a ballot, then drop it in a canister and become the first woman in American history to vote for her husband as President. When the cameramen weren't sure they had caught everything, she repeated it all.

All day the Duchess nervously fingered her necklace of ivory elephants, her favorite Republican talisman, while organizing Warren's fifty-fifth birthday celebration. As the sun began to set, the crowds of curious gathered. "I will not break down," she told Lawler. Her optimism faded into pragmatism, only to rise again: "Well, I begin to see it looks favorable but I still feel that I am in a dream." The Hardings and Harry went next door to headquarters to read returns and telegrams. "You have conducted an unusual campaign, with hardships and abuse," Harry told Warren. "Next to Mrs. Harding you are the best friend I have in the world." Florence chipped in, "Don't count me. You two old cronies take all the credit for everything done in this household."

At midnight a call came from headquarters. The Hardings ran over. It appeared to be a Harding landslide. Lillian Russell wired Warren that he'd "saved America for Americans." Photographers swarmed them. When suddenly Secret Service agents were at Florence's side, she tried to brush them off. "You boys can just return to Washington in the morning." When they persisted, telling her they were there under official orders, she gasped. "I suppose there will be a whole lot for me to learn now." To reporters gathered around her, she repeated her praise for them, gave way to some doubts—"Being a Senator's wife I really like better than I'll like the White House"—and reiterated her promise: "You can walk right in. There'll be no formality at the White House. . . ."

When word reached the Hardings that he had won with 404 electoral votes while Cox trailed along with 127 and that Warren had carried thirty-seven of the forty-eight states in the most overwhelming presidential victory since 1820, the Duchess felt free to celebrate. The Columbus Glee Club arrived and began singing, and the Hardings shook some five thousand hands until two in the morning. The crowd was so exuberant that they lifted a laughing Duchess from shoulder to shoulder. Still, she seemed less than thrilled, saying the nomination had affected her more. "There has been one thought in my mind—just one thing for which I have worked with all my might—victory for my husband. And, after all, helping him will probably sum up my greatest duties in the White House, won't it?"

Meanwhile there was havoc in Wooster. After a barrage of outraged telegrams and letters from livid alumni across the country, Wooster College's board of trustees held an emergency meeting and summoned Professor Chancellor. He confessed to his activities and ranted that Harding would bring blacks to power. He was forced to resign. On election night an enraged mob came to his home intent on beating him. Protected by armed students, he escaped to Columbus.

With crowds in Marion waiting for returns, the three local theaters were packed. One of them was showing *Neglected Wives,* adapted from the play *Why Women Sin.* For those who had talked all summer about the Carrie Phillips affair, there were wicked smiles at the movie's tease: "a melodrama of throbbing emotions and stirring action, an up-to-the-minute story of love and politics." Certainly it was the topic of jokes in the press bungalow over two bottles of champagne, which the Duchess had sent over. As Olive Clapper recalled, the gift "was so inadequate for even one round for the twenty-five or more correspondents and wives that everyone was hilariously joking." The great secret, of course was still unknown to them: On an overnight train speeding from New York to Marion Nan Britton learned from a porter that Harding had won, "sprang out of bed with a thumping heart and dressed quickly." In the silent cold of 7:00 A.M. she disembarked to find Marion a ghost town, recuperating from its night of revelry.

With the greatest challenge of her life now conquered, Florence seemed ambivalent about the prospect of being First Lady. She confessed to a friend, "I don't feel any too confident, I can tell you. I haven't any doubt about him, but I'm not sure of myself. . . ." She may have also worried that she had pushed Warren beyond his competence. She told stenographer Mary Catherine Early, "I always like to succeed in anything I start out to do, but I don't know whether to be happy or sad. The problems confronting us both are so tremendous." She wrote a friend, "The overwhelming victory places a staggering responsibility upon us, personally and as a party. It is sobering in the extreme." To a cousin she confided, "I don't know whether we are to be congratulated or to be commiserated. Look at the condition of the world and think of the responsibility of the Presidency."

Realizing that her remarks could undermine a new administration, she put on her old Duchess resolve. "Isn't it a joke to say such a thing as that when you and I both know if Warren had been defeated I would have been the most miserable woman in the world this morning instead of being the happiest. I am a regular fraud to say that I am scared out of my happiness by the responsibility, even as great as that responsibility is, for I am not. . . ."

Such bravado and those doubts about herself and Warren were nevertheless deeply rooted. Florence had been haunted in the days immediately preceding and following the election. Her determination to "win BIG," her reaction to the "wild tales . . . circulated before" all pointed to the man of her past, the spur of her ambition, the progenitor of her tragedy. "Many, many times," remembered Kathleen Lawler, "Mrs. Harding expressed the wish that her father might have lived through that campaign and to see Warren Harding President of the United States."[11]

22

Prerogatives of a Presidentess

Four days after the election United News Service reporter William McNutt editorialized, "Anyone who tries to figure the Harding of the next four years without counting the influence of Mrs. Harding will get a wrong result. They have been, are and will continue to be full partners . . . She also means to continue her full partnership. . . . She could not avoid it, for he would not permit it. With suffrage a fact in the United States, the first lady of the land, whose husband has been elected by suffrage, will wield an influence second to that of no woman who has ever occupied her position." McNutt was wrong on one account: She didn't wait until the presidency began.

It was not until five months later, in March, that Harding was to be inaugurated. He decided not to name any Cabinet nominees until December, when he returned to Marion after a lengthy vacation and goodwill tour. Still, he began sifting through the promises, recommendations, and connections made by and solicited to the campaign. He told Evalyn McLean, "I want to have a really great Cabinet . . . and [my] one justifiable cause for satisfaction" would be "the record of having made good appointments to public office." Yet he also wanted to place friends he liked in the Cabinet. "I am called upon to be rather impersonal about it and put aside some of my very intimate views of men and give some consideration to the public estimate of available timber." Personally inundated with the sudden lobbying of office seekers, Harding used the Duchess as a liaison, telling advisers to send vital information directly to her, "with a request that she sees that it reaches me."

Senator Pepper observed of Florence Harding during the process of reviewing applicants for public office that she was "a shrewd politician" and "keen judge of men," except "where her personal likes and dislikes were involved . . . she told me that she had kept for years a little book in which she entered the names of those in whom [Harding] might safely confide. I have often wondered what the book would disclose in regard to some of those who later shamefully abused Mr. Harding's confidence." Indeed, if like her husband, Florence was often a good judge of good character, she was also a bad judge of bad character.[1]

Myron Herrick told Evalyn that Harding's election had left the party $1.6 million in debt. Much of the campaign was underwritten by either loans or the fund-raising efforts in their states of five men who were Republican National Committee men: Hays of Indiana, Daugherty of Ohio, Senator John Weeks of Massachusetts, Alvin Hert of Kentucky, and Florence's cousin by marriage, Jake Hamon of Oklahoma. The money, said Evalyn later, was a "mortgage on the presidential power."

Hamon was said to have spent upward of $1.5 million on the campaign, allegedly borrowed in part from Standard Oil banking interests, with the understanding that if he became interior secretary, he would work to have Mexico opened for American oil drilling. Later Hamon's son said Jake was also promised a cut in government oil leases he could arrange at Interior for Standard Oil. Indeed, after the election, when the McLeans joined the Hardings, Sawyers, Daugherty, and Jess Smith in Oklahoma and then Texas, Evalyn recalled how Hamon openly declared that he deserved the Interior post.

At Oklahoma City Hamon feted the Hardings, and at the dinner Florence made a spectacle of patting his shoulder, calling him "Our dear Jake" and telling the gathered guests how deeply grateful she felt "for the terribly hard work he had done to win Oklahoma." Afterward the Duchess was apparently less gregarious, suggests Elmer LeRoy Baker, the careful chronicler of Hamon's life. "It was rumored that Mrs. Hamon had prevailed upon her cousin, Mrs. Harding, to make sure the life that Jake L. Hamon would lead in Washington, D.C. would be a respectable one with his family," he wrote. Told to get rid of his mistress Clara or there would be no Cabinet post, Hamon grew desperately agonized, and the Duchess "sat sadly by and watched Jake's Torment." It was no accident that at the next stop, Brownsville, Texas, Harding conferred with a second choice for the post, Al Fall.[2]

After a disastrous stop at the Scobeys' Texas ranch, where because of bad planning, the entourage had to sleep on cots in an abandoned hotel, and a brief stop at New Orleans, the McLeans returned to Washington while the rest of the party sailed to Panama from New Orleans. At the naval air station of the Panama Canal, Harding refused an offer to fly in a hydroplane with a woman pilot, but not the Duchess. As a public sign of support not only for air flight, but of confidence in women aviators, she gleefully got into a pair of pants, goggles, and helmet, smilingly posed for photographers, climbed into the seaplane, and daringly took to the blue horizon for about thirty minutes, doing what no woman in her position had done or would do for more than a decade. She called the flight "perfectly wonderful!" Florence made sure a newsreel cameraman came with her to capture the view for millions of Americans in the movie palaces back home.

Meanwhile, in Oklahoma, Hamon was interviewed by a transition representative about his potential role as interior secretary and then hosted a wild duck supper to honor the Washington guest. A drunken Clara came into the dinner and began cursing Hamon for leaving her out. He threatened to have her arrested. She threw a duck in his face and left. When Hamon later came to their room, he apparently felt guilty, but when Clara demanded clothes, a car, jewelry, and cash for not being brought to Washington, he whipped her and hit her with a chair. After ten minutes came the inevitable gunshot. Clara got him in the liver. A week later, "holding the hand of his loving wife," Hamon "drifted forth upon that Unknown Sea," as a local newspaper put it. Evalyn surmised that Hamon's death let Harding "right out of the blue" name his second choice for interior secretary. If Florence's visceral reaction to prevent Hamon's mistress from coming to Washington was displaced anger at Warren's adultery, it also sealed the ultimate fate of the Harding presidency, for Hamon's murder resulted in the appointment of Albert Fall as interior secretary. "Too bad he had that one fault," Harding sighed without irony when told of Hamon's murder, "that admiration for women."

Florence ignored the tragedy while living "the beautiful dreams of my girlhood days" during a royal fete in Jamaica by His Excellency and Lady Probyn, caravaned through mountain mist, cheered by natives brandishing machetes, passing beneath a "bon voyage" palm arbor at Port Antonio. After anchoring in Virginia, the Hardings went by train to Washington and were whisked from Union Station by Evalyn to her I Street palace. There a gold-embossed White House envelope waited for the Duchess.[3]

Having read that Florence was due in town as Evalyn's guest, Edith Wilson invited her for tea and a tour, to look over her future home. Florence quickly sent a note back: She would come with Evalyn. Evalyn was confident she would not be received. The list of insults she had hurled at the Wilsons was endless: open gossip about their sex lives and Wilson's affectionate letters to his woman friend Mary Peck, her nasty reply to Wilson's wartime threats to the *Post*. Meanwhile Evalyn and the Duchess left for the Capitol, where Lois Marshall, the wife of the Vice President, was hosting a Senate wives lunch in Florence's honor. The two friends entered the luncheon to thunderous applause and a standing ovation. The welcome stunned Florence. For a woman whose first months in this group had left her feeling isolated and neglected, it was an emotional moment. As she told Lois Marshall, "The luncheon Tuesday was one of the happiest, the most satisfying, and at the same time, most appealing occasions of all my life. . . . The manifestations of genuine friendship on all sides, the kindness showered upon me brought to me a sense of security, and a comfort that nothing else has approached."

The atmosphere at the White House later that day was considerably colder.

Evalyn was not disappointed by Edith Wilson. When Florence returned to Warren's office after lunch, the First Lady's note was waiting, advising her to "come alone." Shoulders squared, veil over face, and pince-nez over the veil, the Duchess was driven to White House and escorted to the Red Room, where the aging vixen Edith Wilson condescendingly noted Florence's rouged cheeks and bobbing blue feathered hat. Uncertain of her worth in such a setting, the Duchess lapsed into loud superlatives. "Her manner," wrote Edith, "was so effusive, so voluble, that after a half-hour over the tea cups I could hardly stem the torrent of words. . . ." Edith made a cutting remark about Evalyn. Florence haughtily stiffened. Edith then said she would not guide her through the mansion but leave that to housekeeper Elizabeth Jaffray, whom she called in twenty minutes earlier than scheduled. Jaffray said that "an unpleasant scene had just taken place" and that Edith, "flushed in the face as I had never seen it before . . . without a word of goodbye, turned and left the room." Florence glared at Jaffray and snapped, "I won't want you for I've already made other arrangements." Jaffray believed that she had just been fired.

Through the rooms, Jaffray guided Florence, who asked that separated twin beds be placed for her and Warren in the Wilson bedroom. Two hours later Edith returned from an appointment and "heard a voice far down in the kitchen. It was Mrs. Harding talking to the cook. She remained until after eight o'clock." Florence told reporters it was "a very pleasant visit."[4]

As she faced the prospect of becoming Washington's leading hostess, the Duchess trusted and depended upon Evalyn. As extravagant and zany as she was, Evalyn had a warm and generous quality she could not suppress. The day before Florence went to the White House, the *Post*'s competition, the Washington *Star,* even praised Evalyn as the "one woman in Washington contributing every week to help alleviate

the sorrows which trail the conflict on European fields" with her continuing work for the disabled veterans in Walter Reed Hospital, arranging outdoor bus trips, volunteering as a nurse, covering extra
comfort and rehabilitation costs. Florence had followed her lead and
now decided she would continue that work as First Lady.

Ned was less successful in what he had hoped would be his influence on Harding. After Warren had named him chairman of the Inaugural Committee, he envisioned an event, said Evalyn, "about ten times
as lively as a Fourth of July celebration combined with the ending of
the victorious war . . . fireworks, displays, bands by the score. . . ." Jess
Smith was made vice-chair, and he wore his bright ribboned badge
throughout the transition. Florence favored such mammoth plans, believing that "after the terrible war and all that had gone on before, they
[citizens] really craved an outlet for their feelings." Alice Longworth's
lover, Senator William Borah, however, declared that ten dollars was
enough to spend to "draw the President and his wife from the Capitol
to the White House." Florence sarcastically remarked that perhaps the
Hardings should ride in their *own* car, but Warren whittled down the
plans to a mere swearing in ceremony. Undaunted, Evalyn arranged for
150 wounded veterans from Walter Reed to attend the ceremony and
planned her own private Inaugural Ball.⁵

Before returning to Marion, Florence and Warren granted a hearing to an agitated Alice Longworth, who had earlier dispatched a note:
"[T]his is to ask you when I may come to see you, as I have several
things I want to talk to you both about." Several Ohio Harding supporters had asked Alice to plead the case that Harry Daughtery not be
named attorney general, as was now rumored. Harry, she said, was a
crook. "It was a wasted effort," she later wrote. "Their relationship,
both personal and political, was too closely involved to permit any words
of warning to take effect."

In Marion the Duchess broke into raging hell over a front-page
Cleveland *Plain Dealer* story by Walter Buel headlined HARRY DAUGH-
ERTY MADE PRESIDENT HARDING. She ripped the paper in two and
dictated an outraged response to Buel. "In fever heat, and in characteristic and vigorous manner, she 'laid out' the writer, saying nobody but
Warren Harding made Warren Harding what he was," according to
Lawler. Florence's only regret was that she was obliged to write instead
of "telling him to his face just exactly what she thought of him." Since
Daugherty had given Buel the interview, she then ordered him to her
and verbally whipped him into silence: "People may say what they want
about me. I do not mind, but when anything derogatory of Warren

Harding is said, I see red. . . . I have been on the warpath about this thing all day long." In this anger, said reporter Harry Price, "Mrs. Harding had counselled against his appointment." Harry insisted, however, rather disingenuously claiming, "The main reason I want to be in Washington is to protect Harding from the crooks. I know how trustful Harding is and I know who all the crooks are, and I want to protect Harding from them."

If Albert Fall's appointment as interior secretary alarmed conservationists, then the idea of Daugherty's running the Department of Justice seemed a contradiction in terms. Many of those who had been stung, outwitted, or simply hoodwinked by Harry as he had slid his way through the Ohio legal system now warned the President-elect that a successful campaign manager does not necessarily make an august attorney general. Feeling he could not "be an ingrate," however, Harding went against advisers, newspaper editorials, and the Duchess herself to make the appointment. There was, however, more to the appointment of Harry Daugherty as attorney general, for it opened a Pandora's box out of which an array of shady characters tumbled. These men were to bring shame to the Hardings in revelations of public and private activities. *Very* private.

The war had created new and expanding opportunities for the crafty operators of the early Jazz Age. German-owned and other foreign manufacturing companies that had been seized during the war had yet to be returned by the U.S. government to their various corporate owners. Lawyers and lobbyists were petitioning for return of the properties or making the case that the owners had not been German; this new class of influence seekers felt justified in employing any method they could to do so, including bribery, payoffs, and blackmail. Prohibition, meanwhile, had rapidly ignited an underworld of bootleggers and middlemen who were easily able to manufacture and sell alcohol illegally, even as they fought over turf and worked to force noninterference from the agents of the Justice Department. At the same time, the "Red Scare," in the aftermath of Russia's Bolshevik Revolution, had left a lingering spy mentality in Washington, where anyone could be investigated for anything in the name of protecting national security. All these factors, said Mark Sullivan, created "an exceptional market for intermediaries and fixers, many legitimate and some sinister."

It was an opportune atmosphere for the well-connected gangster. Even before the inaugural the whisper seeped out that one need not get the ear of Daugherty himself to get a fast decision at the Justice Department but merely needed a word with the man who called the next

First Lady "Ma." Although he used Justice Department letterhead, cars, and offices, he was not an official employee on the payroll. Still, Jess Smith managed to make tens of thousands of dollars by selling his influence and access to the attorney general. "They won't cheat me," Harding assured Mark Sullivan about the sort of men like Harry and Jess.

Among those who wormed their way to the top fast was the red-haired, freckled, hot-tempered Billy Burns, a former Secret Service agent, the self-proclaimed best gumshoe in the nation. For ten years he had been operating the successful William J. Burns International Detective Agency, but with the election he saw the chance to be appointed chief of the Bureau of Investigation at the Justice Department. The "publicity value" it would reap for the Burns Agency was "incalculable," one wag noted. Harry had known Billy since their childhood in Washington Court House. Harry wanted to make the appointment. When rumors reached him that William Chancellor was scheming to assassinate Harding at the inaugural, Billy proved his loyal capabilities to Harry by sending one of the Burns agents to rough up Chancellor in Columbus. Billy was thorough in his pursuit of the federal job. He called in a favor from one of his best former agents, Gaston B. Means. Billy had testified at Gaston's trial for murder of the Chicago heiress Maude King. With half a jury of Klansmen, Means—a North Carolina white supremacist—had gotten off. Now Means was sent by Billy to travel the country gathering letters of recommendation for Burns from people whose secrets, scandals, and skeletons he had a roster on. Good at blackmail, extortion, collusion, maybe murder and at spinning the plain truth into colorful fireworks, the forty-year-old, six-foot-tall, cherub-faced Gaston B. Means not only helped Billy Burns get his job as Bureau of Investigation chief but got one for himself as an agent there. "You'll not only take orders from me," Billy told him, "but from Jess Smith."[6]

The Duchess was focused on who could best help her newly adopted "boys," the nation's wounded veterans. Since they had first met in Hawaii, Charlie Forbes had been a frequent guest at her home and worked hard for Warren's election. She considered his credentials impeccable: He had been a commissioned Signal Corps major, earning the Croix de Guerre and the Distinguished Service Medal in the war. Besides this, he teased and flirted with her, "making frequent passes," which one observer rather harshly thought "may have been a unique experience for her." Warren offered Charlie the appointment of governor of Alaska

Territory, which he turned down. When he accepted the directorship of the War Risk Insurance Bureau, which later formed the Veterans Bureau, Florence was pleased. Hays strongly opposed Forbes's appointment, and Harry Daugherty directly urged Harding not to make it. On having Charlie look after her boys, however, the Duchess ruled. According to one journalist, "it was she, not the President, who insisted."

Forbes's appointment had extra benefits for the Hardings. In their only foray into nepotism, they wanted to find the right place for Warren's capable sister Carolyn Votaw, who was eventually made personnel director under Forbes, while her husband, Heber, was appointed federal prison superintendent.

Among the other appointments on which the Duchess weighed in was that of Pittsburgh financier Andrew Mellon as treasury secretary. When he came to Marion, Mellon's son recalled, the insistent Duchess preempted the President-elect: "During lunch, at which time the question of the secretaryship had not even been broached, Mrs. Harding turned to Father and said, 'I am delighted we are to have you in Washington with us.' Father looked at her anxiously and answered in his barely audible voice that he appreciated her feeling as she did about it but that there was little possibility of his going there." Mellon feared that his holding distillery stock would morally compromise him as a government official in the era of Prohibition, but Harding assured him that he himself owned brewery stock. Mellon relented.

When she did not feel particularly strong about an official position, Florence did not lobby. Although she thought the aged Elihu Root would have been a good secretary of state, for example, she fully approved of Harding's appointment of Charles Evans Hughes to the post. Nevertheless the personal friendships she shared with Warren often formed the only qualification for any number of smaller posts: Reverend Joseph M. Dennig, pastor of St. Mary's, her brother Tal's church, was made consul general at Tangier; their old friend French Crowe became Marion postmaster when, despite Senator Pat Harrison's objections, Warren waived Crowe's civil service exam; Frank Scobey was made director of the mint; even "Uncle Charley" Patton, eighty-three, who used to baby-sit for little Flossie, was named White House gardener. While Warren offered Mont Reily the choice of posts as Cuban minister, Federal Reserve Bank agent, the governorship of Panama Canal or Puerto Rico, the Duchess "urged" him to take the last. Reily did as he was "urged" and took Puerto Rico.

Florence's grudges also manifested themselves. When a Californian who had sat behind her during Warren's nomination reminded her of the insult Corinne Robinson had tossed at her that day, Florence assured him it "did not disturb me in the least." Yet despite Robinson's subsequent campaigning for Harding and her charitable public remarks about the Duchess, the woman permanently became persona non grata to Florence. This capacity for enduring enmity revealed her most fatal flaw. She could forgive political opposition but never personal rejection. Senator Harry New hadn't swung for Harding until the ninth ballot, but because of his and his wife's personal friendship with her, for example, Florence never held it against his later appointment as postmaster general. When she equated personal friendship with political loyalty and applied it to the likes of a Forbes or Fall, however, Florence's otherwise tactical pragmatism failed her and Warren, who suffered from the same sort of genial blindness. "If I err," she had admitted in her diary many years before, "it will be my heart that heralds the way."

Sixty years before, there had been some brief press speculation about Mary Lincoln's influence on political appointments, but not until Florence Harding was a President-elect's wife's role on personnel and patronage so widely known to the public. In the postsuffrage atmosphere, however, she was not criticized for what often was otherwise termed meddling. One editorial even defended the Duchess when leaks linked her to the appointment of a California receivership:

> It must be remembered ... the story that it was the wife of the President who secured the appointment of a candidate for receiver of public money at Oakland ... what is there wrong about it? There is not another woman in the United States who, if she has a pull, is not perfectly free to use it and land her candidate. What has Mrs. Harding done that she should be excluded from the privilege which every other woman in the country enjoys? It is not denied, but on the contrary, it is conceded, that Mrs. Harding is eminently wise, kindly, prudent and above all else unusually endowed with common sense and sound judgment. Are all the personal friends and acquaintances of such a woman as that to be excluded from all hopes of public office for the sole reason that she has a pull alleged to be stronger than the pulls of two Senators combined? When the people elect a President they at the same time elect a Presidentess and it is shocking to assert that she shall not exercise the natural prerogatives of a Presidentess ... we are quite willing to make use of the intuition of the President's wife.[7]

Of the appointments she influenced, two were personally important to the Duchess. Her old newsboy Reddy Baldinger, now thirty-seven, remained doggedly loyal to her. She had put him through Virginia Military Institute, and as an Air Service pilot he was jumped ranks to become the well-salaried senior presidential miliary aide, with carte blanche access to her and Warren. She overrode not only War Secretary John Weeks's recommendation for that post but also his suggestion of the Army's assistant surgeon general for the job of the President's military physician. The Duchess wanted only Doc in that post. Warren backed the controversial appointment, writing Weeks, "I am trying to work out the arrangement for a doctor to meet Mrs. Harding's wishes. She is very anxious to have Sawyer . . . as the White House physician . . . eligible to appointment in the Reserve Corps. I am hopeful that that can be done promptly, and then I can call him to active service. I want to work it in a way which will be very satisfactory."

The President-elect was dependent upon his wife for advice and guidance in the way she had grown dependent upon her doctor. Florence never traveled extensively without Doc. He became not only physician to the President and First Lady but a full-fledged brigadier general in the medical section of the Officers' Reserve Corps. This further gave little Doc, the Washington *Star* explained, "direct authority to make a thorough investigation of the needs of . . . affairs relating to public welfare, such as public health, education and social justice" and to present suggestions that might warrant better operations. Protests were loud since more qualified Army physicians of rank were passed over, and there was a threat the Senate wouldn't confirm him. Democrats, however, couldn't overlook the fact that Wilson had performed similarly when he promoted his own doctor, Cary Grayson. The criticism cut Doc deeply. He was hesitant to give up his lucrative sanitarium work to earn six thousand dollars as "Rasputin to the Duchess," as Alice Longworth dubbed him.

Others, already in Washington and better qualified, were equally eager and began pulling their strings. Dapper with a pencil mustache and groomed black hair, a tad disingenuous about his modesty, thirty-one-year-old naval doctor Joel Boone played his ambition closer to the vest. Cautious and honorable, he was nevertheless ready to be named physician to the President. A graduate of Philadelphia's Hahnemann Medical College, Boone lunched with the dean, William Pearson, to help get the job. Pearson, who knew Doc, inquired of his plans. Doc replied at his cagey best. Boone asked Pearson again to "write him so that he receives your letter in Washington after his arrival [about] something relative to me and the position discussed." Pearson did. But before Boone could be turned down, Sawyer was confirmed as brigadier general, and the press reported that he would also serve as Harding's doctor. Boone backed away, only to wage a subtle but relentless campaign for a White House assignment, with his name already familiar to the suspicious Doc. Both ultimately took monumental roles in conspiring upon history—along with the Duchess.

Sawyer was an odd character. His little pointed white beard, steamy thick glasses, and hollow chest reminded Evalyn of a sparrow. When he dressed in his heavy olive drab military uniform and colorful epaulets, he looked like a cartoon dictator out of the Sunday funnies. His appointment didn't hurt sanitarium business either. Doc hyped its virtues in a new, lavish prospectus, printed and distributed in 1921 by the President-elect's publishing company.[8]

If Sawyer was to guard the health of the new First Lady, the forty-year-old Secret Service agent with the Boston accent, Harry L. Barker, was to protect her from danger—and deliver her flowers, fetch her friends, and help around the house. Although around-the-clock protection for a First Lady had first been authorized in 1919 for Edith Wilson, she rarely left the White House. Florence Harding became the first President's wife to be assigned her own Secret Service agent, and she quickly "adopted" him. While she began cleaning and packing up her Marion house, Barker, bored, asked if she needed help, and she put him to work. In him the Duchess found not only a factotum, handyman, and escort but another son. He had been born only eight weeks before Marshall, in Newtonville, Massachusetts, had worked in Boston's Secret Service operations since 1903, then headed the office, as his father had, before his assignment to Marion.

While Florence developed an affectionate and trusting relationship with Barker, she never warmed to the beefy Walter "Fergy" Ferguson, also of Boston. When she learned that southern Democrat Edmund Starling, chief of the Secret Service advance team, was close to the Wilsons, she decided arbitrarily that he had to go—but later changed her mind. In Agent Jim Sloan she uneasily sensed a barrier. Her instinct was correct. Sloan was one of Warren's boys and never took to her.

When Nan Britton first returned to Marion after the election, it was again Sloan she called, and he brought her to a small house being used as an annex for the transition. Warren arrived stealthily, and after they had settled in a chair, he took Nan in his lap. Between kisses Nan squealed, "Oh sweetie, isn't it wonderful that you are President?" In between glancing at snapshots of their baby and giving her several hundred-dollar bills, he retorted, "This is the best thing that's happened to me lately, dearie!" As she put the money into her bag, she noticed some papers on a table regarding stories of Florence's first marriage, and a "wave of sympathy for Mrs. Harding" swept over her. She sighed her relief to Warren. "They haven't got our story!" The next day, however, Nan boldly took a step further into the public eye when Warren's unsuspecting sister Daisy took her over to headquarters to see him. Displeased, he stiffly shook her hand and signed an autograph.

Never again would Warren risk the chance of devastating his wife by letting his liberties be easily revealed. While she suspected nothing about Nan, Florence remained "a real woman," Kathleen Lawler observed, generally "susceptible to jealousies of the sex." Certainly her role in refusing to permit Hamon's mistress in Washington set a standard of moral behavior. When a friend, Ed Hill, suggested that War Secretary-designate John Weeks's persistent mistress be made Warren's secretary, it set the Duchess "white with rage" and bursting:

> Wouldn't you think Ed Hill would have . . . more regard for the decencies and proprieties? Why, that creature! She has been running wild around here with every man she could ensnare, even with the chauffeurs. I banished her from headquarters because of her conduct, and sent her to the farthest point possible. I permitted her to remain here only because she was brought from a senator's office. Repeatedly, I have been obliged to send my chauffeur at two or three o'clock in the morning to order her off the street, and tell her that Mrs. Harding ordered her to bed at once. The brazen effrontery! She has not a single qualification. Fine White House secretary she would make. That makes me boil.[9]

Florence was solicited by socialites up and down the seaboard with candidates for the position of White House social secretary. The press frequently mentioned Kathleen Lawler for the post, but as the Detroit *Press* delicately put it, she "certainly is not the type that is usually selected." It was not a role traditionally filled by a working woman or a Catholic. Though Florence spoke frequently of Lawler's indispensable trust, and Ned assured her that the job was hers, when Kathleen learned that Florence had been advised against risking the political liability of a Catholic social secretary by Mrs. Joseph, her Cleveland astrologer, Lawler knew she'd not get the job: "I believe that if Mrs. Harding became convinced that . . . a Catholic might in the slightest degree operate against the President, she would oppose and prevent any connection by me with the administration. She was cold as steel, and would allow nothing to interfere with her great goal for her husband and her own ambition." Florence had previously refused to fire Lawler on such intolerant grounds, but now her faith in the stars overrode her other precepts. "Mrs. Harding would take no chances on anything that might harm in the slightest degree," said Lawler, "particularly if it came to her through the science of astrology."

Florence did in fact visit Mrs. Joseph twice in four months, in the last week of the campaign, and on January 17, during a trip to see her dentist—while Warren managed to see Nan. Unlike Madame Marcia, Mrs. Joseph seemed to accentuate the positive. After election day, Samuel Hopkins Adams recorded, Florence's "fears and misgiving had been appeased. She had found a new seeress who described a Star of Destiny burning upon her forehead. The star was to guide her and, through her, her illustrious husband to glory."

Florence was also coping with a deluge of mail. After a reporter remarked on the endless bags of letters Warren received, the Duchess snapped, "You should see mine. That man doesn't know what mail is." In fact, for every five hundred letters that Warren received, Florence was getting eight hundred. Most were from women, many for jobs. The Blackfoot Indians inducted her as "Snowbird" and addressed her as Great White Mother; a decorator told her "it was impossible for anybody coming from Ohio to know how" to treat the White House. Among the more pleasant notes were those from the Vice President-elect's wife Grace Coolidge, who flattered the Duchess by saying she had "contributed in a very large measure" to the victory. They traded ideas on inaugural clothing, and after the Coolidges visited Marion, Grace indulged Florence's spiritualism by remarking, "Somehow, I did not feel it was our first meeting." Florence hoped they would "work shoulder to shoulder." She was less responsive to an unusually unctuous Alice Longworth, turning down offers to stay in the Longworth home on inauguration eve, attend the cornerstone dedication of Theodore Roosevelt's birthplace, or give a job to a favorite old servant of Edith Roosevelt's.

The recommendations of a different First Family did move her. When former President Taft was invited to Marion to meet with the Hardings, he urged Florence to reconsider firing Mrs. Jaffray, and after Nellie Taft wrote her that the White House housekeeper was "capable, intelligent and agreeable," Florence insisted she stay. With Taft she also discussed her plans to entertain at garden parties and informal teas and inquired about protocol direction from the State Department. Accepting Harding's promise to name him to the Supreme Court with the very first vacancy, Taft shared his observations in a letter to Nellie:

Of course, it is easy to see why the McLeans coddle the Hardings, because it will give them an even greater social importance . . . but it is a very dangerous relation for a president to have, and I fear that it is an evidence of the lack of conventional society experience of the Hardings. . . . They were very cordial. . . . The senator was disposed to "chuck" ceremony, to use his own term. Mrs. Harding took a different view, and I stood by her and insisted that it was essential. She is anxious to entertain much, and I am glad she is. . . . When the senator left us for a while, I talked with her and commented on the necessity of insisting that all his friends, except his family, should call him Mr. President instead of Warren as they do now. . . . I had not realized until I talked with them how little they had known of the White House. . . . She is a nice woman, who will I think be all right. She is a little disposed to be anxious not to be backward, but she will readily adapt herself. She is four or five years older than Harding, and I think she tries him sometimes, but he is very considerate. She is not at all bad looking. Her newspaper pictures don't do her justice. . . . I pressed him on the necessity for insisting on three hours in the afternoon for exercise. Mrs. Harding will have to be careful, and her intense desire to do things may be dangerous.[10]

Taft was an astute observer. December found Florence at her most frenetic, "living minute to minute," "the busiest mortal today on this globe," dictating letters while "doing a dozen other things such as having my face artist, hair lady, manicure performer, interviewing the cook, holding telephonic political conferences and getting ready to go to the White House." New Year's Day found her in work gloves, moving items to and from the attic, deciding what to store or take to the White House. She took responsibility for closing both their houses, arranging their travel, chosing their clothes, and interviewing for their personal staff, "quite confirmed in my role as 'dictator,' " she told a friend. In the midst of this Warren left with Al Fall for Florida, where she would go, after a New York trip with Evalyn and Jess to pick her White House wardrobe.

Taft's reservations to the contrary, in these times of Florence's own personal transition into an international figure, it was Evalyn who again kept her steady, considering her every need. On Christmas Warren wanted to give Florence an expensive piece of jewelry and gave money to Evalyn to find something appropriate and purchase it. It was Evalyn who chose a diamond sunburst. Always worn on her black neckband, it was to become the trademark of the new First Lady. "I will not only wear it," Florence told Evalyn, "but I am liable to sleep with it all the time." She signed herself, "with dearest love."[11]

On February 1 the Duchess and her entourage checked into New York's Ritz-Carlton, where Florence's twelfth-floor suite was already crammed with flowers and candy from designers, jewelers, furriers, and milliners anxious to win her patronage. First Ladies had long been a model for millions of American women to copy for each social season's style, but in 1921, as *The New York Times* reported, the fashion industry leaders were, "bending all their energies" to influence Florence because of the "prospect of greater social activity" under the postwar Harding administration. Flattering mentions in print of her "good looks," of her "snow-white hair, pleasant face and trim figure" did not diminish the insecurity of the ungainly Marion teenager of long ago. In sending a copy of her retouched picture to a niece, Florence admitted, "[Y]ou will not recognize it; neither do I, but it is a fine exhibition of what can be done in certain directions. . . ."

In the hall Barker had his first confrontation with women reporters, who volleyed "protests and inquiries as to her activities," while Evalyn and Jess visited shops, soliciting samples for Florence's inspection. Jess was too "sporty" for most people's taste, in his complete gray suit ensemble or with handkerchief, socks, tie, and hatband all in matching purple. Evalyn went for dangerously plunging backlines that nearly reached the derriere. Not much was sent that Florence could wear. "She wants her clothes to be dignified, distinctive and suitable to her position," sniffed one designer, "and she will have nothing else."

The next morning the Duchess held a press conference for about thirty reporters, along with still and newsreel cameramen to whom she self-consciously apologized that if they didn't get a "good picture of her, it's the fault of the subject." She praised the women reporters for breaking into a profession dominated by men and admitted that she couldn't "seem to reconcile myself" to reading "about myself in newspapers." Before they left, she accepted honorary presidencies of both the Girl Scouts and the Campfire Girls, controversial in the early twenties for advocating that young women develop physical stamina. "If I had my life to begin all over again," she declared, "I would begin as a Girl Scout."

Over the next few days modistes lined up with their wares. One day Florence tried on some fourteen gowns and suits in her favorite shade of the delphinium's dark blue-violet, which complemented her blue eyes and gray hair. First called gendarme blue, a cross between Alice Blue and French Blue, it was quickly christened Harding Blue. Of her choices, Harding Blue dominated, and manufacturers took her cue, making the color a brief rage that peaked during the inaugural. Evalyn got a shimmering, plunging silver gown for her inaugural ball.

The evenings were given over to theater. On their first night Will Hays escorted the group to the popular show *Sally,* playing at the Amsterdam Theater, where the Duchess fell under the spell of the hit song "Look for the Silver Lining." There was also *Lightnin'* at the Gaiety and *The First Year* at the Little Theater. Evalyn restrained herself from seeing *Diff'rent,* the "daring study of a Sex Starved Woman," and skipped her regular round of speakeasies. Despite the era's evolving cultural liberations for women, there was already a strong conservative reaction to it. Alongside notices of Florence's and Evalyn's fashion whirl and Broadway nights, for example, was news that the Allentown Federation of Pennsylvania Women planned to "exert all their influence against smoking among women, immodest dress and immodest dancing." The Duchess wanted no publicity in Middle America on her smoking, drinking, jazz devotee companion. Only on their last night, while attending *Green Goddess,* at the Booth Theater, did she permit Evalyn to make her splash by sporting the Hope Diamond.

The next morning, after noticing her picture in *The New York Times* among Jack Dempsey, Doug Fairbanks, and Billie Burke, Florence thanked the hotel staff who lined up to meet her and waved goodbye to the press at Grand Central Station—forbidding photographs. Her first trip in the public eye without Warren had focused attention on the Duchess in her own right, and she relished every compliment. It was also just as well that she wasn't with Warren in Florida.[12]

23

More Women

Just before he left for his trip south, Warren acknowledged to someone other than Nan that her child was also his. To Nan's sister, Elizabeth Willits, he promised to provide five hundred dollars a month for little Anne, as Nan's baby daughter became known, whom the Willitses agreed to raise.

Tales of Harding's compulsive adultery spread widely in the pre-inaugural period. On Christmas Florence had arranged to have dinner in her house with the press corps and Harry, Jess, and his ex-wife and recurrent escort, Roxy Stinson, forgoing the annual tradition of going to Doc's for the holiday. With his own house full of guests eager to meet the President-elect and his wife, Doc absolutely insisted that at the least, Warren put in an appearance at White Oaks Farm. He came by briefly, but rather than focus on the other guests, he remained "very attentive" to the beautiful Roxy, who had come along with him, inviting her to sit in the chair intended for Florence. When Roxy was later quoted in an article about the tête-à-tête, people whispered that it suggested a romantic encounter. To those Harding associates just then coping with a buzzing hive of women trying to cash in on their past affairs, one-night stands, and love letters with the President-elect, the Christmas story was almost humorously tame.

In Florida with Warren, Harry had to rush back to Washington to take care of one such matter. A young woman there was privately trying to sell for one thousand dollars some "sportive" letters Senator Harding had written her. The woman may have been either Nina White, a senator's daughter—for whom Harding signed at least one photograph with "ardent affection"—or Louise Cromwell Brooks, with whom Harding played poker at her Massachusetts Avenue town house. After they had been stuck in a Senate elevator, they had come to know each other well. As Francis Russell discerned, "His roving eye had spotted her and she had responded affably to his egregious maleness." Louise was said to have a cache of love letters from General Pershing as well.

Harding chronicler Samuel Hopkins Adams learned that Harry began efforts to get the letters. "Trusted friends undertook negotiations. The immediate result, as is frequent in such cases, was to raise the price to five thousand." This apparently prompted Doc to telegraph Ned on February 14 with references to "the matters," the "subjects for personal discussion," and "information which you think would be of importance." Evalyn later confirmed that Ned was just at the time providing money for "getting some letters for Harding." As Lasker had served to raise the Carrie Phillips blackmail fund, Harry was now apparently raising a smaller fund to deal with such emergencies, asking very close and rich Harding friends, like Ned, to contribute. Adams then learned, "At this point it was discovered that the bargainer was politically vulnerable through a member of her family. Counter-pressure was brought into play and the documents were surrendered without price." He did not ever reveal the identity of the woman or her family.

Now there was an apparent surplus of blackmail funds at Harry's disposal for any such emergencies that might arise during the Harding presidency. It would be perhaps too indiscreet for the attorney general to maintain such an account, but Jess Smith could, and certainly would, and Harry's brother, Mal Daugherty, ran the bank in their hometown. What is actually known is that an account opened there in 1921 was marked simply as "Jess Smith—Account No. 3," but before federal investigators could examine it some years later, the Daugherty brothers had had all records of deposits and withdrawals burned. It was probably the Harding blackmail fund.[1]

In varying degrees, Jess, Ned, Billy Burns, and Gaston Means, with indirect guidance from Harry and perhaps intermediary efforts by Doc Sawyer, began functioning as a stealth intimidation squad of troubleshooters for Harding, whether the threatened attacks were from racist genealogists, would-be assassins, or spurned mistresses. Led in theory by Harry but administered more directly by Jess, the line was purposefully fuzzy about whether such activities were official or "nonofficial." Throughout the Harding administration, Billy Burns was allowed to maintain his private detective business, while serving as Bureau of Investigation director, and Gaston Means operated as both a bureau G-man and private eye. Moreover, Florence Harding's best friend's husband was legally permitted to indulge in spying, breaking and entering, robbery, blackmail, and other assorted skulduggery when the new attorney general, Harry Daugherty, soon made Ned McLean a dollar-a-year agent of the Bureau of Investigation and gave him its secret code for use in covert telegrams.

The successful retrieval of the Harding letters to the Washington woman was actually the fourth such endeavor assumed by the Harding troubleshooters. The handling of the Carrie Phillips affair had been the first, and it remained successful. Boyden Sparkes recalled how Carrie Phillips "came back early in the winter, right after the campaign." While in Asia, flush with cash, Carrie stocked up on a variety of diamond bracelets, earrings, and necklaces. She still had Harding's love letters, but with her monthly income, she never threatened to go public, sell or publish her letters, or even gossip. The payoff during the campaign of the unnamed "New York woman" for her Harding love letters also proved successful.

The Harding cabal did botch its effort to squelch the blackmail attempts of Grace Cross. Although she did not apparently make a definite threat to disclose her affair with Harding until just before the inauguration, during the campaign she had let enough people know that she had Harding love letters. It was not long before Wilson press secretary Joseph Tumulty, Attorney General A. Mitchell Palmer, Senator Albert Fall, and Harry and Jess knew about them. The attempt to stop Grace Cross from costing as much as Carrie Phillips, in the weeks before the inauguration, apparently involved not only a systematic retrieval of damaging public records on Harding, such as a 1918 District of Columbia police report involving a violent quarrel between Senator Harding and Grace Cross, but the burglary of material from her home, later to become part of an odd collection of items gathered by Ned and Evalyn for their private papers.

One such item is a single scrap of paper, the first page of a scribbled memo, the latter pages missing from the files, and seemingly a non sequitur: "Grace Miller Cross, 1819-or 1821-G. St. from Finley Ohio=30 years old-blonde. is a friend of Harding's Pastor at Marion, his name is McAtee or McAfee. has child ten years old claims—" With the rest of the document missing, no conclusion can be made. Nor is it made clearer by a document dated November 26, 1920, also retained by the McLeans. This is an unsigned affidavit with a blank space for the alleged witness's identity, a document probably fabricated as insurance by Billy Burns, Gaston Means, Jess, or Ned to discredit and frame Grace Cross in the event that her blackmail moved from a suggestion into a formal threat. It may have also remained unsigned because, in the haste to prepare the frame-up, there was a name and address mix-up: Grace lived at the posh Wardman Park Inn as Mrs. James Cross, not at the G Street Akron Apartments as Mrs. George Cross.

———, being first duly worn, deposes and says:

A lady living in this flat called Mrs. Grace Cross came to see me to the best of my recollection six or seven times before the election and asked me if I did not remember Senator Harding coming into her flat. I said I did not know no Senator Harding. She said the gentleman was a very heavy set man and looked a little like a fine colored man. I told her I didn't know anything about him.

She came after me so much I began to get scared. One day she said to me: "You ain't got no sense; if you'll say what I tell you to I'll give you fifty dollars." I asked her who this gentleman was. She says "None of your business who he is." I asked the lady what she wanted me to say. She said she wanted me to say that I had seen this gentleman up in her room with some of his clothes undone.

One morning my wife told me Senator Harding was going to be next President of the United States. I certainly was one pleased man. I got it through my head who the gentleman was and I don't want to be mixed up in any crooked work. I wanted to see Senator Harding get in because I am a Republican and knew my people might get something from him.

This lady certainly does have a lot of different men come into her apartments. Sometimes they go out at twelve o'clock and sometimes I don't know whether they ever go out at all.

I have been janitor of the Akron Apartment House for———, and Mrs. George Cross, the lady you were asking me about has been here for———.[2]

Although it was clear that a delicate effort to discredit Grace Cross in some way rather than pay out more cash from the blackmail fund occurred in the weeks before the inaugural, Florence Harding's arrival in Florida on February 11 apparently put it on the back burner. As soon as she arrived, the Duchess wired her thanks to Evalyn for her help during the New York trip: "I couldn't have gotten along without you." Florence, however, was quite capable of coping with the League in the draft of Harding's inaugural address. When she read his reference implying possible future U.S. entry into some form of a league, the Duchess, "brandishing a blue pencil," cut out the paragraph and was not challenged.

Shortly thereafter the Hardings were back in Marion, staying with

Dr. Harding since the rental lease of their house to a man named Maillard Hunt had already begun. These last days in Marion were upsetting for the Duchess. She had a sad sense that she and Warren would never again live in the house they had built as newlyweds. Writing to a friend to whom she was giving away a set of china, she said wistfully, "I have come to the dismantling of my home—probably permanently. . . ." At one local event honoring him, Warren even wept, fearing, as he put it, that his new "demands upon mind and body might prove too much." On the morning of March 2 the Hardings stood on the front porch to say good-bye to about one third of Marion, some ten thousand people, accepting from them a silver plaque that referred to Florence as an "esteemed helpmate." Warren responded with warm words that, in retrospect, seemed to forecast his own descent into scandal: "Friendship challenges earth's most desirable things—popularity, beauty, honor, education, statesmanship, philosophy. . . . Mrs. Harding and I are going from you with a feeling of sorrow, with that unavoidable touch of regret which comes to every man and woman when they leave the community in which they have developed and lived so long. . . . We go as one of you . . . of the great common people. . . . [F]riendship will be an inspiration and an assurance throughout the term of our public service."[3]

With the Sawyers, the Christians, Florence's niece Hazel, and several other Marionites, the Hardings left for Washington. They were met by the Coolidges at Union Station and were photographed together as the Duchess playfully swung her fur at reporters. After lunch Florence alone commanded a reception room overflowing with "chatting groups of men and—no other woman, and met informally those who had or could devise some claim upon her." Observing her was playwright Zona Gale, creator of the popular *Miss Lulu Bett,* who noted that her "clear, pleasant voice rising when she talks earnestly . . . was audibl[e] above the murmurs." Later that day, when the Hardings paid a courtesy call on the Wilsons, Gale mused that although Florence and Edith were of the same generation, the Duchess "will yet prove so different, as if ages separated them. . . ." That night, after a Willard Hotel party for Marionites, attended by Doc, Evalyn and Ned, Harry and Jess, the Hardings retired early. At least Florence did.[4]

Reporter Ray Clapper later told his wife "the remarkable story of the night before the inauguration." Carrie Phillips was back in Marion, and Nan Britton in New York, so it was evidently Grace Cross who had also checked into the Willard—and found herself a casualty of the new Harding hit squad: "The President-Elect and Mrs. Harding were occupying the presidential suite at the Willard Hotel. Harding's friends were worried about the arrival that night at the hotel of one of his lady friends. They didn't want any scandal on the eve of his inauguration. They cautioned Harding to stay in his room. But apparently they didn't trust him where a pretty woman was concerned, for they kept a vigil out in the hall all night. Sure enough, before the night was over, the President-Elect tiptoed out into the hall. His friends pushed him back into the room. Then they went upstairs, knocked on the lady's door, and ordered her to pack and get out of town, threatening to put the F.B.I. on her trail if she didn't go at once. She was so frightened she left immediately."[5]

March 4, 1921, dawned clear and cold. At ten-thirty the Hardings went from the Willard to the White House, Florence dressed in a Harding Blue blouse and skirt, elbow-length white gloves, her neckband and diamond chosen by Evalyn, a wide-brimmed blue hat turned at a sporty angle with blue ostrich feathers sticking jauntily into the air. She wore a heavy wrap with a deep chinchilla collar. After a brief chat in the oval Blue Room, Warren assisted the fragile Wilson as he shuffled on his cane out into the brisk winds under the porte cochere to the Pierce-Arrow limousine with the presidential seal, the first inaugural in which motorcars drove the principals.

In a second car Edith Wilson, in a cap topped by a gull's wing and covered in black veil, wrapped a thick mink fur across her mouth, conveniently limiting conversation with the Duchess. As their car wound down the crescent drive, they passed reporters and photographers, and Florence "called out in hearty tones first on one side, then the other," waving to the familiar faces, telling a startled Edith that they were "her boys." As the cars proceeded to the Capitol to cheering crowds, the women barely managed a conversation, although satirist R. I. Phillips suggested that they wanted to stop and shop. This ride of the two First Ladies began an inaugural tradition, but when they arrived, Florence "fairly raced up the stairs," liberated from her stifling predecessor.[6]

After the swearing in of Coolidge in the Senate chamber, where Grace wore a bright red picture hat, the officials proceeded to the reserved seating at the east front of the Capitol for Harding's swearing in. The general public had clustered on trees, fire hydrants, wherever they could catch a view, watching a display of daredevil pilots flying in formation above. Special police units were dispatched, on the lookout for anyone consuming alcohol. Earlier in the week several bootleg enterprises, hoping to cash in on the expected crowds, had been stopped by investigators. Street decorations were sparse, but federal and private office buildings were lavishly decorated with flags in different sizes. Among the masses were twenty big Army trucks full of wounded veterans from Walter Reed, courtesy of Evalyn.

As the band played a startlingly modern jazz piece, the Duchess descended the steps of the grandstand to her place, with her sisters-in-law, Daisy and Carolyn, next to the desk where the Bible rested, and a cheer went up from the crowd. When she noticed a woman faint in the crowds, Mrs. Harding asked that the woman be helped. She had also seen to it that every single person—from publicity advisers to typists—who worked on the campaign in Marion had been invited to the ceremony. Warren stepped down, in his dashing cutaway and gray striped trousers, to take the oath. As Warren G. Harding spoke the words making him the twenty-ninth President of the United States, Florence Harding unconsciously took the oath of office herself. A reporter recorded that she was "repeating the words after him." Then she nodded slightly, "confirming her husband's promise," to "preserve, protect and defend the Constitution. . . ."

Now First Lady, Florence, said reporter Constance Drexel, "stood like a soldier besides her husband." During the speech, the first delivered over an electrically amplified loudspeaker, "she watched and weighed his every word." Watching her on the flag-bedecked, sunlit podium, and listening to the themes of the inaugural address, Drexel understood that Florence had had a role in crafting it. Harding stressed both the traditional role of women and her new role of voter, as had Florence repeatedly through the campaign: "We want an America of homes, illuminated with hope and happiness, where mothers, freed from the necessity of long hours of toil beyond their own doors, may preside as befits the hearthstone of American citizenship. . . . With the nation-wide induction of womanhood into our political life, we may count upon her intuition, her refinement, her intelligence and her influence to exalt the social order. We count upon her exercise of the full privileges and the performance of the duties of citizenship to speed the attainment of the highest state." Later in the speech, the Duchess strongly nodded at his injunction against "war profiteering."

As the band played "Hail to the Chief," however, Florence was suddenly struck anew with the terror of Marcia's incontrovertible prediction. While officials filed back to the Senate chamber for Cabinet confirmations, she stared into the eyes of Indiana Senator Jim Watson and said, "I am filled with a fear. . . . It is the proudest day of my life, but we will not live through the four years."[7]

In the Senate Gallery Florence loosened her coat, stared over the railing to see who was where, talking with "jerky little movements" of her gloved hands. The eight women members of the Republican National Executive Committee took their place. One of them, Corinne Robinson, delicately told reporters that Florence was a "woman of strong character, splendid personality and powerful initiative," in contrast with Robinson's sister-in-law Edith Roosevelt who "allowed 'Teddy' to do the talking—Now don't misunderstand me, I do not mean in any sense that Mrs. Harding will interfere in the performance of presidential matters, or even meddle in political affairs. But I do feel that being a woman of unusual individuality, Mrs. Harding will play a great part in moulding the success of her husband's career as president." Congresswoman Alice Robertson seemed embarrassed by the artificial violet corsage someone gave her while Alice Longworth for once removed her hat. Nearby, Gay Nineties icon Lillian Russell sat with Al Jolson.

President Harding addressed the Senate. "I have chosen my Cabinet, in accordance with my best judgment and my personal wishes. I trust it will meet your approval," and each was then confirmed. Near Florence were assorted Cabinet wives who had pursued higher education and careers of their own, including world-traveled writer, public speaker, president of the Girl Scouts and one of the first American women to graduate with a geology degree Lou Hoover, wife of Herbert, commerce secretary; Carrie May Wallace, graduate of Iowa Agricultural College, who had helped develop the tangelo, wife of Henry, the agriculture secretary; and Florence's old Senate wife colleague Emma Fall, who ran the family's lumber and mining interests and New Mexico ranch, wife of Albert, the interior secretary.

Outside, the crowds drifting down the avenue stopped to watch the boys from Walter Reed being lifted back into the trucks. Several in wheelchairs grew somber at the sight of trim marines marching back to their barracks. All attention was suddenly focused, however, on the procession of cars returning to the White House, carrying the new President and First Lady.[8]

It was a quarter to three when the Hardings arrived at their new home. As they stepped onto the North Portico, about to enter the great doors, Florence turned to her husband.

"Well, Warren Harding, I have got you the Presidency. What are you going to do with it?"

He turned to her solemnly. "May God help me, for I need it."

Gathering relatives for a late lunch were met by the humorless Miss Laura Harlan. Just the day before she had been named the fourth social secretary to a First Lady. Debutante daughter of a former Supreme Court justice—but low on cash—she had taken to the samovars of Taft's attorney general and the British ambassador but, according to one paper, was hesitant to "have it known that she was using her birthright as a means of increasing her income."⁹

Just blocks away Grace Cross now was openly in the market to sell her love letters from Warren. She explained this at lunch to her friend the reporter Bertha Martin. Bertha, however, had been briefed beforehand. Managing to make inroads to the Harding damage control unit with the fact that she was a friend of Grace's, Martin had been contacted by Jess Smith some days before the inaugural. Before meeting with her, Jess had conferred with Ned who as publisher of the Washington *Post* could offer the ambitious woman any number of journalistic opportunities if she could get those letters from Grace Cross. Bertha wanted to be *Post* society editor. Jess struck the deal. Martin's colleague and friend Vylla Poe Wilson recalled: "Apparently, Harding wanted the letters and apparently he asked Jess Smith to help get them. Or, possibly, there was no collusion at all. In any case, on the 4th of March, during Harding's inauguration, Bertha Martin took Grace Cross out to lunch and during the lunch asked Grace for the letters. Grace refused to give them up. Bertha offered Grace money for the letters. Grace refused. Bertha said, 'I don't believe you really have the letters,' and Grace Cross opened her handbag and showed them to Bertha. Whereupon Bertha grabbed the packet of letters and hastened from the lunchroom. One week later, she was employed. . . . Jess Smith had gotten the job for her on the *Post*."

Not one to cut all her options, Grace then wrote a sweet congratulatory note to the new President. Amid the avalanche of wellwishing letters from thousands of the anonymous public, Grace Cross immediately received a formal acknowledgment note at her Wardman Park Inn apartment 578, from George Christian, the new President's secretary—on the first day of the new administration: "Dear Madam: The President very greatly appreciates your kind message of congratulations and asks me to thank you heartily for sending it. Sincerely yours, George B. Christian Secretary to the President." The Christian letter, in and of itself, implies nothing damaging, except perhaps the new administration's care not to ignore or alienate the potentially damaging woman. What did make the letter unusual is the fact that it was stolen from Grace Cross's apartment, almost certainly by Gaston Means, and also ended up in the file kept on her by Ned and Evalyn, evidently purloined so that she could have no written documentation in her possession proving any personal connection to Harding beyond having worked in his Senate office for two years. Grace Cross was being carefully watched and slowly defused.[10]

In contrast with such nefarious private directives, the new administration was publicly declaring itself an open house. Harding's first official order fulfilled Florence's campaign promise. At exactly 4:55 P.M. the White House police swung open the White House gates to the American public for the first time since the United States had entered the war on April 6, 1917. The sweeping gesture symbolized a great change. No scene had occurred at the old house like it since the 1829 free-for-all Jackson inaugural. Editorials praised the move and the further announcement that the mansion would again be open to tourists the next week. Masses swarmed across the lawn and headed up to the house; even automobiles pulled up in the driveway. As the public clustered on the North Portico, watching guests come and go, some pressed their noses to the window, looking in. A startled maid immediately began pulling the curtains, but Florence saw this and yelled out, "Let 'em look in if they want. It's their White House!"[11]

As the sun set, across Lafayette Square and down one block, the McLean inaugural dinner and ball was getting under way. Evalyn created hanging gardens in her Babylon with mountains of spring flowers spread on every available table, potted palm trees lining the hallways, and ferns winding up the staircases. In the dining room, amid the museum-high intricately carved wood panels hung with priceless Barberini tapestries, were three hundred-foot tables set with goldware for several hundred guests, with creeper vines and bouquets running the length of them, between several-foot-high gold candelabra with white tapers. Scanning the room, Evalyn felt she had "contrived a scene that I found immensely satisfying." She went upstairs to slip into her silver gown, "made on the prevailing slender lines," and of course the Hope Diamond.

Alice was one of the first to arrive, without Nick, but escorted by her brother Ted, the new assistant navy secretary. With the Coolidges Evalyn and Ned stepped into the smaller ballroom, where a receiving line was forming. Harry and Jess in white tie and tails, Doc in his new military uniform, Charlie Forbes in his military medals, Al and Emma Fall, old Harding friends—houseguests at Friendship—the Jenningses and Scobeys all lined up as one of several dance bands played jazz. Only the Vice President was uncomfortable, but after Evalyn fetched some bicarb and soda, he was relieved. With dancing after dinner, the ball went into the wee hours.[12]

Those not prominent, connected, or wealthy still shared the exciting night of an era ready to dawn bright. Among the curious crowds passing in front of the floodlit open park of the White House was an actress who had been rehearsing during the day at Poli's Theater for her opening in two days in *Whirl of the Town.* Mae West suggested that people "do something new" as a way to become popular. It worked for her as she did "spectacular shimmy gyrations." West reiterated, as if advice for the Hardings, "Do things differently." It was an apt understatement for the times.

The Hardings retired early. Warren wanted a good night's sleep before getting to the Oval Office. Sure enough, the papers said, even "before the arrival of the clerical forces, he was at work." But he must have been taken aback when he entered the office. Smiling and waiting for him, somehow having beaten him with a shortcut in this labyrinth of hallways, was the Duchess.

She had come, she said, to place a flower on his desk. It was time for them to get to work.

If Warren Harding said that he didn't want to be the "best" President, just the "best-loved," Florence Harding had markedly different ambitions.

"Who was the most successful First Lady of the Land?" she asked a senator.

"Mrs. Cleveland or Dolley Madison, I suppose." He shrugged.

She pecked his shoulder with a quick tap and quipped, "Watch me."[13]

Part Five

FIRST LADY
1921–1923

We are just folks, but when I enter the White House I propose to accept all of its social obligations and become First Lady of the land in truth as well as name.

24

"Flo from Ohio"

The first day the White House was again open to the public, tourists were told by guards that Florence Harding was likely to appear and guide them through herself. Strolling through the garden, the public marveled at the newly installed drinking fountains for them and the chirping cacophony from birdhouses she had ordered placed about for the indigenous breeds of the region. Organizations holding their spring conventions in Washington were invited to have their picture taken with the new First Lady and her Airedale dog, Laddie Boy, a gift given to the Hardings the day after the inaugural. Groups and individuals of the sort never previously invited now came to meet the First Lady, from the Waldenstein Society to Albert Einstein and tennis great Big Bill Tilden. For the first time jazz, played by the Navy Band, rang through the grounds, and for the first time in the century the First Lady publicly took to the dance floor.

While Dolley Madison had exhibited such a connection with the public citizenry, in this early Jazz Age of burgeoning public relations Florence Harding made sure the press was well briefed on her open policy. Newsreel photographers chronicled her as they had no previous First Lady. She called most of the reporters by their first names and wisecracked with them. "Never had a president's wife had such a wardrobe. At least, never was one so published abroad," said a Senate wife. "Never had the White House been so free to society reporters invited before state dinners to see decorations, be shown boudoir-gowns, told of Warren's devotion and attentions, confided in, asked advice, and made witnesses to a frank glee, 'We are really here in the White House itself.' "[1]

It was obvious, the President's sister said, that Florence "enjoyed being mistress of the White House better than he did being the President of the United States." Evalyn thought that with her uncertain health, Florence could have assumed a "half-retirement," as Doc and friends suggested, but "for her that was impossible." With the privileges, powers, and symbolism now bestowed upon her, Florence Harding made more than the White House accessible: She opened herself, with a generosity previously unseen. Such activism in the First Lady role was appreciated by the nation but not by the staff.[2]

"She was a strange woman who, hard as she tried, could never quite accustom herself to the greatness and importance of her position," said housekeeper Elizabeth Jaffray of the Duchess. "I believe she had more beautiful clothes and spent more money . . . than any First Lady . . . but . . . she had a temper that was almost uncontrollable at times . . . about as little reserve as any grown person I have ever met." Although she never reconciled herself to this "unconventional and unusual" woman, Jaffray did concede that "there was a rugged honesty and sincerity about her that attracted me deeply." Snobbish Chief Usher Ike Hoover remained stiffly unmoved by such sentiment: "Mrs. Harding was wild and anxious, but so constituted that she could not be a social success. She made most progress with politicians who came to see the President." The distinguished presidential valet Arthur Brooks, a brigadier general in the Negro division of the District of Columbia guard, however, came to understand Florence and defend her against Hoover. "Brooks said Hoover was blasphemous in talking of Mrs. H today," a naval aide noted in his diary. "Brooks dislikes it."[3]

Although the "stuffy" social secretary Laura Harlan aloofly withdrew from defense of her boss, Florence was so loyally supported by her devoted Secret Service agent Harry Barker that she "entrusted numerous confidential missions" to him, according to a coworker. Appreciative of how he had left his four young children in Newtownville, Massachusetts, to serve her, Florence "adopted" him as a surrogate son. "He kept very close to her when she was out of the White House in all her travels," said a worker. "Barker was the only person I knew in my eleven years on duty in the White House who did not have to or would not deal directly on many occasions with Ike Hoover." Because she was often with the President, many of his agents ended up answering to her too, but only one got along well with her and Barker: the head of the detail, Edmund Starling. Barker was so trusted by Florence that she kept him posted outside her room even when she was not there—to make certain nobody except her Irish maid, Katherine Wynne, entered the bedroom.[4]

Since military aides worked as social assistants during events, Warren deferred to the Duchess about any such appointments or transfers, but her "personal insistence" that Reddy Baldinger be transferred from duty under the assistant war secretary to the dual post of "Assistant to the Officer in Charge of Public Buildings and Grounds" and "Assistant Army Aide to the President" added to the Byzantine power struggles among White House aides. Reddy was jumped in rank, was given full access to the Hardings, and assumed the prerogatives usually granted to his superior, Colonel Clarence O. Sherrill. Baldinger was described by a naval aide as a "vicious sort of person" who "had a way of getting out of line and getting into people's hair." He reported in name to Warren but in fact to Florence. He escorted her, formally introduced her and guests to each other, and dispensed flowers from the government greenhouses as gifts to her friends. Like Barker, Florence used him as a liaison to irritable Ike Hoover.[5]

The Duchess got along famously well with the household staff. The largely African-American kitchen, waiter, and cleaning staffers affectionately nicknamed her Missy, and both Hardings were particularly fond of one butler whose son was Duke Ellington. To give comfort to the policemen stationed at the outside gates in cold weather, she had heated stations installed and was so friendly with the florists that she often arranged flowers with them. "She had a very loud voice, yelling from upstairs, hollering over the banisters," recalled Lillian Parks, whose mother, Maggie Rogers, worked as a maid. "She was a character. But Mama said she never once mistreated anybody."[6]

Although Warren, with his late hours, usually slept in his own small bedroom, the press reported that the Hardings shared the master suite, keeping a Bible on the table between their twin beds, above them a gilt crown piece draped with blue-violet damask. On the fireplace mantel were their pictures and one of his mother. Her collection of elephant knickknacks in ivory, brass, bronze, and glass trailed on tables and other flat surfaces not only here but in other rooms. Her necklaces of ivory elephants and coral elephants were displayed with her other neck beads, near a corner cabinet with glass doors covered in blue silk, the side panels revealing rows of spangled, buckled, and pointed shoes. In her sitting room Florence grew her own small potted plants, from Japanese lilies to white violets, rotating them seasonally on a table beside her reading. In the first few months she often breakfasted down in the garden below her window, a chance not only to enjoy the roses but to watch who was coming to meet with Warren in the Oval Office.

Florence decorated the private quarters in the comfortable style of the midwestern matron that she was. She covered the walls of the upstairs oval room in Harding Blue silk. Here she placed chintz armchairs and red velvet davenports, photos of friends and family in silver frames, shaded lamps, and, flanking the fireplace, two "colonial" mahogany bookcases filled with leather-bound volumes, contemporary literature, and her book of press clippings pasted on yellow paper. Her own portrait by Phillip de Laszlo, one of Dolley Madison, and another of James Monroe hung in the room. There was also a grandfather's clock, a huge French vase filled with pussy willows, soft-toned blue rugs, a large bowl of goldfish, her caged pet canary, Pete, and a Baldwin parlor grand piano. The oddest piece in the room was a foot-tall Kewpie doll in a pink dress; it ticked like a "bolsheviki bomb," winked one eye, and would "shimmy" in the breeze, a reporter noted. The single most fascinating item in the room, however, would be installed on February 8, 1922. That day the Hardings became the proud owners of a vacuum-tube detector and two-state amplifier, installed in the bookcases. In the White House for the first time, as in thousands of American homes, the radio had arrived.

In the west end of the upstairs hall Florence padded the dark green walls with long jungle ferns, hung birdcages of canaries, and placed shallow glass bowls of roses. Here she hung the de Laszlo portrait of Warren. Americans also learned that the Duchess was as wild about an early twenties' fad as many other housewives. "Is Mrs. Harding a Mah Jong convert?" a reporter wondered. "We don't know, but we do know there's a Mah Jong set on a table in one of the White House living rooms."[7]

After breakfast at eight and a meeting with Jaffray on menus ("The best, plainly cooked," said Florence. "The idea of strawberries in December never appealed to me much. I believe in the wisdom of nature and prefer to follow her lead"), the First Lady got to work. In a small southeast corner office, seated on a chaise for some three hours, she read mail and dictated her responses to Laura Harlan or one of the executive staff stenographers, scribbled instructions on requests for government intervention, or planned social events amid ringing telephones, scheduling and telephone books, seating charts and bags of incoming letters that might ask advice on how to conduct an international conference or criticize her for using the presidential yacht. While her predecessors had often blandly responded to inquiries about their views on social issues of the day, Florence Harding was the first to send original responses, only using form letters to turn down invitations or requests for money or patronage.[8]

Before the Duchess had lunch with Warren and guests, Maggie Rogers gave her an hour of manicure, massage, and hair wash and set— "the only time my ears get really clean," she genially, if coarsely, joked.

Marcelled tightly in the "horseshoe" shape, her "marvelous pearl gray coiffure" was described by reporter Daisy Fitzhugh Ayres as "intricate, meticulous." Another reporter affirmed that there was no truth to the rumor that the First Lady had to "lay away" the stiff-looking waves "in the dressing table on retiring."

After lunch, if the weather was warm, Florence stood at the south portico for photographs with large delegations, not only women's groups but men's—dentists, Masons, Native Americans—rarely turning down a group of more than a dozen. Other presidential wives may have realized the symbolism of the position of First Lady, but none before Florence had so consciously cared to translate it into actually meeting, touching, and talking to endless lines of thousands of the common citizenry. The New York *Tribune* took note of this and praised Florence for being "far more generous in receiving special groups at the White House than were her predecessors." In the late afternoon the First Lady received "social callers," those who had left their calling cards and were invited to meet her. Her system was to have the individuals grouped into the Green, Blue, and Red Rooms, while she moved from room to room, alerted by Reddy when the approximately ten minutes in each room was up; meanwhile another group was brought into the emptied suite, and the process continued. If she was meeting a special guest, a woman of achievement, or a reporter, her favored salon was the Red Room, overwhelming with its intimidating life-size portraits of George and Martha Washington and its bust of Lafayette. A reporter noted cheekily, however, that the Duchess "dominates every room she enters." Harding's appointment list was longer than his predecessors, said Ike Hoover, but "Mrs. Harding's was even longer."

Dinner was never without guests, and the Hardings rarely got to bed before midnight. Some nights Warren slipped out for poker—or some other activity of dubious virtue—without Florence. When they broke protocol by dining at private homes, she insisted on using the Cadillac "7-passenger" car among the five vehicles available to the Hardings. The car was even photographed for an advertisement promoting the auto industry.[9] The new First Lady also permitted her favored designer, Harry Collins, to print her thanks for the inaugural day outfit she wore, in his book, *ABC of Dress,* along with an illustration of her in it. Collins wrote that "this is the first dress worn by any 'Mistress of the White House' that shows the long waist line . . . this mode will outlast all fads . . . since it is conceived on the principle of correct lines . . . facilitated for the designer by Mrs. Harding's suggestions as to what was becoming to her."

Florence Harding left a distinct visual impression. Evalyn emphasized her "strongly erect" carriage and "her glances and smiles as radiant as when she was a girl." Ike Hoover liked more sedate women: "Mrs. Harding was very fixy, so much so that she looked artificial." Starling thought that she was "well-groomed, neatly dressed and highly marcelled" with a "determined" mouth but that "her eyes lacked decision. They reflected ambition, but they had a clouded, puzzled look, rather than the clear brightness which is associated with an active and logical mentality." Her deep voice, with a crisp Ohio flatness, commanded attention. Jane Dixon recalled it as "quick, decisive and yet musical. . . . The sentences were brief, the tones slightly staccato . . . rattling out orders with the smoothness, the rapidity of a machine gun." Bertha Wilson simply found it a "high-pitched, strident voice."

Florence obsessed about her appearance, favoring beads, sparkles, and spangles, flashing when she turned. "I always felt if I hit Mrs. Harding with a hammer she would go clang," said reporter Vylla Poe Wilson. "She was always heavily made up and she dressed heavily but elegantly in white satin with countless streamers hanging from her waist, studded with jewels which Mrs. McLean had given her. Mrs. Harding, with all these streamers and jewels[,] would make a 'swish' as she walked across the room."

Being scrutinized for what she wore annoyed the Duchess. "I hate clothes," she averred. "I have to be dressed up most of the time." Early in 1921 women's skirts radically rose up the calf, nearly to the knee, a moderated version of the dresses sported by "flappers," those young women whose short skirts flapped against their thighs. *Town Topics* gossiped that the Duchess wore her own dresses no shorter than eight inches from the ground because of her swollen ankles, but she declared, "It is not for me to dictate to American womanhood" how short its skirts should be. "As to the length of skirts, or rather, their shortness," the First Lady felt "the adult woman can settle that for herself and that for the young girl, the mother should be the judge." Her refusal to pass judgment on the new flapper look was even immortalized in bad but admiring verse by a would-be poet.

Florence's trademark black velvet neckband made a mark. A Philadelphia *Ledger* reporter wrote, "Naturally a good many other people are wearing a velvet band, nowadays, who never used to wear anything of the sort. Even the buds and the sub-debs, many of them, seem to feel that they are not quite dressed without their 'Flossie Clings' as they call them, 'because they're flossy and they cling and Mrs. Harding's maiden name is Florence Kling,' as one pretty little flapper explained. . . ." The delphinium-inspired blue-violet Harding Blue trend continued past the inaugural, and Florence fostered it by carrying small bouquets of the flower or wearing corsages of them, complementing her blue eyes and gray hair. There was even a brief competition between "Florentine" and "Alicia" blue, Mrs. Longworth's favored color. So closely did Florence become associated with the color that yet another shade of it was named for her, Duchess Blue.

Florence hadn't stopped being Amos Kling's daughter, however. When perusing fineries with Evalyn, the Duchess was so shocked at their exorbitant cost that she sent the designer away. When an exclusive milliner gushed to her about pricey Parisian wares, Florence harrumphed, "Haven't you any American models? I like them even better."[10]

Being economical in everything she bought also served a highly political purpose in 1921. As the nation went through an economic depression and period of unemployment, and as the President instituted as his first achievement the Bureau of the Budget, which sought to eliminate federal waste and cut general spending, the First Lady started a highly public campaign to do her part in the nation's home. As Ike Hoover put it, while Warren was "inclined to be generous," the Duchess "was close." In her rigid household budget, furnaces were no longer fed coal endlessly, and infrequently used rooms were closed; every alternate electric light was turned off, and often she walked around unscrewing lightbulbs; lawn fountains ran only when there were guests, saving water and easing the strain on the city's antiquated water system. She saved only about two thousand dollars a year from the national budget, but her efforts were priceless in terms of positive publicity.

The First Lady refused the $10,000 House appropriation to redecorate the private quarters, "scrupulously carrying out here their ideals on cutting down expenses," a reporter noted. "I want to get along with what we have," she said in refusing to purchase a new state china, "until we feel the country can afford them better." She also cut food costs for public entertaining but was less successful with personal expenditures. One February her private food bill from Magruder's grocer's was $227.29, from New York Beef, $377.85. Clothing also ran high: a $250 purchase from Harry Collins, a $325 from Hickson. Florence was savvy about ostensibly saving the public a penny but spared no cost for her own presentation and well-being.[11]

Florence fully revived the prewar White House state dinners, massive receptions, even the Easter egg roll, breaking all protocol as the traditionally formal hostess by frankly chatting with guests on everything from her battles with Amos Kling to her belief "in the influence of the stars in human destiny."[12] For her famous late-afternoon garden parties, her own recipe of "squalls" in banana, mint, and lemon, a form of fruit punch with enough flavor to compensate for the absent spirits, was served beneath red and white striped tents. The Hardings stood on a Persian carpet under a large oak tree, greeting guests two by two, as the band blared nearby. Often several thousand guests—people drawn from national and regional government, corporate and social circles, and Harding friends—thronged these events. For the Duchess, the garden parties were a sort of continuation of the Front Porch campaign. For government workers, most of whom had come to Washington during the war, she held a rotation of lawn parties that gave them their first access to the mansion.[13] She also initiated noon parties and sunset dinners of Potomac cruises on the presidential yacht, *Mayflower,* which she had redecorated.[14]

Some of her choices for entertainment following state dinners were fresh and unique for the White House. Besides some eyebrow-raising selections such as "A Lesson with the Fan," "No, John, No," and "Invocation to Eros" performed by a female duo, she showcased the Paulist Choristers, a group of Catholic singers led by Father William Finn, and the "performance art" of comic monologist Ruth Draper. "Paul the American Magician" and "The Zancigs: Two Minds with but One Single Thought" did not make the cut. In the fall of 1921 the new First Lady also initiated a series of musicales "to encourage and develop young American talent."[15]

As for the average tourists not lucky enough to be invited to a social event, Florence was adamant that they be allowed as much access as security would permit, and it helped build her popular legacy. "Manicurists, soldiers, sailors, clubwomen, citizens and their wives from small towns acclaimed her," sniffed a Senate wife. "Society never, as naturally it would not, ceased to regard her as crude in manner, brusk [*sic*] in speech, and lacking in social technique. But I doubt if she knew this or cared."

Florence took personal glee in shocking tourists by coming down the staircase onto the state floor, plucking several from the long lines, and taking them into the florist room, kitchens, and the family quarters. "Wouldn't you like to go up and see the other rooms in the White House?" she asked them. "I know how curious I used to be about it all." She plowed through books on the mansion's history and learned about historic items to point out to the tourists: "I have made myself familiar with every inch of the house so no matter where I go, I am not a stranger. And I love these beautiful big rooms with their high ceilings, their wide spaces, their polished mahogany furniture, carved deep with memories of Lincoln and the Madisons. . . . I thrill to the thought I am sitting in a chair where they once sat, eating from a plate which graced the place of a McKinley or Grant." The new First Lady solicited a portrait of Sarah Yorke Jackson, displayed Civil War era and Lincolnia in an upstairs room, and had Theodore Roosevelt's notes on his renovation transferred from the Library of Congress to the mansion to be kept there as a permanent guide to maintaining its care and historical integrity.

Florence's sweeping decision simply to open the house to streams of tourists got her into political trouble. She had dismissed the previous requirement that tourists receive tickets from their members of Congress as undemocratic and a "needless and burdensome task." Several members up for reelection, however, "felt that they lost in their prestige by not being requested to use their influence in gaining admission for constituents . . . [and able to] continue to harbor the delusion that the President consults them on who enters the White House." Ticketing was restored.

Even when the mansion was closed, the lawn remained a public park. Besides reviving nineteenth-century summer concerts for the general public, Mrs. Harding encouraged motorists to drive through the crescent drives and children's groups to picnic there. She furthermore sought to share White House perquisites, placing limousines and even complimentary theater tickets at the disposal of the city's less fortunate, who either wrote or were referred to her or about whom she read in the newspapers. "No former mistress of the White House ever lived in such close personal touch to the American people," observed a Washington *Star* reporter. "Mrs. Harding had a big conception of what the people of the United States wanted to know about the White House and the people who live in it, and she used every method to let them know."[16]

Such popularity with the people common, however, contrasted with the disdain capital society had for the new First Lady. The woman they favored was the youthful Second Lady, Grace Coolidge, and it was inevitable that a slight strain arose between the two women. Florence was sometimes effusively warm with Grace, sometimes crackling with condescension. When the Second Lady found herself placed in the protocol spot of the First Lady, Grace "breathed in a tragic stage whisper" into Florence's ear, with "intense dismay," that "Oh, I am on the wrong side." Florence looked at her "in consternation" and snapped, "Never mind—what difference does it make to us. Come on." Mary Rinehart felt that "there was considerable strain" in Grace's "attempts to offset the Vice President's complete lack of hypocrisies and social graces. She was genuine, she liked people and she let them know it. But most of us may relax now and then. We need not like all the people all the time. She never dared to relax." Despite what was certainly in part some jealousy of her youthful enthusiasm, Grace was almost universally popular in Washington, even appearing on one of the first *Good Housekeeping* lists of "America's Twelve Greatest Women."[17]

The most beloved figure of the new order, however, was not a person at all. Lacking presidential children, the White House promoted Laddie Boy as a near-human member of the First Family, granting full newspaper "interviews," all actually written by President Harding. Certainly the dog was the first chief executive's pet to receive and respond to mail and be invited as a special guest to social events and fund raisers. There was a special chair for the dog at Cabinet meetings. He was granted plate No. 1 on his dog tag for fetching golf balls for the President. The dog was twice brought up in legal cases, once as the father of a New York dog involved in street fighting, another as the brother of a Denver dog hauled into court for chicken killing. Laddie Boy even came up in a congressional debate over whether the Marine Band was a needless expense, but California Republican Congressman J. H. MacLafferty said the only White House music would then be provided by Laddie running about with a can tied to his tail. Not only did Laddie set off a national craze for Airedales in 1921, but a dog food company even named a brand after him. The dog was further popularized as a mass-manufactured children's stuffed toy. Apparently it all affected the pooch. "We used to call Laddie Boy the 'publicity hound,'" recalled Vylla Poe Wilson, "because Laddie Boy was always around when the photographers were there and the dog seemed to enjoy having his picture taken."

Both Hardings made an emotional investment in the large, shaggy Airedale, their first dog since the poisoned Hub. Laddie often begged for scraps from Warren, eliciting a shout from the Duchess: "Warren, leave that dog alone. Laddie, come here." Then she fed the dog herself. When the couple weren't speaking to each other, they yelled their communications through Laddie.[18]

The canine apparently made up for the Klings, for though Warren's relatives were often at the White House, the visits of Florence's family members consisted of one visit by her daughter-in-law, Esther, and a sudden call by her brother Cliff, when she lay ill. Now when she was at the pinnacle of her achievements, looking back on her Marion life seemed almost to pain Florence. She had no interest whatsoever in even visiting there—undoubtedly in part because of Carrie Phillips's presence. Despite the fact that her old neighbor George Christian worked as the President's secretary, even he and his wife were not easy company for Florence. "Mrs. Harding treated her so mean—unkind— never brought her in, never one of the family," said Evalyn. "Trouble with George, as sweet as he is, how he drinks and how he has been drunk for so many years."

There were press claims that Florence's grandchildren, Jean and George, would be "the children of the White House" and didn't want "Goggy" to leave Marion. In fact, the grandchildren never came to Washington. They attended public school, went to summer camp, and were known in Marion as the grandchildren of its Democratic mayor, George Neely, Esther's father. Esther didn't want them thinking of themselves as "the *President's grandchildren*," said Gilcrest Allen.

Florence told the press, "I want them to do something worthwhile and my mother interest is expended in their direction," but she did so only long distance. "If you are anything at all like your 'Goggy,' " she wrote her granddaughter, "you [have] amounted to a great deal these days and [are] of very great assistance to your mother." Florence wanted her granddaughter raised properly, telling Esther, "[D]o be careful and do not dress Jean too much in silks and satins. I know that makes you smile, but when I look about and see the children of today dressed better to go to school than I did to go to church and Sunday School, I think it is a great mistake, because there is nothing left for them to anticipate in the future." Despite her professed interest, Florence learned that George fell and broke his wrists weeks after the fact, only later reading about the accident in the Marion *Star*, and had to ask, "When is Jean's birthday?" She was also Spartan in her gifts, sending only publicity pictures of Laddie Boy for Christmas. Although she sent their bond dividends in advance and gave money for camp enrollment, she claimed, "[W]ish I could do more towards helping, but it takes about all I can to keep things going because I always must look my best."

Esther remained Florence's great link to Marion. Although she remarried, to Roscoe Metzger, she still called Florence "Mother Harding," and Florence signed her letters, "lovingly mother," writing honestly of the physical toll being First Lady really took on her. There were even faint memories of Marshall's life—and debts: "I note your reference to Christmas greeting from Mr. Barry, of Denver. It took me back to the time when we had the difficult tangle out there to straighten out, but we made the best of a tangled situation." Although she maintained a regular correspondence with her two brothers, they seemed to be more problematic than supportive. Cliff usually wrote querulous notes about the high cost of repairs on their jointly held properties and fears for her health, while her affectionate contact with Tal was underlined with her concerns about his intermittent alcoholism.[19]

The nation of course knew nothing of her strained family problems and the fact that they were not encouraged to join the Washington home circle. Instead the Duchess played out the revival of prewar life in public, a widely recognized symbol of the "return to normalcy" whose "open door policy" made more easily comprehensive newspaper copy than any policy Warren might initiate. "Every other gossip tells you that President Harding comes from Main Street and repeats the story of Mrs. Harding saying: 'We're just folks.' If President Harding is a fair sample of Main Street, Sinclair Lewis has not told us the full story and Main Street is destined to save the world." Such effusive words were written by the worldly H. G. Wells.

Not since Frances Cleveland was the face of a First Lady so instantly recognizable. Florence directly contributed to her own fame by sending out signed black-and-white photos of her White House portrait by Phillip de Laszlo for those requesting her autograph. One photo was even requested of her to be hung in an all-male business office since, she was told, there were "no other pictures of ladies displayed here except in calendar form."

In the giddy atmosphere of the Harding honeymoon in postwar America, the First Lady became a popular celebrity. There arose a Florence Harding chrysanthemum, amaryllis, daisy, sweet pea, pink rose, and a cross between the tulip and tiger lily. Composer David S. Ireland wrote a charmingly silly number called "Flo from Ohio," built on the fact that she had "some smile," better than Mona Lisa's. Her ubiquitous waffles were the lead recipe for *The All-American Cook Book*, among Al Fall's gingerbread and Doc Sawyer's Sunshine Cake. Mrs. H. C. Bush of Pittsburgh, new mother of triplets, announced in *The New York Times* that "the cutest" of the three was named after Florence. The Sunday Peoria *Star* declared hers the best celebrity smile, and D. W. Griffith named her face, and those of British Queen Mother Alexandra and a Pittsburgh scrubwoman, as the three most beautiful he'd ever seen. With the twenties vogue for psychoanalysis prompted by Sigmund Freud, the First Lady's character was examined by psychologist Harriet Robertson in a syndicated newspaper piece, on the basis of interviews and photographs. Robertson concluded that she had "probably missed her calling when she did not take up public speaking" and "might have been a writer of note."

The new First Lady had a double exposure to the American public, for not only did she headline her own appearances, but she was usually with the President in pictures and newsreels: opening day of the Washington Senators' baseball season, reviewing the Atlantic Fleet at Hampton Roads, unveiling the gold statue of Simón Bolívar in the corner of Central Park, dedicating the Lincoln Memorial. At their first Sunday services at Calvary Baptist Church the church was packed to capacity, with one thousand people unable to enter and waiting among the photographers on the sidewalk to catch a glimpse of the Hardings. Police cleared a path, and the President and First Lady passed through the throng.[20]

"It has been a wonderful experience to live in these exciting times," Florence confided to an aunt, enjoying the fads and trends of the Jazz Age along with other mainstream Americans. She tried the new Eskimo pies that became popular with the increased postwar use of dairy products. She cheered on Ty Cobb, who came over to give her "the dope" on a game. She even easily used slang like "Don't you just love it?," "deliver the goods," and "if you get me."

Nothing better pegged the Duchess to her times, however, than her fascination with the new breed of celebrities known as moving picture stars, whom she watched flickering in the capital's "picture palaces," which were being crazily built in small towns and cities alike. Usually with Evalyn, mostly at the nearby Keith's, she would take in matinees of popular hits, including *Orphans of the Storm, Merry-Go-Round, Hunchback of Notre Dame,* and *The Sheik.* She became the first First Lady to entertain guests regularly with after-dinner movies—much to Ike Hoover's disapproval. At one event for various officials from all three branches of government, diplomats, and personal friends, the Duchess had an advance Washington showing of *The Covered Wagon,* with a "special arrangement of music from the '49 days of the Pacific coast" accompanying it. She also screened *Prisoner of Zenda, The Naked Eye,* and *Deep Sea Fishing*—among many other films—in the East Room or on the *Mayflower.*[21]

If Woodrow Wilson had appreciated the possibilities for propaganda in film during wartime, the Hardings fully appreciated not just the power of Hollywood but the political advantages of associating with popular movie stars. Throughout their tenure they welcomed actors, long scorned as vulgar by "society." The record of the first actor invited for a meal with the President was on November 3, 1921, when the

Scotsman Harry Lauder came for dinner. Shortly afterward Al Jolson made the first of many visits, for golf at the McLeans', followed by a White House lunch. There was a visit by child star "Freckles," portrayed by Wesley Barry, who presented a bound volume of *Penrod,* the film version of which he starred in. Marie Dressler came, finding Harding "altogether winning." Evalyn brought her friend Tallulah Bankhead, the stage actress and daughter of a congressman, to meet the Duchess. Warren alone met the stunning starlets Hope Hampton, Viola Dana, and Shirley Mason, but Florence was there to guide D. W. Griffith and Dorothy and Lillian Gish on a tour and host a lunch in their honor. Asked to provide a fund-raising item for an Ohio hospital ward, Florence wove together Washington and Hollywood, politicians and movie stars by providing a pink and white quilt made and autographed not only by her, Warren, Coolidge, the chief justice, and the secretary of state but by many "prominent moving picture and stage stars."[22]

Florence Harding also became the first First Lady to "act" in newsreels in which she was featured as the primary subject. Movie films showed her unique wave with which she favored a crowd, waving not from the wrist but with a full, wide swing of her arm from the shoulder, like a stretching exercise. She would pull and push Warren into the right position for the camera or elbow him to wave. Whether planting a tree, mannishly shoveling dirt way over her shoulders, or whipping through a queue of Girl Scouts, the Duchess appeared regularly in the movie theater. She even tried moviemaking herself under Evalyn's tutelage, learning how to pace the cranking, and then publicly displayed her "art of operating a motion picture camera" by "taking movies of a group of women from the Potomac Park Civic Club" while she was caught on newsreel film doing it. Convinced by Will Hays, who shortly left his job as postmaster general to become president of the Motion Picture Producers and Distributors of America, to develop "a project to link the White House with the motion picture industry" the Hardings even began building a film library at the White House.[23]

If the unabashed interest in the movies by the Harding White House seemed permissible to those Americans who shared the fascination, there was less tolerance of the evil trio of dancing, smoking, and drinking there. Although the Hardings danced in the White House and had jazz music played at garden parties, they never danced to jazz, preferring instead the old-style waltz. When later Florence did a sort of Charleston during a *Mayflower* excursion for congressional wives, it was done for the fun of it, not as a serious attempt to dance jazz. "Nice people did them," noted Mark Sullivan, "only as an occasional stunt under special circumstances." Still, Livingston Johnson, editor of the *Biblical Recorder* newspaper, an established tool of the religious press, hit the Hardings on jazz dancing in an editorial: "Some time ago we noticed in one of our exchanges, for the first time in eight years dancing has been permitted and that the modern dancing has been introduced, the President and Mrs. Harding participating . . . setting a bad example by joining in the modern dance with its 'jazz' music." The White House deftly responded with indirect denial, not from Warren or Florence, or even Laura Harlan's pen, but from that of "Assistant Secretary" Coranella Mattern: "[D]ancing was merely an incident of a couple of informal parties and no modern dancing or 'jazzing' has ever been known there during the present administration."[24]

Florence's views on smoking became known when she was strolling with socialite Helen Pratt, who was smoking a cigarette, saw an approaching photographer, and suddenly grabbed Pratt's arm, and held it down. The caption for the picture taken flattered the First Lady's effort by stating that she was caught "accommodatingly catching the hand of Mrs. Pratt lest the smoke from her cigarette spoil the photographer's effort." When the photo appeared nationally, Florence was sent letters commending her no-smoking policy ("it has caused public comment in your favor"), criticizing any "distinguished man, no matter how handsome a face," who permitted himself to be photographed smoking, and asking her to "use your influence to advance the good cause" of a Woman's Christian Temperance Union purity fight to "overcome the evil habit." Without direct mention of Warren—or any number of her famous friends—Florence replied, again through Mattern, that the First Lady "does not smoke and does not commend it, but she knows a goodly number of people do. She appreciates the excellent motives of those who oppose the use of tobacco, but apart from her example in abstention, she cannot participate in the campaign of opposition."[25]

"You can get no quarrel out of me concerning the dry law," the First Lady wrote an old aunt who wanted "medicinal" whiskey, "but it is a law and the law must be obeyed, and surely your physician will see that you get what is necessary for your medicinal purposes." Such words dramatically contradicted her private behavior, for she freely served alcohol in the private quarters. Without irony, an unsuspecting reporter noted, "The enforcement of the Volstead law or the anticigarette crusade has not caused Mrs. Harding the slightest bit of personal perturbance."

Inevitably, whatever a presidential couple did or didn't do, they were criticized. "Oh, well, the Hardings are so popular they can get away with anything!" said a resentful Democrat. "But really, you know, he's the worst Executive the White House has ever had!" At least one editorial, in the Cleveland *Plain Dealer*, even faulted the Hardings for personally welcoming "every Tom, Dick and Harry who has a business mission or takes a pleasure trip to Washington."[26]

The most encouraging endorsements of the new First Lady came from some of her predecessors. Nellie Taft frequently joined the Duchess at the White House, and they sat together at many public events, but the great turnabout came from the previously frosty Edith Wilson. She sent Florence a cordial note, with hopes that White House life would be enjoyable, and she expressed a desire to return there to see her. Touched by this, the Duchess said it would "be a real pleasure to have you come by . . . without concern for other engagements . . . we do so wish [Wilson] a complete restoration and you the joy of it . . . looking forward with warm anticipation. . . ." In late March the two women got together for an afternoon tea. In some ways only others of that most exclusive sorority grasped the tremendous effort that being First Lady entailed. "My days are so full I don't know which way to turn," Florence wrote Esther Metzger. "Strangers, strangers, most of the time—but it's a great life 'if you don't weaken.' " One afternoon in the Red Room she told Kathleen Lawler, "You think we worked out at Marion during the campaign? Well, I want to tell you that that was not a circumstance to this. If anybody thinks this is just one lovely bed of roses, I can tell you that person is greatly mistaken."[27]

Sometimes it was not the entertaining that might try her patience, but particular guests. On May 18, 1921, at the Duchess's first garden party, 1,537 guests streamed through the east gate: the Cabinet, military, judiciary, Congress, campaign contributors, Ohio political figures, social figures, and the regulars—Evalyn McLean, Alice Longworth, Jess Smith, Charlie Forbes, and Doc Sawyer, even General Pershing, who was rather fond of the new First Lady. Slipping through the politicians, socialites, generals, and captains, sipping a squall in the "Colonial Garden," was one young woman identified on the guest list in a not-so-veiled manner. Her last name was correct. But her first name was listed with that of her daughter, who was also, she said, Harding's daughter. With ice blue eyes that missed nothing, Alice Longworth vaguely remembered after she saw this "girlie" out at Friendship that she had first seen her at a Harding lawn party. At the party, however, Alice did not then know just who was this "Miss Elizabeth Britton."[28]

25

"No Rumor Exceeded the Truth"

If the American people heralded their new First Lady for being candid and making the White House publicly accessible, the palace gatekeeper was distinctly disgusted. Ike Hoover's aversion for the Duchess, however, was based on far darker reasons than his personal disapproval of such a nontraditionalist and her modern use of the mansion he had controlled as chief usher for some two decades. Hoover knew what the public did not—the personal behavior of the President, his wife, and their friends, upstairs in the private quarters—and Mrs. Harding *knew that he knew*. Wesley Stout, who was first given access to Hoover's notes, revealed:

> Mrs. Harding came to dislike him because of his insistence on getting the names of all visitors to the White House, a detail about which he was meticulous, and that . . . feeling came to a point where only the intercession of Ned McLean saved I. H. Hoover's job. . . . That he found it difficult and often impossible to learn the names of guests and callers, and the destination of the President and Mrs. Harding when they left the White House, is evident in the daybook. The first names or initials of guests are missing, question marks are common, names are guessed at or such entries appear as "Lunch, 3 men from office with President." Engagement lists are missing. . . . Mrs. Harding, a dominant woman unused to such monitorship, resented it, and that one thing led to another."

That the Duchess would not want the names of someone like her astrologer or private investigator recorded was understandable; that she didn't want revelations about some of Warren's acquaintances or his excursions outside the White House became an obsession. The vigilance she had displayed about protecting his image during the campaign had only increased. She feared that assassination and blackmail threats—as well as devastation to Warren's public fortunes and her own—would result from too many people knowing of the drinking, womanizing, and other illicit activities of the President and his circle. Her reaction was to attempt to trail and control his every move. Even his Sunday mornings, once prized for golf, were commandeered by the Duchess for public appearances at church. "Well, Warr'n," she often snapped on his tardy return from a horseback ride in Rock Creek Park, "we just missed church again!" When he did make it to church, Warren confessed to the minister he felt "unworthy" of participating on Communion Sundays.[1]

Florence made no attempt to disguise her grasp. Mary Rinehart found her "able and intelligent" but noticed how the First Lady "resented his [the President's] relaxations, feared his friends; she was fiercely jealous of his reputation and of himself." Housekeeper Elizabeth Jaffray concurred: "She could be extremely impatient with the President himself." She was even angry when he spoke freely to editor William Allen White for a story: "Warren, why did he drag in that Saturday night poker game?" Poker, however, was the least of it. "Generally what worried Mrs. Harding," Evalyn confessed, "was her fear of other women."

Absolutely insistent at being beside Warren to "protect him" whenever he left for any announced "relaxation," she even irritated Evalyn. One afternoon, as the President was golfing at Friendship, Evalyn got a call warning that Florence might appear so that the two of them could follow behind him and Ned, demonstrating that they were part of what a reporter later called "the countless ranks of their American sisters, whose husbands worship at the shrine of the fickle goddess of golf." "Nonsense," said Evalyn, "she won't come out here on this hot day just to watch what Harding does. Surely she will let him take an afternoon off!" The Duchess arrived. Evalyn dutifully trotted along with her until she abruptly announced, "Florence, I have had all of this heat that I can stand. Let the men play and we'll sit on the porch.'" Warren then declared that he was so relaxed he "would hate to return to the White House." Evalyn wrote, "Into Mrs. Harding's bossy eyes there came a glitter. She spoke to him in a whisper; he replied in a gruff undertone, and she talked back. Then he began to criticize her dress, her shoes, her hat; it was a kind of fencing game with sharp words for swords. I tried to change the subject several times, to draw the sting of what I saw was smarting in two people's eyes. They continued to rasp each other at dinner. I walked ahead with the President. 'Evalyn,' he said abruptly, 'I'll get even with her if it's the last act of my life. Damn her soul!' "

Such scenes were common at Friendship. According to Evalyn, during a bridge game there Florence suddenly decided that her husband "had a job to do at Pennsylvania Avenue" and yelled at him, "Warren, you should be getting back to work." He kept playing, without response. "Warren, you really ought to be going back to work." Her lips trembled angrily; his brow knitted. With what Evalyn called "undisguised sharpness," Florence snapped again, "Warren!" Only then did Harding turn to her. "I am going to play all afternoon," he said, and then returned to the game. "Five spades doubled."[2]

If Florence worried about protecting the President and his image, he himself certainly did not seem to. As the manager of the Hearst paper in Boston stated, Harding, "liked a game of cards and liked the girls." Unfortunately, he was oblivious to the motives of his fellow poker players, friends of Attorney General Harry Daugherty and his man Friday, Jess Smith, in whose home the President usually played. As Warren's limousine drove him to the home and he walked up the steps, he could not know that standing nearby watching him were those seeking inside government influence; those men were brought there by Harry and Jess's influence-peddling friends, the same men about to play poker with Harding, as evidence of their access to power.

If his slackness about the character of his friends and vulnerability to blackmail ultimately exposed him to gross exploitation, neither he nor Florence ever profited from their nefarious friends' manipulations. Warren lost on the stock market, through one account he set up under Secret Service agent Walter Ferguson's name; Florence played the market herself but never sought insider information. Furthermore, she turned down the loans of houses and yachts from numerous financiers. Even critic Samuel Hopkins Adams admitted that she was "a woman of firm principle, of clear purpose, and of essentially decent standards, possessed of a high heart, a shrewd brain, and a rigid will."[3]

In the postwar era of Red Scares, with bolshevism solidifying its hold in Russia and labor movements growing more mutinous worldwide, the First Lady felt exposed to all sorts of threats, real and imagined; as a result, she clung to Barker. So fearful was she of strangers who had close contact with the Hardings that she ordered that none of the naval personnel on the *Mayflower* be changed without her permission, and if one of the trusted crew was transferred, she sent for the secretary of the navy to rescind the order.

Such anxieties triggered her fears of Marcia's prediction of the President's death in office. "I am always in a terrific fear that he is going to be hurt, that something will happen to him. That he will be assassinated or blown up," she told Evalyn. "You know how he hates Secret Service men, and he is always trying to get rid of them. Lose them!"

In confronting these fears, Florence searched for some method of coping. Traditional prayer did not calm her. Although she assured an aunt that "I have never adopted any of these new cults, Christian Science or Coué," she did let it be privately known that she wanted to meet the famous French psychologist Émile Coué, who led hundreds of thousands in "autosuggestion" repeating the refrain "Every day in every way I am getting better and better." Along with this search came her increased reliance on superstitions and other forms of the occult. Believing that the elephant was an ancient token of protection, she was often sent gifts of elephant items, and she followed a superstitious ritual of sending to the gift giver a penny for each tusk. Evalyn recalled that some astronomical changes drove her mad: "Did you know she was absolutely mentally disturbed when it was a full moon? . . . She would be perfectly frank about it and she said if the moon ever shone on her when she was sleeping and it was full she would go out of her mind completely. Was perfectly frank about it and was convinced of it." Inevitably she returned to astrology.[4]

Despite the fact that there was no further public notice of Florence's consultations with Marcia after the one revelation during the 1920 campaign, the meetings continued, according to Evalyn:

She was going to Madame Marcia, I had known about it for a long time. She didn't go through me. . . . She showed me one day a whole cabinet full of things [written predictions] . . . She didn't go [there] much [but] used to sneak Marcia up the backstairs and that is what burned her [Marcia] up so. . . . One day I went over to see her. Said that she had done everything for Mrs. Harding and that she had been made to sneak up the backstairs . . . that *that woman* [Mrs. Harding] treated her worse than any negro servant in the White House. I protected her [Mrs. Harding], but there was nothing she didn't say about her. "I just despise her!" She wouldn't have said [that] if she hadn't been drunk. I told Madame Marcia that she couldn't talk to me like that about Mrs. Harding and she said all right, but that she despised her.

On some occasions the Duchess did go out for readings—but not alone. Maggie Rogers recalled that since Mrs. Jaffray lived on the same floor with the Hardings, the First Lady often asked the housekeeper to accompany her. "She and Mrs. Jaffray would go to the fortuneteller in the middle of the night," Maggie told her daughter. "After her husband's friends put him in, she worried that they might use him. She would go to this fortuneteller to see what was going on . . . trying to protect him—all the time. She was in on everything. . . . She used Mrs. Jaffray as a companion, as a beard, to go at night." Ike Hoover's notes corroborated Rogers's recollections.[5]

Marcia later recorded her first visit to Florence in the White House:

> I was received in the private bedroom shared by the President and herself, for the Hardings rarely used separate sleeping-rooms. As I stood hesitating in the doorway of the big chamber, which . . . always suggested to me the stiffness and unfriendliness of a great hotel, I saw her standing by one of the windows, gazing out over the lawns. She was alone. Suddenly she turned, and as I advanced holding out my hand, she came toward me with a little rush. Ignoring my hand, she threw her arms around my neck. Her greeting was so unexpected that I stood silent and confused as she clung to me. When she raised her face I saw that she was much thinner than when I had last seen her, with a suggestion of nervous tension in her whole attitude that was rather startling to me. Her first words did much to explain it:
>
> "Marcia, I want to know the rest of the horoscope—the part you did not tell me! Look at me! Don't you think that I already know—or guess? That was what made it so hard for me this summer after the convention—when everyone was envying us and showering us with congratulations, and I had to hide in my own heart the fear of what was really ahead for us so that nobody, not even he, would suspect. You will never know the bitterness of it, Marcia—and something tells me it is not going to be any easier!"
>
> "But you are going to make that fight and you are going to win it, Jupiter. . . . It promises you victory—in the end, and a great work well done!"
>
> "But does it promise happiness?"
>
> "Happiness is always to be found."

The meeting was the first of many to be held in the Harding bedroom, as Marcia promised that a summons from the White House would take precedence over her *paying* customers—despite her private resentment that Florence didn't pay her. Nevertheless, when Marcia fell ill, a huge White House bouquet with the card of the President and

Mrs. Harding was dispatched to her. In a gift shop the Duchess even picked up a gold ornament in the shape of an elephant for Marcia, who shared her belief in the luck brought by the animal. "Looking back," said Marcia, "I think that our relationship was something to which she clung without questioning why, and that often it seemed to steady and strengthen her and to give her new assurance, for . . . she did know when they entered the White House that he would never live to finish the term." What Marcia seemed sure of, however, was that the Duchess didn't know the rest of the "truth" of Warren's horoscope, of betrayal by friends. And Florence suspected even less that she herself would be betrayed—by some of her own friends. Marcia's claim to now be at "the hub of power of the government," and Florence's reliance on astrology to direct Warren's scheduling was known within the government's highest ranks. No less a person than the chief justice wrote a friend in May 1921: "By the way, just as a bit of gossip, there's a curious little story going the rounds to the effect that Mrs. Harding is worrying a good deal. The tale has it that she is a believer in 'High Class' clairvoyance and that for a long time it has been her custom to consult one of the Washington elect of the esoteric circle. Some time before Harding was nominated this soothsayer, grasping at the obvious, informed Mrs. Harding that her husband would be nominated and elected President of the United States. That was very nice, and easy and comfortable to believe. But it is reported that she has consulted the prophet again, since the inauguration, and that the oracle this time indicated that the President would not see the end of his term. This is said to be preying on Mrs. Harding's mind. I have no personal knowledge as to the truth of the story, but got it from some one right close to the throne."[6]

Florence shared her fear of Warren's death with Evalyn, who told some of it to Alice, who considered it all "bosh." When the two women spoke about astrology in front of her, Alice was hard pressed not to break into laughter. In the first months of the administration the Hardings seemed palatable enough for Alice to make herself a friend, once even traveling together with them, the McLeans, Doc, Harry, and Jess to Ohio, although she felt it was more pleasant to be on the "out" list than "in" with the crowd. In some ways the Princess and the Duchess were similar, certainly when it came to ambition for their husbands' prestige. The only time Evalyn ever saw Alice cry was when a negative editorial about Nick appeared in the Cincinnati *Enquirer.* When it came to their husbands' adultery, however, Alice responded to the hurt with a dramatic difference. It was during Evalyn's 1921 Easter brunch that she began her own adultery. Alice left the table to walk in the woods with Senator Borah, and the place went "a-buzz," said Evalyn, who called after her, "Alice, you are a fool. You are hurting your reputation. . . . He is going to get you in trouble." Alice retorted, "I am a Longworth. I can do as I please. You ask Nick if I can't." At this Nick exploded at Alice, "God damn the day I ever married you. I have succeeded not because of you but in spite of you." The next day, at the White House Easter egg roll, Alice told Evalyn, "I am absolutely independent now and I am going my own way."

Certainly having damaged the reputation of her marriage and perhaps her chance of ever becoming First Lady herself, Alice turned some of her frustrated bitterness toward her supposed best friend. Ned warned Evalyn, "Alice Longworth doesn't like you. She doesn't know what loyalty means. You think she likes you. She is jealous of you. She likes you only because of the *Washington Post* and the *Cincinnati Inquirer*."

Evalyn's need for loyalty, for one true intimate friend, however, had been found in the Duchess. And Alice was painfully aware of it. Her resentment of Florence for this was undoubtedly coupled with jealousy of the attention that the President's wife had stolen from the former President's daughter. "It goes without saying that Mrs. Longworth was the center attraction [at a White House reception]," noted reporter Constance Drexel, "that is until Mrs. Harding, released from duty in the Blue Room, came in. . . ."

"The Hardings never liked me, and I can hardly blame them," Alice later wrote. "When I spoke to the President my manner was condescending, if not actually contemptuous. . . . Naturally when they came to the White House, whenever they asked me I had to go. I went there to call on Mrs. Harding . . . a nervous, rather excitable woman whose voice easily became a little high-pitched, strident . . . she told us, rolling an eye that never quite met ours, that she had a little red book which contained the names of the people who had not been civil to her and 'Warren Harding' since they came to Washington. Those people were to realize that she was aware of their behavior . . . her pronunciation of the letter *R* . . . [was] . . . like Wur-r-ren Ha-ar-r-ding.' "

Still, Alice, in her bohemian prints, batik blouses, and trousers, and her cartwheel hat, and with her oversize bag with a copy of the Constitution and a dagger in it, came relentlessly to Harding garden parties, poker games, teas, dinners, screenings. She even called as part of an Ohio Daughters of the American Revolution delegation.[7]

Like Alice, Evalyn reveled in being a White House regular. Even when Ned couldn't make it—for example, at a dinner for the president-elect of Colombia—she went. She was popular with the coat-check staff for her huge tips but was snubbed as nouveau riche by old Washington society, a group that the First Lady snubbed in turn. When Florence drew up guest lists, she emphatically yelled to Warren, "I'm going to invite Evalyn again! And I know the roof is coming off!" In good turn Evalyn made Friendship the Hardings' *other* White House, always welcoming them, their staff, and their guests.

Florence loved Friendship, telling Evalyn, "I always feel that it is the nearest place to Heaven of anything on this earth. . . ." It was a wild place, where Evalyn's pet monkey grabbed a bottle of whiskey and spilled it on Harding's white suit or Coolidge played handball for Evalyn's camera. Throughout 1921, as she spent most of her leisure there with Evalyn and her young sons, the old mothering instinct came out in the Duchess. On occasion she took them to the circus and to a toy shop or for cookies at a Rock Creek Park teahouse beside an old mill. When Evalyn was away and left her infant Emily in the care of a nurse, Florence looked in on the child almost daily; even Alice had to get the First Lady's permission first to come see the baby. "After all, what excels friendship," Florence explained of her bond with Evalyn, "just real, pure, simple friendship?"

Evalyn often bought clothing for Florence. "Oh, Evalyn, I wish you could have been here when I opened that wonderful box," she wrote. "I think I shall wear one gown to the Speaker's Dinner—the other I shall await your coming. . . . I can't tell you how much you are missed." Florence frequently sent huge floral arrangements, small bouquets and boxes of long-stemmed roses to Evalyn, with notes: "My best love this morning," "Just to let you know you are in my thoughts all the time," "in my thoughts as usual." Limiting public speculation about their closeness, however, when asked by reporters about her conspicuous diamond sunburst, Florence never revealed it was a gift chosen by Evalyn. Their intimacy was not without the inevitable gossip that they were a lesbian couple. It was so assumed by Boston Mayor Jim Curley, for example, that he openly mentioned it to people when the Hardings came up in conversation. While their bond might be termed a romantic friendship, there was never a suggestion in correspondence or recollections of those who knew them that it was a physical relationship. Whatever sexual attractions Florence had, even perhaps with men like Barker, remained repressed.[8]

As for Evalyn's heavy drinking, Florence seemed to take it in stride. Few Washingtonians seemed to drink as freely as the First Lady's best friend. The homemade film Evalyn most enjoyed screening for guests was her *Water into Booze,* the story of how, "transmitted by a special machine wire, water could be turned into gin by the invention of John Barleycorn." The film starred Ned. There was even the proud night, she bragged, when "I took a Catholic priest to the speakeasy." After she had watched the Dempsey-Tunney fight in the front row, next to New York Mayor Jimmy Walker, a friend, Harvey Brough, had gotten her a card into the "toughest speakeasy," and she egged on a Father Cunnaham to join her, even offering him a tie to replace his collar. Before she left for Maine in the early summer of 1921, Evalyn surprised Florence by hosting an early birthday lunch for both of them at Friendship, with Alice, Catherine New, and several others in attendance. There was a band—Evalyn tangoed—and a tray of champagne, a glass of which the First Lady sipped but, characteristically, did not finish.

Beyond turning a blind eye to Evalyn McLean's flagrant ignoring of the alcohol prohibition laws Warren had sworn to uphold, Florence allowed herself a comfortable hypocrisy, as did the President. "Once, after he had sent for me and we had sat on the South portico of the White House, talking about a serious railroad strike, he wished to offer me a drink," remembered Mark Sullivan. "He, with Mrs. Harding, took me into their bedroom, saying they felt that since national prohibition was in effect, they ought not to drink in the ordinary rooms of the White House, nor offer drinks to their friends, but that in their bedroom they might properly follow their personal standards." Alice said that "the Cabinet member who did not take a drink when it was offered to him was an exception. . . . It was rather shocking to see the way Harding disregarded the Constitution he was sworn to uphold. Though nothing to drink was served downstairs, there was always, at least before the unofficial dinners, cocktails in the upstairs hall outside the President's room and guests were shown up there instead of waiting below for the President. While the big official receptions were going on, I don't think the people had any idea what was taking place in the rooms above. . . ." During poker, Alice added, "No rumor could have exceeded the truth . . . trays with bottles containing every imaginable brand of whiskey stood about."

Staff members confirmed not only that Harding drank but that he did so frequently. "President Harding was the only man during the four administrations that I lived at the White House who really drank enough to speak of," said Jaffray. "It was also President Harding's habit when he entertained men at dinner often to retire after dinner to the library or study and there play cards and have Scotch and soda served." Starling wrote of Harding's afternoon golf and whiskey. "He played most often at the Chevy Chase Club, and used the house set aside for the President. I kept the key to the desk drawer where three or four bottles of Scotch and Bourbon were stored. When we returned to the house the colored man in attendance, Taylor, brought set-ups, and while the players drank highballs I calculated the results of the bets and announced the winners. The president took a single drink, and when this was finished and the bets were settled he would say to me, 'Telephone the Duchess and say I am on my way home.' " Not only did the White House press corps know of the President's drinking, but some members hosted a private dinner for him at which alcohol was served.[9]

Apart from Friendship, there was a more notorious McLean home, however, where not only the Hardings frequently dined—and he drank—but corruption flourished. The house, at 1509 H Street, was where Harry Daugherty and Jess Smith set up their household for the first year of the administration, gratis of Ned. In the entry-floor office there was a one-way mirror, allowing one to look onto the street unseen but prohibiting those outside from looking in. Decorated by Evalyn, on the second floor, a main salon and back dining room were lined in buff satin. Jess's upstairs bedroom was in pale pink taffeta with a gilt bed, Harry's in chintz. At this same house, visited by the Duchess and Warren, Doc, Fall, and oilman Harry Sinclair, "there were quantities of liquor brought in from time to time and disposed with in the usual fashion," noted Harding chronicler Horace Alderfer. "It was here that appointments were made and deals negotiated. . . . As it frequently happened, appointments for interviews were made from this house rather than the Department of Justice offices." Charlie Forbes later confessed that some of his "best liquor was obtained from the private vault in this house and that all the liquor was delivered under the protection of the Department of Justice."

The house was strategically located two blocks from the White House, one block from the Justice Department and adjacent to the McLeans' I Street house. It was the most accessible of private homes for Harding, and since this was where according to Evalyn "he had all his ladies," he called it "the Love Nest." Evalyn often sent food there for him while "he would be having a party there with these women and she [Florence] would know it." Reporter Vylla Wilson added that Evalyn "had the passage closed" between the Love Nest and her own home because "she suspected that her husband was using it for purposes which irritated her."[10]

What happened in that house and its surrounds was to help shape the infamous Harding legacy. On the corner of the block Jess Smith found his favorite niche, the corrupt vortex of Harding's Washington, the Shoreham Hotel, where thumbs in pockets, the jolly fellow bragged openly to reporters, lobbyists, and political figures of his access to and influence with the Hardings. Indeed he need only be announced to make a surprise drop in on Florence and, according to an anonymous letter circulating in Washington at the time, "does a lot of running back and forth between the D.J. [Department of Justice] and the White House." Despite the fact that he was never an employee, a dollar-a-year man, or even a volunteer, he maintained a seventh-floor office in the Justice Department building, sent correspondence on official letterheads, used department stenographers, and sat in on private meetings with and had unquestioned, immediate access to the attorney general. More alarming was his access to all Justice Department files. With such importance came free trips, meals, hotel rooms—and many offers of cash in exchange for a liquor permit, a pardon or reduced sentence, a stock market tip, the inside track. Jess took them.

Later on, when news of Jess's casual corruption permeated Washington, many observers naturally linked his illicit kickbacks and bribery with profiting the attorney general, who was in turn paying back campaign loans—perhaps even the blackmail funds. Reporter Boyden Sparkes explained: "As he [Harding] moved into Ohio politics he had to join hands with a lot of crooks and became a little too tolerant. Harry Daugherty would say that he was taking money from people not for Harry Daugherty but to pay back the big debt of the Republican National Committee—$1,600,000. It's a lot of money to have to pay back after an election. There was great pressure being put on Harding—but they went into office owing that money. Harry said, 'We will have to get these things fixed up.'—that is where Harding would let his conscience be very elastic."

Of his live-in relationship with Jess, Harry maintained, "We kept bachelor quarters.... I had to have someone to look after me" and felt "I could trust Smith implicitly.... He handled all my accounts. He paid my bills. He looked after my material wants...buying of food—we had a really excellent cook—to everything in connection with our household that had to be done." Said Sullivan: "Smith was to Daugherty at once the object of his affections, the source of his solace.... [H]e was lonely. Daugherty had Smith live with him, his only companion. ... Smith acted as housekeeper and factotum." Alice Longworth suggested that the two men cared for each other, and Vylla Wilson stated on the record that it was "noised about Washington" that "Jess was a homosexual." Often insomniac, Jess enjoyed roaming Washington at night, and within sight of the house he shared with Harry was Lafayette Square, where men interested in discreetly meeting other men could be found. The covert method used to signal such preferences—a colored handkerchief matching a tie—was in fact a signature dress code for Jess, commented upon by many. Even what appears to have been Jess's arranged engagement to the relative of a Federal Reserve Board member ended disastrously when he drunkenly upset her—and she committed suicide four days later, Evalyn recounted.

There remains no evidence of Jess's having a physical relationship with Harry, however, and both men were devoted to Harry's wife, Lucie, who, when not home in Ohio, lay crippled by arthritis in a Johns Hopkins Hospital ward in nearby Baltimore. Daugherty's son and daughter both were alcoholic, in and out of treatment.[11]

Whatever they assumed about the relationship, the Hardings, the McLeans, and many of their circle considered Harry and Jess a duo. "The Hardings," Harry said of Jess, "knew him and liked him. He was popular with everyone. . . . He had grown to love the limelight in the campaign and had his picture taken several times standing beside Senator and Mrs. Harding. I don't think I ever saw a happier man than he was in answering my summons."

The one confidant Jess had in all his nefarious doings was his ex-wife Roxy Stinson, who was disliked by Daugherty and never invited to the Harding White House. Roxie later claimed that she had been sent twenty-five shares of White Motor stock by Jess and told to sell it quickly and quietly, that she saw Jess in possession of seventy-five $1,000 bills, went to "fight pictures" with him in Atlantic City, and she said he planned to make $180,000 from the illegally arranged transportation of the film. While attending a rehearsal of a show produced by a Joe Webber and "Field," the latter asked Jess about a pardon or parole for a Webber brother-in-law, a Mr. Solomon. When Roxie asked Jess about it, he cracked, "Oh, he is sort of a cheapskate and he wants something for nothing. We get a lot of those."[12]

Ned McLean joined Jess in his spying and damage control on behalf of Harding. On April 5, 1921, Harry formally appointed Ned a Justice Department "Special Agent of the Bureau of Investigation," with the nominal dollar-a-year salary. Ned had already proved his skill in helping handle Harding's blackmail problems with women. With approval by Billy Burns, Ned was also appropriated per diem travel and operational monies from a "Detection and Prosecution of Crimes" fund when he did a little out-of-town spying. That the President's friend, the owner of the Washington *Post*, was moonlighting as an FBI agent or that the First Lady's best friend often provided devoted wifely assistance to her Ned troubled neither Ned nor Warren, Evalyn nor Florence, Justice Department officials nor those *Post* employees who knew.

The line between private, illicit high jinks and public, official business was blurred by the McLeans and Jess and their spying activities on behalf of the bureau. In one clandestine—and not entirely clear—transaction, for example, Harry F. Jaeckel, a prisoner in the Raymond Street Jail in Brooklyn, New York, got a secret letter to either Evalyn or Ned, who then asked their valet, Martin Finn, to carry the letter to Jess. Jess passed it on to the attorney general, who requested that Burns take some form of action to help Jaeckel.[13]

Burns—still running his own private eye agency while serving as Bureau of Investigation chief—had a reputation for strikebreaking, intimidation, and flagrant violations of any constitutional rights. Senator Smith Brookhart later declared that the bureau under Burns became a private "government by blackmail." Harding biographer Andrew Sinclair said Burns served as "Daugherty's chief agent in terrorizing into silence those who knew too much about the Ohio Gang. . . . Those who spoke out . . . were immediately investigated by Burns' men in order to force them to be dumb." Even a Brooklyn editor was physically beaten because of his paper's criticism of the administration. "Those of us who were honest," said J. Edgar Hoover, number two man under Burns, "kept quiet about where we worked. We didn't want people to think we were crooks."

Perhaps the single most damaging decision made by Burns that forever haunted Warren and Florence was his hiring as one of his private eye agents for the bureau the master liar, forger, collusionist, and possible murderer Gaston Means, thus placing him within the Harding circle. Burns even attested to Means's deviousness in a recommendation, calling him "the most wonderful operator [I] ever knew." Evalyn was blunter about Means: "Completely different than ordinary people. Always in hot water. Loves to do wrong and love to brag about it. He has the real criminal mind—such a clever one. . . . The best crook I had ever known."

Means made it his business to discover the skeletons in the closets of the powerful circle he now entered. Although Ned knew and used Means, paying out some ten thousand dollars to him, Means in turn knew Ned's vulnerabilities, and could potentially blackmail and extort him. Means had the best gossip on everyone in town and let everyone know it. This included even those who seemed above the fray, like Treasury Secretary Mellon and Interior Secretary Fall. "It looks to me like old Mellon is in bad," Evalyn commented after a whispering session. "Means always said he could get him, you know. . . . Fall went over to the President and said that if he didn't get Means and Burns out of the Department of Justice that [*sic*] he would resign. And they made Fall placated—they told him that they did fire Means . . . but on the other side he was kept on the payroll."

With his status at Justice always vague, it was natural for Means to befriend Jess there. So close did they become that when Jess was too busy to pick up one of his purchases of some personal accessory for the Duchess from a department store, he sent Means. More menacing was how frequently Jess and Burns unleashed their sociopathic colleague to investigate dozens of individuals. Oftentimes Jess conferred with Means at the greenstone K Street house of Daugherty crony and Harding campaign aide Howard Mannington, now a lobbyist, who also ran the capital's most secure bootleg liquor ring from there, with Jess.[14]

Means lived on Sixteenth Street, walking distance from the greenstone house, the Justice Department, the McLeans, Harry and Jess, and the White House. He had innumerable cars and supported his wife and son in a style hardly consistent with that of a Justice Department employee. Julie Means knew nothing about his maintenance of mistresses in Los Angeles, New York, and Boston. "Say anything you can about Means," chirped Evalyn, "but you can't say he is a stupid man."

Harry Daugherty later bemoaned his official appointment of Gaston Means, blaming it on Billy Burns's strong recommendation. When, however, Harry was specifically pressed to declare as fiction *all* of Means's later printed claims—among them that he tracked Harding's continuing adultery for the Duchess—Harry Daugherty recused himself as too busy: "I have no time now to re-read the book in order to answer your question positively Yes." Means was a "human dog," said Harry, but of some of Means's claims, "Many things I knew to be true." He would not elaborate.[15]

In his shocking 1930 exposé, Means insisted that he served as a spy for the First Lady, to trail the President's adulterous activities outside the White House. As he did with all his wild claims, Means lied in details but told a general truth. While he stated that he personally consulted with Florence in the White House, received instructions from her, and reported his investigations directly to her, no tangible evidence exists to support these details. Jess, however, *did* have carte blanche access to her, and it seems certain that while Means may have done the grunt work, it was actually Jess who transmitted orders from and findings to the First Lady. One of Florence's most vociferous defenders,

Warren Sawyer, Doc's grandson, later insisted that while Means was not invited by Florence to the White House, he was familiar to her. "She heard everything about his digging dirt. She knew Gaston Means. He was friends with Jess Smith and the McLeans; that's how he got into that circle. She kind of liked that sort of intrigue, but it also frightened her. She was tight-lipped on secrets, so things he looked into for her through Jess Smith she never talked about, not even with my grandfather."

"Mrs. Harding and Mrs. McLean were very jealous women, and they hired Gaston Means to follow Harding and McLean and report on their actions," Vylla Wilson said. She claimed both women told her "that they had hired Means." Although Ike Hoover did not mention Means by name, his notes confirm that besides Barker, her Secret Service agent, Florence used people as "checkers on the President's movements."[16]

One shocking tale later told by Means was recalled as fact by Evalyn: the story of a girl being killed at the Love Nest during a party attended by President Harding. According to Means, Harding was only a passive witness to a large table being cleared so showgirls—sexually available to the male guests—could dance on it as a "stage." As the table was being cleared, several impatient guests began throwing glasses and bottles off of it. One of two sisters with the surname Walsh, call girls who frequented the house parties but were not related to Evalyn or the senator of the same name, was hit at the temple with a bottle. The President, leaning against a mantel when the accident happened, was immediately hustled out of the house, according to Means. Meanwhile, the girl lay unconscious on a couch as her friends desperately tried to revive her. She was taken to "a little side hospital," where she died, Evalyn related in 1935. "They had this terrible time because the brother started to blackmail Harding, so they turned him over to Burns and were going to put the screws on him, had him locked up at Saint Elizabeth . . . a pure frame-up job. It got all around Washington *before* Means' book was published. . . . They were having hell with that one woman. She was a dope fiend and everything."

Secret Service chief Starling also heard the story, though in his version the woman was killed by another woman when her throat was pierced by the slivers of a shattered champagne glass. Starling thought that since the police had no record, it did not occur. The police, however, did learn of some such event. Vylla Wilson was told by Nina Van Winkle, the chief of the District of Columbia policewomen, that Harding "had drunk too much, and playfully hit a chorus girl who was there on the head with a bottle and killed her. The girl lies in an unmarked grave in 'potter's field.' The bottle was a beer bottle."

It seems incredible that Warren Harding would hit and kill anyone, accidental or otherwise; it was more probable that he was simply present when she was accidentally struck. It may also be that her demise was planned, since any experiences she had with the President would represent the most outrageous risk to his reputation. Evalyn learned that the prostitute was being trailed by Burns's order, and she suspected it was at Harry's bidding since the Walsh woman was a regular call girl for Harding. Evalyn learned of her sexual services because Ned apparently also used her. "I used to try and stop Ned," Harry told her, "and called him down to the office [from the upstairs room at H Street] and told him to stop this nonsense." More incriminating, Evalyn said that when Burns "railroaded" the Walsh woman's brother into a mental institution, the President had approved the tactic. Indeed not long after the debacle he told Harry, "Don't tell Mrs. Harding and don't tell Christian." Boyden Sparkes thought "Harding was ashamed." Indeed, while Florence evidently knew of Warren's general adulterous activities, she must have been spared knowledge of the Walsh girl's death. It would have stricken her with a terror more severe than her reactions to Carrie Phillips's blackmail or Suzie Hodder's child.

Whatever did occur at the Love Nest was handled more discreetly than the activities at the greenstone house of Mannington, the lobbyist colleague of Harry and Jess's. Journalist Alan Hynd noted that "Earl Carroll, producer of the *Vanities* and other Broadway show girls, was entrusted with the job of shipping cargoes of blond bums to Washington on weekends. Pornographic motion pictures, some of them featuring a couple of dolls who later put on clothes, changed their names and became famous in Hollywood, were shown nightly." Despite general suggestions by association that Harding visited the greenstone house, no one ever specifically recollected seeing him there.[17]

Harding associates, from Senator Jim Watson to journalist Boyden Sparkes, feared the President's susceptibility to blackmail because of his adultery, but Ned McLean, Jess Smith, and Gaston Means, apparently at Daugherty's direction, sought to prevent such attempts. Evalyn later found evidence that certain women were paid for their silence by Ned via an open bank account with a large chest of cash. "He would take these great deposits from [one] bank to another," she said later, "pay all of them off in cash—women, so that nothing could ever be proven."

She also said that Florence "lived in terror with him," always fearing revelations of his affairs with women who could not be bought

Flossie Kling was born above her father's store on Main Street, Marion, Ohio, nine months before the Civil War began. (Schermer Collection)

With little brother Cliff. This first photo of Florence shows her as more of a determined miniature adult than a toddler. (Schermer Collection)

A gentle but depressed mother, Louisa Bouton Kling (Schermer Collection)

Tyrannical father Amos Kling whipped his daughter with a cherry switch, but also encouraged her business and musical training. (Schermer Collection)

The gloomy Kling mansion where, according to family legend, Amos made Flossie practice piano so long one day her fingers bled (Schermer Collection)

The teenage Flossie Kling about the time she became pregnant (Schermer Collection)

Henry "Petey" DeWolfe, the alleged father of Flossie's son, who maintained a common-law marriage with her. He died of alcoholism. (Schermer Collection)

Florence's son, Marshall. After Henry abandoned them, Flossie gave Marshall away to her father. (Schermer Collection)

The young Warren Harding, editor of the *Marion Star*. Struck with his virility, Florence ran him down into marriage. They always shared a room, but kept separate beds. (Schermer Collection)

Flossie Kling, about the time she began dating Harding and was supporting herself by working as a piano teacher. She then worked as business manager of the *Star*. (Schermer Collection)

Warren and Florence, Jim and Carrie Phillips, in Venice. On the ship crossing, Jim (*third from left*) and Florence (*fifth from left*) were ignorant of the fact that Warren (*second from left*) was rendezvousing on the quarterdeck with the greatest love of all his mistresses, Carrie (*fourth from left*). (Schermer Collection)

Florence biking in Daytona Beach. Despite the fact that she saw her father in Florida every winter, he refused to acknowledge her for seven years and waited another seven before permitting her to bring Warren into the Kling mansion. (Schermer Collection)

Florence's alcoholic son, Marshall, who was often estranged from his mother. His wife, Esther, grew close to Florence, but she was an absent grandmother. (Schermer Collection)

Despite the fact that she was an occasional morphine user, the millionairess and owner of the cursed Hope Diamond, Evalyn McLean, quickly became the most intimate companion of Florence Harding's life. Attending a December 1920 Senate Wives tribute to Florence (Library of Congress)

The Hardings, Nick and Alice Longworth, on the Hardings' front porch. Openly condescending to the Duchess, Alice lost her best friend, Evalyn McLean, to Florence and later attempted to destroy their friendship by revealing Evalyn's abetting of Warren's adultery. (Smithsonian)

Harding's Senate aide and mistress,
Grace Cross (*at far right*), in newsreel
with Harding outside the Senate Office
Building. Her attempt to blackmail him
with his love letters failed.
(Schermer Collection)

Madame Marcia, the astrologer who told
Florence that if Warren ran for
President, he would win but die in office
of peculiar, sudden, violent death by poi-
son. She came regularly to the White
House by the service entrance.
(Schermer Collection)

Nan Britton, the high school girl whose
crush on Harding led to a later affair
and, she claimed, to her becoming
pregnant at twenty-one with their
daughter, Elizabeth Ann. (Nan Britton,
The President's Daughter, 1927)

Harding's campaign manager and attorney
general Harry Daugherty (*left*), with his
companion, Jess Smith, who helped choose
Florence's clothing, profited from bootlegging during Prohibition, defused Grace
Cross's blackmail, and committed suicide—Evalyn believed it was murder.
Reporter Bertha Martin said it was known
in Washington that Smith was gay.

Florence pins a flower on Al Jolson during the 1920 Front Porch campaign. The gathering there of several dozen actors marked the first use of Hollywood movie stars in a presidential race and was fostered by Florence. (Smithsonian)

Florence Harding becomes the first woman to vote for her husband as President. With women given their first presidential vote, she was the first candidate's wife to speak directly to the new voters about their political responsibilities. (Schermer Collection)

In Panama, Florence Harding became the first First Lady to fly in an airplane. (*Left*) With the woman pilot. (*Right*) Suiting up. Doc Sawyer is at her right. (Schermer Collection)

Inauguration Day, 1921. The Hardings about to enter the White House for the first time. "I got you the presidency," she said to him. "Now what are you going to do?" (Schermer Collection)

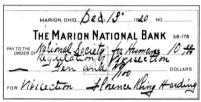

Florence Harding avidly supported animal rights and was a vehement antivivisectionist. (Author collection)

Florence shaking the hand of Laddie Boy, her pet Airedale. To their advantage, the Hardings turned Laddie into a twenties celebrity, authoring articles for the dog and sending him to events. (Schermer Collection, originally from *World's Work* magazine)

In the first White House tennis exhibition game for women, Florence Harding welcomes players. She advocated women's equity in sports, education, employment, and politics. (Library of Congress)

The first First Lady to appear in newsreels without the President. Cameramen record her meeting with women demanding Philippine independence. She even learned to work a movie camera herself. (Library of Congress)

Florence receiving disabled veterans at her party for them. She was responsible for Charlie Forbes's appointment as Veterans Bureau chief (*he stands behind her*), and his corruption was a wounding betrayal. (Schermer Collection)

Florence's political power met little public rebuke, but she was parodied in the above cartoon with Warren as "The Chief Executive and Mr. Harding." (1922 *Life Magazine*)

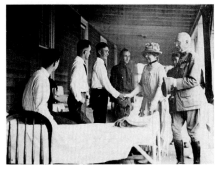

Florence greeting "my boys" at Walter Reed Hospital. Her intercessions on behalf of wounded Great War vets made her a recognized national leader of their concerns. (Schermer Collection)

Evalyn making movies of Ned, the Hardings, George Christian, and a Secret Service agent in Florida, 1922. On that trip, Evalyn let Ned fix Warren up with a society matron and a former chorus girl. (Library of Congress)

Florence and Evalyn in Florida, 1923. By now, Florence knew that Evalyn had permitted Warren to use Friendship for an adulterous assignation. (Schermer Collection)

The garden at Friendship, where Evalyn permitted Florence to burn presidential papers. (Evalyn McLean, *Father Struck It Rich)*

Warren and Florence in Florida, with Florence's Secret Service agent, Harry Barker. He became like a son to her and she trusted him to fetch Madame Marcia for White House zodiac readings. (Schermer Collection)

Florence's first large public appearance after her illness, addressing the National Conference on Social Work, with Reddy Baldinger and Laura Harlan. During this period, she spoke openly of her near-death experience. (Library of Congress)

Florence giving an impromptu speech in Indiana from the train platform during the fatal western tour (Marion Public Library)

Despite Warren's failing health, Florence relished being at the pinnacle of her national popularity on the western tour. She gives her military wave to an immense crowd at the Denver train station. (Ohio Historical Society)

Florence presented with native salmon in Alaska. Warren was already stricken with poisoned crabmeat in Alaskan waters. (Schermer Collection)

The last picture of Harding as he deboards train at San Francisco with Doc, Christian, and Florence (Schermer Collection)

Artist's rendering of Harding's sickroom. Florence was with him at the moment of death and became an accomplice to his negligent homicide and the cover-up conspiracy. (*San Francisco Bulletin*)

The President's widow, escorted by Doc and Christian, on the way to the funeral
(Schermer Collection)

Gaston Means, with his reputed "diaries," before his testimony at the Senate investigation of Harry Daugherty. According to Bertha Martin, both Evalyn and Florence used Means as a spy. Means wrote the book that doomed Florence Harding to a reputation in history as the First Lady who poisoned her husband. Some aspects of it were true—such as the burning of a suppressed book at Friendship, a draft of which turned up in Evalyn's papers. (Gaston Means, *The Strange Death of President Harding*)

Florence at the 1924 dedication of Harding High School in Connecticut. During the scandals, she said she was followed by a spy and that her phone was tapped. (Marion Public Library)

Nan Britton at eighty-five years old. To the end of her nearly one hundred years, she maintained a devoted love for Warren Harding. (*Marion Newslife*)

Evalyn McLean, with disabled World War II veterans at Walter Reed Hospital. She continued her own and Florence's devotion to wounded veterans. (Washington, D.C., Historical Society)

off. Yet even those who were paid still represented threats. Sometime in early 1921 Jim and Carrie Phillips returned from Japan to Marion. Although Carrie no longer claimed to be Harding's mistress and told Marion friends that she had also ended "marital relations with her husband," William Chancellor discovered that "She has visited the White House, not to the delight of Mrs. Warren Harding." Despite her ongoing stipend from the blackmail fund, Carrie had not yet finished getting what she could from her old lover now that he was President of the United States.

Her daughter, Isabelle, had married Count Helmuth Max Alfred Wilhelm Matthees, a German national interned throughout World War I in Florence, Wisconsin. In 1922, with Harding in the White House, Matthees was given his naturalization papers (he would later take the name William Mathee, Jr.) and just three months later was appointed to a post in the American Consular's office at Zurich. Carrie also wangled a federal favor for her brother, John Fulton, a textile salesman who was made a ship inspector at the salary of $3,750 a year. Having enjoyed Japan as much as she did Germany, Carrie hoped to return there in style. Now she audaciously pressed the President to appoint Jim minister to Japan. Harding apparently approved the notion enough to float it to some friends in the Senate, where it was immediately quashed. As Chancellor further discovered, Carrie remained a "rabid pro-German" and "a strong sympathizer with the movements to return all property to the Germans in America taken by the Alien Property Custodian and for releasing the German patents on dyes back to the German monopoly. Her husband has German financial connections."[18]

Other women received money—directly in cash from the President himself. When Ira Smith, head of the mailroom, routinely opened a letter marked personal for Harding, then discovered it was from Nan Britton, he turned it over to the chief executive, who raged at him, "I am President of the United States, but I also have a personal life. If you ever again open a personal letter of mine you will be looking for another job." It was not the last letter from Nan that Smith saw. Reading through a second one, Smith recalled: "The writer was calling upon the President to acknowledge that he was the father of her infant daughter. The letter was signed by Nan Britton. I let the letter cool on my desk while I thought it over and then I took it around to George B. Christian. . . . 'My God!' he exclaimed. 'If the President finds out we opened this he will fire both of us!' " Christian destroyed the letter. Two more letters from Nan were similarly disposed of, with Smith offering his opinion to Christian that it was a blackmail plot.

Nan still found a way into the President's mail pouch. Colonel Starling recalled that shortly after Harding became President, "a man who was close to him approached me and asked me to act as a go-between for some correspondence with a certain young lady, unnamed, in New York. I declined, pointing out that it was not my job and was a private matter which the President would have to handle himself. Later I understood that one of the other members of the Detail [Walter Ferguson] accepted the assignment, and on one occasion brought the young lady to the White House for a brief meeting with the president. This I suppose was Nan Britton." Despite his public declaration that he didn't recall Nan, Ike Hoover stated privately that he had "seen Nan Britton coming into the White House and leaving it after seeing the President several times." Others took note of her presence in Washington. As one of Florence's *Mayflower* cruises was about to leave, Vylla Wilson said, "an unknown woman appeared among them. The press ladies immediately began bussing [*sic*] among themselves inquiring who the newcomer was, and soon, before the *Mayflower* sailed, the new lady was escorted off the ship by the captain. She was Nan Britton."

Gaston Means's claim that he spied upon Nan Britton for Florence Harding in order to purloin Warren's love letters was not entirely a fabrication. It seemed based on a true incident between Nan and Ned McLean at the *Post*. Evalyn recalled, "You know he had a scene in the *Washington Post* one night. Nan Britton had some letters of Harding's. Ned did all the dirty work. He was to get the letters from her. So when she came up to the office he ripped the front right out of her blouse [where she hid some]. But she was smart. She had some others that she didn't have with her [that night]. I have also heard that he hit her. That he was going to be sued."

One of the encounters that Nan herself later chronicled in detail was a visit she made to the President's office, where she said they had a tryst in a large closet, the sitting room actually, adjoining the Oval Office. Still, she complained that she could not understand why Warren made no attempt to see "their" child, although he continued to provide Nan with gifts of cash, several hundred dollars at a time.[19]

Grace Cross's attempts at blackmail had lost their steam after Bertha Martin grabbed the small stack of Harding letters from her at their inauguration day lunch. Vylla Wilson doubted that Harding "had anything whatsoever to do with Grace Cross after [the] inauguration." Still, by continuing to talk of her past relationship with the President, she was a threat to his reputation. Thus in the summer of 1921 and on numerous other occasions she was given the Carrie Phillips treatment—

without the cash. Grace Cross was sent to Europe on an all-expense paid voyage evidently financed by funds given to Bertha Martin, who went with her, although now serving as the *Post's* society editor. That Bertha could take off whenever she wanted from the *Post* would not be a problem for her as an employee of Ned. That she could afford the trip was undoubtedly not a problem with cash from the blackmail fund.

Grace Cross did, however, have an indirect impact on a political decision by President Harding, affecting a Justice Department case. As Mark Sullivan recorded in his diary:

> I met Tumulty in Shoreham Hotel. He told me this: When Harding was Senator, he met a Mrs. Cross. After the nomination and during the campaign, it came to Tumulty's attention that Mrs. C. had some compromising letters from H. Tumulty reported it to Albert Fall. Also Tumulty spoke to Burns (W. J.) and Mrs. Cross was run out of town! Tumulty arranged this through Palmer, who was then Att. Gen. Mrs. Cross, to prove intimacy with Harding, said, "I can describe a birthmark on his back!" She also said that H. once had a heart attack going up the stairs to her apartment. Later, during Harding's administration, they were going to indict Palmer & Orian. The latter had Frank Hogan as their lawyer. Hogan told Tumulty he went to Harding and reminded Harding of how friendly Palmer had been in the matter of Mrs. C. Harding said, "Good God, must I always be followed by that!" Hogan told Harding that Orian and Palmer were innocent and ought not to be indicted. Tumulty said H. sent for Daugherty and had the prosecution dropped. Tumulty thought Harding ought to have given him some little but honorary appointment in return for his kindness in not, as a Democrat, having taken advantage of the Cross matter.

The so-called "birthmark" on Harding's back may in fact have been Grace Cross's reference to the cut she allegedly inflicted on his back with a cut glass during one of their arguments.

It is almost certain Florence knew about Warren's extramarital affair with Grace Cross, if not until some years after the fact. At the least the Duchess knew that this Harding mistress had been under surveillance. During 1924 congressional hearings on Justice Department illegalities, when Senator Burton Wheeler asked Director Burns's confidential secretary, Jessie Duckstein, "Who else did Jess Smith have Means investigating, do you know?" she replied, "Well, I remember a Mrs. Cross." The senator did not publicly ask why, sparing Harding's public reputation, but Florence would have recalled Grace from the Senate office.[20]

Innumerable other women were evidently paid off in small amounts out of the blackmail fund, in exchange for signed affidavits disclaiming rumors of their liaisons with the President. One of these involved the alleged "illegitimate son of the President" resulting from a night's dalliance with a Rosa Cecelia Hoyle, a maid of Spanish ancestry originally from Long Beach, California. With funds, again apparently from the open account, the boy's adoption was said to have been arranged by Carrie Phillips with a family friend. Another affidavit was signed by Augusta Cole, the woman for whose pregnancy and termination of it Warren was responsible, according to William Chancellor. A third was signed by a Ruby Evelyn Randall, about whom no information survives. The affidavits signed by Hoyle, Cole, and Randall came into the hands of Doc Sawyer, who sent copies to the Duchess.[21]

If her reaction to Carrie Phillips's now actually coming into the White House is unrecorded, the Duchess did not miss a beat when it came to women of the past. If she would not respond personally to a letter from "Miss Lutie H. Wheeler" but rather have her secretary do so, the woman's connection to Florence's past was fresh: Underneath the secretarial signature, she boldly wrote "Lutie Hodder," underlined it twice, and decided not to have the letter sent to the niece of Warren's first paramour. To what degree Florence knew details of Warren's ongoing infidelities is uncertain, but she generally seemed to act in denial of any of it, at least on the face of things. When Evalyn sent the Hardings an anniversary gift, Florence told her, "I could wish no more for you and Ned but that you may have as many happy years as we have had together, and as many more on top of that as you could want." Daugherty claimed he "never heard her express a word of suspicion or jealousy about another woman." Even a cousin felt he could joke to her that his mother's love of Harding *"is like that of all women!"* The degree to which Warren was involved with a woman, from love affair to flirtation, seemed to matter less to Florence than the potential for havoc it could wreak on his presidency and consequently on her own efforts.

Around Washington there were subtle suggestions of Harding's habits. Ike Hoover noted that this chief executive "was a sporting ladies' man," a "sporting lady" then being a euphemism for call girl. Starling said simply "he was weak." Around the Washington *Post*, stories of the President's habits were not only common knowledge but sometimes personal experience. Bertha Martin hired a young assistant, a Miss Allicot, who, Vylla Wilson said, "gave the impression that she, Allicot, had slept with Harding." Harding friend Gus Karger blurted in a newspaper that Florence could be "prompted merely by the ordinary suspicions of the wifely person who understands the nature of her husband and distrusts the sincerity of his promises to be good and obedient." Several times the Louisville *Courier-Journal*'s Daisy Fitzhugh Ayres reported that "the President is handsome" and "something of a looker" and even that the First Lady didn't want Warren "to miss seeing the pretty ladies" yet snapped, "I married my husband for his brains." Regardless of what the press knew, however, it never reported any presidential adultery, respecting a zone of privacy, as it was to do for some six more decades. Warren was on essentially safe ground. Before a National Press Club gathering of reporters, he joked, "It is a good thing I am not a woman. I would always be pregnant. I cannot say no."[22]

According to Ike Hoover, "Harding hated to have them [Secret Service] around, for he despised being watched." Eventually he seemed to work out an understanding of sorts with agent Walter "Fergy" Ferguson, who became personally, doggedly loyal to Harding and was willing to explain the President's whereabouts to Florence if necessary. When Agent Jim Sloan was unable to whisk Nan Britton in to see Harding, Ferguson assumed the task. Florence, however, had equal loyal devotion from Barker, a man who appealed to her, as Evalyn noted: "She had the most beautifully complete Secret Service agent at her command I have ever seen." Barker often tipped off Florence when Warren seemed suspiciously occupied.[23]

If over the years the Duchess had learned to endure, if not ignore, Warren's womanizing, she herself was not entirely immune to flirtatious flattery from other men. "If you ever meet Mrs. Harding," said one writer, "don't toady to her or try to flatter her. If you do she will not like you at all, for she has a strong aversion to 'lion hunters,' and other insincere persons who 'bow and scrape.' " This was ironic coming from a woman whose husband toadied to the Duchess, bowed and scraped: Charlie Forbes. Like him, Kate Forbes was cashing in on her proximity to power, writing a series of free-lance articles on the Duchess that appeared in national newspapers. With her weakness for vanity pieces, Florence gave Kate free rein.

Florence fell easily for Charlie's charms, even allowing him to call her Duchess. Vylla Wilson recalled that Forbes always "had a sort of red face as though he had been drinking too much," but the First Lady seemed not to mind. "How about a drink for a thirsty hombre?" he often greeted her flirtatiously. She returned the coyness, quivering her colored feather fan at one reception and whispering, "Good evening,

Charlie, I've talked with so many people today I can't tell you whether you are a general or a civilian." Investigative reporter Carl Dickey wrote that Forbes "had a disarming native charm, an air of plausibility and sincerity, and a way of convincing the most skeptical of his critics on any point on which they disagreed with him."

One person was unconvinced. Evalyn found him fatuous and was immediately suspicious of his motives:

> One day, we were talking, upstairs in the White House, about this and that, and she [Florence] spoke of Colonel Forbes of the Veterans Bureau. She spoke about him with such enthusiasm that I decided I would have to meet him. Not long afterward I had him out at Friendship and saw to it that the butler offered him plenty of whiskey. Forbes talked and bragged until it was revealed to me that he was not likely to do much good to the Harding Administration. Within a night or two, at dinner, I told Harding some of what I knew of Forbes, things I had heard. Some of it was based on the man's own boasting. Anyway, I said to Harding, "He is not loyal to you." "Evalyn, I can't believe it. Anyway I won't turn on a friend because of gossip. This stuff you've heard—forget it." I was so sure, I brought up the subject with Mrs. Harding but she was more set than her husband where Forbes was concerned. She became downright angry with me and for ten days or so we saw nothing of each other. . . . Forbes, beyond all doubt, had been grafting from the millions placed in his custody for the sick and injured veterans. It was malfeasance of a peculiarly low kind; Forbes had been a high official of the American Legion.[24]

Evalyn was a vortex for the Ohio Gang, but if she correctly sensed that Charlie Forbes boded ill for the Hardings, she, along with Florence, remained blind to the morally reprehensible Interior Secretary Albert Fall, lavishing him with social attention. Attorney General Daugherty was not fooled. During the transition he was understandably alarmed when he discovered a telegram under his signature—forged by Fall— had been sent to Harding. In a letter to Fall from his spurned colleague Charles Hunt, kept in a confidential Bureau of Investigation file on Fall, Harry learned disturbing details about the interior secretary: Hunt had lent Fall twenty-five hundred dollars to buy votes in his Senate campaign; Fall had helped in a plan in which a man named A. J. Fountain and his nine-year-old son were murdered; Fall had tried a man for another murder knowing that the accused had not committed it. Hunt was livid at "the high moral attitude which you have assumed since your elevation" and reminded Fall of a night at the Waldorf when Fall rapidly consumed a full bottle of scotch left by Hunt, demanded a check for five hundred dollars from Hunt to cover expenses at a "swell resort" suggested by the house detective. He also recollected for Fall how he, Hunt, had "paid for the transportation of our housekeeper and that you slept with her from Chicago to El Paso then offered to take her to Mexico but she refused because you were too 'short' to interest her."[25]

Still, Harding entirely trusted Fall. When, for example, just two months after the inaugural, Fall proposed the transfer of naval oil and gas reserves from the Navy Department to his Interior Department— with Navy Secretary Denby's compliance, but with opposition from various Navy officials—Harding issued an executive order to that effect. Such a transfer permitted Fall to take government bids—without competitive bidding—on leases from private oil companies that might be interested in drilling the flatlands where oil from adjacent government land was being lost through leakage. With Fall's connections to big oil interests, his lack of moral rectitude in any—let alone government— ethics, and his ambition to enlarge and improve his own real estate in New Mexico, the situation was ripe for corruption.

Fall brought several of his oil friends to the Harding poker table. One such fellow, one of the world's wealthiest oilmen, was Harry Sinclair, a robust, bald self-made millionaire, squat and friendly with the look of a toad. Part owner of a baseball team, producer of a Kentucky Derby winner, for some time "Sinco," as his friends called him, had eager ambitions on leasing the government oil reserves. Sinco had contributed to the Harding campaign and had a passing acquaintance with Daugherty. In a short time Sinclair grew close enough to the Hardings to be invited as an overnight guest several times at the White House and soon became party to the most infamous of Harding administration scandals.

During Sinco's first visit, for poker, another invited guest, Charlie Forbes, sat with the First Lady for some two hours, "talking with her about people and affairs in Washington," when Sinco appeared, and the Duchess introduced them. "It was perhaps a month after Sinclair's first visit when he was there again," recalled Forbes, "and the day after his second visit President Harding told me that the Interior Department was reaching out for a lot more 'territory.' I asked him what he meant by 'territory.' He told me that he meant certain oil lands. . . . In my opinion President Harding acted against his better judgment when he signed the famous executive order transferring the control of the oil reserve from the Navy to the Interior department. He was very easy to impress. Fall put it over on him." In coming months, when questions about Fall's secret leasing of the federal oil reserve in Wyoming to Sinclair Oil were first raised, Sinco's friendship with both Florence and Warren certainly prevented either of them from doubting the credibility of the deal.

Sinco was among the men of nonofficial life whom the Duchess came to know on a personal basis. It was at the poker games, a "combined social and political gathering," noted Charles Hard, that she most frequently gathered her intelligence, when she came in to chat up a little politics with Warren's political and personal cronies. Here, said Robert Small, she was "always at home and thrice welcome in the society of the President's own circle of pals." Frequently she still mixed the first round of drinks for the "gang," among the regulars being Harry and Jess, Doc Sawyer, Charlie Forbes, Albert Fall, and Sinco. Much of the same group gathered at Friendship—without the Hardings, but with Vice President Coolidge and Secretary of State Hughes—to watch the illegally transported film of the Carpentier-Dempsey prizefight, "not . . . one bit less legal than the wine and whiskey that experience told us, our guests would freely drink," Evalyn noted. When an honest Department of Justice official got wind of this, Burns blocked any investigation. "Who would worry much when one's close friends included the President and the Attorney General?" she mused.[26]

At times, the McLeans' Belmont Farm in Virginia proved more of a respite from such shenanigans than Friendship for the Duchess, and she usually spent weekends there in the spring of 1921, often with Warren. Yet even there, they were not left entirely alone with the McLeans. If Florence always went with Warren, then Doc always went too. "Dr. Sawyer is the only man in the world who can really help my wife," said the President. "I am happy he can be near us." Doc openly reveled in his indispensability, desperately seeking to prove his insider status at every turn, once trying to impress reporter Bascom Timmons by revealing the odd confidence that Warren Harding had *three* testicles. Timmons passed this curiosity around his news service office, recalled reporter William MacKay.

Doc had his own secrets. Despite the domestic picture he and Mandy presented from their suite high atop the Willard Hotel, he was frisking through an autumn romance. The claim of the ubiquitous Gaston Means that Sawyer was dating a "Mrs. Whitely," was, again, a pseudonymous truth. Doc's mistress was Berenice Blacksten, Florence's former maid, who now worked at a veterans' hospital at Perryville, Maryland, at an annual salary of forty-five hundred dollars and perhaps free living quarters. Doc was none too careful about covering the relationship. A White House colleague saw him, "arm-in-arm with Mrs. Blackstone [*sic*] walking through the station. They did not see me." Because Sawyer often phoned her, Sergeant John Mattison at Perryville also "knows to whom he [Doc] talks" and told Arthur Brooks, the President's valet. Whether Florence knew of the affair between her doctor and former maid is unclear, but she may very well have been the spur to having Jess Smith direct Means to spy on Sawyer and Blacksten. That Smith and Means kept tabs on Doc and Berenice was a fact that became public knowledge in later congressional investigations into the Justice Department.

Doc's pomposity irritated everyone around the White House, and Hoover said he was "not particularly popular except with the First Lady." The first hot day that the little man appeared in his heavy formal uniform with its honorary medals, White House cameramen asked him to keep walking around. "After about fifteen minutes, while he was panting but still game," recalled Ira Smith, "I asked one of the boys why they were wasting so much film on him. 'Hell, we're just having fun,' he replied. 'Nobody's had any film in his camera since the first shot. But we like to see him strut.' " On another occasion, after Doc dismounted his large horse, it began chewing at his beard, and the press was there to cover it.[27]

In her ambition for recognition, Florence had not only helped put her Warren into the presidency but eagerly encouraged their friendships with an ingratiating, flattering, and supportive circle, Harry and Jess, Charlie, Doc, Albert Fall being the most prominent of them. Neither Harding realized it yet, but these men had already put into motion their own agendas, setting the stage for the ultimate tragedy of their Duchess and her husband. Amid the Ohio Gang revelry, only the guileless Ned and loyal Evalyn proved to have no motive other than friendship. By the summer of 1921, however, the general public still knew nothing of the womanizing, bootlegged liquor, oil leases, fixed deals, or blackmail beginning to shadow their President and First Lady.

During the first summer of the presidency the Hardings had planned on visiting the McLeans at their Bar Harbor estate, Briarcliffe, and the McLeans were even delaying their return in the autumn in anticipation of a presidential visit. "I miss you dreadfully," Florence wrote her, with the news that they couldn't make the trip. Equally disappointing was that the trip to Alaska that Florence had been anticipating for some five years was also postponed. It had been briefly scheduled for the summer of 1921 as a presidential exploration of the region of rich natural resources but by June it was clear that work would keep the President in the capital. Instead there were mid-Atlantic and New England weekend cruises and motor trips.[28]

Moralists might preach that such "rootlessness of a people constantly on the go" would break down family life, but the First Lady found her thrill in motoring in defiance of speeding laws around the city. "Her highly nervous organization gave Mrs. Harding a liking for fast driving which sometimes made an automobile ride with her a thrilling experience," Senator George Pepper said, recalling a near accident at fifty miles an hour when her car grazed a telegraph pole and another car. She simply shrugged and said, "Close call." After another such incident she laughed off the Budget Bureau director's finger wagging, as he "took her seriously to task for permitting her own and other precious lives to be jeopardized." Otherwise Florence's favorite pastime broke no law. She was a vigorous theatergoer, taking in everything from humorist Gelett Burgess, dancer Anna Pavlova, musicals and comedies like *Kiki, Gold Diggers,* and *Bombo,* and the *Ziegfeld Follies* with George Jessel, Fanny Brice (who said her famous nose job was to bring her nose "back to normalcy"), and Will Rogers, a friend of Alice and Evalyn's.

While conservatives might protest the First Lady's watching scantily clad *Follies* girls or the Bolshevik-sounding Pavlova, she vigilantly but vainly tried to protect the Harding public image. Warren's idea of theater was watching strippers from his private viewing box at the Gayety Burlesque, but even with Florence at his side, as when they went to see George M. Cohan's comedy *Mary,* she could not contain his impulses. "Hey, John," he called out to a friend before the entire audience at intermission, recalled Starling. "How do you like the girls?"[29]

26

"Us Girls" and "My Boys"

"Since I have attained it," Florence Harding said in an interview about her role as First Lady, "I feel that there is a great duty and responsibility which I must live up to." If the Duchess manipulated her and Warren's personal images for the press, she was willing to risk criticism of herself when it came to championing social issues. That conviction consolidated itself into a commitment to use her power on behalf of immigrant children victimized by the bureaucracy, international relief, humane treatment of animals, equity in all aspects of life for American women, and her beloved boys, the wounded veterans of the world war. Sometimes her efforts were radical—supporting the "curing [of] drug addicts by vegetable diet"—other times traditional—aiding the "Big Brothers and Sisters" movement of adult sponsors for children in one-parent households—but they were always genuine. She would not lend her name to a cause unless it truly moved her.[1]

On "hyphenated-Americans," Florence felt "citizenship must be without such qualifications," yet she took on troubling cases of individual immigrant children. Reading about a boy from Italy who was being held back on Ellis Island because his entry would have overfilled that country's immigrant quota, she interceded, and the boy was let in. After receiving a desperate letter from a Savoie, France, woman about her young immigrant son, imprisoned for not paying a restaurant tab, the First Lady had New York's Mayor Hylan secure the boy's release. On behalf of young Russian immigrant girls, she even convinced Pennsylvania's governor to override an obscure state law calling for the destruction of aliens' pets. With the expected noblesse oblige of a midwestern Protestant matron, she wanted to effect a positive experience in immigrant "Americanization." After reading about herself in the *Carrier*, a newsletter for mostly immigrant newsboys, the First Lady wrote the editor: "I have heard that a good many people protest that boys ought to keep off the streets and that the work of the newsboys is demoralizing.

It has always seemed to me that boys in cities and towns are certain to spend a good deal of their out-of-school time on the streets anyhow, and if they are usefully occupied, getting some business experience, learning to discipline themselves, developing a sense of responsibility, they are better off than if merely seeking the kind of entertainment that the streets will provide." She also personally tried to imbue hope in immigrants, once coming onto the White House lawn to preach the gospel of the good life in America to gardener Patrick Doherty when she learned he was from Ireland.[2]

While she was willing to have a course cut from her dinners and donate the savings to the Chinese Famine Fund, the First Lady supported international relief only when it avoided issues of state. When prominent Irishwomen asked her to lead emergency relief for Irish families whose homes and farms were destroyed by the British military during the Irish independence movement, Florence demurred because her support could be seen as an anti-Btitish policy statement. When she did undertake a cause, however, it was total. In the aftermath of the 1915 genocide of two million Armenians, she acquainted herself "with the gravity of conditions," personally supported a child with monthly checks, and urged American support of the survivors in one of her typically articulate letters to be printed in newspapers: "From across the sea destitute Christian and Jewish peoples . . . piteously cry to Americans for the crumbs from our tables and the old clothes from our closets . . . to be saved from death by exposure next Winter. Have we not all of us something we can spare or sacrifice?"[3]

The Duchess did not let sentiment get in the way of a policy of which she disapproved. With twenty million people at risk for starvation in Soviet Russia in the first months of the Harding administration, the President asked Congress and the Army for twenty-eight million dollars and Commerce Secretary Herbert Hoover arranged for some seven hundred thousand tons of food, medicine, and other necessities in an attempt to save upward of twenty million people. In a confidential letter Hoover's assistant wrote that it was clear "Mrs. Harding has been one of the Chief's opponents of government relief to Russia. . . ." The First Lady argued that the Bolshevik leaders should have first recanted communism before such a large and decisive intervention from America. Still, when informed of the dire situation of one Leyzer Freidenzohn, an elderly Russian Jew who was trying to emigrate to America, she somehow determined to have the man located in Kiev, then traced to Poland, where he had escaped, and finally given a visa to emigrate despite the fact that his son's American naturalization papers had not yet been processed. "I know how you push things when you take hold," said the woman who first wrote Florence about the case.[4]

Florence had said that had she not been a political wife, she would have worked in animal rights, but as First Lady she proved to have an even more powerful voice. By 1921 such concern was part of a growing movement with the formation of a First Church for Animal Rights and an Anti-Vivisection Society, which fought to ban medical experimentation on animals. In a public letter Florence explained that her interest was not just about animals but about humanity: "Cruelty begets cruelty; hardness toward animals is certain to breed hardness toward our fellow men. Of this, I am very sure from both observation and analogy, the converse is just as true. That is why I am always willing to give every encouragement to humane causes." She initiated measures to protect the wildlife that were drawn to the White House grounds, and in the State Dining Room she ordered the removal of all the animal heads—moose, deer, elk, bear, and bighorn sheep—that Theodore Roosevelt had bagged and hung as trophies. That animals should be killed for sport and displayed repulsed her. The First Lady aligned herself not only with groups like the Animal Rescue League and Society for the Prevention of Cruelty to Animals but with the controversial National Society for the Humane Regulation of Vivisection, phrasing her support as "interest in the subject" with a "wish I could do more." She ate meat but believed that too large a percentage of it was consumed for food, and gave permission for her name to be displayed on the masthead of the National League to Conserve Food Animals.

The Duchess particularly promoted grassroot efforts to educate the general public through the Humane Education Society and its Humane Week activities: "I long to see societies organized all over the country for this purpose, and to have these principles taught to children in the schools." The animal protection community rallied around their celebrity promoter. One editorial, "Mrs. Harding's Way," in the SPCA's *Our Animals,* praised her because she "believes in being active in the humane cause as well as *merely approving* of it. . . . Cruel treatment . . . arouses her militant protest and on more than one occasion she has stopped on the streets of Marion and Washington to reprimand a drayman or cabby for abusing his horse. . . ."

Whenever pain was inflicted on animals for human fancy, Florence said that "it just makes me sick." She would use only ostrich feathers because they could be painlesssly plucked and "wouldn't have a peacock feather in my house" because the birds were usually killed first. She also steadfastly refused to attend Wild West, rodeo, or other cattle shows because she thought they were cruel, and she apologized for her outburst when a woman extended an invitation to one such show: "I hope you did not think me too abrupt about the wild west show . . . [but] in anything that pertains to animals, I fear I am apt to be a little too emphatic." She wore fur but was less than thrilled to be sent the "finest sealskin coat that has ever been produced" when she learned that the government controlled the Alaskan seal industry and killed thirty thousand seals annually. Florence's influence may have also affected public policy when she learned that the federal government had refused to interfere in the "slaughtering of seals in the rocks" by San Diego fishermen because the animals ate fish. In her inquiry of the Commerce Department's commissioner of fish and fisheries, she asked to "be advised" on the policy and left no question of her view: "It is difficult for me to believe that the protection of the fish requires the sacrifice of these seals."[5]

Several First Ladies had been active on behalf of specific causes. Dolley Madison helped launch a girls' orphanage, Mary Lincoln supported a relief agency for freed slaves, and Ellen Wilson fostered congressional legislation to ban local slum dwellings. The innovative activism Florence Harding had for constituencies of women and wounded veterans, however, was political, public, often controversial, and unparalleled, and unlike the work of her predecessors, national in scope. "Your position carries with it unlimited opportunities," a woman urged her on, "and your fearlessness is well-known."

Florence Harding made a conscientious effort to address issues affecting American women of the postsuffrage era, often by drawing upon her own experiences—as a divorced, working mother, business partner, and political worker. The adjustment to the postwar economy, changing moral standards, and increased urbanization were issues the Duchess thought that women could seize as their own, telling reporter Irma Skinner, "I have such great faith in the women of America that I think it is through them that order will come about after the chaotic condition into which our country was thrust as a result of the war."[6]

Florence said she was "particularly anxious" to bring women's organizations into the White House because "I want to help the women of the country to understand their government and their duty to government. . . . I want representative women to meet their Chief Executive and to understand the policies of the present administration." Leading those invited to the White House for the first time were "government girls" who had flocked to town to fill wartime federal jobs. With her emphasis on women's right to higher education, the Duchess also rewarded high school and college women on their graduation with invitations. These included not only groups like George Washington University's Phi Mu Sorority but also all the local Catholic school women students and their mothers superiors and sisters and, on June 7, 1921, the African-American women from Dunbar High School, the first time such a group was invited to the White House.

Theodore Roosevelt's wife had ostracized women she considered socially unacceptable, such as divorcées, by denying them White House invitations. Having personally experienced that sort of bigotry, the Duchess changed the policy. "I lived in Washington alone as a young divorcée," Louise Cromwell said later, thanking Florence, "but I never felt afraid to come by myself and accept your cordial hospitality knowing from that one gracious act that I would be welcome at the White House and I always left feeling better for receiving the kind greetings expended by you." Florence stepped into a minor controversy by inviting the National Council of Catholic Women to the mansion, liberals of the faith disdaining the group's anti–birth control campaign, conservatives aghast that women were active outside "the confines of the home." While she led a fund-raising drive for a controversial Columbia Hospital free clinic providing health care to low-income pregnant women, she did not respond to urges that she condemn Margaret Sanger's movement for birth control, for Florence herself had practiced it in earlier years.[7]

Women's sporting events and interest in physical fitness reached an all-time high in the Jazz Age, but many debated that there were moral, physiological, and emotional reasons why men alone should participate and compete in sports. Not the Duchess. She hosted a White House tennis match between, and was widely pictured with, champions Marion Jessup and Molla Mallory. Under the headline MRS. HARDING WANTS ORGANIZATION TO EQUAL THAT OF BOY SCOUTS, she wrote a remarkably progressive letter to the Camp Fire Girls, of which she served as president: "[G]irls need this kind of inducement to open air life and healthful games and occupations, quite as much as the boys. The part that women play in the world has been greatly changed even in my own generation. It has been broadened and enlarged and we will be wise if we recognize that a larger consideration for the health and physical advancement of the girls will better fit them for the role they must assume." To a Girl Scouts' convention, her message was almost militaristic: "Let us, as in the past, persist in overcoming all obstacles. No matter what the personal sacrifice may be, we must proceed with the great upbuilding work because the girls of America—and our country through them—need the fine, wholesome and stimulating influence of the scouts."

It was natural for Florence to support not only women who dared do as they wished but their right to choose their own directions. "She resented with all the strength of her forceful nature any encroachment upon which she conceived to be her own, or the rights of others," said Kathleen Lawler. "Girls worse than ever? No indeed," declared the First Lady of flappers. "There are as many wonderful women today as ever. Only this. Girls and women should strive harder than ever during these times to be a good and shining example to men." Besides her edict on short dresses that any "woman can settle that [question] for herself, and that for the young girl, the mother should be the judge," she believed that women should not be scorned for using any cosmetic.[8]

With a sense of what captured the public's fancy, Florence was quick to associate with popular women icons of the era. She jumped at the chance to dedicate in Washington a statue of Joan of Arc as a symbol of brave womanhood. After entertaining the Polish-French scientist and discoverer of uranium Marie Curie at the White House, the Duchess pronounced her a "very wonderful woman . . . [of] remarkable discoveries and contributions to science." Instrumental in getting her American sponsorship, the First Lady was given an inscribed book by Curie, breaking her "rule against autographs." Of Curie and scientist Pierre Curie, Florence reflected, "She has been the associate and partner of her husband in their great work of scientific research, and it seemed to me that their relationship was peculiarly ideal and of the sort that must point the way for all of us to the ideal family relationship of the future." She was less effusive when she gave flowers to Margaret Gorman, the winner, at the first Miss America pageant in Atlantic City. Warren held her hand and said she "well deserved" the beauty award, but Florence simply said Miss America's Washington *Herald* photos were unflattering.

In the glow of the postsuffrage atmosphere, the press and public heaped universal praise upon the First Lady for her emphasis on women. "A man's estimate of women depends largely on the character of his wife, and the President's unfailing generosity of spirit toward women is a reflection of you," one Alice Ann Waiter wrote her. "Working outside the home seems never to have offered a problem in the Harding family. It was evidently never a question of husband or career. . . . It was both," observed Florence Davies in a Sacramento *Union* editorial. The Philadelphia *Public Ledger*'s Robert Barry believed that Mrs. Harding was what "history must some day describe as the connecting link between the voteless woman of the Victorian period and the new American womanhood whose indomitable spirit symbolized the new woman." She may not have been as youthful, beautiful, or athletic as the snappy ideal of the new flapper, but Florence Harding was a realistic, if more mundane, model of the progressive woman who had had to work rather than chosen to. Somehow this translated for the public. For her part Florence kept her finger on the pulse of reaction to the status and rights of women, using such items as a profeminist essay by Eugene Debs—with whom she otherwise utterly disagreed—in defense of her views.

Economic freedom was one of the more relevant issues for American women, and again Florence used the White House as a symbol for the power of women who managed household finances. When the price of sugar became exorbitant and there was a move to boycott the product or at least reduce its use, the First Lady signed on. "You and I both know that there are a good many things that the women can do, and that nobody else can do so well. . . . You will have my cooperation [in] the White House kitchen to the last degree . . . [for] diminished consumption is the effective remedy with which to meet all unreasonable prices."[9]

The First Lady raised consciousness about women's fiscal responsibility by using herself as an example. She told the press that she bought the first fifty-dollar bond toward the building of the Women's National Republican Club in New York because "the women intend to handle the finances themselves." Her comment spurred some hundred thousand dollars in subscriptions. "After all, you know, I am a business woman," she told a reporter. "The conviction has come to me that every wife should know something about her husband's business affairs." Florence considered marriage a "partnership or co-operation of plain, practical responsibility." She expounded on this during the transition in a public letter to the Southern Tariff Convention of Woman, defending both a protectionist policy toward American industry and the economic enpowerment of women from even traditional perspectives: "Whatever tends to establish our people on a sound economic basis must be of the utmost interest to women, for they are the makers of household budgets, the managers of the homes, which in the final analysis are the end and aim of organized society."

Such overt politicking brought praise in a *New York Times* editorial:

There have been times, and not so long ago, when there would have been much shaking of heads . . . if the wife of the President publicly had expressed an opinion on a controversial question of political policy and had tried to use such "influence" as she had to guide voters in their action on the subject. . . . [It] would have educed grave criticism and feeling references to "the place of woman." But all that is changed. Mrs. Harding shows, and need show, no hesitation about writing a letter to the women who are attending the meeting of the Southern Tariff Association in Atlanta, or about revealing in her letter that she is with them in advocating and supporting the protection of American industries from foreign competition. This she can safely do now[,] for . . . hers is the pen of a voter—of a citizen with as much power as well as with as much right as anybody else to have and to urge her views on the tariff or whatever seems to her interesting or important. . . . [M]ore cautious than some protectionists, Mrs. Harding refrained from an exact definition of what she wants in the way of duties. . . . Not without acquisition of wisdom has she lived long in a political atmosphere.

Eager to help women who helped themselves, the First Lady assumed the honorary presidency of the Southern Industrial Association because the group of mountain women sold their crafts for their own education and welfare. She was the only Republican to join the board of Sunshine House for "unfortunate and needy women" who worked to pay board and room fee. In one of her more public controversies, she interceded with New York Governor Nathan Miller to commute the death sentence of a Hattie Dixon because she had killed her husband in self-defense. Still a woman of her generation, she believed it was more practical for a husband to support his family, if he was able to, than for a woman to get a job. When a woman wrote that her home was about to be lost because her husband was unemployed, the Duchess contacted a Marion industrial plant to get him, rather than his wife, a job. On the other hand, she thought that women would be respected as breadwinners in future societies. A sense of this ambivalence emerges in one of her remarkably modern letters to an inquiring citizen. It was one she ultimately refrained from sending:

> Sometimes I am not quite sure whether I am entitled to regard myself as the "woman of the day," being afflicted with certain ideas about the relations of women to society and particularly to its economic organization, which some people perhaps do not regard as entirely up-to-date. However, my own feeling is that since it concerns the so-called "woman movement" no harm will be done if there are some measurably conservative influences among the women. I am disposed to take the

attitude of one of the moderate conservatives. I confess that the family, rather than either the man or the woman, has always seemed to me to be the true social unit. In saying this I mean that I have felt that neither the man nor the woman alone can embody all the elements that should go to a properly proportioned career. It is perhaps a little hackneyed, but I think it is everlastingly true, that the man and woman, properly mated—and they should not be mated at all unless properly—are complements of each other, mutually helping, supporting and sustaining. I think we shall come to a time when it will be recognized that one "career" is as many as a single family should undertake. If the career is to be the husband's the wife may very well be content to merge her own career in that of the husband; and I have no doubt the time is coming when the converse will be true, and that it will be accepted that if the career is to be the wife's, as it undoubtedly will in an increasing proportion of cases, then the husband may, with no sacrifice of respect or of recognition by the community, permit himself to be the less prominent and distinguished member of the combination. In the inevitable order of things, I cannot but feel that most of the careers will always be for the man, but that is no reason whatsoever why the woman who has some special talent or capacity, the woman who is peculiarly fitted to gain distinction in literature, or in science, or in art, should not have the privilege of the fullest human and family companionship, and complete opportunity for the development of her special talents. Any other view would assume, it seems to me, that the woman of genius must be excluded from the privilege of a completely rounded and satisfactory life.[10]

The Philadelphia *Public Ledger*'s Constance Drexel noted, "There isn't a bit of doubt that Mrs. Harding will support the appointment of women to important positions in the new administration . . . she is heartily in favor of the promise Harding has made . . . that he will consult with women as well as men in shaping the policies of his administration . . . She herself would have the ability to occupy a very important position 'on her own.' . . . Has she not reached a position of greatest power and responsibility?" Believing that American women had "very great educational and intellectual service" they were "especially postured to render," the Duchess sought to place in the Harding administration several women whom she considered qualified. The best known of these women was Hattie Jewell Anderson, a Northern California single mother who had built a business out of door-to-door sales and soliciting names for political petitioning and causes. During a trip to the Front Porch campaign, Anderson had positioned herself close to the Duchess in pictures, and the two women hit it off as Anderson corresponded with Florence and worked for the campaign. She then openly lobbied for the post of receiver of public moneys, the U.S. Land Office, Department of the Interior for Oakland and San Francisco. "And now she is going to get her appointment through Mrs. Harding and over the heads of California's Senators and Congressmen, who didn't want her or who had other candidates," reported political columnist Edward H. Hamilton.

Anderson kept in contact with Florence, confidentially reporting to her on California Senator Hiram Johnson's "absolute control here" over local appointees and his reelection fight with the candidate backed by Herbert Hoover. "I am sure you will understand me without further words," said Anderson. "I do not feel as a traitor to either faction. . . ." She further revealed that in sending out the employees of her private business, which she continued to operate, to canvass for signatures for various initiatives, she had them give away little novelty gifts and in the process coax voters to reveal their political views. The employees, "alert to political news," recorded everything on cards. Such an enterprise "would surprise many people if they knew of its existence. . . . You can see that with a sales organization unsuspected as having any political affiliations whatever, spreading through the cities and even the country districts, just quietly making investigations, I would have an asset in times of trouble that would be invaluable." The First Lady's reaction to the report, on Interior Department letterhead, is unrecorded.

Ohio suffragist and political activist Mary E. Brown Lee was assured that she would be given a position on the state or federal level by the First Lady's power. "I have enjoyed all your letters immensely and they make me feel very much in touch with everything out there," Florence wrote her. "The position of State Librarian seems an interesting one with all the chance it gives you to get sound conservative literature before schools and clubs, and to wield a really wide influence . . . congenial occupation means a lot in the long run and if the library appeals to you the most, why don't you go right after the job and we will give you as much assistance as possible[?] You do not need to be assured that the president will be happy to find some[thing] for you. . . ."

In one situation Lois Marshall asked for Florence's intercession. When an important position at the Child Welfare League had to be filled, Marshall, a board member, wanted Ida Curry, a recognized children's caseworker and assistant president of the National Social Conference, to have the job. Marshall was told by a male official that Curry would be rejected, that a man was to be given the job. "I feel quite sure on almost anything where children are concerned, especially little children, and there are to be little ones in the institution temporarily, a woman's judgment is better than a man's." Florence agreed. Curry got the post.

On impulse Florence had sent a congratulatory telegram to Republican Alice Robertson, elected as the nation's second congresswoman, having won in the Second Oklahoma Congressional District. Lauding her "magnificent victory," Florence said that she "knew I could pin my faith to the noble women of Oklahoma to do their part alongside" the men. Again the letter was publicly printed. Despite her alliance with the congresswoman, the Duchess did not hold much faith in the President's promise that "there will be more women in public life, and there will be before my Administration is concluded." Florence believed that a majority of women would rise to elected political office only after working through the party system. She responded to one woman who had complained about the lack of women on the Republican National Committee that members had to be chosen on the state level, in the next presidential campaign year, adding, "I was very much interested in what you say concerning women's position in American politics. Of course, you must bear in mind that the entrance of women in the political world was so sudden when it finally did come, we must be willing to bide our time a little."

It was from the most primary level, the informed voter, that the Duchess felt that women would rise in the ranks. "Rejoicing in the enfranchisement of women," she said, "the particular aim and especial pride of women" must be to prove that being given the vote was "no mistake." Inculcation in political process was the way, she told suffragist Anna Churchill Moulton Tillinghast: "The time has passed for discussion about the desirability of having the women actively participate in politics. They *are* in politics, and it is their duty to make their participation effective, and of real service to their country. This necessarily means that much and aggressive effort is needed to maintain their interest, and to inform them concerning issues and public problems."[11]

Florence coped with the factions of politically active women with varying degrees of ambivalence. It was difficult to discern her core beliefs from concessions to partisan expediency, as in the case of the rising efforts of the National Woman's Party. Many Democratic and Republican leaders urged the party to disband and work within their parties to achieve equal rights. The Woman's Party was controversial: The core of its leaders had led the suffrage battle, protested outside the White House, been arrested and imprisoned, and pronounced "disgusting creatures" by Edith Wilson. They planned not only a national headquarters and magazine—to speak to "the interests of women not supplied by any present publication controlled by men or by the old-fashioned women's magazines"—but also "the adoption of legislation by Congress removing all legal disabilities of women under the Federal laws," to "put [women] on a par with men in all things." With the cry "Equal Rights and no quarter asked," the Equal Rights Amendment was being born in the first spring of Florence's First Ladyship.

In words and deeds, the First Lady seemed sympathetic to the idea behind the Woman's Party, if not yet the ERA. During the transition Florence had exuberantly accepted honorary membership on the Woman's Party committee to commission and place in the Capitol the marble sculpture of suffrage leaders Susan B. Anthony, Lucretia Mott, and Elizabeth Cady Stanton, "a gift from the women of the United States. . . ." Asked how she would react to women picketing the President for not appointing women committed to equal rights, Florence phrased her response diplomatically: "On impulse I should say I would probably invite them into tea, so we could talk it over. There is always a correct answer to life's problems if you take the trouble to find it. And what is true of life in general is true of politics in particular."

Unwilling to commit publicly to legislation her husband had not yet embraced, the First Lady still managed to suggest her support. "It is difficult for me to discuss the subject," she cautiously told a reporter when asked about equal rights legislation. "Really—anything like this should come from my husband—don't you think? But I want to say this. In my heart burns a great, a vital message—and that message is for women. If I were in a position to do so—I would hail the women of this land of ours. . . . Women can be a wonderful guiding power to the men of our nation. Let them not force themselves into man's place. Let women do womanly work in a womanly way. In all women is the power to inspire, to call forth the best activities if they will only use that power! Let women know and appreciate the meaning of being an American—free and equal." Ultimately the belief that the ERA would erase the "fallacy that upon marriage a woman lost her identity and submerged her personality" perfectly reflected not only the truths of Florence's marriage but her aspirations for equality for all women.

Generally Florence indicated her belief that the emergence of a Woman's Party and its agenda coming within months of women's first vote was premature and would place them at a disadvantage with more experienced men. She wrote that "the present is a most inauspicious time for a species of political solidarity among the women . . . the activities of men and of women should, and ultimately must, complement each other, in the realm of politics, precisely as the work of women and the work of men contribute in the maintenance of the home and of the entire social fabric." At the time of the National Woman's Party convention Florence joined the Women's National Republican Club, writing for publication not only that this group would be "useful and effective . . . for the propagation of the ideals of citizenship and service" but that "women citizens are going to be able to exercise a large and useful influence through affiliation with and continued interest in the work of establishing party organization."[12]

However, with her husband, Florence accepted an invitation made by their friend Mrs. Batelle—who belonged to both the Woman's and the Republican Parties—and several supportive Republican women to open and dedicate the headquarters of the National Woman's Party. This enraged the Republican National Committee women members who believed that this "third party" threatened the two-party system. They declared that a woman could not belong to both the Republican and "non-partisan" Woman's Party and were so angry that they canceled a Republican rally at which the President had been scheduled to attend, in effect, rescinding their invitation to the Hardings. The First Lady rushed to assure one such woman by backpedaling: "The President is not committed to any participation in the program and he is confident the situation will be so handled that he will sustain his position that women's highest usefulness may be exercised within the political parties." The Hardings "at the last moment were unable to attend" the dedication, but they released to the press the fact that Mrs. Batelle was their White House guest for several days.

Women of the National Republican Executive Committee, led by Ruth McCormick, lobbied the First Lady to join their adamant opposition to the ERA, believing the amendment would destroy legal protection of working women. Florence would not. She tactfully removed herself from the debate by rescinding her acceptance to attend a New York Women's National Republican Club meeting but sending a lengthy partisan letter to be read to one thousand women there:

> If I did not feel that the nation could, and in the long run must be, served best through parties, I should not be a partisan Republican. . . . These are times when the tendency to disintegration of old institutions warns us, on all sides, of the need to hold fast to those that have established themselves as sound, reliable, confidence-inspiring. . . . Surely we women will not permit it ever to be said that, because we came into the full obligation of citizenship, our contribution served to lower the

standard of civic responsibility. Rather, we must seek credit for raising those standards . . . maintenance of those purposes requries that we Republican women shall devote our utmost energies to that work of organization, education, and advancement which is so well typified in your own aggressive and efficient Club.

The President's meek letter merely deferred to his wife's: "I feel it is most appropriate that I should merely associate myself with the expression Mrs. Harding has made and should not present an independent expression of my own."

For stating her views, the First Lady was praised in editorials of party papers like the Waterbury, Connecticut, *Republican*. Following the disclosure of Florence's agreement with Congresswoman Robertson's contention that some Woman's Party leaders were too mistrustful of male statesmen, the Philadelphia *Public Ledger* praised the Duchess for being a "forthright politician and statesman." While her voicing her opinions was praised, however, what she said was not always universally lauded, the Meridian *Morning Record,* for one, claiming that the "hidebound men of the party" held the First Lady back from overt support of the Woman's Party.[13]

While Florence always defended the American political system and never seemed to illustrate any hostility toward men within the parties, she did believe that women must no longer take a subordinate role in government—in any nation—and that the many years of organized women's civic work qualified as political training. She told one such group: "[S]ome people incline to espouse the parliamentary 'group plan' of the European political systems . . . our institutions are not adapted to it. . . . Not only our own country but many others are making the experiment of full participation of women in political duties. Social, economic, and political problems everywhere are peculiarly complex and difficult. . . . I feel that the training they have received through the activities of women's clubs and the benevolent and philanthropic enterprises fit them for a part in political affairs in no wise subordinate to that of men. Women will bring to public life elements of human sympathy, or of understanding, of concern for betterment along social and moral lines. . . . These are not second in importance to any other objects which we may hope to promote through a wiser attitude of our government . . . as woman equips herself for the more thorough understanding of the issues. . . ."[14]

Her party loyalty aside, the First Lady strongly believed that the League of Women Voters was vital to inculcate the average woman politically, and despite Ruth McCormick's plea for Republican women to stay out of that organization—since it also advocated equal rights legislation—Florence refused to disassociate with them. She often invited regional League of Women Voters delegations to meet her at the White House. After one such group had come, McCormick canceled a National Republican Committee women's event Florence had been scheduled to attend. When McCormick then attempted to schedule a meeting with the First Lady "to go over some political questions with you," Florence broke with her and the other anti–League of Women Voters women, saying she appreciated McCormick's "fine work," but as far as her offering positive suggestions to the more conservative women, "common sense tells me that I would do more harm than good."[15]

Florence found herself more comfortable with women in journalism than with those in politics. Though no First Lady had done it before, she had hoped to make herself accessible to reporters in regular press conferences and directly quoted interviews. Edith Wilson had completely denied reporters any access or information, breeding suspicion. Reporter Ishbel Ross said Florence "tried for some rapprochement but feared its consequences and did not carry it far."

"I love the newspaper fraternity," Florence had declared during the transition. "I have talked with a great many of them during the campaign and since, and not one of them has ever betrayed me." Winning a campaign, however, was not the same as being seen to maintain a presidential policy of restricting interviews. As for exclusive interviews, the social secretary revealed to a reporter that while Florence was "anxious to show every courtesy to newspaper workers, especially those of her own sex, for she has a real fraternal feeling for them . . . she is under the same necessary restrictions which the president respects in the matter. . . ."

Despite the stated policy, there were more press interviews, as well as directly quoted ones, with Mrs. Harding than with all the First Ladies before her combined. She just couldn't help talking to journalists and writers she trusted, and so those particularly close to her, like Jane Dixon, the New York *Telegraph* reporter whose career Florence had helped, and Kate Forbes, the free-lance writer and wife of Charlie Forbes, turned out detailed, extensive interviews and profiles of Florence. Forbes was given several days of full access, resulting in a six-part nationally syndicated series running during the holiday season. The articles were flattering, with only the most subtle of intimations of the First Lady's marital woes. "Ladies, she understands your problems. She has experienced most of them," wrote Kate, "she has run the gamut of experiences and circumstances that happen to happen to some people only to broaden them."

Florence cozily referred to the growing women's press corps covering her as "us girls" and told one young woman about the wider and new opportunities for females in journalism by 1921, "You are in a wonderful profession. . . . Ever before you are possibilities to do good— to do the right thing. You are on the threshold of great success." The First Lady related to these working women more than she did to society women and especially respected the woman journalist because, as she wrote, "I feel that I am an Ohio newspaperwoman, in view of my past work experience and always proud of the advancement of my fellow women in a profession for which it has always seemed to me they are especially fitted."

Four weeks after the inaugural Florence gave her first press conference for thirty-six local and national newspaperwomen, at a four o'clock tea, the first such gathering of its kind. It became a regular event. Although she tried to persuade them not to quote her directly, they often broke the rule. It never stopped Florence from continuing to express her opinion on everything from delphiniums to suffrage, while balancing her teacup. By acting the role of the hostess simply entertaining the women, with whom she freely chatted, the Duchess was able to convey her views as she would in a group interview, but she could not be accused of breaking the presidential press policy. Where a "chat" ended and an interview began, neither the reporters nor the First Lady seemed to know, and depending on her mood and the political sensitivity of the question, the parameters were fluid. She enjoyed talking politics and social issues, but whenever she found herself quoted verbatim, she would again try to restrain herself. Despite her attempts to honor the tradition of White House wifely silence, she could not help being the Duchess. "You know I never give interviews," she smilingly told an eager Jane Dixon. "I stood up in front of some callers who were asking me for an interview, not long ago, and when they were insistent, I rebelled. I suspect my 'no' must have been pretty strong because they did look shocked. . . . Just to chat—that is quite another matter." Then Florence proceeded to "chat" for attribution.

As for public speaking, the Duchess declared, "If a woman wants to speak or feels she can speak, let her do so. Personally, I do not feel like a public speaker. . . . The only excuse for public speaking is good oratory." If claiming that she could not "orate" well disarmed potential criticism from traditionalists, it also gave her enough leeway to speak publicly when she wished, for she could not resist a captive audience. While her public words were always impromptu, whether she called them talks, lectures, chats, or a "little patriotic address," Florence Harding was the first First Lady of her century to give regular speeches. In Atlanta the First Lady addressed the Women's Division of the Red Cross Roll Call, a unit of volunteers that had kept working after the war and sought to increase its ranks. The need for Red Cross volunteers had shifted after the war into hospitals around the country as they filled with thousands of veterans requiring short- and long-term care. It is the only full text of one of her speeches to survive: "I know personally Judge Payne, the new national executive chairman of the American Red Cross, and he is a magnificent leader. I believe that under his direction the work of the Red Cross will be as big as it was during the war. There is as great a need of it to meet present conditions as there was in the wartime emergency, and I hope Atlanta will, as always, do her part. My own state, Ohio, has already gone over the top, I hear, and I am very proud of it."[16]

Nearly any effort that aided the Great War veteran, wounded or otherwise, had passionately consumed Florence Harding since the days Evalyn first brought her into the wards. Committed to helping those she called "my boys," she wielded great power on their behalf; the press and public associated her with veterans as her primary cause. When she met with a group of blinded men, whom she permitted to run their hands over her clothes and face, and one impulsively thanked her for being so good to them, she replied, "I only feel the obligation which every other right-minded American woman feels towards you brave boys who have given your sight, and who offered your lives for your country. It is not a matter of goodness, it is a matter of gratitude." To another, who sent her a shepherd puppy—the litter of a dog he had rescued at the front—she expressed her frustration at the limits of what she could do to change their lot immediately: "Your reference to my deeds in behalf of the disabled soldier touches me deeply, for it is a regret to me that there is so little I can do to show my appreciation of the sacrifices they made for all of us. I only wish there were some way in which I could really relieve their suffering and make lighter the burdens they must bear."

Sixteen days after the inauguration the First Lady led the President up the steps of Walter Reed Hospital's Red Cross Convalescent Home, after speaking to each of the two hundred wounded men lining the circular drive in wheelchairs, on crutches, and with canes gathered to greet the Hardings. "[T]he Government will never be unmindful of your condition," Warren promised. The Hardings, along with Evalyn Mc-Lean, went into the wards to speak with the bedridden "boys," and Florence inspected a vocational training center, where the wounded Joseph Yurkunski gave her a silver case he had crafted. Within days she was back and soon became Walter Reed's most frequent visitor and so familiar a housemother that many of the boys called her Duchess. With the First Lady's adoption of the Red Cross Convalescent Home as a national example, problems and issues facing the veterans were on the table.

The Great War left more gruesome scars on its soldiers than any previous one. Maimed by grenades, tanks, and chemical agents like mustard gas, men were left with missing limbs and lung illnesses. The "men with the broke faces," as the French called them, were the most horrific; they had had their facial features simply blown away, holes where noses had been, many left with only an ear or eye. The shell-shocked were being treated with the new "talking cure," an early form of psychotherapy for victims of what was later called posttraumatic stress. The more serious cases received the experimental electroshock therapy.[17]

Florence was more of a substitute mother to the individual Walter Reed men than grand patroness. She sent them notes and letters when a birthday, death, or any other event warranted, and she became very attached to some of them. When Lieutenant Henry Dyson, suffering intense headaches, suddenly just seemed to disappear, transferred without a paper trail, she was so concerned that she had him tracked down and was relieved to learn that the eminent Dr. Harvey Cushing had performed brain tumor surgery on him in Boston's Brigham Hospital. If one of her "boys" died, the First Lady always sent a wreath to the funeral. A Government Printing Office employee, whose son died in the hospital, told the First Lady, "I am proud that my son died for his country—which has a leader who assists in doing honor to the memory of our boys. . . ."

Florence never refused a request from the Walter Reed boys, and a reporter learned that she "personally ministered in scores of cases." If there were genuine financial emergencies in families dependent upon men there, she saw to it that some relief was provided—almost always by Evalyn's largess. Many days when she intended to take a country drive into Rock Creek Park or the new Maryland highways, she suddenly ordered the car to Walter Reed, or sometimes St. Elizabeths, where the shell-shocked were treated. After dinner she might impulsively visit to sit by their bedsides, writing letters for those missing hands, reading to the blind, checking with doctors about their progress. She brought sweets from the White House kitchens, board games, books, even a radio. "If any one is to be denied flowers let it be us here in the White House," she told the gardeners. "My Walter Reed boys first."

Publicity about Florence's adoption of Walter Reed inspired professional women's groups to underwrite material comforts in their local veterans' wards in private or state hospitals, for which the federal government did not appropriate funds. By always bringing visiting celebrities or state leaders to the downtown shops that sold the blankets, jewelry, pottery, utensils, and other handicrafts the veterans made in vocational training, Florence spurred popularity of the shops as gift centers, which often sold out after one of her publicized visits. She even gave permission to Everett Scrivner in an Arizona hospital, who crafted glass "Florence Harding necklaces" to use her name in selling them in mass. It was all good politics, of course, but it was also genuinely felt, the work of a woman of heart.

Socialites thought Mrs. Harding took it a bit far: Why spend extra time in hospitals with the horrifically wounded? She explained simply, "I was in a hospital for eight months with an open wound that had to be dressed twice a day, and I know what hospital life means to a patient." She clearly derived a personal satisfaction from her visits, calling them "one of my greatest pleasures. . . . They have been an encouragement and consolation to me." She treated anything given to her by her boys—from moccasins to an icon rescued by a doughboy from a burning church in France—with reverence. "She treasured everything pertaining to a soldier's life," recalled a Washington *Star* reporter, "and was so affected by their ills that she would be gravely quiet for hours after leaving them."[18]

Florence's worry over her boys' well-being extended beyond the hospital wards, however. While returning from Friendship one day, she spotted a vet on crutches having trouble making his way down a steep hill and yelled out to him to get in her car. Gasping in disbelief, he slipped into the front with the driver, the Duchess leaning forward. "On the way to the city Mrs. Harding plied him with many questions and they had a real friendly chat," a reporter noted. It was not a lone example; it soon became known on the streets that if the First Lady saw a man in uniform walking in the city, she would give him a lift. It was in Washington that she hoped the first national monument honoring the Great War's soldiers, sailors, and marines would be built, and she served as honorary president of a drive to erect the Beaux-Arts National Victory Memorial Building near the new Lincoln Memorial, enlisting some congressional support.

Whenever the President made an appearance honoring the veterans, the First Lady was in prominent attendance. The most moving occasion was in April 1921 at the Hoboken pier in New Jersey where just a few dozen months before, thousands of eager soldiers in khaki had gone off to war. Now, as the *Mayflower* approached the shed, Florence was stunned at the sight of six thousand coffins of men killed overseas, all covered in American flags, their remains now returned home. There were tears in the President's eyes, and he choked as he spoke at the mass service, the most somber, sobering moment of his presidency. "It must not be again," he declared.

The Duchess also made national efforts to improve the quality of ward life, visiting a Georgia insane ward unannounced, a New Hampshire tubercular wing, a Baltimore institute for the blind, headlining the nation's "Lest We Forget Week," a drive for donated clothing, books, records, and other items, and a fund raiser performance of *A Buck on Leave,* the cast of which was composed entirely of veterans. She invited doughboy Mario Chamlee, a tenor whose talent had been discovered in the foxholes of France, to perform in the White House, kicking off national publicity that led him to perform in wards around America. The event that garnered the greatest national publicity to her effort was her annual garden party for several thousand of the wounded soldiers, sailors, marines, and nurses from all area hospitals.

In red and white striped tents dotting the south lawn were gallons of ice cream, trays of cake, bowls of punch, and mountains of sandwiches. Some men sat on the lawn, singing familiar war songs, while waiting to be carried or wheeled over to meet the Hardings. The First Lady wore her old black straw hat, which she had made a part of her uniform during Walter Reed visits "because the boys are accustomed to it and as soon as they see it they'll know where I am." Colonel Sherrill tried to introduce each person on the receiving line, but the Hardings and the vets were so eager to talk that the formality was dropped; some joked about having to offer their left hands—or no hands. Some hobbled in braces; others struggled falteringly with the aid of nurses; some were in wheelchairs. The Duchess was extremely animated, holding two officials in rapt conversation. One quipped to the other, "She is the best politician in the party, just campaigning all the time." The Hardings then went to greet the silent men unable to be wheeled easily, lying in

cots on flatbed trucks. Hovering behind the Hardings—certain to make the publicity shots—was Charlie Forbes.[19]

Although the First Lady tried to read everything from the *American Legion Magazine* to *U.S. Army Recruiting News* to keep informed of the daunting government changes and efforts being rushed into place for the vets, she had to depend on both Charlie Forbes and Doc Sawyer, a member of the Federal Hospitalization Board, to update her. A large part of the immediate problem was that most of the wounded vets were scattered in wards set up in a variety of private and state hospitals and institutions, and there was a lack of any federal standardization of care and benefits. Twenty-five days after his inaugural Harding had appointed a board to investigate existing agencies for the aid of disabled veterans and recommend legislation on their behalf. The 1917 War Risk Insurance Act provided compensation for injuries received during military service, monthly support for dependents, a system of voluntary insurance, medical, surgical, and hospital care, and vocational rehabilitation for those permanently disabled: The Bureau of War Risk Insurance administered the first four provisions, the rehabilitation was provided by the Federal Board for Vocational Education. On August 9 Harding consolidated them into the Veterans Bureau, with one of the largest federal budgets of all government departments. As the War Risk Bureau chief Charlie Forbes now wanted to be director of the new bureau. It was the First Lady who pushed the President against the advice of Sawyer and Daugherty to give Forbes the post. According to Mark Sullivan, "Mrs. Harding liked him and had confidence in him, and that fact had weight in the President's decision." It proved to be the single worst piece of advice she gave.

Forbes glibly, excitedly assured the Duchess and President just how quickly he'd have federal veterans' hospitals built around the country with the $36 million earmarked for it from the bureau's $450 million budget. Both Hardings boasted of the news, Warren to reporters, Florence reassuring her boys that "the Colonel" would take care of them all if anything happened to her. Charlie's bravado was infectious. "Harding—indeed everybody who made contact with the breezy, joke-cracking, hustling, red-headed Forbes—was impressed by him," said Mark Sullivan. "He was of a familiar American type, the go-getter. He had a kind of genius for the sort of enterprise, compound of animal energy and a shrewd workaday knowledge of applied psychology, which a decade later came to be known as 'muscling in.' . . . [T]o his skill at that art he owed his lone-handed capture of one of the best jobs Harding had to bestow." In all the excitement about Charlie's having enlisted as a private, risen to colonel, and earned the Croix de Guerre and Distinguished Service medal, his prewar desertion from the Army escaped notice.

Charlie and Doc, however, were immediately suspicious of each other's motives. Doc, nursing his dislike of Forbes from their initial meeting in Hawaii in 1915, had been Charlie's first visitor in the War Risk Bureau. Instead of greeting Charlie as a new colleague, Doc rudely snapped, "Let's do some real work," and suggested the firing of the bureau's medical director, Haven Emerson, who had once "insulted" Doc. Forbes refused without first seeking other opinions. Doc soon tried to dominate the new bureau's policies and staff and replace allopaths with homeopaths, while whispering to Harding about Charlie. Doc claimed he was Harding's personal representative, pointing out that when the Federal Hospitalization Board was formed, he was made chair and Forbes vice-chair. Some years later Charlie revealed that Doc not only employed Berenice Blacksten but used her as his spy within the government. He was discreet enough not to reveal that she was also Sawyer's mistress, though others did. Of this arrangement, Charlie said:

> When Sawyer came to Washington he engaged as private secretary a young woman who had been Mrs. Harding's cook at Marion while her husband had been the President's chauffeur there. She became the most important operator in his espionage system. He persuaded the President to give her a civil service status without an examination. Her husband was given a roving commission as Inspector of Motor Transportation. ... In this effort to crush the Public Health Service, Sawyer enlisted the support of an Assistant Director of the Veteran's Bureau who was seeking promotion. ... This man engineered the theft of a number of bottles of whiskey from the depot at Perryville and as part of the plot to "frame" me placed them in a closet in my home in my absence from the city. ... I informed the President that if he were not ousted from the service, I would resign. Sawyer again appealed to the President, and the President asked me if I would be satisfied if the man in question were ordered out of Washington. ... I would and he was sent away.

Right away, one of Florence's inner circle had used dirty tricks to foil his rival.[20]

A third figure, Charles F. Cramer, the Veterans Bureau legal counsel, also became important to the First Lady in the most personal way:

financial. Charlie had coaxed his friend, a mousy California lawyer to take the job, and Cramer and his wife, Lila, met the Duchess, who liked them instantly. When Forbes was away from the office, it was to Cramer that the First Lady turned for action affecting her boys. Such personal ties became even more disastrous in the years to come when the public learned that the First Lady sold Cramer the Hardings' Wyoming Avenue house at a ten-thousand-dollar profit and that he had used his .45-caliber pistol within the same walls that she had lived and entertained in during the Senate years.

With Doc, Charlie, and Cramer at her beck and call, the Duchess pushed them, as well as the War and Navy departments, to investigate hundreds of individual veterans' cases. The basic situation of veterans reliant on a strained and disorganized federal effort to help them remained largely unchanged in the first year of the Harding administration, and frequently the women relatives of wounded vets turned for help to the First Lady rather than the Veterans Bureau itself. When she passed along these cases to the War Department or other bureaus, the First Lady always made clear that she found them urgent and that they appealed to her; they were not edicts or endorsements, but she wanted thorough investigations, and proper pension or other compensations made.[21]

The First Lady effectively prompted investigations into the high cost of dining rations at a New York veterans' facility and the status of compensation, poor food, and lack of shoes and clothes at an American Legion sanitarium in Texas. After a complaint about a South Dakota Soldiers' Home, the chief surgeon of the site promised her a "full report." Dozens of individual cases were resolved because of her action. Florence had the mental state of one St. Elizabeths patient, John Collier, reexamined by request of his family; she had another such shell-shocked patient transferred to an institution closer to his Iowa home; Edward Baker, an unemployed Michigan father of two receiving only nine dollars a week in compensation, claimed to have suffered from lead poisoning during his service. Florence contacted Doc, who contacted Forbes, who checked Baker's medical records and Forbes immediately ordered his careful reexamination.[22]

Florence was equally concerned about abuses of the system by veterans themselves. She brought to the attention of the Veterans Bureau's vocational training division a letter she got from a Los Angeles mother who revealed that her son and many of his comrades in a particular vocational program had recovered from their injuries and were simply taking advantage of the government's largess, spending their days at ball games and theaters, to which they were given free admission. It was not just the vets who concerned Florence, but the hospital staffs that served them. She made certain that the salaries of a South Carolina hospital staff were not reduced. When a nurse from a Staten Island Public Health Service hospital complained about the lower compensation service nurses received compared with those in the new Veterans Bureau, the First Lady raised the inequity with the war secretary, who rushed to explain that while the PHS, the bureau, Army, and Navy all paid at different scales, the department "now" was devising "a policy which will pay all alike and will be fair and reasonable as compared with nurse service anywhere."

Typical of the in-depth investigations that the First Lady provoked was a troubling condition at the Perryville, Maryland, Veterans Hospital, which she learned of in August 1921. Some months earlier the medical officer in charge, E. H. Mullan, had received an anonymous letter that male hospital guards had access to women nurses' rooms and "are making a [w]H.[ore] house out of those buildings . . . girls take off their close [*sic*] and run up and down the Hall nicked [*sic*]." Mullan assumed that the women were compliant. Nothing was done. Then a letter, signed only "Colored Help," was sent to "First Lady of the United States," making a personal case to her that "*all* women are due respect from men . . . which [they] know," and clarifying that "There are some decent and respectful women here. . . . If there is one disrespectful character amongst us why should every woman be classed alike. Now Dear Madame I pray that you may give this your direct attention and look into the matter."

Immediately Florence shook the chain of command. She wrote Doc, who spurred an investigation through the surgeon general and Public Health Service, resulting in women being given separate barracks and, during the required inspection, the male guards being ordered simply to pass through the hall there, not to look in their rooms. Furthermore, Mullan now gave the barracks "close attention." Only nineteen days after the complaint letter was sent to the First Lady official action was taken and the problem resolved. One woman thankfully wrote her that everything had changed once "you were cognizant of the fact. . . ."[23]

At times Doc Sawyer resented Florence's complaints that her boys were not receiving the best attention. He responded indignantly to a claim that he wanted to reduce food rations: "You have taken observations enough personally, I am sure, to know what efforts are being put forth. . . ." When a citizen, exasperated with the Veterans Bureau bureaucracy, asked the First Lady to support his plan to build a private hospital for needy veterans, she indicated to Sawyer her desire to co-operate. Angrily Sawyer replied that she should respond that the government was "making exhaustive plans to carry on all services essential" and if it could "only be given the moral support . . . the best interest of the soldier will be properly cared for without having to ask private individuals to finance such affairs." His final advice to her was: "[I]n the language of the street, 'It is up to you.' " At one point he sent her a stack of printed leaflets stating what the government was and would be doing for the vets and told her to mail them out as responses. Florence continued to respond to each case individually.[24]

Aware of the power of his patron, as Veterans Bureau chief Charlie always responded to Florence with exaggerated respect when she made requests of him either directly or those she sent through Doc. Charges of conditions at specific hospitals—such as the Disabled American Veterans' association claim that neuropsychiatric vets at Ohio's Longview State Hospital were forced to sleep on the floor—were met deftly with his personal reassurance that on the basis of what "the inspection report discloses," the charge was false. Unlike Doc, however, who always sent Florence copies of the paper trail, Forbes never bothered to include documentation with his cover letters.

Florence did not pester Doc for the sake of just being heard; despite assurances from him and Charlie Forbes that all was well, she heard continually from hospitalized veterans and their families of gross inefficiency at the bureau. Less than a month after his fierce defense to her of his hard work, she again questioned Doc. America was doing more for its boys than any other nation, he again replied indignantly, but if those who truly cared for the vets "would use their influence to help rather than complain, it certainly would help to make the job easier for everyone concerned." He then suggested that she stop processing the complaints of vets to him; rather, they should gather their "substantiating facts" and take their problems "directly to the Veterans' Bureau." In other words, it was Forbes who should immediately seek to rectify any malfeasance.

Perhaps the complaints from hospitalized veterans and their families of medical care being wrong or inefficient or of claims for compensation not being processed raised questions in Florence's mind about whether her adored and chummy Charlie was the best possible director of the Veterans Bureau. There is no indication that Doc discussed his doubts about Charlie with the Duchess, but with the barrage and blame she fired at Doc for the problems of her boys, a seed of revenge toward Charles was planted in the ego-bruised Doc beyond his initial resentment. Doc now seized on even the smallest of Charlie's oversights.

Weeks after the charges made about Longview State Hospital, Florence again petitioned Doc, for a Mrs. Campbell, who said her husband was not receiving proper medical care. This time, when Sawyer asked Forbes to investigate the case, Doc simply said that his request was prompted by "a friend of mine who referred the case to me." He did not mention the First Lady at all, and he sent a retyped copy of Campbell's letter, but instead of keeping the opening salutation to "Dear Mrs. Harding," he replaced it with a blank line typed with dashes. Forbes replied that a "report of physical examination" proved that Campbell had no legitimate claim for coverage and again failed to include any documentation. In his response to the First Lady, Doc made no reference to Forbes's having made the report to him; Sawyer just passed on the information. Weeks later, on another case, Forbes simply stated that "the report" he had "requested from the Adjunct General of the Army has been received but failed to show any record of the existence of the alleged disabilities" but did not include a copy of it. Again, Doc reported the information to Florence without mentioning Forbes.

That Forbes did not send documentation in the way of report copies was not in itself incriminating; it may have simply been shoddy administrative procedure. Doc had no reason to suspect that any of the claimants were being lied to. Yet to someone like Sawyer, who always provided copies of a case file he referred to, it was at the least a sign of bad management from the very top of a new and highly funded federal bureau. It was certainly worthy enough to prompt a further look into Forbes's working habits. Doc's jealousy about Forbes's closeness to the First Lady also motivated him. If he could limit her blind admiration of Forbes, in the process he could also limit Forbes's sense of rightful access to the woman he was helping look after her boys. By the summer of 1921 Doc had begun planting spies to pay close attention to Charlie's busywork.

If, by the summer of 1921, Florence and Doc were now sensitive to the inefficiency of the veterans' care in hospitals, they did not yet know of scandalous conditions in the actual offices of Charlie's Veterans Bureau. As the Philadelphia *Record* would reveal sometime later, however, "Forbes is of the good fellow type and his free and easy ways are held by some to be responsible for the lax administration. Several younger men in positions in the bureau have been guilty of excesses . . . a room in the bureau had been fitted up with cocktail shakers and other paraphrenalia [*sic*] to make the dull hours pass faster. . . . Girl clerks of the flapper type are reported to have the right of way over the older and experienced women in promotions and this has exerted a demoralizing influence. Hard work and attention to duty are said to have less influence in bringing recognition from supervising officers than do social considerations. . . ."[25]

Charlie and Doc did agree in their opposition to the most controversial federal legislation affecting not only wounded but all Great War vets, the so-called bonus bill, to provide an increased and earlier awarding of their pensions. Although she supported the concept behind the bonus, Florence strongly argued the point that the wounded men must come first and that the congressional bonus bill must be postponed. This opinion was formed in concern not only for the men she saw in hospitals but for the hospitals they were in. Because of the tremendous number of vets who had to be medically treated in all regions of the country, the government had to contract with many private institutions for their care and treatment. The quality of care was inconsistent, and costs were unmonitored. The construction of government veterans' hospitals around the country would solve this, and that was the focus of Charlie's agenda and what Florence promised her boys. She felt that giving out early benefits would increase the budget so that other, new appropriations—like the hospitals—would have to be decreased, and consequently the care of wounded vets would be prolonged.

It was also President Harding's rationale for promising to veto the bonus bill. Enacting it at the time would have added a tremendous burden to the budget, which Harding was reining in; the bonus would have increased taxation across the board. "It has the problem of meeting the call for compensation by the millions of soldiers of the great World War," the First Lady explained in a letter to one woman, "and has, at the very same time, to contemplate diminished revenue receipts which are far short at meeting the current expense of the government."

Florence Harding did, however, win minor federal action for her boys. When she learned of a bright Ohio vet's inability to get a job as local postmaster, the Duchess persistently raised the issue with the President and Postmaster General Hubert Work. Although others discussed it with him, the First Lady's steadfastness was the influencing factor that prompted Harding to issue Executive Order 3560, on October 14, 1921, directing the Civil Service Commission to add five points to the test results of war veterans applying for postmasterships, to count their military service time toward the required period of business experience, and to set no age limit.

Florence continued to clip not only editorials and articles on Harding administration veterans' policies but editorials about herself. In identifying women and wounded veterans as her primary national constituencies, Florence Harding forged a new niche for First Ladies to come. While she balanced her efforts on their behalf between progressive yet cautious words and actions, the public response to such unprecedented First Lady behavior was positive. She noted a particular remark in one newspaper article: that she "has shown equal ability and achievement in the world of affairs next to the President. . . . The White House will not be run by man power alone." In the margin the Duchess herself defiantly scribbled, "Ha-Ha!"[26]

27

"The Chief Executive and Mr. Harding"

On her first day as First Lady, Florence Harding visited her husband's executive offices and advisers, telling reporters that she would be "as frequent a visitor in that end of the White House" as she had been in the campaign offices. "Mrs. Harding was always looking in on us," said Ira Smith, correspondence unit chief, "accompanied by a group of political guests from the Corn Belt . . . lead[ing] a frumpy-looking crowd, mostly women, into the office and [she'd] start explaining things to them in the manner of a Chinatown sight-seeing-tour conductor."

Like Abigail Adams, Julia Tyler, Mary Lincoln, Julia Grant, Sarah Polk, Nellie Taft, and Ellen Wilson before her, Florence Harding never permitted the fact that she was a woman or unelected to office to limit her frank political dialogue with men in government other than her husband. She was, said her friend and former secretary Kathleen Lawler, "a real politician, a born leader. With her scintillating, captivating personality and rapier mind, she waged her political battles in the world of men. She played the exciting game of politics cleverly. She liked it and she gave many good lessons to men who fancied themselves skillful and adroit in the strategy of statesmanship. Nothing gave President Harding more genuine enjoyment than to sit by, and, as he often put it, 'act as referee' while the Duchess went to the political mat with astute politicians and ready debaters such as Senator Henry Cabot Lodge with whom she was ever especially eager to engage in verbal combat. She stimulated him and they had many a hotly fought but merry tilt. She never hesitated to . . . take on all comers whom she regarded as worthy of her steel . . . picked up the gauntlet . . . and frequently provoked the flinging."

Despite such abilities, however, Florence had "not the slightest personal desire or hankering to hold office," preferring instead, as Lawler put it, "to play the game; to stack the cards; to pull the ropes behind the scene, and then to watch what happened."[1]

The most immediate sphere of the presidency that the First Lady successfully manipulated was the press. When friends sent her copies of editorials that were positive toward administration policy, she often dictated flattering thank-you notes to the writer and editor. She buttered up many a journalist. After Mark Sullivan had written a glowing piece on Harding in the *North American Review,* Florence sent flowers to his wife. She was the first First Lady to break the strict rule about privately entertaining journalists at the White House, inviting Ray Clapper and Boyden Sparkes, for example, one night. "Whenever you are speaking or writing of Mr. Harding and me," she told the press, "remember we are doing our best, doing our all. If we make mistakes you may be sure they are not deliberate. We want the people to love and trust us as we love and trust them. And we are grateful—so grateful for this opportunity to serve—for this beautiful home they have provided for us."

She decreed that Warren never be photographed smoking or with even a nonalcoholic drink in his hand. When she saw a natural peg for a story on some aspect of the President, she unhesitatingly pushed it to George Christian or reporters she thought might bite. "I've lived so long in a newspaper atmosphere that I've got the news sense strongly developed," she confessed. "I can see news, feel it, yes, even smell it." And if the McLeans always got the inside story for the Washington *Post,* they could be counted on for a vigorous defense of Harding policy, a fact snidely remarked upon by everyone from other papers' society editors to subscribers. "Why didn't you write something like this when that coon in the White House was traducing, insulting and lying about Woodrow Wilson and other prominent men?" one reader wrote Ned. "If you could only bring yourself to believing the truth you need not kiss his backside every day."

Florence not only managed to soften critics but to have her influence recognized. The San Francisco *Bulletin*'s Washington correspondent wrote: "Warren Harding leaned on 'the Duchess' as no President ever has depended upon his wife. It has seemed to Washington that Mrs. Harding is an integral part of the Presidency of the entire Harding administration."[2]

To everyone the First Lady met, she bragged endlessly of the President. "She asked us to sit down," recalled a visitor, "and after a few words of desultory talk led the conversation to the President—'Warren Harding,' as she called him. 'Warren Harding does this'—'Warren Harding says that'—'Warren Harding thinks thus and so'—'Warren Harding' was the burden of her song the whole time we were in the room." Florence had no apologies for her grand obsession: "Every wife must have her maternal phase. My big job is to keep my husband comfortable and happy in his home, to create an atmosphere of good cheer so that he may go to his duties with a mind and body fit to serve the nation which has so honored him. I regard this as a sacred trust with which nothing must interfere. To slight or neglect it would be rank disloyalty."

Only privately did the Duchess stridently argue with Warren on political decisions. Naval officer Joel Boone observed:

She had no hesitancy in expressing her mind with vehemence and with a positiveness. . . . [S]he had what one would call a 'man's mind.' She was versed in politics and she could express herself clearly and with definite opinion about people participating in politics, and she certainly did. The President shared things political with Mrs. Harding and I felt quite certain that she had no hesitancy in giving him advice . . . [and was] very much at home with any group of men discussing government or politics and personalities related thereto. . . . There were times when Mrs. Harding would take marked issue with the President. When the discussion became too heated and he became displeased, he would . . . leave the room where they had been holding their discussion . . . showing irritation, but I do not remember ever hearing him scold, as it were, Mrs. Harding. . . . [H]e was a man of the most limitless patience. . . .

Daugherty concurred that she "watched carefully to see that he made no mistakes. If he did she was keen to 'pick him up,' though she did it in a way that never nagged. Their discussions were heated at times," he claimed, "but never quarrelsome or bitter."

Even the President thought that she was sometimes "too busy directing the affairs of government. . . . She is full fledged in expressing her opinion as to how the Executive should perform his duties." Sometimes her strenuous admonishments were glimpsed by those for whom they were not intended. "On occasions," a Washington *Star* reporter recorded, "she has been seen shaking a forefinger at her husband."

The press knew that her strength was less as a policy initiator and more as the political adviser. "There are few women who know the details and procedure of government from the city council to the state legislature, the hearings and details of the passage of a bill through Congress more thoroughly than Mrs. Harding. Even during the closing days of Congress with the multitude of affairs piling high, her life training and her keen instinct kept her in touch with things, for few women are more thoroughly in touch with current news and opinions," noted a reporter who covered her. As for her overt political role, the First Lady explained, "All these days it has been a part of my husband's business. It is more interesting and necessary for me to know about these than a lot of things that women draw themselves away from."[3]

The most apparent influence she had on the President was on what he said. In reference to Harding's prominent speeches, dedications, and State of the Union address, *National Magazine* noticed, "When he was making an address, he knew there was one in the audience who was following almost with her lips the words of his speech, which he had talked over with her." On several occasions she argued with him about the message of his speeches. On one occasion she burst into the Oval Office as he was drafting a congressional address with Judson Welliver, his political adviser, and demanded to know what was in the planned speech. Before they could tell her, she snapped up the draft and began reading it. Immediately finding a reference to a proposed one-term six-year presidency, she refused to leave the office until it had been removed.

Such behavior was rare. Rather than having his decisions dominated by her, Kathleen Lawler recalled that the President "never made an important decision without consulting her. He regarded her judgment as infallible. . . . [H]e did consult and advise with her before definitely committing himself." Still, Florence would not ask Warren to defy federal policy in, for example, responding to a plea to halt the deportation of some Assyrians: "It is a thing neither the President nor I can help. . . . If they will come in excess of their quota it is not possible to admit them. . . . I realize there are many hardships . . . my heart goes out to them." Albert Fall admired the Duchess for her "most intelligent interest in government affairs."

As rational as she could be with making savvy political decisions,

Florence Harding remained haunted by the shadow of the death that Madame Marcia had envisioned above Warren as the price for the presidency. Even in the midst of her happiest days as First Lady Florence lived with the fear of losing her Warren to the "strange, sudden, violent" death. She occasionally directed George Christian to rearrange the President's schedule when she feared danger. "The fact that President Harding who is a subject of Jupiter is coming under powerful and favorable influences is believed to augur improved conditions for the country," she clipped from one astrological reading. "The President may have a narrow escape from personal danger and he should watch his health carefully since an inclination toward kidney maladies is indicated in his horoscope," she noted in another note to herself. The First Lady managed to change the dates of several of the President's public appearances on podiums outside Washington and his office meetings with "foreigners." The White House would also direct the State Department that the anticipated Naval Disarmament Conference should begin in the fall—at least two months after the summer solstice but before the winter solstice began—because of the influence of so many "foreigners." Harding initially balked at such changes if he learned of them, then accepted them instead of arguing.[4]

Within the privacy of the mansion, Florence bragged openly that she "put her husband in the White House [and] . . . had had a drive to become First Lady," remembered a maid. She also now spoke frankly of how "she had spent her whole life proving how wrong her dad had been about her husband." Warren even "seemed a little afraid of her." As a close observer of the Hardings later stated, the presidency "meant more to her than it did to Harding himself." Even Daugherty had to admit, "You can say truthfully that she really enjoyed it more than the President; almost anyone would tell you that." As Harding became mired down in the daily problems and decisions he faced, he trusted her to process the inevitable flood of patronage requests for federal positions, realizing that she did so eagerly. "Through the President she tried diligently to keep in touch with public affairs and many times made suggestions about appointments. Her recommendations were frequently adopted, and many appointments that did not turn out so well afterwards were the result of her handiwork," Ike Hoover tartly noted. Evidence of this exists in her correspondence: She pressed Senator Park Trammell to recommend someone of the opposition party whom she wanted to be given a federal post. When she wrote Shipping Board chair Albert Lasker about a man she wanted reinstated, she claimed that Harding agreed but emphasized, "[H]e ought to be reinstated. . . . [I] Am keen about the success of this young man."

Quickly Florence was operating without Warren's direction. "She kept in touch also through private conversations with officials of the Administration," Ike Hoover amplified, "generally unknown to the President and he often wondered where she came into possession of certain information. As he was once heard to remark, 'Mrs. Harding wants to be the drum major in every band that passes.'" Certainly her authority was respected by various levels of officials and political operatives. Texas crony Gus Creager supported without question Florence's choice of a Democrat and former Wilson appointee as the postmistress of Valley View, concluding, "[I]f in any of these cases that come up to you, you take the slightest personal interest, any suggestion you may have to offer will be regarded as a command." Even Doc deferred to her. When he discovered that Paul Tillotson, her twenty-nine-year-old choice for Painesville, Ohio, postmaster, was ineligible until he turned thirty, he presented the dilemma to her, not Warren. "I know you are interested in it, so I am submitting it to you, rather than taking it up with the President."

In judging those qualified for minor patronage positions, the First Lady placed party loyalty above mere personal connection. She would pull no strings for one friend and relative of her grandchildren: "The various states are very jealous about having their own men appointed to positions in their respective states. Mr. Harding . . . does not feel that he could make any more general appointments from Marion." Former *Star* staffers—like old cartoonist Arthur Porter, who was employed by the Shipping Board—were considered only if they had genuine partisan histories. Before she got an appointment for former newsboy F. J. McAndrews, she checked with Jimmie Wood at the *Marion Star* offices because "confidentially, I want to know what family of McAndrews he comes from and can you give me a line on his political persuasion?"[5]

It was at lunchtime, when the President invited guests in public service to join them—from local postmasters to foreign financiers and political leaders—that Florence said she absorbed the most political knowledge and cultivated contacts to seek good candidates for federal appointment. "I have been thinking since our talk on the subject of the head of the Federal Reserve System," Dewey Hilles wrote her, "of some outstanding financier who enjoys the confidence of the country. Reynolds of Chicago, Decker of Minnesota, and Sweeny of Kansas City come to mind. . . ." She gave Columbia University president Nicholas Murray Butler a "parting injunction" as he left the White House one afternoon to "give earnest thought to the question of the best possible successor to the late George W. Aldridge as Collector of the Port of New York. . . ."

With her love of intrigue, the Duchess did not limit her gathering of political intelligence to conventional sources. Upon receiving incriminatory or defaming political information, she carefully clipped off any engraved letterhead or signature. Evalyn did her part to fuel the conspiratorial atmosphere. Since the First Lady couldn't make open inquiries about her suspicions of Commerce Secretary Herbert Hoover's disloyalty, Evalyn, who openly disliked Hoover, acted as a beard. She wrote to Senator Hiram Johnson about the "disagreeable and dirty campaign" being waged for his seat by the "Hoover organization." Johnson said his opponent in the primaries, Charles Moore, who mouthed administration views, was only "disguised as Mr. Harding" but was actually a front for the progressive Hoover stance. He then sent Evalyn a detailed report showing that Hoover instructed his minions—all working for Moore—to frame the fight as "Johnson or Harding." Evalyn turned the report over to Florence.[6]

Florence foremost grasped how much the political climate was shaped by the short 1921 depression and other economic problems of the early postwar era. "The President and I fully realized even in the campaign of 1920," she explained, "that the new administration would be charged with a far greater undertaking in the reconstruction period following the world war than had come in any period in half a century. The next two years will be most critical in reconstruction and in the restoration of a sound economic basis. It was this which made me feel so strongly that we must 'carry on' together." Harding's newly formed Bureau of the Budget questioned government department, agency, and bureau appropriations and whether each of those entities could be consolidated into another to reduce spending, eliminated entirely, or survive efficiently on a greatly reduced budget. The First Lady herself reviewed the budgets of a wide variety of appropriated items, calling for a report of the number and cost of automobiles operated by the U.S. Public Health Service, for example, as well as a detailed memorandum from the Marine Corps on the estimate of cost of uniforms. She even attended an Interior Department conference on unemployment, which reached a high of five million in 1921. To a desperate farmer, she wrote of postwar conditions:

Men who were wicked and men who were unwise, brought the world to its present conditions, and it is not possible with even the utmost sincerity, humanity, patriotism to apply effective remedies immediately. The whole world is involved, and as a whole the world must find the means of readjusting itself to the new conditions in which we find it. You may be sure that suffering and misfortune have not come to any single class of people. . . . The farmers, in our country and elsewhere, are suffering in a way that has certainly made a very special appeal to me, at least, because such special difficulties seem to surround every effort to ameliorate their situation. People who by thrift and saving have secured modest competence find themselves in danger of losing what they have saved. Even the capitalists, whom I beg you not to believe are altogether bad, have had their trouble everywhere. I beg you to feel very sure that the men entrusted with National leadership and responsibility are not blind to these things. Their task is one without precedent, and it will take time, and patience, and above all, ample confidence among all the people to work it out.[7]

Among the Cabinet, it was with the attorney general that the First Lady remained most comfortable being overtly political, and he teased her about it. Writing her that the President had come to confer with him, Harry cracked "Of course you know it—you know everything which he or I do or think. . . . I am loyal to him to—that is as loyal to him as I can be considering that I always give your instructions preference over his." Daugherty fully cooperated with her requests, seeing private citizens, for example, whose cases appealed to her and for whom she scheduled appointments with him. In other cases she directed him to investigate personally such cases as that of three poor sons of a West Virginia steelworker, Andy, Frank, and Teddy Bosko, all serving five-year prison terms for an alleged postal burglary. Daugherty's aide Barney Martin found that the conviction was on flimsy evidence and that the police had forced confessions from the frightened boys. All three were pardoned by the President and permitted to return to their parents.

Florence's iron glove was even flexed within the Justice Department's Prohibition division. "I have this day nominated and appointed Alfred A. King, Lorain, Ohio, a Federal Prohibition Agent, and have forwarded the same to the Federal Prohibition Commissioner," wrote the federal Prohibition director, J. E. Russell, to the First Lady, "asking him to confirm the appointment. It might not be out of order for you to have your secretary call the attention of Commissioner Haynes to the fact that it would please you to have this appointment acted upon at an early date."

Although she worked best with Harry, all the Cabinet members responded to her command. Interior Secretary Fall, after conducting an investigation into Pension Office workers' complaints, assured her, "I will personally see that anything forwarded to this Department forwarded by yourself will receive immediate and prompt attention to that end." She received a similar response from Navy Secretary Edwin Denby: "Please believe it will always be a pleasure to do anything you desire when possible. I hope you will let me be of assistance to you again, and in case of your special interest in matters pertaining to the Navy, that you will express to me what you would like to have done. It may not always be possible but there will always be an earnest effort to do as you desire." She even interceded with the War Secretary when she wanted White House military aides scheduled for transfers to be sent only to nearby stations.

When she exerted her influence outside the executive branch, Florence was more subtle. She might simply send a representative, senator, or governor a copy of an appeal she had received from someone in his constituency, claiming, for example that in her desire to resolve the problem properly and "intelligently," she needed "information on the subject" but that she thought it would be an "unseemly thing for the wife of President to . . . recommend to Congress what its duty is. . . ." As a proper states' rights Republican she tried not to intercede when a final decision belonged not to the federal but to a state government, feeling that it would be "an impropriety" for her "to influence the Governor in a case." When she wanted a death sentence commuted in Alabama, for example, Harry advised against it since Justice had no jurisdiction over the decision.[8]

In the atmosphere engendered by suffrage, the First Lady's power and influence received fairly universal praise, along with some ribbing. In *Life* magazine's large illustration of cartoon drawings of 1922 celebrities she and Warren were pictured front and center and captioned as "The Chief Executive and Mr. Harding." She herself clipped a picture of them captioned, "Our Boss and His Boss" and the accompanying story about a presidential stop in North Carolina, where a farmer stepped up to them, said, "I want to shake hands with the boss," and did so with the Duchess. One true story, widely reprinted, had Swedish immigrant John Anderson taking his oral exam to earn his citizenship. Answering each question correctly, he was finally asked, "If President Harding should die who would assume his duties as President?" The

Swede responded, "Mrs. Harding." The judge smiled. "We'll let you get by."[9]

It was in private conversation with two public servants she highly respected, her brother- and sister-in-law Heber and Carolyn Votaw, that Florence became interested in two particular domestic initiatives. When she learned of Heber's goal of building the first separate federal prison exclusively for women, she immediately grew enthusiastic about the project, speaking about how she foresaw benefits in retraining women in a uniform manner to establish themselves as healthy, working citizens once they were released. Previously women had been incarcerated in state institutions and subjected to many different types of treatment, and by 1922 such institutions had to turn away any more federal women prisoners, for they needed their own space for state convicts. A federal site would also permit the first medical care facility there for the convicts, a large percentage of whom were drug addicts or infected with venereal diseases. The federal prison, however, would be for such women who were considered the most hopeful for rehabilitation, many of whom had actually requested incarceration as a means of changing their lives.

Once a site had been chosen, at Mount Weather, West Virginia, Votaw sent a detailed memorandum to the Duchess. Seven buildings would be converted into the prison to hold about half the population of the nation's three hundred federal women prisoners in the rehabilitative classification—with a seventy-five-thousand-dollar congressional expenditure to conduct the engineering renovation. The bill had been approved by the judiciary committees of both the Senate and House but was being blocked by the district's representative—despite the overwhelming support by his constituents, except for the wary owners of summer cottages near Mount Weather. In sending the report on House Resolution 13927, Heber told Florence, "I will appreciate deeply the help you may be able to give in securing its early consideration by the House of Representatives." She read the report, did some research—scribbling herself notes on the fiscal and geographic suitability of the endeavor—and lobbied Republican House floor leader Frank Mondell to bring it to the floor for a funding vote. It was a long process, but the prison idea would become reality.

The Duchess was equally supportive of Carolyn Votaw's ambitiously progressive long-term goal of carrying out Warren's hope to create a department of social welfare, based on the experimental model she had organized and run as director of the Industrial Hygiene Service at the U.S. Public Health Service and then the Veterans Bureau. With

federal economy the order of the day, however, there was an uncon-
ducive atmosphere for a new executive department; it was an initiative
that might better be achieved in a second term.[10]

Despite the popular surge of the Ku Klux Klan and the views of
some of their friends, no documentation whatsoever even suggests racial
or religious bigotry in either Warren or Florence. Told by a University
of Cincinnati professor about an Ohio Masonic contribution to a racist
organization, perhaps the Klan, Harding had Doc investigate, and he
disapprovingly suspected that the "only one answer" for it was the
Masons' "opposition to Catholicism or anything with which Catholics
have to do." Both Hardings supported a Jewish homeland through the
Palestine Foundation Fund and "the restoration of a real nationality"
and counted the Laskers, Meyer Lissner of Los Angeles, and Rabbi
Joseph Kornfeld of Columbus, whom Harding made minister to Persia,
as genuine friends. When Florence wrote old friend Al Cohen about
her interest in the organization of B'nai B'rith, she declared Warren and
her to be "devoid of racial or religious prejudices."

Within the context of their times and backgrounds, the couple were
remarkably progressive on civil equality, with Harding speaking stir-
ringly for efforts to end racism. Still, both took a qualified, careful tack.
When he spoke in the North, backed by a supportive NAACP and
pacifist black preachers, he proposed antilynching legislation, an inter-
racial commision to initiate social equality between the races, and pulling
the Marines out of Haiti, where Wilson had placed them in an act of
colonialism, but in the South he gently suggested a patient acceptance
of segregation until the arrival of some vague, bright future. While
Florence had black schoolgirls as her White House guests, when she
heard that a black man had obtained an invitation to a private tea honoring the Hardings in segregated Baltimore, she "quickly realized its
importance," and the man's invitation was delicately recalled.

One of Florence's startling habits, after a meal in a private home
or hotel, was her request to thank publicly the chef and cooks, who
were more often than not black. After a luncheon in the Atlanta home
of a prominent hostess, Florence offended white guests when she broke
the social code by asking to meet the black cook in the parlor, then
clasped the woman's hands. After a New Orleans hotel lunch Florence
ended her speech by praising the African-American wait staff, declaring,
"I don't want to leave until I have shaken hands with every one of
these boys," and spoke with each individually. The class distinction
between black servant and white lady remained in place, but in the South

of the 1920s such public recognition was rare from a woman of such status.

After Florence joined Warren in Alabama to hear his most startlingly liberal speech—before an audience segregated by wire fences—supporting legal, educational, and working (if not "social") equality between the races, Florence clipped reams of stories from the black and white press in reaction to the speech. In Birmingham she made a point of loudly applauding a black band that marched before them in a parade, and she stood up to wave to the corps of African-American children who walked the route as a contingent. They saluted back.

Florence fought racism in ways the public never knew. When Warren promised openly racist Katherine Eagan that he would give a political appointment to her friend Helen Longstreet, a Georgia Republican who believed "this country should be, and will be governed by white men," he did so "in the presence of Mrs. Harding." When Longstreet's appointment was long in coming, Eagan wrote the Duchess that "I believe she is being persecuted by the Catholics." After that, Warren was made to rescind the promise, apparently by Florence. Eagan angrily wrote Harding, calling him on his promise, but unfortunately for her she addressed the envelope to Mrs. Harding. The Duchess dictated a terse third-person answer: "*Mrs.* Harding suggests that if you wish a letter of this tone to go to the President, she must ask you to seek some other agency of delivery."[11]

Rarely did the First Lady enter international politics, where her frankness could get the better of her. In receiving the women of the Philippine Parliamentary Mission, then touring the United States in the interest of independence from America, Florence evidently told Jaime de Veyra, wife of the resident Philippine commissioner, that she supported them as women. Press reports that the women "came away delighted with their gracious *sympathetic* reception" upset the State Department, which found its First Lady expressing a view not its own.

In her resistance to any suggestion that America eventually join the League of Nations, the Duchess held sway. "It was Mrs. Harding who finally coerced him," the Frenchman Bernard Fay noted. "Mrs. Harding induced the President to refuse to negotiate any other treaty than that incredible document by which the United States made peace with Germany without signing the Treaty of Versailles." Daugherty said that the "most spirited discussion that I ever knew to take place between them was over a clause in one of his messages relating to the League of Nations. . . . Mrs. Harding was even more tenacious in her opposition." Florence's face "was still flushed" when Daugherty first entered the room, and Warren reread a certain passage in front of them. Harry pointed out that his "interpretation of that would head us straight into the League of Nations, destroy the policy of your party and ignore the pledge of the last election." Florence sat "bolt upright, her eyes flashing: 'Exactly what I've been telling him.' " After arguing for hours, Harding said it would stay as written. The next night he read his speech to Congress, and the disputed section was gone. Daugherty piped up to the war secretary, "A wise little woman!" The Duchess remained a rigid irreconcilable. Passing a news article to the President, she first circled its headline, LEAGUE US NOT INTO TEMPTATION.[12]

At the autumn International Conference on the Limitation of Armaments Florence was highly active. One of Washington's most solemn state occasions preceded it: the memorial service and Arlington Cemetery burial of "Buddy," the unidentified remains of an American soldier brought from the front, representing all those killed in the Great War. While a steady gray rain poured outside, in the Capitol Rotunda the Duchess, dressed in black mourning, attended the service with her head bowed throughout, then joined the President to step up to the flag-draped coffin, where she placed a white rose and satin ribbon. As the President held the rose, she tied the ribbon into a bow. On this overlay, representatives of various countries pinned their highest military honor medals. Florence saved all the newspaper clippings on "Buddy," who was buried the next morning, Armistice Day, at the newly dedicated Tomb of the Unknown Soldier.

The next day, November 12, the conference began, in Constitution Hall, with some thirteen hundred people crammed in to watch the deliberations around a green felt-topped hollow square of tables. There was a flourish of trumpets, and the representatives of the participating nations—Great Britain, Italy, France, China, Belgium, Japan, the Netherlands, Portugal, Belgium, and the United States—took their places. Secretary of State Hughes was the American delegation's Peace Board's acting head, but the President opened the event. "We want less of armament and none of war!" was his speech's famous line. In the viewing box Grace Coolidge knitted while Florence, intent on the proceedings, hunched over the railing. Evalyn was unable to attend; she was six days away from giving birth to her fourth child, Emily (the Duchess won a bet by predicting the right sex).[13]

Before the conference began, Florence studied articles on the complexities underlying conference questions like one in the *Saturday Evening Post*, "Why Germany Drowned Her Credit," which explained

Germany's economic system and problems. She considered her role "of paramount importance, to bring the representatives of foreign nations attending the arms conference into ... a common understanding. ..." She held a brilliant dinner on November 12 for the state leaders, at which she broke protocol by having foreign flags held by American marines, hosted some two thousand foreign notables, a record in White House history, and threw a special reception for one of the few delegation women, Italia Garibaldi, granddaughter of the Italian patriot who had been decorated for battle service in the war. Still, Florence warned reporters, "This coming Conference is such a serious matter that I hope it will not be made a social function."[14]

From the opening session to the last session in late February, Florence missed only one, acting as the President's eyes and ears at the conference. As a reporter watching the First Lady detailed, "She stayed, listening attentively. ... Mrs. Harding has what a Frenchman would call de la tenue. She sits straight as an arrow, listens intently to the statesmen—she owns one herself—and says not a word to the women with her. At luncheon, she is able to tell 'Warren Harding' as she calls your President, everything that happened, down to the expression of W. J. Bryan's face when he heard translated [Aristide] Briand's statement that the dove of peace would have to stay in the coop a while longer." Indeed Florence was disgusted when the French seemed uncooperative. "It is wonderful to think of all the men and women that have been drawn here together," she wrote the governor of Hawaii. "All seemed to go most encouragingly until dear France began acting like a capricious prima donna. I think it is all going to turn out right, but of course it is temporarily rather discouraging, especially, I should imagine, to the other delegates who were beginning to think of going home."[15]

The conference overlapped with the Christmas season, and Florence made the holiday more of a national affair than had any of her predecessors, sending out thousands of engraved presidential holiday cards, kicking off an effort to sell Treasury certificates as holiday gifts, sending greens and poinsettias to veterans' wards, and hosting a yacht party for local African-American children. In the mansion's living quarters she had no tree set up, and she abandoned her announced plan to place lighted candles in each windowsill on Christmas Eve, after being warned that it would set a national example but result in tragic fires from flames torching curtains. As their first White House Christmas neared, Warren gave her perhaps the most political gift a President could give his First Lady.

According to Harding scholar Cyril Clemens, the President presented her with a list of suggested prison parolees, "to select the convicts in the Federal Penitentiaries that she wished pardoned on that day, allowing her much leeway in her choice. The President had great confidence in the judgement of his devoted wife." Grace Coolidge's secretary observed that "the decision was not untypical of the President, allowing her great latitude in this, as in other official matters. Perhaps she demanded it, for she was, beyond any doubt by far the stronger character of the two. She had much the keener mind—and probably knew it; but that never changed her adoration of her husband." The one person she refused to have pardoned, however, was someone whom the President did in fact pardon. Hundreds, including actress Mae West, petitioned Harding for the freedom of antiwar spokesman and presidential candidate Eugene Debs. Florence was fiercely suspicious of Debs's supporters, expecting many civil liberty pickets at the White House. "Duchess," Warren wrote to Mac Jennings, "was very much opposed to any clemency being shown to Debs. However, I was persuaded in my own mind that it was the right thing to do." *He* was still President.

Florence's discovery of the Debs pardon or her hearing about some secret—but legal—impending lease of a Wyoming naval reserve to oilman Harry Sinclair may have prompted the tense holiday season between the Hardings. Charlie Forbes later recalled the Duchess's summoning him and the ensuing days:

> Her first greeting was: "Have you heard any comments about Harry Sinclair?" "No," I replied, "what about it?" Mrs. Harding said: "Why, nothing," and the subject was dropped. . . . On Christmas Day . . . I had a telephone call from Carolyn Votaw . . . who was at the White House. . . . I went over and found the President sitting all alone in his office and evidently very depressed. . . . He said: "This is a hell of a Christmas." I asked him what was the matter and he replied: "Everything is the matter." I gathered from his mutterings that things were not all right with him in his domestic life. In this same conversation the President told me that there were things going on in the public business that he didn't approve—but that he was helpless to stop them. Later that day I met old Sawyer, who was there every morning to feel the President's pulse and advise a new brand of pills. Sawyer laughed and said: "My God, they had a hell of a row this morning." He meant the President and his wife. . . . I met Major Brooks, the president's colored valet. . . . Mrs. Harding then came up and said, "Brooks, mix the Colonel a cocktail." . . . The President came up. . . . Mrs. Harding went on to her bedroom. . . . "Let's take a walk," he said, and we walked down to about

the centre of the grounds and sat on a bench, and he told me how unhappy he was and how empty his life had been. "You know something of it," he said. He wept.[16]

At Christmas the McLeans were lavish with gifts all around for the Harding crew: Jess, Harry, even the Christians. Not to be outdone, Jess sent the McLeans prize corn-fed yearling cattle. But the unexpected gifts on Christmas afternoon at the McLeans were the Hardings. Florence had insisted that she must remove Warren from the mansion after noon—or else.

After reading a confidential report of possible picketing for Debs, Florence had become alarmed by a particular bomb threat to kill Harding on Christmas. Despite the security available to her in the White House, she insisted that they spend the afternoon with the McLeans at I Street. "Mrs. Harding's fears were flavored with a Cassandra quality; from time to time she did predict disaster but none paid her much heed, except to try to keep from arousing her tart anger," said Evalyn. "I remember once when she told me, 'I am constantly in fear that something will happen to him; my dread is that he will be blown up, assassinated. I cannot bear to have him hurt.' " After church, their argument, and Forbes's visit, the Hardings went to I Street for lunch. They talked until an early dinner, and then Evalyn and the Duchess watched Mary Pickford in *Little Lord Fauntleroy*. While Warren's laughter drifted down from an upstairs poker game, Florence "twitched and jumped." When a door slammed suddenly, she "half screamed and almost slid from her chair," Evalyn noted. "There was no comedy about her fears; they were too real." The Hardings finally left at two in the morning, Warren "grateful to my assassins for a very pleasant Christmas Day." It was a case, however, not of paranoia on Florence's part but of her genuine sixth sense. As Evalyn added in airy epilogue to the day, "They found the bombs you know." Terror about Marcia's predictions of Warren's death as President often made the Duchess look absurd, but she was not so ridiculous as always to be paranoid. Sometimes she was justified.

On New Year's Day, at the annual White House reception, Evalyn made her first public appearance since Emily's birth, Florence having invited her to receive guests along with Cabinet wives. After the Hardings greeted legislative, judicial, diplomatic, and military leaders and their spouses—including Alice Longworth, of course—there was a lunch break. Then the doors were opened for the general public. Approximately 6,575 citizens streamed through the receiving line, one woman lamenting to Florence that the hose and shoes she had worn for the First Lady had been ruined by the slush, a small girl loudly yelling, "Mrs. President," at her.

"I wish you could have been here for the closing days of the Conference," Florence wrote some weeks later to Evalyn, now with her family in Florida for the winter. "It was the most impressive scene it has ever been my privilege to witness, and I do not mind saying to you that 'that man Harding' didn't do so bad." Eventually eight treaties, seven by the United States, were signed, including the five-power Naval Limitation Treaty, five-power Submarine and Poison Gas Treaty, six-power German-Pacific Treaty, and four-power Pacific Treaty defining Japan as a mainland.[17]

As Harding's first year in office closed, the press began making political assessments of his administration. One analysis concluded, "In all his work as Chief Executive, Mrs. Florence Kling Harding, has continued [as] his helpmate as in the past, traveling with him and following with keen interest the swiftly-moving current of events. She has listened to every utterance with a knowledge of details equal to that of any man in public service." Another said the Duchess was one of the best things about the President. She even received her own admiring editorial, "Mrs. Harding's First Year in Office," and the Philadelphia *Public Ledger*'s Constance Drexel in a three-column analysis concluded that "Mrs. Harding has brought with her the middle Western conception of woman's role. She thinks of herself as an individual with personal responsibilities, yet as the complement of her husband. . . . Yes, Mrs. Harding has been a success during her first year in the White House. She has personified the new American woman. . . ."

Less welcome was the public disclosure that came out of a House Appropriations Committee hearing on the independent offices appropriations bill. Florence Harding had opened the White House to so many people in her first year that the allotted budget of $50,000—from which earlier she had so proudly saved money on heating and electricity—was nearly depleted. By the end of fiscal year 1921 only $88.64 remained. Asked if the budget could be reduced to $35,000, as it had been in 1918, Colonel Clarence Sherrill, head of the Office of Public Buildings and Grounds, testified that no, it could not: The wear alone of reopening the house to tourists was high, and the $3,000 in repairs to the greenhouses were a must because of the heavy use of flowers. Sherrill's testimony infuriated the Duchess and earned him her permanent enmity: "Mrs. Harding, of course, is doing a great deal more entertaining and we are having a hard time to make ends meet and get enough flowers, because a lady does not appreciate how much money is involved. They see the White House decorated and so on, and they just call for flowers and we must provide them." He made matters worse by asking for an extra $10,000. The committee ruled that such an addition would have to be approved by the new Bureau of the Budget. Sherrill never pressed for it.[18]

As the winter of 1922 ground on, Florence grew eager to join Evalyn in Florida. Warren was optimistic about leaving after Congress moved some of the treaties out of committee, though Jess Smith noted that Florence was "more apprehensive about Congress." Congress did ratify the treaties by early March, and the Hardings, Sawyers, and Harry and Jess joined the McLeans in Floridian waters, on the *Nahmeoka,* a houseboat with four double staterooms. The friction between the Hardings since winter, however, bloomed as colorfully as the tropical flowers decking the boat. "Mrs. Harding was very jealous of Warren," asserted Evalyn. "[S]he used to tell me that society women were trying to get him away from her." In Florida, however, it was Warren who was trying to get the society women. He not only flaunted his womanizing but did so drunkenly in a woman's hat. Reporter Boyden Sparkes recalled how the President "walked out onto the pier of some town . . . and the newspaper men had been asked to stay away and Harding was wearing a woman's hat with a girl on either arm, singing, 'Good-bye Girls, I'm Through.' "

Evalyn later vividly recalled Harding's extramarital escapades— and Florence's tirades—on the Florida trip, in conversation with Sparkes and the unpublished draft of her autobiography:

> The President, George Christian and Ned got off to play golf one morning and we were going to steam on up and meet them on a place further up. Mrs. Harding and I stayed on the boat. They got a secret service man to tell us that they had been delayed and wouldn't be back to lunch and would be back later. Mrs. Harding was furious. . . . They had played more than golf, I afterward suspected. . . . Around four o'clock . . . this little launch . . . pulled up and Ned was standing on the front with his shirt pulled open and braving the waves. . . . I knew then what their condition was because ordinarily my husband was none too daring around water. . . . They were hooping and yelling and the Duchess was furious, and raging. . . . [W]ith her chin uplifted, [she] watched them from the deck. Her nostrils flared and she wet her lips a time or two but she held her fire until the President was within a yard of where she stood; then she spoke. . . . "Warren[,] you come down into the stateroom immediately! You ought to be ashamed to let people see you in

this condition. Practically, you are ruined now." They went downstairs and you can say they had a bitter disagreement in the stateroom because you could hear it all over the boat.

At dinner time, the President was in a very disagreeable mood. They began talking about the pretty girls they had had. . . . She [Florence] started in and Ned called them [the girls] by their first names. . . . Mrs. Harding grumbled a bit more and Ned by no means helped the situation when he became loquacious about some pretty girls they had encountered when they had reached the golf course. . . . She wanted to know how come they had missed the boat. "We never said any such thing," [the men replied]. Which was a deliberate lie. Mrs. Harding was furious and Mr. Harding feeling very happy. . . . She sputtered and Ned asked the President which one of two ladies he had liked the best. . . . The President and Ned in spite of all reproofs continued drinking and neither cared one damn [that] the Duchess was so furious.

At Palm Beach . . . where we had leased a little cottage connected with the hotel . . . Ned came up and said, "Now Evalyn, I think the president has had a pretty hard time and it is only fair that he should meet a couple of pretty women. Will you take care of the Duchess and let me take him up to a friend of mine?" . . . [Ned's friend was] a society woman—Mrs. E. Clarence Jones, now Mrs. Wilson, one of the leaders down there. She was the end girl in a theatrical show years ago. Named Blossom. Then married this E. Clarence Jones, old enough to be her father. She was perfectly beautiful. And Maizie Haywood, Bill Haywood's wife, she was Mrs. Phil Plant. Ned said, "Now will you send word on up to the two of them to get a luncheon up for Harding?" I said, "I'll get the girls and take care of her [Florence]." So we arrived at Palm Beach and we go up to the little cottage and the President said, "Now what are you going to do this afternoon Evalyn?" I said, "Well, I think it would be awfully nice if you two men go off and play golf and have lunch at the golf course, and I'll take the Duchess for a ride.' " Very innocently, the President said he didn't think he wanted to [play golf] so then she [Florence] wouldn't oppose it. . . . And sure enough she said, "Oh, you go on, you and Ned—have your golf game. Exercise is what you need."

So they go on and Mrs. Harding and I have lunch. . . . I had a dull time all that day inventing things of semi-interest for Mrs. Harding's benefit. . . . I drove her until I was dizzy—just dizzy. Finally she said, "Evalyn, we got to get back—Wurr'n will be back." I had my doubts about "Wurr'n's" being back, but finally we started around and coming back we had to pass my friend's house. All of a sudden she grabs my arm—I am black and blue for days—"Look! It's the Secret Service man." The damn fools left him outside. . . . There stood Colonel Starling on guard in front of my friend's house. Under my breath I cursed Ned and his distinguished friend for a pair of fools. . . . "Whose house is that?" she asked. "I don't know." I, her Palm Beach guide, grew awfully dumb. "There is something doing somewhere. There is something wrong somewhere," said Mrs. Harding, looking at me sharply. "We'd better stop and ask that Starling. Hurry." I protested that would not look well and gained my point. I was burning because I had talked my head off and driven for hours and the darn fools left Starling outside. Well, we got back and it came six o'clock, and no Warren. We waited and waited and no Harding and no Ned. "Evalyn, do you know where to reach 'em?"

"No. They'll come along, without our searching for them."

"Well, we better send for them to that house."

"Oh, that would never do. Suppose they were not there? It might get in the papers." That shut her up for a little while and in about half an hour more they came and both were fixed beautifully. Then I heard Harding's whistle break as he stumbled on a step. I knew the top was about to be blown off. Oh, but he was gay and hearty. He goes in and said, "Well, Duchess, you look beautiful tonight." She said, "Warren, go upstairs this minute. I want to talk to you."

"Oh, no, I am boss in this house."

"Warren, you have been drinking," she was raising her voice— you know how she did when she got excited. "Why Duchess, you know I have been out playing golf."

"Oh, no, you haven't. Where have you been? Out with a lot of hussies."

"Well, what of it?" Then he ordered something to drink right there and said, "Now, listen—I am President of the United States. You think you are most of the time, but by God, I am tonight." Poured himself a whale of a drink. I was shivering. He said, "Ned, old boy, we are going out tonight. We are going out to Bradley's [casino]."

I was terrified. I knew if he crossed into Bradley's gambling house, it would really injure him. . . . Mrs. Harding had fought Palm Beach from the start—"Warren we are going to be ruined if we go to Palm Beach." Thought it was the sinkpot of the world. When we'd go under the bridges she'd make us put our cards away when we were playing a little innocent bridge so the people couldn't look down and see the cards. . . . I had become impatient. But what Harding was talking about was an entirely different matter. I had begun to acquire some of Mrs. Harding's understanding of the situation. Previously I had thought that she was foolish to fight as she had against Palm Beach. . . . I had sense enough

to know that if it were noised about that he had gone to such an establishment as Bradley's gambling club the whole trip might be transformed
into a national front page scandal. By then, too, I knew that Harding
had some vicious enemies, men who for a longer time had been the
enemies of Harry Daugherty. I got worried. . . . I took Ned upstairs and
said, "What are the plans for tonight?"

"Well, the two girls are going to meet us and going down to
Bradley's later."

"No, you cannot let the President go down there." Then I got hold
of him and I said, "Now, Mr. President, you have had a nice day and
I want you to take some coffee and stay right here with me. You are
leaving on the 12:30 train. You stay and we will play poker or bridge."
. . . She [Florence] came back. They kept wangling, finally he [Harding]
promised he would stay. Ned and Daugherty went down to Bradley's
and they determined Blossom and Maizie would go right out [with them].
. . . I didn't believe Maizie would yell &%*#, but there was a terrific
scene. . . . They got Daugherty and put him on the train and then Harding and Mrs. Harding came down and got on. I don't know what time
Ned came [home]—I went right to bed.[19]

The press corps that covered Harding saw or heard of such incidents but never breached the zone of privacy to report it, and thus the
general public never knew the President's marriage was so troubled.
Rather, newspapers highly praised the union. "Much has been said and
written in recent years about the breakdown of marriage," announced
the Rochester, New York, *Democrat and Chronicle*, "but the case of Mr.
and Mrs. Harding shows that marriage and the home have not altogether
been wiped out even in the highest places, and that loyalty between
husband and wife have not yet become an unknown quantity." An unwitting editor undoubtedly caused twitters among those who *did* know
the state of the Harding marriage when he declared, "There is nothing
erotic about the Hardings . . . they go arm-in-arm, she a half step behind
him, but never farther away." The President was actually the most
honest, if also the most subtle. The Duchess, he just shrugged, was "the
best pal a man ever had."[20]

28

The Summer of '22

When the Hardings returned from Florida, they dined at the Willard as guests of Interior Secretary Albert Fall and his wife, Emma. They already knew Fall's friend Harry Sinclair, but at this dinner they met another oilman whose fate was to intertwine with their own, Edward L. Doheny. The Dohenys were close to the Falls. After one dinner Doheny came up and put his arm around Fall's shoulders. "I love this man," he said. "That's a queer thing to say, but it is true." So close were Doheny and Sinclair that they had even been houseguests together at the Falls' Three Rivers Ranch in New Mexico. The ranch had recently undergone extensive expansion; not only was there a sudden burst of development and more cattle, but there was more land. On his twelve-thousand-dollar salary, Fall had vastly multiplied his landholdings by buying a neighboring property he had long coveted.

Doheny and Sinclair had good reason to be friends with Fall. Known to only a handful of people, including the President, that April the interior secretary had finally arranged to lease some of the naval oil lands to Doheny and Sinclair so that their respective oil companies, Pan-American Petroleum and Sinclair Oil, could begin offset drilling on the areas being drained of their reserve. Doheny's high bid had won him the rights to the reserve at Elk Hills, California. Sinclair got the one in Wyoming he had long been itching for—an oddly bulbous piece of land called Teapot Dome.

The leases were not public knowledge because Fall claimed that disclosure would compromise national interests. Word did get around, at least in Navy and oil circles. That summer, Charlie Forbes recounted, "after the signing of the Teapot Dome lease the oil matter came up again and the President said, 'Well, I guess there will be hell to pay. But these fellows seem to know what they are doing.' . . . I am satisfied that President Harding did not profit by the oil transactions and did not suspect Fall of profiting by them." Harding did not profit, but Fall did.

In the late spring tentative plans for the Hardings' summer trip to Alaska were again announced—if Congress adjourned before August 1. "I'll believe in that Alaskan trip when I've taken it," the pessimistic First Lady admitted. She was right, as she had been the summer before, but she did have her *Mayflower* cruises and—that May—a new and welcome face on board, the assigned naval doctor, Joel Boone.[1]

Decorated in the war, Boone took pride in being in the presidential social circle. He had served in the Navy Department's Bureau of Medicine and Surgery and as the Red Cross director of the Bureau of Naval Affairs, but it was only after the Duchess first approved of him and his wife that he became medical officer on the *Mayflower*. On May 27 Sawyer went over the Hardings' medical histories with Boone, who thought "Mrs. Harding most remarkable woman for years and physical condition." Days later Boone wrote of his meeting with her: "Said she was so pleased to find me a 'modest man' as they were scarce now days in public life. She expressed confidence with me on the *Mayflower* and said that Gen'l. Sawyer would not always accompany them on trips; when he did not I would be charged with the President's health. She was assured that I realized my responsibilities." Boone observed that "to an untrained medical eye" Harding appeared "as an individual in the best of health." As he became more familiar to her, Florence confided in him about "mean bridge players, experiences in travelling, guests invited requesting extra invitations for friends, etc." He also noted that startlingly "Mrs. H. talked very frankly of things at the White House (spies)."

Just twenty-five days after meeting Doc, the ambitious Boone declared in a luncheon speech to the Glen Cove Country Club that Sawyer was a " 'God-sender' to this administration and this Nation." Privately, however, Boone soon grew disturbed by the truth behind Doc's declaration of the President's exercise regimen and excellent health. Playing golf the way he did was in fact not helpful to the President's health, Boone assessed: ". . . he played too many holes on a single outing when under great mental strain and pressure of official responsibility. Sometimes he would eat hurriedly in his rush to keep golf appointments. He crowded a game in between serious and busy afternoon office hours. Healthful and much needed relaxation was impossible under such practice." Poker was also damaging: "He loved to play cards and there were times, when doing so, he lost too much needed sleep." Boone had desperately wanted a White House assignment since the transition, and in his trying to obtain one was probably remembered by the cagey Doc. He would do nothing to threaten his plum appointment. Boone did not challenge his superior, especially considering the Duchess's confidence in Sawyer's abilities, but he did make a pointed journal note without naming Doc. "In other words, his [Harding's] recreation unfortunately was not directed nor supervised."

Boone's disapproval of Jess Smith's health care was unqualified. During a cruise on the *Mayflower*, while recuperating from appendix surgery performed some weeks before, Jess turned to Boone for treatment of abdominal discharge. Complicating matters was Smith's diabetes, a condition he ignored. "He couldn't afford to neglect his health as he did," noted Boone, who re-dressed the wound, then joined the Duchess to watch the two-reel film *Missing Husbands*.[2]

On May 12, the day before Jess had undergone surgery, he had written a new extensive twenty-four-part will. Half of his $400,000 estate was to go to various relatives and charities, the other half to Roxy and Harry and Mal Daugherty. Harry later said that Jess was "indispensable to my personal comfort" and that he "relied absolutely on his honesty and loyalty," but both Daugherty brothers were more secretly tied to Jess. Although it was two years after the fact, the Harding campaign bank account in Jess's name at Mal Daugherty's bank remained active. Harry never explained this when later questioned but said only that the deposits "involved men and women whose names, and the amount they contributed could not be divulged without a breach of trust." Such an avowal of honesty seemed to be belied by Jess's constant bellowing of his own version of "My God, How the Money Rolls In," his trademark song: "My sister sells snow to the snow-birds, My father makes bootlegger gin . . . My mother she takes in washing, My God! how the money rolls in!"[3]

Although still recovering from his surgery, Jess refused to absent himself from the Duchess's June 7 garden party for veterans. After being besieged by vets waving their name tags for her autograph, she signed a few, then told the others to write their addresses on cards that she would sign and mail later. Knowing of her superstitions, one vet gave her a four-leaf clover he found on the lawn for good luck. Amid the crush constantly around her, the First Lady held the clover carefully between her index finger and thumb and was still holding it when she went back into the house. She had it preserved as a memento in a small water-enclosed glass bead and wore it around her neck.

At this party, as at the one a year previous, Charlie Forbes had been prominently photographed with the First Lady; now he was so closely associated with her that some believed he reported to the First Lady more frequently than to the President. When finally the men lying on cots and the boys in rolling chairs were carried back onto trucks and buses, they were brought to an auditorium to hear Charlie assuredly pontificate to them that the Duchess had been "dee-lighted" to have them at the White House and that "the government is bending every effort to help the nation's incapacitated men."[4]

Also in attendance was a fuming Doc Sawyer. Two weeks before the party a crack was visible in the happy facade of Florence's men working for her boys. On May 24 Boone scribbled, "General Sawyer says Col. Forbes is an autocrat. There is apparently friction." Others at the Veterans Bureau deeply resented Sawyer's own autocracy. "Visited Bureau," wrote Boone. "Magruder made insinuating remarkings about keeping appointment with Gen'l. Sawyer, saying he 'was not running this ship.' Captain said to consider summons from him [Doc] as from White House. Magruder a bull in a china shop at time."

Evalyn's appearance at the party was one of the few White House events she attended that season. The McLeans remained longer in Florida than usual and were to leave early for Maine. Early in June they hosted a Sunday brunch party, to celebrate the second anniversary of Harding's nomination. When Boone congratulated him, the President muttered that his "troubles dated from then." With the onset of railroad worker and coal miner strikes now among his other presidential woes, Warren was losing enthusiasm for the presidency. "Frankly," he wrote to diplomat Dick Child, "being President is rather an unattractive business, unless one relishes the exercise of power. That is a thing which never greatly appealed to me. . . . I would rather be an ambassador than to be President. . . . I would like the one you occupy. I love Italy and I particularly love the environs of Rome. Probably I should be a very poor ambassador."

Having friends who had an estate like Friendship went a long way in aiding the troubled Warren—and not just for relaxation. With threats to his presidency out of his direct control, it helped to have friends who were not only willing to undertake yet another covert operation, like a quasi-official suppression of a scandalous publication about the President's personal life, but who also had the place to carry out the task.

As a special agent of the Bureau of Investigation Ned got more than his dollar a year. He was sent the weekly "General Intelligence Bulletin" assembled by the new "Special Assistant to the Attorney General," young J. Edgar Hoover. Issues of the mimeographed bulletin were numbered and distribution was controlled. It was sent to specific individuals, marked "Strictly Confidential," and had material culled from bureau spying activities. One issue, for example, reported on "Communist Matters, at Home, Abroad, Anarchist Matters, Syndicalist Matters, Individuals, Mexican Matters, Japanese Matters, Negro Matters" and contained a special supplement on "The Proletarian Party of America." The President also used Ned as a cash conduit. Whether it was for the blackmail fund for the continuing monthly payments to Carrie Phillips or some other woman or for child support to Nan Britton, Harding enigmatically wrote Ned on White House stationery that he was "enclosing herewith my check for $200.00 covering matter we discussed the other night." It was, however, in staging a massive book burning on the lawn at Friendship that Ned earned his dollar.[5]

The tip had come from William E. Baum of Saugus, California, who received a brochure in the mail from the Sentinel Publishing Company of Dayton soliciting his subscription for a book. He sent a copy of it to his congressman, Walter Lineberger, who read it and alerted George Christian, who, in a "personal and confidential" note, informed Attorney General Daugherty. The name on the brochure was familiar. Daugherty underlined it: William Estabrook Chancellor.

At six dollars a book—or six for twenty-five dollars—autographed copies of *The Illustrated Life of President Warren G. Harding*, "A Review of Facts Collected from Anthropological, Historical and Political Researches by William Estabrook Chancellor," would soon be available to the public. Among many claims the brochure promised that the book would reveal how Harding, with a "notable absence of public achievement," had become "the foremost man in America," deal "scientifically with his ancestry, record and mental characteristics," include a "report as to whether his parents were ever married," provide a "record of his wandering life," and give the "story of his marriage to a divorced woman and of her father's opposition to him which was not for the reason, falsely alleged, that he was a 'poor painter.' " The book would answer the question, "Why, on Christmas Day, 1920, did Mrs. Harding entertain at dinner six newspaper correspondents without their wives while the father of Mr. Harding ate alone in a Marion restaurant and his sister went to Columbus?"

Chancellor had planned to print his book during the inaugural, but Billy Burns, of course, had arranged to have him harassed while private detectives watched until Chancellor burned the papers thought to be the manuscript. Chancellor then fled to Montreal with twelve hundred dollars. And the *real* manuscript. Later in 1921 he returned to Ohio and researched with a vengeance, uncovering new information on Carrie Phillips, on Warren's heart condition, and on how Florence was head of "The Regency" government. By spring 1922, in an empty Dayton loft, he typeset the plates and began printing the expanded book and advertisements promising that "bona fide subscribers" would be "accorded full opportunity to examine original records." There was no price listed, no copyright notice, no mail-order address, no listed author. The Sentinel Press, which printed Ku Klux Klan literature, was listed as publisher. Baum in California had received only a brochure, but the actual books were being surreptitiously sold in Dayton, Columbus, Cincinnati, and Cleveland. John O'Dwyer, a Toledo Democrat, urgently wrote George Christian to report that the warehouse storing the books was in Toledo and suggested the White House "send out a Secret Service man to see where it is being published and who is financing it. You might be able to bust it up."

With this new lead, Christian again alerted Daugherty, who told Burns. Jess Smith and Gaston Means were sent to do the dirty work and were backed by dozens of official Bureau of Investigation agents and Burns Agency private eyes, sweeping through Ohio, seizing every copy they could door to door by asking to examine the book, then purchasing it for a higher price or demanding it by government order. Since the suppression of such a book in peacetime was absolutely illegal, the boxes of the book were not brought to a federal property but rather carried off by Smith and Means. To Friendship.

Though much of what Means wrote in his later scandalous book must be dismissed as exaggeration, he told the truth about the books' destruction: "I myself had helped to light a bonfire that burnt up the entire edition of this book—copyright and all—bought at a price. . . . The bonfire was made in the rear grounds around the palatial home of Mr. Boyd [alias McLean]. These books and plates had come to Washington in a guarded express car. The car was packed full."

Not only were the books brought to Friendship for destruction, but so too was a copy of the book with Chancellor's handwritten notes, and pages of new research material that he planned to use for an even larger and more salacious version. This copy was not destroyed. For no stated reason, Evalyn kept it herself, secreted away but preserved for history in her papers. Later riffling through it, she said, "Mrs. Harding said to me that she had something on Harding. I'll bet this was it because she knew about the woman [Carrie Phillips] but it was too well-known. I remember once when they had a bon fire out there and burned all this stuff, and this must have escaped."

Chancellor, now harassed by the Justice Department "with a vengeance," moved to Maine with a college friend whose son, Ralph W. Bentle, recalled, "When Daugherty started opening Chancellor's mail Dad brought him here to hide and protect him. They believed there was reason to fear that he was to be committed as insane in order to discount any evidence he might submit to the public."[6]

The Chancellor book notwithstanding, the First Lady had other reasons to be afraid. Since it seemed certain that the strikes would not see an early end, and workers were unemployed for longer than expected, threats were made against the life of the President. Yet again Florence's anxiety rose as Madame Marcia's predictions preoccupied her. On July 24 she learned that Colonel Sherrill questioned the loyalty of White House food handlers seriously enough to order an examination of their backgrounds. A week later Doc learned that an unemployed "Red" had aimed a rifle at the President's office near West Executive Avenue. Under such increasing tension, the Hardings left for a road trip back to Marion, Ohio, for its four-day centennial celebration. Along the 215 miles of Pennsylvania and Ohio bituminous coal districts that the Hardings traveled, there were no staged demonstrations, but rather, as one reporter put it, "striking miners lined the streets of their dingy little mining towns and waved their hats [at] the President and Mrs. Harding. . . . Pennsylvania state constables were scattered along the route."

Marion was drastically different from the dusty village where Florence had been born sixty-two years before. It was now a small city that had, in 1919, produced more then twenty million dollars in manufactured products. Despite the trip's being a vindication for the defiant youth who had wrecklessly married against her father's wishes and the reassuring presence of Harry and Jess, Florence had been "dead against" returning. Her brother offered the use of the Kling mansion, but the irony of Warren's being barred from it for so many years was too much for Florence; they stayed instead at Warren's father's home. Although she ran into her granddaughter, Florence could not bring herself to spend time with her grandchildren. Despite the thrill of riding in the limousine emblazoned with the presidential seal down the soft summer blacktop past old friends and foes, the fairgrounds band concert, parade review, even the playing of "Flo from Ohio" in her honor, it was as she made her way into the old Marion fairgrounds that Flossie came home in grander fashion than Amos Kling could have ever imagined. "I could not tell whether I was most proud and happy then," she said, "or when I used to ride up on my own white horse to the judges' stand at the same spot years ago to receive the blue ribbon." Warren gleefully turned to the crowds with his familiar description: "And now I want to introduce to you the best scout a fellow ever had—my wife."

As she climbed the steps to take her place next to the President, the First Lady's eyes scanned those Marionites chosen to sit in the stacked seating behind them. As she waved to old friends, her face was stricken when her eyes met those of Carrie Phillips. Once it was certain, however, that Carrie would not be permitted near the Hardings, Florence relaxed, later cryptically writing, "I appreciated the apparent clearing of the atmosphere in and about Marion. Although I went out under great pressure . . ." Thus, when a young blond woman nervously approached her later that afternoon, Florence folksily extended her hand with a "Why how-do-you-do, Nan? How are you?"

Nan Britton later wrote of how the President told her that Florence would "raise hell" if she even faintly suspected his adultery with the young woman. Secret Service agent Jim Sloan was more ominous, warning Nan that the Duchess would seek "some form of retaliation." Although Florence was "patronizing" to her ("Yes indeed, I keep Warren Harding the best dressed man in Washington"), Nan was now disabused of any fear that Mrs. Harding knew about the love affair. Although she had no idea of breaking up the marriage, Nan never "cared whether or not she did discover" the affair. Nan's pursuit of the President was to become dangerously bolder.

"I rejoiced at the apparent good feeling that prevailed through all the mining districts of Pennsylvania, West Virginia and Ohio," the First Lady wrote about the return trip. "I know of the desperate conditions that exist but I feel sure that none of these laborers, with but two or three exceptions, have any unkind feeling towards the Chief Executive, and I am sure they know they have a champion of their cause when it is right." If she now had less fear of assassination, she was "full of anxiety over the state of affairs," she wrote Evalyn, now in Maine, provoked by hundreds of letters from rail and miners' wives who told of their family hardships as a result of the strikes. With her secretary and housekeeper on vacation, the First Lady was also managing all her affairs.[7]

Evalyn had invited the Hardings to relocate to the cooler and roomier Friendship for the duration of the miserably muggy summer, but Harding's constant rounds of meetings prevented the move. When a columnist sniped that the McLeans were trying to sell Friendship to the government as the presidential retreat and that they were insulted that the Hardings hadn't come up to see them in Maine, it greatly distressed the Duchess. Evalyn assured her: "[D]on't worry about the horrid old newspapers! You are doing so wonderfully and no one can really hurt you or our friendship for each other. You know I love you, and I can't begin to tell you how proud I am of you. . . . This has been hard on you both but you are coming out of it with flying colors, and the respect of the whole country! I miss you every day and I do hope you can get up here some time this summer. Remember, Friendship is yours if you ever feel like using it. . . . I know how busy you are and I will write you every week . . . do take care of yourself."[8]

Besides her personal concerns and duties, throughout the strike crisis Florence solicited advice from her business and political contacts. When she sent Charles Hilles in the New York headquarters of the Republican National Committee a copy of the President's response to an impudent telegram from the Railway Employees Publicity Association, Hilles advised her to have the White House issue a formal statement that it would not "permit a group of men to freeze our people or to starve them," and that if the workers didn't resume their work by a certain date, the government would seize coal storage and operate the railroads. Then he added yet another worry to her list: "I fear we are again in trouble in the prohibition enforcement office here. . . . It is an almost impossible task. The office is full of dynamite, always. I think the next directing head should not be the nominee of a political organization." Days later financier Birch Helms, who underwrote some of the Army Nurse Corps' needs at Florence's request, advised her, "Concerning the railroad strike, do you not think that it would be expedient for the President to ask Mr. Loree and a few of the most conservative railroad executives to meet for an informal chat in somewhat the same manner as the President talked with the various union officials. . . . If so and the President and you so wish, I would be glad to talk with Mr. Loree."

There was some public knowledge of the First Lady's role during the strikes. The Washington *Herald* reported: "Both of them have been concentrating on the business at hand. Mrs. Harding works and thinks with the President on his major problems constantly. . . . [H]is eating has become irregular and at times almost uncertain. His sleeping has been interfered with. . . . Mrs. Harding in her natural anxiety for her husband's welfare has abandoned everything save arranging for his comfort." Another paper said that she "had been upset for many weeks over the violence and vicious attacks occasioned by the mine and railway strikes, all of which she had followed closely, and with apprehension," noting her cancellation of a long-anticipated inspection of the biochemical bureau of the Animal Division of the Agricultural Department. "The days are most trying," Florence revealingly wrote Hilles. "I have made up my mind that the days of the war had no harder problems to meet than the present time." Her stress was unwittingly increased, moreover, by Evalyn's report of her conversation with a railway executive who insisted that Commerce Secretary Hoover was giving the President bad advice on dealing with rail workers.[9]

The strikes also provoked the first public humiliation of the First Lady, for her interest in a horse. The incident began with a letter on August 1 from the Hudson County District Society for the Prevention of Cruelty to Animals in Connecticut. It tipped off the Duchess to the situation of an impoverished preacher, a Dr. Myers, who owned what was reputed to be the "oldest living horse in America," fifty-one-year-old Clover, a workhorse that had served the community. Myers would have to sacrifice Clover in order to survive himself. Moved by the "sense of justice and gratitude and faithfulness which impels you to sacrifice your comfort rather than kill a splendid horse," Florence sent a hundred-dollar check to Myers to keep Clover fed and housed. As inevitably happened, the letter found its way into a local paper, was picked up by a national news service, and was widely disseminated across the nation. With mining and railroad families desperate for food and in danger of being dispossessed, charity toward old horses made the "just folks" Duchess seem like a Marion Marie Antoinette, sorely out of touch with the reality of American life.

Under the heading "The Human Mule and the Horse," a cartoon showed a figure labeled "old and broken worker" on "poverty road," remarking, "Having been only a working mule all of my life, no one cares for me in old age," while on the other side of the fence in "Field of Plenty for Old Age" stood Clover, above him the caption "This Old Horse to Be Cared for the Rest of His Life. Mrs. Harding sends a check to help care for him." When, in reaction to the publicity, Florence withdrew Laddie Boy and Oh Boy (a bulldog who was briefly part of the Harding White House menagerie) from appearing at a fund-raiser, a sarcastic cartoon showed both dogs locked up in heavy neck chains by an outside gate, shedding human tears, with Florence's shriek from the White House, "You both stay home!" The most critical editorial, printed on her birthday by the New York *Call*, was titled "On the Advantages of Being a Horse":

> ... A noble sentiment dear lady, and none so flint-hearted as to say you nay ... a fine and beautiful world where superannuated horses can find ladies of high station to take an interest in them. ... But it will take more than $100 worth of clean hay and sweet oats to get the rest of your message across, Mrs. Harding. ... [I]t is not a beautiful thing that horses and men are cast away when they have exhausted their strength ... dear lady, a horse has no soul, he has no appreciation of art or music or lit-

erature; a horse has not even a vote. But horses aren't thrown out to starve when the summer's work is done, to beg or to live on the savings from an all too meager daily provender; and even though the loving God may not want to see self-sacrificing men consigned to mother earth after a lifetime of work . . . the masters of jobs decree otherwise, and what they say goes, not what a loving God might require. . . . Clover will live in easy luxury for the rest of his remaining years. If the $100 had not come, the worst that could have happened to him would have been a quick death by shooting. But those workers who have done their work and are cast aside, they are condemned to live, and their sentence is for life. And in this system in which we live there can be no more cruel sentence. Do you want to do something, dear Mrs. Harding, to ease the declining years of all aged horses—and men? Then join us in our battle against this system against which any loving God would cry out in protest! There is no other way![10]

While the Clover incident was unfolding, a series of public attacks began on Doc Sawyer specifically and the Veterans Bureau generally. Sawyer had taken a public stand that bureau personnel should be all civilian instead of largely military since it would keep salary and pension rates lower, and from all state chapters of the American Legion he was vilified. More dramatic, however, was the tension between Doc and Forbes, which finally burst into public view. As chair of the Federal Hospitalization Board, Doc not only resented but was highly suspicious of the fact that vice chair Forbes called board meetings whenever Sawyer was out of town and pushed through rubber stamp approval of the sites Forbes had chosen for federal veterans' hospitals. Doc publicly criticized this, stating that the money should first be spent on building semipermanent housing for permanently impaired vets, not on huge veterans' hospitals, the need for which, Doc claimed, would rapidly diminish. Thus he refused to release the funds for the hospitals that had been appropriated by Congress. Rather than build new hospitals, he proposed to ship vets by train to different government hospitals—from New York to North Carolina in several instances. As a result of the impasse, thousands of shell-shocked, tubercular, and injured vets around the country continued to languish in overcrowded ad hoc wards, even boardinghouses, in all varieties of institutions, unattended, unsupervised, still in desperate need of professional medical care. The war had ended four years before.

Little Doc's massive ego was under the greatest personal attack it had ever experienced. One cartoon, "Sawyer Visits His Home Town," had him as a smug commissar, leaning back in his rocking chair, smoking a pipe with his foot propped up against a potbelly stove, surrounded by an assortment of goony Marionites all impressed by his boast "An' then I told them hospitalization experts where to get off at!" In the corner stood a veteran with a crutch under his arm and a piece of steel for a leg. Legion commanders around the nation papered their representatives and senators with telegrams. "Further withholding help cannot longer be justified by any one interested in welfare of the great army of the *unburied dead*," a Georgia Legion leader argued. The South Dakota Legion accused Doc of "obstruction towards the Veterans Bureau Building Program" and ordered him to give Forbes "a free hand." A South Carolina Legion passed a resolution that Sawyer's opinion "is at variance with the opinion of Colonel Charles R. Forbes . . . and other expert investigators" and that "Sawyer has seen fit to interpose himself between Forbes and the President, thereby delaying the overdue hospital building program. . . ."

Amid this conflict the Senate passed the bonus bill, and now Harding had to sign or veto it. While he had continued to support it in theory, he had also warned that passage would come at the expense of a national tax hike, a step he was not willing to take. The issue not only fueled the fire but brought forth anonymous threats to Doc Sawyer: "Say what the hell [do] you think we soldiers are? . . . [W]e'll shoot every one of you sons of bitches . . . we can do a lot of dirty work as well as you, so take warning. We want our Bonus."

Since Doc owed his job to a First Lady who was publicly viewed as the champion of wounded veterans, the controversy reflected poorly on her and made much of her previous efforts seem to be a sham. Such continuing conditions, along with the furor pressing for his resignation, did not bode well for Doc. On August 24 he initiated a wholly illegal Justice Department investigation. As Joel Boone noted, Sawyer "would have Daugherty investigate attacks on him. Mr. H[arding] dislikes A.L. [American Legion] and resents attacks on S." At the same time Doc would do his own personal spying on his bête noire, chummy Charlie Forbes.[11]

In May Forbes had pushed through his site recommendations to the Hospitalization Board when Doc was out of town and unable to voice his dissent. Doc's daily efforts to confront Forbes were always denied, and when they finally met, Doc accused him of manipulating the board. Rumors about Charlie's drinking, spending, and indecorous behavior were rife in Washington that summer. By now his wife had obtained a quick divorce. In his first trips around the country to inspect sites, Forbes had taken along Carolyn Votaw as an official of the Veterans Bureau, Elias Mortimer, a wealthy building contractor who footed the bills and his wife, Kate. When Heber Votaw's jealousy over his wife's and Forbes's relationship led him to threaten to throw Charlie out a window, however, Carolyn was not invited to join a western caravan.

This next junket proved to be the most outrageous of all of Forbes's gallivantings, a constant flow of liquor, movie stars as party guests, and occasional swims in full evening dress. Forbes met with various construction firms, awarding government contracts only to those who "loaned" him tens of thousands of dollars. When he met with property owners, Charlie engaged in graft by first inflating the value of their land to be sold, then getting a cut. Mortimer was getting a chance to see the sites, make a carefully prepared bid for the construction— and peek at the sealed bids of competing firms. Jealously, however, the President's absent sister had kept track of the partying and learned that Charlie had spent much time with Kate Mortimer in closed hotel rooms. Kate in fact began talking of separation from Elias, and by the time the deals were sealed, Mortimer was livid with Forbes. Carolyn not only knew too much but she was also the President's sister. She tipped off Doc about Forbes's drunken caravan.

Doc's mistress Berenice Blacksten also told him of the beehive of activity at the Perryville, Maryland, warehouse where the vast surplus of medical and other hospital supplies was kept, part of the Veterans Bureau complex where she lived and worked. Doc wanted to see it with his own eyes. On two separate weekends that August—ostensibly as fishing trips in the country with his teenage grandson—Doc went to Perryville and uncovered one of Charlie's schemes in action. Warren Sawyer recalled, "He told Mrs. Harding about everything we went to check out, what was going on at those warehouses. Forbes was very crooked. It was a pathetic moment, because Mrs. Harding had so liked Forbes. They all liked him in the beginning."

Charlie had persuaded the Bureau of the Budget to give him blanket approval of the sale of a three-page list of supplies he claimed were damaged goods at Perryville. He added a long list of his own, emptying the warehouse of accumulated supplies and equipment. Many of the goods—sheets, blankets, towels, gauze, bandages, soap, drugs, and alcohol—were perfectly fine, but he wrote them off as unusable and proceeded to sell them cheaply to the Boston supply firm of Thompson & Kelley at prices far below their value. Boston freight trucks moved daily out of Perryville with the supplies. Then Forbes would order "new" supplies from Thompson & Kelley at marked-up costs. At one point new sheets were brought in at one end of the warehouse and sold as surplus from the other end. All told, Thompson & Kelley bought about seven million dollars' worth of goods while paying only six hundred thousand dollars. Forbes and his legal counsel, Charles Cramer, raked in kickbacks from Thompson & Kelley, but they were trivial compared with those Charlie got from the hospital construction contracts. Other firms competing for bids against Thompson & Kelley to buy and sell to the bureau approached Doc with complaints of unfairness, and he reported them to the President. Harding called in his great poker pal. Charlie boldly suggested Warren send investigators; they got no farther than Forbes's office but reported back to Warren that they could find nothing wrong.[12]

Apart from what Sawyer told her and Warren, however, the Duchess had her own sense of the malfeasance at the Veterans Bureau. She had yet another spy of her own. In early 1922 Florence met Stella Marks, an assistant in Charlie Forbes's office, after she wrote the First Lady about "your boy" Joseph Wright, a veteran on whose behalf the First Lady had interceded. Marks pledged "renewed loyalty" to Florence, adding, "Please call me when you are confronted with problems concerning your boys. I can help in this way." She kept the First Lady posted about various Veterans Bureau activities, including a riverside camp dubbed the Florence Harding Retreat. The same time that she spoke of "that fine big hearted Colonel of ours," however, Marks also reported on his strange behavior. Not long after a Mrs. Soper was made head nurse of the retreat, Forbes abruptly rescinded her earlier announced appointment to a formal post. Soper was privy to incriminating information about him. "A word from the 'Mother of all these soldiers' to Colonel Forbes in the interest of the [Soper] appointment being renewed would be effective I am sure," Marks wrote the Duchess. "This is more necessary than my words imply." Shortly thereafter, Marks wrote again, this time with a more ominous warning about Forbes: ". . . please advise Colonel Forbes that he and his assistants as well as others of lesser rank must be prepared to defend the interests of the Administration when the Sutherland Committee opens fire on this Bureau. I got a tip that the Veterans of Foreign Wars and the Legion are agreeing . . . to challenge [bureau] functioning. . . . Matters here are sometimes of national moment and I realize that you should not be annoyed with them but I know that the Veteran's Bureau which is in itself the greatest Asset to the Administration . . . becomes its greatest liability when its policies are perverted and [an] indifferent attitude [is] taken. . . . If you could be spared to this issue and then delegate the work to us in your name, much could be done."

Amid the distracting crises of the summer, the First Lady depended on Marks to keep her eyes and ears—and the line of communication—open. "I am going to ask you to come in some day and talk about some of these things face to face rather than write," Florence scribbled cryptically. "I want you to keep me in touch with everything that is going on 'around and about.' "[13]

Eleven days after writing Marks, at four o'clock on August 22, Florence met with Charlie for an hour. Despite her knowledge of his rivalry with Doc, she probably did not reveal any of the intelligence she herself had been gathering on him. Her schedule seems to indicate that she was indeed conducting her own investigation. Just hours before she saw Forbes, Florence met with Carolyn Votaw. The next day at one-ten she met with Doc, the Disabled American Veterans' Commander Cook, and the National Rehabilitation Committee's Captain Dikes. Whether she was gathering more information or sharing what she had learned from Forbes and Votaw is open to speculation, but clearly she was up to something. "No one is going to impose on Mrs. Harding," Kate Forbes had written some months earlier. "That is, not more than once, anyway."[14]

Three days after her meeting with Doc, he was sitting behind Florence, ensconced in the front row of the House visitors' gallery, to hear the President address Congress on the increasingly destructive coal and rail strikes. A reporter noted that seated near her were "half a dozen flappers" who "flirted harmlessly with anything in trousers that would respond." The Duchess focused on the person in the seat dead across the chamber from her, Princess Alice.

The strikes were now pushing the insecure chief executive into a state of near terror. In his attempts to cope with what was increasingly perceived to be a threat to the stability of government, according to accounts gathered by the Bureau of Investigation, President Harding calmed himself by excessively drinking whiskey in the Oval Office. Unfortunately one such episode of this occurred in front of a railroad union leader brought in to speak with him.

Rail workers' union president B. M. Jewell recalled that in meeting with the President, he couldn't do any business with him. A Mr. Klein recounted the scene for Bureau of Investigation agents: "[Harding] couldn't talk but barked; he was so drunk he couldn't talk, he had a bottle of good whiskey on his desk and instead of doing business with brother Jewell, he kept taking shot after shot, an argument started, brother Jewell told Mr. Harding that he won't let his men go to work unless they'll sign national agreement and give us what we want, and Mr. Harding told him that he will make them go back to work on the old scale. He couldn't do anything with the President, he was too drunk." Klein reported that Jewell said Harding didn't "run this country or strike, the railroad officials are running the country. They [the officials] told Harding that it cost them 25 thousand dollars to make him." Strike representative Frank Hammerlein repeated these and other details in a Buffalo speech before three hundred strikers: ". . . he is not my President and he is not President of our union. I don't know what you would call him, I know I would not call him a President . . . he has to do what the Wall Street gang tells him and whatever they say he has to do, so he . . . could not settle this strike so we are not going to mind him at all. . . . [W]hen we get through with President Harding there won't be much left of him . . . I would not say that you should kill President Harding, but . . . we are going to fight our own way and to Hell with President Harding. . . . After he has sobered up he will go out and play golf. . . ."

When handbills with this propoganda were distributed on New York Central trains, Burns sent two F.B.I. agents to investigate, the White House considering it all anarchistic. Harding told Evalyn that the nation "would never know how close we came to a desperate revolution." Meanwhile Burns sent out a "discreet agent" to get affidavits on who had first revealed the President's drinking: "It is of the greatest importance that we make a thorough investigation of this and I will leave it to your judgment to see that nothing is left undone to run this man to earth."[15]

Under such extraordinary pressures, unable to escape what he perceived to be his sole responsibility for the government's survival, Harding took a dangerous risk to his reputation. Nan Britton still "took many tears down to the White House" from Chicago, about once every two months. Her love letters to him now got through smoothly, the mailing envelope addressed to his valet Brooks. Within this first envelope was another addressed in the code name A. Y. Jerose, which matched the sexual anatomical nickname he had used for Carrie Phillips, "Affectionately, Your Jerry." These were given directly to Warren. Harding placed everything related to Nan, letters, photos, notes, in the vast drawer of his office desk. Only George Christian had access to it, and he was instructed, according to Nan, to "burn everything in that particular drawer if anything should happen to the President."

Whenever she inquired about the Duchess, Nan thought Warren

had a "certain deprecatory attitude which he seemed to reserve for Mrs. Harding . . . his affectional interest in his wife had ceased long, long before Mr. Harding and I met in New York in 1917 . . . he did not even value her casual companionship." When Nan noted that he kissed his wife when they were reunited after an absence, he wrote her, "You need give yourself no concern over that, sweetheart. My kiss for her is most perfunctory, I assure you!" Florence was, he joked to Nan, as safe "as though she were in jail." He had hoped Florence would take an overnight out-of-town trip, so he could spend a night with Nan, but since he became President, the Hardings had been separated only one night and Warren had spent it camping with Thomas Edison, Henry Ford, and Harvey Firestone.

Since she was a hometown girl, when Warren allowed Nan to tour through the White House, she had nothing to fear if she ran into the Duchess. The Brittons remained friendly with the Hardings, and when Nan's sister went to Washington, bringing along the three-year-old "President's daughter," she was taken to lunch by Carolyn Votaw in the Senate Dining Room. In Carolyn's office, even Charlie Forbes took to the winsome child. Warren was in a meeting, Carolyn told Nan's sister, as they went through the White House; otherwise she would have taken the child to see him. It was the closest he ever came to seeing the child reputed to be his daughter.

Gossip about the state of the Harding marriage was particularly rife in the Secret Service. Jim Sloan was the agent disliked most by the Duchess. "He was frank to express his feelings toward Mrs. Harding which amounted to much more than mere dislike, and on one occasion revealed his resentment toward her which had been aroused by the occasion of one of his visits to me," said Nan of Sloan's excursion to deliver money and a love letter from the President. "He said Mrs. Harding, knowing he was going to make a trip to Chicago, but not of course knowing why, had said to him, '[J]im, where are you going? . . . what are you doing for Warren?'" Sloan replied, "[N]othing at all." Florence was suspicious. "Well, you are! And what's more I'll see to it that you are put out—I'll make you lose your job!" Sloan left the service before she fired him, going to an investment house where Warren played the market in a secret account.

According to several individuals close to the Hardings and McLeans (including Alice Longworth), during the strikes the President had a woman, alleged to be Nan Britton, met at Union Station by Secret Service Agent Ferguson and brought to the White House for a tryst—not walked past the careful eyes of Ike Hoover but driven through the southwest gate. Repeating his pattern of taking dangerous chances that seemed to have begun with his amorous adventures on a ship deck with Carrie Phillips while the Duchess slept nearby, Harding made love to this woman in the small private chamber just off the Oval Office.

If Warren had his loyal Fergy, Florence had her loyal Barker. With her fears particularly roused that summer, Florence had Barker keep his eye on the President. Maggie Rogers, working in the house that August, told her daughter that "she [Florence] told him [Barker] to watch very carefully. . . . She was in on everything." Sensing Florence's growing fears and stress, Barker had become especially "dictatorial . . . taking his job too seriously or rather has a tendency to overstep," as Boone scribbled in his diary that summer. And Barker knew what he was looking for and how to get the truth about Warren Harding to his wife.

Ferguson fetched Nan at the station, her train arriving late, and brought her to the President's office. When Harding flushed with anger at him for being late, Ferguson reflected, "I knew right then and there that this fellow was crazy in love with this girl." Ferguson stood in the hallway outside the door. The other door into the office was through an anteroom where George Christian sat and worked, and that door was already closed. Tipped off about the woman's presence by Barker, within five minutes the Duchess rushed up and demanded entry into the office. Ferguson told her the door was secured by Secret Service regulation, even to her, that she could only gain entry through Christian's office. He recalled: "She was furious and demanded entrance through my door. I repeated the Secret Service instructions. She turned and dashed into Christian's office. As she disappeared, I ran into Harding's office and grabbed the girl, telling them what was happening. We got out before Christian got around to letting Mrs. Harding in. I don't know whether he knew the score, but . . . he took his time opening the door to the President's office. I showed the girl the way out and told her to find my car and wait for me. I was standing at my post by the time Mrs. Harding came rushing out. She stood and glared at me like she couldn't believe it. Finally, she spun around and returned to the White House by the back, private route. As soon as I thought it was safe, I went to the car and took the girl to a hotel."

"I don't think the Duchess ever found him, *in the moment*," Alice Longworth recalled many years later, "but that summer afternoon in his office, I understand—it was really rather a close call. Stumbling in closets among galoshes, she pounding on the door, the girlie with panties over her head. *That* sort of thing." Alice, who heard the details through

Ike Hoover, delighted in withdrawing her cigarette long enough to peal through the smoke, "My God, we've got a President who doesn't know beds were invented, and he was elected on a slogan of 'Back to Normalcy'!"

When or if Florence confronted Warren about the incident and what excuse he might have provided are unknown. That such incidents still occurred and upset her was no secret. As Madame Marcia told a reporter, "Mrs. Harding's serious illnesses were brought on by distress about her husband's affair with 'that woman.'" Even if she had grown accustomed to coping with such incidents, they still took a toll. At the same time, late August, Florence received an envelope that said, "If you think best, open and read." She did so, and to her sensitive state of mind, it was a menacing letter, suggestive of some other Harding mistress being harassed by Gaston Means or Jess Smith. Titled "The Handwriting on the Wall," it referred to "real crooks" and historic abuses of power, asking if it was "the prerogative of any said 'Officer of the Law' to handle a delicate woman as if she were made of Iron and Steel," offering that "certain things should come under the observation of our President, Warren Harding, that are being done against him." It ended with the warning "Remember the Ides of March," possibly suggestive to Florence's mind of Marcia's prediction of Warren's death before his term ended, on March 5, 1925.[16]

On an overcast Saturday, August 26, on a long-delayed *Mayflower* voyage, the Hardings screened *The Prisoner of Zenda* for their guests, but when the lights came up for the change to the second reel, the Duchess was gone. She did not appear at dinner. Hours after they docked, Boone noted in his diary, "Mrs. H sick." On September 6 Florence scribbled alarmingly to Evalyn, who had been pleading that the First Lady come rest in Maine with her, "I doubt very much my being able to leave home . . . the next three days ought to determine my condition. I do long to see you. . . ." Two days later Boone noted in his diary, "Mrs. H very ill."[17]

29

The Valley of Death

On Wednesday, September 7, the White House announced that the First Lady's cancellation of appearances was due to an illness "neither alarming nor serious," but the next day Doc informed Dr. Boone that she had a dangerously acute illness. Florence's right kidney had shifted slightly and twisted the canal between it and the bladder, the fluid accumulation in the pelvic region causing sharp pains, a dilation of organs, and such a strain on the left kidney that it inflamed and was also unable to expel urine. This was the fatal danger. Unrelieved of such bodily toxins, the general blood system would absorb them and cause uremic poisoning. Surgical incision to straighten the kidneys, however, would strain Florence's weak heart. The only immediate measure that could relieve her was to try to sweat the liquid out of her system through her pores. As had been done in all her attacks since the surgery, Florence was wrapped in heavy blankets and hot towels to keep her perspiring.

The next day, after a brief rally, the First Lady rapidly declined. "This isn't going to be a short illness," said Warren. "I've gone through these before." Boone enlisted naval nurse Ruth Powderly and gave Florence a hypodermic needleful of codeine. Doc called in America's leading physician, Dr. Charles Mayo of Rochester, Minnesota, who advised that nearby surgeon Dr. John Finney of Johns Hopkins come in immediately. Still, even in the midst of this crisis, Doc Sawyer was jealous of those growing close to the Hardings. The President was so concerned about Boone's being immediately accessible to Florence that he wanted the doctor to stay in the mansion, but, noted Boone, "Sawyer had not made that suggestion."

Harding also wanted honest public disclosure and had Sawyer release a medical bulletin. Thus, one of the more astounding aspects of the illness came on Friday, the eighth, when George Christian gave out mimeographed pages of a single typed paragraph. For the first time the seriousness of a President's wife's medical condition was presented to the country: "It is admitted that her life hangs in the balance. Hope has not been abandoned by any means, but it is realized that the physicians in attendance are battling against tremendous odds. Mrs. Harding's optimistic nature, her indomitable will and the manner to which she is helping in the fight for life are all on her side. Her mind is active." Each day thereafter bulletins were released, the Philadelphia *Public Ledger* editorializing that the effort was "striking in comparison with the attitude of the previous Administration as to compel notice. Recognition of the intense popular interest in the President's wife . . . have prompted a policy of frankness with the public."[1]

From her White House room the First Lady still played the Duchess. "Warren," she commanded, flat on her bed, "be sure to have one of your cars take Dr. Finney to the station." Another time, when he anxiously gazed down upon her still body, she opened her eyes and told him to go play golf. "Don't worry, Warren, I am going to get well. I want you to go right on with your work." The President now confined himself to pacing between his study and the sickroom, sometimes taking a chair and sitting just inside the door to watch her as she slept. "Mrs. Harding was supposed to be dying. We sat around her bedside not knowing that she was conscious that we were in the room," a friend later recollected. "Suddenly Mrs. Harding spoke. 'Have you any thought of getting a room ready for Dr. Mayo? Have you seen to it that he will have every comfort?' We were dumbfounded. We did not realize that she knew that we had sent for the great Mayo. We thought she was sinking. But she was 'on the job' even then."

By the time Mayo arrived on Saturday, the First Lady was jeopardized with septicemia and slipped in and out of consciousness. During a three-hour consultation of the doctors in the private quarters, Dr. Finney said he was certain the liver was involved and recommended an operation for relief of the infection. "Mrs. H assented to operation," Boone noted. "My view—watch blood count during night but still had margin to wait. . . . Sawyer took strong stand against operation feeling she could not withstand mental and physical shock."[2]

Meanwhile a national vigil spontaneously arose. The third women's conference on the League of Nations, meeting at Geneva, Switzerland, the Veterans of Foreign Wars, African-American jazz societies, the Senate, Seventh-Day Adventists, newspaperboy leagues, the Girl Scouts, Boy Scouts and Camp Fire Girls, the Union League Club of New York all joined in group prayer. Some four million members of various Christian churches offered prayers. Prayer sessions were announced on Saturday in synagogues for the next day. Maids were given Sunday off so they could go to church for the "dear lady." Anthracite coal miners, reaching a settlement with coal operators in Wilkes-Barre, wired their prayers. The entire population of Washington was asked to pray by city commissioners. Sunday matinees at the theaters, vaudeville, and movie houses were punctuated with standing silent prayers. The national commander of the Disabled American Veterans, comprising some 171,000 members, asked that each "join me in prayer to Divine Providence for the speedy and complete recovery of Mrs. Harding, who has always been deeply interested in our welfare." As one paper reported of that Sunday, not "since the stirring days of the great war, [when] the whole nation united in one prayer—success for the Allied armies—has the country bowed its head in common appeal to the Almighty as it did yesterday."

An outpouring of love for the dying Duchess gushed forth. Dozens of editorials appeared, discussing the value of a First Lady and praising the way Florence handled the role. When a rumor spread that she had died, the *Marion Star* was inundated with calls and telegrams. "She is just beginning to live. She has worked so hard," wept one woman into the telephone. "How terrible it is to think that death may take her at such a time." Everyone from Inez McWhorter, Florence's old cook, to Texas Guinan sent telegrams, with Warren signing each acknowledgment. Advice from doctors around the country also came fast and furious: Use "Biofeed"; place copper and zinc disks on the kidney attached by wires stuck in vinegar, water, and milk; use a "Vitonitt" electric blanket to sweat her; inject calomel, sulfuric acid, alcohol, and perspiration.

Of all the expensive wreaths brought to the North Portico, all of the reporters were most touched by the simple gift of one man, Julius Jones, an African-American veteran, who hobbled up with one rose. "I lost my leg," he explained. "I didn't have a friend in the world who cared. But Mrs. Harding one day found me recovering from the operation in the hospital. She seemed interested when I told her I had no friends. Next day she came with a big bouquet of flowers." At Florence's order the gates had remained open, and thousands of well-wishers flooded in to kneel in prayer on the driveway. A Senate page arrived with a framed psalm. Harry and Jess, Cabinet members, congressional, judicial, military figures, Woodrow and Edith Wilson in a horse-drawn victoria, even a stone-faced Charlie Forbes all came with hope that Florence would survive. One person did not visit throughout the crisis. Detesting sentiment, with no belief in an afterlife, Alice Longworth didn't cope well with the specter of death.[3]

Just before midnight a car raced up under the porte cochere, and a thin woman with bulging eyes and jangled nerves, eyebrows arched into a look of permanent surprise and stray dark hair, jumped out and ran to the North Portico. Frazzled, frightened, she was waved through the entrance, into the elevator, up to the family floor. She was the only one allowed to see Florence besides Warren and the medical staff and remained the most vigilant visitor, coming several times a day, even taking her meals there.

Evelyn had arrived.

"The news had come to me at Bar Harbor and, after an exchange of wires with Sawyer and a long distance talk with Harding, I had started for the Capital on a special train. We broke all [speed] records," she recalled. "I was taken directly to the office [study] of the President. . . ." He broke the news to Evalyn: "I am afraid Florence is going."

"Surely," she protested, "there is something we can do. We can muster all the doctors—"

Harding told her that Mayo and Finney thought surgery was the only chance for survival but that Doc refused to agree. Warren asked Evalyn to intercede. She consulted first Mayo, who was so disgusted that he was ready to leave, then Doc, who, "pacing up and down the floor just outside the bedroom where Florence was lying, quite out of her senses from the effects of self-generated poisons . . . seemed to me [to be] trying to take power through the silver stars on his shoulders, to make them testify afresh each minute that he was after all a general . . . there was something ridiculously bird-like in his striding." She chastised him: "Now look here, General, do you realize the load of responsibility you have taken on yourself? You are standing out against Finney and Mayo. Good Heavens! Think of who they are." Sawyer squinted at her from behind his thick spectacles: "I realize much more sharply than you can just how the country will think of me if . . . anything happens to her. . . . I have pulled this woman through many and many a time. I know her constitution. I know what she can stand and I know she cannot stand another operation. . . . I am gambling on my reputation: I am facing ruin, almost, just because I am convinced that if her heart holds out the kidney stoppage will open up. I tell you, I'm their *family* doctor." Evalyn calmed down. Sawyer took her in to see the Duchess. She recalled thinking that Florence was already dead.[4]

At the next consultation Finney insisted on immediate surgery; Mayo and Doc's son, Dr. Carl, thought it could wait a little. Doc stayed opposed. Boone hesitated, worried that if he gave poor advice, he would have "ruined my professional career." Harding insisted. Boone said her blood and urine tests suggested that surgery could wait overnight. "I should never have voiced an opinion," Boone thought shortly after. At one point Carl also had second thoughts, fearing for the reputation of the prosperous Sawyer Sanitarium. Even at this, Doc refused to agree. Ultimately, he told the press, the decision was "left entirely to Mrs. Harding," at this point lucid. After Warren told her of the views, she advised against surgery. Outside, the press and public kept vigil through the night as friends came and went, putting up a good front. "Mrs. Harding seems better," Evalyn told reporters. "That is just why I am going home." With tears in his eyes Harry said "pluck and will" would save her. One friend not identified by name, however, couldn't help remembering the ominous prediction Florence had obsessed upon at a time that now seemed so distant: how she, "in the very early days of the Harding boom for President, expressed a premonition that, if her husband were elected it would mean tragedy for one of them, or for some one they held dear."

Through the night into Sunday Warren obsessively repeated the 121st Psalm, then, said Mayo, "made frequent visits to Mrs. Harding's room, and talked with her, but she was so sick it was impossible for her to carry on a conversation." At one point when her fever reached 105 degrees and her respiration was two and a half times its normal rate, and death was expected at any moment, her eyes opened. "Don't worry, Warren," she said, "I am not going to die."[5]

As the wee hours went by, Florence's condition worsened. At times, discomforted by the fever—a bad sign that the poison was spreading through her system—she tugged nervously at the bed clothing around her. The opium was not killing the pain. Around four in the morning Mayo and Boone went in to see her; the latter noted that "she had a very strange stare on her face directed right at both of us." As she kept gripping her fingernails into her palms, he was alarmed to see them bleeding. Doc moaned in grief, "Her last chapter is being written."

Only later did Florence Harding reveal in vivid description what seemed to be a sort of near death experience: "I saw two indistinct figures standing at the foot of my bed. . . . These figures were rapidly fading away into the distance and it seemed as though I were looking through the small end of an opera glass. I realized I was dying, which I was determined not to do. . . . When you [Boone] were disappearing from my view, I knew that I was losing consciousness and I also knew that, if I did lose consciousness, I would die."

As she lay on her deathbed, Florence said Amos Kling and other relatives who had died came into her consciousness "because they just gave up." According to what Florence later told her niece Louise, her spirit was "floating," she was "going. . . . But she fought back, through sheer will." As a *National Magazine* writer, with whom Florence later spoke, said, "It seemed as if she were on a moving platform with voices in the distance at the foot of her bed which was gradually fading farther and farther away. She clenched her little hands with determination." To herself she repeated, "I must live. I must live." Suddenly, she stated, she "felt a sort of change" and "passed off into a deep sleep."

Having entered into what she called the "Valley of Death" or "the Shadows," Florence said it was a life-changing experience from which she emerged with new understandings. "The one thing that counts when you are down in the Valley of the Shadows is: What have you done for human beings? What have you collected or gathered in the way of knowledge? Reading, material things, collections or hobbies all count for naught in the Valley of the Shadows. It is this: How much have you done for human beings, for those you love?"

At the moment she fought back, there was a sudden, dramatic physical change. "It was then that the nurse discovered that she needed instant bed care. . . . She had spontaneously relieved the obstruction. . . . She began to drain spontaneously from the kidneys voluminously, and began to clear mentally. As Dr. Mayo and I observed this amazing episode," Boone wrote, "I have never experienced such a positively definite exhibition of mind over matter as eventuated in Mrs. Harding's case. . . . [S]he demonstrated that, when death was on the threshold for her, she kept herself from dying truly by pure willpower."[6]

Poisoning remained a threat if the slight improvement slowed. Surgery to remove the bad kidney, rather than merely drain the liquid still remained the only way to save her, but the toll on her "treacherous" heart condition, aggravated by the use of opiates, could kill her. The Duchess continued the refrain "I must not die, Warren needs me," clenching her fists. As the sun rose on Monday, the swelling was subsiding, the kidneys starting to function. Surgery was again delayed. Warren took his first walk on the lawn in days, but all business remained suspended. By Tuesday her condition relaxed enough that Mayo thought he could leave. Dr. Carl also left, but not before jealously insulting Boone for his sudden closeness to the Hardings, as if they were the Sawyers' personal property. "Disliked his remarks prior to leaving in talking to me of attention to Mrs. H. He confesses to a suspicious disposition," noted Boone. Each day that week, with Warren taking every meal with and reading to Florence, she improved. Sunday, the seventeenth, was, Boone noted, "Mrs. Harding's best day to date." By month's end she still had many uncomfortable nights, but by mid-October she was able to sit up. Not until December, however, did the doctors feel assured she would survive. On October 1, at her request, the White House was again opened to tourists.

Life had indeed gone on. On Tuesday, September 19, the President finally vetoed the bonus bill, but other issues affecting the veterans were beginning to accumulate and become problems not remedied by a veto. In the last days of September the contents of an important letter were gently brought to Florence's attention from one of her California "spies," Edythe Thompson, who had disturbing news about Veterans Bureau affairs.

In the midst of Florence's crisis, on September 14, Doc put in writing to the President the extraordinarily alarming news that Forbes had given the nod for construction to begin on hospitals, despite the fact that the Federal Hospitalization Board had yet to approve them. In the case of a Minnesota site, Charlie hadn't even mentioned it to the board, saying simply that Harding had approved it. One Massachusetts hospital was budgeted at $1.5 million, but under Forbes it ultimately cost twice that. "If the policy of making these great, ornate, elaborate and high-powered hospitals is pursued, we shall finally find that we have wasted a large part of the money," Doc ranted, projecting a $15 million overrun. The time had come, he urged, "when frankness is absolutely necessary." Why did Forbes want new hospitals built instead of renovating those already existing, and where were the overrun costs going?

Even in illness, Florence had similar questions after learning from Thompson the peculiar details of an awarded contract for a California veterans' hospital's construction: "Confidentially, the man who got the commission for the plans at Livermore knows less about hospitals than any man on the coast . . . it will make a nasty piece of campaign material besides making the soldiers uncomfortable. . . ." Florence passed the information on to Doc. Forbes glibly responded to Doc's inquiry that "without any question all of the difficulties regarding Livermore will have been eliminated in a very short time." Still, Doc wisely advised Florence to tell Thompson if "the apparent evils have not been eliminated that she had better let you know further about the subject."[7]

Sawyer remained indispensable to Florence as a political operative and the man who could keep her alive, but Joel Boone now had privileged access to the grateful Hardings. He was given use of the White House tennis courts and the First Lady's personal car, consulted on naval medical services over dinner with the President, sat in the presidential box to hear Harding address Congress. He now was, said Florence, "one of the family," and she arranged that he be retained in the mansion instead of being sent out on the *Mayflower* when it went out of town. In every way, however, he carefully protected such access by never contradicting Doc. As the First Lady grew to rely on Boone, Doc inevitably grew envious. "Talked with Gen'l. Sawyer relative to our relations," Boone noted at the time. "I assured him of my loyalty." Still, he now found himself Florence's unwitting confidant as she shared her thoughts and observations about Sawyer and his behavior and asked Boone for his views. "G.S. [General Sawyer] vs. Mrs. H. and our conversation," Boone cryptically recorded. "Peculiarities explained."

There was evidence of the old Duchess the day after the midterm election when Warren reported the results of Republican losses, and she belligerently piped up, "Warren Harding, don't you tell me such an untruth. [Senator] Frank Kellogg couldn't have been defeated and I know that is not true." Meanwhile national newspapers shifted from stories on the housebound First Lady to her substitute at events of the new social season, the "very popular" but uninterested Second Lady ("I find it hard to start in on the social round," Grace Coolidge confided to a friend. "I went to a tea this afternoon and wondered, why?"). This spurred Florence to orchestrate efforts ensuring that she was remembered, kicking off a national "Forget-Me-Not" drive for the Disabled American Veterans by buying their first flower from her sickroom and thus prompting the sale of hundreds of thousands in office buildings, theaters, and department stores; sending gargantuan bouquets with her handwritten cards to social affairs, and making certain the press office released reports of her progress, such as her first steps walking again.[8]

Of the few visitors permitted to see her, Evalyn was the most diligent. On one occasion she brought an amusing gift of a crown made of Belgian lace, another time a Czechoslovakian vase stuffed with *four dozen* roses. At Harding's November 22 address to Congress, Florence asked Evalyn to go in her place. "I think it was one of the best he has ever made, and the appearance when he came in the room would have done your heart good," Evalyn reported. "I missed you so, the place seemed so queer without you. I wish now I hadn't gone. Do hurry up and get well so we can have our good times once more. With all my love always affectionately."

Evalyn wrote Warren too, after he sent a "sweet note" about Emily, adding "some day, if you ever have a minute to spare, I would love to have you see her." He would come to see Emily, but he also had another *girl* in mind—considerably older—whom he wanted to see, at Friendship.

Despite confinement to her room, the Duchess still managed to keep tabs on who was coming into the mansion and visiting with the President in the west wing, likely through her loyal aides. There was at least one incident when Harding was slipping out, and she shouted loudly within earshot of all the staff, "Warren, you're not going out of this house tonight!" The New York *Herald* significantly noted his stag status: "It is not a record that he has appeared at any function to which women were among the guests . . . lately he has been going quite freely to men's parties." Parties at the Love Nest were always stag—except for chorus girls and prostitutes.

What motivated Evalyn McLean to permit the President, the husband of her best friend, to use her home Friendship for an assignation can only be speculation. At face value, it was unbelievably cruel. Harding may not have been in love with his wife, but in his way he loved her. In concern for her calm and complete recovery, Warren would certainly not want to do anything to upset her, nor would he expect that Evalyn, as her best friend, would want to encourage any such thing. There could be no risking of any further assignations at the White House, which may have been suggested to Evalyn, not by the President himself but by Ned, as a liaison. It was most likely a passive situation: Warren may simply have arranged to play golf at Friendship one late fall afternoon, while Ned arranged to have Nan Britton brought there discreetly to rendezvous at the vast estate with the President.

All that is known is that the rendezvous took place while Florence Harding was confined by convalescence to the White House and that among several who learned the details of it—probably from Evalyn herself—was Alice Longworth. Reporter Hope Ridings Miller later wrote: "A number of capital residents had glimpsed her [Nan Britton] in Washington and some knew that she had visited the President at the White House. Furthermore, Means' statement that Harding and Nan sometimes met 'in the house of a very accommodating lady who was supposed to be Mrs. Harding's friend but appears to have played both sides' could be verified by several individuals. They were well aware that 'the accommodating lady' was a veiled reference to Evalyn McLean, in whose home Harding and Miss Britton occasionally met." Mitchell Palmer's wife saw things herself: "He used to drop by Evalyn McLean's house to visit that woman. He would just walk in and go right upstairs. Evalyn completely ignored him. I was appalled the first day I saw him there. 'I think we should rise when the President enters,' I said. 'Tut, tut,' said Evalyn, 'he doesn't want to be noticed.' I should think not—when I realized what was going on!'"[9]

Regardless of any possible lack of malice in Evalyn's complicity with Warren and Nan, if Florence were to learn of it, the betrayal would be utterly devastating.

At the time Florence knew nothing of such visits, particularly since, as late as July 1922, she did not know of Warren's affair with Nan specifically, nor is there evidence that she suspected it was Nan with whom she nearly caught Warren in the Oval Office in August. Also, the First Lady was undoubtedly distracted by a continually distressing situation in which she had a vital interest. On November 22 Doc told Boone that he was looking into the background of Commander C. R. O'Leary, who was in charge of the Supply Corps, which serviced the Veterans Bureau warehouses. Sawyer was "fearful that there is some crookedness in the Veteran's Bureau. Forbes and O'Leary do not look like good combination." Leaving Florence in Boone's care for the day, Doc explained that he was going to the Perryville warehouse the next day.

Despite what Boone perceived to be "certain suspicions," Florence convalesced calmly: "I have had my meals up in my room, and on the nights I am able to sit up he [Warren] dines with me here on a little table." On Thanksgiving she was allowed to walk to the hall and then, in a wheelchair, descend in the elevator to the state floor, where she presided over her first table meal in weeks, with Warren and Harry. It was only a brief flash of joy for the day before Doc reported a new Forbes dilemma to Warren: "I am sending you a list of surplus Army supplies [sale catalog], including among other things, canned goods, now stored in Washington, which, I am told, they can well use at St. Elizabeth's. Why should it be sold to go elsewhere?" Harding permitted the sale to go on after the government need for such items was determined, and he still saw no evil: "I can not escape the conviction that the management of St. Elizabeth's is quite as much at fault in omitting to make a justifiable bid for desirable supplies as is the War Department for selling to the greatest financial advantage. It is a great pity that the selfishness of departments results in a lack of coordination [and] . . . loss to the Treasury." Coming revelations made the 18,104 cans of No. 2.5 pears and 10,000 boxes of russet shoe polish pale in comparison.[10]

On December 7 the First Lady pushed her recovery—with a slight setback when she sought to resume her position and greet Georges Clemenceau, who lunched at the White House with Harding. Persuaded against her instinct by Dr. Boone, she greeted the legendary French wartime leader outside her room, dressed in blue, seated in a chair. "I stood beside her. She was nervous and did not have a good hold on herself," said Boone, "much disturbed that she had not introduced me to Clemenceau. Seems to feel terribly. Said she does not know what possessed her except that her illness accounts for lack of composure. . . . [S]he was much upset." A quiet Christmas was held that year, Florence relying on friends to shop for her and being permitted downstairs only for Christmas dinner, though she tore through her wrapped gifts like a happy child.[11]

Her lengthy convalescence left Florence in such frustration that she finally arranged a session with the world-famous pyschologist Emile Coué, having "taken an active interest in his writings," a reporter noted, and being "in a receiving frame of mind for treatment." But the Duchess was still the Duchess, and Coué's optimistic mantra of "Day by day in every way I am getting better and better" was not enough. That she had looked death in the face more closely than ever shook her, and she unequivocally believed she had been spared by the "prayers of the people . . . the thought as I was lying there, hovering so near the borderland, that so many thousands of so many creeds and all denominations . . . were offering up their prayers." She had always been conscious of how quickly life passes and "struck anew with the fact that time is creeping on space," but now seemed more spiritual, and that for her meant even more absolute faith in the supernatural. Even when bedridden, she shot up and snapped at Dr. Boone for placing her slippers on her bed; "very bad luck," she told him. It was only a matter of time before Barker was on R Street fetching Madame Marcia and escorting her into the west wing, down the hall and up the elevator, avoiding the inquisitive Ike Hoover at the North Portico. Marcia melodramatically recalled:

> During her long and critical illness, my visits to her were necessarily lessened, although we kept in frequent touch with one another. I knew that her sickness was not to be fatal, a fact which she was insistent upon knowing for her condition at times was more dangerous than was generally realized, and her constant prayer was to be spared during the remaining days of her husband. When she rose from her bed the conviction was stronger upon her that these days were not to be long. . . ." How short a time?" she insisted. And I knew that evasion was no longer possible. "Death will claim the President before the year is ended!" I told her. Slowly she turned back to me. Her eyes were filled with a curious brooding light. "You are certain, Marcia?" "It is not I who am

certain—it is Destiny that is certain!" I answered. The brooding light deepened in her eyes, and she flung out her arms in a bitter gesture. "Power, glory—they make us slaves, Marcia—slaves! They are killing my husband—they are killing me! The price is too great, Marcia, too great, too cruel for us to have to pay!"[12]

Florence's illness had also taken a toll on Warren. Evalyn remembered, "Time after time each night the nurses had to attend to her; and every time they did, of course, the President was disturbed. . . . When she was sick or not, he always had to sleep in the bed next to hers." Warren did show genuine concern and gentle care for Florence, often taking her by the hand, but he also craved freedom. Whether concerned for his health or paranoid about his being with other women, Florence tried to pin him to her side even once her recovery was assured. Maid Maggie Rogers observed that this made him "stay away even more. . . . Mrs. Harding spoke of ingratitude and said that she could see now that her happiest times had not been at the White House but when they worked shoulder to shoulder at the newspaper. She said *he* thought he didn't need her any more, but he *did*. . . ." Florence often fumed: "I wish he would listen to me. I wish he would pay attention to me."

To friends, however, she insisted that her enforcing such time together improved her marriage, that "this illness has been a blessing." She declared, "We have had more time with each other than at any period since the beginning of the campaign . . . it was a treat to be able to take advantage of my condition and sit upstairs in the evening and talk to my husband." After their dinners alone together Warren still read to her, once reading her proofs of a forthcoming book on Yellowstone National Park, where they had honeymooned and hoped to visit again along the way of their still-anticipated Alaska trip. "We hope that her health has been steadily improving," the French ambassador wrote the President in the new year, "and that you will be able to enjoy free of all serious cares that journey to Alaska so earnestly desired by her."

When Florence retired after a dinner, Warren revealed to a friend that her health might further delay the trip, but he spoke almost mystically of his dream to see the land of the Aleutians, "plunge boldly out into the open ocean and approach the Arctic Circle . . . up into that far northland greeted by a midnight sun." Florida with the McLeans was more certain. Although away, Evalyn continued to lift her friend's spirits, writing openly, "I don't think you realize how much I miss you and how often I think about you. I always liked you from the first evening

I met you at Alice's, but now I love you dearly . . . you have my unbounded respect and admiration."

Besides Evalyn, it was Doc in whom Florence had "complete confidence" as she looked ahead. If she chose to ignore his petty jealousy of Boone (Doc was "not enthusiastic" for him to come to Florida, although Florence was "very desirous" of it), Doc bravely endured character attacks while doggedly tracking the culprits of misdeeds against her boys. Warren felt similarly, boasting that Doc brought "my wife back to life after she had literally entered the shadow. I owe him everything I have." That her little Rasputin could keep her alive against the nation's leading physicians now utterly "vindicated her feeling that he was possessed of supreme medical skill."[13]

30

One Suicide and Two Resignations

By the new year it was the President's turn to be ill. A virulent influenza, accompanied by high fever, chills, and disorientation hit Harding hard, peaking on January 17 and requiring Boone to sleep at the mansion and check on him every two hours. He was bedridden for weeks and did not feel good for three months. Doc insisted he was too weak to go to the west wing, and for a month Warren worked upstairs in his study. When Doc did insist that Harding rest, he did as he was told. When Florence insisted that Warren not assume too much work, he also followed her orders, as when she found him going through a work folder with George Christian and in a "direct and candid fashion" commanded George out and Warren back to bed. She wanted him well in part because she wanted to make the Alaskan trip. "Out west they don't know they have a President," she wrote an aunt, "and I am anxious to have them see Mr. Harding."[1]

Both Hardings were on edge about Charlie Forbes. At the end of January Doc informed them that several veterans serving in Congress were "exceedingly anxious to introduce a bill calling for an investigation of the Veterans Bureau." Doc hoped to stall them, but the press was now on it, making an investigation inevitable. Doc confided Charlie's criminality to Boone, who recorded, "Things look rotten." If Warren still held out hope that Charlie was merely a sloppy administrator, Florence now seemed convinced that she and her boys had been betrayed. On January 22 Boone went directly to the Duchess: "Talked to Mrs. H. about Forbes—am pleased that she seems to have had her eyes opened to him." When Doc confronted Charlie in what Boone termed a "very hot conversation," Forbes threatened that Doc "would be slandered," perhaps about his affair with Berenice Blacksten.

Forbes's betrayal stunned not only Florence but other women who had loyally supported him. "I cannot put my information on paper," California informer Edythe Thompson, unable to comprehend the criminality of Forbes, wrote the First Lady, but "my own private opinion is that someone very close to Colonel Forbes has perhaps put over in his name some very irregular things. . . . I do not believe that he would violate the confidence that you and the President have in him. If you could talk to him confidentially and get him to see the great danger he is in . . . If an investigation is to be made by you, allow me to suggest this: the investigators be not from the Department of Justice. . . . [I]t is so easy for people to get into a government office and have so little regard for their country. . . ." Florence's spy Stella Marks wrote her urgently but honestly: "Conditions here in the Bureau are such that someone must dare to hint at least that a conference be arranged whereby the President will be at liberty to advise the immediate hospitalization of Colonel Forbes. He is certainly a sick man and this Bureau is not the place for him at this time. In view of the circumstance, other matters have accumulated which involve executive action and I certainly hope Mr. Harding will intervene. . . ."

The Duchess unequivocally wanted Forbes fired. "Warren's friends and chums, knowing that she would not sacrifice her bigger ends to their graft, avoided her," a friend of Florence's noted. "Cabinet officers and financiers never discovered that she was the brains of the partnership. They were not accustomed to meeting women like her. Nor was she accustomed to dealing with men like them." Boone wrote at the time, "Forbes apparently on the descent, his record besmirched by his actions. He is and always has been a 'nut' in my estimation. Believe his record will reflect adversely on Administration. President am sure will handle situation wisely."[2]

He did not. On innumerable occasions Doc and Boone together

or alone pressed Harding to fire Forbes. He remained "loath to believe anything ill," insisted on getting, said Boone, "unbiased facts and fair and accurate facts, as far as he could, before he was willing to take drastic action." When they returned with more incrimination, Harding still "would not commit himself, listened patiently, [but] gave no evidence what action he might take. . . . I must say I was impatient for him to act more expeditiously," Boone concluded. Doc had even desperately turned to his perceived enemy Harry Daugherty, then contending with a dangerous bout of flu, to intervene. When Harry reeled off the allegations against Charlie, Harding became enraged, denying their truth. Harry was adamant. Harding was so angry that for the first time he failed to ask Harry to stay for dinner, a usual custom when they met at day's end. The next day the direct line from the Oval Office to the attorney general's office did not ring once—something that had never happened before. Some days later Harry prompted the Duchess into action by writing her, "Your distinguished husband was not very kind to me Thursday night."

It was only when the Duchess forced the issue of dismissing Forbes in a formal meeting, also attended by Doc, that Harding faced reality. The next day he apologized to Harry, admitting that Forbes had betrayed him, adding, "I am heartsick about it." A day later the President finally took his anger out on the right person, summoning Forbes to the Red Room, where Warren throttled him by the neck, yelling, "You yellow rat! You double-crossing bastard."

Forbes asked permission to make an immediate inspection tour of the British veterans' hospitals. Harding agreed on the condition that he first submit a written resignation. The administration announced a bureau "reorganization," and the next day, February 1, Charlie's cohort and the bureau's legal counsel Charles Cramer resigned. It was too little too late. In less than two weeks, on February 12, the Senate voted to investigate the "waste, extravagance, irregularities and mismanagement" of the Veterans Bureau. The House was poised to follow suit. Harding, having been aware of Forbes's malfeasance well before he reacted, could technically be tried for a felony. Forbes's ship reached Liverpool, but before he disembarked, he was handed a cable. He stepped ashore stripped of all official status. Public rage against him remained high through the long months before investigations and actions were taken against him. Florence Harding later said that she and Warren "never recovered from Forbes' betrayal."

While Florence appreciated Doc's effort to rid the bureau of corruption, his continuing affair with Berenice Blacksten made her realize that he would not disclose anything to her that reflected poorly on his own reputation. After he slipped out of town with Berenice for the day, the First Lady revealed what she knew of the affair to Boone. "His secrecy about trip not approved by his patient," Boone noted. Doc himself never acknowledged his affair to Boone, who recorded, "There seemed some embarrassment when I met him at gate in Union Station" with Berenice in tow.[3]

As Washington buzzed with gossip about the impact of Charlie's betrayal on the First Lady, she had to contain her anxiety lest her illness recur. "I am much stronger," she reported to Evalyn in Florida, "but my heart is still very uncertain." In the midst of her doubts about even Doc's being entirely truthful, just five days after the congressional inquiry was announced, Florence received a note from spiritualist Bertha Eldred that "Marcia has a message for you." It was not the personal but the political health of the Hardings that prompted Marcia, who had already done a tarot reading on Forbes. Now there was to be a fuller accounting of others Florence had equally long presumed to be friends: "Oh, Marcia, I had to see you! I am surrounded by traitors! Terrible things are happening. I must know who are Warren Harding's friends and who are not. I have a plan. I will let you know when I am ready for you to help." The same month Florence placed a reading from Marcia in her account book: "The President is coming under some very powerful influence and needs to safeguard his health. . . . The opposition of the Moon to the Sun and Saturn in his horoscope shows that he cannot depend upon his friends. He should be suspicious of the ones he *should* trust and *trust* those he *should* be suspicious of."

Publicly the First Lady now seemed a shadowy figure, her only public act being a fuel curfew in the mansion during the national fuel shortage. When she ventured outside, it was only for some crisp air on the south portico, hidden from the public who strolled the lawn below. The only glimpse of her by outsiders was brief and accidental: As Warren was being photographed and she wanted to make certain the lighting was correct, she entered a state room and yelled out, "Hello boys!" to photographers, while ordering Warren, "Now, Mr. President, look pleasant please!" Even after being seen by the photographers, however, gossip about her health prevailed. "Of course, every time the White House is mentioned someone leans forward and asks earnestly, 'Well, really, and on the level—how is Mrs. Harding anyhow?' " wrote a columnist. "Another woman—who often has inside information—said that she had talked to Dr. Sawyer, and he didn't seem at all optimistic." Another rumor had her recuperating on a world cruise, and she was besieged with telegrams criticizing her for planning to leave America. She finally called a press conference for February 24.

The thirty-six women reporters from large newspapers, wire services, and magazines and several free-lance writers were brought upstairs into the oval room, where a fire blazed below the First Lady's portrait. Sun streaked through the three long windows, the light glinting on the silver tea set on the large oval mahogany table, laden with flowers, cakes, and scones. Laura Harlan poured tea, and Reddy Baldinger stood nearby. Sitting on a Roman bench, Florence was dressed in a red robe with pink roses, "pasty white and heavily made up as she could be," thought Vylla Wilson.

Florence's eyes may have had a "wonderful light" when she told of her near-death experience, but a reporter said, "It wasn't altogether the old vivacious Mrs. Harding." She chose her answers carefully, "now and then she had to think for a word," and went into such detail about her illness it "revolted" one reporter. The stunning news was her public acknowledgment that she was "backing the movement to establish a Federal institution for women prisoners." The New York *Evening World* reported that an "indication of Mrs. Harding's recovery is her re-entry into public affairs. It became known today that she is using her influence to obtain passage in the present Congress of a bill to permit the Government to take over a hospital in the Blue Ridge to be used for women drug addicts. She sent for Republican Leader Mondell and asked him to hurry the bill through, but so far the way has been blocked, and it is doubtful if she will have her way."

Florence also chided those who had incorrectly reported that she had used a cane. She opened her clippings book, into which she had pasted "every single scrap of copy" about her, "with the names of the authors written neatly beside each clip—and she had to go to a great deal of trouble to find out the names of the authors since few Washington newspaperwomen had bylines." That she would go to such an extent, thought Vylla Wilson, "made your blood run cold." She spoke of how the scheduled March trip to Florida would "renew" her and showed the reporters a blue gown sent up from Evalyn, but there was only a veiled reference to the Forbes scandal in a private aside to Wilson. "You can't fool me," she said. "I know what's going on."[4]

And what she didn't yet know she was about to find out. "I thought I would like a little gossip myself," Florence wrote Evalyn in Palm Beach. "The pity is the things I would like to say cannot be put on paper!" Evalyn did her duty, in several letters:

I have a great many things to tell you. . . . Dorothy Dalton the moving picture actress is making one of her big pictures near here, and I have been up several times to see it taken. . . . David Elkins is here with his brother Steve and is hitting the high places. Their girls were put out of the hotel the other night and there has been a great deal of scandal about it. . . . Senator Dupont [*sic*] is up to his old tricks—leaves Mrs. Dupont [*sic*] in the Hotel and runs around with lovely young girls! There are a lot of 'Follies' girls here and they are wonderful. May Howard looks very stylish, is hitting the high spots. She drinks likes a fish and never gets to bed until daylight. She is a wonderful woman for her age—of course, here you are nothing unless you have a beau. You must never be seen with your husband, and never go to bed until morning! Everyone here says W. R. Hearst will not live a year! That he is dying! I told that to Mrs. Hearst the other day and she was very pleased! . . . I can't tell you how much I miss you and how anxious I am to see you.

Significantly, Evalyn added a reference to one of the society women the President had enjoyed an assignation with the winter before: "Maizie Haywood left last night."

Evalyn sent her yet another gift, a shawl, in anticipation of the Florida trip. In thanking her, Florence made clear just how ill Warren had been. When it [the shawl] was brought in, "Mr. Harding was on one bed in my room and I on the other, a proper setting don't you think. . . . Mr. Harding is up today with his clothes on for the first time since Tuesday. He looks fine in the face, but of course is very weak and his legs very wobbly. The aftermath of grippe is far more annoying than the disease itself." Evalyn was also ill, having developed an alarmingly large lump in her neck and sudden weight loss, signs of a thyroid condition. Florence said the Red Cross flag would be flown in Florida: "between Mr. Harding and myself, Harry Daugherty, Jess Smith and Evalyn McLean! I am sorry to hear you are not well, but we will discuss that when I go down there. . . . Mr. Harding says I look twenty years younger. Of course that is not so, but I am glad he thinks so."[5]

At the same time the two friends were corresponding, there was a strangely urgent tone to be found in a thank-you note sent to Florence from Alice Longworth for anniversary roses. "We are going away tomorrow for a few days and as soon as I get back I am going to find out when it will be convenient for you to see me," Alice wrote. Apparently it was inconvenient for Florence. Days later Alice persisted in her *second* thank-you letter: "I am so glad that you are really better and do hope that you will feel up to letting me come and see you before you go South. It is such a long time since I have seen either you or the President. May Miss Harlan telephone, if it is possible?"

Before Florence saw Evalyn, the Princess had something important to tell the Duchess. Alice relished her access and curried favor for it. Sending Florence a blue scarf to mark the first inaugural, she had added: "[D]id enjoy cards the other day and outrageously successful wins too. Thanks for all the good times at the White House during the past year." Florence responded that she was "happy if you enjoyed with us some good times here. . . ."

That Warren had a sexual liaison at the McLean home in the fall of 1922 was no secret by the winter of 1923; although Alice later confirmed that Florence learned of the encounter, she would not take credit for being the "first person" to tell of it. But during her brief and only call on the First Lady in the winter, Alice recalled that she told Florence how during her illness Evalyn had been "so kind" in letting the President use Friendship to meet with "women friends from Marion."

Certainly with her long-simmering jealousy over Evalyn and Florence's friendship, Alice had a motive for revenge, for despite her superficial camaraderie with Evalyn, the two had a habit of stabbing each other in the back. For several years after the fact, the White House seamstress, Lillian Parks, for one, heard not only that Warren came to Friendship to "meet Nan Britton over there" but that Alice used her knowledge to sabotage Florence and Evalyn's friendship.

Whether Alice provided Florence with the details of the liaison or merely gave the initial tipoff, maliciously hurtful damage had been done. Florence had already been lied to by Forbes and doubted Doc's complete honesty. Now, she must have felt at least a deep suspicion about Evalyn's loyalty, and at worst, a cutting betrayal. The incident must have chillingly reminded her of what had happened a decade earlier, with the last best woman friend she had had, Carrie Phillips.[6]

What Florence did with the information is not certain. By the time they arrived in Florida, Warren was "physically and mentally tired . . . not what one would call a robust individual," reported David Lawrence. She did not cancel the trip, but while she may not have fiercely confronted Warren, Harry wrote her just days before their departure, "If this is the day you are on speaking terms with him, give him my regards." At the same time Warren also made a veiled reference to Ned that their adulterous behavior of the year before couldn't be repeated this time. "I understand the party is stag," Warren wrote Ned of the guest list, "outside of Evalyn to look after you and the boss to keep me right." As was her habit, Florence threw herself into distraction, seeing to Ruth Powderly's promotion as chief naval nurse, hosting a movie screening, talking obsessively of Ohio politics, being fitted for a new wardrobe. She left herself not a moment to dwell on Evalyn's betrayal. If she chose to confront her, it would not be by letter. Even the day before leaving for Florida, she hastily organized a dinner for an old friend and departing Cabinet member. Al Fall was leaving Interior to go into the red belly of Russia itself—as an agent of Sinclair Oil.[7]

Florence was aghast when she learned that Fall wanted to leave. She had planned on his being appointed to the Supreme Court when an opening occurred, and before accepting his resignation, Warren had told him, "Go over and talk to the Duchess. Let her talk to you." Even she could not convince him. "I will be of more help to the President and to you," Fall told her, "outside than in. If you ever need me I will know it as soon as you do, and you will not have to send for me. I will come to you without call." To anyone who would listen, Emma Fall would read a January 4 letter from the Duchess in which she said she "can't find words to express her regrets on hearing of his determination to leave the Cabinet because the administration needed him so badly and he was so loyal in his friendship," which she knew he "would continue to be." Yet even the possible future appointment to the high bench was now refused by Fall: He was completely finished with any public service.

On Monday, March 5, as she emerged from the White House, the Duchess paused for the long row of clamoring cameramen. Coming along, but suffering from a shot nervous system and lingering flu, were Harry Daugherty and his nurse. He wrote Florence, "We will say nothing [about his illness and the presence of a nurse] to anyone—only the President and you, [and] of course, Jess knows it, but we can trust him." Displeased with the division of quarters was Dr. Boone, assigned a room with the messy Jess Smith, who was living high again and neglecting to care properly for his appendicitis wound and his chronic diabetes. Boone was, however, wide-eyed at the McLeans' posh private rail car: "I never could have imagined any rolling stock on rails could be so elaborate. Mrs. McLean always carried pink sheets and pink pillow cases, not only to have on her bed on the McLean special car, but for any sleeper that she occupied in any of her travels."[8]

The next day Harry, Jess, and their entourage went on from Ormond to Miami's Flamingo Hotel, while the Hardings and Doc were whisked away by the McLeans to their rented 120-foot-long yacht, the sleek *Pioneer*. Descending from the train into Evalyn's arms, Florence saw for herself just how ill Evalyn had become, shaking nervously, dangerously underweight, her eyes bulging, her skin translucently pale, her neck thick with a goiter. "Evalyn is not very well," the Duchess later wrote to a friend. "Dr. Grile is coming from Cleveland this week to examine her neck and decide whether the goiter is to be removed or not. Dr. Finney of Johns Hopkins telegraphed her that her heart was such that she cannot take an anesthetic."

During a stop at Cocoa Beach, Florence visited with her brother Cliff and his family, pointed out historic sites to Evalyn on a motor tour, and, when residents gave the Hardings a choice property lot, a reporter noticed that she "took the deed." Mostly she remained on board, lounging in a blue and white kimono and head kerchief, spending hours in conversation with Evalyn on the canopied decks adorned with palms and flowers. Alone with her, despite her illness, Florence seems at least to have hinted that she knew about Evalyn's having provided Friendship as a presidential trysting site. Boone sensed a strained atmosphere on the yacht, innocently noting that "everyone seemed to have been gossiping about one another, for some unknown reason." As she had in the early part of her life, however, Florence seemed to have repressed her hurt, this time because Evalyn seemed to be in such precarious health.

Coming down the gangway to the Flamingo Hotel dock, the Duchess yelled good morning to those gathered to see her but went directly to their cottage, covered in purple bougainvillaea. She instantly loved Miami, in the midst of its Jazz Age boom, taking in palm-lined Collins Avenue, Lake Pancoast, the rising Ocean Drive hotels, and the fence-enclosed Firestone estate. "And such a place as this must be so interesting to live, to work in. . . . There must be a wonderful opportunity to study human nature, where so many people of many kinds come. . . ." That night, whisked away to a late-night drinking and poker party hosted in a new hotel by Miami developers, Warren gave a glowing statement for public release on the promise of Miami. With the Florida vacationland property boom of the Jazz Age, the President helped anchor Miami as a prosperous center for fun, sun, and sin.[9]

Joel Boone, in a cottage room with Jess, was repulsed by the odd man. "Jess Smith's way of living and my way of living and our interest, except in the Attorney General," he noted curtly, "were almost the opposite." Boone also worried about the exhausted President. "Harding was very fatigued for some time with a post-influenzal rebound after he had been the victim of a very severe cold if actually not an influenzal infection with all its manifestations," he noted. "I might observe that influenza toxemia definitely affects the musculature of the heart, which accounts for a lot of the fatigability that accompanies it and follows it."

Harding's frequent complaint of "indigestion" was also a bad sign. Momentary deficiency of oxygen in part of the heart provokes an odd pain—angina pectoris—pinpointed just below the breastbone, left shoulder and arm, and upper abdomen, but longer periods of deficiency cause cardiac infarction, death. At times the pain was only in the abdomen and often mistaken for indigestion. Hardening of the coronary arteries— kept in check with a nonfatty diet and exercise—when progressed to a certain point was further exacerbated by physical and emotional stress, but an "extraordinary mental shock" or "unusual physical strain" could cause an acute occlusion. Even had he not had a mysterious history of heart troubles, the President was now a prime target for just such a death. Although Doc had no worry about Warren's weak heart, it was evident to even strangers. That winter, when Harding shook hands with Emmanuel Libmann, the highly respected and prominent cardiologist noticed a shortness of breath in the President and abrupt pauses in his conversation. Libmann immediately diagnosed a cardiac condition and predicted Harding would be dead within six months.

Florence remained blissfully unaware of Warren's true health. In the first interview in which she authorized full quotations, with reporter Edith Dunton, she said she was "particularly anxious to go to the territory of Alaska to see what could be done to bring the great national wealth of that vast territory to the door of the American people." It was the first official statement that the Alaskan trip would be made.

Meanwhile back in Washington tragedy reverberated in the wake of the Veterans Bureau debacle. The resigned legal counsel, Charles Cramer, shot himself. According to his wife, Lila, he had not come down for breakfast as usual, and the cook went upstairs only to find him sprawled on the bloody bathroom floor, a gun nearby. "For some reason the butler had carried the body from the bathroom where the dead man had shot himself, to an upper back porch," recalled his friend the writer Mary Rinehart, "and I shall never forget the strangeness of seeing him lying there, in the early morning sunlight." They moved the body again, to his bed. Then Mary left with many unanswered questions. "He had spent almost all of that night writing letters. There were many of them, but they disappeared that morning. One of them had been addressed to the President. What had he thought about, as he sealed the last one and picked up his revolver? What about that dark moment when any man, any woman, draws the long breath which is to be the last?" It was later suggested that Cramer had been on the take for millions of dollars with Forbes, but no investigation of his suicide occurred. To the press, however, there was something lurid about the suicide's having taken place in Florence and Warren's old Wyoming Avenue house. The only word from Miami was that the Hardings and Cramers had been "mere acquaintances." The suicide letter he left for the President mysteriously disappeared.[10]

In Miami, Florence soon tired of long walks, receptions, and the daily Cola Santo's Band numbers such as "Hot Lips," "Give Me All of You," and "Bohemian Girl." She worked on mail, sent from the White House, and even managed a patronage dispute between California's senators. She had extraordinarily limited contact with Evalyn. After ten days in Miami, the Hardings went north first to St. Augustine and then to Jacksonville. Jess left for Ohio, "on personal business." Boone said, "I had no idea about his affairs, business affairs, but recognized and knew he liked to get his nose into all sorts of things, at least to find out what was going on. I did not encourage him in any way to discuss his interests with me." As for Harry, he was devouring news reports, said Boone, "about the elections of 1924, suppositions and predictions as to whether or not Harding would seek renomination."[11]

The news that Harding had purchased his family's original farmhouse in Blooming Grove and would build a golf course on the property was interpreted as his having "served notice that he will not again be a candidate for the presidency." Even Mark Sullivan wrote for publication at the time, "If for personal accounts—which personal reasons might readily take account of Mrs. Harding's health—Harding should step aside." To be sure, there were some private signs that he might not run. "I am always interested in South America," Florence wrote with suspicious prematurity for someone planning to be First Lady for another six years; "we are looking forward to a trip there after we leave the White House." Warren's hand was suddenly forced, however, by Daugherty's unscheduled announcement that Harding would stand for reelection. Privately he was heading off intraparty opposition, but publicly it made Harding into a partisan candidate instead of just the august President. Boone and Doc conferred, the former writing, "Rather chilly atmosphere . . . Sawyer . . . surprised me by saying A.G. [attorney general] did not always speak for the President and overestimated his accomplishments in President's behalf. Insinuating story re: relations between Pres. & A.G."

One headline proclaimed WARREN A CANDIDATE, SAYS MRS. HARDING, and seasoned observers deduced that Harry's announcement was

Florence's doing and that the attorney general's presence in Florida was calculated to do more than help him recuperate. Political columnist Edward Lowry made the case that by having his attorney general and First Lady "nominate" him, and make it seem merely like a spontaneous act of devotion, the President could not be accused of politicking:

> Nothing that affects Mr. Harding's political fortunes is ever undertaken or set in motion without their participation and advice. Mrs. Harding holds Daugherty's skills in politics in the highest esteem. . . . The two of them have not had a chance to talk together with Mr. Harding since last September, when Mrs. Harding fell ill. . . . [N]either of the Hardings realizes, and certainly they would resent being told that Daugherty is a handicap. . . . And the President always listens to Mrs. Harding when either his personal or political affairs are concerned . . . persons who have been about Mrs. Harding . . . take the circumstance into account. It makes Mrs. Harding a factor in considering the probable course of public affairs. . . . One undeciphered figure is in this Florida group. He is Jess Smith. . . . He is always spoken of as "Mr. Daugherty's friend, Mr. Smith." The President so refers to him. . . . Smith is attached to Mr. Harding on the theory that the course of the satellite is the course of the planet. Mr. Smith's functions seem to be many, but [are] not clearly defined to the public gaze. At any rate, he is now a member of the presidential party, and that implies a certain consequence.[12]

Evalyn's reflection that the trip had been weirdly still was stating the obvious. Even in Miami the air had been oddly cold for days on end. For Florence, it was particularly threatening in the most unnerving way imaginable. As she had been reaching out to a massive crowd of cheering Floridians, some thoughtful person tossed her a gift. "They had given Aunt Florence a large bouquet of flowers, but her Secret Service agent Barker grabbed them away from her," recalled Louise Kling. "Inside that bouquet was a vial of acid. If she had smelled the flowers, she would have been burned."

And it was to be a considerably chillier spring in Washington.[13]

31

Astral Premonitions

Alaska, Alaska, that was all the Duchess talked about. As a test of her endurance she joined Warren on a packed two-day trip to New York, visiting the New York *Tribune* plant, going to the Music Box Revue on Broadway, missing only a Yankees game at which her favorite player, Babe Ruth, hit a homer. "And I not there to see him!" She even organized another press conference for women reporters, now always speaking for attribution. "I am talking to you because I am interested in women," she told them. "I like to see women succeed."

In telling reporters how she read character by physical features, Florence admitted that her large hands showed her to be an active woman and that with her returning health she was anxious to "start doing things." Indeed that month she successfully blocked federal legislation with her lobbying skills. When she heard of the government appropriation being considered for the purchase of the "castle" of Senate widow Mary Henderson as the first official residence of the Vice President, the Duchess raged as in old times. "Mrs. Harding, who had been growing obviously impatient," recalled Nicholas Murray Butler, "burst into flames and almost shouted, 'Not a bit of it, not a bit of it. I am not going to have those Coolidges living in a house like that? An hotel apartment is plenty good enough for them.' " The bill was defeated.[1]

The President was equally fit, or so Doc maintained in a bizarre, rambling interview in which he credited Harding's Anglo-Saxon race as the reason for his "physical and mental strength" and claimed that Harding "obeys all orders explicitly" and "knows much of medicine and consequently many of the causes which lead to disease. Because of this he is often able to see for himself a red light indicating danger, which he avoids simply by changing his course." As for himself, Doc boasted that he kept Harding in excellent health "by watching closely for every sign or symptom" and every morning made "any medical or clinical examinations which may be necessary" because he "wants to know the exact physical condition of this human machine. . . . [A]s long as they [the Hardings] are in his care he is not going to take any chances." All this proved tragically untrue, for Doc never detected Harding's cardiac weakness. Doc's only correct observation in the interview was his fear that Harding could not sustain any serious illness: the President was not in the most robust condition because of a lack of exercise.

Meanwhile commitments were made for the western trip, from fishing at Bill Wrigley's island of Catalina to the Hardings' being "Head-liners" at the "Historical Review and Motion Picture Industrial Expo-sition," in Hollywood, "an extravagancy by the greatest entertaining force of all ages, the motion picture industry." Although they were to tour the Midwest, plains, Northwest, and West Coast, Florence was fixated on Alaska. "It will be a fascinating trip," she told her cousin, while poring over a book chronicling the territory's history and geog-raphy.[2]

Al Fall and his successor, Hubert Work, insisted that Alaska's resources were best exploited under the Interior Department, but Har-ding refused to act on this recommendation before seeing the region. Until he left for Russia in June, Fall remained a close companion to Warren, his colorful wife, Emma, quoting the President as telling Al, "I want you to go and I hope you will make some money. I know that whatever you do in Russia will be in absolute agreement with my policy." If Fall's working for Sinclair was not directly embarrassing to Harding, his recent quips to the press *were*. "Though President Harding likes to drink as much as I do," Fall told London reporters, "he is prepared to stand or fall by the enforcement of prohibition on the ground that it is the law and must be enforced."

Florence had come to know Sinclair personally. She had enter-tained him just weeks after Florida, the oilman writing his thanks to her for "the delightful hospitality extended to me on the occasion of my recent visit to the President. Your courtesy was deeply appreciated." Ingratiation was also one of Florence's most effective methods for gath-ering secrets. By the spring of 1923 the First Lady, like most insiders, knew of Fall's seemingly legal leasing of Teapot Dome to Sinclair. But that Fall would even refuse the idea of later accepting a prospective post on the Supreme Court to take a lucrative oil job in Russia stimulated her old suspicions. Even if Fall bragged endlessly about his newly en-larged ranch, he kept mute about the source of his windfall. When Olive Clapper began to hear the "gossip of crooked deals" involving Fall's oil leases, she asked her husband, the national political reporter, if the First Lady "in her secluded corner" knew anything about it. "She's not secluded," said Ray Clapper. "She knows more about what's going on than he does. Why, she's known Albert Fall for years and Sinclair and Doheny too. She's not fooled!"[3]

What the political gossip could not answer, the stars could confirm. Before the First Lady permitted any formal announcements of who would be accompanying her and the President to Alaska, she finally summoned Madame Marcia for a usual twilight session, anticipated since her illness. Florence was lying on a couch in her room, clutching a sheaf of papers. "I have a list here of the men who are closest to the President," she told her astrologer. "I want you to write out the horoscope of each one. I should have had you do it before the Cabinet was formed. That's where I made a great mistake. I pray God it may not be too late now." For three days Marcia worked with the information the Duchess had gathered, the birth places and dates of friends and officials of whom she was now suspicious. When Marcia returned with the charts, Florence told her, "I will study each one myself, alone." Marcia was surprised when Florence reported her own surmisings on Fall. "The most immediate and dangerous menace that I can see centers around this one man. What is he doing—right now? Try clairvoyance, Marcia."

"I was lying on the President's bed," Marcia later related—after what was perhaps the most bizarre scene to take place in the mansion's 122-year history—"the First Lady, was lying in her own bed beside me. She wore a white Philippine-embroidered nightgown, with a pink silk negligee over it, and pink mules on her feet—but for all her finery, she looked worried and drawn, and suddenly old. . . . We were both too tired to talk, or even to stand. I had just finished one of my most exhausting clairvoyant readings. She had heard terrifying things about her husband."

Marcia said she went into a clairvoyant state and began to see barren country, then fields gradually rising, until she saw one steep one, rather like a dome, "and all of a sudden, I was gazing into a vast field of oil wells." Florence yelled out, "I knew it! They are trying to keep it from me, all this scheming about oil leases. They lie to me. Why? I am frightened." She then mentioned her fears about Jess Smith: "I am as afraid of him as I am of that other man [Fall]. But I'll save Warren Harding from them all—if it kills me!"

Although Marcia told her story after the scandals broke, she didn't need clairvoyance to learn about Jess Smith and confirm his nefarious doings. The circles of spies and loyalties of the Harding crowd had become even more byzantine. Although Florence disliked Roxy Stinson and refused to invite her to any White House events, Roxy confided her suspicions about Jess's activities to Evalyn. The two women had met through Jess. Through Evalyn, Roxy met Marcia and through her was able to transmit to Florence incriminating personal information on Jess. Marcia was nothing if not a clairvoyant in the loop.

That spring the nation had its own first blast of titillating capital scandal when a private letter of Senate wife Mrs. Poindexter was leaked in the press. Harding Cabinet wives were humiliated when the letter revealed that for their private parties Marion Denby used Navy Department cars, boats, and bands and Martha Weeks used War Department aides. Unnamed were a senator's pregnant wife "dizzy with strong drink" and another who boasted of knowing the safest place to get bathtub gin tested for purity. Some outraged citizens began a petition drive featuring a list of questions—"What are the names of high officials of the government in whose homes gambling at bridge is permitted . . . [and] in whose houses liquor is served to guests?"—and a demand for public answers from none other than Attorney General Daugherty. He gave none. Luckily Mrs. Poindexter had not mentioned Jess Smith—or Warren Harding.[4]

Evalyn, for one, had given up drinking. Upon her return from Florida in early May, she was so ill that Dr. Finney finally decided to perform risky surgery and remove her goiter in her room at Friendship. It was there that Ned received a May 19 letter from Jess Smith. It seemed a desperate grasp for security, coming from one who had just spent several weeks with his friends: "You have always been so nice to me and I have such a deep affection for you that I really get homesick for you. . . . I want you to know how much I appreciate your kindness to me in every way. I probably will never be able to repay you but I am always willing and ready to do anything I can for you at any time." Jess wrote similarly to Joel Boone that week.[5]

Days later Jess joined Harry out at the Shack, their Ohio cottage. Jess told Roxy that a Columbus man identified only as a friend who would "arrange this or that" arrived and insisted on seeing Harry. Jess woke a tired Harry, who, said Roxie, "abused Jess unmercifully . . . swore at him and talked disgracefully." Harry dressed and departed, leaving Jess alone. Used to receiving telegrams from Harry that read, "I am awfully lonesome without you," Jess felt the incident was an outright rejection. "Jess adored Harry," Roxy sympathetically confessed, "he loved him." Not understanding why Harry was now spurning him, Jess retreated into plaintive paranoia. "They are going to get me," he told Roxy in Columbus. "They pass it to me. . . . Let's go home before dark." He suspected strangers of listening to his conversations and following him and asked friends to stay with him at night. "Tell me what the trouble is," Roxy said, trying to comfort him. "No," he responded. "Just cheer me up. . . . Do *you* miss me when I am gone?"

Meanwhile, suffering the critical fallout of headlines like PROHIBITION LAW HARD TO ENFORCE, SAYS DAUGHERTY, Harry was summoned to see the President privately in his office. Although he did not mention the Duchess, Marcia, Roxy, or Evalyn directly, Warren said he had "been informed" that Jess was "running with a gay crowd, attending all sorts of parties." Coming just after the Poindexter revelations, such a small thing—Warren told him—as Jess's "using the Attorney General's car until all hours of the night" had wider implications for scandal now. Harding paused, then said sadly but firmly, "I suggest that you tell him it will be impossible for him to go with us on the trip to Alaska. The party is already filled." Harry knew Jess would be deeply upset but nevertheless confronted him when he returned the week of May 21 to the new apartment they shared at the Wardman Park Inn, where they had again frequently entertained the Duchess and Warren at dinner. Boone, also present, recalled that "there had been much gossip brewing in regard to Jess' appearing to speak for the Attorney General . . . and [he had] bumptiously irritated a number of people. He . . . overestimated his importance." Boone said a "word of praise" from Harry would cause Jess to "purr," and he "tried in every way to keep close to him. Daugherty . . . realizing that Jess was overstepping the bounds of propriety and using growing bad judgment, the criticism levelled being intensified, became convinced he had to 'lay down the law' to Jess." He spoke bluntly: "Jess, if you do not discontinue your seeming assumptiveness [*sic*] and do not change your ways down at the Department of Justice, and in and outside of Washington, you will have to cease to live with me and move out of this apartment." Herbert Hoover heard about a more dramatic ultimatum, that Harry told Jess he would be "arrested in the morning" for his two years of pardon fixing, trafficking in confiscated liquor, and influence peddling. Boone said Jess stood there "stunned . . . subdued, less hyperactive, less voluble, and appeared to 'draw into his shell.' "

On Saturday, May 26, the two men were in Columbus for the weekend; Harry suggested that Jess stay there and check into a sanitarium. Jess begged to return to Washington, see friends, and close some unspecified "little business." Harry acquiesced but thought Jess was "acting queer" on the train returning to Washington. A few weeks before, Roxie told Evalyn that Jess had "started to turn green" when he looked into a store window and saw a gun, and recalled, "Once Jess fainted—passed out cold—at the mere sight of a gun. I don't know why he was so afraid of guns; I just know he was." Now, however, whether to protect or to harm himself, Jess had some urgent enough reason to buy a gun while in Roxy's company. She said Jess "came down the street his old self, his head up, and just like as if he were happy and everything, and I saw such a change in him, and I said, 'Are things all right now, Jess?' And he said, 'yes, they are all right now.' "

On Monday, May 28, Florence invited Harry without Jess to sleep over at the White House. Harry arranged to have his aide Barney Martin stay with Jess. Jess assured Harry that he "felt much better than he had for several weeks." Harry, however, told Martin that he was "uneasy" about Jess. Martin passed this information on to the man who lived in an apartment on the floor below Jess and Harry—Billy Burns.[6]

On May 29 Jess, Harry, Martin and Boone played golf at Friendship. From there Jess went to the Justice Department but made no attempt to clean out his office. Harry went to the White House, to sleep there again. Martin and Jess walked to the Wardman Park. Jess said he felt tired, but there was no discussion of his going to a sanitarium. According to Martin, they both retired to separate suites at nine. Sometime around nine the phone rang in the McLean bedroom at Belmont Farm. Ned answered. It was Jess, hoping he could join the McLeans for several days. "Oh, damn," said Evalyn, "I don't feel good; but tell him all right." The phone rang again, at ten. It was Jess, saying a rainstorm was raging in Washington but he would be at the farm in the morning. Evalyn was suspicious: "That's awfully funny, never knew that to happen before." At one in the morning the ringing started again. This time Evalyn answered. Jess was "a little upset." Evalyn ascertained Martin was with him and reiterated that he could come to the farm. "Anything worrying you?" she asked. "No," he quipped. "Just scared to death." He hung up. Evalyn went to sleep. "I thought maybe he's getting drunk—he was a heavy drinker."[7]

Details of what happened in the next few hours appear muddled. The version that Washington read the next day went as follows: There was a shot in Harry and Jess's apartment, reported as having occurred at 6:40 A.M.; Martin was awakened by it, rushed in, and found Jess dead on the floor, next to the bed, a .32-caliber revolver in his right hand. A bullet had plowed through his right temple and embedded itself into the upper portion of the doorframe.

Martin was then publicly reported as having called Burns, who rushed up from his apartment. Sergeant J. D. Marks and policemen Mills and Keech of the Tennallytown subprecinct station took charge of the police investigation. Coroner J. Ramsay Nesbitt was called, viewed Jess, and signed a certificate of suicide, explaining why he did so without any further examination: "The District Code provides that where there is not even a reasonable doubt but that the case is one of suicide, no inquest shall be held. I was called to Daugherty's apartment in Wardman Park Hotel by the police. Smith was lying dead on the floor. The body had not been touched. He apparently had shot himself while sitting on the edge of the bed. His body slumped off on the floor, the head striking a metal wastebasket at the head of the bed and overturning it so that the head was partly in the basket."

The local press report, written on the scene, stated that Harding was phoned the news—by whom it was not stated—and then ordered Boone to the scene. "[T]wo hours later [Boone] returned to the White House to report to the President the details." It was certain that "Boone came to the White House after his visit to the Hotel." An important variation, however, came from Elmer Dwyer, the Wardman Park manager. Dwyer wanted to call Herbert Schoenfeld, the house doctor. Burns said no, it could wait. Instead Burns called Harding in the presence of Martin and Dwyer—at 6:45 A.M. In "a little while" Boone appeared, pronounced Smith dead, and only then allowed Dwyer to call Schoenfeld, who later admitted that the "atmosphere in the suite seemed to discourage a thorough examination of the body."

Boone's version differed further. He said he had received a six-thirty call *not* from the President but from Dwyer and been told to hurry to the Wardman Park. There he was taken to the apartment, and Martin told him Jess had shot himself. He saw two policemen in the room but "did not get their names." He noted how the body had fallen oddly, the head in the wastebasket, the hole in his temple—blackened, he thought, from "powder burns"—and he saw the bullet in the doorjamb. It was only *then* that Boone said he saw Burns enter the room, but he "learned that Martin had immediately called Mr. Burns." It was then that Nevitt was sent for. Boone "was told" by Martin that Jess "*had* been holding a pistol in his right hand"—implying it had been removed—that nobody else had been in the suite and he "had no idea what time the suicide had been committed." To one of Burns's Investigation Bureau agents Nesbitt, however, stated: "The body had not been touched." He offered to testify before a congressional committee. He was never called.[8]

In Boone's version, he then went from the apartment to the White House to tell the President, and both men then went to Harry's room. "Harry," a composed Warren told him, "Boone has some news for you

and it's very bad news, so get hold of yourself." Boone further recounted:

> And then I said as quietly and calmly as possible, "General, Jess
> Smith has shot himself." All the color left the Attorney General's face.
> Most terribly impressive stare came across his countenance as he looked
> at me and then looked at President Harding as though he couldn't believe
> what he had heard. He dropped his head into his two hands. There was
> a terrible silence in the room. The President and I did not utter a word.
> The Attorney General was shocked speechless. I felt his pulse and it
> showed that he was stunned, so that his circulation was disturbed. I
> feared that he might have a very profuse cerebral hemorrhage as we
> stood there. He leaned way over toward the floor with his head in his
> hands. As we stood quietly, it seemed quite a while before he raised his
> head. The Attorney General said: "Why did he do it? My God, why
> did he do it? Why did he do it?" and repeated himself. I said: "None
> of us has the slightest idea." Then he wanted to know who was there
> at the time, who found him. He wanted details. I thought it was well to
> narrate all that I knew.

Warren told a silent Florence, after which Boone came in to give
her details, saying that "in the absence of knowing any other cause"
Jess had probably done it because of his health.[9]

Martin told Boone that Jess had dated a "so-called will on brown
wrapping paper" on Monday, May 28, presumably after the golf game,
which eliminated beneficiaries of an earlier will. He had told a friend
that he had written a new will that day, but there were no other signs
of a planned suicide; in fact, he had several scheduled meetings for the
next day. The press reported that the new will, found in his jacket, left
nearly all his fortune to his sister-in-law and nephew. After Harry ordered Jess out of Washington, he was no longer the primary beneficiary
of Jess's will; in the new one Harry was not even mentioned. Ignoring
this, Harry wrote Ned McLean, "I will send you a copy of the will.
This is the will that I think will stand. The one made last week is not,
I am confident, a valid will," he said. "I know the whole story now
and some day I will tell you enough of it to convince you that he did
not commit an act of cowardice; what he did is traceable to his sickness.
Everything will be all right and his soul is safe because he was the soul
of honor and integrity. . . . I did not go to the funeral because I did
not feel so well." Later, under investigation, Harry groused that Jess's
suicide "was the very worst thing he could have done to me, for it

deprived me of a living refutation of the charges and innuendo levelled at me."

With Harry leading the pack, the party line of the Harding White House quickly assembled itself. Boone's official statement said that Jess had "practically lost his reasoning by his continual worrying about his health." In reality Florence had been accurate in her suspicions that Jess had been up to no good—with or without Madame Marcia's charts. He had been terrified by the rising tide of financial troubles and the widening knowledge of his tangle of illegalities. Losing money on the stock exchange, he often went into debt, then borrowed from shady lobbyists and lawyers, who were hoping to cut back door deals with Justice on behalf of their clients. The most notorious bribe had Jess receiving about $200,000 for "expediting the claim" of the American Metals Company. Harry had approved it in forty-eight hours, and he and his brother allegedly received $40,000 from the deal. Jess had also accepted $50,000 to have Harry quash two hundred indictments against coal operators. How Jess's schemes related to Harry's decisions was never provable since none of Jess's financial or personal papers or even the green notebook he was always scribbling in were found. Harry later conveniently explained that Jess burned all their mutual financial records until "there was hardly anything left."[10]

Believing that Jess's covert deals and role in silencing Harding's mistresses and critics were motivations for his *murder*, Evalyn McLean hired two private detectives to investigate. They reported that Gaston Means was likely involved, but the only witness they could produce was a bellboy who, "after spending most of the night in the room of a lady guest on a floor below that of the Attorney-General's suite, had been sneaking down a flight of fire stairs when he had passed a big man who had smiled at him. The bellboy recalled that the big man had had dimples when he smiled." Means's dimples were his most obvious physical trait, but dimples are not enough to convict a man. When Evalyn began talking about her suspicions, Means confronted her at Friendship. She insisted "it's true," but Means would only state at the time that Jess had not been shot by the gun found near him. Fourteen years later— six years after his sensational book and serving none of his usual exploitative purposes—Means said a frightened Jess came to talk with him and Burns in the latter's apartment, drank heavily, and was walked up the stairwell to his apartment by them. Burns left, and Jess began fighting with Means, who punched him out, above the temple. Then Means said he shot Jess with a rifle and silencer, used paper to keep his own fingerprints off Jess's gun and then placed it and an empty bullet cartridge nearby. While the official account made much of the fact that Jess's head hit a wire basket, Means pointed out that the bruise, a reported fact, could not have occurred from the basket; that would have resulted in a cut, not a bruise.

Evalyn had other suspicions that linked Means and Burns to the Daugherty brothers in Jess's death. "He didn't kill himself," she later emphatically stated; "they murdered him—the Daughertys themselves gave it away to me." When she first heard details of the death, she zeroed in on the fact that Harry had decided not to sleep in their apartment that night—for a second night in a row—but at the White House, with no stated reason for doing so, yet somehow knew that Jess was drunk at the time. Although Jess had recently bought a gun, Evalyn didn't believe he would use it on himself. "There was no post-mortem examination of the body," she went on, "and I have often wondered why. Jess Smith was scared to death of firearms; I know that for a fact. I always have a gun around and any time he saw me handle one he would say, 'Hey, put that thing away. It might go off. I don't even want to see it.'" Then there was the question of his appendicitis wound: "Mal Daugherty . . . told us over and over about an unhealed wound on Jess Smith's abdomen. [Harry] began talking about . . . [how] Jess was scarred. . . . I questioned W. F. Wiley, general manager of the *Cincinnati Enquirer*, who had been in [Florida] with us during the winter [and] . . . shared a bathhouse with Jess Smith. 'How was that appendicitis scar of Smith's?' [Evalyn asked him]. 'It was healed as smooth as the back of your hand,' said Wiley." She also emphasized the strong rumor that the bullet wound had been on the left side of Jess's head—but that Roxie and others confirmed that Jess was right-handed; it would have been virtually impossible for him to shoot his left side.

When Evalyn tried to pinpoint details of Jess's death from Barney Martin, she said he "never once told me the same story twice." She concluded that because "Smith got in so bad" on his shenanigans, which adversely affected the Daughertys, Means, and Burns, Jess had to be killed. "He certainly was scared that night. . . . Now, you take that and you take the wound and take Wiley and it's a different sort of notion. Smith wasn't that kind of man [to shoot himself]."[11]

Although no one ever printed the allegation, Vylla Poe Wilson bluntly recalled the "hints of homosexuality regarding Jess and Harry," and gossip linked Jess's death to his being romantically wrought up over Harry, that Jess's jealousy over the devoted attention Harry began receiving from Boone—strictly medical care—and Harry's rejection and order to move out of their home drove him to suicide. More dark was the whisper that Jess was killed because of the severe taboo of their sort of relationship and the potential blackmail that it posed to the attorney general. "I know Harry Daugherty had loved Jess Smith better than a brother," Evalyn reiterated. "I know that Harding and Daugherty were partners if ever two men were. I am convinced that some of the pieces of this picture puzzle are missing." Doc Sawyer's grandson recalled, "Jess was 'not the marrying type,' but he committed his life to Daugherty and the whole crowd accepted it."[12]

When Florence gently pressed Harry about Evalyn's insistent theory that Jess was killed, an exhausted Daugherty said sarcastically that women were too suspicious to be in politics. What the Duchess really thought of Jess's death is strangely unrecorded. Having recently survived so much unexpected sickness and betrayal, she probably viewed it with her unique brand of sentimental practicality. Some weeks before, she told a friend who had unexpectedly lost her mother, "Time helps us to adjust ourselves to new conditions." If she was stunned mute by the loss of her dandy arbiter, Florence "sensed the gloom" that enveloped Warren and Harry, "with their intimate memories of Smith and happy times." The night after the death she had the Boones join them for dinner and a movie. Warren and Harry spoke only in monosyllables, and during the movie the only sounds were long, moanful cries from Harry.

If the Forbes resignation and Cramer suicide raised the first flurry about scandals in the administration, Jess's death set off a buzz of rumor. Alice Longworth quipped that he died of "Harding of the arteries." In front of Harry, Doc berated Boone that Jess could have been saved with better medical care. Senator Tom Heflin was the first to link the death publicly to Harry when some months later he declared in the Senate: "Jess Smith is dead, some say by his own hands, and some do not know how he died, but he died in Daugherty's apartment. Some people will a long time inquire why Jess Smith was brought here by Daugherty, and put into the service of the Department of Justice—a plain, dry-goods clerk. I am told, he had no knowledge of law, and no experience in the work to which he was assigned. I repeat, why was this man brought here by Daugherty? And, oh, how conspicuously he has figured in all the terrible things now being uncovered. He is dead. *Some* say he killed *himself.* Some think he was murdered. He remembered some of his friends in his will. And of course, those *who were remembered in his will profited by his death.*"[13]

Florence evidently thought it wise now to distance herself from Harry's promise to make her money. Initially as First Lady, she had handled her own investments through brokers, but in early 1923 she had turned to him for advice on management of some of her holdings. "I do not know just how many shares of stock you have and what the stock is," he wrote her. "I wish you would let me have this information. It might be of advantage to you in some developments if I knew." Wisely, Florence withdrew any further discussion with Harry of profiting from the boom market or inside tips. She also seemed to be distancing herself from Evalyn. There was no attempt made by either woman to see each other at the time of Jess's death. Despite her flow of flowers, notes, and phone calls to the still-bedridden Evalyn, Florence would not venture to Friendship, to which Evalyn returned from the Leesburg farm in the first week of June. Perhaps she would have found it trying to be pleasant with the woman who had betrayed her in the very home where that betrayal took place.[14]

In the wake of Jess's death and amid the gathering but unseen storm of scandal, Florence had to prepare for the fateful 15,057-mile transcontinental journey. Through fifteen plains, midwestern, western, and northwestern states, Harding was to give seventy formal speeches in auditoriums, at luncheons, and following motor parades, and dozens of informal train whistle-stop addresses. From Tacoma the party was to sail to Alaska and along its coast, train through its interior, sail back south, resume the train trip down the west coast, sail from San Diego through the Panama Canal, stop in Puerto Rico and Cuba and return home.[15]

The advice sent to Florence from Birch Helms was put into action on the trip: major speeches only in several large cities, limiting the President's appearances to avoid his becoming politically mundane and to force people to make an effort to come to him. He must not stay at the houses of wealthy citizens because locals would resent his cavorting with the rich. The press must receive breaking news so as to justify the cost of their travel. There must be an element of surprise to proposals in his speeches. "I have found it necessary to restrict my speaking engagement to one in each city," Warren wrote the advance man at Florence's urging, "and have also found it necessary to forego [*sic*] the acceptance of all teniers of private or personal hospitality." She told Esther Metzger: "All my efforts are now bent towards our trip to Alaska." Florence was now determined that nothing stop her, and she was taking along a nurse to be sure. In a draft of a third-person letter, she affirmed, "The Pres. has said he will not make the trip unless Mrs. H. is able to accompany him."[16]

The great diversions from preparations were the First Lady's speeches to the Big Brothers and Sisters and the five-thousand-member National Conference of Social Work, and her role during the national convention of the Nobles of the Mystic Shrine in the first week of June. She waived the ticket requirement for White House tours, and some twenty thousand people passed through one day, breaking all records. Tens of thousands of Shriners and their wives packed Washington that week. Although appalled at the government's "burning [of] money" to light the capital's streets through the week, she graciously accepted baskets of California fruit, visited encampments, swung her arms as a baton to lead a lively band concert in songs she knew, and used such a potential mass market to push her cause, suggesting that the Animal Rescue League sell pictures of Laddie Boy as souvenirs to the Shriners. At the parade, which she reviewed with Warren, the First Lady stood up some 110 times, whenever the flag passed. "Why shouldn't the women of America pay the same respect to the flag as the men do? No citizen of this country is a better American than I am." Like a scene from some comic opera, everyone in the stands soon followed her example.

Knowing that some branches of Shriners were anti-Catholic and in that sense sympathetic to the Ku Klux Klan and that the Klan itself was holding a huge demonstration less than half a mile from Washington, Harding censured hate groups in his Shriners speech. The press "considered [it] to be a direct attack" on the Klan, particularly in light of his criticism weeks earlier of "factions of hatred and prejudice and violence" that "challeng[ed] both civil and religious liberty." During Shriners' week, the Tall Cedars of Lebanon had a secret induction ritual, complete with pyramidical skullcap, making Harding one of them. Either in retaliation for his remarks or just for publicity, the Klan then spread rumors that Harding had in fact been secretly inducted into *the Klan*. Since his induction was only vaguely reported in the press, to retain the secret Shriner rites, the Klan story was made credible. Klan Imperial Wizard Alton Young said, "Harding agreed to be sworn in as a member of the Ku Klux Klan. A five-man 'imperial induction team' headed by [Wizard] Simmons conducted the ceremony in the Green Room of the White House. Members of the team were so nervous that they forgot their Bible in their car, so Harding had to send for the White House Bible. . . . Harding was permitted to rest his elbow on the desk as he knelt on the floor during the long oath-taking. Afterwards, the President appreciatively gave members of the team War Department license tags that allowed them to run red lights all across the nation."

The story spread rapidly. In Charleston, West Virginia, Klansman Reverend Basil C. Newton told ten thousand people that "the Klan held one initiation in the dining room at the White House." Reports came back to the White House from Texas, Oklahoma, Oregon, and Illinois that Harding's membership was evidence that the Klan controlled the government and was used as an inducement to sign up new members. The President had Christian deny any membership. It was an ironic legend for a man elected President despite rumors he was of mixed racial blood.[17]

By the time the Shriners left, Harding was not only politically troubled but personally spent. He put his finances in order and prepared a new will, sending copies to Marion lawyer Henry Shaffner, asking him to "hand same to your Uncle, Charles D. Shaffner, in case of my death." Helping compose the will, Harry noted that Harding did not remember any children other than nieces, nephews and Florence's grandchildren. He later used this as proof that Harding did not father a child by Nan Britton.

On her last visit, in January, just as Warren developed his influenza, Nan had been incessant in her demands for attention. She remarked that she hoped Florence would fully recuperate. Warren said he did too yet—according to Nan—added that Florence would "very probably pass on before I go" and he would then marry Nan and "adopt" Elizabeth Ann. He also mentioned that Sawyer really "doesn't doctor me much" but that Florence "has lots of faith in him." They kissed, but there was no sexual intimacy between them. Nan was to leave for Europe the day after the Hardings headed west.

Among many Harding loyalists there was later a concerted effort to print denials of Warren's relationship with Nan and fathering of her child. The single most significant person, however, would never deny it in print or otherwise. No one person had been more frequently in the public and private presence of Harding than George Christian. He was the one voice of authority who could unequivocally disprove the stories of Nan Britton and many other women. Although loyal to Florence, George knew the true state of the Harding marriage. Moreover, as Harding's Senate and presidential secretary, he was the single person given access to Harding's office desk, where Warren kept everything related to Nan.

Christian not only did not deny the charges but confirmed their truth. He did not leave a written record, but others did, while he was alive. In a private letter to Charles Hard, Kathleen Lawler was shocked at how George defended Nan Britton: "Would you believe that George Christian, of all living persons, would insist that all that miserable scandal is true? I have myself heard him repeat it many times in public and private, and twice in public he tried to force me to agree with him and say it is all true, and that I know it." Confronting him, Kathleen retorted, "Mr. Christian, if it were true, you are the last person on earth who should admit it."[18]

In his new will Harding conveyed the farm he had recently purchased to his brother. He had spoken earlier with excitement about retiring there, playing golf, working on his memoirs. In his letter regarding the purchase, he admitted that "it is my hope that I'll last until 1925. . . ." Carolyn Votaw was stunned when she heard about his new will. "Your will, Warren! Why, what for?" He sighed. "Oh, I don't expect to come back from Alaska." Weeks earlier Harding told the American Society of Newspaper Editors that he'd hold on to the *Star* as chief owner, but the day before he signed his will, he sold it for $500,000 to Louis Brush and Roy Moore. Given the evidence of the will and the *Star* sale, his brother thought, "Warren evidently sensed danger." Since he had never made such decisions without Florence's approval, the Duchess must have found it equally ominous.

The talk of congressional inquiries into alleged and assorted Administrative illegalities shook Warren. Old friend George Cortelyou was shocked during a June visit when the President bluntly snapped, "The people may think I don't work hard, but this place is hell at times. I am doing the best I can to give the country a good administration." Whether in reference to Albert Fall and Teapot Dome, Harry Daugherty, Jess Smith, and corruption at the Justice Department, or Forbes and the Veterans Bureau scandal, the President did not say as he then spewed his anger "with still greater emphasis," in admitting that he knew what was "going on" and would do something about it. "They think that I do not know of some things thought to be going on in my administration, that I am weak and too tolerant and all that; but they will find out when I get back to Washington that there will be such a shake-up in some places as will show that they have misunderstood and misjudged me."

Harding's anger in the weeks before the trip was evident. He told Mont Reily, "[I could kill] Harry Daugherty and you for getting me into such a mess as President of the United States, as it is all grief and no joy." When Senator Howard Sutherland asked whether he still enjoyed the presidency, Warren said plaintively, "You know I always like to do all I humanly can for my friends. The greatest trouble I have with this job is that I often find my so-called best friends instead of putting themselves in my place and protecting [me] at every point, putting things over on me." Evidence indicates that Harding was speaking not only of Forbes, Harry, and Jess but of Fall.

There are suggestions that Harding now questioned the motive for Fall's oil leases. He turned ashen when he read a letter that Starling passed on to him from a friend out West regarding the arrangements, but it was not clear whether they related to Fall's ranch improvements or the actual leased lands. The most definitive statement on the matter, however, came from Reily. Just prior to going West, as Florence later told Reily, Warren "had been informed of the Teapot Dome affair, and . . . he was a crushed man, after that. You know Governor Reily, that Warren Harding was the soul of honor, and *that* exposure crushed him so completely, I feared all the way on our trip that he could not survive the disaster."

That Emma Fall claimed that the Hardings believed her husband to be honest by pointing to their June luncheon for the Falls was not necessarily proof, however, that *Florence* trusted him, for just four days before she left for Alaska, at 2:45 P.M. on June 16, she met with Forbes, then under preliminary investigation, but whose presence was registered in the visitors' log. Having "friends" in for probing conversations didn't mean the suspicious Duchess considered them innocent.[19]

Whether because of Forbes or Fall, Jess and Harry, or Warren's drawing a new will and selling the *Star,* or her own health, Florence yet again summoned the guidance of Madame Marcia in early June. Marcia told her of "death stalking the air we breathed in Washington," of the "little white powder" (a veiled reference to the gunpowder burn on Jess's face) and that among some of the men in whom Warren "reposed unwise confidence were some who dealt death." It had been almost exactly three years since Florence had first heard Marcia's predictions of Warren's "sudden, peculiar and violent" death as well as of her own demise, to occur soon after.

The sensible and optimistic side of Florence that served her well— and was in evidence most of the time—abandoned her completely when she was stirred by the supernatural. To her the June reading was all the more believable because she knew the real state of both her own and Warren's health, indeed poor in both cases. "You must take back what you predicted to me! You must!" Florence yelled at Marcia in this briefest of meetings. "Study your charts again! Be *very* careful!" Marcia repeated what she had said before. Her astral premonition of "dark clouds" around Harding unequivocally proved to her that he would not live to see March 4, 1925.

From the man in whom the Duchess placed her absolute trust about her and Warren's health was concerned, however, Florence got a contradictory message. There would be no dark clouds over Harding during the trip, according to Doc Sawyer. On April 16 he assured Boone that "The Presidential family are in very good condition. . . . They are both doing splendidly. In fact, I have never known them to be better since coming to Washington than they seem to be now."

Warren, however, thought distinctly otherwise. Promising former Congressman James Burke that he would visit his Pittsburgh home in the autumn, Harding confessed: "I cannot yield to one-tenth of the demands that are now being made upon me in connection with this trip. The grade is too steep. I need rest, but at the same time I want to see my country and its people." He continued to feel severe fatigue. He could no longer sleep flat, his valet recalled, but only if his head was propped high. The most persistent problem he had was pain in his chest, described invariably as heartburn and indigestion. Doc prescribed a daily dosage of gelsemium, uritone, and coryza tablets for what he considered unthreatening digestive and bronchial bouts.

Dr. Boone, however, actually tested the President's health. The simplest but in retrospect the most astounding of little notes that Boone kept for himself was one that never made it into his diary, the draft of his memoirs, or even his later oral history. Transcribed from "Record (medical record)" of President Harding—the original of which somehow was surprisingly missing from Boone's otherwise comprehensive, detailed papers—it is an unambiguous five lines showing heart trouble: "E.C.G. before departure on transcontinental + Alaska trip—left axis-deviation no other distortion of the tracing reported. Tracing at White House."

The professional competence of Doc Sawyer to diagnose and treat Harding properly should have also raised alarm. Through the spring Doc was himself so ill he had to return home to be treated by his son. Boone also knew more than he let on, recording that Doc, "when walking on the street when there was heavy traffic . . . seemed to have difficulty seeing the curbing and he would misstep. To read and see objects he had to hold reading material and the objects very close to his eyes. . . . [Eye] Doctor Trible found his superficial retinal vessels showed quite advance tortuosity. Trible thought that he had cerebral symptoms of irritation. I thought so, and being suspicious that was the cause of some developing personality changes."[20]

Florence made no attempt to see Evalyn before the latter left for Maine, a lapse that neither of them would have permitted a year earlier.

The Duchess claimed that Doc did not want to expose her to possible illness from Evalyn—even though the First Lady had been out in public in New York, greeted thousands of Shriners, and was soon to encounter tens of thousands of more people on the trip. Evalyn claimed that "the Hardings urged us to go with them to Alaska, [but] Dr. Finney told me he must forbid my making such a trip." Alice Longworth, however, later claimed that the Duchess now feared that having encouraged Warren's alcohol use and adultery, and having had an intimate friendship with Jess, the McLeans were a public relations risk in the presence of the twenty-two reporters who were to travel with the Hardings for two months. Indeed, this gossip seems confirmed as fact by Boone. Boone recorded that Warren had drawn up a list, but "with criticism subsequently being voiced and many eyebrows raised" about it, some unnamed friends were removed from the final list of twenty-two guests and twenty-seven staff. There did now seem to be a gulf between the old friends, Florence's letter to Evalyn, the day before departure, reading like a final good-bye yet a longing for their old camaraderie:

> I am just distressed beyond words that we have not been able to break bread before my leaving. As far as I, myself, am concerned, I would have taken a chance but Dr. Sawyer seemed to be fearful of subjecting me to any possible danger however remote because of my being worn out with my power of resistance lowered. When I look back on the year just past it has been such a disappointment because of my condition and yours we have not been able to have our good old times together. I want you to know that I am not unmindful of the many courtesies and kindnesses you and Ned have extended, and not only to me but Mr. Harding. Should I live to return from the trip I do hope this fall we can be more together and again cannot refrain from voicing my regret that you and Ned cannot be members of our party, for while I know the trip will be very trying and strenuous I am sure the trip will be most interesting.

If the trip would have been strenuous for a woman like Evalyn, it was absolutely dangerous for someone with health as uncertain as Florence. "I fear she will never come back from this trip. She would never dare to let him go alone. She does not dare," said a friend of the President's. Doc asked Boone to relate all of Florence's medical history to the naval doctor who would be on the SS *Henderson*, which was to transport the party to Alaska from Washington State. "I realized that such a trip as she was going to undertake [would entail] varied altitudes, frequent changes in climate, tremendous heat of the summer in the middle portion of the United States, varied dietetic changes, nervous emotional and great physical strain," recalled Boone. "I was apprehensive that she might have a recurrence of her kidney ailment. Very secretively then, I requested [that] . . . one of the medical officers assigned to the ship [be] a surgeon . . . that it would be well to have a radiologist on the ship, since an x-ray machine was being installed especially for this trip at my request. Then very secretively, I had [naval officer] Parham place aboard the ship a coffin. No one ever knew of that . . . certainly not the President, the First Lady, or any of the Presidential party."

Boone said of the jealous Doc, "I did not feel that he was particularly enthusiastic to have me go," but Florence demanded he come—though not for herself alone. She was alarmed by Warren's mysterious bouts of "indigestion." On May 27, she wrote Esther, she had stayed up "until three this morning with Mr. H. A case of indigestion—I have no use for that trouble. It acts too quickly . . . those that have the most robust picture can stand the least." Boone said Warren also wanted him to go: "He emphasized that I knew his physical condition as well as General Sawyer."[21]

At a June 18 press conference Harding soberly announced, "Only death or serious illness will cause any delay or postponement of this trip." With a more ironic fatalism, Florence earlier remarked that unless "the stars have gone out of their course," they were going.

With the trip confirmed, friends became alarmed. "It required no medical expert to determine that President Harding was a very sick man," recalled Kathleen Lawler. "I knew it. Everyone about him knew it. He was ill and completely exhausted." Senator Sutherland "strong [sic] advised against it" because of the "high temperatures he was likely to encounter and the impracticability of his saving himself." Virginia Speel, Washington Republican committeewoman, told him, "You are so weary and look so ill. Mr. President, is it necessary for you to undertake this taxing trip?" Charles Hard grew frustrated: "We have all said everything we saw or dared in opposition to this trip. The President is not able to make it. He ought not to go." George Christian, "on the verge of breaking down and weeping," made his feelings known as well. "The President ought not to make this trip. It is a mistake. He is not equal to it. I have told him so, told Dr. Sawyer so, and opposed it with all my might. He is too sick and it is too hot for him to undertake this long journey." Gus Karger was chilled by it all: "It is a gruesome mistake. . . . I can see nothing but a coffin in a funeral train coming back across the country." Elizabeth Jaffray thought that Warren himself "knew something was going to happen to him."

"Wherever we are to stop I want the doctors . . . as close to the president's room as possible," Florence directed Starling. "It is not for myself that I want this done but for Warren." Only later, in retrospect, would Florence state, "Warren Harding was a sick man, a very sick man, when we left Washington for Alaska, and I knew it well. He had given his promise to the Alaskan people to go out to see them, and he was determined to do so. . . . You know when he made up his mind to do anything, the case was settled. He would not break his word to them. He said, 'I have promised the Alaskan people. I am going.' He would listen to nothing to the contrary. "[22]

Others on the scene at the time, however, said that it wasn't quite that way, that it was she who insisted that the trip go ahead as scheduled, despite his health. Once again her overpowering insistence wore him down. Although she would go because she wanted to watch him, her presence added anxiety to Warren's mounting stress. As Boone noted, "Mrs. Harding insisted on accompanying him on the trip. There was grave doubt that her health could bear the ordeal of long travel and the demands of public appearances and her participation in the program arranged for the Presidential tour. This fact worried the President." Reporter Ross Bartley added that Harding was "strongly opposed to Mrs. Harding's accompanying him. She insisted, however, upon realization of what had been the hope of a lifetime. . . ." When Lawler asked why Doc didn't "set his foot down" and order Harding to cancel the trip, Christian curtly replied, "[I]t's no use." If it was clear that Doc saw no risk, it also seemed certain that Florence was willing to take all risks.

If she knew the truth about the President's health and what the trip could do to him, why did the Duchess still insist on the trip? It had been nearly a year since she had been out continuously among an adoring public. In the interim she had coped with more adultery, a near-death illness, betrayal by her best friend, a terrible abuse of the wounded vets she had professed her dedication to and the humiliation of the political fallout, and the shocking suicide of a friend. And all this was shadowed by a prediction of death she desperately tried to elude but believed in. Out across America, up to Alaska, along the California coast, it would be easier to escape. She would be respected, celebrated, admired, and ultimately loved by an entire nation. As one reporter on the trip reflected, "She seemed to relish being amongst them, greeting them by the hundreds and hundreds on single occasions. She said she liked to look in their faces and feel the warmth of their handclasps, try to understand what their feelings were about life and the issues of the day. . . ."

But it was more than the limelight or keeping an eye on Warren that drove her: "I have been wanting to go to Alaska for six years and they are not going to talk me out of it." The New York *Tribune*'s White House reporter, as did others, found it a strange urge: "For six years, Mrs. Harding had longed for a trip to Alaska. Why that rugged Northland held so great an attraction for her was a thing her friends never understood, but she had wanted to make that trip since long before Warren Harding was seriously considered as a presidential possibility." From her frame of mind, the trip was her destined fate. She was simply possessed to go regardless of the consequences.

In the end, making the trip to Alaska, even at risk of his health, was truly the President's decision. But, as always, he was "eager to do anything that his devoted wife wished."[23]

Part Six

THE WESTERN AND ALASKA TOUR, 1923

. . . I never expected to get him out of there alive. I knew how sick Mr. Harding was, even before he left Washington.

32

The Duchess of America

If she would never possess the passion of the President of the United States, Florence Harding would be heaped with the affection of a nation as the Duchess of America. None of her predecessors had undertaken a trip of such record-breaking length, and few other woman in the world would be seen, met, and heard by so many people, not to mention be captured in as many newsreels and in photographs. No First Lady had been so physically demonstrative, hugging, kissing, even backslapping, using both hands to shake and greet as many as possible. "It is no secret on the train," a reporter noted, "that she is as popular as the president himself." For a full month and a half—despite severe weather changes, the President's deteriorating state, ominous signs of death and danger— the Duchess burned an indelible, engaging impression on her country in her great shining moment on the world stage.

On June 20, at two in the afternoon, and in ninety-degree heat, the ten-car presidential train left Washington, speeding and chugging through the torpid air, across the blistered plains on its grueling schedule.

The Hardings' parlor car was the *Superb,* which they had used in the campaign, furnished with pale green chairs, a chaise longue, a dining table, small electric fans, and a buzzer to summon staff members. At the end of the car were an observation platform and amplifier for speech-making. Telephones were plugged in at stops along the way with local switchboards. Whether the train stopped in a station or cornfield, the crowds were unbelievably enormous, with most sidewalks five rows thick, thousands of schoolchildren usually in the front waving flags and dressed in white, workers spilling from factory windows and hanging on fire escapes, crowds lining streets and viaducts, cramming into the lobbies where the party stopped, waiting for hours just to get a glimpse of the Hardings. New York *Times* correspondent Richard Oulahan observed, "There is as much curiosity to see her as the President. Mrs.

Harding has a way of her own in responding to cheers in her honors. It is a wave of . . . a full-arm gesture, half suggestive of the smartness of a military salute . . . hand and arm are brought . . . sweeping above the head and then back to the right . . . downward, then up. The people like her and respond with hand-clapping, cheers and waving of flags and handkerchiefs."[1]

With women reporters who boarded the train at stops, the enthusiastic Duchess was good copy, as she chatted while peering out the windows at "those little towns of the Middle West" where "Democracy is being made," while dressed in the geometric patterns of bronze, black, and blue colors of the current Tut vogue, inspired by the recent discovery of King Tutankhamen's treasures in Egypt. Women that season, Alice Longworth recalled, were all "nuts for Tut."

So enthusiastic was Florence that starting in Washington, Indiana, she herself began to give "little talks" from the rear platform to the crowds calling out for her. This was not lost on the male reporters, who provided her with good political press, in part because of her constant leak of inside information. "It is Mrs. Harding who is having the fun of the trip, the time of her life," wrote one reporter, "eager, democratic and still ambitious . . . the first of all the wives of our presidents who takes an actual hand in politics and is just as intense and enthusiastic in the game as if she were herself a candidate for re-election . . . the social as well as the political center of this expedition."[2]

It was not long before the Duchess was managing things, slowing the train down because "I want the people to see their President," and getting Warren to speak as often as possible, from seven in the morning to almost midnight. Dubbing this her "back porch campaign," she encouraged talk of his running in 1924 despite his "little talks" with her that his health was bad and his fears expressed to Doc that the "Alaska trip meant death." Whenever his morbid premonition did not preoccupy Warren, he privately expressed his dismay at friends who had been "selling him all over this town, and all over the country" and made clear his desire to clear the administration's name. "And the people will believe me, when they hear my story." In the first presidential speech carried to both coasts by radio, Harding spoke of his support for a World Court, but one audience member, Warren Flynn, was more alarmed at what he saw than what he heard: "He looked very, very tired. He did not walk with the vigor that I had expected of so robust a man. As he spoke, he leaned upon a desk . . . his attitude suggested that physically, he would welcome nothing so much as a rest. . . . [T]he physical strain and fatigue he was [*sic*] under was very apparent."[3]

At times the First Lady seemed to be stepping in for her husband. As Boy Scouts passed before a Kansas City reviewing stand to be pinned with medals by Harding, Florence stepped up to the only Scout in the line who was black, Damon Bass, to decorate him herself. When a woman told Warren that she had voted for him, Florence interrupted, "I hope he'll not disappoint you," while Warren appeared to be suffering from a rash (which the Associated Press's Ross Bartley was told was an allergic reaction to strawberries), and his lips were blue. That day editor William Allen White recorded that Harding's "lips were swollen and blue, his eyes puffed and his hands seemed stiff when you shook hands with him." Cardiac asthma, in which the heart is unable to pump blood from the lungs, causes difficulty in breathing, depriving the body of oxygen, and results in blue-tinged lips. Furthermore, Harding's valet, Brooks, said, "He has to be propped up on pillows and he sits up that way all night. If he lies down he can't get his breath." A person suffering from cardiac asthma must be kept in an upward position in bed, permitting gravity to pull the blood down.

Doc began spinning the first of many tales, telling the Kansas City *Post*, "Harding is feeling fit and in splendid physical trim to undertake the Alaskan trip. Both the President and Mrs. Harding are standing the trip and the warm weather splendidly. We are used to warm weather in Washington, you know." In the hotel, however, Doc insisted that the President skip all events preceding that night's speech. Florence, packing ice on his lips, piped up, "I'll take your place," and, despite his protests, became the first First Lady to substitute for a President at scheduled public events, a meeting of war mothers and a two-hour parade. People were dazzled. Said one: "She is the sort of woman one would pick out of a busy crowd to ask a direction or street number."

While dining that night with Senator and Mrs. Arthur Capper, Harding was briefly visited by Emma Fall. Capper saw Harding emerge "perturbed and obviously shaken" and assumed that Emma had "told Harding something that was a wallop on the jaw." Emma later protested that she was with Warren "alone for one minute," and talked of her life in New Mexico but she did not state whether she had mentioned the Falls' expanded property and ranch improvements, which may have led Warren to suspect Fall of having taken bribes for the oil leases. Later that night, to Mont Reily, Warren predicted that he would die before the trip's end. The next morning, traveling to Hutchinson, Kansas, William Allen White speculated that Harding was speaking of Fall when he said, "I have no trouble with my enemies. I can take care of them. It is my friends. My friends, that are giving me my trouble!"[4]

In Hutchinson Florence pushed him to act for publicity. "Warren, have your picture taken with that little baby," she snapped, insisting then that he pick up the child. "Now don't be afraid to hold it." When a ten-foot wheat binder came toward them in the field, it was "at the urging of Mrs. Harding" that the President drove it around the hundred-acre farm for newsreel cameras and photographers. Boone later insisted that the heat was dry, not humid, so that driving the binder was not "physically harmful," but considering his knowledge of Harding's heart condition, it is odd that he neither prevented nor later commented on the risk in having the President then exert himself by shoveling with a pitchfork the wheat he had just cut.

If Warren thought that his death was imminent, he also seemed to believe that he had nothing to lose by making the trip: If he was going to die soon, he might as well continue doing what he had himself committed to do. Florence, worried not only about his health but about Marcia's prediction that he wouldn't live past March 1925, placed blind faith in Doc's control and reassurances. At times Doc seemed to be completely oblivious of Harding's true condition; it seems almost sinister how he simply ignored the risk of having his patient make a fifteen-thousand-mile public tour. Boone did know the true condition of the President's health, but as a naval physician he would risk not only any future promotions but his very post if he were to challenge a brigadier general of the Army Medical Corps and the chairman of the Federal Hospitalization Board. There was no greater example of Doc's incompetence and Boone's acquiescence than what happened in Colorado Springs. At a University Club dinner for Secretary Work, Boone scribbled in his diary, "Admiral Rodman take[s] ill at table. Gen'l. Sawyer sitting next to him immediately called, 'Boone, Boone.' I ran and laid the Admiral on the floor. Sawyer said, 'He's gone,' but he soon regained consciousness." That the President's personal physician should misdiagnose an admiral as dead, in front of observers, his assistant, and his two most important patients and that no person should question his authority and ability illustrated the grip Sawyer had over both Hardings. It made ironic Doc's boast in Denver that Warren "obeys implicitly the instructions of his physician."[5]

In Denver Harding vigorously declared that Prohibition might be an "invasion of personal liberty," but it must be obeyed as law. The United Press's Lawrence Martin then wrote an explicit article stating that Harding privately drank liquor from his stock but had recently turned down gifts of liquor from friends. Worried about political ammunition from the opposition, the First Lady cornered the President and pressed him to "live up to its precept in practice." Warren relented, and his vow to stop all drinking was announced.

Tragedy began to plague the trip when the press corps went for a drive into the mountains, and one car swerved over the embankment, free-falling into Bear Creek Canyon. Thomas French, the historian Thomas Dawson, and National Republican Committee representative Sumner Curtis were killed. Curtis, former Washington *Post* and Associated Press reporter, editor of the *National Red Cross Bulletin,* and executive secretary in the Senate during Harding's years there, had been Florence's friend since her arrival in Washington. Overcome with grief, she canceled all her appearances. That same afternoon a tram car, ignoring a warning signal, had headed at full speed toward the car carrying Warren and Florence, halting just four feet away. A collision would have killed both Hardings. "Death cast a pall," noted a reporter.

By Cheyenne, Wyoming, the Hardings' spirits seemed revived. A large group of people with ten-gallon hats, sitting on horses, was gathered on the outskirts of the waiting crowd. As the train neared, they came into focus: They were cowgirls and had a bouquet for the Duchess. Florence made a little speech and held out her arms to them. Not missing a beat, she asked the cowgirls to repeat the ceremony, this time with the newsreel cameras set up to record it. From the platform Warren eyed them carefully. "I can reconcile myself to the departure from the west of the cowboy," he said, "but never would I stand for the disappearance of the cowgirl."[6]

The stop at Salt Lake City was diverted nearly three hundred miles south to a vast state holding, Zion Park, at Cedar City. "The President was loath to make the trip," recalled Boone. "He knew it would be a hard one." The First Lady, however, wanted to inspect the site as a potential national park and had her way. Utah Senator Reed Smoot had been lobbying for the visit, Boone continued, "so he had conferences with Mrs. Harding and successfully prevailed upon her to use her influence with the President to get him to visit." Warren's consolation would be some horseback riding—without the Duchess—but this too proved disastrous. The hard ride badly aggravated his hemorrhoids. Meanwhile on a lodge porch Florence gave a speech to Boy Scouts on obedience to the law. When Warren, irritated and sunburned, returned, she yelled, to the embarrassment of all, "Warren, you look just like a great big Indian!" Florence Harding, however, made a historic contribution: Zion became a national park. In Idaho the First Lady continued to prevail over the President. At one stop a reporter said Warren sighed that he "had enough" and dropped an event, while Florence sent him back to the hotel, then went on with the full program herself.[7]

At the Anaconda Copper Mining Company near Butte, Montana, the Hardings stared out at the belching black smoke rising into the sky from stacks, snow-capped mountains in the distance. Unable to hear above the deafening roar of dumping ore carts, the Duchess warmly stepped forward to greet miners, ignoring their grimy hands, laughing at the idea of her white gloves being sullied. Yet again she eclipsed Warren, some people complaining that he didn't wave but pleased that she always did. Noted a reporter: "She seems to have stood the trip better. . . ." Warren perked up at Yellowstone National Park—and not because it was an idyllic reminder of his honeymoon trip. One editorial at the time praised the Hardings as a "congenial, middle-aged couple, sharing each other's aspirations," but there was no evidence of that to those who witnessed an angry Duchess berating Warren publicly for his wandering eye. As they headed for a lodge, a dozen young attractive waitresses stopped the car, carrying flowers and ukeleles. The Secret Service tried to pry them off the running board, but Warren ordered, "Let them stay!" As they serenaded him, he burst into a smile, winking at them all, and insisting on staying for another song. At the last song Warren asked if he could return later to the girls, but scheduling prohibited it. Florence bawled him out in front of everyone: "Warren, I watched you while those girls were here! It took you just as long to say good-bye to those girls as it did for you to run through 3,000 tourists yesterday at Old Faithful!"[8]

Women along the way did spark Warren's interest. At a Spokane veterans' hospital he leered at the nurses. After a patient told him life there was "fine," Harding cracked, "I don't wonder with all these pretty young girls around." After dinner at the Marie Antoinette Hotel, the "Princesses of the Reclaimed Deserts" of "youthful grace and beauty" performed and then lined up to meet him. As he looked them over, Warren quipped, "I wouldn't mind always living in a desert which produces such beauty." He summoned waitresses Anna Kelley, Maria Stewart, and Nora Brewer, gave them tips, and worked his seductive warmth on them, leaving the girls speechless, save for the occasional long moan. Warren, living what he thought might be his last days to the fullest degree he could muster, was pleased that he still had his magic. "The last girl who waited on me," he told the manager, "was so flustered she dropped plates all through the meal."

The most colorful stop was in Meacham, Oregon, where the Hardings participated in the dedication of the old Oregon Trail. As they shook hands with five thousand people, Dr. Lee Johnson noted how vulnerable Harding was to assassination and that "he was put through a series of exercises which no person, not even a president, should have had to endure. He was carried from the trainside to the celebration grounds perched atop a shaky stagecoach hauled by fractious horses over rough ground. Then there were two speeches to be made. . . . And lastly the barbeque at which he had to . . . ingest the horror of bear steak and similar viands of undomesticated nature . . . cooked in the proper pioneer fashion over open fires and amidst the dirt and confusion that reigned there that day, open certainly to all manners of contamination. . . ." As usual the Duchess was fired up, a "marvel of mental strength and will power," one observer said as she walked, talked, shook hands, and shouted out to admirers, even climbing up on an old stagecoach for a rough ride. "Of the two, Mrs. Harding is making the most votes," said a reporter, "Mrs. Harding has more ginger at the end of the day than any other member of the party."[9]

At Portland, where the Herbert Hoovers joined the party, a sense of danger returned to haunt the Hardings before a hotel reception. At some stop in the West a small middle-aged woman had looked strange enough as she neared the Hardings to attract the attention of the Secret Service. In the atmosphere of unconstitutional union strikebreaking by Daugherty's command and the paranoia of "Red" anarchists, she was classified as a "fanatic." She showed up at a second stop along the way and was given "maximum attention" by agents determined to "take her in tow" on the "slightest pretext." She appeared again in Portland, where she planted herself at the foot of steps leading to a hotel reception for the Hardings. This time four agents surrounded her while two others held her down as the Hardings passed. Asked by a reporter about the scuffle, an agent flashed photographs that proved she was following the President and First Lady. Since she made no assassination attempt, she was released but was now "being kept under surveillance."[10]

There is no record of Florence's reaction to the threat, but she shook some forty-five hundred hands at the reception with a few slaps on the shoulders, then dashed off to a luncheon, "like a steam engine," said Boone. She "received great ovations and was noticeably extremely popular with the people. This trip made me appreciate her great value to the President of the United States more than I had ever realized. . . ." Even after the President gave his speech, she won points, cracking in front of the crowd, "That was a wonderful speech, Warren." He snapped: "Well, why shouldn't it be? You wrote it, didn't you?" She shot back, "Yes, I did"—then realized where she was—"not."

In Portland, as in Denver and Tacoma, Florence toured a veterans' hospital, and she seemed to move beyond whatever humiliation she felt about the still-unfolding Forbes scandal, reaching out in renewed effort, albeit with less concrete promises of how the government would care for the veterans. Of all the citizens she met on the trip, she said, disabled vets were "uppermost" in her mind. The Spokane *Journal* noted that she "lost no opportunity to visit the disabled men, running away from the official party on one occasion to greet a small band in a hospital."[11]

Riding her popularity, Florence even began selling a sanitized version of her life as an unquoted source to reporters, claiming that Henry De Wolfe had simply been a bad businessman, that once Amos Kling accepted Warren, her father had given them a "belated wedding gift of $100,000," even that she'd been to Asia. To a Tacoma paper she did admit that her one poignant "matter of regret" was that Amos Kling "did not live to see his son-in-law and daughter take their places in the White House." If she had blossomed in the White House, however, Flossie Kling of Marion triumphed on the western trip. "It can be said without fear of contradiction," noted a Washington reporter, "that no living woman is more popular in the west than Florence Harding."

Still, at the very last moment before heading to her dreamland of Alaska, Florence could find signs that fate was closing in on her. Their train, on its way for maintenance in preparation of the return trip, was caught in a sudden rock landslide, and Edward Roddy, the engineer, whom the Hardings had befriended, was instantly crushed to death. Escape into Alaska, away from such ominous signs, was desperately what the Duchess needed. As they boarded a transport, they were overcome with a thick rain, the first rain of the trip.

As the SS *Henderson* headed into the sea to the strains of "Yes, We Have No Bananas," Florence, whom Boone called "pleased as a bride," gathered the cards from masses of flowers already on board for her from friends and admirers. But the President desperately declared that the heavy schedule must be abandoned. "Unless it is radically modified and changed in many respects following my Alaskan visit, it will kill me."[12]

33

Poison

Along with three Cabinet members, the House Speaker, friends, military aides, staff, and reporters, there were also now in the Hardings' presence the strange faces of 460 sailors, 72 marine guards, 21 officers, and a Navy band. Seventy-five of Hollywood's latest films were provided for entertainment, Warren usually watching through the glass-enclosed observation deck from outside, where he smoked alone. Also on board were an X-ray machine and pharmacy and naval nurse, Sue Dauser.[1]

Although the *Henderson* had brought marines to France, the superstitious among the party soon considered it a "ship of ill omen" because it had been engulfed in flames and abandoned at sea, only to be retrieved and the hull refitted. Now, in these treacherous waters it would have to navigate about a thousand miles of inland channels, and along the way were the tales of fishermen capsizing into a freezing death and of two hundred spirits haunting the site of the wreck on reefs, camouflaged by fog, of the *Princess Sophia* in 1914. One night, as Captain Allen Buchanan tried to anchor, a sailor clanged a bell, shouting, "Twenty fathoms and no bottom!" An atmosphere of near surrealism consumed the vessel, the silent, increasingly icy waters ruffled only by eddying tides, the sun a fierce red until almost eleven at night. Towering snow-capped cliffs and dwarf pine trees flanked the narrow passage. Only occasionally was there sight of a thatched wooden bungalow or an abandoned cannery factory or a lumber camp set in the rich, wet peat, "wonderful fairylands," thought Boone. When anchorage was found, the Hardings went on deck to see the unearthly midnight sun, which silhouetted them against the shimmering endless ocean of gold and purple. The eerie stillness was punctured by the Navy band's blaring of "End of a Perfect Day."

At about ten at night, on July 8, the great dream of the Duchess had finally been achieved: She was in Alaska, a land as wide and long as the continental United States, exceeding by thousands of miles the entire square footage of Western Europe. The Hardings first glimpsed the territory as they stepped onto the deck after a movie and saw the outline of Annette Island. If reaching this mark was a pinnacle of an ambitious life for Florence, it also proved to be its waning. It is a tragic irony that the achieved dream of Alaska would take such a deathly toll.

All were roused the next morning by a loud "Star-Spangled Banner," played by a barefoot Alaskan band on an approaching launch, along with Scott Bone, the Alaskan governor, a former Harding campaign manager. The first president to visit Alaska, Harding toured with his party through Metlakatla, a village of four hundred, and went to church, surprised to find natives waving American flags, the women in short skirts and their black hair in bobs. The next stop was Ketchikan, the entire town being one large wharf, the houses on sidewalks made of wood planks laid upon green waterstained pilings, rising from the loam. Tricolored bunting and misspelled signs dotted the few wood houses scattered on a mountainside, and there were tours of a new baseball park, freshly painted salmon canneries, a paper factory, and a cold storage plant holding four million pounds of fish, some of them two-hundred-pound halibut. The next morning the *Henderson* was met by Alaskans wrapped in colorful blankets who glided up in painted ancient canoes. The party then spent three hours in Wrangell. Ceremonies became routine, the Hardings performing as if in a haunting montage, accepting salmons, berries, and uprooted wildflowers, bouncing in a jeep-like wagon down muddy streets past crudely crafted welcome signs. It was, said Boone, "like a great moving picture."

At the capital, Juneau, the Hardings were formally entertained at the governor's mansion, a small version of the White House on a desolate hill, complete with five hundred guests, at an outdoor dance in a hot fog and under the opalescent sunshine. The party lasted until midnight. Will Steel, editor of the *Sunday Capital*, spoke with the Hardings and later recalled, "The President freely expressed himself on matters of state and politics, with frequent observations on the part of the First Lady of the Land, whose mind is always alert and particularly keen on matters that concern her husband and his administration."[2]

From Skagway the *Henderson* navigated through the channels and out to sea, passing mammoth glaciers and mountains en route to Seward. Mist enveloped the ship, and the ocean became extremely rough, with many passengers becoming seasick. By July 12 they were so far out that all land disappeared from sight. The ship's heat had to be turned on for four days. The sun still set at midnight, but it now rose at three in the morning. Despite Warren's heart condition, Doc did not discourage his endless rounds of shuffleboard. After crossing the unfathomable Gulf of Alaska, the party disembarked to explore inner and northern Alaska by train.

Florence was given briefing materials that stated that native Alaskans took "more kindly to our ways and customs" than Native Americans, but after one native Alaskan expressed "grievances about the white man's canneries" and another said that if they organized to "smash up a cannery," there would be more attention to Indian fishing rights, the Duchess lost her cool: "If I were just an ordinary citizen and not the first lady, I would have a few things to say to you from the heart."

Despite this outburst, she propounded on Americanism, declaring that "nowhere in the world have I seen such expression of it as in Alaska." An editorial noted her "alertness in grasping the fundamentals of American society as composed of the masses" and how she "readily emerges from her exalted station to enter into a bond . . . with all with whom she comes into contact. When Mrs. Harding gave voice to her estimate of Americanism as applied to Alaska, she was not saying something just to be nice." Florence clearly saw the economic benefits to "Americanizing" Alaska: "One of the most essential steps is a new opening of the natural resources of the country and the restoration and development of transportation particularly in the great territory of Alaska. The nation has in this storehouse, woodpulp, lumber, oil, coal and manifold metals and minerals that are necessities. Some way must be found to get them out in order to check the decline of the territory in development and even in population, and to deliver its wealth in the states."[3]

On Friday, the thirteenth, under a midnight sky of pink, yellow, and green, light enough to read the newspapers, the party headed toward Fairbanks. Like a Christmas toy, their train curved into deep tunnels, twisted through snowsheds, precariously glided atop spindly bridges with bottomless gullies below, squeezed through cathedrals of stone, close enough to touch from the windows, often dwarfed by monster glaciers that reached into the tracks. Deeper into the supernatural territory, the vistas burst like painted postcards through the large train windows: green meadows flaming with all forms of native wildflowers, distant mountains lost in clouds.

Inevitably some boredom took over. Warren occasionally poked through Edgar Saltus's *The Imperial Orgy* but more often insisted on numbing rounds of poker. From Wasilla to Willow, he drove the engine twenty-six miles while the Duchess sat in the fireman's seat, but after a spat between them she rode in the baggage car. "If he wants her, he knows where he can find her," noted the Fairbanks *Daily News-Miner,* "and he will have to come to her, just as all of us old timers have to go to Mother for comfort." Behind the train was a steel-wheeled Dodge roadster, run on the rails, which the Duchess preferred riding in alone for the view. Occasionally she called for the company of James G. Steese, chairman and president of the Alaska Railroad. They had met some months earlier in the White House when she first summoned him to confer on the itinerary.

On the train Steese said he fed Harding "game and fish, after I had my veterinary surgeon pass upon its palatability," but "refused to let him have any of our famous Cordova cracked crabs" because "it was too risky in the summer time for him. . . . Those same crabs poisoned Cherikov and all his crew when he was second in command on Bering's voyage of discovery of Alaska 200 years ago."

Steese later claimed he had been told by Doc that Harding "had an iron stomach, but a weak heart," a statement that indicated Sawyer was aware of Warren's heart condition and blatantly chose to ignore it. While Boone said he and Doc suggested to Harding that he not partake in "acts . . . which we felt unduly taxed his vitality," only Doc had the power to order Warren to desist from such activity. Doc didn't stop Harding from driving a golden spike at Nenana to mark the completion of the railroad or laying a Masonic temple cornerstone in Ketchikan. The single most alarming incident was permitting the President to climb 190 steep, endless wood stairs at Chickaloon. Steese, trying to "spare him all the climbing I could," guardedly escorted Harding, who looked exhausted and breathless halfway up. A smiling Sawyer lagged behind.[4]

As the Hardings finally reached Fairbanks, ninety miles from the Arctic Circle, the greatest fear of the Duchess was realized. Atop the world, out in the Alaskan wilderness, her illness kicked in. Boone said that throughout the trip. "She just did not wish to miss any entertainment or attention that the citizenry seemed to wish to bestow upon her," but the fewer people there were as they headed farther north, the more subdued she became. Quite the opposite, Warren thrived on the isolation, eager for the long days of the highway trip back to the coast. That could now be made only by placing Florence's life at risk. Sawyer ordered it canceled, Boone noting, "We dreaded to tell the President." With her precarious condition the train return had to be slow, and it, Boone said, "seemed infinitely longer to me, and I am sure it did to the President." On July 17 they reached Seward and reboarded the *Hen-*

derson. Doc insisted that Florence avoid climbing and a canvas-covered platform lifted by crane from dock to deck was made for her. Despite Warren's heart condition, neither Doc nor Boone suggested he use the platform too.

Two days later they were out to sea, headed west, nearly touching old Russia. As Florence grew healthier, however, Warren began to spiral. Unable to sleep, even with sedatives Doc gave him, he obsessively played cards into the night. Entranced by enormous icebergs dropping with a roar into a river and the resulting tidal waves, Warren sat silently staring, said Steese, and "it was nearly three hours before Harding could be, almost literally, dragged away to continue his very crowded itinerary." He piped up to ask "how the bull seals controlled their extensive harems."

Florence stayed on board at Valdez and Cordova, sending thank-you notes to flattering reporters and editors. By Sitka she was touring the ancient Orthodox St. Michael's Church, set amid the red tile spires and green onion-domed architecture of the Russian settlers, drawn with Warren by the church's Father Pontelarf past the Russian icons, gold goblets, into the inner sanctuary to see ivory crucifixes set with gems from the age of Peter the Great, after which they strolled through a forest dotted with totem poles of Alaskan history figures. Meanwhile, the *Henderson* crew was loading up fresh food for the voyage south. Reporter Lukin Johnson noted: "Harding, from the upper deck, had watched the seamen carry up the companionway the heavy boxes containing the fresh crabs...."[5]

At nine-thirty in the evening of July 22 the Hardings left Alaska, now shadowed in what a reporter called an "opalescent sunset," sailing from the "land of loneliness," its "somber, solitary, melancholy mountains" fading away. As they headed south from the midnight sun, darkness again began to descend more frequently upon the Hardings.

For decades to come, historians debated whether there really was a mysterious seaplane that flew in from the coast to give Harding some ominous message about impending scandals in Washington. There was in fact a seaplane message: official greeting from Vancouver's minister of public works as the *Henderson* crossed into Canadian waters, but it had nothing to do with Harding's sudden "collapse" shortly after. The simmering scandals, however, certainly were on his mind. Several days later Washington State Senator C. C. Dill recalled how Harding "tearfully lamented the betrayal of two of his Cabinet members, Interior Secretary Albert Fall and Attorney General Harry Daugherty...." Herbert Hoover corroborated this less explicitly:

I found Harding exceedingly nervous and distraught. As soon as we were aboard ship he insisted on playing bridge, beginning every day immediately after breakfast and continuing except for mealtime often until after midnight. One day after lunch when we were a few days out, Harding asked me to come to his cabin. He plumped at me the question: "If you knew of a great scandal in our administration, would you for the good of the country and the party expose it publicly or would you bury it?" My natural reply was, "Publish it, and at least get credit for integrity on your side." He remarked that this method might be politically dangerous. I asked for more particulars. He said that he had received some rumors of irregularities, centering around Smith, in connection with cases in the Department of Justice. Harding gave me no information about what Smith had been up to. I asked what Daugherty's relation to the affair were. He abruptly dried up and never raised the question again.

Evalyn McLean reflected that Harding "loved to feel he could trust his friends. When he saw his friends dropping by the wayside—that was his life, friends. He reached the point where he didn't care." Indeed even during his happier moments in Alaska his premonitions of death revealed themselves. Talking to Governor Bone about the past spring's Gridiron Club dinner, Warren had said that in 1924, "President Coolidge will attend that dinner." Other mounting tensions about Harding's health now finally surfaced. The only open confrontation between Boone and Sawyer came on July 23, after the younger man lanced a minor infection on Warren's finger. Warren sent for Boone instead of Doc because of his "poor vision." As Boone treated the President, he became aware that Doc slipped in and stood staring at them: "I felt a chill in the air and suspected that General Sawyer was critical that I was treating the President. When I had finished . . . I returned to my stateroom. General Sawyer followed me . . . [and] in my stateroom very curtly told me never to go to the President or treat him without his knowledge. . . . I impressed upon General Sawyer that I was a Regular Naval Medical Officer, the President was my Commander-in-Chief, and if any time he sent for me I would respond with alacrity and without announcing that I was doing so to anyone. . . . Nothing more was said of this incident."[6]

A turn of events far more consequential, engulfing not just the doctors but the entire presidential party, was set into motion some time after the *Henderson* left Sitka but before it arrived in Vancouver, either on Monday or Tuesday, July 23 or 24. The President ate some shellfish, almost certainly crabmeat, and was poisoned.

Where the President consumed the tainted seafood is difficult to discern, for almost daily he consumed some form of shellfish. Boone publicly claimed that there had been no such food, but when someone wrote him about "those crabs . . . at Sitka" he made a correction for himself in the margin, "at Valdez, not Sitka." Reporter James Nourse said the crabs were put on board at Cordova but kept in cold storage. It was reported at the time that at *both* Cordova and Sitka crabs were sent on board and served, but whether they were tainted with ptomaine, noted one reporter later on, "the doctors do not agree." Who brought the crabs on board remains a mystery. A newspaper at the time provided only one vague clue, quoting an unnamed source on the ship that the crabs had been "the gift of Alaskan fishermen." Reddy Baldinger, however, recalled that at one brief stop after Sitka, he also "bought a mess of giant crabs" and had the cook boil them for him late at night. An insomniac Warren found Reddy in the deserted dining room, and joined in the crab feast. How much was consumed is uncertain, but Reddy recalled that they ate the crabs with butter for over an hour. The poison almost certainly came from the crab brought on board "anonymously" since Reddy didn't become ill, but some of the larger party—Lou Hoover, George Christian, and Ross Bartley among them—did. "Don't let anybody kid you about ptomaine poisoning," Bartley later admitted. "We were all sick."

The others soon threw off the effect, but on Wednesday, July 25, however, Harding had sudden, sharp abdominal pains, without vomiting. There was "weakness . . . some fever and increased pulse rate associated with the pain and distress." Doc Sawyer applied some unnamed "treatment," probably a purgative, and "the symptoms were somewhat ameliorated," according to a later consulting physician. Sawyer would not call in Boone. Doc handled it himself.[7]

When the *Henderson* landed in Vancouver on July 26, Harding addressed forty thousand citizens in Stanley Park and attended a lunch but revealed to Vancouver Mayor Tisdall that he had "indigestion from eating crab meat." Again among an adoring public, the Duchess was "full of the joy of living," said one reporter. "I am here only because I insisted," she told the press of the trip. Throughout that night, as the *Henderson* headed down to Seattle, the fog grew denser than the passengers had ever seen it. The white clouds hung on the decks themselves; it was often impossible to see the water at all. Meanwhile in his stateroom Harding suffered some sort of attack and went to the Duchess, who fetched Doc. They did not send for Boone. At about eight in the morning of July 27, as Harding was shaving, there was a sudden jolt.

The boiler room started flooding, steam escaping as a result, and a panicked scream went up for "All hands on deck!" The crew and passengers rushed out, barely able to see the *Zeilen,* the smaller ship that the *Henderson* had just hit, before it was swallowed into the fog and began sinking. Warren remained alone in his cabin. Brooks returned, and recalled, "He was lying down with his face hidden in his hand. I told him it was a slight collision and everybody was ordered on deck." The President did not look up but said simply, "I hope this boat sinks."

As the party went into breakfast, they learned that the fog remained so thick that their scheduled morning arrival in Seattle would be delayed indefinitely. At times, when the ship simply stood still in the white clouds, passengers were unable to see one another on deck. There, through the fog Interior Secretary Work—a doctor—found Boone, safely out of what he thought was any hearing range of Doc. "I hear the President was sick last night."

Boone was stunned. "If he was, I was not informed. I'll see about it." He went to the Duchess. "Was the President sick last night?"

"Yes, 'Old Doc' was up with him most of the night and into the morning as we traveled into the fog," she told him. "Warren was very sick last night and all today." She admitted, "You should have been informed, you may have been able to help him—you may have seen the thing differently than 'Old Doc.'" Jealously guarding his status, particularly after the argument over the infected finger, Doc sought to block Boone from access to Harding throughout the day. "I was not asked to see him," Boone remembered. Finally, Boone had to approach Sawyer to get any confirmation; Doc was hardly forthcoming. "I inquired of Sawyer the nature of his ailment, and he said he felt it was an intestinal upset."

As the ship inched toward Seattle, the Hardings emerged to ascend the upper deck. Boone immediately noticed that Warren "looked very pale" and "tired and not well." Harding was now told that they would arrive at about 1:00 P.M., some three and a half hours behind schedule. At this the President ordered a dispatch sent to Seattle officials, stating that he could carry out only the afternoon events, but was unable to try and make up the morning ones as well. "Regrettably," said Boone, "the request to cancel the morning schedule was never carried out, but it was dovetailed into the heavy afternoon schedule and even that afternoon schedule was added to . . . a terrifically exhausting program for the President. . . ." Why the order was ignored was never explained.[8]

As they came into the harbor, Harding stood on the *Henderson* bridge to review the American battle fleet, shimmering in colorful, tiny flags. Florence grasped his arm: "Warren, please cancel our going ashore. You are not physically up to it since you were sick last night." Just then the fog rapidly broke, and within view were hundreds of thousands of people, standing on roofs, in windows, and lining the waterfront and roads in merciless heat. In the eleventh hour Doc finally joined Florence and others in urging Harding to "modify his program very radically" and rest, but in this instance he "refused to listen." In need of the adulation as much as rest, he said simply, "we are going to go ashore."

A telegram did somehow manage to reach the First Lady at sea: an unexpected message of concern from Evalyn. Florence's reaction is unrecorded, but it must have been touching, the first clear signal of renewed loyalty from Evalyn since the strain in their friendship. Counteracting this, however, was an incident that undoubtedly shook the superstitious First Lady: Just after the Hardings disembarked in Seattle, the *Henderson,* on its way out, rammed mightily into another vessel. Soon even stranger news arrived: Having business on the West Coast, Harry Daugherty decided to come see Harding. The Duchess felt fate could narrowly be escaped only so many times. "When we were in Seattle, I never expected to get him out of there alive," she later revealed. "I knew how sick Mr. Harding was, even before he left Washington."[9]

34

The Heart of San Francisco

Laden with delphiniums and roses and twirling a Japanese parasol on her shoulder, the First Lady paraded in an open car through the teeming streets of Seattle, while the President doffed his straw hat. The "constant use of his right arm as he waved his hat added to the concern of Doctor Sawyer and myself," said Boone. Sometime before a three-thirty picnic Harding had a clandestine meeting with Harry Daugherty, who seemed to have rather suddenly "turned up and had an hour with him," recalled Hoover. No report of the private conversation is extant, and only Hoover made a record of the contact. How, or even if, the talk with Daugherty upset the President is unknown. The most daunting task, however, still lay before Harding: a speech to the largest crowd that had ever gathered to hear a President. Every one of the sixty thousand seats at the University of Washington stadium was filled, and several thousand folding chairs jammed the field around the podium. Via loudspeaker, thousands of others cramming nearby streets would also hear it. Reporters noticed how intensely focused the Duchess was on her husband.

During the speech, scheduled for four-thirty, Florence, Doc, Boone, everyone on the stand were stunned when Harding's voice grew "husky" and his breathing "labored." Disoriented, he referred to Alaska as "Nebraska," then suddenly "dropped the manuscript, and grasped the desk," wrote Hoover, who shot up to the podium and picked up the speech. Harding continued. Doc did not stop him, and Boone—even though he likely knew he should—didn't dare cross Doc. Being unable to stand upright for a long period of time was a clear sign of Harding's weakened cardiac system, which was unable to pump the necessary blood flow upward to the brain; hence his swaying and disorientation. The inability to withstand the heat was also typical of a person who was operating on a limited blood flow. He had likely suffered a mild heart attack right then and there.[1]

Praising the poised First Lady, the Seattle *Evening Record* noted her concern over the President's condition, as she "arose from her chair several times and straightened her dress in a nervous manner and never once during that speech lasting more than an hour did she take her eyes from the nation's chief executive." At first she declared, "Warren must speak no more. He is sick and I must take care of him." When the Hardings proceeded to a children's hospital, *The New York Times* noted, "Mrs. Harding was doing most of the honors in greeting the knots of people gathered at every corner along the route. . . . Harding did not leave the car." Once his "attack of weakness" passed, however, with the Duchess confident of his recovery, the President pushed his luck even further. All the missed morning events were crammed into the six-hour schedule, along with innumerable requests Harding would not refuse—quick, unscheduled stops for the crowds and continued parading. Although he "felt it almost impossible to hold his hat and wave his arms when he was greeting the crowds," he pushed himself, said Boone, until "his arm was practically paralyzed," further affecting his heart. Yet that night he addressed the Seattle Press Club and a crowd at the train yard.

Severely fatigued, he went into his stateroom, followed by Doc. Doc shut out Boone from the room. The train lumbered out into the dark, headed south to Yosemite Park.[2]

Through Friday night into Saturday, July 28, Harding's temperature rose, and he was unable to keep food down. Doc still maintained, as did Warren, that it was seafood poisoning, and to flush it out, Sawyer began his first full day of flooding Harding's system with purgatives, the homeopathic ingredients of which he never revealed. When a scheduled stop at Eugene, Oregon, was passed, the press grew suspicious. Doc told them that it was poisoning, but that Warren's condition wasn't serious, nor was there "the slightest apprehension . . . that the President's illness might end fatally." That subversives apparently sought to bring the rushing train to a dangerous short stop by placing tree trunks on the tracks outside of Roseburg, Oregon, undoubtedly preyed more on the paranoid First Lady's mind than did her husband's condition.[3]

Doc specifically kept Boone out of the loop as long as possible. "I wondered why I had not been summoned to be of assistance in professional care," Boone reflected. "Sawyer had been taking care of him. . . . The day wore on, I was aware that the President was staying in his bed in his stateroom. I thought it was strange . . . Sawyer didn't inform me. I spoke to Work and Hoover about the President's condition, and they wanted to know what I thought about it. I then informed them that I had not been informed that he was sick by Sawyer. Thought it was very strange and late, toward evening, they went to Mrs. Harding [since] she had become very concerned about the President and [it was finally decided] that I should be brought into the picture."

Pressed by the Cabinet officers, she confessed to Boone that she had stayed up all night with Warren, along with Doc, as he plied the President with the purgatives. She told Boone that she would not stay awake another night in a row if he "would stay up all night with the President and not let him out of . . . sight. . . ." Boone promised to "absolutely not take my eyes off of him." After this conversation Boone was finally permitted to see Harding a few times, but always "in company with General Sawyer at the latter's request."[4]

On such matters, when the Duchess took control of decisions, she was not questioned by even Doc. After she and Doc had encouraged Warren to continue on after the danger signs of heart trouble in Hutchinson, Vancouver Harbor, and Seattle, Florence finally ordered a cancellation of the trip and "compelled the president to yield," wrote reporter Steve Early. She also, "in conference" with advisers, decided to release Harding's planned speech in Los Angeles. Florence had even wanted to "go back to Washington at once" but was convinced otherwise by Boone. Instead, they would rush straight to San Francisco and settle there for the moment. Along the way to San Francisco, H. L. Denton, a railroad superintendent of police, recalled that "at every point Mrs. Harding would greet the crowds and speak a few words to them." The San Francisco *Journal* even called her the "acting President." At Dunsmuir, Florence "captured the crowd by her charm and warmth," but if Doc's Rasputin hold on her was ever in place, it was now: She called him forward and to the crowds announced her allegiance to "the man who saved my life."[5]

That night, with Florence and Doc asleep, Boone was finally alone with Harding. "I sat there watching the President hour after hour[;] at times he was quite restless and seemed very uncomfortable . . . his breathing was quite heavy," he recorded. When the train stopped in the wee hours for servicing near Redding, Boone seized his stethoscope to examine Harding: "There seemed to be a dead silence. I felt very much alone. I was aware of the great responsibility that was suddenly upon me. I became instinctively conscious that there was more wrong with the President than we had foreseen. . . . I didn't like what I felt in taking the President's pulse. . . . I found that the left border of his heart was well to the left of its normal position. It was almost midway between the usual left border and the right axillary line of his left chest . . . well out beyond . . . one and a half inches to the left, and abnormally moved over. . . . Sounds of his heart were muffled, with some irregularity as I heard it and as I noted through his pulse. I then decided that the President had a dilated heart. At that time of my examination the train began to move, picking up speed quickly and making considerable noise, so that I could not . . . continue. . . ."

The next morning Boone courageously told Sawyer that Harding had heart dilation. Doc fiercely disagreed, insisting it was poisoning. Boone saw the futility of arguing and, to his great credit, finally decided to override Doc but circumvent Florence. Herbert Hoover recalled how Boone "came to me and stated that he believed that the President was suffering from something worse than digestive upset, but that Dr. Sawyer would not have it otherwise. . . . Boone was much alarmed, so I took him to Secretary Work. . . . Work insisted on going into the President's room and soon sent for Boone." They took a percussion tap of Harding's chest; it was easy for anyone with a basic understanding of the body to note the size of an enlarged heart by differentiating the sound of the hollow lungs. Work realized the truth. "They came out," said Hoover, "and asked me to arrange that some heart specialist should meet the train in San Francisco." He immediately wired the Stanford University president and the former American Medical Association president, Ray Lyman Wilbur, who then contacted a leading San Francisco cardiologist, Charles Cooper.[6]

Doc certainly resented Wilbur, who was no friend of homeopathy. In reaction he vehemently asserted his indispensability by trumpeting Florence's support for him. Wilbur understood why Warren continued to place absolute and now dangerous trust in Doc: "Friendship with him meant that lapses of his comrades were overlooked. His simple human nature seemed to lack discriminations regarding his comrades." Doc, of course, was also nearly blind, and Boone had seen signs of a small stroke—although he said nothing of it to Sawyer.

As the train neared San Francisco, however, even Doc told Harding not to dress or walk, but that he would be carried off in a stretcher to a car carrying him to the Palace Hotel. Harding scowled at this, went into his room, and emerged fully dressed. Harding angrily snapped, "I am [not] going to receive the Governor . . . and Mayor . . . in pajamas. . . . I will not be carried off this train!" Neither doctor stopped him or asked the Duchess to intervene. Harding emerged, gray in color, Florence following, smiling, giving her military wave to curious passengers on a departing train, pulling Hoover by the arm to pose with her. After a brief ceremony the party ignored the waiting ambulance, got into a limousine, and went to the Palace Hotel in the heart of downtown. There Harding walked up stone steps into the lobby, to the elevator, and down two long corridors. "I thought he might die walking the required distance from the elevator to the special suite," said Boone. Led into the paneled room 8064, Harding threw his arms in the air and fell across the walnut four-poster bed. Only his shoes were then removed as he was covered with a blanket. Noted Boone: "His pulse was irregular and he was very short of breath." He fell right to sleep. Florence took an adjoining suite of mahogany furnishings and gray tapestries, Boone directly across the hall, the Sawyers on the floor below, near the Hoovers, Wallaces, and Works.[7]

The hall became a temporary White House, a screen blocking the view of it from the curious, while right outside the Harding suite, choked by the cigarette and cigar smoke of dozens of reporters loitering for news, sat bellboy "Gold Braid Joe." Doc told the press that after two days' rest, Harding's schedule in the city "will be carried out completely as planned," that the poison attack had been "violent," with severe diarrhea and sick stomach, and claimed "the information given out has represented absolutely everything there was to tell." A Riverside

Daily Press reporter thought, "Many of the questions were evaded." When Doc was out of the room, Boone immediately examined Harding's heart, found him "suffering with Myocarditis," and hastened a meeting with Wilbur and Cooper, both of whom "knew that we were in trouble and that the President was a very sick man," said Boone, and "interrogated General Sawyer and myself in much detail, and they made an examination of the patient. . . ."

Doc told Wilbur that Harding was suffering from a lingering fatigue from his winter flu, "attacks of indigestion," and a "history of pain in the chest." After his own examination Wilbur noted the shallow and irregular breathing, a heart rate up to 130 with extra beats, and an enlarged heart, both left to right. Boone was secretly relieved that Wilbur and Cooper "gave support to my opinions." Hoover put it bluntly: "The doctors, despite Sawyer, at once diagnosed the case as a heart attack."

It was inevitable that Doc would resent the intrusion of such a highly respected medical expert on his previously exclusive turf. In an attempt to prove his power, Doc concocted the first public bulletin on Harding's health. But, said the decisive Wilbur, it was "superseded later by one drawn up by myself indicating . . . the state of the cardiovascular system." Avoiding open confrontation, a compromise was struck the next morning with the issuance of a joint public bulletin. Filled with highly medical information, it was carefully manipulated to minimize alarm. Doc's medical notion of "poison" was now presented as "digestive disturbance." Omitted was any reference to the "purgatives" that Doc still insisted on applying—and mentioned to reporters. Nor did the doctors mention Harding's having had a heart attack, only that he had "temporarily overstrained his cardiovascular system." As Boone later admitted with understatement, the doctors "joined together in wording the bulletins, and many times suggested changes were made by different members of the consultant team." Boone had his own work to do on the President in the wee hours.[8]

Hospital care would have allowed for Harding's heart damage to be detected by the large, untransportable ECG machines, but it was Florence's decision to keep him out of a hospital, where Doc would have even less control. "Keeping the President at the hotel permits Mrs. Harding to stay near him," said Doc, and "that is an advantage." She didn't want Warren at the Palace long either, saying "the place for a sick man is home, and home in this case is the White House." Despite day and night nursing care, Florence refused to leave the sickroom: "I'm not even going to church . . . all the newspaper boys who had advance copy [that] had me in the role of resting . . . will have to change their stories." With what a reporter called her voice of "color and authority" she yelled at the press, "No noise at the end of that corridor!" After meeting with the mayor and police commissioner, she held an informal women's press conference, the sickroom partially visible through the door, which she quickly, firmly shut. Although she declared, "I like the job . . . I believe in women in politics," when asked if she was a "feminist," she put up her hand and snapped, "I don't get into politics with reporters. You must not question me like that . . . I am entranced with California. . . . Now I must bid you all good-bye and return to my husband."

When she was not in the sickroom, the Duchess was thriving on intense work in the small office, directing aides, helping to cancel every scheduled event and reservation of the aborted trip, dictating thanks for previous events, responding to hundreds of telegrams and phone calls. Such energy further dazzled the press, one editorial claiming, "Mrs. Harding is deserving of a big place in the heart of America." To those who best knew her, however, such frenetic activity masked fear.

On that Sunday Wilbur recalled, "We had a frank discussion of the case in front of Mrs. Harding at the time of our first consultation, so that she was familiar with our point of view and our fears and hopes." Through the "cold medical facts" she kept "her head up and her eyes dry." Perhaps out of uncertainty, certainly out of loyalty, she never contradicted Doc's belief that Warren just had food poisoning and would soon recover. "I did not share the belief," she later revealed, "that it was just a slight illness." Indeed she forced a bravado. "Everything will come out all right," she told George Christian.[9]

In the face of doom the First Lady continued business. After she met with Ann Godfrey, the federal immigration officer reported, "I have never seen a better helpmeet, a wife to whom a husband could turn to and find such support as Mrs. Harding." Florence announced later that as soon as Warren was recovering, she would go as his "personal representative" to veterans' hospitals at the Presidio and Palo Alto, "in order not to disappoint the boys."[10]

Meanwhile the delayed release of Monday night's bulletin—without the words "poison" or "heart"—sparked the first public suggestion of disagreement among the doctors. The Anaheim *Plain Dealer* noted that it was nearly two hours before they released the bulletin, "after there had been considerable discussion as to its wording. It was rewritten several times. What the new symptoms were, Dr. Sawyer declined to state. It was considered important that Dr. Cooper, a noted heart specialist, had been called in. His presence was interpreted as meaning that the president's heart had been affected following his illness from ptomaine poisoning." Which doctor leaked this news is uncertain, but there is a clue in a San Francisco *Call and Post* disclosure that Harding had been panting when he came into his room and collapsed on the bed—a description that exists in only one other place, Boone's diary. Boone's apparent press tips fueled a war of words with Doc. Reporters followed up persistently. It was Boone who likely told the Chicago *Tribune*'s James Nourse that "the doctors" said that "recovery depends entirely upon the response of his heart." The Los Angeles *Record* carried the bluntest headline: HEART ATTACK COMPLICATES HAR-DING ILLNESS.[11]

Doc had his own tactics, independently emphasizing elements of the joint bulletins that corresponded with his own theory and mitigating those that did not. Given his savvy timing, the press on deadline simply quoted Doc verbatim without trying to interpret the bulletins. "Calling visiting and local newspapermen together," the *Call and Post* reported on another of his techniques, "Sawyer discussed the case from beginning to end last night *before* the final consultation of the staff of physicians resulted in the last bulletin. . . ." And when one bulletin was released before he could pontificate, Doc simply "declined to answer reporters' interrogations." He also gave reporters the names of other doctors to contact for their opinion of his professional treatment, doctors who also happened to be friends, who naturally praised him; like Illinois Medical Board examiner Dr. Gilbert Fitzpatrick and Burton Hazeltine, surgery chief of U.S. Hospital 28. Doc also politely put down the other doctors, calling Boone a "laboratory technician" and quipping that "no doctor" could predict potential complications.

Doc's most skillful technique to be seen as master of the case was capturing the public's fascination with the word "poison." Alongside his initial claim of tainted crabmeat thus were his references to "copper poisoning," from crabs that might have been taken from copper cans, or caught in copper-rich waters, or served from copper utensils. When the alarmed Copper and Brass Research Association wired Boone that it was "impossible to eat food containing sufficient amount[s]" of copper to poison, Boone carefully replied that it was not Doc's "intention to convey" that. A correction was requested by the Copper Association in one of the subsequent bulletins. No such clarification was forthcoming.

Although Boone believed firmly that Doc misdiagnosed Harding's heart trouble as indigestion, he conceded that poisoning "may have been so." When someone asked Boone whether it was berries or crab that poisoned Harding, Boone scribbled "not so" to the former but wrote a question mark next to the latter. If he conceded that Harding *might* have been poisoned without permanent effect, however, it was Doc's treatment of it that became the truly alarming point for Boone. In another apparent blind quote to the press Boone now raised the largest red flag of all.

The "most important" factor in Harding's precarious condition that continued to "weaken him" was "the administering of purgatives to rid his system of the poison."[12]

While Boone insisted that Harding have "one small drink" of whiskey to stimulate his circulation, every two hours Doc also fed him a steady diet of eggs, milk, toast, chicken broth, and "homeopathic eggnogs." Although infinitesimal traces and safe amounts of poisons like arsenic (which homeopaths used to reduce fever) and belladonna (also called deadly nightshade) were possibly in the heart stimulant that Doc did use on Harding, the homeopathic purgatives he still insisted on pumping into the President's system were never disclosed. A single page of Harding's clinical chart does exist, however, and records the use of the heart stimulant digitalis. It was injected at 3:00 A.M. and at 9:00 A.M. from at least Sunday through Tuesday—by Boone. This being done when Doc was off his shift it suggests that Boone did so secretly. Boone later explained that he "always tried most zealously to be loyal" to Doc, but although he was "older in my profession, and also with a senior rank," the younger man continued, it was "quite natural that I did not agree with him at times and many times professionally, as I was schooled in the most modern forms of medicine. . . ."

On Tuesday, July 31, Doc announced that the "poison had not yet been eliminated," and Harding had "failed to respond" to three days of purgatives. Although they were potentially at cross purposes with the digitalis, he increased the dosage of purgatives. Whether his motive was premeditated or not, Doc further drew Florence to his defense in a manner that would suggest her tacit approval of his treatment. "Mrs. Harding knows everything," he announced. "I have given her every detail in the case of the president just as I did when she herself was ill." That morning, when Doc ran in to see Harding and then out to talk to the press, a California reporter noted that "he did not wait for the morning consultation of specialists but passed the word of good cheer on to the Nation. . . ." Doc got his message across clearly. George Holmes wrote that "Sawyer's voice is the determining one in the plans and he is strongly of the opinion that the president is getting along so well."[13]

On Tuesday Florence announced that at the President's request she would soon assume some of his canceled appearances, and she greeted Captain Buchanan of the *Henderson,* which had arrived ready to complete the tour home. Otherwise she stayed at Warren's side, encouraging him with the news that a brief bout with pneumonia was over. Harding even shook off his premonitions for a while, talking of his hope to be ambassador to Italy someday, thankful for the blackberry juice he requested. Doc announced that Harding had "utmost confidence" in the Sawyer homeopathic treatment and understood the "scientific side of his case," which read as *Warren* now tacitly approving of Doc's poison diagnosis and the purgatives. Florence, however, revealed later that she was pessimistic: "When we reached San Francisco, I knew that he was desperately ill, and that is why I declined to ever leave the Palace, or to accept any . . . invitations . . . to get me away and find some rest . . . when they reported that the President was in no danger. I believed that the President was in danger."[14]

That night, as Doc went for a drive, he prophesied to reporters, "The chances are nine to one that the President will make a rapid recovery." He mentioned the heart only to dismiss fears about it— "heart action was definitely improved"—and said that the "great strain" on it was only a result of the continued presence of poison. When "questions of a technical nature" were posed to him, he "asked to be excused from answering." Reporters were frustrated. "So much seemingly irreconcilable information has filtered through," Ernestine Black complained. National newspapers were also beginning to see through Doc's spin and the coded bulletins, leaving some doctors who read the reports with no doubt about Harding's condition. Boston Dr. Samuel Levine was "convinced that President Harding had an acute coronary thrombosis with myocardial infarction. I felt so firmly about this that I suggested to Dr. Harvey Cushing, the celebrated brain surgeon . . . that we should telephone Sawyer. . . . Cushing replied that it was not our business and that we should not interfere. . . . None of the medical attendants knew about coronary thrombosis, or the patient never would have been moved from city to city as he was during the illness. He finally had a shock with paralysis of one side of the body which is one of the complications of acute coronary thrombosis. This helped to confirm . . . that the entire illness was a coronary attack. . . ."

Other less scientific prognosticators had similar opinions. In Washington reporter Harry B. Hunt, recalling his 1920 interview with Madame Marcia and her prediction that Harding would be President but "not live out his term," returned to get her reaction to his reported recovery. Poring over the President's horoscope, she shook her head. "It is the end. He will never recover. The crisis will come Thursday night." Hunt smiled, but Marcia was insistent. "He will be dead by Friday." Not everyone worried. Evelyn in Maine was relieved by news of the recovery, and in Vermont Vice President Coolidge returned calmly to farm chores.

The charade continued into Wednesday, August 1. "Even though the President had a bad night," Boone later confessed, "the bulletin issued by us five physicians at 9:30 A.M. on August 1 stated, 'The President is fairly comfortable this morning after a few hours of sleep.'" Once again Doc's iron hand prevailed. "[W]e have reached clearer sailing," he told a reporter; "we have passed the peak load of trouble," he told another. He even wired his son that a "train could be made up in a short time for the return to Washington." As for the purgatives, Doc publicly offered that he was "keeping the system at work throwing off poisons." He further boasted that the doctors "are now a unit in diagnosing the trouble." They were not. That night, as Doc "demonstrated his confidence" that Harding was "past the crisis" by going for another drive, Boone took advantage of his absence to tell reporters *on* the record that "I will not say that all danger is past."[15]

Even Boone's small efforts to protect Harding, however, seemed futile. Since he hadn't wanted Harding to see headlines predicting his death, for example, Boone read around them, but, as *New York Times* reporter Richard Oulahan noted, "It was not Dr. Boone's office to determine whether the President should have his way. That was for General Sawyer, as the physician in charge, to decide. When Sawyer was summoned and saw the situation he handed the newspapers to the President." Doc continued to tell Harding that "no organ has been impaired" by the poison, but that was not what Oulahan learned around the sickroom. "Every little set-back has a detrimental effect upon the President's already over-worked heart." Doc was livid about the leaks now challenging his judgment, and, Oulahan continued, "took to task certain newspaper men who, he said, had ben printing unwarranted stories of what went on in the sickroom. . . ."

Meanwhile, announcing that she "had the President now where she could boss him," Florence met with "several important visitors and committees in the President's name." She still refused to leave the hotel because "I know this husband of mine better than anybody in the world and he needs me." Oulahan thought she "thrive[d] on responsibility" and was in a good mood. Warren's mood was less certain. Reporter Carter Field said Harding was "inwardly dejected" but did not regret the trip, saying it was "the best thing I ever did." Boone said he "showed no interest in public comment relative to his illness," but Wilbur claimed he was "very much interested in the newspaper reports of his illness." Harding did sense what truly threatened his life. When Wilbur assured him that his lungs had cleared, Harding replied, "I am not so much worried about them, but what about this dilation of my heart?" Said Wilbur: "[H]e was conscious of the fact that he had overstrained his heart," but the distinguished doctor made no effort to affirmatively seize professional control from Sawyer or attempt to advise the First Lady. After all, Florence had decisively canceled the trip at the right time, and with pathological passivity he felt, Wilbur said, "he could make his way" under the "watchful care of a devoted physician who knew every detail of his life."

It was now predicted that December would be the earliest Harding could work again (in which case he said privately he would resign). Hoover began making efforts through friends "to take a private residence for him on the California coast." Florence got into the decision by meeting with Ralph Palmer Merritt, president and managing director of the California Associated Raisin Company—then called the Sun-Maid Raisin Growers—which was then under Justice Department investigation for violation of antitrust laws. Merritt told an astonishing story:

> I had met the lady before. She was a hard and very realistic type of person. She said to me, "We are being asked to go down to Pebble Beach Lodge and to have the President convalesce there, but we have no [personal] money. We spent all of the money of the President's salary on the travel here, and we have no money. Can you get us the money with which to pay the expenses of going down there?" With that amazing request I went back and discussed it with Dr. Work, Mr. Hoover, Mr. Wallace, and it was decided that I should find out how much it would cost to lease the Pebble Beach Lodge and I would then go out and collect the money necessary to the expenses of the President's convalescnce. The total bill came to between $25,000 and $30,000 on the estimate. I went down Montgomery Street to Mr. Crocker's Bank and called on various people whom I knew were the heads of banks and corporations, and I came back with $25,000 in checks to pay this bill. I then went to Mrs. Harding and told her what I had done and told Mr. Hoover, Dr. Work and Mr. Wallace. They were all very happy and Mrs. Harding said she would tell the President. The President sent for me and I went in to see him as he lay in bed. Mrs. Harding was sitting beside him reading a story . . . "I want to thank you very much . . . you are about

to be indicted by the Federal Grand Jury for the violating of the Federal Anti-Trust laws . . . my Attorney General [is] bringing this action against you. . . . You need have no worry about this matter at all. Your books will be restored to your business office, the indictment will be dismissed and . . . I, personally, the President of the United States, apologize that this action should ever have taken place." . . . I thanked him very much. I left the room. . . . I had left all these checks and money with Dr. Work.

The money was never returned to Merritt, although his case was dropped, and he implied that the Duchess held on to the funds as personal assets. If true, it made the First Lady a direct party to an illegal payoff for personal profit.[16]

The only visitor to see Warren alone that Wednesday was his sister Charity Remsberg. After a meal with Florence, the refreshingly candid Charity told reporters that Warren didn't realize how near death he was and that Florence was now insisting that if he recovered, he must not challenge the stars and seek reelection, that they must leave the presidency as soon as possible. She also was "amazed" by how unaffected the Duchess seemed by the crisis: "She has not looked better in years than she does right now." The daughter of homeopathic doctors, Charity openly opposed Doc's treatment, bluntly telling the San Francisco *Call* that the "purgatives to rid it [the body] of the poisons . . . was [*sic*] one of the barriers" to Harding's recovery. This was the second press reference to the danger being posed by Doc's purgatives, and still no one dared attempt to stop him—or ask Florence to stop him.

Charity also learned something nobody in the press managed to print: that Warren was upset that day in somehow realizing that "his so-called friends plotting against him . . . would tear down the administration." Harding perhaps had one particular man in mind when he told her this. That same afternoon the *Princess Charlotte* had docked in San Francisco, coming from Seattle, and Harry Daugherty had returned unbidden. One reporter learned that Harry's attempt to confer with Harding in the sickroom about railroad deregulation had been thwarted by Doc. As Wilbur noted dryly, anything "troublesome was kept away." As the ever-artful Harry passed a cluster of reporters on his way out, however, he claimed no meeting had taken place because " 'I don't think he ought to try to talk today. . . . I had to go.' " Still, as Wilbur recalled of Harding the next morning, "the first thing he asked was, 'Has Daugherty issued any more bulletins during the night?' " in reference to "interviews on subjects of controversy"

Harry had granted after trying to see Harding. Without irony, Wilbur added, there was "a slight increase in the blood pressure" of the President.

The Duchess did meet briefly with Daugherty, but what transpired in their conversation was never revealed by either of them. Whether they discussed Justice Department affairs, the Veterans Bureau investigation, and the imminent investigation on the oil leases can only be speculated, but it was not out of the range of possibilities considering their history of working out damage control together. They planned to meet again on the evening of August 2.[17]

On Thursday, August 2, Doc gave his boldest declaration to the press—that "The President will not be an invalid"—but counteracting this was the ominous leak to *The New York Times* that Harding had suffered an "indigestion" attack the night before, that this "endangered the President's already weakened heart," and that "the President's heart remained overstrained." The most important warning in the press that day was mention yet again of the purgatives, now having been plied into Harding for six days. Even Dr. Work, who had focused on the President's gallbladder, stated that damage to that organ resulted from the purgatives. In the most explicit language to be printed to that date, one of the doctors—again, likely Boone—leaked to George Holmes that Harding was "badly impaired" by the "purgatives administered so freely during the first few days of his illness."

Doc's urging to get Warren back to Washington soon had the implied backing of the First Lady, who had first voiced that opinion as the train had sped down to San Francisco. Yet this morning it was the Duchess herself who was more frightened than she had ever been. "Every morning I arose early and went into his room adjoining mine, in negligee, and combed his hair and helped freshen him up," she recalled. "He always liked me to do that for him, you know. The instant I looked into his face that last morning I was struck by the change in his countenance. I was horrified. Death stared back at me, looked me in the face."

Meanwhile, after their last conference for that Thursday, undoubtedly frustrated that their services seemed to have no bearing on the treatment, Cooper and Wilbur withdrew. Cooper told Doc, "There is no need for me coming in for conference every day," and after going with Work down to Hoover's suite, Wilbur declared, "I shall go back to the High Sierras."

As the clock neared seven that night of August 2, editor Alfred Holman visited Florence, and when two little girls came by with flowers, she emerged to see them in the hall, which echoed with the distant sound of a phonograph. She returned to Warren, closing the door behind her. From that point on, confusion, conflict, and curiously shifting details reigned in the room where President Harding lay dying—and Florence Harding stood at the center of the intrigue.[18]

35

Negligent Homicide

In the details of who was in the President's sickroom after 7:00 P.M. on August 2, and at what time, a conspiracy involving his doctors and his wife to cover up those very facts emerges.

According to Boone, as evening set in, he went into Harding's room and found Warren's head raised on pillows, Doc sitting on the bed, "resting his body about the ankles of the President," nurse Ruth Powderly in a corner chair, Florence reading an article—not Samuel Blythe's "Calm Review of a Calm Man," as history persists in reporting, but an article about Henry Ford in the Dearborn *Independent*. Without warning, Harding "stiffened out and had a very frightened expression and became pale and broke out in a profuse perspiration, showed irritability," said Boone.

Doc immediately took Warren's pulse, and Powderly and Boone found his body soaking. "I don't know what happened to me," said Warren, "very strange, sinking feeling that I have never experienced before." Told to remain still, he shot back, "But I'm so damn wet!" Powderly dried him and changed his pajamas. "Florence," he ordered, "please go on with your reading. I don't know what happened to me. It was a very strange experience. Came on unbeknownst to me. Now I feel perfectly comfortable as though I had never had such an experience." Wilbur was not summoned. Warren's pulse stabilized. The "seizure, whatever it was," said Boone, only "seemed a transitory situation," though he wouldn't say later whether the "restoratives" were used. He then claimed that he asked Doc, "If you are going to be here, General, do you think it would be all right if I just went downstairs and stepped out in the street to get a little fresh air?" Doc assured him, "By all means, Doctor, get out there."[1]

The most detailed record of the next hours was left by Boone in his handwritten and typed diaries, his oral history, his drafted memoirs, and marked newspaper clippings. As assiduous a chronicler as he was, however, inconsistencies of basic facts make some of his claims suspect. He said Charity had been the only sickroom visitor, but Starling of the Secret Service had also come in. He said that when George Christian returned on Thursday, he saw Harding, but Christian didn't return until *after* that dramatic day. In what he planned as public memoirs, Boone claimed he passed General Pershing in the lobby reading newspapers but didn't stop to speak with him because "I did not want to disclose this seizure." This conflicts directly with an equally definitive version in his oral history: "I stopped, spoke to him, and he solicitously inquired for the President." More peculiar than his own conflicting versions, however, is the *New York Times* report that not only was Boone *dining* with Pershing, but he had "left word where he could be found." Stranger yet was Ross Bartley's confirmation that Pershing was being honored at a large private dinner at the home of Congressman Julius Kahn when the President expired.[2]

Boone's claims about his precise whereabouts at crucial times is faulty as to be suspect. In his projected public memoirs, he states, "I spent practically all the day hours and all the night hours with the President, very rarely going to my room even for a cat nap. . . . I scarcely left my eyes off him at any period." Yet more incriminating than published photographs of him posing on the hotel roof through the week is his own August 1 diary entry: "Col. Filmer has been most kind and generous with his car. Took a little ride with him after dinner—first time I had been out of the hotel since arrival." Despite the fact that he used his diary to write his memoirs, he rigidly repeated to historians through the decades, "I was never away from his bedside [but for] even a few minutes." Why would an otherwise upstanding naval physician blatantly prevaricate?

Many sources verify that Boone had indeed left the sickroom after Harding's first attack on August 2, but the scientific doctor, not usually given to supernatural beliefs, claimed, "I had a subconscious feeling that I should return to the President's sickroom," and he did. Was this just an excuse to get himself back to the room, along with his claim that he asked permission to go out for a walk, and thereby formulate a cover for some disastrous treatment administered by Doc? His repeated willingness to acquiesce to his superior suggests this is within the range of rational possibility—particularly in light of conflicting reports of Doc's whereabouts at the same time.[3]

There is no conflict in numerous accounts that while Boone was gone, sometime between seven and seven-thirty, a panicked Florence Harding came bolting out of the sickroom shouting.

All the local reporters there in the hall corroborate that Doc was not in the room at the time that Florence came out of it. The San Francisco *Call and Post* reported that only she and nurses Sue Dauser and Ruth Powderly were "in the room at the time." The San Francisco *Examiner Extra* had her yelling to Barker in the hall, "Get *all* [emphasis added] the doctors, for God's sake!" The paper noted that Work and Wilbur were in Work's room and that Doc was "in his room and came rushing in." The San Francisco *Chronicle* said Doc was "absent from the room for a few moments." The San Francisco *Journal* said Doc "was found" and then "hurried at once to the President's side."

There was no dispute in any account of what had just preceded her yelling in the hall. In one abrupt moment bedridden President Harding died.

But the First Lady did not believe it.

In his first, immediate report Ross Bartley, the careful Associated Press reporter, confirmed the San Francisco reports that Florence, Powderly, and Dauser were "the only other persons in the room." However, he also declared that Doc was "able to reach the room before the nation's leader passed away." In his second story Bartley said Doc "worked desperately within the room, applying restoratives." It was only "later," the *Call and Post* pointed out, that "a correction was issued on this bulletin stating that Sawyer also was present" at the time of death.

After the immediate reports of the three women being in the room at the time of death were printed, however, their accounts became contradictory. Dauser first stated to Boone that she did not witness Harding's death. Just before her death, however, Dauser admitted to the San Diego *Union* that "I had just come into the room to relieve Ruth Powderly on the night shift" and was "one of five persons who witnessed the death of Warren G. Harding."

The only recollection by Powderly had her asking Florence, "Doesn't he look fine?," then turning to see Harding shudder just as Florence "attended to some thing around the bedroom" and "had her back turned to the President, picking up the magazine she had been reading." She did not address who else was or was not in the room but an important clue was that she "had gone for a glass of water to give him with his night medicine." This would suggest that Doc was about to give Harding his medicine. What kind of medicine is not described, but there is no account of Harding's being on any kind of regular medication through his illness except for Boone's digitalis and Doc's persistent purgatives. And Boone was not in the room.

This scenario makes all the more strange a quote of Doc's, saying that Florence had told the nurses to take a break and that *he* had "gone for a brief walk, which took about 10 minutes, and returned to find the President dead," thus suggesting that he had left Harding alive and alone with Florence from about seven-twenty to seven-thirty. However, because we know absolutely that Boone had left the eighth floor for at least ten minutes, it would mean that Doc was actually in the room with Florence but playing fast with the facts. This appears to corroborate the most peculiar of all possible versions from Florence Harding herself. Some weeks afterward the Duchess told it to her friend Dolly Gann, who recorded, "There was no one else in the room. When she looked at him an agonized look of pain was on his face. He tried to speak, but no word came. She screamed for help. He was gone before any one could reach her."[4]

As events unfolded, it proved to be beneficial for Doc's reputation to have himself removed from the sickroom at the moment of death, and there was no person whose confirmation of this would be less questioned than the First Lady herself. Nor would anyone find something amiss about briefly leaving Warren with his attentive wife, who could not and did not ever give him any medication. What, however, was Doc's motivation to create such an account, and why would Florence go to such lengths to confirm it?

As Wilbur, Boone, Work, Cabinet members, staff, and other reporters now frantically clustered as close as possible to the sickroom, an "official" account of the President's death began to take shape, crafted with skill to exculpate the witnesses. In his unpublished and dictated recollections of the death, made shortly after the fact, Herbert Hoover seemed unwittingly to capture some more of the truth than appeared in the official account and his own later published version. According to him, Wilbur had placed Doc as present—"sitting on the other side of the bed actually feeling the President's pulse—when the President had stiffened up and without a struggle had fallen back. Dr. Sawyer at once jumped up and felt of his heart and exclaimed: 'The President is gone.'" Hoover also learned that Mandy Sawyer had phoned for Wilbur. This made obvious the fact that Doc had left the sickroom briefly but suddenly to fetch his wife since she was never in the sickroom.

Wilbur said he was there "within a minute" of the death (Hoover said it was more like "three or four minutes"). When he got there, it was clear Doc had been applying medicine—not purgatives but stimulants—which he had not had at hand: "In the meantime, Dr. Sawyer had rushed for stimulants and prepared a hypodermic." Despite Doc's presence, Florence turned to Wilbur and pleaded, "Can't you do something, Doctor?" Doc had apparently told her that Harding was not dead or at least could be revived, for she was not convinced of his demise for nearly an hour. Wilbur also could not help noticing how controlled the usually tense Doc seemed: "Sawyer had occasional attacks of breakdown, but was clearheaded clinically and saw the whole situation." At this point Wilbur took over.[5]

Boone's version claims that at this point he returned to the eighth floor, vaguely heard his name being shouted, and spotted the AP's Steve Early, who yelled, "They want you right away!" He bolted into the sickroom and saw Florence leaning over Warren's body. "They tell me the President is dead, but I do not believe it. I know that you can assure me that that is not a fact," Boone wrote that she said to him. Then she "grabbed me hysterically, shook me by the shoulders, looked me in the eye with a very startled expression and said, 'Doctor Boone, you can save him, you can save him! You can bring him back! Hurry, hurry, hurry!' " He saw the nurses, Doc, Work, Wilbur, and Hoover there and "instinctively knew" Harding was dead. He raised Warren's eyelids, touched both corneas, closed the eyes, then "took Mrs. Harding in my arms. She looked stunned as I said, shaking my head: 'No one can restore him to life. He is gone!' " Doc told the barely composed Boone, "You had just left but a very few minutes when the President had a terrible seizure. He shook the bed violently, body quivered, his color left his face completely in what was a twinkling of an eye." Sawyer added that he had been on the bed itself, lying across the President's ankles, and "was in the same position when the terminal . . . accident occurred," contradicting the Hoover version of Doc's taking Harding's pulse at the time of death.[6]

Raising even more questions was the lapse between the actual time of death and the doctors' futile treatment. Wilbur said that he had been called to the sickroom "shortly after seven." Hoover said that when they all were gathered there, the clock said 7:20. At 7:35, Wilbur abruptly stated that Harding was dead and wrote the death announcement for release with no medical details, and Judson Welliver had it typed and handed it out to waiting reporters. The San Francisco *Journal* said that three reporters first heard a woman shout for a doctor at about 7:30, while the United Press claimed that it was just "shortly after 7" that Florence's scream was heard.

In a later edition of *The New York Times* on August 3, Richard Oulahan pointed out that "The exact time of the death of President Harding remains a mystery. Officially, it is given at 7:30 o'clock, but according to some of those with whom he talked, General Sawyer, the president's chief physician, said that after it was realized that the President had passed away, he looked at his watch and it was only 7:20 o'clock." Oulahan further learned that Harding had first "collapsed" at 7:10 and it was "probably several minutes after the President passed away before Sawyer thought of ascertaining the time." Oulahan concluded: "Reports of what happened in the sick room when the President's sudden stroke came are still somewhat confused" and "comparatively few of the details had been noted." One thing Oulahan did ascertain was that "General Sawyer was either in the room with the President, or just outside the doorway when the fatal stroke came."

By the next day Oulahan noticed that he was getting different accounts from different people. "There have been several versions of the incidents surrounding the death of the President," he reported; "it was told by some of those in the vicinity that Mrs. Harding rushed to the door of the bedroom and called for help from her husband's physicians." Now, however, he was told that "Sawyer was not in the room when the President died." Oulahan did not disclose his source.

The next day Oulahan wrote another story reflecting a "complete and accurate version of the circumstances" that he managed to pull out of someone who knew the truth but who obviously felt he had something at risk if he spoke on the record—probably Boone. According to Oulahan, he "believes that the following is as nearly correct a version as can be obtained. This account was the outcome of efforts of a member of the President's party to get all the facts. He talked with those who were in position to know what happened and checked up on discrepancies."

While he mistakenly wrote that Mandy Sawyer yelled for the doctors—she had telephoned—Oulahan did confirm that she had been tipped off about Harding's attack by Doc, supporting the notion that Doc ran from the room. He also had some startling new facts:

... information appears to show that the official bulletin announcing the President's death was in error in its statement that Mr. Harding died at 7:30 o'clock in the evening. The evidence indicates that his passing occurred at least ten minutes earlier. . . . Mrs. Harding and General Sawyer were alone with the late President at the time. Ruth Powderly, the nurse had left the sick room. Mrs. Harding was reading . . . Sawyer was sitting by the bedside holding the President's hand, not for the purpose of feeling his patient's pulse or for any other professional reason, but purely an act of affection. . . . "That's good, go on," [Harding] said. . . . At that moment his body slumped forward. General Sawyer still held the President's hand. Almost instantly he said in a startled tone, "The President is dead!" Mrs. Harding came quickly to her husband's side. "Do something for him, give him something," she cried. General Sawyer grasped a hypodermic syringe *kept near at hand* [emphasis added] for use in an emergency. It was filled with a stimulating liquid. He gave the President an injection and at the same time called to Miss Powderly, just outside the room, to bring hot water bags.

Oulahan also learned that Work reached the room nearly seven minutes after Harding's collapse, and "he or some one noted by a watch that it was about 7:26 when he entered. . . . Wilbur came next, a minute or two behind." Cooper was contacted and was there next.[7]

Oulahan's information appears accurate. For whatever motive, in their public bulletin, the doctors decided to announce that Harding had died at seven thirty-five. On the final death certificate, however, they put down seven-twenty. Again, the period of at least a ten-minute gap was raised, now for the historical record but confirmed also by Oulahan's source.

The certificate had not been filled out by the time Edmund Starling of the Secret Service questioned the doctors. He asked Sawyer if he "knew the cause," and Doc didn't hesitate: cerebral hemorrhage. "Do the other doctors agree?" Starling pressed. "Yes," Doc shot back.

"But they had not signed a certificate to that effect," Starling noted. Although it was after midnight, he assembled the doctors. "I talked with them, trying to reduce medical terminology to terms I could understand," said Starling. Sawyer immediately began talking and pointing to his head: "It was a clot on the brain right here . . . the same that happened to Woodrow Wilson but more severe." No one mentioned that a human could not die instantly from such a clot, though he could from a heart attack. The other doctors did not speak, but when the question arose of signing the death certificate, there appeared one more telling bit of evidence suggesting that Doc wanted to distance himself from the place, time, and cause of death.

Despite the fact that he was the reigning power over the Hardings and the other doctors, Doc would not sign to the cause of death as he stated it; if he had, he might have technically convicted himself by willful misrepresentation of fact and committed perjury on the legal document. Wilbur finally signed it because, Boone said, "he was a practicing physician of California" and thus gave the certificate added legitimacy; if Doc, as the officially recognized nonresident President's doctor had signed it, however, the certificate would have been equally valid. Wilbur had not been witness to the death; legally, as far as he knew, it could have been cerebral hemorrhage—or anything else for that matter—that the President's doctor told him it was. "If Starling had any suspicions that the doctors—voluntarily or involuntarily—had conspired with Sawyer to cover up the real cause of death," noted a medical historian, "he did not pursue them." The conspiracy to cover up the true nature of the President's death had begun. The only accomplice absent from the room as the certificate was prepared was the First Lady.[8]

Clearly, besides the fatal heart attack, something embarrassing had happened in the dying of Warren Harding.

The evidence from firsthand and press accounts—the shifting versions of the death scene, questions about whether Doc was in or out of the room at the moment of death, the vague references to syringes of "stimulants" and Sawyer's touching Harding's body at the time of death, whether holding his hand or lying across his lower legs, the fact of the First Lady's disbelief that Harding had died and her asking Wilbur and Boone to perform some medical act to counteract whatever provoked his collapse, the discrepancies in time, the processing of the death certificate—indicates that the participants conspired to protect Doc from charges of "killing" Harding.

What *did* Sawyer do those very last moments before the sudden heart attack? Evidence makes plausible that Doc accidentally provoked the death of the President with a final, fatal overdose of his mysterious purgatives, pushing the man's already weakened heart into cardiac arrest. For nearly a full week Doc had been pumping Harding full of purgatives. It is a medical fact that purgation with loss of potassium from the body, combined with the digitalis, could increase the risk of heartbeat cessation. On August 2 Doc probably applied one too many. As he gave Harding a dose of the purgatives in Florence's presence, Warren suddenly shuddered and collapsed. Doc rushed to reassure her and then went to get a stimulant, leading her to believe Warren could be revived and accounting for the "missing" minutes as he rushed away from the death scene back to his room for some other medicine or to find Boone for help. This also explains the later, sanitized claim reported by Oulahan that the syringe of *stimulants* was *"kept near at hand,"* when, in fact, it was not. The medication that was "kept near at hand" was the *purgatives.* Publicly revealing such incompetence would humiliate Doc, the other doctors, memory of the beloved President—and Florence Harding herself. Innocent and accidental it was, but Warren Harding's death was a case of negligent homicide.

Florence's complete support of Doc's treatment and Boone's informed refusal to stop it made both of them complicitous with Sawyer. Thus they had all the more reason to protect him. Her claim that she was alone with Warren when he died does implicate her in the conspiracy—although she may have been reassured by Doc, before he dashed out, that Warren hadn't died, only to realize later what she had witnessed. There is evidence of this in Dauser's remark that when she entered the room, she found Florence placing her finger in Warren's mouth, believing he had just choked on chewing gum. With Doc now out of the room, this is how perhaps Florence felt she was not disingenuous in saying Warren "died" alone in her presence.

In many respects Harding was more culpable for his own death than his wife. By institutionalizing Doc's personal influence, he officially sanctioned blind faith in the physician and his methods, investing absolute access and authority in Sawyer through his-high ranking appointment. Entirely apart from Sawyer's endless purgatives or inability to detect heart trouble, Harding refused not only to follow the suggestions for rest of Boone but to respond to signs of danger in his own body. He simply turned that responsibility over to others. Harding knew full well his condition, but he consistently, consciously made the choice to continue straining his heart and general condition, choosing to weaken himself increasingly at each juncture, never acquiescing to professional advice. He stopped this behavior only when the Duchess canceled the remaining trip. He had often listened to Florence beneficially during their life together, but when she was too distracted to guide him during the final illness, he seemed to give up on himself. His own mistakes and the betrayals may have also provoked a fatalism.

On the other hand, Florence's thirst for public affirmation and a personal need for attention drove her to push herself and Warren too hard—especially on the trip. Despite her genuine concern for his health, her primary attention was focused on her own interaction with the crowds on the trip; with Doc and Boone along, she seemed freer to ignore, as she never had, Warren's personal needs. Before she finally canceled the trip, Florence Harding could have earlier taken steps to prevent the further deterioration of Warren's bad health. While Boone's motive not to defy his superior is clear, why Florence was so unusually passive is not. Her most probable motive actually stemmed out of affection for Warren, simply realizing that although his health was bad, he might as well be allowed to do what he most enjoyed—with some limitation—rather than prevented entirely from doing so. One thing is certain: She believed that his death was imminent and, in retrospect, happened at just the right moment. Apart from her belief that it was astrological fate that he die before his term ended, in light of later statements she made to Evalyn, she could not have wished him dead at any more opportune time. The scandals of his administration were at a breaking point and there were later suggestions that impeachment might have occurred. And in times of marital strife, she undoubtedly wished he would die. If she was a passive accessory to negligent homicide, however, her motives were never evil. She did not poison or in any other way murder him.[9]

The Duchess, however, became even more deeply enmeshed in the conspiracy by adamantly announcing an important decision furthering the cover-up. Boone later claimed Florence's reaction to the death was so severe that she was sedated to sleep, unable to make decisions: "Mrs. Harding dropped her head on my shoulder, sobbed all over. Miss Powderly took her into her bedroom and gave her sedatives and put her to bed." His image of such a distraught widow contradicts every other report. Wilbur said that when he said she "must hold herself together," Florence replied with control, "I won't break down." Added Hoover: "This was typical of the iron will which maintained her." Doc told reporters that while she was "unable to realize that she had lost the husband who had made up all the interest in her life . . . there was no collapse, no hysteria. Just a brave rally to face the duties devolving upon her at this hour." For some six hours after the death she was conferring and making decisions.

What others later termed Florence's unsentimental coldness was just a result of her having "prepared herself" according to Doc. With her sense of death stalking the trip stemming from both the irrational terror of Madame Marcia's prediction and the rational reality of Warren's health, it seemed like the fulfillment of fate, perhaps some form of relief, certainly a validation of her faith in astrology. Moreover, it had been perhaps almost twenty years, probably before her 1905 hospitalization, since Warren had been as emotionally intimate and demonstrative to her as she certainly was to him. With his death she had lost an ally, comrade, and partner but certainly not a physical companion whose ardor had sustained her. Increasingly problematic as a living man, he would, to her, be more manageably adored as a precious memory. "He was magnificent in life," she repeated weirdly over the next few days, "but he is more wonderful in death."

Now, for the man she had helped propel into the presidency, she would make certain that she not only lavished her own respects to him but provided an opportunity for the nation to do so. She focused on the business at hand. "Still," she said, "I have something to do." First, she asked that the Cabinet wives, Mandy Sawyer, Ethel Jennings, and Charity Remsberg be brought to her. Sobbing, Charity "broke down completely," and Florence hugged and calmed her. The gathering was to delegate some duties with funeral arrangements, but it also served the purpose of posthumously providing good press for Harding's political achievements on the trip, to augment the inevitable flood of fond Harding recollections that would now come. She spun stories of how in his "last hours" Warren had "said kind things . . . of the newspaper correspondents . . . and paid a tribute to the fair grounds they had given of the President's speeches and the incidents of the tour." This meeting also enforced the public image of herself she wanted. "She is going to be terribly upset if she sees in the newspapers that she collapsed," Lou Hoover warned reporters.

In between meeting with General Pershing and San Francisco Mayor James Rolph, Florence decided to get the body out of San Francisco quickly: "Let us leave as soon as possible. Before he became President my husband and I talked over just what we wanted done when the end came . . . the simplest service . . . a private funeral. But my husband died as the President. . . . [T]he funeral must be part of his public life . . . fitting with the high office. . . ." She agreed that like McKinley, Warren should lie in state in the Capitol, where the public could file by to view him. "But after that," she said, "he belongs to me." She insisted on a private burial in Marion. She also sent out two dresses to be dyed. "Strange, I only had one little black dress to my name," Florence later told her daughter-in-law. "Fortunately, I was able to have a red gown and also a yellow one colored black. Saved me quite a bit, too."[10]

Following the custom of casting a death mask of incumbent Presidents, the Harding Cabinet members contacted local sculptor J. Earl Cummings. When they informed the Duchess, however, she was "quick to make her decision" to deny permission, saying, "I want to remember him as he was in life, not in death." The other decision affecting the corpse over which Florence had sole prerogative as widow was the most controversial. It was one she made only after Doc had privately conferred with her. There would be no autopsy.

It remains unknown what Doc said to Florence to prevent an autopsy, but he told his grandson it was a "very disgusting thing" to have done and "all sorts of complications could arise and then delay the whole trip back and the funeral." An autopsy, however, would also establish an absolute cause of death, and Cooper, an expert in identifying instances of cardiac arrest, was available to perform it. Yet with the fact of the brain hemorrhage affirmed, and no autopsy to disprove it, Doc could never be totally incriminated by the other doctors or publicly rebuked for his failure to detect and treat heart disease and safeguard the President during his last few days and weeks. As subordinate to his superior Boone once more acquiesced. One medical historian thought that despite their professional reputations, Wilbur and Cooper "went along with Sawyer to avoid an unseemly and publicized dispute."

There is further circumstantial evidence of the apparent paranoia of Doc and the Duchess regarding close but unauthorized examination of the body. A Palace Hotel newsletter carried a picture of the six armed private guards whom Florence had asked be placed about the corpse, to make certain it was not moved, touched, or in any way disturbed. Her faith in spiritualism may have been the cause of this decision since she believed a body must rest overnight to permit the spirit to release itself completely. However, after a tearful Powderly and Dauser had pulled a white sheet over the corpse and robed it in white, Wilbur was asked by Florence to summon an undertaker quickly. Beginning at nine, and working until three the next morning, morticians from N. Gray and Company embalmed Harding in the sickroom, then placed the remains back on the bed, "the dressing for burial deferred until late in the day."[11]

Although Coolidge had been telegraphed in Vermont with the news of Harding's death, it spread slowly across the country. In nearby Maine, for example, at five in the morning, Evalyn wired that she was "happy over the good news of the president." Not receiving a response from Florence, when she finally learned the truth, she felt it "as a clap of thunder." It was nearly sunrise when church bells in Marion awoke the senior Christians, who first thought that Florence had died.

As dark fell on the West Coast, the Reverend James West made his way through the dense but silent crowds gathered at the Palace, having been called to say a brief prayer in the presidential suite. He noticed how the Duchess "was clearheaded and made prompt decisions on every point brought to her." When he told her that Warren died as "most men want to die, suddenly and without pain," she seemed to turn on Sawyer, snapping to him, "You keep me alive as long as you can. Don't let me go if there is a spark of life left in me." She also took pride in her "instinct to bring her sick husband to San Francisco instead of taking him to the Yosemite." Daugherty noted the same cool demeanor. "She was not one who easily revealed her feelings. I had never known her to weep in public . . . in the lonely hours which followed in her room . . . I asked her to tell me how the end had come. And she did in a quiet restraint, more terrible to me than a paroxysm of weeping."

Florence went to bed at one, "slept fitfully," rose early, inquired about "poor George" Christian's reaction to the news—he had been in Los Angeles—and was soon "directing all affairs." Powderly "marveled at the will with which she came back to the world from which her husband had suddenly been taken." As she made more decisions, some superstitions dictated them. For example, she decided that the body should rest in the White House for just one night, wanting it placed there "while daylight lasted." She now revealed to others her belief that it was Warren's fate to die in office, openly recalling to friends Marcia's prediction preceding the 1920 convention that if "Warren went to the White House something will happen to one of us," and "now it has come true."

Florence worked uninterrupted in the parlor overlooking Market Street, responding to condolences from kings and Marionites alike, reviewing the funeral train's guest list and itinerary, "as poised as though she were approving plans for some happier event," noted a reporter. Meanwhile in the same room undertakers laid out Warren against the wall, in a bronze casket lined with white silk. The corpse was dressed in a formal black cutaway jacket and striped trousers, but Florence told the morticians, "He always wanted me to pick out his ties," as she handed one over. "Let him wear this one. . . ." The facial features were carefully painted with a smile, and after Florence spent time alone with the body, it was sealed under glass. Before it was sealed, she noticed that the corpse still had a Masonic ring on its finger and asked that it be removed for her. As people called on her, Florence led them to the coffin. "Look at him," she told reporters as they gazed at the corpse, "more magnificent still in death!"[12]

With his body dressed, embalmed and magnificently safe under glass, the true reason for Harding's death could never be discerned from examination. That did not mean, however, that many—doctors, journalists, private citizens, conspiracy theorists—did not begin to grow suspicious.

In the Palace Hotel itself, "rumors began to fly about, each wilder than its predecessor and all denied soon after by official bulletins." Even a Baltimore *Sun* eulogy thought that the medical and final death bulletins pointed to "an obscure and puzzling malady." Pennsylvania's Pottsville *Journal* asked why if Boone and Doc knew about Harding's bad health, he was permitted to make the trip—and if they did not know of his true condition, why not? Dr. Walter M. Thorne publicly called Sawyer "incompetent," and a Fresno *Bee* editorial stated that "the most competent who could have been secured" as doctors were not. Homeopath Alexander Markey was the most direct, saying that "not a single" public account "has given us the real cause of Harding's death; they dared not come out with the obvious fact that it was due to medical ignorance, intolerance and incompetence." He believed that the "medical trust" of allopathy—represented by Wilbur—had "billions of dollars invested in the business of catering to and maintaining a state of disease," yet it was Sawyer he charged with being "way behind the times in medical education. . . . What transpired behind closed doors between these four allopaths and lone homeopath may never be known."

Other diagnoses seemed to get close to the truth, but without cooperation from the doctors, there could never be any confirmation. The medical details of the death, the respected judge A. A. Hoehling wrote Boone, were "certainly confusing to me since the testimony doesn't seem to point to a dying man, far from it, or one with advanced arterial sclerosis. . . . I am certain there was no foul play concerned with Harding's death—I am equally convinced there was 'covering up' during those last 7 days of what was really happening to the President, and I know why."

Although no one at the time stepped forward to state he suspected that Doc's excessive use of purgatives may have provoked the fatal heart attack, rumors circulated that Harding's death was really due to cardiac arrest and not to cerebral hemorrhage—rumors that made incompetents or, worse, liars out of the doctors. Just fifteen months after Harding's death, for example, *The New York Times* stated unequivocally that it was due to heart attack, but that it was "kept a close secret by those who knew of it." First hearing such claims, George Christian, indignant about the indirect attacks on Doc Sawyer, declared, "There is absolutely no foundation for the statement that the President had a weak heart.

He was a splendid specimen of physical manhood . . . always in excellent health." Those who knew the facts remained silent.[13]

The doctors themselves always maintained a united front to protect Sawyer publicly, but privately in conversation and correspondence, the conspiracy unraveled. The first to demur was the doctor least quoted in print but the bluntest in private, Hubert Work. He believed that the credibility of Wilbur's American Medical Association presidency and Cooper's prestige were the crucial factor in the success of the cover-up and told Boone so. As Boone wrote in his diary, "Work said that I would have been in 'a hell of a fix' without consultants to assist me do things at S.F. for President Harding. Work said G.S.[awyer] did not know modern medicine and was not in step with the times." Some weeks after the death Work wrote Wilbur that it was only after "you and Dr. Cooper got into it" that there was any competency in Harding's treatment.

Indeed, lost amid the August 3 headlines blaring Harding's death was a statement signed *only* by Wilbur and Cooper, intended to separate themselves subtly and point up related causes of death different from Doc's claim of apoplexy: "As already indicated in the bulletins, the heart was enlarged and probably the blood vessels which carry to it its nutriment thickened, for his history shows that previously he had anginal manifestations . . . nocturnal dyspnea and a Cheyne-Stokes type of respiration." Wilbur and Cooper concluded that Harding died of a "sudden epileptic seizure," with no mention of brain apoplexy.

In probable reaction to what was Doc's certain anger at their being too honest for comfort, Cooper softened his stance in a personal note to him five days later—but did not capitulate on the cause of death, saying that "under your wise, experienced and devoted Captaincy" they had "worked together so harmoniously." Cooper added that they had "tried so hard to save the late President," suggesting that Harding had obviously died some moments before efforts were made to revive him and that "victory [had been] snatched from your hands by an unavoidable and coincidental happening," suggesting that Harding had died perhaps as Doc was in some way touching him and that the moment of death was coincidental to that.

When Cooper wrote Wilbur on August 13 with an airtight case as backup of the public version they had agreed to, he began by listing Harding's symptoms from the *last* consultation that day to support the claim that "the sudden ending was not anginal." Yet his letter suggests that neither he nor Wilbur could ever be said to know the true condition of the heart at the moment of death since it was not they but Sawyer who "was present and saw the President die" and that it was he who "*said* [emphasis added] that the ending was definitely apoplectic in character." After Sawyer was dead, Cooper released himself from the conspiracy. He admitted to his associate Dr. Roger B. McKenzie that Harding's "death was due to coronary occlusion."

In the following weeks Wilbur began obfuscating the diagnosis that protected Sawyer. In a *Saturday Evening Post* article, he praised "devoted" Doc for guarding Harding "in every way possible under the conditions" but referred to "the infection that interrupted his long trip" and added most oddly that Harding "lost his gallant battle against death from pneumonia." Almost in afterthought, Wilbur mentioned: "We had been fearful of complications because of the enlarged heart." In his later memoirs he dropped heavier hints:

> One of the most troublesome problems for physicians in dealing with the illness of a prominent person is to present to the public an honest and accurate picture of just what is going on without developing too much alarm, if the illness is serious. Always to be kept in mind is that there may be recovery, complete or partial, of the patient—or a fatal termination. In the Harding illness we had to face constantly the attitude that we should not disclose the exact condition surrounding the illness. We determined, though, to present the actual findings as to temperature, heart rate, respiration rate, and leukocyte count, describing symptoms about which there could be no dispute, and let the physicians of the country draw their own conclusions. That was particularly important, since an incomplete diagnosis had already been passed out to the press which had led many people to think that the problem was a form of food poisoning and was both insignificant and transient. It was necessary to bring out the evident arteriosclerosis and the heart condition. All five members of the medical staff agreed to all parts of every public statement made, except for the final one prepared by Dr. Cooper and myself. . . . We shall never know exactly the immediate cause of President Harding's death, since every effort that was made to secure an autopsy met with complete and final refusal. . . . With the history of cardiovascular disturbance the sudden death could also have been of the heart type. . . . [I]here was no way of final determination as to whether it was a heart attack or cerebral apoplexy.

Wilbur never explained what he meant by "we had to face constantly the attitude that we should not disclose the exact condition surrounding the illness." Wilbur's unqualified opinion may be reflected in a blunt remark by the later President whom he served as interior secretary. "The cause was undoubtedly a heart attack," said Herbert Hoover, reflecting a private opinion that might equally have come from Hoover's own White House doctor, Joel Boone.[14]

Boone, who had the most to risk if revelation of the conspiracy leaked, remained vigilant about maintaining it. He even seemed potentially willing to censor Wilbur, writing him, "[I] would very much like to see and read the references you are making in your autobiography to President Harding and will give you my frank opinion of it."

Perhaps with guilt for not overtly blocking Doc's grossly unprofessional behavior, Boone said he "never recovered" from Harding's death. "It stunned me so violently as to exact permanent health scars on me . . . a President who lay there dead before my eyes, for which I bore some responsibility." Boone had done his best. From the start of the trip he knew Harding was "anything but a well man" and dared confront Doc about the necessity of limiting activities and acutely monitoring heart rate, blood pressure, and diet. Boone tersely recalled, "It was a great misfortune that my efforts to practice preliminary professional safeguards were stalemated."

Not long after the death, however, many in the White House circle heard inklings about the cover-up to protect Doc. In front of Boone, President Coolidge's chief of staff, Bascom Slemp, sarcastically asked why Boone was along on the trip if "Mr." Sawyer was there as doctor. Rudolph Foster, the White House executive clerk, cracked, "Someone had to wear the spurs and someone do the work." Slemp tried to prompt the truth out of Boone by stating, "Then the Hardings did realize the situation as it really existed," but, Boone recorded, "I maintained an absolute silence." To Boone's pat repetition that Harding died of apoplexy, Daugherty retorted cynically: "I thought his heart went back on him because of exhaustion. . . ." Boone recorded that Daugherty "realized the time I have had with the General" and said that "people here would [soon] feel unkindly towards G.S. as the Marion people do." Harry advised Boone "not to jeopardize [his] career in S.'s defense." Some months later Boone was again confronted with Doc's continuing incompetence when the old man put his ear to the chest of a suffering Brooks, declared "no heart disease," and gave him sugar pills. Yet a "complete examination substantiated my beliefs" of heart disease, Boone recorded. After Doc similarly misdiagnosed his own secretary and Boone then did so correctly, Boone revealingly noted, "Had my suspicions [of Doc's misdiagnosis]—at other times and with others [patients]."

Boone nevertheless spent decades evading the truth, refusing to confirm or provide medical details and dismissing any death "theory" put forth by inquirers. To those like Clare Boothe Luce who wrote that Harding died of heart attack, he dashed off enraged letters. He was equally abrasive when other witnesses to Harding's deteriorating health offered their opinions. After Colonel Steese revealed his observations about what seemed to him to be clear signs of Harding's heart trouble to researcher Cyril Clemens, Boone snapped that Steese was "off the reservation" when he spoke of a "known weak heart" and "conditions supposed to have existed within the President." Steese retorted, "If the President did not have a weak heart, why does not Boone categorically say so, instead of hinting at some mysterious disclosure he is to make at some future date?" Even when scholarly medical historians asked for clarification in their careful analysis, Boone evaded telling the truth: "I do not believe it contributes anything to history," "I shall be pleased to assist you restricted somewhat by . . . the professional confidences that I hold," "I wish to withhold certain knowledge." When Harding's physician nephew told a historian of "the possibility of coronary thrombosis," Boone was mute, scribbling on this historian's inquiry: "Gave him no medical information."

The only recorded capitulation of Boone to the truth emerged in his private conversation with Harding's physician nephews, George Harding and Warren Harding, at—by utter coincidence—the Palace Hotel, some years later. As George Harding recounted, "Boone is certain that Uncle Warren had a coronary occlusion followed by enfarction of the heart wall due to diminished blood supply to the heart muscle, and that his sudden death was due to rupture of the heart. . . . This condition was seldom recognized except at autopsy prior to 1928 or 1929 and is certainly more convincing than any other explanation that can be given." Dr. Warren Harding recalled a May 1923 dinner when his uncle was "complaining he couldn't sleep at night. That he got short of breath . . . that was nocturnal dispeia [*dysphea*] that comes with a coronary condition. . . ." Dr. Harding also told diplomat Jay Moffat that Sawyer "did not seem to realize that [Harding] was threatened with coronary thrombosis and did not keep him absolutely quiet . . . [so that] when he sat up in bed, having not been warned to stay motionless, the heart ruptured. . . ."

In reality, Boone would not convict Doc to others because he wanted to do it himself—in memoirs never published: "To definitely modify that earlier opinion would require much research which I intend to undertake at sometime. Presently, the material I will need is not available nor am I able to make certain contacts indicated. . . . With the passing of time before it is too late, I fully realize my responsibility to the American people and to historical accuracy."[15]

Doc of course was always steadfast in claiming that his colleagues agreed with his diagnosis and treatment. "There has never been a difference of opinion between the five physicians who have handled the case thus far," he told reporters. That Boone *had* very much disagreed with Doc permanently unnerved him during Boone's high official profile in the time to follow. "Sawyer thinks I would make good in private practice, making complimentary statement and being unusually pleasant to cause me suspicion," Boone recorded.

After Harding's death there were indications that Sawyer realized that Boone's assessment of Harding's heart was valid yet in a manner that illogically never incriminated himself. On August 8 Doc slipped, for example, telling a Washington *Star* reporter that during the Seattle speech "he [Harding] was attacked with a dilation of the heart." Weeks later, in a melodramatic speech, he claimed that Harding sighed, "I wish we were back in Marion where you and I would have this case in our own hands," and that he responsibly replied, "It would be very unwise for me to proceed in the care of your case without every possible source of information being used in determining the cause of your trouble." He then stole credit from Boone for examining Harding's heart on the train to San Francisco: "I discovered that his physical engine, his heart, which had been operating his human machine for more than a half century, was faltering. This big heart had gone beyond its endurance and this comparative physical giant had joined the invalid list."

Doc never publicly recanted his poison theory since it exonerated him from misdiagnosing Harding's condition, nor regretted his permitting Harding's strenuous activities at the end, and further justified the heavy daily purgative dosages. Colonel Christian claimed, however, that in private Doc told him that "there was nothing in the stories of serious ptomaine poisoning, that the president recovered promptly and apparently returned to his usual form with but two days of cessation from his usual activities." This surprise then suggests that Doc simply continued a vigorous regimen of purgatives because he didn't know what else to do to reduce the "abdominal" pain that was really heart trouble. The alternative to this is more ethically troubling, for it would mean he knew of the serious cardiac condition yet treated Harding as if there were none.[16]

Conspiracy theorists did not blame Doc alone, however. One theory had Hoover behind it, since he later appointed Boone President's physician, Walter Brown (who advanced the western and Alaska trip), post-master general, and Wilbur interior secretary. At a Geneva dinner for Edith Wilson, the story was that friends like Daugherty poisoned Warren "to save him from embarrassment of political scandals." Wilbur said that even he and the other doctors had been accused of "plying him to death with pills and purgatives," although it had been Doc alone who applied these.

"The Harding Poison Murder Case" took three volumes of 350,000 words, index, illustrations, and court exhibits to prove that Harding was poisoned first on the way to Alaska, then before arriving in Seattle, again on the train rushing down from Seattle and finally in San Francisco. Strikingly close to the true timing of Harding's heart seizures and Sawyer's overapplication of purgatives, it may have been based on inside information, since it was assembled by a Harding administration Secret Service agent, former Burns Agency and FBI agent Walter Thayer, who had the support of Charity Remsberg. While in the Secret Service, he worked on a twelve-million-dollar counterfeit bond case, an "inside job" using Treasury plates, that had perhaps involved Gaston Means and Jess Smith. Thayer claimed that Harding was "himself directing an investigation" of the scam through Assistant Attorney General Charles Brewer. Harding died when Brewer was in San Francisco on this case. He further claimed that Secret Service Chief W. H. Moran had "sent out a squad of their men to get something on William J. Burns." J. Edgar Hoover said Thayer was "mentally unbalanced" and had all of his voluminous research and data destroyed.[17]

Pop theories about Harding's death became a national pastime. An employee at the Seattle Press Club, the site of Harding's last public meal, recalled that the cook there, George Brown, bragged "how he could make everybody sick" with "a few drops of croton oil in the stew or salad" and "doctors would not be able to find out what the cause was." A Sacramento woman said Madame Marcia did it to prove herself a genuine sorceress. Nome housewife Mrs. Hugh O'Neill thought Gaston Means "hounded [Harding] like a yellow cur" and killed him. The Klan said it was a papist plot. Others said it was the Klan.

The conspiracy to cover up the circumstances of Harding's death was motivated by ego alone. There was not even circumstantial evidence to suggest evil intent, yet in the vacuum of honest disclosure, sinister overtones of a plot between Doc and the Duchess were inevitable and the most widespread and believed. The pretext to this was that they wanted to be together in love. When one journalist questioned why Harding felt the need to appoint Sawyer to such a high rank as brigadier general, the writer received a note suggesting, "Perhaps 'some news-paperman who wishes to remain anonymous' informed you that he held that post incognito, so to speak, because he was the secret lover of Mrs. Harding." There was even a Marionite who spoke of discovered love letters between Doc and the Duchess plotting Warren's death. While certainly Florence psychologically depended upon Sawyer, any notion of a physical love between them was ridiculous, and even had it been true, there was nothing to gain by killing Warren.

The two most popular fables were that she poisoned him as a mercy killing (because Daugherty told her that Warren's felony stemming from his knowledge but failed disclosure of Forbes's misdeeds meant impeach-ment hearings) or in revenge for adultery with Nan (an affair about which she knew nothing). Bernard Fay even made the case that she killed him with love, that Warren "belonged to the feminine sex, not to Mrs. Har-ding . . . she directed the life of her husband with merciless affection, zeal and care. Whatever any one may say, even if she did not actually give him a dose of arsenic . . . it was she who killed him."

Florence revealed no concern about any rumors about Warren's death. Wilbur said she appreciated that the doctors had been "quite frank in the whole discussion of the illness" with her and had "full confidence in us, saying that she looked at people's eyes instead of listening to what they said in order to see if they were telling the truth, and that we had passed her assay."

Before the funeral train left, Florence asked that Reverend West re-turn to conduct a service "not to exceed fifteen minutes." Beforehand, she described Warren to West "as she knew him emphasizing his bigness of heart, kindness of spirit. . . ." With the white quilted silk of the open cof-fin bathed in rose light from the lampshades, the sobs of many reporters and Daugherty, a controlled Florence refused a chair during the service and was, said West, "familiar surprisingly to several Scripture passages . . . particularly 'I have fought the good fight . . .' " She led West to the casket and repeated her "magnificent in death" line. There "crept over her pale face a smile." Then she was left alone with the body for a few minutes. While the coffin was closed, taken to a service elevator, and car-ried to a street cortege, she lingered, with Wilbur. He later remembered:

> Mrs. Harding came and joined me where I was standing at the window in order to watch the funeral procession leave the hotel. We stood there for over half an hour looking out across Market and up Geary Street. As my hand was on her left arm to steady her I could feel her enlarged heart beat against the back of my hand . . . she was still

brave and undismayed. She said, "I'll have to get used to all this spectacle, and this will help me to do so ... this is a wonderful city. . . . Warren and I had looked forward to greeting the people of San Francisco. We had been urged by Republicans and Democrats alike not to come; but Warren felt that if he could bring his message to the people he could accomplish much." ... Her mind was going back over a lifetime of incident and detail regarding "her Warren." Florence said she "had nothing to live for now, that life was empty, that the bottom had dropped out." When Wilbur suggested she write a memoir, the Duchess said bluntly, "I know only two things: politics and publicity."[18]

At seven the Hardings left San Francisco, their destiny, reputations, and historical legacies changed forever. Florence's final word on what she really believed was the cause of Warren's death seemed summarized by the general information sheet of his will; the response for "How long ill" was listed as "about two weeks." Evidently she too privately believed it was a heart attack, not apoplexy. Whenever she later spoke of the death, however, she avoided details. As Colonel Christian said, "There was no spirit of faultfinding."

After all, Doc was still the man who could keep her alive. And she wanted to stay that way.[19]

Part Seven

THE WIDOW
1923–1924

I am rearranging my life, as I inevitably must.

36

The Fires of August

As Mark Sullivan explained, Harding's funeral train across America "enabled scores of separate communities to have a direct part in it . . . an event not before duplicated and not in the future likely to be." There was hardly a mile along the route that wasn't at least spotted with a few individuals. Through canyons, desert, and plains, cowboys, farmers, Boy Scouts, and Civil War vets stood in the dusty heat and pouring rainstorms, in cars, on horses, on foot. The observation car window was removed to permit the flag-draped coffin, raised high on a catafaque, to be placed there, always guarded by two soldiers, a sailor, and a marine each standing at attention at a corner. The car was flooded by pale electric light, visible for miles around in the open night prairie along parts of the same route it had traveled thirty-nine days before. It was a forest of purple and white flowers, reaching the ceiling. As the train passed into towns, bells from churches, schools, and other public buildings were tolled. Out of respect for the President, all men removed their hats, but it was Florence's "boys," the veterans of the Great War, who turned out in droves, forming honor guards to salute her. Despite the Veterans Bureau mess, she was being praised as their "real friend who never forgot them."

Peculiarities still seemed to haunt the party. In Cheyenne vast dust clouds blew about, followed by a fierce lightning storm. As it made its way through Chappell, Nebraska, a tire of the forward driving wheel on the locomotive slipped, and the train jolted and nearly wrecked as it approached a crowded station. A spontaneous rain of huge hail rocks then smashed the train roof and sent screaming crowds running for shelter. The rain was followed by a "high wind of near cyclonic intensity" and finally a rainbow, all of it "strange phenomena" for those on the train, said a reporter. Gathered at one station were the same group of cowgirls on horses with whom Warren had mildly flirted on the way coming out; tears streamed down their faces.

Using the same car she had shared with Warren on the trip west, Florence permitted only Daisy Harding to board along the way. Never negligent of the press, she asked secretaries to pass out candies to the reporters. The trip was emotionally difficult for all the passengers, who now treasured their dusty ribbons reading "The President's Alaska Party," which they wore until the actual burial. The most broken up was Daugherty. On the coffin lay a bouquet that said simply, "Harry to his old friend Warren."

In Omaha the Duchess left her car for the first time, reported Robert Barry. "She was calm and cool when she passed into the car to gaze without weeping upon her husband's bier." In Chicago she observed, "I can understand what a shock my husband's death has been to the nation. . . . It wasn't until our western trip that I fully appreciated the nation's respect. Really, you know, when we were in Alaska I was electrified time and again by the murmur that so often rose. . . . 'There he is!' the crowd would say. And now," she concluded, pointing to the coffin, "there he is!"

More than three million Americans along the 3,100-mile trek jammed urban rail stations hung in black crepe or stood on the remote plains to see the train. They were playing dirges, carrying signs, repeating prayers, even placing pennies on the track as the train passed, to keep as souvenirs. Reporter Carter Field wrote, "[H]alf a dozen times during the night Mrs. Harding, lying in her bed, peeped through the shade at the crowds gathered. . . . At once she sent out peremptory orders that the train must be slowed down while passing through Ohio towns. . . . [T]here were occasionally cries from the crowd for her to show herself. . . . They did not see her."[1]

Beyond the train's route were other mourners. In Marion, Philamen Gregg recollected how "the entire town" silently trudged to pray at the Harding house. Ships halted mid-sea to hold memorial services, and on the *Leviathan* Labor Secretary James Davis delivered a eulogy. In London, there was a Westminster Abbey service. Edith Roosevelt attended an Episocpal service in Oyster Bay, Long Island, while her niece Eleanor Roosevelt issued a public statement of bereavement for her and her husband, Franklin. Babe Ruth wrote Florence that Warren's "interest in baseball and his many kind acts towards individual players was deeply appreciated by all of us." The International Council of the Women of the Darker Races, led by Mrs. Booker T. Washington and Mary Bethune, issued a resolution of sympathy to the Duchess. African-Americans alleged to be Harding cousins attempted to form a memorial society to him, although it was "not encouraged" by Chicago politicians, according to a woman of mixed race whose parents were Harding friends.

Meanwhile, Assistant Attorney General A. T. Seymour asserted that Harding's greatest legacy to Americans was appropriately relaxation. He emphasized how Harding fought for a reduction in work shifts and an eight-hour workday, arising from his "deep and abiding belief in the necessity for recreation" and because "he also loved to play." The steel industry immediately eliminated its twelve-hour workday and credited the move to Harding. Others just struck while the iron was hot. Samuel Blythe rapidly marketed the fib that his story "A Calm Review of a Calm Man" was the last thing Harding heard. The story was bound and copied and sold for sixty-eight cents by Macy's.

The crowds were greatest in Chicago. For miles around people, from groups of Slavic factory workers to Michigan Avenue high hats, thickly lined the route. Crossing into Pennsylvania, Boone noted, "Crowds in the greatest number in the history of Pittsburgh thronged hillsides, bridges, and even every point of vantage. . . . Most striking, it seemed to me, was the tribute paid by steel mill toilers as the train passed the big industrial plants on the river front. Even the din of the mills was stilled as the train went by. Toilers unmindful of their soiled clothes and besmeared faces and hands . . . stood with bowed heads, crushing their caps to their breasts."[2]

The Duchess rarely left her bed but called various associates to her. One night Boone showed her a single farmer about a mile ahead, standing beside his plow and horse, bowing in anticipation. He pointed out that it was also a tribute to her and quietly wondered to himself how she would deal with her loss of power. "[S]he never mentioned . . . the fact that she had ceased to be the First Lady . . . [that] that honor had been removed from her." To Harry, she spoke of Warren: '[H]e did too much. It was a strain no human body could endure. I warned him. . . . But he was a man . . . [w]ho really never took any care of himself. I couldn't get him to lie down and take naps to break the strain. He wouldn't lie down in the day-time and he was always late in turning out his reading light at night. He thought he could stand anything and everything."

Senator Watson thought she "sat throughout the days and nights like a grim warrior guarding the body of her dead . . . heroic and unflinching." To pass time, Florence read and saved articles for her clippings book, such as an interview with Marcia predicting the time of death and Sir Arthur Conan Doyle's statement that since Warren's was a "high" spirit, it would take longer than the usual three days to "communicate through an earthly medium." Florence now frequently repeated the predictions of 1920 that the "presidency would bring just this disaster." The San Francisco *Chronicle*'s cover drawing of nubile young women scantily clad in robes, draping their arms over his coffin, was perhaps the most titillating tribute. Other articles were presumptuous. Just two days after Harding's death, Carl Sawyer told the press that Florence would be moving to the Sawyer Sanitarium as a permanent patient. She had no such intention.[3]

Meanwhile the stunned White House staff raced to prepare the mansion, rushing to remove all the summer white linens covering the furniture. Evalyn stopped by, just in time to see the mourning bunting placed in the East Room, then went to Union Station to be there for Florence when she arrived. From Maine, she had raced down the East Coast in a railroad special in record time. As the Harding train neared, low-flying planes sprinkled rose petals on it. At the station a reporter thought the coffin was lifted from the train "in a dimness that gave play to odd shadows, strange thoughts."

The scene in the dread of night when Florence asked Evalyn to bring her down to the East Room so she could speak with Warren in his coffin became part of White House lore and one of the strangest moments in the life of the Duchess. When the incident was later described to her, Mary Rinehart mused that since he had died, "only then, after all those years, he was truly hers." Through the ordeal, Evalyn said, she "never saw her shed a tear . . . there was no sign of . . . weakness, of collapse. . . ." Christian was with both women, and it was him that Florence ordered, "Put back the casket lid." For two hours she had rambled on to the corpse in the vast, echoing room. Evalyn vividly recalled it all:

> In the nighttime what was no longer the President appeared quite alive; rouge and lipstick touches, that in daylight were ghastly, with a softer illumination made him seem almost himself. Then I began to shiver, because I heard Mrs. Harding talking to her husband. The heavy scent of flowers cloyed my nostrils as we stayed on and on and Mrs. Harding talked. A chair was placed for her and she sat down. "Warren," she said, her face held close to his, "the trip has not hurt you one bit." That poor thing kept right on talking, as if she could not bear to hear the silence that would so poignantly remind her that he could not speak to her in turn. "No one can hurt you now, Warren," she said another time. That one remark helped me to understand how she was weaving strands of comforting philosophy out of grief. I know how she had feared

that some crank might do him harm; I too sometimes am conscious of a feeling of warmth when I think that my own dead are now beyond the reach of harm. Before we left she looked about at all the flowers, the costly sheaves of roses, the wreaths and the usual collection—oversize of course—of those stupid fabrications that the florists make, and then buy back, withered, from cemeteries for further use. Somewhere in those mounds she saw something that she wanted, and she stooped down as if she were in a growing garden to pick it up—a small bouquet of flowers, of daisies and nasturtiums. These she placed directly on the coffin after she had told George Christian to close the lid. It was three o'clock in the morning when we started back upstairs.

Some later speculated that Florence had suffered a nervous breakdown or other type of mental instability. On the contrary, she was quite sane, her comments and activities in the days preceding and following the East Room vigil showing her capable, if a bit formal. She was so dignified in fact that one maid thought Florence had "turned to ice." Her remarks to the corpse were more a philosophical response to Warren's repeated remark on the trip about how his friends were betraying him, but Florence never did reveal who the "no one" was to whom she was referring.

At breakfast the next morning Florence found comfort in eating only with Laddie at her side. When she sobbed slightly, it spooked him, and he began barking loudly and jumped into Warren's favorite chair. She then bent down, talking to and calming him, and brought the dog with her to the coffin. There he sniffed at the flowers, walked to the door, and sat, waiting. As the funeral procession began, Laddie was returned to the kennel, never to see Florence again. She got rid of him, giving the dog away. Nor did she receive any of the friends who called, among them Al and Emma Fall.[4]

Shortly after breakfast officials gathered at the White House to escort the caisson carrying Harding to the Capitol. There thousands stood for hours in the mercilessly muggy morning heat, filing past the open coffin until five—thousands still waiting in line—when the funeral began. A single large wreath of red, yellow, and white flowers was placed over the wreath of wilted and dead flowers that Florence had arranged on the coffin in San Francisco. The Duchess had had to be convinced to permit this official funeral since Warren had wanted a simple service. Throughout the ceremony Florence showed "iron determination." Said Christian: "Had it not been for Mrs. Harding's bravery we would all have collapsed."

Provided with no escort car, Florence's limousine got stuck in the traffic jam back to the White House. It was astonishing to observers that she was so cool. Only once did she fall prey to darker sentiment. That Evalyn had impulsively raced down the coast from Maine to be waiting at the station for Florence without having even wired ahead seemed to have as emotional an impact on the widow as her husband's death. Any betrayal of the previous spring seems to have been forgotten. Evalyn was a friend for life. At Union Station, as she was boarding the funeral train that was to travel to Marion through the night, Florence held Evalyn's hand tightly and asked, "What will become of me? May I not go with you?" Evalyn assured her she could share her "home and fireside." Then Evalyn sent her off, with the promise that she would be there for her when she returned. Evalyn's doctor prevented her from going to the crowded funeral and burial in Marion.

Ever suspicious, however, Evalyn did ask the President's valet about the truth of Harding's death. Arthur Brooks began sadly, "If he had turned back when he was first told to why—" He didn't finish his thought. "How about that awful sunburn in Kansas when he rode around under a broiling sun on a reaper in a wheat field; when his lips were so swollen?" Evalyn interrupted. "That wasn't sunburn," said Brooks, "that was heart."[5]

Amid the remarks made about Florence's stoic behavior during the funeral, only the New York *Tribune* thought it revealed the "ice that binds her heart." Otherwise there was universal praise. A tough old Army sergeant who had served under Pershing observed the widow throughout the Washington services and told reporter Carter Field, "Mrs. Harding is the nerviest woman I ever saw. Maybe her lips quivered a bit yesterday when she leaned over the body of the President, but she did not give way. . . . Strong willed, I call it. That's the kind of stuff you find in good women anyway. Men ain't there when it comes to that kind of suffering. They don't stand up."

Such "manly" toughness was seen as an attribute in the case of Florence Harding. Now, before the burial, the nation's newspapers ran hundreds of editorials praising her in a political context. "Warren Harding leaned on 'The Duchess' . . . as no president ever has depended on his wife. . . . Mrs. Harding was an integral part of the presidency of the entire Harding administration," said the Kansas City *Star*. "Mrs. Harding has been a fighter all her life. . . ." The Associated Press wire story noted, "Mrs. Harding made her husband President."

The highly political role the Duchess had played as First Lady, all the more overt during the trip, raised a new consciousness about the old role, and in light of the increased profile of women in all phases of public life during the Jazz Age, she was universally hailed for her work.

The Boston *Evening Transcript* thought that "the American people have come to appreciate the mettle of Mrs. Harding's womanhood. . . . They have begun to realize, what her friends and associates have known for many years, how completely she fitted into her husband's public life, how priceless was her help in the career which brought him from a farmer's boy to the highest office. . . . A President's wife does not ordinarily appear on the stage of public affairs. The Constitution places on her shoulders none of the cares of State. . . . Yet her share of these burdens, as in the case of Mrs. Harding, may be great, and it may require a great emergency to show how large a share of these burdens she may take it upon herself to carry." Five days later the paper added: "If the Constitution permitted . . . she could take the chair vacated by her adored husband and life pal, and pick up the reins where they fell from his lifeless hands and administer the affairs of this great nation with ability, wisdom, justice and in a statesmanlike manner." The *Idaho Statesman* said: "There have been first ladies of the land before, honored and beloved first ladies. But no wife of a president ever before meant so much and taught so much to America as did the wife of President Harding . . . she took the high office to which he climbed . . . they will go down into American history as the most perfectly mated couple of the executive mansion. . . . And the Harding administration will be remembered . . . as that of Mr. and Mrs. Harding. . . ." The Sunday following Harding's death in pulpits across the entire nation it was Florence Harding who was exalted for her sacrifices, steadiness, ambition, and intelligence. At a Bronx Episcopal church, the Reverend A. E. Beatley called her "a symbol of universal sisterhood for women and a sign of democracy's advance . . ."[6]

In Marion, concealed behind drawn shades from an upstairs room at her father-in-law's house, Florence watched the endless line of citizens waiting to come in and pass by the coffin, two large electric floor lamps shining on his familiar features, the rest of the furniture moved out of the parlor. She insisted that the house remain open straight through until the very last moment before the funeral. At the time Cliff and Tal were again not speaking to each other, and she whipped off a note ordering them to bury the hatchet; she didn't want a Kling family rift making news now. The Duchess was regal with the Coolidges, wishing Grace "success as the new mistress of the White House" and telling him, "Mr. President, I could not think of having you come to our home without extending to you my personal greeting." During the day she greeted old friends in the kitchen; "this is a good place to talk," she said, "cheerful as could be expected." Florence refused to permit anyone to make her decisions. She spoke of a hope to travel to Europe soon, how she would not ask the current tenants of her Marion house to vacate it, and how she wanted *Star* employees to march in the funeral procession. She was almost matter-of-fact. After one too many people had expressed their sympathy, she snapped, "Yes, it is too bad, but I am not going to break down."

The Cabinet returned to the house the next morning, when the casket was closed and carried to the hearse. The last to leave the house was the Duchess in her black dress and dramatic veil blocking her features and reaching to the ground. "Through the silent, face-walled streets the cortege passed and around the corner to the quiet cemetery," recalled Joe Chapple. The family, friends, and officials proceeded to an ivy-covered vault. There was a military gun salute, final prayers, and hymns of burial. The casket was carried into the vault. As "Nearer, My God, to Thee" softly came to a close, the Duchess bowed her head in prayer. Now the sound of heavy sobs could be heard, but as *The New York Times* noted, "Mrs. Harding stood dry-eyed." She walked into the vault, alone with Warren one last time, directing two Secret Service agents to flank the doors of the vault "and stay until the entrance is sealed." When she emerged from the vault, Starling noticed, "Her face was lifted, and her eyes shone with a light I had not seen in them before."

Before returning to Washington, Florence went to the vault again. As the sun set, before boarding the train, she ordered that the car that had taken her and Warren west, and the coffin back east and to Marion, be detached. She said she "never wanted to see it again."[7]

Florence was angry at the moment—at Coolidge. She thought his early-morning swearing in "a bit hasty," and before Harding's body had been returned to the White House, Coolidge sat for a formal picture at Harding's desk. There were reports that when she had been ready to leave the White House for the station, Coolidge's aides had neglected to have an official car called for her and that Reddy Baldinger had already been fired. So angry was George Christian that despite Coolidge's announcement that he would retain him, Christian told reporters immediately after the funeral that he was "through, right now" and quit. The Coolidges did invite Florence to stay in the mansion as long as she wished and dined with her the night she returned. "It was a magnificent performance," said Coolidge's biographer Claude Fuess, "for a man who knew how little Mrs. Harding had thought of him." Thoughtful Grace had insisted on it, and as *The New York Times* noted, Calvin "always has a willing ear for any ideas of Mrs. Coolidge on any subject." She was already credited with influencing him toward "sympathy for the League."[8]

Florence's train arrived at Union Station at nine-twenty in the morning on August 11. She stayed in her private car for "some minutes" and called all the reporters who had been with her since the Alaska trip to tell them of her appreciation, wish them luck, and say farewell. Still veiled, she again walked firmly through the station, Doc, Christian, Reddy, and several military aides in her wake, a few bystanders pausing to watch her. The funeral was over; people had trains to catch; life went on. A single car brought her to the White House.

On the North Portico steps, Barker ran over to open her car door and give her his arm. Grace Coolidge hugged her. Once in the front door she nearly broke into tears when she saw Laura Harlan and the entire household staff lined up to offer their condolences. She had been a hard boss, especially in her first weeks as First Lady, when she was suspicious of the maids and butlers who nervously darted like mice about her family rooms. After her illness, however, she had seen their loyalty, and they had earned her affection. She went down the line to each one, but after it was over, she lifted her veil. "Reddy," she said, "come along. Bring Laura and Harry and let's get to work. Everything has to be sorted and packed. The furniture, Warren's clothes, his papers."

Florence went first to her room, put on an old day dress, and, with Reddy, began going through Warren's closets. She pulled out a suit and dispatched it to the Smithsonian later that day. She snipped buttons from his coats as practical and inexpensive gifts for friends and family. The bulk of the clothes went into storage boxes, to be sent to a Marion warehouse. Then, to Laura, she designated the pieces of furniture to be packed. They worked into the early morning.

The endless train rides, the ceremonies, the dirges, and her own complex grief—all had taken their toll on the sixty-three-year-old woman. Still, she had a formidable task ahead of her: salvaging her husband's reputation. It was no small goal. Florence Harding was now ready to attack the overwhelming task of finding, reading, and sorting through all of President Harding's papers—not only private and official letters sent to him but his public messages, private memos to Cabinet officers and White House staff, friendly letters to the public, private correspondence locked in a wall safe in the Oval Study, and a secret file marked "Heart-Throb Letters"—and destroying everything that she thought could be, as a friend later told the press, "misconstrued." Meanwhile, *The New York Times* reported, Christian immediately "spent some time" getting the Oval Office and executive wing cleared. Christian had frantically gone through the drawers of Harding's desk, "feeling that it might contain personal documents"—namely, the Nan Britton love letters and pictures—until there were only left "papers of casual importance." Only then did the Duchess go down to the office to take "some of the papers."

She began at the wall safe, which she opened by its combination, and commenced reading from these "Private Office" files. She told Reddy to light the fireplace, and though the air was hot and thick, he did as he was told. She began to hand him papers. Often she came over to look at the burning papers and stir the ashes herself with a brass poker. Sometimes she didn't even trust Reddy, making sure some letters went directly from her hand into the fire. This went on for five nights, the Duchess thrusting into the flames other "confidential and personal papers" that she had rummaged from the Oval Office during the day.

It was not just personal but official letters that were to be destroyed. In the west wing, the executive offices were in an uproar as George Christian ordered the staff to gather rapidly all papers, especially those with Warren's handwriting or signature. Although the press reported that this gathering was "under the widow's orders," the public had no idea that he was stuffing it all into ten-foot wood crates, a foot wide and a foot deep. As the papers accumulated, the overwhelmed Duchess realized that she couldn't possibly scan, let alone read, everything she might want burned. She had a plan. She would take the boxes with her. She called Evalyn.[9]

Florence paused long enough to respond to Rose Hoes, who created the Smithsonian exhibit of First Ladies dresses, and sent a white dress for the collection. She also began quickly to divest herself of other items. The strangest gift was her unceremonious turning over of Laddie Boy to Barker; she never wanted to see the dog again or the bronze statue being sculpted of him, paid for by newsboys' pennies. She gave feather fans to Maggie Rogers, hats to Mrs. Jaffray, and riding crops and Warren's engraved buttons to the McLean children. "I can never forget your unfailing friendship," Florence wrote from the White House to Evalyn two days before joining her at Friendship, "and especially during these days when your thoughtfulness in every way has been such a comfort to me, and so I am sending you this line just to tell you a little of my deep appreciation and gratitude which I cannot trust to put into words."[10]

Evalyn yet again came through for Florence. In a "rainy chill as though early November," in the early evening of August 17, leading several other empty McLean cars, Evalyn came to take the widow forever away from the mansion she had fought so hard to enter. Gripping a suitcase that she insisted on carrying herself into the limousine despite the attempts to take it by Reddy and Harry, both of whom left with her, Florence Harding walked out of the White House in black but with no veil. As she did so, Evalyn noticed, "she lifted up her chin in a characteristic gesture." When the wide black iron gates swung open onto Pennsylvania Avenue, Florence and Evalyn, in "a dismal downpour at dusk," headed out to Friendship, followed by a convoy of cars loaded with possessions and the gasping wooden crates crammed with Warren's papers. There were no curious pedestrians, no staff on the lawn, only three reporters. Before she left, Florence looked out for a moment over the wide lawn, then glanced back once at the mansion, a setting, a reporter thought, "as sombre as the epilogue of a Greek tragedy."

Although Evalyn was planning to return to her children in Maine, she welcomed the chance to let Florence use Friendship for her own secret purposes, as she had once permitted Warren to do so. Through September 4 it was to be home for the Duchess. On her first night there, after the rainstorm ended, she and Evalyn strolled through the dark gardens. "Cicadas were singing with their wings, as we walked beneath the trees that shade the lawn," Evalyn said. "Now that it is all over," the Duchess told her, "I think it is all for the best. I could not wish him back to all that strain." Back in Maine several days later Evalyn wired Florence, who responded: "Of course I miss you but I am getting on very well, with days full of looking over my papers and repacking some of my things. I have only been able to walk in the grounds once for about ten minutes but can't begin to tell you how much I enjoy the porch upstairs. I am out there most of the day and manage to do a lot of work *in that way* out of doors. . . . I think of you all many times a bday. . . . It does help me to carry my burden, as much as is possible, to live in such an environment. The grounds are so beautiful and it is all so peaceful that it must inspire the beautiful thoughts I need to help me."

In her absence Evalyn asked various officials to attend to the Duchess. "We found Mrs. Harding just as brave and fine as she has been all along," Grace Coolidge reported to Evalyn after a visit to Friendship. Charles Evan Hughes was especially kind, arranging to give Florence Warren's Cabinet Room chair, each Cabinet member contributing to replace it with a new one for Coolidge. When Al Fall first heard of Harding's death, he had wired the Duchess that he was taking "the first boat home." Emma came up from New Mexico, Al from New York. They went directly to Friendship. "I am here, just as I said I would be to do anything in my power for you," he told her. "Command me." The Falls took a room at the Wardman Park Inn to be on call to her— and for Al to respond to the growing congressional inquiry about the oil leases made on his watch at the Interior Department. At least to their faces Florence did not betray any doubts about Fall's reputation, but neither did she ever take him up on his offer to perform any favors for her.

With Kathleen Lawler and maid Katherine Wynne helping her sort through her clothes—many of which she sent to her granddaughter to fix for her own use—and the Sawyers staying with her, Florence was not entirely alone. She reflected on her life there to Esther Metzger: "I can hardly realize two weeks ago today we laid Mr. Harding away. I have been very busy—guess it's just as well because it gives me no time to think in the daytime but my nights are awful. I have no idea when I am coming home or how long I will stay when I do come. . . . The days are pretty dark to me and I see absolutely nothing for the future. Well, I will just have to wait. Time will adjust some things that I cannot see now. You have much to be thankful for. . . . Three fine children & such a splendid husband."[11]

Removed from curious eyes, the Duchess was able to continue examining the boxed papers and burning what she thought incriminating on a pyre in the garden. One morning she took Reddy down to the Riggs Bank, where she had maintained a safety-deposit box since the Senate years, returned, then burned the box's contents. Another morning out from the McLean basement came boxes of the government-suppressed Chancellor book, which had threatened to reveal all the Harding skeletons. The copies had been stored there by Gaston Means and Jess Smith. Now they were thrown onto the bonfire. Still another day she brought out the suitcase she had carried from the White House, handed it to Reddy, and told him to throw it on the fire without opening the lock. As the fire devoured it and air pockets broke, it burst open and the papers inside it were consumed. Reddy did not ask about the contents, but she shot him a look not to question what she was doing. "Reddy, we must be loyal to Warren," she said, "and preserve his memory."

While at Friendship, Florence was notified by lawyer Charles Shaffner that Warren's most recent will had been located in a safe-deposit box in Marion. She wired that she wanted "nothing done about the will" until she returned. Florence had the remaining crates repacked and sent ahead to Marion. She left Washington on September 5, writing Evalyn about "how much the stay at Friendship has done for me. I am much better, and everyone comments on how well I look considering what I have been through. I owe it all to you. . . . I do not know how long I will stay in Marion. My business will govern the length of time. Please keep me advised of your movements. . . ."[12]

Arm in arm with Grace Coolidge, dressed in black cape and hat, waving a handkerchief to friends gathered to see her off, Florence left for Marion on September 5 in a steady rain. She was cheerful, beaming a smile, and had "never looked better than at any time" since her illness a year before. Only one reporter showed up at Union Station, but another wrote, "She has been so intimately associated with affairs of international importance and she is a woman of such keen acumen that it does not seem likely she would be willing to settle down very far from the political center of gravity."

Although ostensibly in Marion for the will probate, Florence was determined to complete her culling of Warren's papers. From a room at the Sawyer cottage at their sanitarium, she wrote to dozens of friends asking them to return to her all original letters sent them by Warren over the years, explaining that she was trying to amass a collection of Harding's papers to be opened later to researchers. There seems to have been no resistance to or suspicion of what the widow was doing by those who complied, although there is no record of just how many people did cooperate and what they sent. If any of the letters were incriminating, Florence burned them. It was clearly not a matter of a bereft widow trying to keep a few past incidents private, as Martha Washington had done in burning letters between her and her husband. Florence did not want the general public or press to know what she was doing. When one citizen inquired about some Harding correspondence to Florence, one of her temporary secretaries responded on October 1 with an outright lie that Florence was not "in a position to have access to the President's papers." Every morning of the next six weeks she was driven down to Warren's old private *Star* office, where she had the crates placed and the old pot-bellied stove fired up as she continued her burning.

Hoping to return to Washington by November 1 and make a temporary home in a Willard Hotel suite, she wrote Doc: "I started on Mr. Harding's papers this week and I find it a very trying job. I am sure it's going to take me much longer to go through them than I anticipated. Do you suppose the Management at the Hotel would mind if I did not take those rooms until December 1? If it inconveniences them at all we

will let it stand as agreed. . . . I work like a dog each day as it is."
Florence didn't justify her burning to Doc, nor did he question it.

Soon enough Florence asked Reddy to take an extended leave of
absence from the Army—and personally paid him—to continue processing the papers she brought from Friendship as well as some sent by
Christian to a Marion warehouse from the onset. There were about eight
crates to get through now. Every day they were at it again, she first
reading the papers, then handing to Reddy those she wanted destroyed
in the stove and placing those she would keep back in a crate. It might
be a single page to be burned or saved, or an entire file. Only once did
Reddy speak out that these documents had historical value, that the
worth of Harding's signature alone was reason enough to stop burning
indiscriminately. She listened for a moment, then continued burning.
Reddy apparently said something to the *Star* editor and old Harding
friend George Van Fleet, who gently interceded. Burning the papers,
she snapped, was "what Warren would do."

Usually by noon each day Florence's hands, face, and arms were
covered in soot, as she repaired to the Sawyer cottage for a break. The
mind-numbing tedium of reading through tens of thousands of typed
and handwritten documents was not only exhausting her but playing
tricks on her mind. She lost any sense of proportion, of system, of
common sense, intent only on finishing as quickly as possible. In the
process, she tore off the names and addresses heading some letters, but
kept the contents, tore parts of carbon copy documents from one box,
yet preserved the original typescripts of the documents, which were
packed in another. She kept letters written to Harding about rumors of
his African blood and his drinking alcohol, for example, but not the
undoubtedly whitewashed responses to them—which would have at least
preserved his official response.

Van Fleet recalled that after it was all over, there were only two
crates. In the end a full half of the papers had been burned. The loss
resulted in gaps chronicling Harding's state political career, but Florence
destroyed even more of her own record. None of her correspondence
before 1915 was left, nothing in her own hand related to her life with
De Wolfe, as a mother, piano teacher, or business manager, all records
of her education and Amos Kling's business transactions. Very little of
her incoming White House correspondence was kept, yet she preserved
various drafts of her outgoing letters, social schedules, astrological notes.
Letters from her informants on Forbes were often kept with their names
torn off. It was a peculiar puzzle that would never be complete.[13]

Throughout the autumn delegations of visitors descended on Marion to visit the Harding vault. Although she attended a civic memorial on Harding's birthday, Florence otherwise kept a low profile, turning down an offer to do an Armistice Day radio address to American women and receiving only British Prime Minister Lloyd George. When Colonel Christian poked around the Sawyer Sanitarium to see how she was doing, he was asked in. She had just finished signing responses to more than ten thousand sympathy notes, letters, and telegrams. She had already exceeded sixteen thousand stamps. According to Christian, she expressed her "determination to examine every one of these missives and decide on the nature of her reply." Somehow, he thought, however mindless, the "incessant work" distracted her from mourning.

Financial minutiae also occupied her. Although the government paid for the funeral and mail, Florence had to pay other expenses, and she kept a precise account, from the $50 to ship her piano to the $76.15 for "Packing household goods." She wanted government reimbursement on $275 worth of postage and stationery, and she wanted the Treasury check for Warren's salary for the first two days of August. Once Warren's will was probated, her security was more than assured. She got the lion's share of cash as stated in his will—$25,000—property, stocks, bonds, dividends, and interest "absolutely and forever." He left $2,000 each for her grandchildren. However, she had to confront the huge debts and stock losses racked up by the President, which were now privately pressing the estate. "Sawyer told me of Pres. H's losses thru Ferguson— S.S. man," Boone wrote in October, "wherein his estate will have to pay more than hundred thousand on obligations." In fact, there was not only the $30,000 or so that Warren invested with Ferguson but also a $180,000 loss to the brokerage firm that former Secret Service agent Jimmy Sloan ran. It was settled with a $30,000 offer in compromise.

Still, Florence inherited cash, property, and investments totaling about $500,000—this in addition to her own Kling inheritance and investments of $100,000. With over a half million 1923 dollars, Florence Harding became the wealthiest presidential widow to that time, rivaled only by Julia Grant, who died in 1902 with an estate of $250,000. Although Congress did not grant her the usual $5,000 presidential widow's pension, Florence did take her $13,300 annual salary early, as contributing editor of the newly organized Harding Publishing Company, with the opportunity to write *Star* editorials, wanting to maintain her "financial, official and editorial" connection.[14]

She also attended to plans for a formal memorial to Warren, refusing her support from hundreds of proposed ideas like San Francisco's Harding municipal golf course. Doc told her that with Coolidge's support, he was planning one effort, although he often threatened that it would not be in Marion unless the city provided more support. On October 8 the Harding Memorial Association was founded as a nonprofit corporation under Ohio laws, its stated purpose to build and maintain a mausoleum for both Hardings, converting the Harding house—willed to the association by Florence—into a historic site. Gathered for an initial meeting, Doc, Coolidge, Hughes, Weeks, New, Work, Davis, Mellon, Daugherty, Denby, Wallace, Dawes, Payne, Upham, Freling-huysen, McLean, Hammond, Prendergast, Christian, Donithen, and Dick Crissinger were elected as board trustees—first approved by Florence. Significantly absent was Albert Fall.

Doc had to push Florence to contact wealthy friends for donations. As "your doctor and friend" he rather demanded this of her, stating that her gathering papers for a biography to counteract those that were appearing as a "disgrace" was not as important as raising money: ". . . if you are to benefit by the acquaintances . . . you have had here [Washington] then it will be well for you . . . to come back here . . . if you have decided in your own mind that you do not care to again participate either directly or indirectly in affairs of the nation, then there is no reason . . . avail yourself of the possibilities which are still yours. I have to admonish you that minor matters of detail are of little importance compared with the . . . creation of a Shrine in honor of the President . . . you have your own mind but . . . there is always a time and place in which to do things which are really worth while . . . such time and place are now at hand."

As talk of scandal in the Harding administration began to circulate in October, the Duchess may have realized that despite her best efforts, Warren's reputation was inevitably to deteriorate. She was, said Kathleen Lawler, "keen enough to be sure if the Memorial fund was not raised then it might never be." Still, she remained removed and inactive on the project.

The Senate committee investigation of the Veterans Bureau began formal hearings on October 22. The next day erstwhile bureau contractor Elias Mortimer began telling sordid tales of drinking parties, corruption, and kickbacks involving Forbes, including his attempt to seduce Mrs. Mortimer and how Mrs. Forbes then emptied Charlie's checking account, went to Europe, and divorced him. After two months of hearings, Forbes and Mortimer went on to be tried for conspiracy to defraud the government in a nine-week trial beginning in 1924.

Washington social columnists assumed that Florence did not immediately return to the capital because of her embarrassment over Forbes or, just two days after the Veterans Bureau hearings began, Albert Fall's appearance before a Senate committee headed by Thomas Walsh of Montana. Fall was questioned on why the Teapot Dome oil-drilling lease to Harry Sinclair and the Elk Hills lease to Edward Doheny had been secretly arranged by him, with no public disclosure after the fact. Fall claimed that national security on naval policy was the reason for what he called his "discretion" and that he received no money nor had he ever worked for Sinclair or Doheny before being appointed to the Cabinet.

Neither investigation, however, is what delayed Florence's return to Washington. She was housebound by a severe parasitic infection and being treated at the sanitarium by Carl Sawyer, a fact held as a secret. The scandals, however, did fuel the rumor about Harding's "strange death," and Harding friend Mac Jennings—certainly with Florence's prior approval—finally addressed it publicly in a Rotarian speech: "I want . . . to give lie to the absurd and vicious story that he was the victim of a poison plot. There is not a shadow of foundation for this canard." On details of Harding's death, Doc remained mute.[15]

Florence saw Doc during his rare autumn trips back to the sanitarium. He refused to relinquish his position as White House physician, even in light of press speculation that he was "being forced out." A Coolidge naval aide called Doc a "smooth hombre and tricky," warning Boone to "keep [his] eyes open . . . be cautious . . . & to assert [himself]" with him. Despite Coolidge's preference for Boone and his revolting fears about Doc's incompetence—as well as Doc's own thought of resigning to run the Memorial Association full-time—Sawyer's need to control Boone obsessed him. On December 13 there was a confrontation and the first sign that Doc was talking to Florence against Boone, who knew the truth regarding Harding's death and therefore remained a threat. Boone wrote that Doc "wanted to talk 'frankly with me'; he was very white. Resented my having exam. President during his absence. . . . Became very nasty. Said he had discussed it with his son & Mrs. Harding. . . . I never knew how to please him." Doc's professional treatment of the new President began to raise startling questions about his treatment of the late President. "I insisted that laboratory examinations should be made of [Coolidge's] nasal and other respiratory system," Boone wrote. "Expressed myself as disapproving of chlorine gas for a President when it was merely in the experimental stages. I did not feel the President should be used as a guinea pig."[16]

Florence seemed to be trying to distance herself from the Sawyers, choosing to spend the weekend before Christmas with her grandchildren before going to Columbus to celebrate the holiday with Ethel and Mac Jennings, on whom she relied as sounding boards. "Many are the times I need your good advice," she later told him. To Evalyn, she afterward wrote that she "had a restful time seeing only a few friends and avoiding public appearances. Then I went back to Marion to find thousands of letters, telegrams, Christmas greetings, and parcels."

Arriving in Washington on January 2, 1924, Florence went directly to her suite on the top floor of the Willard, taking with her the thousands of pieces of correspondence she planned to respond to. This, along with her "business and private affairs," occupied her immediately. She knew the McLeans would already be in Palm Beach, but she missed Evalyn, who proposed that she come live with them in Florida for the winter. "I do not feel I could so at present," Florence wrote, "although I feel more at home with you than with almost anyone I know." The McLeans would not be back in Washington until early spring. By that time they, along with Daugherty, Fall, Sawyer, and Forbes, would find themselves the subject of accusatory and sensational national headlines in scandal. As would the Duchess herself.[17]

37

Spies and Scandals

"I don't feel like ever going to Washington," Harry Daugherty had written Florence in the fall. "My heart is not there like it was. I don't seem to be able to get started to get over this blow and loss. . . . When you think of anything I can do for you call upon me. You know how willingly I will respond." The note from the abrasive old pol was heartfelt, but written to Florence, rather ironic. The Duchess needed neither Harry's nor anyone else's comfort. "[I am] rearranging my life as I inevitably must," she wrote the governor of Hawaii. In fact, Florence determined that having "laid the dead to rest," she must "devote herself to the living" and ignored social expectations that she indulge in mourning. Ray Clapper observed: "Mrs. Harding, always a most practical, capable woman, for all her feminine charms approaches her new life just as she has the past difficult tasks or trying situations, with a determination to make herself mistress of the situation rather than let it make her."

Days after her return to the capital the "Ladies of the Senate" passed a resolution honoring Florence for her "conscientious performance" as First Lady. It was a promising start. She wrote Esther nine days after arriving:

I am very nicely situated down here. Think I am going to be fairly well satisfied, or at least, as near as I can anywhere. I don't like the board as well as that I get at the "Metzger house." My new secretary started in this week, but I have my doubts when it comes to her being a howling success. However, I am going to be patient and give her a chance. My friends have been very kind, coming to see me, and my rooms have been full of flowers, from the day I arrived. Fact is I am never alone. Every moment of my time has been taken since I started to write you this morning. Am now waiting for my dinner. I have very nice rooms here and my dining room is about the size of yours. My, how I used to love to skate. The weather was not very cold here when you were having that very cold snap . . . never very cold.

She also referred to an underlying irritation: "Mandy Sawyer 'drops in' three or four times a day."[1]

As people came to see her, it was clear that the Sawyers were not only watching out for Florence's well-being but monitoring her visitors and her conversations with them. Undoubtedly fearing any discussion of medical details about Harding's death, Doc was especially alarmed when Boone came to see her. Boone recorded that despite Sawyer's claims that she was in delicate health, she was in fact "looking very well and seemed to be in good spirits. Had about 15 minutes with her . . . we could have had better talk . . . a more intimate conversation . . . if I had been alone with her, rather than with Mrs. Sawyer. . . ." Doc, said Boone, showed "evidence of growing hot and cold, as it were, when we [Boone and Florence] were together."[2]

Besides his fear of being replaced by Boone, Doc had other troubles. Just three months after its formation the Harding Memorial Association "has been allowed to sag," Mac Jennings reported to Florence, and Doc engendered a "great deal of bitterness" in Marion when he began "talk of the removal of Warren's remains" from there. Even after he was subpoenaed that spring to testify against Forbes for conspiracy to defraud the government, he remained reckless in his associations. Sawyer, Boone noted, "said that he was to have a mtg. with KKK representative relative to a contribution to the Harding Fund." Some citizens, offended at the million-dollar price tag for the Harding Memorial, wrote Florence about Doc's misguided ambition for a grand mausoleum instead of a scholarship fund, an institute of study, or some other living memorial. In the face of continuing revelations about the conduct of Harding underlings, the memorial grew to seem a disproportionate effort. The Duchess willed items as well as the remaining presidential papers to the association but thought she could not afford to write a large check to it.

Despite her wealth, Florence wanted to "relieve her mind" about the cost of her Willard suite. Doc told the manager he should take $50 off her monthly bill of $350: "You will find Mrs. Harding one of the most saving guests you ever had." Then, showing his true colors, Doc referred to the former First Lady as the commodity he now viewed her: "Her presence here has already demonstrated that she is really a great acquisition to the guest list of the Willard Hotel."[3]

Newspaper accounts of Florence's wealth, however, raised a red flag in the new atmosphere of scandals. The first accusation that her money was ill gotten was made by retired New York banker Frank A. Vanderlip. Valentine's Day headlines carried Vanderlip's claim that Warren had sold the *Star* at a suspiciously high price of $550,000 as a covert vehicle for a bribe on the oil deals, that it had been purchased for a price higher than its value because oil kickbacks were laundered through the profits Harding received, in thanks for his condoning the Sinclair and Doheny leases. With Vanderlip hauled before the Walsh Committee in its wide-net search for scandal, the unraveling of Harding's reputation began.

Naturally Vanderlip's false claim enraged the Duchess, but she became suspicious when she learned of what she called the "pretty penny" he paid to former reporters, Secret Service agents, and Scotland Yard investigators for what he claimed was a private investigation. She feared that Vanderlip was trying to uncover not just political but personal scandal on Warren under the guise of fair investigatory journalism. "Vanderlip's lawyers have asked for an extension of time in filing their answer," Florence wrote Jennings. "V. is now in Washington. They say he is going to write for the *New York World*. I say he is here for another purpose. Everything is in a terrible chaotic state down here but the people are getting very tired of it all." At one point the former First

Lady decided to appear before the Walsh Committee as a witness against Vanderlip, to give her estimate on the value of the *Star*, recount discussions with Warren on its sale, and mention other previous large offers for it. Jennings warned that while her appearance would have sentimental appeal, the investigators would carry the inquiry "into matters outside the case itself." He advised her not to get "needlessly involved" and to "write no letters relating to matters in litigation without the advice of an attorney."[4]

Besides the momentary anticipation of the Duchess's testifying, there was also persistent talk in Washington that she was going to write her autobiography, a remembrance of Warren, or the story of his life based on his papers. She received at least one solicitation from a free-lance researcher to aid her. "It is my intention, ultimately, to undertake this work myself but . . . will do so only after I have made a careful study and arrangement of the vast amount of material I have long been gathering," she responded. But her gathering of papers in Washington had less to do with using them for research than with sanitizing their contents. "I think of her most pitifully as she came back to Washington long afterward to get Warren's papers from the White House files, read them over word by word, discovering at last the things she had only guessed," recalled a Senate wife. "There are those who say unkindly that she came back to open a salon and continue as a dowager queen. But I doubt that. What she came for was to burn Warren's papers in an effort to save his posthumous reputation. What bitter thoughts were hers we can not know. Poor Florence Harding! If only she had married differently, or if she could have dared for herself, as in some other day she might!"

The matter of Harding's papers arose days after her arrival when she permitted Charles Moore of the Library of Congress's Manuscript Division to come see her. Moore had written to her in October, when he first heard rumors of the papers' being destroyed and urged her to at least consider donating them to the Library of Congress for eventual public use. The library would take care of "classifying [and] arranging" them but use them for research only "on your order," and she would have "complete control." Despite the gargantuan work this would have spared her, she wanted no other eyes culling through these papers. Now she dismissed him by saying she had "burned them all." A few days later, hoping to publish a selection of Harding's letters, Frank N. Doubleday of the publishing family visited her. Florence blankly repeated what she told Moore. She had burned everything because, she said, she "feared some of it would be misconstrued and would harm his memory."

What Moore and Doubleday could not know was that in the very same suite where she sat and told them this, she was *still* burning letters. "Have spent busy morning with my Sec'y," she wrote Mac Jennings, "but even after the destroying of 67 letters could not clear my desk."

Besides the President's papers, however, the Duchess had burned her own "personal file," correspondence from the campaign and White House, confidential letters, carbon copies, and even applications for federal positions. As she began gathering material for "an intimate biography" of herself and Warren, she regretted having destroyed some material. "It never occurred to me that my file would be useful for that purpose," she said in retrospect.[5]

Ensconced in her suite overlooking Pennsylvania Avenue, the former First Lady attracted appeals like homing pigeons. Hundreds of what she called "beg" letters poured in on her: appeals for money or requests that she lend her name to this or that society, cause, movement, or event, from paying for a boat for missionaries trying to reach isolated Alaskan natives to supporting the Constitutional League in its efforts to pass the Equal Rights Amendment. She no longer had the assistance, access, time, and resources even to consider most requests, let alone help each. Often asked to use her influence with Coolidge, Congress, or other officials in patronage cases, for example, she could now only pass on such appeals to those still in power with whom she had been personally close. Doc helped to place a Charles Baumgardner at the Veterans Bureau, and Postmaster General Harry New reinstated a fired Scranton postmaster. In light of the various ongoing Harding administration investigations, she explained in a third-person draft, a letter from her "would be resented by those in authority and it would hurt rather than help. She greatly regrets that conditions preclude her from attempting in any way to influence matters . . . you will realize the impropriety of her doing so."

Kathleen Lawler had returned to help Florence with the backlog. She not only structured a correspondence system but even drafted her formal letters. "Miss Harlan was not a bit of good or help to me on such matters," Florence remarked. Lawler wrote Florence's highly regarded sympathy letter to Grace Coolidge on the untimely death of her teenage son, and the former First Lady then copied it in her own handwriting, hiding it when Catherine New came to call. Florence used old Western Union Telegraph notepads to scribble out dozens and dozens of her own form letters, mostly in the third person for a secretary's signature. She remained careful with money, privately contributing to Ohio flood relief and the preservation of George Washington's birth site. In one letter she made the closest to a public revelation that she ever would of Warren's stock losses: "There has been no settlement of her estate, and her means have been greatly exaggerated. . . ." To requests for her clothes, she had two different responses: ". . . has long since made provisions for the wearing apparel that she does not need," and "all her things are at present in storage . . ."[6]

Among her own outings, the Duchess often dined at the home of friends like George Christian or went for winter drives with Mandy Sawyer, slipping out to visit historic sites in Maryland and Virginia. During a visit to the Smithsonian to inspect her gown, now being prepared for display, she got rather testy. "She had many criticisms," recalled Rose Hoes, "her ambition being apparently to have it as perfect as possible." She saw herself as the first of the "moderns" among the First Ladies, at least in fashion, said Hoes, and "It was Mrs. Harding's own suggestion that feet would be necessary for the figure which was to represent her, as it was one of the short-dress periods." Something about seeing herself as a mannequin brought the Duchess back for return visits a little too frequently for the nervous curator. She recalled her habit of taking Ohioans during the Senate years to see the collection and told Hoes that "it seemed rather strange that she was now going to form part of it." Hoes noticed how Florence glared at herself paired with Edith Wilson's mannequin in a double glass case, but "evidently bore no malice or hatred in her heart." Poker-faced, the Duchess cracked, "How happy I am to know that I am to be in the same case with that lovely woman." Edith Wilson, however, invited Florence to attend the National Cathedral funeral of Woodrow Wilson in February. The Duchess sat with Nellie Taft and Eleanor Roosevelt, behind the Coolidges.

Through all the months after Warren's death, Florence had distracted herself in work to prevent any grieving, but the Wilson funeral seemed to prompt a brief reflection. Dolly Gann, Senator Curtis's sister, recalled how during a visit the Duchess "received me with the old cordiality, but I could see she was crushed." She spoke endlessly of Warren—his rise, his accomplishments, the campaign—and his end. "She seemed to live over again the scene in the hotel room in San Francisco, and told me how she had been sitting by Mr. Harding's bedside at the last, reading aloud to him." She did not, however, discuss the cause of his death.[7]

Florence had hoped to break away and join the McLeans in Palm Beach sometime in March. Two weeks after the widow arrived in Washington, Evalyn had wired: "When are you coming down to us? You know how much we want you and this lovely weather here would do you good . . . let me hear how you are and that you are coming down to us . . . all my love." As fate had it, Florence's delay in being with the McLeans was fortunate.

Throughout the fall Senator Walsh's Committee on Public Lands investigations had not proved that Albert Fall had done anything wrong. Geologists debated whether his leasing of Elk Hills and Teapot Dome were really necessary in terms of oil drainage from the government reserves and whether in fact, as Fall claimed, the leases actually made money for the government by selling drilling rights instead of just letting the draining oil go to waste. But it was during the break over the holiday season, when Walsh began to receive reports of Al and Emma Fall's improved ranch, his purchase of a vast tract bordering it, and the development of both properties—all on Fall's relatively small salary—that the senator's suspicions grew. Doheny was subpoenaed. Was his oil company behind the sudden Fall windfall? No, Doheny declared, he had never given Fall either a gift or loan. Walsh was getting warm, and Fall nervous. Fall asked Price McKinney, a wealthy mining friend, to say that he had lent the money for the ranch. McKinney refused. Fall began drinking heavily. The committee asked to see him again. A doctor signed a statement saying he was too ill to appear. He checked into a hospital in a most unlikely place to find peaceful recuperation, Atlantic City.

Over Christmas Emma, grasping for even the remotest kind of tangible proof of Albert's character, wired the Duchess, expecting a response. It was lucky for the public reputation of the former First Lady, who was inundated with mail, that she did not reply. Evalyn then received an urgent telephone call from Emma. Could Ned please come visit Al? The McLeans delayed their Palm Beach trip, and Ned went up. Fall begged him to say to the Walsh Committee that it was he who had lent one hundred thousand dollars for the ranch improvements. Fall assured him that it had nothing to do with Sinclair or Doheny. Without any questions Ned wrote out a predated check for the amount. Fall then wrote Walsh that the "gentleman" McLean had lent him the money for the Harris ranch and furthermore that Sinclair and Doheny had never given "one cent on account of any oil lease or upon any other account." From Palm Beach, Ned wrote a corroborating note, claiming that he had made the loan, unwittingly committing perjury.

Walsh, still suspicious, not only demanded that Fall be called for committee questioning again but asked that the former interior secretary be put under surveillance by none other than Billy Burns and the Justice

Department. If there was anyone Attorney General Daugherty disliked more than Doc or Forbes, it was Albert Fall. As FBI memos confirmed, Justice feared that Fall would slip out of the country. Burns put agents on Fall's trail while he was in a hotel, and they were ordered to stop "Mr. Fall's probable departure from New Orleans by steamer for some foreign port. . . ." Agent Orville Dewey was careful about how he might approach Fall because "if he was cornered and his past record brought up he was liable to shoot someone. . . . Fall is known to have been connected with the shooting of a man at Alamagorda [*sic*], New Mexico. . . ."

Concurrently Senator Walsh called for Ned to be questioned. Suddenly Ned's sinuses began acting up, and his lawyer, former Attorney General Mitchell Palmer, informed Walsh that Ned couldn't travel. Walsh said he'd come to Palm Beach and get the testimony. Then Fall headed to Palm Beach. He now admitted to the McLeans that Doheny had "loaned" the money. Evalyn retorted, "[Y]ou have got to go before the committee and tell them the truth," and pestered him nightly to do so. "He was trying to protect Doheny and the stockholders. Finally, I told him, 'If you don't release Mr. McLean from his promise I am going over and tell Senator Walsh who it was.' Doheny was one of Walsh's best friends. [Fall] almost had a heart attack when he heard that." Ned told Evalyn with loyalty, "I won't go back on him." She had the final word: "Look here, you have gone far enough for a friend." Walsh was on his way to Florida.

To keep himself informed of Walsh's movements toward Palm Beach, Ned then did something even more stupid. He began sending and receiving telegrams to and from his office at the *Post*, via his confidential aide William Duckstein and his wife, Jessie—Billy Burns's private secretary—regarding inside information on Walsh from the Bureau of Investigation. All this was done in the bureau's weird secret code, Ned still being a dollar-a-year gumshoe. When some of the telegrams were intercepted, the secret liaison between the former First Lady's best friends and the Bureau of Investigation was publicly revealed and instantly raised wild suspicions. Burns was hauled before the Walsh Committee. He immediately wired Daugherty, "I promptly sent for Mrs. Duckstein and suggested to her to wire her husband and suggest propriety of McLean resigning." Ned finally confessed that he had not made the loan, and Walsh asked him now to get a similar admission from Fall, who was hiding in a red robe in his hotel suite just blocks away.

"Evalyn has tendered me a closed car, driver, footman, for my special use," the Duchess wrote with understatement to Jennings at the time Ned was the object of national opprobrium, "but, just now, I decided not to avail myself of the offer till some of this mess blew over." In the public's mind, the oil leases, Bureau of Investigation, Forbes and the Veterans Bureau, Fall, the McLeans, Harry's hijinx, Jess's suicide, Warren's strange demise, and Florence all were entangled and came to be known to history as the Teapot Dome scandal.[8]

Fall relented only to say that he had not gotten his money from Ned. Some days later, on January 24, Doheny admitted before Walsh's committee that he had "loaned" Fall the $100,000, delivered in a little "black satchel," but he argued that that amount was the equivalent of fifty dollars for an "ordinary" person. He also insisted that the "loan" had nothing to do with the Elk Hills oil lease. As proof he showed a promissory note for the "loan"—with his signature torn off, he said, because if he and his wife died, he didn't want his executors to press his friend Fall to pay it back. The next day came the admission from an aide that Sinclair had given about $30,000 worth of Liberty bonds to Fall. Fall finally appeared but declined to answer questions on the ground of self-incrimination; Sinclair also refused and was indicted for contempt of the Senate in criminal court. Coolidge then shocked Harding loyalists by appointing a special commission of two men, a Republican lawyer and a Democratic Ohio senator, to handle all necessary prosecutions. When it was sometime later discovered that Fall had received a combined near total of $400,000 from Sinclair and Doheny at the time of the leases, charges of conspiracy to defraud were handed to Fall, Doheny, and Sinclair, as well as bribery charges to Fall and Doheny.

In a public relations effort to sway their verdict, the latter two men, after consulting with Will Hays in Hollywood, pitched none other than Cecil B. De Mille to make a film of "the long history of intimacy and complete trust between Doheny and Fall, as shedding light on the informality of their financial transactions," to dramatize how "the naval oil leases actually benefitted the country." Teapot Dome, the film spectacular, never made it to the silver screen.

Florence was disgusted—not by what her friends Fall, Doheny, and Sinclair had done but by Senator Walsh's behavior. If she believed that Forbes deserved the indictment he received in February of 1924, she couldn't bring herself to speak against Fall. Recalled Kathleen Lawler: "Mrs. Harding went to her death believing in Secretary Fall." When the widow wrote an encouraging note to him in the midst of his trial, she was hurt not to receive a reply. "Surely Albert Fall knows that I know him, and that I do not believe any of the things said about him, or that he is guilty of any wrongdoing. Warren Harding had faith in him, and believed in him, and I do." She recalled how Warren had wanted Fall to stay in public life and how she herself tried to convince him not to go to Russia on behalf of Sinclair. In a note on February 15 she assured Emma of her "unbroken friendship."

Harding's friends continued to look for any alternative to Fall's guilt; one even claimed that Sinclair himself had initiated the investigations "with the idea of having his leases cancelled because he had found an insufficient supply of oil." Mac Jennings recited the loyalist line when he assured Florence that "the oil leases were not corruptly made," and perhaps "a good thing for the government," only that Fall was "an *indiscreet borrower* and, through sickness or drunkenness, turned yellow and tried to save himself by lying, and induced his friends to lie for him." He told a mutual friend, "I do not think the country is tremendously disturbed over the Teapot Dome thing. . . . Nobody has really been caught except Fall and I doubt if anything can be proved against any one else." Still, Florence left Fall's name off the permanent Harding Memorial Association board of Warren's "warm friends or admirers," while not excluding Navy Secretary Denby, also under investigation for having approved Fall's transfer of the oil lands from Navy to Interior Department jurisdiction. She even had Denby and his wife, Marion, call on her.[9]

During the Teapot Dome hearings, when Sinclair Oil executive Archie Roosevelt brought forth the news that Sinclair had made a $68,000 payment to a foreman on Fall's ranch, Alice Roosevelt Longworth caused a stir by marching into the room as a sign of support for her brother. Evalyn took fiendish delight in this, noting that Alice "got so frightened when she thought she was going to be called in the *Means'* trial."

The so-called Means trial, actually the Senate committee investigating the activities of Attorney General Daugherty, did not send Harry to jail nor is it even recalled as well as Teapot Dome, but it did more damage to the Harding reputation than the oil scandal, and it even implicated the Duchess. The case against Daugherty was complicated and fractured with shaded areas of ethics, built over time as various accusations attached themselves to him. In essence the charges were influence peddling, kickbacks, and bribery, the accusation that for a fee the attorney general refused to pursue and prosecute criminal activities and manipulated federal rulings in favor of the payee. The web became all the more tangled because many of the illegal activities were pinned on the late Jess Smith, who was assumed to have acted with the knowledge and authority of the attorney general. The most sensational claims had Smith selling liquor permits to bootleggers, some vague evidence being stocks, bonds, cash, and other rewards tucked away in accounts in the Washington Court House Midland Bank owned by Daugherty's brother, Mal. The Senate investigation was ruled over by the colorful Senator Burton Wheeler, who had a good eye for a sensational head-line—and was being trailed by Bureau of Investigation agents.

During a February conversation Dr. Boone noted that Daugherty "did not seem worried about investigation on his Department," but the attorney general craftily lined up support for his cause. He even turned to Boone: "If this case of mine comes to trial, I might want you to testify in regard to the peculiarities, if any, of Jess Smith, his nervousness and general condition for the last two years of his life. I hope to talk with you personally before the case is tried. I have no doubt in my mind that Smith was practically crazy part of the time. Of course, he never said anything to me about the matter in which his name is in-volved. It was the understanding that he was not to become connected in any way with any government matter, and he never did that I knew of, unless it was in this and I learned of his connection with this matter long after . . . you might be called upon the testify as to my illness . . . and to what extent I was able to keep track of what Jess Smith was doing." He further told Boone, "I am all right as far as I am concerned, but I don't know what others did and what others did may cause concern or give reason for suspicion." In reply Boone hedged about volunteering as a character witness for Harry. "In any event," Boone asserted, "I must speak out the truth . . . so far as my knowledge goes, [it] will do you no harm." On advice of his counsel, Daugherty never had Boone summoned.[10]

On March 12, with Senator Smith Brookhart as chairman, the Wheeler Committee called as its first witness the perennial flapper Roxy Stinson, now presenting herself respectably in horn-rimmed eyeglasses. Angry at the Daugherty brothers for their refusal to turn over the full amount of an $11,000 bank account she claimed Jess had left for her alone—and not to share with Harry and Mal—she was willing to spill some beans. Roxy was also being trailed by a G-man, and her hotel room was being bugged. During the hearings she talked about Jess and Harry drinking and dealing at the K Street greenstone house of Ohio lobbyist Howard Mannington and at Ned McLean's H Street town house. She told of seeing Jess with thousand-dollar bills to share with the Daughertys and carrying valises of purloined whiskey, courtesy of Justice Department medicinal permits. Harding was suggested as one of five recipients sharing in a $33 million Sinclair Oil deal, but Roxy claimed that Jess and Harry had been sore that they hadn't been let in on it. While she said she "felt certain that Smith had died by his own hand because he had been so thorough in 'putting his house in order,' " she also left the door open to a more dastardly possibility, asserting that "Jess Smith was deathly afraid of a revolver." She denied Harry's claim that she was a "vicious woman . . . a disappointed woman and all that stuff."

Burns and Daugherty began receiving notes from Ohioans disparaging Roxy's character. One called her a "notorious liar." Another wrote Burns that she had "numerous men friends and that she made an effort to get $5,000 from one of them at blackmail." One "negro preacher" wrote Daugherty that Roxy could not be telling the truth because she was "a divorced wife" trying to "revenge her former husband." Yet another told of a wholesale tobacco buyer's "love nesting" with her for a week at Cleveland's Gibson Hotel. Harry received his share of hate mail, some of it reflecting a prevalent, if extremely expressed, cynicism about the Harding administration. An anonymous "ex-soldier" thought that all the "big crooks" opposed the bonus bill because "they are afraid there won't be any money left for them to steal. That goes for all that whole Cabinet including Harding, Coolidge, yourself and Mellon. . . . If you had any self-respect you would do what your friend Smith did, but you are too yellow to do that. . . . Harding died for being crooked and I hope that God will punish you the same way."

Roxy was but an appetizer for the tabloid press. On March 14 Gaston Means took the stand to build on some of the ground she had laid, regaling how Forbes, Fall, Smith, and Daugherty attended drinking parties at the K Street house of Harding crony and lobbyist Howard Mannington. RUM AND HARDING AIDE IN STORY OF GATHERING PLACE, cried the New York *Daily News*. Means gave details: Jess and Mannington, in tandem with Harry, sold liquor permits to bootleggers, and Jess and Harry got huge kickbacks after fixing a deal between the alien property custodian and a Swiss manufacturer whose American factory had been seized. Means told the investigating committee that the Hardings had knowingly attended the McLeans' screening of the Dempsey-Carpentier prizefight film, illegally transported across state lines. They had not—though Coolidge, Daugherty, Hughes, Fall, and most of the Cabinet *had*.[11]

The colorful story about the fight film made national headlines and particularly enraged the Duchess. As a director of the board of the reorganized *Marion Star* she felt she had a voice in the wire stories and reporting printed in the newspaper by the new owners, Louis Brush and Roy Moore, and her old friend, the editor George Van Fleet:

> I was furious at Van Fleet for an article I saw in the *Star* about Hughes seeing the prize fight pictures etc., but they had dragged Warren into it too. Then, they weren't satisfied with that, but Moore in his crazy idea "to feature stunt" had it placed on top of first page and in brackets. Just quoting what Means said. In the first place, Warren Harding was not there. 2nd place, Hughes was telling how he had gone to this dinner but knew nothing about what picture, if any, was to be shown. It was a large dinner and you know Evalyn gets all these pictures before they have been released. Be that as it may, why drag Warren Harding in? All a lie to begin with & it would have been a very easy thing for Van or Moore to have telegraphed me. When the *Marion Star* has to publish such rot, I think things are coming to a pretty pass. Supposing it did come over the wire? Warren is not here to defend himself. Well, what I told Louis Brush was aplenty and I told him I wanted him to take it back to Moore and Van.[12]

One by one, other witnesses chipped away at Harry's reputation by focusing on the antics of Jess Smith. Harry's stenographer, Mary Yeager, testified that on numerous occasions she took dictation on "personal matters" for Jess at Justice since he was "a friend of the administration" and that he traveled on government funds. The imprisoned bootlegger George Remus testified that his meetings with Jess were to procure whiskey permits, at which he was successful, and for protection against potential trouble with law enforcement agents. He estimated cumulative payments of nearly $300,000 for protection alone, and almost three dollars on each case of whiskey covered by the permits, for a total in excess of $500,000. The payments continued after Remus had been arrested and convicted, with Jess having promised that if the Court of Appeals or even the Supreme Court sustained the lower court in the conviction, arrangements would be made to obtain a commutation of sentence so that Remus would not have to go to the penitentiary. Jess had assured Remus that Harry was kept fully abreast of every detail by him. Daniel E. Smith, Mannington's house manager, testified that twice in 1921 there were shipments of twenty cases of liquor delivered there, for which Jess had signed. A receipt proved one of the deliveries.

Confiscated liquor was also revealed to be part of the H Street booty. When large trunks that leaked whiskey at Union Station were discovered by the baggage master, they were reported to the Justice Department, which confiscated the liquor. The stockpile was eventually placed in a storage security warehouse, and largely under the administration of Frank Burke "withdrawals were made, and liquors given promiscuously to a host of officials and citizens."

The former First Lady was then dragged briefly and indirectly into the hearings, tied to Jess and his liquor supply. One George Clark claimed that she "had stopped a trip of the *Mayflower* until Jess Smith, who had boarded the boat against [her] protest and without [her] knowledge, had been routed out and put ashore with his bootlegging supplies." What did not come out in the hearings but was gathered by Burns's agents for him was far more damaging to the Hardings. A March 23 memo stated that the representative of a "certain New York interest" had told the Burns agent in a secret Majestic Hotel room meeting on March 19 that the representative "under the direction of Mr. Jess Smith and Mr. Harry Daugherty had taken whiskey from the Department of Justice to President Harding at the White House and to Dr. Sawyer, the president's physician . . . that he also overheard confidential conversations between Mr. Harry Daugherty and Mr. Jess Smith regarding certain money[s] that were to be received from Mr. Orr and others in New York coming from illegal withdrawals of whiskey, under false permits. Also, that he had declared, under oath, that he had knowledge of certain females who were intimate with Mr. Daugherty and they could give damaging testimony regarding his official and private conduct and this messenger had given the names and location and addresses of several of them."

A hint of Harding's private life came as Smith's activities were reviewed in detail. An audit of his Riggs Bank account showed securities worth almost $300,000, and one in Ohio with $80,000 in securities. Access to "Jess Smith Account No. 3" in Mal Daugherty's bank, however, was blocked by the brothers. Publicly this was described only as a "political account" stemming from the 1920 campaign used jointly by Daugherty and Jess and assumed to be a deposit spot for $50,000 worth of a Liberty bond payoff. Under oath Daugherty refused to testify about it, in part, he said, because he had been the personal attorney of Warren and Florence Harding and didn't want to betray them.

A year later Harry admitted that he had burned the records of this account, and he pleaded the Fifth when asked about them. That news not only fueled the idea that Jess had been killed because he knew too much but stirred speculation that Harry was hiding a dark secret about Harding to protect his reputation. Harry's lawyer suggested this to reporters: "It was not anything connected with his case that impelled him to refrain from [testifying]. . . . If the jury knew the real reason for destroying the ledger sheets they would commend rather than condemn Mr. Daugherty." In further implying that Harry did so out of loyalty to Harding, his lawyer said that the account had held at the ready funds to deal with Warren's "affairs of the heart." He was likely referring to the blackmail fund, from which Carrie Phillips had been reputedly paid monthly until Harding's death.

There was, thankfully for the Duchess, no revelation of the blackmail fund. Time also spared her the knowledge of attempts to establish a similar fund for another woman. Nan Britton, still struggling financially, made a quiet inquiry to Jimmy Sloan asking if he knew if Harding had made any private arrangements in the way of $50,000 for little Elizabeth Ann. Sloan discreetly approached Dick Crissinger about the possibility of Harding friends' contributing a fund, similar to the arrangement Daugherty made in 1920 for Carrie Phillips, with which Sloan was familiar. Crissinger wanted to help, but when Sloan called again, Sloan was shut out. Nan's effort was seen by loyalists as blackmail and, if it were learned of by the press, a potentially more explosive scandal than Teapot Dome. Nan was certain that Crissinger had "approached someone in the meantime" who talked him out of it. Boone noted in his private diary on February 8, 1924, "G.S. [General Sawyer] told me Crissinger had sent for him late this P.M. and told him some things that made his 'teeth chatter,' " although Nan placed this as occurring a year later. She was also unsuccessful in her attempt to find work as a secretary with the Harding Memorial Association. In a routine acknowledgment the Duchess turned her down.[13]

As the reputations of the Harding cronies seemed to deteriorate through the spring, so too did America's love of its late President. The former First Lady was herself under suspicion, rumors circulating that much of her wealth had been illegally earned. With the McLeans and Daugherty under fire, Florence herself was placed under surveillance by the Wheeler Committee. "You know," she later confided to a friend, "my door was watched constantly. My telephone was plugged, detectives were watching every act of my secluded life." She fretted to Jennings, "Congress is in an awful mess. If Warren could only have lived, I feel sure some of this would have ceased long ago." In despair, Florence yet again turned to the metaphysical, hoping to contact Warren through a medium. When Sir Arthur Conan Doyle began declaring that he spoke frequently with President Harding from the other side, Evalyn went to smoke him out when he lectured in Washington. "He got crazy in the end," she recalled, confronting him by telling him: "I think you are absolutely on the wrong track and had better go back to writing detective stories." There was no evidence that Florence ever did get to "talk" with Warren after his death.[14]

Meanwhile the mounting claims against Daugherty placed the attorney general under unbearable heat, particularly since his self-defense was so vehement. He refused to permit a "fishing expedition" through Justice's confidential files, and he attacked the Wheeler Committee for detaining Gaston Means in Washington when his trial for larceny and conspiracy was about to begin in New York. Jennings told Florence that he hoped Daugherty would "not make the mistake of talking too much," for it would not help either "him or his chief."

"Coolidge was loath to believe that such things were possible" about Daugherty, according to Herbert Hoover. "From this man's long-time character, he should never have been in any government. Finally Hughes and I went to the President and urged Daugherty's removal. Coolidge had a high sense of justice and asserted that he had no definite knowledge of wrongdoing by Daugherty and could not remove him on rumors. We urged that Daugherty had lost the confidence of the whole country and himself should be willing to retire for the good of public service." Doc Sawyer turned his knife into Daugherty as well, speaking to President Coolidge about how Harry's mental and physical health prevented him from effectively doing his work. "President thinks A.G. unbalanced," Dr. Boone scribbled two days after Sawyer's meeting.

"If he [Coolidge] is disposed to allow this persecution of me to continue," Harry told Boone, "that's his business. I don't see how he can do it, considering the respect he has for me and that I am entitled to from him. . . . He knows all the facts, unless he is being lied to, as I suspect, by certain persons whose malicious activity and deceitful treatment I am surprised have not been detected. " Coolidge, however, made it clear that the continuing trial and troubles dogging Daugherty would drag into the November election and threaten a Republican victory. The "strange man," as Harry called Coolidge, finally requested his resignation as attorney general. He agreed but later demanded a statement from Coolidge absolving him. The forced resignation, Harry wrote the President, was the "only thing that did me an injury that lasts, and unless by some act or utterance of yours, while you are yet in office, you remove a suspicion, it will go on forever to my great detriment

and injustice. . . . [T]rials and court actions and findings, as well as un-
questionable facts, have proven my integrity and faithfulness." Coolidge
refused.[15]

Harry asked the Duchess for a similar letter attesting to the fact
that his innocence and ignorance of Jess's misdeeds were always believed
in by President Harding and her. Florence wrote Mac about the request
and her ultimate decision to send a letter of personal support—short of
what Daugherty needed:

> I have been facing a most trying situation. I did not see Harry when he
> was here, but he sent George [Christian] and Dr. Sawyer down with an
> outline of what he wished me to say. It was impossible. Harry had
> worked on both George's and the Dr.'s feelings to such an extent that
> I made up my mind I would have to fix things up by my "lonesome
> self." After lying awake half of the night I decided on what I finally sent
> to Judge Sater. This morning George arrived with a message but he
> thought mine very good and perfectly safe. Poor Harry my heart aches
> for him and he is broken in body and spirit. I have never set eyes on
> him since the first time of his return from the South. No use talking,
> Mac, if he ever needed friends he needs them now. Right or wrong, I
> could not refrain from sending those few words.

Jennings dosed her with reality by pointing out that "While no
direct responsible testimony has been produced connecting him with any
crookedness, personally, his affiliations with people of unsavory transactions and repute—men Warren had to banish from Washington—has
been developed." Florence believed, "Notwithstanding all the vicissi-
tudes Attorney General Daugherty has experienced, his letters to the
press have been most dignified and have shown great understanding,"
but she soon reported on the sad, final break between the two old
campaign comrades. "Guess Harry did not care much for my message—
he was in Washington two days ago. Did not call me up, nor have I
had a word from him." They never spoke or wrote to each other again.
Shortly after, when she greeted a student at her apartment, Florence
reflected, "I have only a year or two more at the most. But you are
young—young enough to live to see how many of my husband's friends
will be loyal to him."[16]

Florence refused to consider the possibility that there existed jus-
tification for the inquiries into Fall or Daugherty. "I regret to say the
same disgraceful performances still continue on Capitol Hill," she wrote
Alec Moore, the ambassador to Spain, "but from all over the country

are coming protests now[,] and the official body [Congress] are insisting that the tax laws must be passed. It is very apparent that certain people have been hearing from home!" Florence had developed a political blind eye. Nor did she seem to find irony in her own activities, which, if publicly learned, would have cast her in a negative light. In response to the same letter in which Jennings railed against charges that Harding's health had broken because of his "too sudden stopping of the use of intoxicants," she pointed out no hypocrisy in Mac's invitation to also dine at a friend's home who, Mac further wrote, "proposes to serve some Sparkling Burgundy he has preserved from pre-Prohibition days, with a view to your entertainment."

Tucked away in her suite away from the practical realities of the scandals, the Duchess angrily crumpled the daily newspapers' accounts of the hearings, after reading every detail, every editorial. "Greatly distressed" about the efforts to attack Warren's character, she termed those disreputable people mentioned in testimony as his friends to be "the merest casual visitors." On several occasions she was at the point of appearing on Capitol Hill to testify in "a response to what was being said by witnesses and others prominent in the inquiries with respect to her husband" and give "the public an understanding of Mr. Harding's part in certain acts that had figured in the testimony far different from the apparent popular impressions." After consulting Mac, Evalyn, and Christian, the Duchess decided that her appearance might make her "the centre of a public controversy." She ultimately decided to "bear these insinuations in silence" since going to the trials would compromise her dignity.

Mac tried to calm her with what proved to be a prescient, if historically ambiguous, notion: "Cultivate philosophy, be patient and long suffering, knowing that every president of the United States has run the gamut of calumny and been vindicated by time, with the exception of those few who were too weak to leave an impress upon the minds of men or upon the pages of history." On a personal note he urged her to "not soften yourself by leading a cloistered life" in the capital, despite the scandals. Otherwise, he suggested, she might as well live among the familiarity of Ohio. As the hearings went on into spring, however, and more sensational revelations popped up with each new session, the Duchess refused to socialize casually about town: "I am going to sit tight until this storm flows over. It certainly can not go on much longer."[17]

The widow's most public appearance during her stay in Washington was at the February 28 Congressional Memorial Service to Warren, held at the Capitol. At the service Charles Evan Hughes mentioned the Duchess, who prominently wore her mourning ring fashioned after Queen Victoria's, and all eyes turned to her in the gallery: ". . . he was most blessed of fortune, winning the woman of his choice—Florence Kling—his partner in all his struggles and achievements, who with sagacity and never-failing loyalty worked by his side when opportunity was slender and only increased her efforts as his interests broadened; who brought rare grace and distinction to the discharge of the highest responsibilities, the sharer of every burden, his most trusted counselor, the companion of his soul. . . ." The service marked open resentment toward the Harding crowd by the Coolidge crowd. "Miss Harlan saw to it that I got a ticket," said Boone, who sat behind the Duchess. "I felt Mrs. H should have thought about this herself. I got Capt. Andrews a ticket thru Mrs. Coolidge. He likewise incensed at improper evidence of gratitude."

Although she was willing to see the new First Lady, the former First Lady commanded her to the Willard. "Mrs. C. told me Mrs. H. has set a day & hour for former to call at Willard Hotel but resented such under circumstances," Boone further recorded. "There has been no meeting to date but have talked to each other on phone." Neither Coolidge ever did call on her. Nor were White House invitations extended to her, though Edith Wilson received them.[18]

The Duchess still had her circle, however narrow its reach. On Easter Sunday Evalyn sent her huge buckets of spring flowers and fruit, as did other friends and family members, and a Supreme Court justice and General Pershing called. With spring Florence's spirits seemed to lift. On March 23 Florence, "affable and in good spirits," had Boone up for lunch. In April there was a curious boom to nominate Florence Harding as Ohio's Republican gubernatorial candidate, with the plan of nominating her for President in 1928. Several Ohio political leaders asked Jennings about the story, and while he responded that Florence had "no personal political ambitions," he was not so sure. "I trust this [her lack of ambition for office] is not an unwarranted statement," he wrote her, "although I said that I had not any word from you about it." No, she was not running for office anytime soon.[19]

Spring, however, brought more personal humiliations. An April 15 headline, BURNS ACCUSES KIN OF HARDING, detailed how Harding's brother-in-law, Heber Votaw, as superintendent of prisons, had been suspiciously lax in permitting the narcotic drug ring to flourish in sales within the Atlanta Penitentiary. The "Federal Prison Dope sensation" made for garish and embarrassing headlines: VOTAW FOOT ON PRISON

DOPE RING LET HIGHER UPS ESCAPE. The former warden, superintendent, and guard all testified that Votaw had blocked investigation of the dope ring—and fired the guard for aiding an investigation. The guard also revealed that the Harding in-law had let Jess's friend the imprisoned bootlegger Remus live in a private apartment with bath and actually be served dinner in the chapel. More embarrassing to Florence than Heber's troubles or the breaking stories of Carolyn Votaw's gallivanting about with Forbes was the publication of a private letter written by Doc to the committee investigating the Veterans Bureau saying that Harding had known about Forbes's misdeeds while he was still serving as bureau director, meaning that the President had committed a felony. The Duchess made only a pale defense of Doc to Jennings: ". . . when he sent his letter to each member of the committee, he never dreamed it would be given for publication."

Sawyer said he "still felt the responsibility for those at W.H.," yet he frequently left Washington for Marion—much to Coolidge's relief. Boone recorded that "Pres. said he always felt better when 'old Doctor Sawyer away.'" Coolidge was a difficult patient who didn't like his doctors to tell him much about his health as he was being treated. Meanwhile Sawyer held fast to the prestige of the White House and, whenever he returned, became suspicious of anything he could construe as a scheme to replace him. His resentment of Boone ran deep. The young doctor had quickly pursued a friendship with Grace Coolidge and was openly hoping to succeed Sawyer as White House doctor. Nasty behavior by Sawyer was not uncommon. One morning he was "too mad to talk" to Boone for his conversing with the Coolidges about pollen and allergies and held open his office door for Boone in a rude gesture that indicated the younger man should just leave.

There was also the first serious questioning by the Coolidge crowd about the gross misdiagnosis of Harding's death. Secretary Work now flatly stated that Sawyer had not been competent enough in homeopathy advances to treat a President. Boone recalled of Doc: "His personality had changed very much the latter months of our association. He became hypercritical, ultra sensitive, [having] imagining[s] just made of suspicions. Seemed to have lost the grip of himself, showed a sense of insecurity, of appearance noticeably. Sometimes he seemed to wander around rather aimlessly. Of course, I felt he was never at home during the Coolidge regime. . . ." Doc even told Work that he was going to quit because he "could not be responsible for a 'self-medicator,'" meaning President Coolidge, who took pills on his own.[20]

As the walls started closing in on Doc, Florence made a concerted effort to distance herself from him and branch out on her own again. Although she "grew shy" about attending a dinner for Girl Scouts whom she had earlier greeted in her apartment, she made several trips outside Washington. Bestowed with a number of honors, including an L.L.D. from the Ohio Northern University College of Law, she attended no such ceremonies. In April, however, Florence spontaneously agreed to attend the laying of a cornerstone of a modest vocational school in Bridgeport, Connecticut, named for Warren. She stood the train trip quite well, and it gave her confidence to join Evalyn—upon her return from Florida—on a trip to New York without guards or any other aides. Traveling in the McLean rail car, given the use of John Wanamaker's limousine through an arrangement by George Christian, who now worked for him, and escorted about by one of Harding's old friends, a Mr. Kellar, the two women took in plays and shopping.

Florence also began entertaining as a single hostess—without the Sawyers around—and had a stream of friends and visitors into her suite, sometimes treating them to dinner in the hotel dining room. Despite the speculation about how Harding's death had affected her, the state of her own health, and the embarrassment over the assorted scandals, the Duchess was vital. In April she decided she would not only attend the Republican National Convention but make a summer trip to Europe. "I am still thinking very seriously of crossing the water this summer," she wrote Alec Moore. "Should I go, in all probability my dear friend, Mrs. Tod [Evalyn's secretary] will come along. . . . We would not go until after the convention and should this trip really come to pass, you will be duly notified in time to meet us in France."[21]

Now making longer-term plans with her own life, she made clear her intention not to retire to Marion and live with any family members. If she was not particularly close to the Klings, neither was she to the Hardings. "I hear Deacon's wife has been visiting in Washington," she told Jennings, "but she staid [*sic*] clear of my domicile." There was now friction with Warren's family, thanks to Doc's "unworthy criticism" that Carolyn's agreement to become a trustee of downtown Pittsburgh Harding Memorial Hospital damaged the Marion memorial fund-raising effort, and his pressing Florence to write Deac to chastise his sister. Carolyn and Deac were thoroughly insulted, she questioning the "influence [on Florence] of some persons" who were "prejudiced and unreliable." Deac wrote Florence that despite her "ambition, your experiences, your judgment and your devotion to the life of my dear brother," his siblings had "the freedom to use our best sense" without the "attempt of others to tell us what not to do." Although he "mingled with feelings of kindness" this rebuke, he barely veiled his distrust of Sawyer by concluding that perhaps the family's reaction might also be "useful to you in some way."

Planning to settle in Washington, Florence was to buy a house there—she had Catherine New scouting for one—and finally get to writing *her* book. So many people with the slightest connection to Harding were claiming to be his official biographer that Florence finally had the executor issue a statement to the Associated Press that "Ultimately, a biography will be prepared and published either by Mrs. Harding or someone acting under the direction and approval of herself. . . ." Realizing that her initial idea of self-publishing Warren's Alaska speeches would be a "costly and uncertain proposition," she finally gave permission for Kathleen Lawler to begin a book on the 1920 campaign, which they had initially discussed doing together. Florence was just not ready to begin writing. She admitted to Mac Jennings, "It seems to me, some of my friends, unthinkingly, or otherwise, are lying awake nights trying to think up something for me to do. . . . There goes the bell and I think it is Evalyn. . . ."

Interestingly she returned to an idea of doing some work for animal rights, as she had considered doing had Warren not been elected to the Senate. Despite a warning from Mac that her support of a radical antivivisection group not only was wrong because of the medical advances experimentations on dogs provided but would "bring upon your head the displeasure of those who know the necessity" of them, the Duchess retorted on this issue just as strongly: "You did not know it, of course, but I have been fighting vivisection for years and particularly since coming to Washington. Outside of Baltimore there is a real terrible place. In the animal kingdom there are plenty of animals of a much lower type than an intelligent dog for them to do their experimenting on. I am dead against it, and I am for the dog, and I am going to fight on, and if I have any money left (which I won't if I keep staying at the Willard) some of it is going to go to that cause. . . ."[22]

Meanwhile not only Doc's status at the White House, but sixty-four-year-old Doc himself were deteriorating. "General Sawyer never seemed the same, physically or in disposition," recorded Boone. "He seemed to build up quite a wall about himself. . . . Not as mentally alert and as keen as he had been. He seemed to tire readily, evidenced little mental quirks, particularly of a suspicious nature . . . he wanted very much to be retained at the White House . . . but . . . there was kind of a . . . wishing to be back home in Marion. . . ." Getting the message by the increasingly infrequent calls for his services by the Coolidges and their reliance on Boone, Sawyer told several people he was resigning, but Boone learned only from the morning papers on June 25 that Doc was returning to Marion. Boone offered his appreciations to Doc and said he would be willing to care for Doc's surviving prize patient, the Duchess. The older man did not respond kindly. Three days later he took bitter pleasure in telling Boone that Coolidge had decided to name James Coupal, who had served him as Vice President, as the new White House physician.

Florence got the first inclinations of Doc's deeper intentions when she received several letters from Dr. Carl asking her to join his parents and spend the "summertime" at White Oaks Farm. "Many thanks for a renewal of your kind invitation to return to your roof," she replied politely but formally, on July 8, turning down the offer.

In the early summer an unsigned pamphlet began circulating in Washington. This anti-Republican leaflet was now trying to link the octopus of Harding administration scandals with a sensationalized version of Harding's death by raising questions about Doc's newspaper quote at the time of the death that he had been out of the sickroom for ten minutes only to return and find the President dead with Florence there. In July, when a reporter tried to find Doc and ask him for his reaction to the quote in the pamphlet, Sawyer was suddenly unavailable, said to be leaving for or already on his way to Marion. That such a misquote from a newspaper account during the time of Harding's death went unanswered of course only increased the already existing undercurrent of suspicion. A clear and direct statement from Sawyer clarifying the misquote would have put it to rest. Instead the question was simply ignored. And Doc got out of town.[23]

Florence seemed to relax considerably. She spent the July Fourth holiday at Friendship, laughing, dancing, enjoying herself with Evalyn, the young McLeans, and their menagerie. As the first anniversary neared, she could dispassionately ruminate about Warren's death with Kathleen Lawler, objectively assessing the situation by saying he "would have lived a little longer" had they not made the arduous western tour. "He was determined to go and while we knew that he was a sick man, we thought that if we could once get him across the continent, and on the boat to make the trip through the Panama Canal, he would recuperate. He would have had a month away from all the worries, have been where he could not be reached, and would be obliged to relax and rest. It was thought that the water trip would restore his health and put him on his feet."

In mid-July, however, there was the slightest recurrence of her kidney ailment. "My old trouble has been giving me some annoyance, and I don't mind telling you I was quite discouraged for a few days," she admitted to Mac Jennings. Instead of asking to be treated by Doc Sawyer, however, Florence strenuously insisted that he not be called. With Kathleen Lawler at her side every day, the Duchess tried to will her health back. She knew that if the Sawyers discovered her ailment, they would insist that she return to Marion. She did not want to go back. In the six months she had struggled through the scandals and depression, she had also carved out the beginning of a new life in Washington.

"She loved to be there," wrote Lawler. "Her old spirit was still dominant. She strongly combatted the arrangement, stoutly contending that she could and would soon regain her health. . . . She lost strength steadily. On many days, only her will power enabled her to leave her bed. She insisted always that she was equal to the exertion. She was so ill, however, by Friday, July 18, that we became alarmed and advised Dr. Sawyer at Marion of her condition. He arrived at the Willard Hotel the next morning. After an examination the doctor said that she must go back to Marion, at once, accompanied by a nurse. Dr. Sawyer was insistent." Doc wanted to take control and told her, "[Y]ou must have a nurse. You are unfit to travel without one." Florence became enraged. She had no intention of being brought back to Marion and, said Lawler, "prepared to defend her position." She justified that if she were to leave Washington with a nurse, it would be reported that she was about to die. "And I have not the slightest notion of dying yet, Dr. Sawyer. I shall not have a nurse."

Sawyer countered her. "Very well, you must either take a nurse or Mandy must come down tonight and take you back on Monday." Again the Duchess was insistent on not being forced back to Marion. "Mrs. Harding voiced her disappointment in no uncertain terms," said Lawler. "She repeated again and again that it was unnecessary for her to leave Washington." Sawyer would not leave until she agreed. Lawler said that since Sawyer was still officially her doctor, the former First Lady "was obliged to agree," but after Doc finally left with his ultimatum, the Duchess let loose, her hard-won mastery of her daily life and emotions both now at risk. "I cannot be reconciled to going back to Marion. I do not want to go. It is wholly unnecessary. I will be all right. I much prefer to remain here. We are accomplishing so much and we'll have a nice time together. I want to stay here now that we have my work so well in hand. For the first time since I entered the White House, I have my own affairs properly arranged and as I want them, and it is my purpose to keep them as nearly current now as possible.

For the first time since we started for Alaska my personal correspondence is up to date."

The Sawyers were relentless. Mandy Sawyer arrived at the Willard on Monday, July 21, and lunched in the suite with the Duchess and Kathleen. Then they headed downstairs to Florence's car, and she went in without help, along with Mandy. In the end Florence had to make the choice she had always believed she would have to make when faced with her ailment. Whether the Rasputin in Doc had truly brainwashed her into believing that he was in fact the only person who could keep her alive or she realized she could have searched for another, more expert specialist is unknown. But if Evalyn kept her happy, Doc kept her alive.

"I tucked her into her automobile at the entrance to the hotel, for the last time," remembered Kathleen. "Though she was suffering intensely and had grown daily more spirituelle, she looked wonderfully well and never more attractive. She was handsomely outfitted, keen, alert, sparkling and responsive as ever. With her old time buoyancy of spirit and a happy smile, she waved her hand as she began the journey over the route she had so often joyously travelled."

Without fanfare Mandy and Florence boarded a train at Union Station. It was the last time Florence Harding was in the familiar station, the last she saw of Washington.

Evalyn had written Florence just before she returned to Ohio: "I think of you so often, and dread the thought of what it will be for you to go back to Marion!! You are so wonderful I know you will go through with it, but I know how hard it will be for you! We loved having you at Friendship and you know you will always have a home with us as long as either one of us lives!! . . . Take care of your self and don't do too much! You know how much we all love you."[24]

38

Life at the Sanitarium

When Maillard Hunt heard that Florence Harding was back in Marion, he offered to vacate the Harding house and break the lease so she could resume occupancy. "No, I will keep my bargain," she said. "I would not think of disturbing you. I can be perfectly comfortable meanwhile, in my brother's home when in Marion." She did not plan to retire here, just spend the summer where she would stay with Cliff Kling—usually. She believed that her being at the sanitarium was only to be treated by Doc, now and whenever she came to town suddenly or needed careful treatment. She still intended to return to Washington, yet as long as her life depended on Doc, she was essentially trapped in Marion.

The Sawyers claimed that Florence was there to stay. They said she had gone to Washington "just to finish up all the heavy correspondence." As Warren Sawyer told it, "She always planned on just coming to Marion and living out her days there. She wanted to come live with my family on the farm. They had a connecting bedroom on the downstairs floor of a nice bungalow for her. It was too hard for her to walk up and down stairs, so she was set up on the main floor." At White Oaks Farm the President's widow was treated like other patients. One week she was charged $7.90 for her long-distance calls, and $1.25 for an express shipment of apples. Except for "visits to old friends and neighbors or an occasional business trip" in the region, she was considered permanently "retired" to the sanitarium, "attending few functions outside those of the immediate Sawyer family." As one Marion resident later put it, "Florence was very much in the control of the Sawyers." She did make at least one visit to her grandchildren. Said their half sister Helen, five at the time, "I remember her because she gave me a quarter. A lot of money in those days. But she was just an old lady."[1]

On her return to Doc's care the Duchess kept busy by resuming a political battle she had begun in Washington. She wanted to have the long-term, loyal Harding attorney Hoke Donithen appointed to be Sixth

Circuit court judge. In the presence of Ohio's senators Frank Willis and Simeon Fess, Harding had promised to do so just before leaving for Alaska. When a vacancy occurred in July, the former First Lady wrote a straightforward letter to President Coolidge, with the request that this last Harding intention be fulfilled, citing that President Roosevelt had done so with every similar promise made by McKinley. She had her letter hand-delivered from the Willard and asked Willis and Fess to send corroborating letters to Coolidge, along with their support for the appointment.

"Recognizing and admitting the presidential prerogatives," said Kathleen Lawler, "Mrs. Harding was stunned by the response President Coolidge returned to her letter." Coolidge decided that he wanted to make the appointment from Kentucky, which had had no judge on the court for a great while. The Duchess raged against Coolidge. She wrote again to the Ohio senators with a new plan: "[I]f Kentucky cannot agree as to the judgeship, let's make every effort to secure Hoke's appointment." Then Coolidge refused to consider Donithen at all. This, said Lawler, "worried her to the last."

In Marion Florence could no longer escape the ghost she had managed to evade for a year. "Every Wednesday night I would take her for a ride in the country," said Warren Sawyer. "I didn't know why Wednesday had to be the night for some time, until I realized that the church bells were rung in Marion on that night. The day they brought President Harding home to Marion to bury him, they tolled the bells all day long. She couldn't stand the memory."

As "that fateful August 2nd" neared, Florence wrote Dr. Boone that life had become "so trying. Each day I have lived over those San Francisco days. The old adage that time softens grief is not true, so far as I am concerned, but I have had to meet it somehow, some way. I was ordered home peremptorily, by Doctor Sawyer, and my last visit in Washington suddenly terminated. I had a very narrow escape from a recurrence of my old trouble, and have been quite unable to understand the cause. However I am now coming out of it, and on the whole, am fairly well. . . ."

On the the first anniversary of Warren's death the heat was oppressive. "I have been only fair since coming home," she wrote Kathleen. "I have just been to a memorial service for Mr. Harding which was most trying." The event did, however, prompt her grieving process. Depending long-distance on Kathleen to help process correspondence, the widow was once again burdened with telegrams, cards and letters reminding her of Warren's death. "I find myself completely overwhelmed," she wrote. To mark the date, she composed a rare but heart-felt poem, "Gone but Not Forgotten," had it engraved in a small folder and tied with a half bow of black ribbon, and distributed it to friends:

> In the graveyard softly sleeping,
> Where the flowers gently wave,
> Lies the one I loved so dearly,
> And tried so hard to save,
> Husband how hard I tried to keep you,
> Prayers and tears were all in vain,
> Happy Angels came and took you,
> From this world of sorrow and pain,
> I would love to see your smiling face,
> And kiss your fevered brow,
> I would love to clasp you in my arms,
> And have my husband now,
> In my heart your memory lingers,
> Tenderly fond and true,
> There is not a day dear husband,
> That I do not think of you.[2]

As August went on, she rallied. "I am not up to my usual self because of this heavy cold along with my other troubles," she wrote Lawler. "My days are full and I look upon it as a blessing, because it gives me no time to indulge my grief, although this past week has been very trying." At the time she indicated her hopes to travel, writing a cousin, "I am slowly recovering from my old trouble . . . if I go anywhere it must be to Mrs. McLean at Bar H., pursuant to an invitation long ago accepted. Of course everything depends upon my condition and response to the Doctor's care and treatment. So far he has given me no encouragement whatsoever when I talk about going East and you know the summer is going very fast. It soon will be too cool for me to go up there. These are trying days for me, and the past two weeks especially have been difficult living over the anxious and sorrowful hours in San F. . . ." If Doc kept Florence from Evalyn, there were frequent attempts from Maine to boost Florence's spirits: ". . . you have the respect of the whole world!" Evalyn told her. "Don't work too hard. If there is anything in the world we can do let us know and we will do it with pleasure!"[3]

The sudden turn of events on September 21 changed everything. "My grandfather always got up with the sun, and he went to the farm and picked the eggs and milked the cows," Doc's grandson Warren Sawyer remembered. "And there was a big crescent drive of gravel in front of the main house. He went out then and raked the gravel. So on this one morning he came back around six to get breakfast. He talked to my father and grandmother. Then he went and talked to Mrs. Harding. She was the last one to see him." Charles E. Sawyer died at his sanitarium in Marion on September 23, outliving his most famous patient by one year and seven weeks.

"He never seemed to recover from the shock of the President's death and I could notice a great difference as time went on and how greatly the weight of that tragedy poured," Dr. Carl told Boone. Without realizing the irony of his statement, Carl added: "Father's passing on was almost identical with that of his friend, President Harding." Dr. Carl asserted that his father died of a heart attack, but in a curious twist, Boone scribbled a note to himself on September 23. "I believe from 'cerebral hemorrhage.' "

"It was strange about Mrs. Harding in a way," Mac Jennings wrote a mutual friend. "She bore her bereavement wonderfully at first and was her brave, practical, competent self. But month by month I could see that she was feeling her loss more and more and that it was robbing her of her power of resistance and the spirit with which she had fought the onslaught of her disease. The sudden death of Dr. Sawyer, almost in her presence, depressed her greatly." Publicly Florence made herself a strong presence at Doc's funeral and burial, shocked, but not defeated.[4]

The autocratic Dr. Carl claimed that Florence was only "making the best of the situation," and that, in fact, she was utterly devastated at the abrupt death of her protector. The prospect of living without the psychological comfort of Doc's seemingly magic power did provoke considerable anxiety about her returning to Washington. "The suddenness of the calling was a shock I was little prepared to meet and made me feel in connection with my sorrows of the last year, that my 'world was going to bits,' " she wrote her cousin after Doc's death. "Unless my health soon improves I do not see much in life for me. Each week I think—the next [week] will find me in Washington and here I am." Still in all, it was soon clear that Florence had no intention of making a home in a bungalow room on the grounds of a sanitarium for mental patients. Despite the pessimistic warnings of Dr. Carl, she now planned to return to Washington. She wrote Lasker that while Doc's death was "a great shock to all of us and his loss means much to me as he was not only my faithful physician, but my devoted friend," and although she was "making a very slow recovery from a recurrence from my illness and am not as yet able to make any plans for my return to Washington," she was "anxious to get settled there before winter comes."

Indeed there were more signs that she was interested in living rather than dying. The Indianapolis *Star* reported that the Duchess was finally to begin work on her memoirs. She was considering the offer of Nancy Christy, wife of the illustrator Howard Chandler Christy, to visit New York because "the change might be good." She kept current with her accounts, signing her checks for October, clearing her recent purchases from Uhler-Phillips. Starting on November 1, she wanted to stop having the rents due to her from the Star Building and the Mount Vernon house sent first to Harding estate manager and instead go directly to her. She continued fussing about her Smithsonian mannequin, requesting that a Harding Blue opera cloak be added to it.[5]

She certainly was no recluse in Marion—especially when it was a public appearance on behalf of her boys. As the parade of veterans went down Main Street on October 16, Defense Day, the former First Lady not only reviewed it but got out of her car and, a drizzle soaking her, stood in the curb to review the marchers. Later that afternoon at old Garfield Park the Duchess, swathed in black, sat with some friends under the covered Chautauqua pavilion and listened to the concert organized by the local Kiwanis. She went to Warren's tomb to hear a funeral dirge played for him, then engaged the Tenth Infantry guard detachment there in lively conversation for some time. Making regular visits, she came to know personally the officer and twenty-six enlisted men detailed to guard the vault—"my boys," she called them. Forrest Dotson, an eighteen-year-old guard there at the time, recalled, "Mrs. Harding would drive by very slowly. But she never got out of the car."

Several days after Defense Day, Florence learned that Harding Agriculture Secretary Henry Wallace had died. She had followed his slow demise in the press. On October 15 Boone had performed gallbladder and appendix surgery on Wallace, who died of "bacteriaemia" ten days later. "A most terrible case to lose," as Boone put it. This came on top of the tragic news that Laura Work had driven her motorcar off a new highway and been instantly killed.

A more public loss quite insulted her. According to reporter Robert Small, the Duchess "suffered a keen disappointment" when she "lost her vote in the presidential election." Having forgotten to register to vote in 1924, she was "much chagrined" when she learned that she had missed the deadline. When Florence appeared for a "special dispensation" from Ohio's secretary of state, the matter was given full consideration, but no loophole was found. "Only those who knew Mrs. Harding's deep interest in politics could appreciate how this dilemma hurt her," said Small. When President Coolidge refused to make the exception, she was deeply wounded. The incident was frustrating for this feminist who had so vigorously advocated the vote as women's civic duty, and it was also strangely ironic: The first vote of the first woman to vote for her husband for President became her only vote. After the deaths of her friends and the humiliation of being denied her vote, she "went to bed almost immediately and never left it alive," as one newspaper put it.[6]

She did leave it. Just once more. Sensing that Dr. Carl was keeping the former First Lady isolated, Evalyn went out to Ohio in her private train car, ostensibly just to have dinner with the Duchess but to probe gently the situation at the sanitarium, "where many of the patients were mental cases," and see if she could pry Florence away and back to Washington; "[Y]ou know you always have a home with us where ever we are," she had recently written her. Having been there for the Duchess upon her return from San Francisco and then permitting her to burn Warren's papers at Friendship, Evalyn had proved her genuine loyalty to, and her love for, Florence in a way that no other friends had. Although there was no evidence that Florence ever confronted Evalyn about Warren's trysts at Friendship, she had obviously been forgiven. And the embarrassing but brief brush with scandal that the McLeans experienced during the Teapot Dome trial in no way changed Florence's view of her tried and true companion.

"I persuaded her to come down to the car and have dinner. We tried hard to have a pleasant evening," wrote Evalyn. "When she was leaving, there in the railroad yards where she had come and gone in triumph so many times, she spoke with finality. 'I will never see you again.' 'Now, now,' I protested. 'You are going to get better and visit me.' 'Evalyn, this is the end.' "

Days later Florence developed a severe abdominal pain. When Carl released a public bulletin on November 3 that she was suffering again from nephritis, she became angry; she had wanted as little information as possible to be divulged. Cards, letters, and telegrams flooded White Oaks Farm. As had not been the case with her illness in the White House, the news of her condition was discouraging from the start. George Christian immediately left Washington and rushed to her side. Even she seemed to sense the inevitable, sternly refusing to let Carl call in specialists; he did "venture her displeasure" by summoning Dr. John Woods of Cleveland. Carl finally decided to perform surgery to adjust her twisted kidney tube days later, but the operation weakened her heart. On November 7 she became increasingly restless; the surgery had not resolved the blockage.

At her bedside daily Christian carried out many of Florence's requests, ordered with the kind of gentle finality that the dying give. She managed to scribble a note and had him pin it to some clothes: "If I die put these things on me. If anything happens to me use these articles to lay me out in, with a winding sheet. Think it too trying to put a dress on." She had a new will drawn up. After it was completed, she seemed to lie back in what Christian called "perfect comfort." As she worsened, she exercised no will whatsoever to grasp as tenaciously to life as she always had.

By November 14 her pulse had weakened, and there were signs of impending coma. Two days later, however, she was fully conscious again, able to eat, her pulse rate returning to normal. By November 20, however, she was failing rapidly, her breathing labored. Through the night she went in and out of a coma. Early the next morning she was read a get-well message from the Coolidges. Fully comprehending the message, she whispered her appreciation. It was her last moment of consciousness. With Carl and Mandy, Cliff Kling, and Christian beside her bed, she died at five minutes to nine. Sawyer listed her death as the result of myocarditis and chronic nephritis. Just before she had slipped away, she wrote out a check for $125 to provide a full Thanksgiving dinner for her boys guarding the Harding vault.

From a distance Evalyn, also confined to her own bed in illness, had reached out to Florence one final time, asking her to "have someone drop me a line how you are getting along." Florence had been read the letter but been too weak to reply. Evalyn was reflectively making her peace. "I think of you so often, and of the wonderful times we have had together and it just seems like it can't be true, that they are all over! You were so wonderful in the White House. As Mrs. Hale said yesterday, 'No one ever filled the place like Mrs. Harding did.' It must be a great comfort to know you have made such a success of life. . . ."[7]

Since the Kling mansion already had been closed for the winter by Cliff, Florence's coffin was placed in the large drawing room in the home of her niece Hazel Longshore. Initially the Klings would not permit the public to view her remains, but after strident protests that the Duchess had "never denied the public a privilege that she thought belonged to them," they relented. For two days Florence's body was on view and one Mose Ruth had to be hired to police the twelve thousand mourners who paid their respects—among them her old nemesis

Carrie Phillips. The Ohio Association of Newspaper Women, to which Florence had belonged, placed pink carnations in her coffin. Boone noted of the remains, "Amusing dress & posture in coffin—glasses left on."

The sky was leaden on November 23, the day the Duchess was buried. The Cabinet sent a wreath, and Secretary Hughes remembered her publicly as "a woman of extraordinary strength of character and her husband's most faithful counselor." The Coolidges did not come to Marion. Grace delayed the release of the official social schedule, and the President had the White House flag lowered to half-mast and issued a message: "We are disappointed that her brave fight was in vain, but it is a source of pride to know that she made it, and so valiantly as to arouse the admiration of her countless friends." Appropriately enough, there was a touch of spiritualism in the public mourning, with Arthur Conan Doyle declaring that Warren's spirit "called out to his wife while she was on earth and actually summoned her to him and she went." The *Daily Editorial Digest* said it straighter when it said her death "marks the passing of a President Maker."

Amos Kling would have puffed up with his peculiar brand of pride at how important his little Flossie had become. The streets of Marion were packed on the day of the funeral, thousands of men, women, and children standing silently, their heads bare and bowed as the coffin passed them. The directors of the Marion Retail Merchants' Bureau ordered all stores closed for business between twelve-thirty and five-thirty and asked that its members drape their windows in black. All town flags were at half-mast, tied with black crepe. It was the least they could do for the former Miss Kling.

The "mite wild" little girl who used to sled with vigor down Gospel Hill was carried in her coffin out of the Longshore house by Marion names that would have been familiar to old Amos—Rapp, Van Fleet, Sawyer, Prendergast, Uhler, Shaffner, and Schroeter—to the Kling church, Epworth Methodist, where at two o'clock her pastor, Jess Swank, conducted a brief service, opened by the singing by the Columbus Glee Club. After a prayer by Warren's Baptist preacher, the Reverend George Landis, the flower-laden coffin, escorted by a delegation of one hundred soldiers and officers ordered there by Coolidge from Fort Hayes in Columbus, made its way past spots that had been familiar to Florence since childhood.

The soldiers proceeded into the cemetery and were joined by the twenty-three guards at the Harding vault; the Duchess was surrounded, one last time, by her "boys." Also in force were Ohio newspaper publishers, who considered her one of their own. As they stood around the gray stone vault, a chilly wind swept the air, snowflakes starting to flurry. Crammed into the tiny vault were Klings and Hardings and friends—the Christians, Van Fleets, Jenningses, Reddy Baldinger, Harry Barker, Ned McLean, Hoke Donithen, Mandy Sawyer, along with Edwin Denby, John Weeks, Hubert Work, and Catherine New—as Florence was laid beside Warren. Eternally nearby were her parents, her first husband, and her only son. Just as Landis pronounced the final benediction the sound of the Columbus Glee Club softly rose in her signature song, "The End of a Perfect Day." As it ended, the calm was snapped by a bugle sounding taps. Everyone emerged into the rapidly accumulating snow. The vault was sealed, and with it so many of the secrets of the Duchess and her Warren.[8]

Alice Longworth, who hated nothing more than sentiment, was unable to get through to Evalyn McLean during the 1924 Christmas season. Mrs. McLean was not seen at any teas or balls or dances or receptions. "I heard that she just sobbed, for several weeks straight through. No hysterics, just weeping. For weeks on end."

The day after Florence's death there appeared an unsigned, if sentimental, remembrance of the Duchess in the Washington *Post*, quite different from the stiff obituaries of the era, drafted by one hand, that of Evalyn's, for no person had ever come to break the facade and know the wife of the Marion editor as well as the Washington editor's wife: "Florence Harding was a good woman, as good as gold, as true as steel, as brave as a lion, as gentle as a dove, as sweet as the flowers . . . she wrote simply to two friends who loved her as she loved them. . . . 'I know that you understand what is in my heart.' Foremost among this remarkable woman's personal qualities were courage and resoluteness, but even these paled before her inflexible fidelity to her friendships and her friends."[9]

39

Remembering

Before the pink Florence Harding roses planted by the Duchess on the White House lawn withered and died the first summer after her death, her reputation had already begun to unravel. If Warren Harding's stature started to slip seven months after his death with the burgeoning scandals, it took only five months for Florence's to do so.

Just weeks after Florence was buried, Madame Marcia began peddling her story as fortune-teller to "senators and Cabinet members and congressman, and judges, bankers, lobbyists, diplomats," crowned by her role as First Seeress to the First Lady. Her first article, in *Collier's*, published in May 1925, reprinted her letters from Florence, complete with her zodiac code name Jupiter signature. Marcia even said that she had been accurate in predicting poverty for herself because she had turned down $50,000 for four missing oil leases! Later, in 1938, even from a hospital bed, crippled by an operation, an ice pack against her head, Marcia confabulated: "For a quarter of a century I, Marcia, had been the hub of the wheel of our national government—and, now, through this woman who was the power behind the throne of her husband's administration, I ruled a nation of 120,000,000 people." During the 1926 McLeod Committee's investigation of the capital's "astrologers, seers, soothsayers, palmists, psychics and other fortuntellers," examining whether to hike further their annual $250 licensing fee, Marcia was called to testify. In the caucus room Marcia confronted the great Houdini, who favored higher fees, before a crowd of photographers and newsreel cameramen. "You're a smart man, Mr. Houdini. But perhaps I can tell you something you don't know. . . . When November comes around and the license is due, you won't be here." Houdini's grin fell. "You'll be dead." She was right. He died on October 31, 1926.

Marcia died of cancer as a welfare patient in the Washington Home for Incurables in the mid-1940s. She had been visited by Evalyn, who brought her healthy, home-cooked meals. And liquor.[1]

Six months after Marcia's article, America woke up on Christmas Day to the headline HARDING PAPERS BURNED BY WIDOW and read that the Duchess had "burned practically all the letters he had left concerning political and national affairs." She had unwittingly incriminated herself and Warren when she admitted to Frank Doubleday that she had destroyed the papers because she "feared some of it would be misconstrued and would harm his [Harding's] memory." Of course she hadn't burned everything. There were two boxes of letters locked away, but as the new president of the Memorial Association, Dr. Carl refused to make copies even for the Library of Congress, even after Daugherty insisted on it. Five days after Christmas 1925 Van Fleet told reporters that the papers destroyed were only "letters which may have been misconstrued by others than those for whom they were intended." As she sorted and prepared the letters for the furnace, Van Fleet added, Florence had repeated that she wanted "to do just what Warren wanted done." What had been intended as a clarification only deepened the controversy.

Other papers had been saved. George Christian had kept a box in the White House basement instead of sending them to Marion. Discovered during the Hoover presidency, the carton was sent to Marion, to join the papers that sat on the precarious wood shelves of Hoke Donithen, who agreed that they belonged in the Library of Congress. Fearful that some papers might incriminate his father in Harding's misdiagnosed health and death, however, Dr. Carl took decades to cull through each item himself, all the while denying access to the late President's family—many of whom were highly respected leaders in the medical profession. Harry Daugherty termed it a "rather peculiar situation."

Furthermore, Dr. Carl refused to permit any of the family, including Deac Harding and his son George, to be represented on the Harding Memorial Association. George Harding finally demanded to know why the family had been shut out. Carl "answered that he was in charge and that he wanted to handle it in his own way. He said he didn't want anyone to tell him what to do. He wanted to run things. . . . [W]e were not even invited to come to meetings, until Carl Sawyer died," said George.

How much Carl might have destroyed is unknown. It is known that he "separated the correspondence of a purely personal or private nature" from "official" papers. It is also known that he removed all medical records and references to Harding's health that reflected on Doc Sawyer in any way. Well into 1991 Carl's son, Warren, held on to medical records in a back room of his dilapidated house, overrun by cats, and stray folders of Florence Harding's papers showed up at central Ohio barn auctions. In 1964 Carl finished purging the remaining papers tucked in the bowels of the old White Oaks Farm and sent them off to the Ohio Historical Society in Columbus in a truck preceded by state troopers so "Teapot Dome people"—his reference to historians researching the scandal—couldn't hijack them. As archivists went through them, they noticed many gaps, only some of which Dr. Carl filled with suddenly "discovered" boxes. Soon after he died.[2]

There were other letters, however, that Dr. Carl never torched. These of course included Warren's missives to Carrie Phillips. The attorney for her estate said, "If old Doctor Sawyer had got hold of those letters, he'd have made a bonfire fast enough." The irony was that Harding had been given possession of the letters by Carrie but that he had chosen not to destroy them and returned them to her. And by the terms of Florence's will, all of Warren's writings were deeded "to the public for the benefit of posterity."[3]

Nan Britton insisted that Warren had asked her to destroy his love letters to her, so she did not publish any when she scandalized the nation in her book *The President's Daughter* (1927), revealing Harding as her lover and the father of her child. That Nan was an intimate partner of Warren's is hard to deny; among other things, her descriptions of Harding's lengthy letters to her on Senate stationery match the factual evidence of Carrie Phillips's similar collection. Whether her child was also his, only he and she knew. Daisy Harding, for one, believed Nan and provided lump sums for the child's support until Deac Harding halted the payments, disclaiming Nan as a blackmailer. Nan's book was countered by sycophantic Harding loyalist Charles Klunk with his booklet *The Answer;* in turn she sued for defamation of character. A sensational trial ensued in 1931, with Klunk's lawyer, Grant Mouser, calling Nan a "degenerate and pervert" whose move to "that vitiating and depraving atmosphere" of New York City had made her fall "in bad company."

Mouser brought the Duchess into the conflict, using Warren's "love for his good wife" as evidence against "distorted . . . deranged . . . demented . . . diabolical" Nan, who "had no respect for the sacred marriage tie" and "wished to undermine or distress the wife of Warren Harding." Mouser condemned Nan for pursuing a man "whom [*sic*] she knew had a beautiful home in Marion, who had lived with his devoted wife for 32 years, and who lived that long with that one woman whose heart was wild for children, but [with] no possible chance for realization."

In quoting from *The President's Daughter,* in which Warren complained of "a hell of a life with my wife," Mouser denounced it in orotund terms: "I have heard the soft inclinations of love coming out from his heart filled with deep emotion, as he called her, his wife, the Duchess, that was his love term for her. . . . I cannot believe that he would break his marriage vows, disregard the sacred obligations to that fine character. . . ." At one point the lawyer passed a picture of Florence around to jurors to compare her "trusted and true" face to Nan's "demented" face.

In later years defenders of Harding referred to the case as proof that Nan lied since the Ohio jury of three voted against her. In fact, even a defender of Harding's presidency admitted that she lost not only because she did not turn over any love letters but because of a "highly prejudiced jury." More interesting was that many Harding defenders refused to testify against Nan Britton or help defray Mouser's legal fees. When Daugherty was asked by reporters about Nan's claims, he said enigmatically, "I have no information, and I have no doubts."

The one person who could have convincingly and unequivocally dismissed Nan's claims of visits to Warren's Senate and White House offices resolutely refused to do so. As Harding's secretary George Christian knew his every move and visitor, but he could not be budged into refuting her on the stand. Although he was aware of Harding's schedule and visitors, he sought to protect himself by claiming ignorance of her activities with Harding. He could never be accused of lying if further evidence backing her claim surfaced. Christian praised Mouser's "untiring efforts" to defend the Harding marriage but added, "My attendance at Toledo would be of no help to you." He told Mouser that "it would be quite futile to approach the Washington friends of the President" to help his case and that it was "the Hardings that should pay for it." Of equal importance was the reaction of Warren's sisters and brother. Daisy, however much she later publicly revoked her complete support for Nan, refused to swear against the claim that Elizabeth Ann was Warren's daughter. Even more surprising was the reaction of Warren's brother, George, who had steadfastly refused to continue financial support for the putative Harding child. Mouser frustratingly wrote that George "will in nowise assist us." However much the family resisted the contention that Elizabeth Ann was a Harding or an heir to any of Warren's estate, they all refused to renounce her and her mother.

Nan never wavered. "He wasn't a philanderer. He loved me and

I loved him." Nan Britton was a genuine survivor. She died, nearly one hundred years old, in 1995. Well into her last years she was winsome, even in a short skirt. "It has really occupied much of the thoughts of my lifetime," she recalled at age eighty-three. "He was, I think, one in ten thousand who father children out of wedlock and continue to accept responsibility. He never once thought of repudiating his fatherhood and only wished that he could tell it openly. So I have stayed with this because his untimely death left me to solve my own problem. I realize what it must be [like], especially in these days, [for] girls in their teens who are becoming pregnant. It was just one of those things that's happened so many times. . . ." Nan was then writing a book on historical figues and illegitimacy. "My daughter carried the name Harding through high school up until the time she married."

As for Elizabeth Ann, Nan described her as "conservative." Nan's three grandsons did not learn about their grandfather the President until 1964. "My mother speaks for the family," said Elizabeth Ann of her Harding parentage, "where that is concerned." She was philosophical: "My mother told me when I was very young that President Harding was my father. I'm not ashamed, but I don't like the publicity. . . . I had a normal childhood, but then, I didn't go around telling people about it. I do recall that when she spoke of President Harding she always talked of him in glowing terms. Mother wasn't bitter. All through the years she never spoke badly of him. It was all love, adoration and affection. She told me she loved him very much." Nan's first grandchild was named Warren.[4]

Florence too loved him, and it was she who lay beside Warren Harding beneath the open dome of the magnificent Harding Memorial in Marion. Their bodies were reinterred there in 1927, and the tomb was dedicated on June 16, 1931. The Duchess was fondly remembered by Coolidge and President Hoover. "He had the advantages too, of the deeply interested and watchful care of a wife," twanged the Yankee. "No record of his work would satisfy him which failed to recognize the helpful influence of Mrs. Harding." Hoover told the crowd, "[L]et us not forget the very large need of praise rightfully due that wonderful woman here by his side—a fitting companion in death even as in life, Florence Kling Harding, whose loving devotion and untiring energy played such an outstanding part in the shaping of his life and career. . . ."[5]

Damage, however, had already been done. A year earlier the book that condemned the Duchess's reputation appeared on the market and scandalized the nation. In his craftily assembled *Strange Death of Pres-*

ident Harding, Gaston Means charged that *the Duchess* had killed Harding with *Sawyer*'s complicity. Around this myth the strands of several truths were spun. And while the book's ghostwriter, May Dixon Thacker, repudiated Means in a *Liberty* magazine article, "Debunking the *Strange Death of President Harding,*" she stated that apart from the claim that Florence poisoned Warren, the book was "founded on many facts" and that "even the high officials in Washington referred to had conceded that there was much truth in the story." As Harding friend and reporter Boyden Sparkes remarked, "How many of his statements were true? He's smart enough never to let you know." Evalyn added, "He tells enough truth in that book to be able to get off with his lies. He'll bring just enough truth in it." Across America, Gaston's book was read with gasping gullibility. Some libraries wouldn't circulate it. In others, like the Handley Library in Winchester, Virginia, it was "preserved in a locked case with other curiosa and erotica." The day after Florence's death the United Press had stated, "Probably no other woman in the history of American national life ever held so securely the admiration of the country as did Mrs. Harding." Seven years later she was reviled in caricature as the First Lady who poisoned the President.[6]

After a lifetime of tight living Florence's financial legacy dissipated fast. Save for about $56,000, her $500,000 estate was left to her two grandchildren, but there were many smaller gifts to devoted staff like Harry Barker, Laura Harlan, Kathleen Lawler, Katherine Wynne, and Ruth Powderly. Joel Boone, for one, was angry, scribbling in his diary, "Read Mrs. Harding's will. She unmindful of my services, but remembered many others. Had not thought of being remembered in will." He scratched out the further notation "—until I saw who she did leave [money to]. Sawyer responsible for her ingratitude. He knifed me on every level" and scribbled a substitution: "During the Coolidge Administraton Sawyer became cool and seemed embittered toward me and probably was critical toward me to Mrs. Harding—over whom he had great influence." Boone died in 1969, never having published the memoirs he promised.[7]

Unfortunately the alcoholism that had claimed their grandfather Henry De Wolfe and father, Marshall, also affected Florence's grandchildren, George and Jean. Each worked at a variety of engineering and aviation jobs, spending most of their lives in or around Marion. By Jeanette LaMarche, George had two sons, Peter and David, and both of them had children and grandchildren. By George Weil, Jean had a son, who lived in Puerto Rico, married a resident there, and had three daughters. After briefly living with him there, Jean moved to Seattle, where she lived with her brother. George died of self-inflicted gunshot wounds in Hagerstown, Maryland, on February 6, 1968. Ten years later, still living in Seattle, Jean died, said a close relative, "without a cent. They both inherited a lot of money. Spent it all." Their mother, Esther Metzger, died in 1977. The Harding sister closest to Florence, Carolyn Votaw, died in 1951; Heber followed a decade later.

In his last years Tal Kling was quite ill, but his brother came to visit only briefly, instructing the taxi driver to wait for him. Tal died at age seventy-three, on July 1, 1938, leaving his dog Trixie, and widow, Nona, who died in 1968. Tal never formally converted to Catholicism, but a priest conducted a mass for him, and he was buried in St. Mary's Catholic Cemetery. Although the Kling family plot remains highest on the hill of the Marion Cemetery, still looking down on Hardings, Sawyers, and Phillipses, and the huge monument has "Children" engraved on it, Cliff was the only one of Amos's children to lie there. He died on July 11, 1937, leaving the bulk of his fortune to his daughters, Hazel and Louise, neither of whom ever visited or sent a card to their aunt Nona. The Klings had equal disdain for Jean and George, the more rightful heirs of Florence. After Florence's death Cliff tried to get jewelry for Hazel that had been willed to Jean. Neither Kling niece had any children. After Louise's 1984 death what remained of the Kling fortune was designated by her to establish annual full scholarships for music students from Marion, a highly appropriate tribute to Florence. Louise was generous with information about her aunt, proud of her accomplishments, and eager to preserve her memory. Despite her dislike of Harding, she gave Florence's piano to the True Museum and some family china to the Harding Home. Much of the remaining Kling items were scattered into flea markets across central Ohio.[8]

In 1926 the lower floor of the Harding Home was opened to tourists by the Memorial Association. It was adorned with original furnishings, presidential gifts, Florence's linens, fans, slippers, hats, shawls, and several gowns, all of which Florence had had carefully stored, down to Warren's folded socks. Initially Reddy Baldinger was caretaker. Near the end of his life Reddy finally talked—to Francis Russell—revealing Florence's remarks about having to "be faithful to Warren's memory" and the burning of the papers. He married late in life, never had children, and died at age ninety-four, in 1978, the last survivor of the loyal retainers of the Duchess.[9]

Harry Barker returned to Boston, where he resumed his post as Secret Service operative in charge until 1937, when he was promoted to supervising agent of the New England District. He retired in 1945 and died in 1957. His son Russell adopted Laddie Boy as his own. The famous pet died in Newtonville in January 1929 and was buried in nearby Marshfield, having lived out his dog days as celebrity mascot of the Newton High football team in the fall of 1924 with an orange and black bow on his collar. His copper statue, cast from 19,314 newsboys' pennies, remains in Smithsonian storage. When someone asked Barker to breed a pup from Laddie, he refused, to the end loyal to his Duchess: "I can't do it. Mrs. Harding made me promise never to breed Laddie Boy, because she wanted his line to die with him. Don't ask me why."

George Christian, going blind in later life, stayed in Washington, where he died in 1951. Often invited back to the White House, during the Truman years he ran into Ira Smith, chief of the mailroom, who had been uncertain how to handle Nan Britton's love letters to Harding. "Remember, Ira, when we tore up the President's letters?" George reminded him. "Good thing, too."[10]

Although Charlie Forbes's betrayal devastated the Hardings most, he suffered the least. After his 1925 trial he was sent to Leavenworth for two years, managing to delay his incarceration for a year with claims of "ill health." Resourceful as ever, out of the pen, Forbes immediately signed a lucrative deal to print his sensationalized memories for the New York *World* tabloid. He never remarried and returned to Washington State. Less lucky was Albert Fall, who had the distinct honor of being the first Cabinet officer ever to be imprisoned. In the end it was decided that Doheny's hundred-thousand-dollar payment to Fall was a "gift" to an old friend, and Doheny got off without penalty. It was also judged that in accepting the "gift" the former interior secretary was guilty of graft. He was fined—ironically—one hundred thousand dollars—and sentenced to a year in the state penitentiary at Santa Fe.

In her barely decipherable scrawl slanting in all directions across any scraps of paper she could find, Emma wrote endless pages of letters with her "absolutely true facts" about Albert's innocence, hoping to write a "true" version of Teapot Dome. At an El Paso lecture she whipped out a letter from Dr. Carl Sawyer "saying Harding died of natural causes," although an astrologer asserted that he had "most assuredly" been poisoned. She was conspicuous at the 1940 Republican National Convention and died three years later. In 1944 Albert died penniless in an El Paso hotel. Decades later, in a dusty crate in the Interior Department's storage, his picture was found, damaged. Restored, it was hung in 1967, the first time since the Teapot Dome trials.[11]

Although a hung jury let Harry Daugherty elude conviction, his reputation remained tainted. For years, sprinkled with his anti-Semitic remarks, he railed against Reds, who he thought were behind the plot to get him convicted. Evalyn shrugged. "Nobody is going to believe him—whether he spoke the truth or not." His wife was buried the day after Florence, but having survived breakdowns, alcoholic children, his companion's suicide, and his brother's imprisonment, Harry died of simple old age in 1941, taking his secrets to his grave. When pressed about Harding's "woman scrape," he retorted, "I never talk about dead men or living women."[12]

Someone who *did* talk forever regretted doing so. William Estabrook Chancellor had finally fled to Canada in 1922 to escape further intimidation by Billy Burns's boys. He returned to Ohio only after the Duchess had been dead for three years, and he lived to the age of ninety-five, dying in 1963. While his remains the only book ever to be suppressed by the federal government for political purposes outside wartime, it is now forgotten, with only a handful of copies known to exist. The rumors he spread of President Harding's black ancestry persist, however. One African-American, Eva Thorton Wells of Chicago, "as fair as was President Harding," who "passed" as a white person, insisted that her black grandfather was a cousin of President Harding's father. A branch of a black Richmond, Indiana, family by the name of Harding declared themselves presidential kin, and eventually an organization was founded in Greenwich, Connecticut, based solely on the premise that Harding was "our first negro President."

Also courtesy of Chancellor's book, Carrie Phillips had the distinction of being the first of Harding's mistresses to be mentioned in print. After Harding's death she had returned to Berlin during its most decadent era and was alleged to have become the mistress of a former prince of Germany and to have been lent a castle on the Rhine to live in. She returned to Marion with a bed bearing a silver crest of the German royal family. Back in America before Hitler's Third Reich, just in time to see Jim's investments wrecked by the Depression, she became a rabid "America Firster," bitterly opposed to fighting Germany. Not long before Jim Phillps died in 1939, she threw him out, and his last months were spent in a single back room at the run-down Hotel Marion. During World War II the FBI was again said to send agents twice a week to report on Carrie's activities. She was harmless, her only Germanic legacy being the shepherd dogs from the royal kennels she bred without control. The diamonds she had purchased with Harding hush money in 1920 were long gone.

By the Eisenhower era Carrie Phillips had deteriorated into a senile hermit, dozens of unhousebroken dogs her only companions. Still, as with Nan, remembering Warren warmed her. In the fifties some Marion women went to a nearby medium who had a message for a "friend" of theirs from the spirit of Warren Harding: "Don't worry. Everything is alright.'" Shortly after, one June day, one of the women spotted Carrie walking with a fur coat over her naked body. Taking pity, the woman gave Carrie the message. She burst into a joyous smile, wailing, "You don't know how long I've been waiting for that message!" Eventually she was placed in a nursing home by the county. When her home was finally entered, her lawyer came across a shoebox crammed with dozens of love letters and poems from Warren. She died in 1960.

Harding's various other mistresses scattered, aged, and passed on, none leaving memoirs. Grace Cross died in 1944, still beautiful, an accomplished singer, having enjoyed a happy family life with her husband and one son, who later recalled that Warren Harding had been a guest in their home. Jess Smith's ex-wife, Roxy Stinson, died at eighty-two, her obituary recalling how in 1924 she had "shocked the nation with her testimony on where the bodies were buried in the scandal." Just before she died, a Columbus *Dispatch* reporter found her. "She stood behind a screened door at the front porch," he wrote, "a grey-haired, gaunt woman wearing a faded housecoat, wearing a sweater over her shoulders." She was terse: "I've had so many writers here. I'm sorry. I can't help you. Sometimes even students. I'm a rock-ribbed Republican, but I can't stand politics. It's so dirty. I drew a lot of notoriety once, and if I were to say anything it would start all over again." Another woman of the Harding saga had a more grisly exit. After society editor Bertha Martin (who helped Jess blunt Grace Cross's attempt to blackmail Harding) enjoyed a stint bootlegging liquor from the embassies, she was "found with her head on the gas stove and all the gas jets on. . . . clothed in white gloves, a fur coat and her jewels."[13]

After the Duchess's death, the two women most closely associated with her, Evalyn and Alice, never fully resumed their earlier friendship. It was Evalyn whom Alice called one day in 1925 from White Sulphur Springs with shocking news. "She screamed it over the telephone. I thought she was kidding. Said she was going to have a baby but that it was a secret—with all the telephone operators listening in! Ned was sitting in the room. Before I said anything, he said, 'She is going to have a baby and Borah is the father.'" The child, whom Alice is said to have borne by the famous Idaho senator William Borah, was named Paulina, born in 1925. Nick Longworth was at least officially the child's father. Some years later, when Evalyn asked Alice to join her in an air flight to Cincinnati, she responded, "Oh no Evalyn, I couldn't leave little Paulina. She is my only child and it really wouldn't be fair to her!" Evalyn laughed at that. "Here Alice had been leaving the poor child every second that she felt like it, and now she had suddenly developed a case of mother love."[14]

With Nick's sudden death in 1931, Alice Longworth's ambition to return to the White House as a President's wife was dashed, but she created a cottage industry as critic when her cousins Franklin and Eleanor Roosevelt stormed the place in 1933. Living to age ninety-six, dying in 1980, she was not only mentally agile but generous when it came to assisting eager history students, answering the smallest details of their endless questions about the Hardings and McLeans, enjoying her retelling of the old jokes and gossip, with no bitterness.

By the time Eleanor Roosevelt had been First Lady for a dozen years, a book, a novel, and a play using Florence Harding as a character had all appeared, finally reducing her to a hatchet-faced cartoon. Yet it had not been Eleanor Roosevelt but Florence Harding who had first flown in an airplane as a President-elect's wife, spoken publicly on equality issues for women, personally looked after the welfare of men wounded in a world war, whose marriage had been portrayed as a political partnership, who had appeared in her own newsreels, welcomed black women to the White House, and been so familiar with the Washington press corps as to be on a first-name basis with many of its men and women. Still, in the postwar era the Duchess was dismissed by Clare Boothe Luce as "iron-jawed" and "grim," and Margaret Truman irresponsibly declared her "the worst First Lady." A peculiar 1982 Siena College poll of history professors to "rank" First Ladies in such categories as "value to country," "courage," "intelligence," "background," "integrity," and "public image" placed her at the bottom, the result of Warren's famous rating as the worst President, not her own achievements.

If Florence Harding was not quite an Eleanor Roosevelt, she was even less a remote and mute Bess Truman. As discourse grew on the roles of First Ladies, there was eventually some appreciation of earlier women who had the courage to record or discuss their convictions. Thus Florence Harding became a link in the continuum of a long tradition, succeeding the likes of politically active Abigail Adams, Mary Lincoln, Julia Grant, and Helen Taft, preceding Lady Bird Johnson, Betty Ford, Rosalynn Carter, Nancy Reagan, and Hillary Rodham Clinton.

There was also a permanent legacy for the nation, those institutions for which the interested First Lady used the prestige and visibility of her position to lend support—Zion National Park, for example, and the federal women's prison system—and the hundreds of individual Americans on whose behalf she interceded, resolving problems of immigration, housing, pension, and equal rights, furthering the concept of an accessible democracy. Her largest legacy, to the American veterans of foreign wars, covered both the public and personal. The Veterans Bureau she had so eagerly anticipated—though devastated for a time by the scandals generated by its director—evolved into a full-fledged Cabinet-level department. The great irony was that the Veterans Administration was built directly across the street from Harry and Jess's little house on H Street, where a prostitute was allegedly killed by the President. For her, federal concern for the wounded vet would have been her proudest legacy, but by World War II Mrs. Harding's work was all but forgotten except by the woman who had sparked it.

Evalyn McLean lived on, for another twenty-four years. Five years after Florence died, she began drinking heavily again. It began with a glass of claret, "under doctor's orders," she said. "Then I started wanting something stronger." It may also have been because of her deteriorating marriage. Trying to stop again was "like going through the tortures of the damned." But she did. Ned's alcoholism, however, only worsened. Evalyn explained:

> He went out of his mind. . . . He had his smash here and I came up from Florida. We worked like dogs over him. He was completely gone. I took him back to Florida and [Dr.] Betcher said he was still crazy. Then we came back and things went from bad to worse, and that's when I got suspicious about the women. Before then I said, "I am going abroad with the children. I've got to get a rest." . . . Dr. Betcher . . . said, "if you leave Ned McLean he is going to end up in an insane asylum or in the gutter. . . . [G]ive him one more chance. You will never regret it if you do." So I said all right, and it was a hellish trip. He said he had no money, so I had raised about $50,000 [for the trip] some way— borrowed it. I was hard up then too, don't know why, but I was. We started over and he was so fiendish that I started drinking on the trip. . . . wouldn't let me sleep, accused me of this one and that one, and I thought he was going to kill me two or three times. . . . On another night I went into his room and there he was sleeping quietly. . . . I thought it was awfully quiet in here and I looked and he had stuffed the bed full of pillows and gone out. . . . That old, old trick. Oh God! We had lots of fun.

Unwilling to endure his adultery, Evalyn initiated divorce proceedings, but by the early 1930s Ned was committed to a Towson,

Maryland, insane asylum, where he meandered around in pajamas and danced the hokey-pokey with Zelda Fitzgerald. When addressed directly by name, he cried. She still visited him: "If I didn't do that, there wouldn't be one living soul to look after him." In the end Evalyn couldn't bring herself to go through with the divorce.

Untroubled by her eccentricities, Evalyn thrived. She went on to write a column in the Washington *Times-Herald,* exploring, in her seriocomedic style, political and social issues of the day. And it was Florence's endeavors for "our boys" that Evalyn kept alive. During the Depression, although she lost about one third of her fortune, when thousands of vets stormed Washington, pressing early for their promised bonus, she drove herself to their camps to offer some of them gardening jobs at Friendship. Realizing that many were starved for food, she promptly showed up at three in the morning with a thousand sandwiches from Childs restaurant, then bought hundreds of Army cots and watched them delivered to a temporary shelter. Her sense of justice was wounded when she learned that President Hoover had let General MacArthur burn the Bonus Army camps and drive the vets out of town. Evalyn turned her rage against Hoover—and MacArthur—and publicly chastised them for the action. "When they turned the tanks and gas on 'em I was in California—but when I saw that movie reel I darned near tore the place down. If I'd been here I'd have led them right straight out to the White House."[15]

Evalyn was again in the headlines in 1932 when she hired Gaston Means once more—after his first stint in prison—and both became enmeshed in one of the most infamous stories of the Depression era, the Lindbergh baby kidnapping. Remembering her from the Harding era escapades, Means approached Evalyn, saying he could lead her to the kidnapped child with his underworld connections—for a fee of $100,000. She said, "Means, the Department of Justice are beginning to get on to us until you get me that child, but, so help me God if you double cross me you are going to the Penitentiary. I am going to slit it wide open to the public." For two months the odd duo skulked around the country at sites where Means claimed the kidnappers promised to leave the child. The baby—and Evalyn's $100,000—were never recovered, a trial ensued, and Means was sent up the river again.

Realizing that the FBI was reading his mail, Means instigated more mischief from his cell at Leavenworth, in letters to his sister Belle. He went on endlessly in his old conspiratorial way about how "Pres. and Mrs. Harding had contributed $100,000 to the much larger fund in my present indirect custody" and that this fund "in part belong[s] to Nan" and her daughter. He died in prison in 1938. One FBI memo later reported that Evalyn's $100,000 ended up in the hands of gangster Max Hassel "to be used in rum-running activities."[16]

During and after World War II Evalyn became the godmother of the wounded servicemen and women in Washington, hosting countless parties at Friendship on their behalf, letting them toss around her Hope Diamond for kicks. Hundreds of them kept in touch with her after they were sent to regional VA hospitals, sending letters, pictures of their families, and reports on how their various therapies were working. In her newspaper column, "My Say," she vigorously asserted America's debt to the veterans. When she defended women in the military against allegations of immorality and received an anonymous obscene letter, Evalyn was undeterred—and simply got J. Edgar Hoover on the case, having the letter sent to the FBI labs for fingerprints.

Whether Evalyn had some secret on J. Edgar Hoover or suspected his homosexuality through his association with Jess Smith, she struck some terror in the heart of the man who succeeded Billy Burns as head of the FBI. Whenever crazy Mrs. McLean demanded protection from imaginary threats by thieves and kidnappers in a flashy Miami nightclub ("she is desirous of a spectacular appearance rather than protection," one agent reported to Hoover), he complied. When it was gently suggested that she wouldn't need FBI protection if she didn't wear her jewelry out, Evalyn retorted illogically that "she is not afraid of wearing the Hope Diamond because of the proverbial curse attached to it for anybody who touches it." During Cheyenne's Frontier Days an agent reported that Evalyn, because of "excessive drinking, became somewhat careless in permitting various persons attending this rodeo to handle the Hope Diamond."[17]

Meanwhile her fortune continued to dwindle. On April 26, 1943, Evalyn offered the Hope Diamond, her pigeon-blood ruby, a collection of medium-size emeralds and sapphires, and a diamond and emerald–encrusted snuffbox that once belonged to the sultan of Turkey for sale as security for a loan. "I am trying to raise some money from the Hope Diamond and some other jewels of mine to try and to save my children's estate," she stated. She lost the Washington *Post* and Friendship but remained gleefully optimistic. Even though the Hope Diamond was often in hock and she couldn't pay for her storage units crammed with her relics, she didn't hesitate to phone a California plant that made artificial limbs for disabled veterans and ask that samples be sent to her, for the boys.

In the end the Hope Diamond seemed to curse mostly J. Edgar

Hoover. He went into a frantic fit when, upon Evalyn's death in 1948, it was given to him, wrapped in brown paper, marked by her for his care. Hoover rid himself of the cursed jewel swiftly, ordering a bank vault opened on a Saturday. Eventually it found its way to the Smithsonian, the most famous relic of the Harding era, not far from where Florence's white gown with Harding Blue sash was on display.

"What bothers me," Evalyn wrote of the Hardings, "is that so many, many persons find it easy to believe that he was a sort of monster and that his wife was worse. Actually I wish the record in the case enabled me to make a complete defense. I know too little to do that and, furthermore, some things that I know are not defensible. Was he the father of a misbegotten child? . . . I am prepared to admit that he probably exposed himself a time or two, as have so many, to such a plight."

At the very end Evalyn McLean shared a tragic epitaph with Alice Longworth. Both their daughters committed suicide. Little Emily, Florence's goddaughter, who had renamed herself Evalyn after her mother, was only twenty-six years old at the time of her death in 1947. After that jolt Evalyn suddenly stopped looking back on the Jazz Age in which the girl had been born, the year of living high, making movies, the year the Hardings had come to the White House. Perhaps she was embarrassed. Perhaps she was pained. Or maybe the liquor and morphine had destroyed her memory. She died just months later. "All of us forget much more than we remember," she noted with as much wit as wistfulness, "and that's a blessing."

In the end, however, it was Evalyn who had managed to best understand and capture the paradoxical personality of her friend the First Lady Florence Kling Harding. The day after she wrote the unsigned eulogy of Florence, Evalyn expanded her tribute to consider the Duchess beyond being a personal friend, to review the theme of her existence: "The life story of Florence Kling Harding, like an epic of sturdy American womanhood, was a chronicle of continual struggle against great odds, and of continual accomplishments. From the day she first faced the world . . . she encountered hardships before which a less courageous spirit would have weakened . . . she not only kept her courage and her vigorous individuality, but she retained as well a depth of human understanding and a confidence in herself . . . that endeared her to many thousands. . . . In her thoughtfulness for the interests of others and in her loyalty to her friends she was outspoken to a degree that won for her recognition as one of the most vigorous-minded women who ever presided over the household of a President."

Florence Harding defied the strict conventions laid out for a woman of her time and background. Even in making the traditional choice of marriage, she found an outlet for her drive to the summit, however ill suited was the vehicle to carry her there. In another age she might have grasped her goal alone without its crumbling tragically in her hands. Still, her ambition had been requited. "The happy wife is not the woman who has married the best man of earth," she had written to herself halfway through her life, "but is one who is philosophical enough to make the best of what she has got."[18]

Even Amos Kling would have had to grudgingly concede, it had been a practical solution to living.

Acknowledgments, Sources, and Notes

Acknowledgments

My interest in the Hardings was prompted by a phone conversation with the late Alice Roosevelt Longworth in the winter of 1976 for a history research paper, and she continued to spice my efforts through college with further conversations in 1977 and one in early 1979. A year later it was Louise Kling of Marion, Florence Harding's niece, who furthered my interest, providing information on her aunt's early years, following Miss Kling's interview in a local newspaper. A third figure, historian Francis Russell, author of *The Shadow of Blooming Grove*, also made himself available to my many telephone inquiries, and he provided many finer details on Florence Harding and Carrie Phillips and the love letters between her and Harding. Agent Mike Hamilburg immediately saw promise in my book proposal. At William Morrow the book was initially contracted in 1986, and through the years editors Lisa Drew and Will Schwalbe kept a patient watch. It was editor Zachary Schisgal and assistant editor Anne Cole who finally shepherded this project through to the end with generous amounts of tolerance. Zach always went to bat for the book when the noose tightened. David Groff edited the manuscript to completion with a keen eye, judicious pen, and humor, asking the right questions about Florence's story and helping clarify the choices of her life. Dr. Kenneth G. Berge of Rochester, Minnesota, reviewed the new medical details of President Harding's controversial death. Without the help of Craig Schermer, whom I met at the Harding home in 1991, this book would be missing vital components. Craig has the foremost collection of Hardingiana, including hundreds of original letters, photographs, and other items, which he has generously shared without asking for any return. Dr. George Harding kindly provided insight into his collateral ancestor and his wife. Gary Cohen permitted me to draw from his archive of Evalyn McLean transcripts, and John Alford provided copies of correspondence between Florence Harding and Malcolm Jennings. The late Ray Pierman provided his recollections of Madame Marcia in her later years, and Hilla del Re provided information on German law that permitted the male head of households to apply physical punishment to his family members. Marion natives Glenn Elsasser and Dick Halberstein provided their help and memories. Joan Cross provided information on Grace Cross in a November 21, 1991, letter. In Marion it was Carroll Neidhart and Scott Crider who served as my guides around town, bringing me to a number of residents who had known the Hardings and/or their circle: Warren Sawyer, Miriam Stowe, John and Betty Bartram, Jack Kellogg, Mary Elizabeth Moore, Philamen Gregg, and Helen Brashares. Also in Marion, Charlton Myers, Dick West, and Madge Cooper Guthrie were of tremendous help in providing local lore, as were natives John Schroeter, Rick Halberstein, Hugh Cleland, Glenn Elsasser, and Gilcrest Allen. Two residents of Marion also helped but requested anonymity. Eric Braun kindly permitted me to have a suite in his offices during the early research stages of this project when paper was rapidly accumulating.

I want to thank friends Byron Kennard, Meredith Burch, John Dowd, Dale Eldridge Kaye, Richard Sullivan, Ellen McDougall, Ed Purcell, Jennifer Farley, the late Martha Schermer, and my father for their reading through sections of the manuscript, assisting with research, and general support. Once again, Raul Escuza's genius computer assistance helped. Mary Wolfskill helped shepherd through my successful effort to have the sealed papers of Dr. Joel T. Boone opened at the Library of Congress. At other institutions I would like to thank Linda Seidman at the University of Massachusetts, Jeff Thomas, and Durayea Kemp of the Ohio Historical Society and Carol Bowers of the American Heritage Center at the University of Wyoming.

Selected Manuscript Collections

Florence Kling Harding Papers within the collection of Warren G. Harding Papers, Ohio Historical Society. Within this collection are also the papers of Dr. Charles Sawyer, Kathleen Lawler, George Christian, Charles Hard, Malcolm Jennings, Cyril Clemens, Ray Baker Harris, and others. The various stages of Lawler's, Clemens's, and Harris's manuscripts of Harding biographies (the pagination is often confusing and nonexistent), and E. Mont Reily's original manuscript, "Years of Confusion," are in this collection. The manuscript of George Christian, Sr.'s proposed Harding book is on Roll 249. The Florence Harding Papers are available on microfilm rolls. They are organized as follows: Roll 242, 1916–1923, correspondence, letters filed chronologically; Roll 243, 1923–1926, and undated, correspondence and miscellaneous materials; Roll 244, 1920–1922, clippings; Roll 245, 1922–1923, clippings; Roll 246, 1922–1923, clippings; Roll 247, 1923–1924, clippings. Unfortunately many of the FKH clippings have no date or publication information but are identified in the notes as fully as possible.

Evalyn Walsh McLean Papers, Library of Congress, Washington, D.C. This collection includes the McLean manuscript, only a portion of which was used in Evalyn's memoirs, correspondence, notes, materials on Grace Cross, and William E. Chancellor's original manuscript with his new information on Harding

Joel T. Boone Papers, Library of Congress, Washington, D.C. This collection includes Boone's handwritten diary, his typed diary, a copy of his oral history at the Hoover Presidential Library, correspondence, medical information on Harding, and a typescript of Boone's memoirs.

Francis Russell Papers, American Heritage Center, University of Wyoming, Laramie, Wyoming. Excerpts of Warren Harding's letters to Carrie Phillips are available in this collection.

Marion County Records, microfilm edition, Marion Public Library, Marion, Ohio. The divorce decree of Florence and Henry De Wolfe and the wills of Florence and her father, Amos Kling, are available here.

Mark Sullivan Papers, Library of Congress, Washington, D.C., and Herbert Hoover Presidential Library, West Branch, Iowa. A copy of Sullivan's diary held by the Hoover Institution at Stanford University is in the collection of the Hoover Library.

Dean Albertson Papers, Special Collections and Archives, W.E.B. Dubois Library, University of Massachusetts, Amherst, Massachusetts. Albertson's interview with former Harding reporter Vylla Poe Wilson and the recollections of reporter Bertha Martin are part of these papers.

Federal Bureau of Investigation. The files on Warren Harding, Florence Harding, Evalyn McLean, Jess Smith, Harry Daugherty, Gaston Means, and Albert Fall.

Craig Schermer's Harding Papers. The largest private Harding collection. It includes the diary of Florence Harding.

Gary Cohen's Boyden Sparkes–Evalyn McLean Transcripts. Private collection. This collection includes the transcripts of interviews conducted by reporter Boyden Sparkes with Evalyn McLean in preparation for her memoirs.

Charlton Myers' Harding Papers. Private collection. This collection includes many rare newspaper and magazine articles on the Hardings and a copy of the Chancellor book.

Will Hays Papers, Indiana State Historical Society Library, Indianapolis, Indiana.

Anna Tillinghast Papers, Schlesinger Library, Radcliffe College, Cambridge, Massachusetts.

Harriet Upton Taylor Manuscript, Schlesinger Library, Radcliffe College, Cambridge, Massachusetts.

Mary E. Brown Lee Papers, Ohio Historical Society, Columbus, Ohio.

Irwin A. Hoover Papers, Library of Congress, Washington, D.C.

Calvin Coolidge Papers, Library of Congress, Washington, D.C.

Edith Wilson Papers, Library of Congress, Washington, D.C.

William Howard Taft Papers, Library of Congress, Washington, D.C.

Charles Moore Papers, Library of Congress, Washington, D.C.

Herbert Hoover Papers, Herbert Hoover Presidential Library, West Branch, Iowa.

Selected Bibliography

Adams, Samuel Hopkins. *The Incredible Era: The Life and Times of Warren G. Harding.* Boston: Houghton Mifflin, 1939.

Alderfer, Howard F. "The Personality and Politics of Warren G. Harding." Ph.D. dissertation, Syracuse University, 1935.

Allen, Frederick Lewis. *Only Yesterday.* New York: Blue Ribbon Books, 1931.

Atlas of Marion County, Ohio: From Records and Original Surveys. Philadelphia: Harrison, Sutton & Hare, 1878.

Bagby, Wesley M. *The Road to Normalcy: The Presidential Campaign and Election of 1920.* Baltimore: Johns Hopkins Press, 1962.

Baker, Elmer LeRoy. *Gunman's Territory.* San Antonio, Texas: Naylor Co., 1969.

Boughton, James. *Bouton-Boughton Family.* Albany, N.Y.: Joel Munsell's and Sons, 1890.

Britton, Nan. *The President's Daughter.* New York: Elizabeth Ann Guild, 1927.

Brogan, Hugh, and Charles Mosley. *Burke's Peerage and Baronetage American Presidential Families.* Toronto: Maxwell, Macmillan, 1993.

Brough, James. *Princess Alice.* Boston: Little, Brown, 1975.

Brown, Dorothy M. *Setting a Course: American Women in the 1920's.* Boston: Twayne Publishers, 1987.

Butler, Nicholas Murray. *Across the Busy Years*. New York: Scribner's, 1939.

Chancellor, William Estabrook. *Warren G. Harding: President of the United States*. Privately printed by the Sentinel Press, 1922.

Chapple, Joe Mitchell. *The Life and Times of Warren G. Harding: Our After-War President*. Boston: Chapple Publishing Co., 1924.

————. *Harding the Man*. Boston: Chapple Publishing Co., 1920.

Clapper, Olive. *Washington Tapestry*. New York: McGraw-Hill, 1946.

————. *One Lucky Woman*. Garden City, N.Y.: Doubleday, 1961.

Collins, Herbert. *Presidents on Wheels*. New York: Bonanza, 1971.

Colman, Edna M. *White House Gossip: From Andrew Jackson to Calvin Coolidge*. Garden City, N.Y.: Doubleday, Page, 1927.

Cottrill, Dale. *The Conciliator*. Philadelphia: Dorrance, 1969.

Cox, James, M. *Journey Through My Years*. New York: Simon and Schuster, 1946.

Crockett, Fred E. *Special Fleet: The History of Presidential Yachts*. Camden, Maine: Down East Books, 1983.

Cuneo, S. A. *From Printer to President*. Philadelphia: Dorrance, 1922.

Daugherty, Harry M. *The Inside Story of the Harding Tragedy*. New York: Churchill Co., 1932.

Downes, Randolph C. *The Rise of Warren G. Harding, 1865–1920*. Columbus: Ohio State University Press, 1970.

Felsenthal, Carol. *Alice Roosevelt Longworth*. New York: Putnam, 1988.

Ferrell, Robert H. *The Strange Deaths of President Harding*.* Columbia: University of Missouri Press, 1996.

Fuess, Claude M. *Calvin Coolidge*. Boston: Little, Brown, 1940.

Gilbert, Clinton. *The Mirrors of Washington*. New York: Putnam, 1921

Greene, Laurence. *The Era of Wonderful Nonsense*. Indianapolis: Bobbs-Merrill, 1939.

Gross, Edwin K. *Vindication for Mr. Normalcy*. Buffalo: Privately printed, 1965.

Harris, Ray Baker. *Warren G. Harding: An Account of His Nomination for the Presidency*. Washington, D.C.: Privately printed, 1957.

*Ferrell's study was published as the manuscript for this book was being completed. Although his sources were consulted—leading, for example, to study of the Dean Albertson Papers—the text was not read, to avoid altering this author's specific views on the medical cause of Harding's death. Once the manuscript for this book was completed, the Ferrell text was read. Ferrell drew on Dr. Boone's papers but found no contradiction in his accounts of the days preceding Harding's death, which this author did find, nor did Ferrell suggest there was a link to the death with Dr. Sawyer's use of purgatives, which this author does. Ferrell also makes a case questioning Nan Britton's veracity and does not consider the Susan Hodder child by Harding; this author believes the Britton and Hodder relationship (if not entirely the issue of their daughters' paternity) in the context of the general laxity Harding had about his adultery. In every respect, however, the Ferrell study does assiduously make the case that Harding should not be considered the worst President.

Hearings Before the Select Committee on Investigation of the Attorney General, U.S. Senate, 68th Congress.

Hicks, John D. *Republican Ascendancy.* New York: Harper, 1960.

History of Marion County. Chicago, Ill: Leggett, Conaway and Co., 1883.

History of Marion County, Ohio, and Representative Citizens. Chicago, Ill: Biographical Publishing Co. 1907.

Hoes, Rose. *The Dresses of the Mistresses of the White House as Shown in the United States National Museum.* Washington, D.C.: Historical Publishing Co., 1931.

Hoover, Herbert. *The Memoirs of Herbert Hoover,* vol. 2. New York: Macmillan, 1952.

Hoover, Irwin A. "Ike." *Forty-two Years in the White House.* Boston: Houghton Mifflin, 1943.

Jacoby's 1908 History of Marion County. Chicago, Ill.: Biographical Publishing Co., 1908.

Jaffray, Elizabeth. *Secrets of the White House.* New York: Cosmopolitan Book Corp., 1927.

Johnson, Willis Fletcher. *The Life of Warren G. Harding.* New York: John C. Winston Co., 1923.

Kern, Ellyn R. *Where the Presidents Lived.* Indianapolis: Cottontail Publications, 1982.

Keyes, Frances Parkinson. *Letters from a Senator's Wife.* New York: D. Appleton & Co., 1924.

Kittler, Glenn D. *Hail to the Chief!: The Inauguration Days of Our Presidents.* Philadelphia: Chilton, 1968.

Kohlsaat, H. H. *From McKinley to Harding.* New York: Scribner's, 1923.

Kurland, Gerald. *Warren Harding: A President Betrayed by Friends.* Charlottesville, N.Y.: SamHar Press, 1976.

Leighton, Isabel, ed. *The Aspirin Age: 1914–1941.* New York: Simon and Schuster, 1949.

Longworth, Alice Roosevelt. *Crowded Hours.* New York: Scribner's, 1930.

MacMahon, Edward, and Leonard Curry. *Medical Cover-Ups in the White House.* Washington, D.C.: Farragut Press, 1987.

McLean, Evalyn Walsh. *Father Struck It Rich.* Boston: Little, Brown, 1935.

Means, Gaston. *The Strange Death of President Harding.* New York: Guild Publishing Co., 1930.

Means, Marianne. *The Woman in the White House.* New York: Random House, 1963.

Medved, Michael. *The Shadow Presidents.* New York: Times Books, 1979.

Mellon, Paul. *Reflections in a Silver Spoon.* New York: Morrow, 1992.

Michelson, Charles. *The Ghost Talks.* New York: Putnam, 1954.

Miller, Hope Ridings. *Scandals in the Highest Office.* New York: Random House, 1973.

Murray, Robert K. *The Harding Era: Warren G. Harding and His Times.* Minneapolis: University of Minnesota Press, 1969.

Parks, Lillian Rogers. *My Thirty Years Backstairs at the White House.* New York: Fleet Publishing Corp., 1961.

Pepper, George Wharton. *In the Senate*. Philadelphia: University of Pennsylvania Press, 1930.

Randolph, Mary. *Presidents and First Ladies*. New York: D. Appleton Century Co., 1936.

Rinehart, Mary Roberts. *My Story*. New York: Farrar & Rinehart, 1931.

Romine, Trella H., ed. *Marion County 1979 History*. Marion, Ohio: Marion County Historical Society, 1979.

Ross, Ishbel. *Grace Coolidge and Her Era*. New York: Dodd, Mead, 1962.

———. *Ladies of the Press*. New York: Harper and Row, 1936.

Russell, Francis. *The Shadow of Blooming Grove*. New York: McGraw-Hill, 1968.

Russell, Thomas H. *The Illustrious Life and Work of Warren G. Harding*. New York: International Business Library, 1923.

Sadler, Christine. *Children in the White House*. New York: Putnam, 1967.

Sautter, R. Craig, and Edward Burke. *Inside the Wigwam: Chicago Presidential Conventions, 1860–1996*. Chicago: Wild Onion Books, 1996.

Sawyer, Carl. *The Sawyer Sanitarium: A Prospectus*. Marion: Harding Publishing Company, 1921.

Scanlon, Nelle. *Boudoir Memoirs of Washington*. Philadelphia: John C. Winston, 1923.

Sinclair, Andrew. *The Available Man*. New York: Macmillan, 1969.

Smith, Ira T. *Dear Mr. President: Fifty Years in the White House Mailroom*. New York: Messner, 1959.

Starling, Colonel Edmund. *Starling of the White House*. New York: Simon and Schuster, 1946.

Stoddard, Henry L. *As I Knew Them: President and Politics from Grant to Coolidge*. New York: Harper & Brothers, 1927.

Sullivan, Mark. *Our Times: The Twenties*, vol. 6. New York: Scribner's, 1937.

Swanberg, W. A. *Norman Thomas: The Last Idealist*. New York: Scribner's, 1976.

Teague, Michael. *Conversations with Mrs. L.* New York: Doubleday, 1981.

Teichmann, Howard. *Alice: The Life and Times of Alice Roosevelt Longworth*. Englewood Cliffs, N.J.: Prentice Hall, 1979.

Thompson, Charles Willis. *Presidents I've Known . . .* Indianapolis: Bobbs-Merrill, 1929.

Trani, Eugene P., and David L. Wilson. *The Presidency of Warren G. Harding*. Lawrence: Regents Press of Kansas, 1977.

Wade, Wyn Craig. *The Fiery Cross: The Ku Klux Klan in America*. New York: Simon and Schuster, 1987.

Watson, James E. *As I Knew Them*. Indianapolis: Bobbs-Merrill, 1935.

Werner, Morris R. *Privileged Characters*. New York: R. M. McBride and Co., 1935.

White, William Allen. *A Puritan in Babylon*. New York: Macmillan, 1938.

Wilbur, Ray Lyman. *Memoirs*. Stanford: Stanford University Press, 1960.

Wilson, Edith. *My Memoir*. New York: Bobbs-Merrill, 1938.

Selected Articles

Ackerman, Carl. "How the President Keeps Well." *Saturday Evening Post* (May 5, 1923).

Boroson, William. "America's First Negro President." *Fact Magazine* (January–February, 1964).

Chaumprey, [Madame] Marcia. "What the Stars Told Mrs. Harding," *Collier's National Weekly Magazine* (May 16, 1925); "When an Astrologer Ruled the White House," *Liberty* (April 9, 1938, and June 11, 1938); "The Tragic Love of Mrs. Warren G. Harding." *Home Magazine* (January 1934).

Dickey, Carl. "Plundering the Wounded Men." *World's Work* (June 1924).

Downes, Randolph, and K. Walker. "The Death of Warren G. Harding." *Northwest Ohio Quarterly* (Winter 1962–1963).

"The Duchess of Center Street," Special issue, Marion *Newslife*, May 5, 1980.

Ficken, Robert. "President Harding Visits Seattle." *Pacific Northwest Quarterly* (July 1975).

Forbes, Charles. Memoirs, *New York World*, December 4, 1927.

Jennings, Malcolm. "Washington-Alaska-Marion." *Rotarian* (November 1923).

MacAdam, George. "Harding." *World's Work* (September and October 1920).

"Mrs. Harding Dies After Long Fight." Obituary, *New York Times*, November 22, 1924.

O'Hagan, Anne. "The Woman We Send to the White House." *Delineator* (November 1920).

Russell, Francis. "The Four Mysteries of Warren G. Harding." *American Heritage* (April 1963). "The Harding Papers: How Some Were Destroyed and Some Were Saved" *American Heritage* (February 1965); "A Naughty President." *New York Review of Books* (June 24, 1982); "The Shadow of Warren Harding." *Antioch Review* (Winter 1978).

Sawyer, Warren, ed. *Harding Star* newsletter, bound and reprinted by Harding Home, 1960s.

Schruben, Francis W. "An Even Stranger Death of President Harding." *Southern California Quarterly* (March 1966).

Stephenson, Francis M. "President Harding," New York *Sunday News*, August 2, 1964.

Stratton, David H. "The Memoirs of Albert Fall." *Southwestern Studies* (1966).

Thorpe, Will J. "Details of President Harding's Funeral." *Mortician* (August 1923).

Warwick, Jack. "Growing Up with Harding." *Northwest Ohio Quarterly* (Winter 1955–1956, and Summer 1958).

"Washington Wife," "The Other Presidents." *Good Housekeeping* (February 1932).

White, William Allen. "The Other Side of Main Street." *Collier's* (July 30, 1921).

Wilbur, Ray Lyman. "The Last Illness of a Calm Man." *Saturday Evening Post* (October 13, 1923).

Interviews

The author spoke to the following individuals either by telephone or in persona: Gilcrest Allen, June 2, 1987, July 20, 1987; Bill Barnett, July 22, 1991; Betty Bartram, July 17, 1991; John Bartram, July 17, 1991; Betty Beale, February 24, 1992; Elizabeth Ann Harding Blaesing, September 10, 1996; Helen Metzger Brashares, July 22, 1991; Hugh Cleland, July 10, 1991; Lucille Davelli, October 19, 1991; Hilla del Re, July 16, 1991; Glen Elsasser, April 22, 1991, May 29, 1992, July 8, 1992, February 2, 1993; Herbert Gary, July 17, 1991, July 10, 1991 (extensive and recorded tour of Harding Home and its contents), July 21, 1991, July 30, 1991; Philamen Gregg, July 20, 1991; Madge Cooper Guthrie, April 24, 1991, July 29, 1991; Clare Holland, August 5, 1986, August 18, 1986, September 16, 1986; Lois Hughes, July 31, 1991; Jack Kellogg, July 20, 1991; Louise Kling, May 10, 1980, May 22, 1980, May 23, 1980; Bruce Lackie, February 27, 1992; Alice Roosevelt Longworth, March 1976, September 1977, January 1979; Mary Elizabeth Moore, July 22, 1991; Charlton Myers, July 20, 1991, April 8, 1992; Bernice Norwood Napper, July 11, 1991; Carroll Neidhart, July 17, 1991, July 18, 1991, July 19, 1991, July 20, 1991, July 21, 1991, July 22, 1991; Lillian Rogers Parks, June 21, 1991; Ray Pierman, December 21, 1984; Barbara Pryor, September 19, 1991; Francis Russell, September 13, 1984; Warren Sawyer, July 20, 1991; Craig Schermer, July 18, 1991, August 1, 1992; John Schroeter, June 2, 1987; Jurado Solares, July 12, 1991; Dick West, June 15, 1987, July 18, 1991.

Endnotes

Code: Florence Kling Harding [FKH], Warren G. Harding [WGH], Evalyn Walsh McLean [EWM], Charles E. Sawyer [CES], George Christian [GC], Alice Roosevelt Longworth [ARL], Harry Daugherty [HD], Joel Boone [JB], Malcolm Jennings [MJ], Kathleen Lawler manuscript [KLM], Jack Warwick memoirs [JWM], papers [P], interview [I], oral history [OH], *Harding Star* [HS], Washington *Post* [WP], Washington *Star* or Washington *Evening Star* [WS], Washington *Herald* [WH], New York *Herald* [NYH], *New York Times* [NYT].

Prologue: Talking to the Dead

NYT, August 7 and 8, 1923; *WP*, August 7 and 8, 1923; *WS*, August 7 and 8, 1923; *WH*, August 8, 1923; Washington *Daily News*, August 9, 1923; Solares I; Colonel C. O. Sherrill, military aide to the President, August 6, 1923, Headquarters of the Metropolitan Police, August 7, 1923, "Coolidge" file, and EWM manuscript, EWMP; *Liberty* magazine, June 11, 1938; Britton, pp. 267–69; Holland, Guthrie, Russell, Schermer Is; KLM, chapter on Harding's funeral, pp. 17–18.

Chapter 1: A Proud Family, a Shrouded Family

1. Florence Kling was born on the second floor of the commercial building. It has traditionally been placed at 127 South Main Street, but legend also claims with no tangible evidence it may have been at 162 South Main Street, *HS*, October 8, 1966, and April 1, 1969; *NYH*, February 20, 1921; "The Commencement Annual, 1898, The Marion High School"; *1883 History of Marion County*, Kling biography, p. 600; *Jacoby's 1908 History of Marion County*, Kling biography, pp. 632–33. The names of the Kling sisters are not recorded. The brothers were Michael, Henry, George, Jacob, and Amos.

2. Christian, Sr., manuscript, pp. 34–35.

3. *History of Marion County, Ohio and Representative Citizens*, 1907, pp. 131, 489; GC manuscript, p. 42; microfilm edition of Last Will and Testament of Amos H. Kling, probate court records, November 17, 1913, Marion Public Library; Elsasser I. Henry H. Kling, born on February 13, 1835, served as captain of Company D, ROUI and was killed on November 25, 1863, at the Battle of Mission Ridge in Tennessee, in the Civil War. Michael Kling, born on March 23, 1829, also served in the Civil War for the Union. He was wounded and died in Van Buren Hospital at Milliken's Bend, Louisiana, on May 27, 1863. Jacob H. Kling, born on October 13, 1837, lived only to fifty-two years, dying a bachelor, of apoplexy, on December 16, 1889; U.S. Census for Marion Town, Township and County, 1860 and 1870; *Atlas of Marion County, Ohio, History of Marion County, Ohio and Representative Citizens*, p. 131; Cleland I.

4. Neidhart I; *NYT*, November 22, 1924; KLM, no page, no chapter, WGHP; clipping, Eleanor Margaret Freelander "Mrs. Harding as I Know Her," syndicated column, "The Girl Next Door," n.d. [1920], n.p., WGHP; 1883 *History of Marion County*, Kling biography, p. 600; *Jacoby's 1908 History of Marion County*, Kling biography, pp. 632–33; Ohio county residence and census research on Klings, courtesy of Glen Elsasser; Elsasser I. By 1908 Elizabeth Kling had also died in Lucas County, never having come to live with her rich and famous son in Marion.

5. Chancellor, p. 225, Margaret E. Kling, *Genealogical History of John Ludwig Kling and His Descendants, 1755–1924*, p. 8; Clifford Neal Smith and Anna Piszczan-Czaja Smith, *Encyclopedia of German-American Genealogical Research* (London: R. R. Bowker Co., 1976); for information on Jews in southwestern Germany and the towns of the Palatine and Württemberg where they lived, see pp. 160–61. *Delineator* (November 1920); John D. Hicks, biography of Florence Harding, *Prominent American Women;* Louise Kling I; for information on German Mennonites in America, see Smith & Smith, op. cit., pp. 47–48.

Florence's Kling family was also referred to as Mennonite, a religious sect that is part of the general Pennsylvania Dutch population in Lancaster, but the Klings were Lutherans. There is a suggestion in *The Genealogical History of John Ludwig Kling and His Descendants* that the Amos Kling ancestors, different from her, more prominent line, may have been Jewish. She notes that two other Kling families came from Württemberg as well, also to escape, as she put it, "religious persecution." Yet she carefully says that they were "mostly" Protestant, rather than *all* Protestant. If they were not Protestant, the persecuted Klings were certainly not Catholic, for the entire reason for the persecution was that the Germans in this region, controlled by France, were non-

Catholics. Just as the Protestants were persecuted because of their faith, so too were the Jews who were primarily from the southwestern part of the country, where the Klings originated. Tracing specific Jewish families in the seventeenth and eighteenth centuries is extraordinarily difficult. The feudal system in which they lived was, as one historian writes, "complicated . . . as regards to citizenship and allegiance even in a small village. . . ." Jews had been in Germany since the Holy Roman Empire, and their fate shifted from era to era, town to town. Sometimes they were protected by the precarious power of the kaiser, but always they were repressed, whether by legal limitations on their professions or by the sword. In the mid-1700s, when the Klings emigrated to America, the Rhine-Palatinate regions—where the Klings originated—ruled by the noble house of Wittelsbach, was a haven for Jews, and most villages were permitted a quota of Jewish families. In 1743, for example, Pfalzgrafschaft had 488 Jewish families; in 1722, 10 Jewish families lived in Billigheim, and 7 in Leimen. No records exist, however, of how many such families lived in the many other towns of the Palatinate or of their surnames. In the region of Württemberg where the Klings were from, in the period just prior to their immigration, five of seven cities permitted Jewish residents to live there, but they had only a relative few because of severe anti-Semitic attacks in the region. Freudental, for example, had 24 families as of 1731, but Stuttgart only 5 in 1779. As Florence's niece later recalled and clarified, without irony of bigotry, "The Jewish story hurt us most. Besides, the story was that they were highborn German Jewish, not persecuted. And if they were Jewish, it was in ancient times. The story couldn't possibly be true, so it hurt." Margaret Kling did record the story that one George Kling, who migrated to a southern county of Pennsylvania that became part of Delaware, but not Lancaster, County, *may* have been an ancestor of Amos Kling. A false genealogy of Florence Kling based on this assumption was created. The mystery of Amos Kling's origins is obfuscated by just two generations. There are twelve Klings listed in the 1850 Ohio census index, but none in Richland County, where he claimed his parents moved that year and none by the names of Michael and Elizabeth. There was Daniel Kling in Ashland County, Milton Township; Davis Kling in Wayne County, Green Township; George Kling in Wayne County, Canaan Township; and Moses Kling in Crawford County, Lykens Township. A Rosalia Kling lived in Lucas County, a William in Gallapolis, an Adam in Guernsey County, and a Christian in Middletown.

   6. KLM for references to "Vetallis" grandmother "born in southern France"; *Delineator* (November 1920); Huguenot reference from text of Cyril Clemens speech at Webster Grove, Missouri, Reel 254, WGHP; Amos referred to his 1867 business trip to the Paris Exposition as a visit to "the old country." Yet he later obscured a further reference to his mother by identifying her as being "of German extraction." *Jacoby's 1908 History of Marion County*, pp. 632–33; Elsasser I.

   7. A French historian recorded that the Boutons were of "noble ancestry" and a family marked with "patriotism, education and religion" that was "seen in the race all down the ages." With nearly a millennium missing from its history, the family is next chronicled from 1350, when military and court records abound with Boutons. Somewhere in the past thousand years the Catholic Boutons had become Protestant or, as the French Protestants were called, Huguenot. Nicolas Bouton, Count Chamilly, Baron Montague de Naton, said to be born in about 1580, was the father of twins

Harard and John, born in 1615, and another son, Noel. During the Catholic persecution of the Huguenots, the Boutons escaped to a nearby mountain range. John fled first to England, then to America. He landed in Boston, went to Watertown, then moved to the new settlement of Hartford, Connecticut. In 1651 the Boutons—with their son and daughter—relocated to a newer settlement, Norwalk. By his wife, Abigail Marvin, his eldest son and namesake, born in 1659, helped establish New Canaan. During the American Revolution John Jr.'s grandson Ezra served with the Westchester County militia. Ezra's son Jakin married Rhoda Richards, and her father, Edmund Richards, was a captain in the First Regiment of the Continental Army, was taken prisoner by the British, and escaped. See James Boughton, *Bouton-Boughton Family* (Albany, N.Y.: Joel Munsell's Sons, 1890); FKH application for membership in National Society Daughters of Founders and Patriots of America, No. 1394; Nellie Hanford Furman to FKH, n.d. Roll 243, WGHP.

8. "Why Mrs. Harding Will Help Carry Connecticut," n.d. [circa summer–fall 1920], Reel 244, WGHP. Benedict mistakenly recalled that when he courted her, Kling was already "a prosperous manufacturer of farming implements," Norwalk *Hour*, August 18, 1923; Lawler manuscript. When the Boutons moved to Ohio, they sold their home to Lester Messinger, who later sold it to Allison B. Walker, a famous New York artist who founded a retreat in New Canaan.

9. GC manuscript, p. 35, WGHP; *NYH*, February 20, 1921; 1870 Marion census.

10. Advertisement, courtesy of Judge Myers collection; Christian, Sr. manuscript, pp. 42–43, Reel 249, WGHP.

11. *Delineator* (November 1920) *WP*, June 15, 1920.

2. *The Girl on the Horse*

1. *NYH*, February 20, 1921; FKH to Mr. W. H. Houghton, January, 31, 1921, WGHP; *WP*, June 15, 1920; KLM; childhood photo of Florence and Clifford Kling appears as a single frame, in "Romance of Louisa Bouton, Mother of Mrs. Warren G. Harding," Norwalk *Hour*, August 10, 1923, an undated clipping on the Kling family trip to Connecticut; FKH clippings, WGHP; San Francisco *Bulletin*, August 4, 1923; JWM.

2. "The Commencement Annual, 1898, The Marion High School"; *History of Marion County*, pp. 223–24; Neidhart, West Is; EWM, *Father Struck It Rich*.

3. For information and background on Amos Kling's business activities in Marion: *NYH*, February 20, 1921; *Atlas of Marion County*, 1878; "The Commencement Annual, 1898, The Marion High School"; *1883 History County*, p. 600; *Jacoby's 1908 History of Marion County*, pp. 632–33; KLM; *History of Marion County*, 1907, pp. 126, 131–32, 141, 155, 173, 216, 266; Romine, p. 527. The initial importation of the horses was made by Wallace, Watkins & Kling, the subsequent ones by the Marion County Importing Company, of which Amos was a member.

4. JWM; descriptions of the Kling mansion, Kling, Gary, Schermer, Elsasser Is. The piano used by Florence as a girl was donated by Louisa Kling to the Stengle-True Museum in Marion.

5. *Delineator* (November 1920); Neidhart I; *HS*, November 1, 1969; Christian, Sr. manuscript, p. 35; "Recalls Mrs. Harding as Noted Horsewoman," Marion *Newslife*, May 5, 1980; clipping, n.d., n.p., Reel 260, WGHP; FKH to Jennie Nichols, American Humane Education Society, March 27, 1922, Reel 242, WGHP.

6. *NYT*, June 20, 1920; *Delineator* (November 1920); Thomas H. Russell, p. 131; Chapple, *After-War*, p. 56; *NYH*, February 20, 1921; Colman, pp. 381–82; *Atlas of Marion County, 1878;* Neidhart, Kling Is; Romine, p. 544.

7. KLM; Baltimore *American*, September 17, 1922; clipping, Zoe Beckley, "No Wedding Ring on Mrs. Harding's Hand; Hates Kitchen, Adores Editor-Husband," n.p., n.d. [1920], WGHP; FKH to Esther De Wolfe Metzger, January 17, 1923, copy in collection of Craig Schermer; Richard Halberstein to author, January 25, 1993; article by Kate Forbes, Boston *Post*, January 1922; Boston *Globe*, February 26, 1922; Christian, Sr. manuscript, p. 35; Washington *News*, September 9, 1922; Neidhart I.

8. Christian, Sr. manuscript, p. 35; Chapple, *After-War*, p. 56; San Francisco *Bulletin*, August 4, 1923, McKinley information from June 14, 1920, clipping (n.p. but possibly Chicago *Tribune*), Reel 257, WHGP; Louise Kling said that her grandfather met Rutherford Hayes several times in the Ohio capital. Kling I.

9. "Local Woman's Impressions of Mrs. WG. Harding Told," n.p., n.d. [1920], Reel 260, WGHP; Kling I; Christian, Sr. manuscript on the Hardings, p. 35; Newspaper clipping, n.p., n.d. [1920], "Mrs. Harding: The Woman," WHGP; *Delineator* (November 1920); manuscript page, Reel 260, WGHP; Chapple, *After-War*, p. 56; Zoe Beckley, clipping, "No Wedding Ring on Mrs. Harding's Hand; Hates Kitchen, Adores Editor-Husband," n.p., n.d. [1920], WGHP hereafter cited as Beckley clipping; *WP*, June 15, 1920.

3. *Whipped with a Cherry Switch*

1. *NYH*, February 20, 1921; Kling I; *WP*, June 15, 1920; "Local Woman's Impressions of Mrs. W. G. Harding Told," n.p., n.d. [1920], Reel 260, WGHP; *Delineator* (November 1920); Johnson, p. 124; *NYT*, November 24, 1924; clipping, Margaret Freeland, "Mrs. Harding as I Know Her," syndicated column, "The Girl Next Door," n.d. [1920], n.p., WGHP; Johnson, p. 124.

2. Communiqué of the Performing and Media Arts, College-Conservatory of Music, University of Cincinnati, Fall 1990 issue; articles on history of Conservatory and College, B. J. Foreman and editors. There are no records of Florence Kling's studies there, interview with Lois Hughes, University of Cincinnati Librarian of Archives and Rare Books Department: "The Cincinnati Conservatory of Music merged and changed so many times and records were lost"; "Local Woman's Impressions of Mrs. WG. Harding Told," n.p., n.d. [1920], Reel 260, WGHP.

3. *NYH*, February 20, 1921; Thomas H. Russell, p. 131; Chapple, *After-War*, p. 56; Birmingham *Post*, October 26, 1921. One account later claimed that as a child she had "failing eyesight"; another even stated that in her early teens she had to take a leave of school because of "threatened loss of eyesight. . . ." She was always dependent upon spectales. Photographs of the young Florence Kling, courtesy of Craig Schermer; author interview with Judge Charlton Myers, July 20, 1991; Johnson, p. 124;

WP, June 15, 1920; Kling I; KLM; Adams, pp. 18–19; Chancellor, pp. 225–26; Warren G. Harding to Sarah Harding Dickerson, February 12, 1883, and description of Merry-Roll Round from Francis Russell, pp. 52–53.

4. KLM; author conversation with Dr. Bruce Lackie, February 27, 1992; Chancellor, p. 227; *NYH*, February 20, 1921; del Re, Kling, Lackie Is.; *Delineator* (November 1920).

5. FKH to Minnie Kirby, February 7, 1922, Reel 242, WGHP; KLM; Thomas Russell, p. 131; Chancellor, pp. 225–26; Adams, p. 19; Francis Russell, p. 82; Stowe, B. Bartam, Kling Is.; *Atlas of Marion*, 1878; *HS*, April 1, 1969; Washington *Post*, June 15, 1920; information on Emily Hanford Bouton's death, from Marion Cemetery records; euphemistic descriptions of Florence's behavior leading up to her pregnancy, from the Lawler manuscript; FKH diary.

4. *Living in Sin*

1. KLM; Christian, Sr., manuscript; Kling, Stowe, Kellogg, Gary, Allen, J. Bartram Is; Marianne Means, p. 181; Simon Eugene De Wolfe family chart, courtesy of Miriam Stowe; Adams, p. 19; material on FKH activities prior to WGH marriage in Francis Russell's books, from interviews with Ada Denman, a cousin, Francis Russell, p. 83.

2. Except for two scraps of paper, there is no material record providing unequivocal evidence of the events during her pregnancy and marriage to Henry De Wolfe. Most knowledge of this most difficult period of her life has been told by three generations of Marion residents to three generations of reporters and writers, historians, and chroniclers. Some of the tales may be yarns spun romantically, or unflatteringly, but all of it, in some form, began as whispered secrets and town gossip. The claim that Amos might have been the father of his own grandson appeared on a draft page of a typed manuscript of William Chancellor, stating that "Mayor Neely is one of the two grandfathers of the two grandchildren of Florence Kling Harding, the other being her father Amos Kling . . . ," Chancellor typed manuscript page, "Insert 28 A," Harding File, Campaign memorabilia, EWMP. The claim of Henry De Wolfe disputing his paternity of Florence's child is from Chancellor, p. 83. The claim that he merely agreed to name himself as father is from Chancellor, pp. 225–26; JWM; Stowe, West Is. FKH never explained what happened, referring to her pregnancy only in oblique cursory remarks pointed enough to make her painful reactions to it clear but abstract enough to keep details hidden. Colonel Christian explained with succinct clarity that there were "attentions" from Pete to Flossie, "resulting as such affairs generally do and as might be expected from a high spirited girl like Florence," Christian, Sr., manuscript.

3. Francis Russell, p. 83; KLM; Stowe, Myers Is; Affidavit of Search, December 23, 1991, Franklin County, deputy clerk of the probate court Tamara L. McManauay to author; author conversation and notes with office of Crawford County marriage indexes, probate court records, January 23, 1992. There is no record for a De Wolfe marriage as far back as 1831 and until 1969; records of Marion County marriage indexes, checked July 24, 1991.

4. West, B. Bartram Is; Christian, Sr., manuscript, pp. 36–37, Reel 249, WGHP; microfilm copy of record of births, probate court, Marion County, 1880, in Marion Public Library.

5. KLM; Downes, p. 13; Francis Russell, pp. 32–47; Bartram, Stowe, Schermer, West Is; *NYT*, November 22, 1924; Ada Denman quote from Francis Russell, p. 83; Adams, pp. 19–20; Marianne Means, p. 181.

6. *HS*, April 1, 1969; Christian, Sr., manuscript, pp. 36–37; Adams, p. 20; Norman Thomas to Ray Harris, September 17, 1957, Reel 257, WGHP; Francis Russell, p. 21.

7. Francis Russell, pp. 82–83, see also for Denman quote; Adams, pp. 20–21; J. and B. Bartram Is; KLM; newspaper clipping, n.p., n.d. [1920], "Mrs. Harding: The Woman," WHGP; Beckley clipping, WGHP.

8. Warren G. Harding III to Ray Harris, n.d., Reel 257, WGHP.

9. KLM; Downes, p. 13; Francis Russell, pp. 32–47.

5. *Divorce*

1. *Delineator* (November 1920); KLM; J. Bartram, Elsasser, Kling Is; Christian, Sr., manuscript, Reel 260, WGHP; *Marion Star,* December 2, 1884, May 13, 1885, October 5, 1887, December 15, 1887, July 1, 1938; Schedule H, Estate of FKH, Reel 241, WGHP; FKH diary; Adams, pp. 21–22.

2. JWM. The story of her being a widow before she married Harding even appeared in her obituary *NYT*, November 22, 1924, Stowe, West Is.; *Washington News,* September 9, 1922; *NYT*, June 20, 1920; *Marion Star,* February 5, March 4, and July 27, 1885, December 11, March 11, and October 12, 1886, April 25, June 9, and December 11, 1887.

3. De Wolfe's testimony against Florence became part of the public record, and in 1920 William Chancellor obtained a copy. Once the Hardings were in the White House, the original testimony disappeared. Chancellor, pp. 80–83; Marion Public Library court records, Florence M. De Wolfe against Henry A. De Wolfe, civil action (divorce), June 12, 1886, p. 52.

4. General biographical material on Harding, from Francis Russell, JWM, Adams, Cottrill, and Murray; quotes of Dr. Harding, from an Associated Press story, November 1, 1925; on his purchase of cornet after selling Kling insurance, Colman, p. 393; Christian, Sr., manuscript, pp. 184–85; reading late from Harry Daugherty to Cyril Clemens, October 25, 1939, Reel 254, WGHP; reference to Nettie Hecker from Cottrill, p. 254; *WP*, November 23, 1924; picnic reference, from Kling I; reference to her catching him at train station, from Francis Russell p. 84–85; "Warren, it's a good thing you wasn't born a gal . . ." was told by President Harding himself at a National Press Club banquet in 1922, reprinted in Adams, p. 8.

6. *"The Thirst for Love"*

1. JWM; Christian, Sr., manuscript; Swanberg, p. 6; *NYH,* February 20, 1921; Clapper, *One Lucky Woman,* p. 82; Colman, p. 382; KLM; *NYT,* June 20, 1920; Beckley clipping, *World's Work* (September 1920); *Delineator* (November 1920); Stowe I; *WP,* June 15, 1920.

2. Charity Remsberg to Cyril Clemens, July 19, 1942, Reel 254, WGHP; Napper, Kellogg, Moore Is; Downes, pp. 25–26, 554; Christian, Sr., manuscript, pp. 39–41, 52–53, Reel 249, WGHP.

3. JWM; Christian, Sr., manuscript; Chapple, *Harding—The Man,* pp. 68, 82; Kellogg I; Carolyn Votaw to Cyril Clemens, March 27, 1935, Reel 254, WGHP; Beckley clipping, *HS,* September 1, 1969; FKH diary.

4. Charity Remsberg to Cyril Clemens, March 19, 1948, Reel 254, WGHP; "Questions to Mr. Miller Relative to Early Life of President Harding," Reel 241, WGHP; Kansas City *Post,* August 10, 1923; letter of Carolyn Votaw to Cyril Clemens, n.d.; HD to Cyril Clemens, October 25, 1939, Reel 254, WGHP; Warren G. Harding III to Ray Harris, n.d., Reel 257, WGHP; West I; *World's Work* (September 1920); *Delineator* (November 1920); Thomas H. Russell, p. 132.

5. Gary, West, Neidhart Is; *HS,* July 4 and September 5, 1966, January 10, July 1, and September 1, 1967; *NYH,* February 20, 1921; *World's Work* (September 1920).

6. *HS,* July 1, 1969; Kling, Stowe, West Is; Chancellor, p. 87; Christian, Sr., manuscript, pp. 39–41; Francis Russell, pp. 85–86.

7. *MS,* July 8, 1891; Thomas H. Russell, p. 132. On her marriage registration with Warren, she is listed as Florence M. Kling (volume 10, p. 169, marriage records, Marion Public Library). In the *Star* story, written by Warren, the groom was noted as "Warren G. Harding," the bride referred to only as "Florence." Quote of Florence saying she "would make him President," *WS,* August 7, 1923; Beckley clipping, Gross, p. 48.

7. *Business and an Illegitimate Baby*

1. KLM; JWM; Neidhart I; *HS,* April 1, 1969; *NYT,* June 20, 1920.

2. Thomas H. Russell, p. 64. Chancellor, p. 226; *Delineator* (November 1920); *NYT,* June 20, 1920.

3. Francis Russell, pp. 80, 89–90; Thomas H. Russell, p. 138; San Francisco *Call and Post,* July 31, 1923; Baltimore *American,* September 17, 1922; *Delineator* (November 1920); JWM.

4. West, Kellogg, Sawyer, Stowe, West, J. Bartram Is; *WP,* November 23, 1924; San Francisco *Call and Post,* July 31, 1923; *Delineator* (November 1920); Baltimore *American,* September 17, 1922; clipping, n.d., n.p., "Recalls Mrs. Harding as Noted Horsewoman," Reel 260, WGHP; Thomas H. Russell, p. 134; Beckley clipping, Marion *Newslife,* September 2, 1979; Marion *Newslife,* May 5, 1980; *HS,* December 1, 1966; Swanberg, p. 7; Thomas H. Russell, p. 138. Reddy Baldinger became *Star* newsboy in 1893. Ora Baldinger to Cyril Clemens, July 9, 1939, Reel 254, WHGP.

5. Chancellor manuscript, EWMP; clipping, n.d., n.p., "Recalls Mrs. Harding as Noted Horsewoman," Reel 260, WGHP; *NYT*, June 20, 1920; Baltimore *American*, September 17, 1922; Thomas H. Russell, pp. 133, 290; *WP*, November 23, 1924; Beckley clipping, n.p., n.d. [1920], Reel 260, WGHP; San Francisco *Bulletin*, August 4, 1923; Ross, p. 194; Washington *News*, September 9, 1922; *Modern Maturity* (February–March 1975); *Delineator* (November 1920); Chapple, *After-War President*, p. 59; "Local Woman's Impressions of Mrs. W. G. Harding Told," n.p., n.d. [1920], Reel 260, WGHP.

6. JWM; *Marion Star*, September 15, 1895, and July 16, 1910; New York *Evening Telegram*, June 18, 1921; *Daily Oklahoman*, August 6, 1923; *NYH*, February 20, 1921; J. Bartram I; KLM.

7. Beckley clipping; *HS*, September 5, 1966, August 2 and January 1, 1968, June 1, 1968; Charity Harding to Cyril Clemens, October 10, 1937, Reel 254; FKH coming home an hour before Warren, Daughtery, p. 170; Florence on duty to housewife as part of marriage contract, New York *Evening Telegram*, June 18, 1921; Florence on the equality of work in a marriage, from her letter to Minnie Kirby, February 7, 1922, Reel 242, WGHP; *HS*, November 1, 1969, September 5, 1966, May 1 and September 1, 1967; JWM; Thomas H. Russell, p. 132; *Marion Star*, February 10, 1910, October 24, 1891; San Francisco *Call and Post*, July 31, 1923; Stowe, Allen, Elsasser, Schermer, West Is; Christian, Sr., manuscript, p. 210; *WP*, November 23, 1924; *NYH*, February 20, 1921; for theory that Harding perpetuated the idea of Florence Harding completely running his business and life, see Kurland, pp. 7–81, and Sinclair, p. 37.

8. Norman Thomas to Ray Harris, September 17, 1957, Reel 257, WGHP; *NYH*, February 20, 1921; *World's Work* (September 1920); Chapple, Harding—The Man, p. 82; Harding's crack about Kling running for office, Marion *Mirror*, September 19, 1894; Alderfer, pp. 109–10; Marion *Republican Transcript*, January 19, 1898; *WP*, June 15, 1920; WGH and mother-in-law, JWM and Christian, Sr., manuscript, p. 43.

9. Colman, p. 383; Edward W. Townsend. *Chimmie Fadden Explains*. New York: United States Book Company, 1895, pp. 22–23, 55, 83, 110, 166.

10. Marion *Newslife*, September 2, 1979; legend of Harding's first experience, from West I; Harding familiarity with Lizzie Lazalere, from Francis Russell, p. 75, and Cleland I; quote of William Allen White, reprinted in Russell, *New York Review of Books*, p. 30, and reference to Harding's letter in which he admits to having had STD, p. 33; Chancellor, pp. 82, 85; Cunningham quote, from Stowe I; Elsasser I.

11. Schermer, Moore Is; Chancellor, p. 227; FKH diary; *History of Marion*, 1907, p. 358; Gross, *Vindication for Mr. Normalcy*, p. 47; Gary tour I. The idea that Florence worked at the *Star* only to keep an eye on Warren was first forwarded by Mark Sullivan. Samuel Hopkins Adams and Francis Russell agree. This author does not. *Marion Star*, March 1, 1907, February 2, 1907; Clara Wallace quote, from West I.

12. *Marion Star*, December 28, 1896; KLM on "keen regret." The "mumps" defense was used by many, including Grant Mouser, in the later attempts to discredit Nan Britton's claim that Harding was the father of her child. All that is known of Harding's affair with Susan Hodder and his fathering of Marion Hodder derives from two articles and one author conversation with Francis Russell. Russell read about the Hodder relationship in a later letter Harding wrote to Carrie Phillips, and he confirmed it in the early 1960s in a conversation with the granddaughter of Susan Hodder, the

daughter of Marion Hodder. There is also precise information in a Harding genealogical account that appears in a non-American publication of British genealogists. See Russell, *New York Review of Books* and *Antioch Review* and Brogan and Mosley, p. 606. No Marion, Ohio, record of Hodder child birth there, Davelli I; FKH diary. This diary, discovered in 1997 and in the collection of Craig Schermer, contains written material from approximately 1895 to 1914, before FKH left for Washington. There was a hodgepodge of notes, ranging from Christmas messages she used in cards to recipes for removing wax from carpets to proper grammar and phonetic guides to French, Italian, and Spanish phrases. It also revealed a highly literate side, with frequently recalled quotes from Shakespeare, Emerson, and Eliot.

8. Friends, Neighbors, and the Mental Institution

1. Ray Baker Harris manuscript, p. 19, reel 260, WGHP; Downes, p. 6. Harding had actually made a brief trip to the sanitarium before his marriage, but on January 7, 1894, he checked in and stayed for forty-six days, until February 22. Only forty-nine days later he was back, checking in on April 12. Three years later, on May 12, 1897, he had to return. Battle Creek Sanitarium to Ray Baker Harris, June 9, 1939, Reel 257, WHGP. The chronicle of Phoebe Harding's troubles and CES's role in saving her is from Francis Russell, pp. 100–01.

2. *Time* (September 25, 1995); West, Bartram, Is; Sawyer atheism, Moore I; *History of Marion County*, 1907, pp. 156, 198, 202. The Sawyers had married on August 11, 1879; Sawyer signed letters to the Hardings as "The Doctor," but he was also known as Doc. CES was friends with Dr. Kellogg and reputedly escorted Harding there, Sawyer I.

3. "The Commencement Annual, 1898, The Marion High School"; Francis Russell, p. 140; KLM; West, Kellogg, Sawyer, Stowe, B. Bartram, Gary tour, anonymous Is; Marshall Kling graduation essay, courtesy of anonymous Marion resident; Christian, Sr., manuscript, pp. 34–35, 57; Marion *Newslife*, May 5, 1980; *HS*, February 1, 1968.

4. George Christian, Sr., to FKH, June 7, 1922, Reel 249, WGHP; Neidhart, Gary tour Is; *HS*, September 5 and December 1, 1966, January 10, 1967, September 1, 1968, and February 1, 1969. Doc gave her a dictionary for Christmas with the advice to "read between the lines," Gary I; *Marion Star*, January 1 and 4, 1906. "My family, as long as I could remember, always had a party on Christmas night," recalled Warren Sawyer. "Well, she had to have one then before ours—on Christmas Eve. Just to keep up, you know. And they had those so-called 'Tom & Jerry' parties with pretty well-spiked punch," Sawyer I.

5. *HS*, September 5, 1966; Sawyer, J. and B. Bartram Is; background on Samuel Britton from *Marion History*, 1907, p. 325, and on Jim Phillips, p. 689.

6. FKH was extremely generous with the most downtrodden of Marion society, helping dicker down the cost of medical care at a sanitarium for neighbor Madge Fell, gave out food baskets to the poor. She also played the piano at the weddings of young people she liked and had open houses for students when they were home on break. Thompson; Marion *Newslife*, September 2, 1979; Francis Russell, p. 140; Moore, Sawyer, B. Bartram, Elsasser Is; *HS*, September 5, 1966; *Star* information, Francis Russell,

pp. 102–03; note about George Van Fleet's becoming managing editor because of FKH, Adams, note 1, p. 20.

9. Political Wife

1. KLM; J. Bartram, Stowe Is; *Marion Star*, June 16, 1931; Michelson, p. 228; *NYH*, February 20, 1921; *NYT*, November 22, 1924; T. A. O'Leary to Cyril Clemens, October 19, 1939, Reel 254, WGHP.

2. Johnson, p. 125; Kansas City *Post*, August 5, 1923; Downes, pp. 554, 557.

3. Chapple, *After-War*, pp. 74–75; Dixon recollections in *NYH*, February 20, 1921. It is interesting that among the notices Harding chose to carry in the *Star* were editorials on the death of First Lady Caroline Harrison, Ida McKinley's illness delaying a presidential trip to San Francisco, and praise for Julia Grant during General Grant's final illness. In noting that a little girl wanted to kiss President Cleveland, who granted her wish, Harding said, "Such incidents make big girls sing, 'Backward O! Backward . . . ,'" *Marion Star*, November 9, 1892, May 5, 1901, July 29, 1885, November 17, 1885. FKH's disks also included Chopin, Bach, Handel, the romantic and emotional Italian operas, a *Madama Butterfly* disk, but almost no Wagner or more heavy music. She continued to collect contemporary and popular dance music, including, "Oh, You Beautiful Doll," Schermer I.

4. HD's memoirs, *The Inside Story of the Harding Tragedy*, chronicles their first meeting; other background material on HD is from Francis Russell and Adams; HD to Ray Baker Harris, June 7, 1938, Reel 259, WGHP; descriptions of Jess Smith, from Adams, pp. 42–46; Columbus *Dispatch*, January 7, 1973; Columbus *Citizen-Journal*, November 12, 1973. With a long porch overlooking the Deer Creek Lake, one and a half stories high and shingled in redwood, the shack had five bedrooms, ample space for Harry, Jess, and their guests, and there was a ten-room house nearby for overflow. Reporters dubbed it the "playhouse" for "Us Boys," meaning Ohio cronies. A boathouse protected a launch that piloted guests up and down the narrow creek. There was a walk-in cooler in the basement lined with wine racks. Roxy Stinson later recalled the Shack as "rather crude. I didn't think much of it. I was only there a few times on errands, and never alone. I was always with Jesse [*sic*]. As far as I know, there were never any women there for parties. Just men. Some of them, real celebrities . . . I won't name anyone who was there. I could tell a lot of stories, but I won't. . . . I know a lot that was never written that would be of interest to women. I didn't know about women," from Roxy Stinson testimony before 1924 congressional investigation of Attorney General Daugherty; *NYT*, June 9, 1920; Gross, p. 47; Kern, p. 57; Ora Baldinger to Cyril Clemens, July 9, 1939, Reel 254, WHGP; Colman, p. 397; Adams on Florence's work at the *Star* during the Columbus years, pp. 54–55; *HS*, September 9, 1966; postcard owned by Bartrams, September 22, 1911; Columbus astrologer, Sawyer I.

5. Alfred M. Cohen to Cyril Clemens, September 19, 1939, Reel 254, WGHP; Kellogg, Schroeter, Sawyer Is; Sullivan, pp. 97–98.

6. Francis Russell, pp. 91, 104, 134; KLM; *NYH*, February 20, 1921.

7. Francis Russell, pp. 145–46; Charles D. Hilles to Cyril Clemens, October 26,

1938, Reel 254, WGHP; Chautauqua, Cottrill, pp. 101, 125, Francis Russell, pp. 161–62, *NYT*, June 13, 1920; Warren's first desire to see Alaska, Ketchikan, Alaska, *Chronicle*, July 8, 1923; Dixon quotes, *NYH*, February 20, 1921; Kling quote, Moore I.

8. *HS*, November 1, 1968; Sinclair, p. 44; Kurland, p. 9. Warren's own health seemed to improve in this period. His last recorded visit to Battle Creek, for example, was for seven days, starting on November 19, 1903; *Grant Medical Center Network* (Fall 1989), pp. 4–9; *NYT*, November 22, 1924; Ray Baker Harris manuscript, draft chapter 1907–1914, Reel 260, WGHP; Francis Russell, pp. 165–66.

10. Adultery

1. Francis Russell, pp. 167–71; all Warren Harding letters to Carrie Phillips, from Francis Russell Papers, American Heritage Center, Laramie, Wyoming; author conversation with anonymous, Marion resident who knew Mrs. Phillips, read through the entire correspondence between Harding and Phillips, and knew the details and chronological progress of the affair, July 20, 1991; one poem from WGH to Carrie Phillips is quoted by Russell in his article in the *Antioch Review*, p. 66. Other excerpts have appeared over the years in publications including the Columbus *Dispatch* and Washington *Post*.

2. Sullivan, pp. 97–98; primrose path quote from Adams; Chapple, *After-War*, p. 82; Harding editorial on driving, from *Marion Star*, August 30, 1910; quote from Blacksten, from Thomas H. Russell, p. 289; Warren Harding to Carrie Votaw, September 21, 1905, WGHP; Heber Votaw obituary, n.d., n.p., frame 398, Reel 259, WGHP. Besides Carolyn, other Hardings had departed. Young George or Deac, as he was called, married and practiced medicine in Columbus, and Charity and Elbert Remsberg moved to California, while Daisy went to Vassar for some teaching courses. Florence was cordial but distant to her socially prominent sister-in-law, Suzie Kling. *NYH*, February 20, 1921; author interview with Dick West, July 18, 1991; *HS*, September 1, 1967; *History of Marion County*, 1907, pp. 201, 215; Kellogg, Gregg Is.

3. FKH to "My dear Alice and Nick," n.d., The White House [February 18–24], 1922; WGH to Ada Denman, February 8, n.y. [1906], Reel 241, WGHP; WGH to Carolyn Votaw, September 21, 1905, WGHP; microfilm edition of last will and testament of Amos H. Kling, probate court records, November 17, 1913, Marion Public Library; Chancellor, pp. 87–88; Stowe I; CES to WGH, March 18, 1907, *HS*, July 1, 1968. Kling rewrote his will on June 29, 1907.

4. WGH to Carolyn Votaw, August 4, 1907. They set sail from New York on August 1, 1907. WGH to Carrie Votaw, August 7, 1907, Reel 257, WGHP; WGH to Coonie Christian, August 8, 1907, Reel 241, WGHP; Kling, Gary Is; With his love of Napoleon Harding visited Waterloo on his first and second trips to Europe, New York *Tribune*, September 25, 1910.

5. Christian's report on Marshall, from Francis Russell, p. 181; *HS*, January 10, 1967; Sawyer, Moore, Brashares Is.

6. *HS*, August 1, 1967; WGH to George and Coonie Christian, Christmas Eve 1907, Reel 249, WGHP.

7. Francis Russell, *Antioch Review*, pp. 63, 66; *NYT*, July 10, 1964.

8. *WP*, June 15, 1920; Italy events, Gary tour I; WGH to the Christians, 1908, Reel 257, WHGP; "Egypt, Alaska Trip 7-Year Dream of Mr. and Mrs. Harding" clipping, n.p., n.d. [April 1923]; WHG to Coonie Christian, February 14, 1909, WGHP; West I; bracelet was later property of Hazel Longshore, Kling I; Francis Russell, pp. 194–96.

9. *WP*, June 15, 1920; author interview with confidential Marion source, July 20, 1991; *NYT*, March 26, 1972; CES to WGH, March 18, 1907, *HS*, July 1, 1968; West, Gregg, Gary tour Is.

10. Britton, pp. 5–7, 10–11, 15; transcript of *Britton* v. *Klunk,* 1931, Reel 250, WGHP.

11. KLM; Francis Russell, pp. 196, 201, 207–09, 212–13; Longworth, p. 180; article on FKH, New York *Tribune,* September 25, 1910; Cottrill; Britton, pp. 17–19.

12. Russell, *American Heritage* (February 1965); Francis Russell, pp. 217–18.

13. *NYH*, February 20, 1921; Chancellor, p. 226; KLM, chapter 1, p. 7; Francis Russell, pp. 214, 218; Russell, *Antioch Review,* pp. 63–64.

11. *Betrayal and Confrontation*

1. "At one point" quote, from Russell, *Antioch Review,* pp. 63–64; "Florence Harding knew of her . . ." quote, from Kenneth Duckett in *Marion Star,* January 20, 1972. Although the exact date when Florence first learned of her husband's affair is not clear, the reference to her offer of divorce seems to dovetail with Carrie Phillips's final anger with Harding's refusal to divorce and her threat to move to Germany. The Phillipses and Hardings had gone to Bermuda together, happily, in March 1911. Carrie left in September 1911. When the Hardings went to Germany that autumn, they did not visit Carrie there. Thus the affair was first confirmed for Florence sometime between March and September 1911. "Everybody in town knew about Carrie Phillips, even though Mrs. Harding had ignored it," Moore I. "Family conversation in those days didn't run to subjects like Carrie Phillips and Mr. Harding. Everyone shut up about it for a while, but it was in the wind." Allen, Schroeter, Is; KLM; FKH quote, from *National Magazine* (March 1923); FKH diary and clipping in it.

2. Fragment of Warren Harding letter to Carrie Phillips, July 1911, with code, private collection. Other parts of the code included: "Cloudy—message not clear . . . ; Capitulate—I can't wait any longer; Revoke—answer at once by cable to—; Glorious—I am coming to you at . . . ; Gallery—I need you at earliest possible day . . . ; Grateful—all my love to the last precious drop . . . ; Guide—Will meet you at— . . . ; Mist—No letter has come since yours of the— . . . ; Multiply—I send you a thousand fond caresses; Matrix—I am utterly and gladly all yours—today and always; Maternal—I'd like make your favorite picture a rapturous reality tonight; Magistrate—I am ready to put all else aside and seek our need of happiness together; Martyr—Honestly sorry, but can't come now; Malat—Hotel Manhattan, New York; Dissent—Boston and the Boston Kiss; Deplore—Paris . . . ; Deliver—I am asking for your embrace; Desire—I send you the night kisses . . . Despite—All you are concerned about are well; Design—I am mad to hold and possess . . . ; Constant—I love you more than all the world; Universe—*All* (*when there are no words.* If you can't translate, I'll show

you); Delude—I crave you every day and hour"; Russell, *Antioch Review*, pp. 64, 74; Francis Russell, p. 220.

3. *Delineator* (November 1920); background on "End of a Perfect Day," Sullivan, *Our Times*, 1900–1925, vol. 3, New York: Scribner's, 1930), pp. 357–58; clipping, Eleanor Margaret Freeland "Mrs. Harding as I Know Her," syndicated column, "The Girl Next Door," n.d. [1920], n.p., WGHP; *WP*, June 15, 1920, for quote on "deeply interested in the study of labor questions . . ."; FKH supports violence of English suffragettes, Jane Dixon, " 'Talk It Over at Tea; Mrs. Harding's Principle of Diplomatic Services," New York *Evening Telegraph*, June 18, 1921. Columbus march, Gary I.

4. Francis Russell, p. 219; Romine, Neidhart, Sawyer Is; Carl W. Sawyer. *The Sawyer Sanitorium: A Prospectus.*

5. Sawyer, Kling Is; KLM on science of astrology study; Sparkes-EWM transcript, n.d.

6. Adams, p. 75; Francis Russell, pp. 222–30; Longworth, pp. 202–03.

7. Russell, *Antioch Review*, p. 64; Russell, *New York Review of Books* (June 24, 1982); *Marion Star*, November 5, 1981; Francis Russell and Kenneth Duckett, *American Heritage* "The Harding Papers . . ." (February 1965). The poems are presented in general chronological order, by season and year, as pieced together from the above sources.

12. Marion Exodus

1. Britton, pp. 19–20; West I; interview with Nan Britton in Marion *Newslife*, September 2, 1979; Ellen Metzger Stoll interview in Cleveland *Press*, April 12, 1969; *Quiver* (November 1912, January 1913, November 1913, June 1914), Marion Public Library.

2. Information on Marshall is from Russell; WGH to Carolyn Votaw, October 29, 1913, quoted in Ray Baker Harris manuscript draft, p. 14, Reel 260, WGHP. Although Amos Kling's gravestone said he died on October 21, 1913, probate court papers list date as being the death date twentieth. In any event, on the twenty-ninth, Cliff, as acting executor, pressed for probate court processing of the will, microfilm edition of last will and testament of Amos H. Kling, probate court records, November 17, 1913, Marion Public Library; KLM.

3. Adams, pp. 63–64, 75–76; HD letters of spring and fall 1912, quoted in Russell, p. 241; *HS*, September 1, 1969. According to Warren Sawyer, Florence nearly died five times because of the ailment, saved by his grandfather as "a heroic lifesaving measure," Sawyer I; FKH, "You can do it . . . ," from KLM, chapter 1, p. 7; Florence on her role in Harding's decision to run for the Senate, from *Delineator* (November 1920), but the reference is to the HD visit in Florida, not Texas, which was after the election; Russell, p. 220.

4. Russell, *New York Review of Books*, p. 32; Russell, *Antioch Review*, p. 64; Francis Russell, pp. 245–53; Christian, Sr., manuscript, pp. 110–12, Reel 249, WGHP; FKH influencing Warren to use anti-Catholicism in 1914 campaign rhetoric, Gary, Sawyer Is.

5. Francis Russell, pp. 250, 253; Britton, pp. 20–21; Russell, *New York Review of Books*, p. 32; Russell, *Antioch Review*, p. 64; Gary, Sawyer, Russell Is.

6. Although a Marion death date lists Marshall's demise as November 23, 1915, it was actually the date his ashes were buried; West I. She noted them and their kindnesses to her—for example, Warren Givens, "sent me flowers—he knew Marshall"—in her address book and remembered them at Christmas. For her grandchildren, she invested Marshall's remaining inheritance—some in Kersey Lumber Company, run by a friend of his, FKH Senate address book, WGHP; KLM; *NYH*, February 20, 1921; B. Bartram I; Sparkes-EWM transcript, 1935.

7. WGH to CES, July 10, 1919; Clare Murdoch, Library of Hawaii to Ray Baker Harris, September 10, 1962; *World's Work* (June 1924); CES reaction to Forbes and FKH attraction to Southern California climate and interest in Chaplin, Sawyer I; Francis Russell p. 254–256; Charity Remsberg to Cyril Clemens, November 5, 1941, Reel 254, WGHP.

8. *HS*, July 4, 1966, and author's collection, FKH to Jim Woods, June 10, 1922; NYH, February 20, 1921; Moore, West Is.

13. Fish out of Water

1. Quote from FKH on arrival in Washington, *WP*, June 15, 1920. They first rented the furnished house of Hilary A. Herbert, the navy secretary under Grover Cleveland, at 1612 Twenty-first Street; KLM, chapter 3, p. 3, on illness of 1915–1916; FKH illness, WGH to CES, December 15, 1915, January 11, 1916, February 1, 7, 1916, 16 and 19, 1916; CES to WGH, December 20, 1915; CES to FKH January 24 and 27, 1916; FKH to CES, January 12, 1916, n.d [circa February 1916], all WGHP; Harris manuscript, "The First Months in Washington," Reel 260, WGHP; Marion *Newslife*, May 5, 1980; Frank and Berenice Blacksten in Washington, CES to WGH, February 9, 1917, WGHP.

2. Kern, p. 57. They moved into their second home, at 2314 Wyoming Avenue, in June 1917; Chancellor typed manuscript, "158 A," Harding, campaign material file, EWMP; clipping, "Washington Residence . . ." n.d., n.p. WGHP; WGH to CES, March 30, 1916. She also recorded "good cook" Mary Hawley, a "Swedish cook for luncheon and dinner" Mrs. H. Boyson, private waiter Adough Byrd. In a notebook she kept during the Senate years, she even listed her own pronunciation guide to a generic Asian language to deal with servants: "Pilikie—Trouble," "Pau—Finished," "Kapu—Keep Out," and "Puku-puku—Broke." FKH sent for what she needed from specialty shops: She had the Pecan Roll in Cleveland to mail-order her candy gifts; Great Western for dustless wax; "the nuns" for fine lingerie; Breck-Weiss Millinery in New York, which did Lillian Russell's hats; Martha Griffiths in Marion for dandruff soap; Gaultier & Petit on the Rue de la Paix for Parisian dressmaking; the Women's Exchange in Cincinnati for women's products; Schlesinger Shoes in Baltimore; Edith Daniels in Columbus for "that cold cream"; and Gullabi Gulbenkian in New York for imported rugs. Locally she shared a hatmaker with Princess Alice, Madame Agasta; had "payment under protest" with Robinson's Good Chickens; and relied on "the

oyster man" at Twelfth and E streets, Ticer the tinner, London the plasterer, and Andrews Paper Store for metal egg carriers. Florence Harding address book; WGH to ES, December 23, 1917, WGHP; *HS*, December 1, 1967, and May 1, 1968.

3. FKH to Ada Denman, April 29, 1916, Reel 241, WGHP; First Lady exhibit, Hoes, p. 31; incident at White House, KLM, chapter 29, p. 40. "The world is full of reverses, so we all should be glad to extend a helping hand.... I have used Royce's goods for fifteen years and have always found them exceedingly satisfactory ... ," FKH to Jimmie Olofson, Royce's Extracts, August 22, 1919, WGHP; on access to reporters, Philadelphia *Public Ledger*, June 20, 1920.

4. KLM, chapter 5, p. 12; Ada Denman to Ray Baker Harris, July 20, 1938, Reel 259, WGHP; on Votaws, Chancellor, p. 235; Chancellor, Downes, pp. 556–57, Francis Russell, p. 372, Gary, Sawyer Is; Boroson, *Fact* magazine, pp. 53–55; on FKH influence, KLM, chapter 32, p. 20; WGH to MJ, June 24, 1920, from his Washington office, WGHP; on suffrage, typed scrap, n.d, n.p., Reel 257, WGHP.

5. *WP*, June 15, 1920; Scanlan, pp. 26–27, 36; *Good Housekeeping* (February 1932); this article lists no author by name, although it reflects observations made by a woman who observed Florence closely as a Senate wife during their gatherings and conversations.

6. Parks I; William C. Spragens, ed., *Popular Images of American Presidents* (New York; Greenwood Press, 1988), p. 277; Sullivan, p. 145; Stratton, *Southwestern Studies*, pp. 6–7, 20–21, 26, 42–45, 54–55; FKH and political friendships, KLM, chapter 20, p. 5; chapter 5, pp. 6–8; chapter 7, no page number.

7. On WGH golfing, including game with Franklin D. Roosevelt, FDR to Ray Baker Harris, September 5, 1933; July 29, 1921, notation, Reel 259, WGHP; Ray Lyman Wilbur to Cyril Clemens, October 11, 1937, Reel 254, WGHP ARL, pp. 320–21; Ray Baker Harris manuscript, "The First Months in Washington," Reel 260, WGHP; Sparkes-EWM transcript, December 11, 1934.

8. WGH to MJ, April 24, 1916. The Hardings left Washington for Chicago on June 4 and stayed at the Blackstone Hotel for the convention, WGH to CES, May 27, 1916; quote on FKH at 1916 convention, KLM, chapter 3, p. 4; Downes, pp. 252–53.

9. FKH autobiographical sketch, Reel 232, frame 1014, WGHP; horse incident, support of animal rights groups, West I; FKH and cars, *Delineator* (November 1920), WGH to J. Harry Denman, January 18, 1917, Reel 241, June 14, 1920, news clippings, n.p., WGHP, and Cuneo, p. 119.

10. WGH to Charles Hard, May 14, 1915, Reel 256, WGHP; Downes, pp. 252–53. The Hardings were so often always together that there exists almost no correspondence between them. FKH never proved to be a good correspondent, rarely writing any personal letters, usually asking WGH to send a message from her to friends in his letters; in at least one such note he called himself "The Secretary to the Duchess," WGH to Coonie Christian, Christmas 1920; long Senate letter from Hotel Bon Air, WGH to FKH, n.d., Reel 241, WGHP; on letter to Carrie Phillips, Russell-Duckett, *American Heritage* (February 1965).

14. *The Morphine Addict and the Hope Diamond*

1. The Longworths did not move into their more famous Massachusetts Avenue house until 1925. Hard was also a mutual Harding-Longworth friend from Toledo; EWM manuscript, pp. 302–03; ARLI.; *WP*, August 18, 1986.

2. Sparkes-EWM transcript, December 11, 1934; past beauty of FKH, EWM manuscript, p. 307; overall general biographical information on EWM, from her autobiography, *Father Struck It Rich;* ARL, Holland Is; Clare Holland to author, August 18, 1986.

3. Quote on Florence telling about circulation of newspaper and "I love people . . ." Sparkes-EWM transcript, December 10, 1934; EWM manuscript, pp. 304–07.

4. Clipping, n.p. [Washington], n.d. [1916], WGHP; EWM's unsigned obituary of FKH, *WP*, November 23, 1924; Sparkes-EWM transcripts, December 10 and 11, 1934; J. Bartram I.

5. Alcoholism and drug addiction, Sparkes-EWM transcript, April 2, 1935. ARL alluded to her own enjoyment of cocaine in recalling her visit to a Boston doctor to have necrotic bone removed from her jaw. "The doctor used a great deal of cocaine, a drug I could learn to like," ARL, p. 171; Holland, Beale Is; Clare Holland to author, August 18, 1986.

6. For quotes from EWM on making movies with D. W. Griffith assistant, ARL, Sparkes-EWM transcript, n.d.; CES to WGH, April 1, 1916, on movies, WGHP; information on FKH enjoying Keystone Kops and Chaplin, Sawyer, Gary I; Holland, Parks Is.; EWM manuscript, p. 363; ARL encouraging affairs of her cousin Franklin and brother Ted, Felsenthal, pp. 138, 144.

7. WGH to CES, April 20, 1917, CES to WGH, February 1, 1917, WGH to CES, February 5, 1917, WGH to CES, January 3, 1917, CES to WGH, December 24, 1916, WGH to CES, February 19, 1918, WGHP.

8. WGH to CES, March 30, 1916, WGH to CES, March 9 and December 21, 1916, CES to WGH, February 16, 1916, WGH to CES, March 23, 1917, WGH to CES, March 15, 1916, and January 20, 1917, WGH to CES, February 16, 1916, WGH to CES, March 23, 1917, WGHP; Sawyer I; Marion *Newslife*, September 2, 1979.

9. "Mandy and the Doctor" letter to WGHs, n.d. [1917], Roll 262; WGH to CES, December 21, 1916, WGH to CES, December 23, 1917, *HS*, December 1, 1969; WGH to Ned McLean, July 6, 1917, EWMP. In the summer of 1917 the Hardings motored to New England, the Duchess insisting that they stop "for pottery (Lenox) and go to Corning for glass. Seems foolish," WGH to CES, postcard, Roll 262.

10. "Riley Grandin" information and suggestion of McAdoo, from Sparkes-EWM transcript, December 11, 1934; Peck letters, EWM manuscript.

11. Felsenthal, p. 190 on Ned McLean's mistress; pp. 134, 146, 151 on Nick Longworth's affairs, and pp. 117, 145–49, 155 on ARL affair with Borah; last quote on FKH's jealousy over Warren and other women, from EWM manuscript, p. 306.

15. *Lust and War*

1. Felsenthal, pp. 130, 133, 135, 146, 151, 155; EWM manuscript, p. 337; CES to WGH, November 3, 1919, and WGH to CES, November 1919, *HS*, November 2, 1967; ARL, p. 315; WGH to Harriet Taylor Upton, December 13, 1916, and March 16, 1917, Reel 241, WGHP. WGH voted against Philippine autonomy, the urging of British clemency toward Irish political prisoners, and the confirmation of Brandeis to the Supreme Court. He voted for a literacy test for immigrants, overriding Wilson's veto.

2. Russell, *Antioch Review*, p. 64, lists the date of this letter as January 23, 1917, but it is dated February 4, 1917, in the WGHP; Francis Russell, pp. 279–81. In the first session of the Sixty-fifth Congress, Harding voted not only to declare war on Germany, but for the espionage law, foodstuffs, and fuel control measures (the Food Administration Act), to requisition foreign vessels of enemies, prohibit trading with the enemy, and provide war risk insurance. He later voted against sending relief to Europeans suffering for lack of food.

3. Britton, pp. 25–36. Louise Beiderhause wrote to WGH: "When Nan Britton was in my class three years ago, you came to the YW in 15th St. to see our school and we had a nice half hour's chat—so ever since I have followed your speeches in the newspapers . . . ," Louise Beiderhause to WGH, October 30, 1920, WGHP.

4. Schroeter I; Marion *Newslife*, September 2, 1979; quote on "During the world war . . . ," from Chancellor typed manuscript, page "A 90," Teapot Dome Affair file, EWMP.

5. *NYT*, March 14, 1921; Colman, WGH chapter; clipping, "Washington Residence . . ." n.d., n.p., WGHP; clipped a newspaper article, "Towns and People in War News: Can You Pronounce Them?," FKHP; FKH war activities, Sawyer, Gary Is; Felsenthal, p. 138; *NYH*, February 20, 1921; "Senate Wives Club Tribute to Mrs. Lyndon B. Johnson," program Katie Louchheim P, LC; Lois Marshall and Senate wives, *Our Vice Presidents and Second Ladies* (Metuchen, N.J.; Scarecrow Press, 1988), p. 203; clipping, "Mrs. Harding Very Fond . . ." Boston *Post*, January, n.day, 1922; FKH quotes on war and women, *Delineator* (November 1920); Scanlan, pp. 120, 131–33, 139. Harding's voting record to aid the disabled soldiers would be significant in light of his future commitments to them—and the Duchess's. He voted for vocational rehabilitation for disabled soldiers but against pension increases for their care in rest homes or for those who had incomes exceeding a thousand dollars. He later supported giving pensions to soldiers of the Spanish-American War, the Philippine insurrection, and the Chinese relief expedition.

6. Britton, pp. 39–53. There is further confirmation in her story through a letter of WGH to George Van Fleet in which he sends Carrie Van Fleet a box of Martha Washington chocolates from Washington; this is the same candy Nan reports in her book that WGH often sent her; Carrie Phillips in Washington, Francis Russell, pp. 296–98; on ARL spying, Felsenthal, p. 139; Sparkes-EWM transcript, January 4, 1935; MJ to WGH, March 13, 1917, on Wurlitzer family, WGHP; Sawyer I; on French ancestry remarks by FKH, text of Cyril Clemens speech at Webster Grove, Missouri, Reel 254, WGHP; "100 percent Americanism," *NYH*, February 20, 1921; WGH on

German spies in America, WGH to George Van Fleet, February 22, 1917, Reel 241, WGHP.

7. WGH did not hide his weakness for beauty, writing in the *Star*, "Howard Chandler Christy is accused of having kissed his models. Those who have seen the pictures he has produced will hardly blame Howard." Ziegfeld Follies "chickens," WGH to FKH, October 23, n.y. [1916–1919], Hotel Touraine, Boston, WGHP; Martha Lane to Cyril Clemens, February 2, 1940, WGHP; Chancellor, pp. 109–10, 235. The police records of the District of Columbia Metropolitan Police are now kept at the National Archives. The records for 1918 are missing, August 27, 1987, author conversation with Mary Ronan, National Archives; story of New York women, Gregg, Gary, Guthrie Is; story of woman at Big Moose, West I; on Grace Cross, Sparkes-EWM transcript, January 4, 1935; scrap paper of background on Grace Cross and Chancellor notes in Harding file, EWMP; Bertha Martin recollections of Harding at Grace Cross's apartment, from Dean Albertson interview with Poe Wilson, October 2, 1964; regarding James E. Cross, WGH to Charles Hard, February 11, 1918, Reel 256, WGHP; Maurice Maschke to WGH, April 3, 1919, WGHP; Schroeter I; Senate wife quote, from *Good Housekeeping* (February 1932).

8. Quote on Mrs. Phillips, Sparkes-EWM transcript, March 20, 1935; *American Heritage* (February 1965), letters quotes are on page 102; WGH to Jim Phillips, April 22 and May 1, 1918, Reel 257, WHGP; the date of the first letter is different from the date listed in the *American Heritage* excerpt, as is some of the text of the May 1 transcription.

9. On visiting the Fultons, WGH to FKH, October 5, 1916, WGHP; the "difficult tasks" quote, from a United Press story, September 1, 1923; FKH as using cusswords, WGH to FKH, Monday, March 24, n.y. [1916–1919], Hotel Bon Air, Georgia; WGHP; quote on FKH, "despising . . . ," from *NYH*, February 20, 1921; FKH quote on herself as peacemaker, *WP*, June 15, 1920; scene between Florence Harding and Carrie Phillips, from *NYH*, February 20, 1921.

10. Russell, *Antioch Review*, p. 62. The 1918 register of the Hotel Witherill is now missing, Clinton County Historical Association, Helen Allen, director-curator to author, October 29, 1991; on WGH, August 17, 1918, letter to Carrie Phillips, Francis Russell, pp. 304–05; on heart trouble, WGH to Frank Scobey, May 5, 1918, WGHP.

11. WGH to Frank Scobey, November 18, 1918, WGHP. WGH's "natural reluctance to leave Washington when she was confined to her bed" forced him to skip an important Republican meeting in Ohio, but at the end of November he noted, "I am very hopeful that her condition will be such that I can go to Ohio next week without any misgivings." On December 7, WGH reported that "Mrs. Harding is showing a slight improvement and I think the circumstances will be such that I can presently venture to come to Ohio," WGH to Charles Hard, November 27 and December 7, 1918, Reel 256, WGHP. Earlier that year, at the end of February 1918, she had a minor spell. WGH reported, "Mrs. Harding is getting along quite nicely and I feel very certain that a week later I shall have no reluctance in leaving for Ohio . . . ," WGH to Charles Hard, February 29, 1918, Reel 256, WGHP; WGH to CES, November 25, 1918; WGH to CES, December 7, 1918.

12. Britton, pp. 68–76; Adams, "The Timely Death of President Harding," in Leighton, p. 85. There are innumerable small details in Britton's book that perfectly

correspond with factual information in the private papers of WGH that she could not otherwise have known or learned and that confirm her version of the affair, if not the parentage of her daughter: that WGH sent Martha Washington candies, that he stayed at the Hotel Manhattan in New York, that Nan knew about Mrs. Harding's 1918 illness, and corresponding dates in her book with Isabelle Phillips's decision to marry.

16. *"I Do Not Permit Him to Run"*

1. Watson, pp. 225–26; for Fall incident, KLM, chapter 7, no page number.

2. EWM manuscript, pp. 327–32; EWM, pp. 178–79.

3. Vetallis Kling married Nona Younkins Hinamon on July 30, 1919. *Marion Star*, July 1, Nona and Tal Kling photos, courtesy of Glenn Elsasser; Elsasser I; ARL and Wilson, Felsenthal, p. 136; FKH hates League, Gary I; two letters on the League, WGH to FKH, March 23, 1919, March 24, 1919, Downes, p. 323; WGH to Harriet Taylor Upton, September 6, 1919, and February 28, 1920, Reel 241, WGHP; WGH to Charlie Forbes, October 24, 1919, Reel 241, WGHP; WGH to George Clark, October 30, 1919, and WGH to Charles Hard, October 21, 1919, Reel 256, WGHP; Harris, p. 25; Charles E. Hard, "The Man Who Did Not Want to Become President," *Northwest Ohio Quarterly* (Summer 1959); KLM, chapter 7, no page number.

4. CES to WGH, October 8, 1919, and WGH to CES, October 8, 1919, WGHP; FKH on queen of Belgium, *Delineator* (November 1920); Kling I; ARL, p. 292.

5. Thomas H. Russell, p. 134; material on Lawler, from Detroit *News*, December 7, 1920, and KLM, chapter 8, p. 2. Lansing, Michigan, native, Kathleen F. Lawler started as a stenographer and became the indispensable aide to Connecticut Senator Orville Platt, then formed her own agency, coming to know well many senators and representatives and counting the Supreme Court, Justice Department, and U.S. Shipping Board as clients. A Republican, she found conventions particularly lucrative, having worked those in both 1912 and 1916.

6. Sinclair, p. 114; Sullivan, pp. 45–46; HD, pp. 15–17.

7. Downes, p. 306; CES to WGH, October 12, 1919, WGHP.

8. Baker, pp. 300–07; Ardmoreite, March 14, 1921.

9. Britton, pp. 77–130; Russell-Duckett, *American Heritage* (August 1965), p. 21.

10. Stowe, Sawyer, Allen Is; Thanksgiving, WGH to CES, November 22, 1919, WGHP; *HS*, November 1, 1968. Although they spent Thanksgiving with the Sawyers in Marion, the Hardings again spent Christmas with the McLeans in Washington that year. Though he regretted not being able to partake in the intoxicating "steaming cup" as tradition always had it, he said that if he returned to Marion, he might also have been tempted "to indulge in various reunions" which he now wanted to avoid, perhaps in cryptic references to Carrie Phillips; *HS*, December 2, 1968; the Hardings had remained in Washington in 1918 because of FKH's illness, and again in 1919, WGH to CES, December 22, 1919, WGHP; on Carrie Phillips before Harding decided to run for President, Russell, pp. 298, 344.

11. For support of friends and Harding's fearing a loss of fun and distrust of HD, see Francis Russell, pp. 309–16; Watson, pp. 225–26; Sparkes-EWM transcript,

December 11, 1934; ARL, pp. 320–21; on Florence's health at the end of 1919, WGH to Carl Sawyer, October 8 and November 3, 1919, WGHP; HD quote on "two of us . . . ," from Sullivan, pp. 45–46; Sinclair, p. 119; Adams, pp. 27–28, 100.

17. *The Zodiac of Jupiter*

1. Harry B. Hunt story, August 8, 1923, run on wire by NEA Service, Inc.; *Home* magazine (January 1934), *Liberty* (April 9, 1938, and June 11, 1938); *Collier's National Weekly* (May 16, 1925); Sparkes-McLean transcript, March 20, 1935; KLM, chapter 17, p. 12.

2. KLM, chapter 7, no page; HD to FKH, n.d. [circa winter–spring, 1920], WGHP; ARL, p. 241; Charles Hard to Cyril Clemens, November 23, 1939, Reel 254, WGHP; HD to FKH, from the Shack, n.d. [spring 1920], Reel 241, WGHP; Charles Hard to WGH, March 19, 1920, Reel 256, WGHP.

3. According to Warren Sawyer, her health had been a primary reason WGH had "hesitate[d] in pushing his campaign for the presidency," but WGH wrote his cousin after a Columbus event, "Florence was not ill, as the newspaper stated, but was detained here for various reasons and someone started the story of her illness in order to explain her absence." Warren Sawyer quote, *HS*, November 1, 1968; WGH to J. Harry Denman, February 28, 1920, Reel 241, WGHP; Pepper, p. 62; FKH letter to Scobeys, from Downes, p. 396; on FKH and destiny of WGH, Sawyer I and Christian, Sr., manuscript, pp. 54–55, 88; Gary, Gregg, Sawyer Is; EWM blind quote on FKH, *WP*, November 23, 1924.

4. Sullivan, p. 100; Britton, p. 102.

18. *Blackmail*

1. Francis Russell, p. 345. A portion of WGH's response to Carrie Phillips's blackmail appears in Russell, *Antioch Review*, p. 65, Russell, *New York Review of Books*, p. 33. The remaining portions were provided to the author from the private collection of a Marion resident.

2. Various versions of Marcia from 1920 to 1938 overlap on some dates; thus the accounts are grafted from her recollections in aggregate, Harry B. Hunt story, August 8, 1923, NEA Service; *Home* magazine (January 1934), *Liberty* (April 9 and June 11, 1938); *Collier's National Weekly* (May 16, 1925). KLM confirmed that it was FKH who convinced WGH to attend the convention, KLM, chapter 8, p. 11.

3. Christian, Sr., manuscript, pp. 85–86.

19. *Chicago*

1. "Tragedy" quote, Downes, p. 417; on Marcia's prediction at convention, Harry B. Hunt story, August 8, 1923, NEA Service.

2. FKH to Mrs. Speyer, October 23, 1920, Reel 254, WGHP; *NYT*, June 13 and 20, 1920.

3. Quote on Hiram Johnson, *NYT*, June 13, 1920; Congressman Fess quote, KLM, chapter 1, p. 7; FKH recollection of the convention is from *Delineator* (November 1920).

4. *NYT*, June 11, 1920; FKH reaction to suffragist parade, Gary I.

5. Sinclair, p. 150; HD, pp. 37–38; KLM, chapter 9, pp. 2–3, 11; Chancellor, pp. 190–91, 206–07.

6. Britton, pp. 130–34; Sautter and Burke, pp. 141–44.

7. Francis Russell, pp. 371–91; HD to Ray Baker Harris, June 29, 1938, Reel 259, WGHP; Harris manuscript, "Convention," pp. 29–31, Reel 257, WGHP; "If he hadn't filed . . ." quote, from Harris, p. 25; material on WGH's condition, from Sautter and Burke, p. 144; WGH remark on "living longer," *NYT*, August 4, 1923; on FKH's role in filing for Senate election, HD to Ray Baker Harris, July 7, 1938, Reel 259, WGHP; Fess quotes, from KLM, chapter 1, p. 7.

8. Sinclair, p. 150; J. W. Wadsworth to Cyril Clemens, November 14, 1947, Reel 254, WGHP; on the questioning of WGH on his adultery, Clapper, *Washington Tapestry*, p. 55, Francis Russell, p. 383; Leighton, pp. 86–87.

9. George T. Harding to Ray Baker Harris, July 26, 1937, Reel 259, WGHP; account of WGH and FKH notes on withdrawing on Saturday, from Hunt story, August 8, 1923, NEA Service; J. W. Wadsworth to Cyril Clemens, November 14, 1947, Reel 254, WGHP.

10. "Society row," KLM, chapter 9, pp. 15a, 16, 18; ARL, pp. 304–11; Charleston *American*, November 5, 1920; Kansas City *Star*, October 8, 1920; HD, p. 53; FKH on following ballots, *WP*, June 15, 1920; FKH remarks to Reily, from E. Mont Reily to Cyril Clemens, n.d, Reel 254, WGHP; Britton, p. 135; FKH acknowledging power of astrology in nomination, Hunt story, August 8, 1923, NEA Service; FKH on watching for Kansas delegation support, *WP*, June 13, 1920; "hysterical" reaction, from KLM, chapter 9, p. 21; quote of FKH on reaction, *Delineator* (November 1920).

11. FKH back to headquarters, clipping, "Mrs. Harding Will Make Golden Rule Watchword," n.d., n.p., Reel 257, WGHP; FKH on going back to headquarters, *Delineator* (November 1920); Britton, p. 189; victory reception scene in Congress Hotel headquarters, *NYH*, February 20, 1921; Beckley clipping, WGHP; WGH to photographers, from June 12, 1920, AP story.

12. *Good Housekeeping* (February 1932); Detroit *News*, December 7, 1920; GC to FKH, July 30, 1920, WGHP; HD, pp. 27–28.

13. FKH letter to Ethel Jennings and one beginning, "I have faith . . . ," from Harris, p. 26; "I shall never forget . . ." quote, Beckley clipping; Harris manuscript, "Convention," p. 30, Reel 257, WGHP; FKH to Nellie Kling, June 1920, Reel 257, Harris Papers, WGHP; Norman Thomas to Ray Harris, September 17, 1957, Reel 257, WGHP.

20. *Women*

1. Sinclair, p. 160; Boston *Post*, August 29, 1920; newspaper clipping, n.p., n.d. [1920], "Mrs. Harding: The Woman," WHGP.

2. EWM manuscript, p. 340; Gregg I; *Delineator* (November 1920); KLM, chapter 15, p. 2; Boronson, *Fact Magazine* (January–February 1964), pp. 53–55; Chancellor, pp. 208–09; Chancellor typed manuscript page, "Insert 28 A2," Harding file, campaign memorabilia, EWMP.

3. WGH to Carrie Phillips, July 2, 1920, copy in private collection. "She was considerably talked about," he said enigmatically, adding that she was "under some investigation," but mentioned only her "being pro-German during the war," and in that context, "Harding himself never suspected Carrie as being disloyal," HD to Ray Baker Harris, July 21, 1939, Reel 259, WGHP. The progression from WGH to Donithen, Daugherty, Hays, Lasker, and then Carrie Phillips is from author interview with anonymous source, Marion, Ohio, July 21, 1991; Gary tour I; Sawyer I. The progression was apparently learned from Carl Sawyer; Russell-Duckett, *American Heritage* (February 1965); on actual amount of payment, *Marion Star*, November 5, 1981; EWM quote on Ned's giving money to blackmail amount, Sparkes-McLean transcript, March 20, 1935; on "New York woman," Russell, *New York Review of Books*; Britton, p. 351; Grace Cross blackmail letters, Bertha Martin recollections, Albertson P.

4. Another voter wrote wondering if WGH hadn't progressed to a higher level of Masonry because of his "bad reputation," Downes, pp. 524–25, 556. Hirsch recollection is from Francis Russell, p. 402; July 25, 1920, clipping, "A Little Picture of Mrs. Harding at the Notification."

5. "Candidate for Position of First Lady of the Land," clipping, n.d., n.p.; *Good Housekeeping* (February 1932); on Lasker's liking FKH, KLM, chapter 15, p. 3; Kansas City *Star*, October 8, 1920; publicity efforts, Downes, p. 487.

6. Downes, pp. 468–69; San Francisco *Bulletin*, August 4, 1923; Chattanooga *Times*, n.d. [1920], WGHP; "Nominee's Wife Knows the Game," clipping, n.d., [October 1920] n.p.; Myrtle Mason, "Nebraska and Iowa Citizens Are in Love with Mrs. Warren G. Harding," n.d., n.p.; HD, p. 58; Smithsonian Division of Political History, WGH photo book; Cuneo, pp. 108–12; EWM, pp. 239–40; newsboy day at Front Porch, *NYT*, September 27, 1920, and Johnson, p. 126.

7. Newspaper clipping, "Mrs. Harding: The Woman," n.p., n.d. [1920], WHGP; "Local Woman's Impressions of Mrs. W. G. Harding Told," n.p., n.d. [1920], WGHP; KLM, chapter 15, p. 2, and chapter 22, p. 6; Philadelphia *Public Ledger*, November 7, 1920; *NYT*, June 20, 1920; Clapper, *One Lucky Woman*, p. 83.

8. "Nomination" quote, Philadelphia *Public Ledger*, June 20, 1920; KLM, chapter 4, pp. 3–6, 8, 29, chapter 25, p. 8; two FKH notes, n.d. [1920], Reel 256, WGHP.

9. Background on special "days" at Front Porch, from Downes; Charles Hard to Helen Minster, December 21, 1920. Women staff included Edna Blair, Edith Shipman, Grayce Wall, Ellen Talbot, Edith Watkins, Hortense Fies, Mary Yeager, Bess Mason, Stella Fischer, Eva Uhl, and Coranelle Mattern; Yeager and Mason were also Catholics, *Virginia Pilot*, November 18, 1920. FKH in headquarters and orders to staff,

KLM, n.p.; Chancellor, pp. 208–09; Chancellor typed manuscript page, "Insert 28 A2," Harding file, campaign memorabilia, EWMP.

10. The permanent press corps that lived in Marion that summer covering the Front Porch campaign included Robert Small, Ray Clapper, Boyden Sparkes, Byron Price, Charles Michelson, W. N. Price, Phil Kingsley, and Ed Hill; Philadelphia *Public Ledger*, June 20, 1920; Clapper, *One Lucky Woman*, p. 83; clipping, "Recalls Mrs. Harding as Noted Horsewoman," n.d. [1920], n.p., Reel 260, WGHP; article, n.d. [1920] n.p., Roll 262, WGHP; Beckley clipping; *WP*, June 15, 1920.

11. Clapper, *One Lucky Woman*, p. 84; Sparkes-McLean transcript, March 20, 1935; Hirsch incident, from Francis Russell, pp. 401–02; EWM manuscript, p. 340; Chancellor, pp. 212, 219; *Marion Star*, November 5, 1981; Olive Clapper, *Washington Tapestry*, p. 59; Britton, p. 102; Charles Hard to Helen Minster, December 21, 1920, Reel 256, WHGP; Chattanooga *Times*, clipping, n.d. [1920], WGHP; Gross, p. 44; Russell, *Antioch Review*, p. 71; Downes, p. 523.

12. Rickenbacker parachutes, from clipping in WGH scrapbooks of Marion Public Library; Bess Furman Papers, Container 75, LC.

13. The Chattanooga *Times*, n.d. [1920], WGHP; *Delineator* (November 1920); *WP*, November 23, 1924; clipping, Eleanor Margaret Freeland, "Mrs. Harding as I Know Her," syndicated column, "The Girl Next Door," n.d. [1920], n.p.; WGHP; *WP*, June 15, 1920.

14. *NYH*, February 20, 1921 *Delineator* (November 1920); "Mrs. Harding: The Woman," newspaper clipping, n.p., n.d. [1920], WHGP; *NYT*, November 7, 1920; Beckley article; *WP*, June 15, 1920; Colman, pp. 383–84, Edna Colman was a correspondent for the Baltimore *American*.

15. FKH clipped a laudatory editorial on one such speech, noting that it was being "commented upon all over the country, and we have received perfectly splendid reports upon it. It is being quoted widely, and it is regarded as a really marvelous piece of work," KLM, chapter 4, p. 25, chapter 21, pp. 59–60; Nathan William MacChesney to Cyril Clemens, October 12, 1939, Reel 254, WGHP; Kansas City *Star*, October 8, 1920; FKH writing campaign literature, Colman, pp. 383–84; FKH to Helen Cannon, September 2 (?), 1920; Harry Price quote on League letters, interview with FKH, "bales of letters," quoted in KLM; Ira Bennett to FKH, August 24, 1920, WGHP; FKH to Ned McLean, September 8, 1920, EWMP; Blair quote, from *WP*, October 10, 1920; Drexel quote, from Philadelphia *Public Ledger*, November 7, 1920.

16. Gregg I; *NYH*, January 2, 1921; *NYT*, June 20, 1920; text of Cyril Clemens speech at Webster Grove, Missouri, Reel 254, Chapple, *Harding the Man*, p. 83; *NYH*, February 20, 1921; *Good Housekeeping* (February 1932); "The Girl Next Store Says," clipping, n.d., n.p.

17. FKH making "countless addresses," Colman, pp. 383–84; FKH to Mrs. Pardee, October 31, 1920; FKH to Harriet Taylor Upton, October 31, 1920; *NYT*, November 5, 1920.

18. Upton and WGH dispute on WGH's lack of interest in strong lobbying of the governors of Vermont and Connecticut to call their legislatures into special session and vote on suffrage, Downes, pp. 502–09; Upton wanted to avoid a repeat of 1916's "Billion Dollar Special" of Vanderbilt and Whitney heiresses who toured the country

for Hughes, Downes, pp. 511–13; on Falls and Longworths at "Woman's day," KLM, chapter 4, p. 34, and chapter 9, p. 19; Rinehart, pp. 318–19; Downes, p. 521; on ARL's not wanting to speak during campaign, W. F. Wiley to EWM, September 25, 1920; clipping, Harding scrapbooks, Marion Public Library; ARL, p. 322; KLM, chapter 4, p. 21, chapter 29, p. 40.

19. KLM, chapter 4, pp. 45–48, chapter 5, p. 6; *NYH*, February 20, 1921; KL to GC, January 2, 1932, Reel 249, WGHP; HD to Cyril Clemens, August 15, 1939, Reel 256, WGHP; Charles Hard to Cyril Clemens, November 23, 1939, Reel 254, WGHP.

20. Denver *Post*, August 13, 1920; *Collier's* (May 16, 1925); Beckley clipping; *WP*, June 15, 1920; WGH to Coonie Christian, Christmas 1920.

21. *Racism, Scandal, and Movie Stars*

1. Gary I; on use of Hollywood in campaign, FKH to Mabel Bennett, August 31 and October 11, 1920, WGHP; on EWM interest in movies and actors, Ben Atwell to EWM, January 21, 1920; Tallulah Bankhead to EWM, March 20, 1945, D. W. Griffith to EWM, February 25, 1921, EWMP; Chaplin, Pickford, Fairbanks, and Norma Talmadge had sold war bonds in Washington and met with the Wilsons as patriotic wartime duty, not for partisan campaigning. Philamen Gregg recalled that "for Doug and Mary, Mrs. Harding was arraigned in her cloak and best bib-and-tucker. And there was no darning socks," Gregg I. On crowd excitement over Jolson, John and Betty Bartram Is; photo of CES from clipping, Harding scrapbooks, Marion Public Library; WGH and actresses, from Smithsonian, Division of Political History, WGH scrapbook; Downes, pp. 470–71; Marion *Newslife*, September 2, 1979.

2. Elsasser I; KLM, chapter 15, p. 2; excerpt of Harding's B'nai B'rith speech, KLM, chapter 25, p. not listed; Downes, pp. 524–25. Bigotry toward KLM, KLM, chapter 9, p. 43, chapter 15, pp. 6–16. Weeks had been so blatant about having "taken up" with this woman that she was standing at his side to welcome Harding in the Senate following the nomination, "and she was very much in evidence presenting her so-called claims to recognition," said Lawler, at Washington headquarters. Weeks then "conceived of the happy idea of turning her loose [as a manager] in Marion," where he could date her without the threat of his wife's interference, KLM, chapter 17, pp. 1–11.

3. About the only notice paid to FKH's brothers was: "There is almost a streak of the hermit in the 'Kling boys,'" *NYH*, February 20, 1921. Tal and Nona Kling lived at 643 Ballentine Avenue, *Marion Star*, July 1, 1938; clipping "Faith, Morals and Politics," n.d, n.p., Reel 37, Calvin Coolidge Papers, LC. Text of Cyril Clemens speech at Webster Grove, Missouri, Reel 254, WGHP; *Delineator* (November 1920); *NYH*, February 20, 1921; Chapple, *Harding the Man*; Charlotte Chambers Hall to WGH, n.d., WGH to Charlotte Chambers Hall, January 16, 1921, reprinted in KLM; Chancellor, pp. 225–27.

4. Downes, pp. 488–89; *NYT*, June 20, 1920; *Delineator* (November 1920); *WP*, June 15, 1920; *Modern Priscilla* clipping, courtesy of Bartrams; *Outlook* (August 25, 1920); J. Bartram I.

5. Chancellor, pp. 111, 178–79, 182, 219, 212, and 356; Chancellor typed man-

uscript page, "Insert 28 A," Harding file, campaign memorabilia, EWMP; KLM, chapter 4, pp. 18–21; Ted Morgan, *FDR: A Biography* (New York: Simon & Schuster, 1985), p. 228; Downes, p. 524; Chapple, *After-War*, p. 56; Johnson, p. 124.

6. HD, pp. 57–58; KLM, chapter 21, p. 60; *NYT*, October 8, 1920; *Daily Oklahoman*, August 6, 1923; "Nominee's Wife Knows the Game," clipping, n.d. [October 1920], n.p., Chattanooga *Times*, n.d. [1920], WGHP; Rochester event, clipping, n.d., n.p., WGHP.

7. FKH to EWM, July 16, 1920, EWMP; EWM manuscript, pp. 337, 377–78; Clapper, *Washington Tapestry*, p. 58, and Clapper, *One Lucky Woman*, p. 86; KLM, chapter 21, p. 69.

8. Christian, Sr., manuscript, pp. 110–12; Chancellor, pp. 208–09, 258; Downes, pp. 553–59; George Cook affidavit, October 13, 1920, EWM manuscript, pp. 337, 339, FKH to EWM, October 17, 1920; Chancellor typed manuscript page, "Insert 28 A2," Harding file, campaign memorabilia, EWMP; EWM, pp. 243–44; George Clark to Charles Hard, October 13, 1920, Reel 256, WGHP; *Fact Magazine* (January 1964), p. 55; ditty, from Cleveland *Press*, April 11, 1969; Cox flirting, Britton, p. 179; WGH reaction, George Clark to Charles Hard, October 13, 1920, Reel 256, WGHP, and KLM, chapter 21, pp. 62–63; *Fact Magazine* January, 1964 pp. 56–59; Dayton *Journal*, October 29, 1920; FKH making decision to issue no denial on the story, from Michelson, p. 227; various color flyers of Chancellor rumors, Gary, Moore Is. When interviewed, Chancellor hedged and obfuscated: "He admitted that he had absolutely nothing. He says further that the typewritten propaganda being circulated by the Democratic Party is absolutely false. He thinks that the 'color taint' if anywhere is in the paternal side. The typewritten copy circulated fixes it in the maternal. He thinks that there might be something to it, but that the admixture of blood was so far back that nothing could be proven," George Clark to Charles Hard, October 13, 1920, Reel 256, WGHP.

"Certain mysterious home folk" who had lived in small locales near the homes of different Harding relatives made statements on affidavits. Some of the campaign managers traced the stories to local Marion residents as well. One "proof" raised was the same tale that a Helen Harding Meredith used as "proof" it was all a false rumor: that blacksmith David Butler had killed a man who, said Mrs. Butler—a Harding— was black. The Chancellor tree went back three generations from Warren and listed his parental great-grandparents, George Tryon Harding and Ann Roberts, as "BLACK." The affidavits were an organized effort, Cook, for example, serving as a witness to the affidavits of two others, the stories all coordinated and all made within four days. George Cook recalled that the story had been made "repeatedly" but "never been denied either publicly or privately. . . ." Calvin Keifer recalled that a cousin of an older generation, a Mr. Starnes of Blooming Grove, had been killed by one David Butler because Starnes had remarked that Butler's wife was black. Mrs. Butler was the sister of George Harding, therefore Warren Harding's aunt. Lindsay stated in detail that his schoolteacher had been one Rosalindy Harding, a first cousin of George's, and that she "had the features and color and resembled a negro" and that her brother "was a colored man of very high coloring." When once her brother came to visit Rosalindy at the school, in Scott Township on the old farm property of one James Miller, the sight of such a dark-skinned man frightened some of the smaller children who had never seen so deeply hued a person, as one student, Washington Sickel, vividly re-called. Lindsay also remembered being caught in a fierce rainstorm with his mother, near the Galion and Bucyrus Pike, and that they took shelter in a nearby one-and-a-half-story home of a "colored man," who was George Harding's uncle.

The one possible hole in the extremely aged Lindsay's affidavit is the use of the term "Harding families," an ambiguity of which side of George Harding's family Rosalindy and her brother were cousins. A remark that it was George Harding's father's family, not his mother's, that had African blood puts it in contrast with other contemporary reports claiming it was George's mother, not father, who had African ancestry, Calvin G. Keifer affidavit, October 9, 1920, Montgomery Lindsay affidavit, October 13, 1920, EWMP. On Dr. Harding's false genealogy, Downes, pp. 3–4, 260, 554–58; *History of Marion County*, 1908, p. 810. A "perfect record" was drawn up that Harding could "present to the public," Christian, Sr., manuscript, p. 53; Chancellor, p. 42. Hays was told by a reporter that "the reason the Hardings are childless" was that WGH was "too much of an American to bring any children into the world with a negro strain," "Potter" scrap, n.d., H. R. Mengert to EWM, October 16, 1920, Will Hays to Ned McLean, October 17, 1920, "Billy" to obscured name, October 16, 1920, EWMP; WGH on meeting with black groups during campaign, WGH to Charles Hard, June 24, 1919, Reel 256, WGHP; on WGH's attitude of segregated equality and how it affected campaign, Downes, pp. 552–53.

9. "We are going to win . . . ," FKH letter of October 4, 1920, excerpted in Anderson Auction scrap, January 20, 1937; "my own way . . . ," from FKH to Mabel Bennett, October 11, 1920, WGHP; EWM, p. 245; FKH to Joe Cannon, KLM, chapter 18, pp. 2–3. Partisanship didn't prevent FKH from generously writing the wife of Democratic Senator Mrs. Atlee Pomerone when she underwent surgery, "I know all about what it means from a pretty full experience myself, and my sympathy is with you," FKH to Mrs. Pomerone, October 1, 1920; recollection from William Wile, from *WS*, November 22, 1924; HD, pp. 64–65.

10. On arrival back in Marion, KLM, chapter 21, p. 70; FKH to Joseph Freling-huysen, November 1, 1920, WGHP; FKH to EWM, October 23 and 31, 1920, EWMP; FKH to Catherine New, November 1, 1920, Reel 241, WGHP; "There had been . . . ," clipping, "Mrs. Harding Will Make Golden Rule Watchword," n.d., n.p., Reel 257, WGHP. FKH told one reporter that it was a good omen that the election fell on WGH birthday, Philadelphia *Public Ledger*, June 20, 1920; Downes, p. 559.

11. FKH during election day from the various unnumbered pages and chapter draft by KL; Cuneo, pp. 147–49; HD, p. 67; Lillian Russell telegram, from *Marion Star*, November 1, 1968; *NYT*, November 14, 1920; on movies in Marion on election day, Marion *Newslife*, November 3, 1980; Clapper, *One Lucky Woman*, p. 84; Britton, p. 135; on letter to cousin, Abby Gunn Baker, "With the Hardings in the White House," n.p., n.d. [1921]; "Well, I . . . ," from *NYT*, November 7, 1920; "I believe in my soul . . . ," FKH letter of October 4, 1920, excerpted in Anderson Auction scrap, January 20, 1937; "Many, many times . . ." KLM, chapter 4, p. 22; quote to Mary Catherine Early, from *Virginia Pilot*, November 18, 1920; FKH to Miss Phelps, November 11, 1920, WGHP.

22. *Prerogatives of a Presidentess*

1. "Mrs. Harding Due Share of Honors." United News Service story, November 6, 1920, Marion, Ohio; EWM, p. 253; WGH to MJ, December 14, 1920; Pepper, p. 62; *NYH*, January 2, 1921.

2. Weeks, HD, and Hays were appointed to the Cabinet. Hert died, EWM manuscript, p. 353; Hamon and FKH, Baker, pp. 307–09, *Daily Ardmoreite*, November 26, 1920, and March 18, 1921, and Chancellor, pp. 192–93, Baker seems to suggest that either WGH or FKH spoke directly to Hamon; FKH to Senator Frelinghuysen, November 4, 1920, WGHP.

3. EWM p. 248; EWM manuscript, pp. 364–65; Sparkes-McLean transcript, December 10, 1934. FKH held the distinction of being the only First Lady–elect to fly until Eleanor Roosevelt began her globe-trotting by air in 1933. It may have surprised WGH, who, thirty-five years earlier, had written that a woman's "right to wear pants and make the night hideous on the streets is questioned." Photograph and caption from clipping, n.p., n.d., WGHP, also photograph from Chapple, *After-War*; *Marion Star*, September 15, 1885. Five months after Hamon's murder, Clara Smith was found not guilty, Baker, pp. 307–09, *Daily Ardmoreite*, November 26, 1920, and March 18, 1921; Chancellor, p. 198, Francis Russell, p. 422, and EWM manuscript, pp. 353–54; train, *WP*, December 6, 1920.

4. Edith Wilson to FKH, December 1, 1920, FKH to Edith Wilson, December 6, 1920, WGHP; EWM manuscript, pp. 307–09, 320–21; Chancellor, pp. 355–56; Eugene Smith, *When the Cheering Stopped* (New York: William Morrow, 1964), p. 112; *City Paper* (Washington, D.C.), October 3, 1986; FKH to Lois Marshall, December 9, 1920, WGHP; Edith Wilson to FKH, December 6, 1920, WGHP; Wilson, p. 316; Jaffray, pp. 78–80; *WS*, December 7, 1920. ARL hated the Wilsons more than EWM, Teague, pp. 168–69.

5. *WS*, December 5, 1920; 1920 correspondence file, EWMP; EWM, pp. 250, 254; FKH and inaugural, KLM, chapter 4, p. 42; WGH to Ned McLean, January 12 1921, January 28, 1920, n.d. [early January 1921], Harding file, WGHP; EWM, pp. 254–55; Warren F. Martin, clerk, U.S. Senate, Committee on Rules to Ned McLean, February 25, 1921, EWMP. Response to some of Ned's editorials: One anonymous writer asked why he never printed anything negative about "that coon in the White House" who was "traducing, insulting and lying about Woodrow Wilson . . . ?" Furthermore, "If you could only bring yourself to believing the truth you need not kiss his backside every day." Julia Summers of the "Woman's Made in America League" praised FKH when she "announced that the sheep had to give up their royal posture," while offering hope that FKH would wear American-made clothes only, unlike Edith Wilson, who wore gowns by Worth of Paris. When Ned reported the praises, FKH was thrilled: "Ned you are one dear boy. 'The Boss' [meaning herself] is going to be thinking about you," Francis King to Ned McLean, November 15, 1920, James Williams to Ned McLean, November 19, 1920, Julia Summers to Ned McLean, November 24, 1920, Robert I. Miller to Ned McLean, December 29, 1920, anonymous to Ned McLean, E. V. Raye to Ned McLean, n.d [postelection], all in

"1920 correspondence file," FKH to Ned McLean, n.d. [1920], signed "The Duchess," and FKH to EWM, n.d. [December 1920], EWMP.

6. ARL to FKH, December 6, 1920, WGHP; Brough, p. 260; ARL, p. 322. Price quote, from KLM; Sullivan, pp. 101, 226–28; HD, p. 69; *NYT*, May 31, 1923. Ned congratulated the "Boss" on HD's nomination, Ned McLean to FKH, December 26, 1920, EWMP; Francis Russell, p. 427; information on Burns and Means, *Fact Magazine* (January 1964) p. 57, and Alan Hynd, "The Man Who Swindled the President," *True* magazine clipping, late 1940s, JBP.

7. Dickey, *World's Work* (June 1924); Adams, p. 429; Charles L. Mee, Jr., *The Ohio Gang* (New York: M. Evans & Co., 1981), p. 149; Raymond Benjamin to Will Hays, November 16, 1920, Will Hays Papers; HD, pp. 179–184; Marianne Means, p. 169; on Votaws, Francis Russell, pp. 523, 525, and Chancellor, p. 41; Mellon, p. 104; FKH to George Harvey, October 20, 1920, WGHP; on Root and Harvey, KLM, chapter 16, p. 9, chapter 17, p. 7; *NYT*, November 14, 1920, February 3 and 12, 1922; Mont Reily to Cyril Clemens, n.d, WGHP. Her nephew remembered her "irritation" at the Robinson snub, George T. Harding to Ray Baker Harris, July 26, 1937, Reel 259, WGHP, typed page, no page number, II, Reel 257, WHP; FKH friendship with the News, James. E. Watson to Cyril Clemens, August 7, 1941, Reel 254, WGHP; editorial in defense of FKH's patronage role in personnel, from a clipping, n.d., n.p., clippings files, WGHP.

8. *Marion Star*, June 15, 1978; "Dr. Sawyer to Have Important Role," *WS*, March 10, 1921; ARL I; John Weeks to WGH, February 17, 1921, and WGH to John Weeks, February 20, 1921, Reel 155, WGHP; Sawyer. JB was born on August 29, 1889. CES to W. A. Pearson, February 1921, W. A. Pearson to JB, February 26, 1921, JB to W. A. Pearson, February 28, 1921, JBP.

9. George O. Barker had served as the Secret Service's operative in charge of the Boston District until his death in July 1903. Two months later his son Harry joined the force. For thirteen years he loyally toiled there and was promoted in 1916 to fill the position his father had held. After four years in Boston, he was put on the special tour of duty to guard FKH, Robert Snow, assistant director, Office of Government Liaison and Public Affairs, U.S. Secret Service to author, December 20, 1991; Starling, p. 168; Britton, pp. 135, 139; FKH on mistresses, KLM, memorandum, p. 1 and chapter uncertain, p. 15.

10. FKH to Miss Phelps, November 11, 1920, Elizabeth Lodge to FKH, November 20, 1920, WGHP; Detroit *News*, December 7, 1920; KLM memorandum, pp. 1, 4–5; chapter 17, pp. 8, 10; Leighton, p. 90; KL to Ned McLean, January 20, 1921, EWMP; *NYH*, January 2 and February 20, 1921; Grace Coolidge to FKH, November 4, November 11, December 20, 1920, January 10, 1921, and FKH to Grace Coolidge, January 12, 1920, WGHP; Cuneo, p. 70; William Howard Taft to FKH, December 16, 1920, Taft Papers, LC; ARL to FKH, December 15, 1920, FKH to ARL, December 16, 1920, FKH to Mrs. Leonard Wood, December 11, 1920, WGHP; FKH to Helen Taft, December 17, 1920, Helen Taft to FKH, December 17, 1920, WHT to HHT, December 26, 1920, Taft P and WGHP; Jaffray, p. 80.

11. FKH to Charlie Kling, December 1920, Chas. Hamilton Autograph letter, listed in undated catalog from 1970s; FKH to Louisa Kling, January 2, 1921, FKH to Mary Hale, December 24, 1920, WGHP; going into attic, clipping, n.d., n.p., courtesy

of Bartrams; KLM, chapter 25, page not listed; FKH to EWM, January 9, 1921, WGHP; FKH to EWM, December 27, 1920, EWMP; FKH on WGH's clothes, KLM chapter 25, p. 8.

12. The favored designers included Hickson, Lucille, Farquharson & Wheelock, Elsie, Joseph, Harry Collins, and Otto Kahn. From Hickson she ordered a suit for the inauguration ceremony, several dinner and evening gowns, and a tricorner hat, *NYT*, January 18, January 31, February 2–7, 1921; Adams, p. 215; Mee, pp. 23–24; Ishbel Ross, *Ladies of the Press*, pp. 194, 312; New York *Evening Sun*, February 1, 1921; FKH to Louisa Kling, n.d. [1921], WGHP.

23. *More Women*

1. Britton, pp. 142–43; Adams, p. 208, Francis Russell, p. 432; on Nina White, author conversation with Barry Landau, December 17, 1994; Louise Cromwell, Francis Russell, p. 448; Roxy, KLM and Francis Russell, p. 429. The only official "matters" that had concerned Ned was the Inaugural Committee, but it had been disbanded two months earlier, CES to Ned McLean, EWMP, 1921 correspondence.

2. Various documents in the McLean papers in the files from 1920, 1921, 1922, and 1923, as well as the one marked "Harding and Campaign memorabilia," were stolen from the homes of Chancellor and Grace Cross. There are background reports and scraps of paper that provide clues to the identities of those who were under surveillance. There is also correspondence between the McLeans and Burns, Smith and J. Edgar Hoover, including special reports on Bureau of Investigation problems; Carrie Phillips, Sparkes-McLean transcript, March 20, 1935, and Marion *Newslife*, September 2, 1979; materials on Grace Cross, 1920 correspondence file, EWMP. There was another technical mistake on the bogus affidavit: Mrs. Harold Cross lived at the address, but not a Mrs. George Cross, the name on the affidavit. Listed in the 1919 and 1920 and 1921 city directories of Washington, living at the Akron Apartments at 1829 I Street, NW, Apartment 9, was "Harold M. Cross, clerk," not George Cross. A "Winifred Cross" was first listed at No. 9, in 1918, but she disappeared from the directories until 1921, when she was listed two blocks away at 2030 G Street, District of Columbia city directories 1918–1921. Grace Cross, however, was married to James Cross and lived at the Wardman Park Inn.

3. FKH to EWM, February 13 and 28, 1921, EWMP; Adams, pp. 193, 245; FKH to Mrs. William Fell Brown, January 29, 1921, KLM, pp. 27–28. In the FKH clippings, an unidentified newspaper scrap from the 1920 fall campaign is an anti–League of Nations statement in language similar to that used by FKH in her correspondence at the time, though it cannot be certain it was not made by WGH. It begins, "I have so much faith in . . . American womanhood, so much confidence in the intelligence of the women of America, that I do not fear their final judgment in the 'solemn referendum' on the course of our nation in its foreign relations . . . ," Myrtle Mason, "Nebraska and Iowa Are in Love with Mrs. Warren Harding," n.p, n.d. [1920], WGHP; see also FKH stand on League in the Edwin Hill article "Lincoln and Roosevelt Form Standard in Harding's Selection," January 2, 1921, *NYH*.

4. *NYT*, March 3, 1921, March 4, 1921; Zona Gale, famous author, creator of

Miss Lulu Bett, "Drab Inaugural? It's Rich in Color, but Quiet in Tone," n.p., n.d. [probably March 5, 1921], WGHP; Edith Wilson. p. 316.

5. Clapper, *Washington Tapestry*, pp. 59–60; Britton, p. 153. Neither Carrie Phillips nor Nan Britton attended the inauguration; Grace Cross, however, lived in Washington. The Willard guest registers were sold at public auction in 1969, author conversation with Anne McCracken, Willard Hotel public relations office, October 20, 1986.

6. Murray, p. 11; Edith Wilson, p. 318; *WP*, March 5, 1921; Wilson, p. 317; R. I. Phillips, March 21, n.d. [1921]. n.p., WGHP.

7. *NYT*, March 5, 1921; William Martin to Ned McLean, February 25, 1921, EWMP; FKH reaction to "war profiteering," clipping, n.d. [March 5, 1921], WGHP; inaugural details, Prohibition agents, *HS*, March 1, 1969; campaign staff invited to ceremony, Charles Hard to Helen Minister, December 21, 1920, Reel 256, WHGP; Winifred Van Duker and other assorted articles; "Women Dominate Factor for First Time in History," *WP*, March 5, 1921, Constance Drexel, "Mrs. Harding Shares Task of Presidency," *NYT*, March 5, 1921.

8. Interview with Corinne Robinson on FKH clipping, n.p., n.d. [March 1921], WGHP. Other committeewomen present were Kentucky's Christine South, Utah's Jeanette Hyde, Minnesota's Mrs. Manely Fosseen, and New York's Agnes Livermore. Two days earlier they had obtained a separate department and budget within the Republican party headquarters. "Mrs. Harding Keeps Open House," *NYT*, March 4, 1921; *WP*, March 5, 1921; Watson, p. 227; *WS*, March 7, 1921.

9. Marianne Means, p. 166; FKH to Lousia Kling, January 3, 1921, WGHP; "Mrs. Harding's Job," *NYT*, February 13 and March 5, 1921; *WP*, March 5, 1921; *WS*, March 6, 1921; *NYT*, March 3, 1921.

10. Albertson-Wilson interview; George Christian to Grace Cross, March 5, 1921, EWMP.

11. Johnson, pp. 127, 380; Randolph, pp. 228–29; Chapple, *After-War*, p. 167; *NYT*, March 5, 1921; *WP*, March 5, 1921; *WS*, March 7, 1921. Stores along the F Street clothing corridor displayed Harding Blue clothing and carried ads for it, *WS*, March 6, 1921.

12. *NYT*, March 5, 1921, EWM, pp. 254–56; *WS*, March 5, 1921; Albert Fall to Ned McLean February, 21, 1921, Emma Fall to Evalyn, August 30, 1921, EWMP; *WS*, March 5, 1921; Harding Blue predominated. The Marine Band, graciously allowed by Florence to perform at this unofficial event, played dance music as waltzing and cakewalks worked up a sweat long past midnight, *WP*, March 5, 1921.

13. *WS*, March 6 and 7, 1921, review of *The Whirl of the Town*; *WP*, March 7, 1921; Cuneo, p. 152; *Good Housekeeping* (February 1932).

24. "Flo from Ohio"

1. Ray Baker Harris, March 5, 1921, Reel 260; clippings of White House social office entertaining for March and April 1921, Reel 237, WGHP; Starling, p. 18. The other visitor was Grantland Rice. On her first day as First Lady she accepted from Charles W. Quetsche of Toledo a champion Airedale, Caswell Laddie Boy, *HS*, Jan-

uary 1, 1969; Ray Baker Harris, "March 5, 1921," Reel 260; *Good Housekeeping* (February 1932).

2. Charity Harding to Cyril Clemens, October 10, 1937, Reel 254, WGHP; *WP*, November 23, 1924.

3. Jaffray, pp. 86–93; JB typed diary, January 27, 1924, and February 8, 1924, JBP; Hoover, pp. 274–75.

4. Albertson-Wilson interview; Barker, newspaper clippings; n.p., August 11, 1923, and n.p., August 16, 1923, Secret Service Files; JB memoirs, chapter 21, p. 273; Starling, p. 168.

5. JB memoirs, chapter 21, pp. 97–98; memo to Mrs. Howard Sutherland, October 11, 1921, File 50, Folder 8, Reel 155, WGHP; JB typed diary, November 13, 1922; JB memoirs, chapter 27, pp. 84–86. Part of Baldinger's new job made him responsible for maintaining the White House and grounds, furnishing flowers to the White House, the correct functioning of the household staff, purchase and maintain items for White House, escorting the First Lady, attending the President at formal events, Peyton March, special order, War Department, June 1, 1921; Colonel C. O. Sherrill to WGH, May 17, 1921, Reel 155, WGHP; newspaper clipping, n.d., n.p., frame 206, Reel 259,

6. Clipping, n.p., n.d. [circa spring 1921]; *NYT*, December 22, 1921; New York *Evening Telegraph*, June 18, 1921; Parks I.

7. JB memoirs, Chapter 17, p. 55; "President's Room Was Formerly Lincoln's," Washington *Times*, September 12, 1922, clipping, n.d., n.p., Marion Public Library, and *WP*, January 1, 1922; "Tales of Well Known Folk in Society and Official Life: Her Garden Lore and Deep Affection for Little Nook Where She Plants Own Flowers," *WS*, n.d. clipping; *National Magazine* (March 1923); FKH to CES, August 30, 1921; *HS*, November 1, 1969; *WP*, December 25, 1921; clipping, New York *American*[?], May 6, 1923; Olive Clapper, *Washington Tapestry*, pp. 62–63; on De Laszlo portraits, FKH to EWM, September 8, 1921, EWMP; "Mah Jong at the White House" clipping, n.d. [circa April 1923], n.p.

8. "Women Writers Glimpse White House Sanctums," clipping, n.p., n.d. [February 1923]; New York *Evening Telegraph*, June 18, 1921; *WS*, August 26, 1923; "Mrs. Harding wastes no time over the selection of food. . . . The Hardings eat to live, not live to eat," Jaffray told a reporter. FKH correspondence became so heavy that eventually ground-floor offices were requisitioned for stenographers William Rockwell and R. W. McGee, *WP*, January 8, 1922; *WP*, December 25, 1921; Baltimore *American* [Fall 1922]; New York *Evening Telegraph*, June 18, 1921.

9. Parks I; "Almost every day a hairdresser and a facial masseur would come to the White House and spend an hour or more working on Mrs. Harding." Jaffray, pp. 89–90; "President and Mrs. Harding Often Slip Out for Potluck," Louisville *Courier-Journal*, January 22, 1922; *WP*, December 25, 1921; *NYT*, June 18, 1921; Wesley Stout, "White House Newsreel," *Saturday Evening Post* (January 26 [n.y., circa 1930s], p. 22, clipping, JBP; *WP*, January 8, 1922.

10. Harry Collins, *The ABC of Dress* (New York Modern Modes Corp., 1923); FKH to Esther Metzger, February 25, 1922, Schermer collection; JB memoirs, chapter 7, p. 113. Large shoes and lengthy skirts "quite well concealed" the true nature of her health, observed JB, and "she did not complain about them being swollen nor confess

to that disability"; clipping of *Town Topics*, January 27, n.y., *NYT*, April 23, 1921; Kate Marcia Forbes, "What Goes Around the White House Fireside," *WP*, January 1, 1922; Sarah Kanuras, New York City, to FKH, n.d.; Philadelphia *Public Ledger*, "Dolly Madison's Letter," January 8, 1922; article by Minnie Brown, Boston *Sunday Advertiser*, August 19, 1921; *WP*, November 23, 1924; Hoover, p. 279; Starling, p. 166; New York *Evening Telegram*, June 18, 1921; Albertson-Wilson interview; Boston *Sunday Post*, January 8, 1922; *NYH*, February 20, 1921.

11. Hoover, p. 254; newspaper article, n.d. [February 3, 1932], n.p., Roll 262, *WP;* "Mrs. Harding's Business Management of the White House," clipping, n.p., February 3, 1923; two scraps of lists of bills, not in FKH's handwriting, one on White House stationery, the other marked "January" through "May" in columns, FKHP, New York *Evening Telegraph*, June 18, 1921, and *HS*, November 1, 1969. She directed that the Wilson china be used. A Lenox set in blue with the seal of the United States was used as the private service. A large crystal set rimmed in gold was donated and used as the Hardings' personal set. Gary tour I; KLM, chapter 4, p. 15; "White House to Save," clipping, March 18, 1921, n.p., "President's Room Was Formerly Lincoln's," clipping, n.d., n.p. Marion Public Library; Colman, p. 384; Jaffray, p. 81.

12. *NYT*, April 18, 1922, and April 23, 1923; *WH*, April 18, 1922; clippings of White House social office entertaining for January, February, April, May, and June 1922, Reel 237, WGHP; clipping from "—Woman" magazine, n.p., n.d. (full title of magazine obscured in clipping).

13. Clipping, *WS* [?], June 27, 1921. Just eight days after her first garden party on May 18, 1921, FKH held another massive one, this time for 1,604 people. Again, EWM, ARL, and Jess were present. A third large garden party was held five days later, this one for more than any others, 1,906 people. Guest lists for May 26 and June 1, 1921, garden parties, Reel 237, WGHP; n.p., n.d. [circa spring 1921]. FKH instituted an annual "School Girl Reception" for young women students in nearby schools and greeted them en masse, school by school, the May 10, 1921, reception totaling over 700, clippings of White House social office entertaining for May and June 1921, Reel 237, WGHP; government workers, *NYT*, March 14, 1921.

14. Other musical selections included "Menuetto—All'antico," by Karganoff, "Les Millions d'Arlequin," by Riccardo Drigo, "Le Cinquantaine," by Gabriel-Marie. *Mayflower* dinner, musicale program, May 29, 1922; Louisville *Courier-Journal*, September 25, 1921. The 273-foot-long ship had been built as luxury yacht for Ogden Goelet, in 1896, used by the Navy in the Spanish-American War, refitted as a presidential yacht in 1904. TR negotiated Russo-Japanese War treaty on it. Taft put in enormous marble bathtubs, Crockett.

15. *HS*, November 1, 1969; *WH*, December 16, 1921. Draper performed "a program of monologues," which included a high society matron, a Jewish girl, a hillbilly woman, and a Maine Yankee wife all in dialogue, December 8, 1921, social office notation, Reel 237, WGHP. May 3 and 17, 1923, social office notations are samples of classical music entertainment, Reel 237, WGHP. FKH also enjoyed the work of Russian, Polish, and Slavic composers Taskin, Tchaikowsky, Napravnik, Moussorgsky, Koshetz, Dargomijsky, Leoncavallo. Mark Sullivan Papers, Container 7, FKH letters to Mrs. Sullivan, LC. WGH wrote an inquiring musician that FKH "determine[s] all entertainments at the White House," WHG to H. R. McDonald, Reel

235, December 16, 1921. FKH signed a photo for Carrie Jacobs Bond, "To one who has given to me such exquisite joy as I have experienced over and over again in her 'Perfect Day,' " Jane Palmer to Ray Baker Harris, October 1, 1933, Reel 259, WGHP; GC to FKH, March 29, 1921, Samuel O. Paul to WGH, March 26, 1921, and Julius Zancig to GC, March 14, 1922, File 50, Folder 9–10; "Artists Who Wish to Perform at White House," Reel 155, WGHP; *WS*, August 7, 1923; [city unknown] *Times-Star Dispatch*, October 15, 1921.

16. Cyril Clemens typescript chapter, "The Hardings at Home," Reel 254, WGHP; HD to Cyril Clemens, September 8, 1939, Reel 254, WGHP; Scanlan, p. 74; clipping "Mrs. Harding Very Fond of Dogs, Says Mrs. Forbes," Boston *Post*, January [n.d.], 1922, clipping; *WS*, August 7, 1923; "Mrs. Harding's Tact Saves Situation," clipping, n.d., n.p.; New York *Evening Telegraph*, June 18, 1921; Lincolnia, KLM, chapter 4, p. 17; Laura Harlan to Charles Moore, May 16, 1921, LC. Tickets for tours, *NYT*, October 11, 1921. She placed drinking fountains on the south lawn, *WS*, May 6, 1923. "Open Gate Policy, White House to Save" clipping, March 18, 1921, n.p.; "no former mistress . . . ," *WS*, August 7, 1923; generosity, Scanlan, p. 73; "Never were . . . ," *Good Housekeeping* (February 1932); "First Lady Declared for Open Door Policy . . . ," Universal News Service story, March 6, 1921; Colman, p. 387.

17. "Washington Plans Brilliant Season," *NYT*, October 8, 1921; FKH to Grace Coolidge, October 17, 1921, Reel 237, WGHP; *NYT*, April 9, 1921; "Senate Ladies Tribute to Lady Bird Johnson, program text, April 26, 1966," Katie Louchheim Papers, Box c34, LC; *Christian Herald*, August 27, 1921; Rinehart, p. 365; *Good Housekeeping* (February 1932).

18. "Warren G." Rex to Laddie Boy, March 24, 1922, Reel 254, WGHP; *HS*, November 1, 1969; Philadelphia *Public Ledger*, n.d. [February 1921]; Chapple, *After-War*, pp. 142–43; Thomas H. Russell, pp. 223–24; *HS*, March 1, 1968; *WP*, February 16, 1923; *WP*, May 20, 1921. The Cuban Army polo captain Eugene Silva even offered Florence a pony after she spoke of its beauty, while watching a match, *NYT*, July 10, 1921; Ira Smith, p. 115; Albertson-Wilson interviews.

19. Allen, Schroeter Is; FKH encouraged the Lett sisters to open a Washington shop, Moore I. Evalyn was jealous of FKH's Marion friends, Marion *Newslife*, September 2, 1979; EWM on Christians, Sparkes-McLean transcript, December 17, 1934; De Wolfes came to Washington but missed seeing the Hardings, Stowe I; Jean and George De Wolfe, New York *Evening Telegraph*, June 18, 1921; *NYH*, February 20, 1921; Brashares, Betty Bartram, Allen Is; FKH to Esther Metzger, March 27, 1923, June 24, May 31, August 24, May 11, 1922, postmark, FKH to George and Jean De Wolfe, November 23 and December 31, 1921; FKH to Esther Metzger, January 17, 1923. Jean and George went to grade school in Marion, spent summers in camp. Jean then boarded at the Bennett School for Girls in Poughkeepsie, New York, George at a private school in Cleveland. Neither child was ever confirmed. George W. Neely, elected in 1922, was the father of Esther De Wolfe Metzger, FKH to Esther Metzger, November 29, 1921, postmark; FKH to Esther Metzger, July 28, 1921; FKH to Esther Metzger, January 1, 1923. FKH seemed personally closer to Tal, Elsasser I. FKH business relationship with brother Cliff, assorted receipts for Mount Vernon Avenue home, 1912–1923, Clifford Kling to FKH, July 30, 1921, Reel 241, WGHP. The Hardings avoided any nepotism. Except for Heber and Carolyn Votaw, no Hardings

or Klings were given special treatment or tried to parlay their connections for perks, Scanlon, *Boudoir Memoirs*, p. 73; recollections of Louise Kling, Marion *Newslife*, May 5, 1980.

20. Marion *Star*, November 21, 1924; H. G. Wells, "Finds Belief in Harding Growing," November 13, 1921, n.p. DeLaszlo was painting WGH in "Pink Room" when FKH came in about a letter, needing information from WGH. DeLaszlo sketched her as she talked, dressed in an pale yellow organdy wrapper, and then developed her portrait. When he unveiled it, FKH was struck by the facial structure—a "sort of composite," with as close a resemblance to her own mother as to herself, and for this reason she highly cherished the painting, *WP*, December 25, 1921. FKH sent out her formal photograph for press stories, Jane Palmer to Ray Baker Harris, October 1, 1933, Reel 259, WGHP; request from all-male office for photo, MJ to FKH, February 9, 1922, private collection; "Flo from Ohio," copyright 1922 by D. S. Ireland. The march "Keeping Step with the Union" was likewise dedicated to her by composer John Phillip Brown, John Phillip Brown to FKH, August 24, 1921; cookbook, *HS*, October 1, 1968; *NYT*, March 25, 1921; "For People Who Think" column, n.p., January 23, 1922. Robertson further said: "She has eyes in the back of her head . . . and an unusually creative imagination . . . that sees the deed accomplished while it is yet a dream. . . . Her reasoning powers are remarkable in a woman . . . aggression and literary ability of a high order . . . power to influence people . . . strong patriotism, benevolence. . . . Mirthfulness, friendship and hospitality . . . Idealism and loftiness of character . . . conscientiousness and firmness . . . ," "Shows She Might Be Lecturer or Writer" clipping, n.d., n.p., Reel 237, WGHP; first Sunday at church, *NYT*, March 14, 1921.

21. FKH to Nellie Kling, November 19, 1921; news clipping, n.p. The Hardings met Cobb in Augusta in early April 1923, during their return trip from Florida; slang, Boston *Post*, January 1922; Wesley Stout, "White House Newsreel," *Saturday Evening Post* (January 26 [n.y. circa early 1930s]), p. 22, clipping, JBP; Will Hays to WGH, April 13, 1923, File 789, "Motion Pictures, WGHP; April 14, May 21, and June 14, 1923, social office notations are samples of such entertainment, Reel 237, WGHP; various undated social notes and clippings from unmarked newspaper social columns.

22. Wesley Stout, "White House Newsreel," *Saturday Evening Post*, January 26 [n.y. circa early 1930s], p. 23, clipping, JBP; "Happier Days Here for Gish Sisters," clipping, n.p., March 28, 1922; *WP*, April 25, 1921; *Screenland* magazine (December 1933); Griffith and the Gish sisters came on March 27, 1922, following *Orphans of the Storm* premiere; quilt, *NYT*, September 15, 1921.

23. Various film shorts of FKH, private collection; Jean Eliot "Postponed Tennis Matches on at White House," clipping n.d, n.p.; WGH to Mr. Cohen. May 8, 1922, File 858, Reel 231; WGH to Will Hays, December 18, 1922, quoted in December 15, 1922, article, n.p., Reel 254, WGHP; Declaration of Principles of Motion Picture Theater, File 858, Reel 231, WGHP.

24. ARLI; Sullivan, p. 489. Johnson excoriated the Hardings on a variety of issues, including the fact that WGH read some papers, "thinking them through," on a Sunday, *Biblical Recorder*, August 21 and November 16, 1921, and n.d. [circa January 1922], and Coranella Mattern to Livingston Johnson, January 5, 1922.

25. Clipping, Harding scrapbooks, Marion Public Library; Louise H. Rumpf to FKH, September 22, 1921; Coranella Mattern to Louise Rumpf, January 5, 1922.

26. FKH to Aunt Carrie, January 29, 1923; "The enforcement . . . ," *WP*, January 1, 1922; "Oh, well . . . ," clipping, n.p., n.d. [circa spring 1921]; Cleveland *Plain Dealer*, April 24, 1921.

27. Edith Roosevelt turned down FKH, saying she rarely left "my hilltop" when in fact she traveled extensively, and FKH had no contact with the remarried Frances Cleveland Preston, Edith Roosevelt to FKH, January 9, 1921; Eleanor Roosevelt to FKH, n.d., WGHP; Helen Taft to Laura Harlan, November 9, n.y. [1921 or 1922], WGHP; FKH to Edith Wilson, n.d. [March 1921], Edith Wilson P, Container 20, LC; FKH to Esther Metzger, February 22, 1922; KLM, chapter 4, p. 10.

28. Also at the party were "Major and Mrs. Matthew Cross" and "Mr. and Mrs. Whitman Cross," although it is not clear if they were relatives of Grace Cross. "Miss Elizabeth Britton," listed on guest list for May 18, 1921, garden party, Reel 237, WGHP. In the 1918 register of the Witherell Hotel, Nan signed as "Elizabeth Christian" while WGH signed his actual name, Francis Russell, p. 669. When speaking about Nan Britton's notorious visit to Friendship and her assignation there with President Harding, which she witnessed and later hinted at to Mrs. Harding, ARL remembered seeing her once at a White House lawn reception, ARL I. In her book Nan Britton does not leave an account of either the garden party or her later secret visit with Warren Harding at Friendship. At the time *The President's Daughter* was published, EWM was not only still the leading hostess in Washington, close to J. Edgar Hoover of the FBI, and the wife of a powerful publisher but a public figure known across the country in her own right. No doubt for fear of libel—and the power of the McLean money—she left the McLean house incident out. With other unknown figures, Nan carefully veiled their names. As for the date of the garden party, she claimed that she had burned all records of her contact with Harding upon his suggestion. In her memory she recalled her first White House visit as being "June, in the spring of 1921." Without reference to any datebook, it is possible that she remembered the visit being thirteen days later than it was—less than a two-week difference. Although she described only two White House visits in detail, she recalls a visit in 1923 as being more emotional than "on *any* previous visit to the White House," indicating that there had been more than one previous visit, Britton, pp. 170, 233.

25. *"No Rumor Exceeded the Truth"*

1. Ike Hoover's dislike of FKH is hidden in the cryptic notation of June 28, 1922, following mention of a private dinner: "Chief Usher Hoover absent by order of Major Baldinger." The next day there was a more direct message, again written in the third person by Hoover, after mention of another private dinner: "The Chief Usher ordered not to return for same. Order given by Major Baldinger as coming from Mrs. Harding." Later there were doubts cast on the claims of Nan Britton, Madame Marcia, and Gaston Means that they had come into the White House (or that WGH had visited the Crow's Nest, and FKH had visited Marcia at home) because there was no

notation of their coming through the door or of the Hardings leaving, as registered by the chief usher in his record book. In light of FKH's effort to confound Hoover's recording incoming guests and her and WGH's movements, this could not be used to discredit them. Often guests were noted as coming in but didn't give their names to Hoover, leaving him to guess. His record of "Mr. Ox and Mr. Oulegan" were the *NYT*s Adolph Ochs and Richard Oulahan. "White House Newsreel," *Saturday Evening Post* (January 26 [n.y. circa early 1930s], p. 23, clipping, JB files; Gary tour I; golf, Howard Sutherland to Cyril Clemens, January 12, 1940, Reel 254, WGHP. The first Sunday he was President, WGH went out to play golf. On March 11 he hosted his first White House poker game, "White House Newsreel." On Communion Day at Calvary Baptist, WGH did not participate, confessing that he felt "unworthy of that," Olga Jones *Churches of the President*, (New York: Exposition Press), 1961, pp. 115–16.

2. Rinehart, p. 364; Jaffray, p. 87; White, p. 622; clipping, Harding scrapbooks, Marion Public Library; EWM manuscript, pp. 361–62; EWM, p. 262.

3. ARL, p. 320; any inside information, scrap note on ECT stationary, n.d., William Wrigley to FKH, December 18, 1922; rumors of a lavish vacation, FKH to Ada Denman, January 17, 1923, Reel 241, WGHP; Adams, p. 26; Sinclair, pp. 262–63.

4. Edna Heffley to Hardings, August 10, 1922; JB memoirs, chapter 27, p. 109; Sparkes-EWM transcript, December 11, 1934; scrap of letter, FKH to Aunt Carrie, n.d.; superstitions, FKH to Russell Moore, October 18, 1921; ghosts, New York *Evening Telegraph*, June 18, 1921.

5. Sparkes-EWM transcript, March 20, 1935; Parks I; Ike Hoover, p. 274.

6. *Collier's* (May 16, 1925); William Howard Taft to Gus Kreager, May 2, 1921, Taft P, LC. Taft's gossip was correct in theory but wrong in specifics, for all evidence states that the presentiments of WGH's death were told to FKH before the 1920 convention.

7. ARL p. 313; ARL I; *WP*, April 27, 1922. When EWM told ARL that Ned thought she liked EWM only because of the *WP*, ARL responded that she liked EWM "despite the *Post*," Sparkes-EWM transcript, January 4, 1935, and March, n.d. [1935], p. 471; EWM manuscript, pp. 362–64; ARL at White House, Philadelphia *Public Ledger*, April 23, 1922; ARL, pp. 323–24; April 18, 1922, guest list, Reel 247, WGHP, and various undated social clippings mentioning Longworth as White House guest.

8. Parks I; guest list of May 3, 1922, dinner, Reel 237, WGHP; description of Friendship, Starling, p. 175; FKH to EWM, November 1, 1920 EWMP; Sparkes-EWM transcript, February 27 and March 20, 1935, transcripts; *NYT*, April 23, 1921; FKH to EWM, February 8, 1922; *National Magazine* (March 1923); Marion *Newslife*, May 5, 1980; article by Minnie Brown, Boston Sunday *Advertiser*, August 19, 1921; Pryor I.

9. Sparkes-EWM transcript, March, n.d. [1935]; ARLI; Sullivan, p. 244; ARL, pp. 314, 324; HD said that he told WGH, "I would not touch liquor while in government service—it would have been too hypocritical," typescript of second of several articles on HMD by Edgar Mels, n.d, n.p., Reel 256, WGHP; Wesley Stout "White House Newsreel," WGH to unnamed senator, April 26, 1923, Reel 259, WGHP; Jaffray, pp. 83, 85; Starling, p. 169.

10. Starling, pp. 171–72; Sallie Pickett, "President and Mrs. Harding Visiting and

Being Visited in a Friendly, Homey Way," n.d. [circa 1921], n.p.; Alderfer, p. 333; Sparkes-EWM transcript, December 10, 1934; Albertson-Wilson interview.

11. Sullivan, p. 231; Sparkes-[first name unclear] Todd transcript, March 30, 1935; HD by Edgar Mels, n.d, n.p., Reel 256, WGHP; Albertson-Wilson I. Jess Smith's habit of wearing matching colored handkerchief and tie is mentioned in Francis Russell, Adams, and Sullivan. What this may have signified was mentioned in *Before Stonewall* film documentary, WETA-PBS airing, June 17, 1997. Much of Jess Smith's access to the Justice Department is encapsulated in an anonymous letter circulated in Washington, a copy of which was obtained by a Bureau of Investigation agent. This letter appears in the FBI files not as an original document but as a black copy. There is no date and further identification, but it is obviously from between March 1921 and May 1923 because it refers to Smith in the present tense. A partially obscured photostat date seems to read "9-?-22." It is located within a background file on Means, 62-7824-99x1. HD's hospitalized wife, Lucie, of eighteen years was paralyzed. "When she was in the hospital in Baltimore, I drove from Washington every night in the week, returning after midnight and being back at work the next day as usual," typescript of second of several articles on HMD by Edgar Mels, n.d., n.p., Reel 256, WGHP. "She has been given up many times, but never by me, for I never give up anything," HD to William Jennings Bryan, January 5, 1923, Reel 259, WGHP; Sparkes-EWM transcript, December 13, 1934.

12. HD, p. 69; FBI file 62-7824-1, Part I, 62-7824, Part II.

13. Ned was given food, travel, and operating expenses from a "Detection and Prosecution of Crimes" appropriation, HD to Ned McLean, April 5, 1921, Reel 259, WGHP; Sparkes-EWM transcript; March 20, 1935 Jaeckel incident, paper scrap, Secret Service file, Reel 147, WGHP.

14. Sinclair, p. 262; quote from Hoover, *True* magazine clipping, late 1940s; Sparkes-EWM transcript, December 17, 1934, and February 27, 1935, Alderfer, p. 337.

15. *True* magazine clipping, late 1940s, p. 132; Sparkes-EWM transcript, December 17, 1934; HD to Cyril Clemens, February 12, 1940, Reel 254, WGHP; HD to Ray Baker Harris, May 29, 1939, Reel 259, WGHP.

16. Means later claimed that he was spying on Nan Britton, but he may have merely used her name since she had already published her book and she could not sue him for libel, as could Carrie Phillips, Grace Cross, or Augusta Cole, whose adulteries were not yet printed. Means even dated his consultation with FKH as March 3, 1922, *True* magazine, p. 129; Sawyer I; Albertson-Wilson I; Ike Hoover, p. 240.

17. The Means account, originally from his book, is summarized in *You.S.A.* magazine, April 1963, p. 6; EWM further stated of the circumstances in which she later learned of the Walsh woman's death: "I heard these rumors . . . I would see them drink too much—drunk, never—[but] never let down their guard. Remarkable, isn't it? Because I am not easy to fool. . . ." She also suggested being in on a meeting with the President, discussing the problem: "Look up Walsh at St. Elizabeth's. Brother of those two girls was railroaded in there by Burns," Sparkes-EWM transcript, January 4, 1935. Starling could not recall WGH's ever going to the greenstone K Street house, Starling, pp. 171–72. Vylla Wilson said the death occurred at the K Street greenstone house: "Harding was at a party at 1625 K Street, NW . . . ," Albertson-Wilson I; *True* magazine clipping, late 1940s, for Hynd quote on K Street house, p. 132.

18. Watson reflected euphemistically that WGH's "lovable nature carried with it certain weaknesses that led him easily into temptation and sapped his power of resistence when beguiled," Watson, p. 228. Sparkes said WGH was "very susceptible to blackmailing plots," Sparkes-EWM transcript, December 10, 1934, and January 4, 1935; Carrie Phillips, Chancellor typed manuscript, page "A 90," Teapot Dome Affair file, EWMP. A perusal of Hoover's usher's book on who came to the White House shows the mention only of one guest listed simply as Mrs. Phillips, at a private dinner for twenty-one guests at the Willard, hosted by Henry and May Wallace, entry for February 28, 1922, White House guest register, Reel 237, WGHP.

19. Smith, pp. 111–13; Starling, p. 170; Albertson-Wilson I, p. 5; Sparkes-EWM transcript, January 4, and March 20, 1935.

20. Albertson-Wilson I; Mark Sullivan diary, entry for August 2, 1923, Hoover Institution Collection, Herbert Hoover Presidential Library Archives; Hearings before the Select Committee on Investigation of the Attorney General, U.S. Senate, 68th Congress, pursuant to Senate Resolution 157, p. 2543. There are no longer any records on Grace Cross in the FBI.

21. Marionite Madge Cooper Guthrie, who later spoke with Rosa Hoyle's son, recalled that the original birth name of his mother was changed to Warren Hardy, and he claimed, "I am one of the many illegitimate sons of Warren Harding," Guthrie, Gary Is; Gary said that there were other women besides Phillips, Britton, and Cross whom "Senator" Harding had been involved with, at least three others [besides Britton] "claiming that they had children by Harding. Jess Smith fixed it up and they all got something out of it financially. How much, when—I don't know, but they had to sign off on it." CES sent the affidavits with an oddly cryptic cover letter "relative to the cases presented by Judge Brown," CES to FKH, August 17, 1922, WGHP.

22. Unsent letter signed by Laura Harlan to Lutie H. Wheeler, January 3, 1922; FKH to EWM, July 9, 1921; HD, p. 28; Charlie Kling to FKH, n.d.; Gus Karger, "Sway of the First Lady's Scepter Is Supreme," Hoover, p. 237; Starling, p. 171; Albertson-Wilson I, p. 3; Cincinnati *Times-Star*, January 30, 1923; Louisville *Courier-Journal*, January 15, 1922, December 18, 1921, June 25, 1922; Starling, p. 166.

23. Ike Hoover, p. 234; Ned McLean to Samuel J. Prescott, November 22, 1921, EWMP. Fergy, thirty-one years old, was the best "all-around athlete" of the agents, excelling in boxing and wrestling, "alert and agile," typed scrap on Walter Ferguson, n.d., EWMP; EWM suggested that Nan's reliance on Sloan developed into a brief affair, Sparkes-EWM transcript March 20, 1935; quotes on Barker, Sparkes-EWM transcript, December 10, 1934, p. 23. FKH became "accustomed to the secret service," Chicago *Daily News*, July 7, 1922.

24. Albertson-Wilson interview; Boston *Post*, January 1922; *World's Work* (June 1924), p. 169; EWM manuscript, pp. 388, 393.

25. Emma Fall to EWM, August 30, 1921, EWMP; HD to Cyril Clemens, April 29, 1940, Reel 256, WGHP; Charles F. Hunt to A. B. Fall, November 30, 1921, R. W. Tinsley to J. Edgar Hoover, October 27, 1925, FBI file on Albert Fall.

26. Ike Hoover, p. 238; New York *World*, December 4, 1927; San Francisco *Bulletin*, August 4, 1923; typescript of second of several articles on HMD by Edgar Mels, n.d, n.p., Reel 256, WGHP; Poker games usually ended by one in the morning, *NYT*, March 26, 1972; Jaffray, p. 81, 82; Ike Hoover, pp. 249–50. If he played cards

at a private home, Harding finished at about twelve-thirty, had a scotch, and then said, "Starling, telephone the Duchess that I am on my way home," Starling, p. 169; Charles Hard to Cyril Clemens, November 23, 1939, Reel 254, WGHP. Charlie Forbes recalled that at one poker game Ned tried to solicit funds from Albert Lasker to pay the fine of a prisoner about to be released from Leavenworth until WGH announced he would remit the fine, Alderfer, p. 353; EWM manuscript, pp. 359, 362–64, 369, 374–75, 394; Sparkes-EWM transcript, February 27, 1935, John L. Thover, ed., *Politics of the Nineteen Twenties: Issues, Alternatives, and Decisions in 1924* (New York: Girin Blaisdell, 1970), p. 38.

27. "Mrs. Harding Succumbs to Long Illness," clipping, November 21, 1924; United Press story; Ginger Garner MacKaye to author, June 5, 1991 (Mrs. MacKaye's husband, William, was an employee of Timmons); JB typed diary, for November 12, 1923, and January 11, 1924, JBP; Smith, p. 115; New York *Globe*, January 7, 1922; Hearings before the Select Committee on Investigation of the Attorney General, U.S. Senate, 68th Congress, pursuant to Senate Resolution 157, p. 2543; Sawyer I.

28. "President Hopes to Go to Alaska During Summer, n.p., n.d. [1921]; *WP*, June 21, 1921; FKH to EWM, September 8, 1921, FKH to EWM, August 8, 1921, EWMP; July 29, 1921, notation, Reel 259, WGHP. The weekend before the Hardings went to dedicate the relocated Plymouth Rock, WGH joined Thomas Edison, Henry Ford, and Harvey Firestone for an overnight campout near Hagerstown, Maryland, without FKH, who was ill, July 23–24 1921, notation, Reel 259, WGHP.

29. J. G. E. Hopkins, ed., *Album of American History*, vol. 5, 1917–1953 (New York: Scribner's, 1981); Pepper, p. 63; *HS*, November 1, 1969; ARL I, on music and books enjoyed by her circle. FKH "probably" read *Miss Lulu Bett* by Zona Gale, *Alice Adams* by Booth Tarkington, *One of Ours* by Willa Cather. Francis Russell, p. 463; Starling, pp. 174–75;

26. "Us Girls" and "My Boys"

1. CES to FKH, August 8, 1922; *NYT*, April 15 and October 6, 1921. Initially FKH said she would decline appeals from new organizations because she could not give "sufficient study to warrant acceptance of membership or any opinion" and lend her name to causes "of national public scope," Indianapolis *News*, October 13, 1921; n.p., March 3, 1921, clipping.

2. "I was asked to adopt a French orphan—a splendid work, a fine idea, though if I did follow it out I would adopt one of our American orphans," New York *Evening Telegraph*, June 18, 1921; "Mrs. Harding's Fad," clipping, Philadelphia *Public Ledger*, n.d., and other n.d., n.p.; French boy, *NYT*, November 24, 1921; "Mr. and Mrs. Harding Save Dog Condemned to Death," clipping, n.p., n.d. [July 2, 1922]; FKH to John Pasta, June 20, 1921; FKH to Lou Hoover, August 17, 1921; Margaret Doherty to author, June 4, 1990.

3. *NYT*, March 14, 1921; FKH to Mrs. Cabot Stevens, March 29, 1921; *NYT*, April 3, 1921; Near East Relief, *NYT*, May 31, 1921; Irish relief, *NYT*, March 18, 1921.

4. Christian Herter to Perrin Galpin, February 13, 1922; "U.S. Airlift to Re-

publics Pales Beside 1920s Aid," *WP*, January 27, 1992; FKH to Herbert Hoover, February 6, 1922, Mary Lee to FKH, March 28, 1922, FKH to Herbert Hoover, April 1, 1922, copy of letter, Herbert Hoover to FKH, n.d., forwarded with W. N. Haskell to Walter Brown, March 20, 1922, Herbert Hoover Library.

5. "Mrs. Harding's Fad," clipping, Philadelphia *Public Ledger*, n.d.; reference to animal rights groups, *NYT*, March 14, 1921; FKH to Mrs. Jennie R. Nichols., March 27, 1922; animals at White House, Washington *Times*, August 12, 1921; Harry Hunt, "Shades of T. R.! His Trophies Move!," clipping, n.d., n.p.; tree was planted on east White House lawn and plaque on the State, War, and Navy Department Building, *WS* and *WP*, October 16, 1921; support of various animal groups, n.d., n.p., Reel 246, clipping files, WGHP; National League to Conserve Animal Foods, *WS*, November 18, 1922; "makes me sick," New York *World*, October 23, 1921; quote on feathers "Mrs. Harding Very Fond of Dogs," Boston *Post*, clipping, n.d. [January 1922]; sealskin coat, clipping, n.d., n.p.; rodeo, FKH to Mrs. Campbell, December 14, 1921; FKH to Mrs. Baldwin, April 24, 1922; San Jose *Mercury Herald*, April 13, 1921; education, FKH to Mrs. Campbell, December 14, 1921; seals, FKH to Henry O'Malley, June 3, 1922.

6. Clapper, *Washington Tapestry*, p. 58; *National Magazine* (March 1923); *NYH*, February 20, 1921; "I have great faith . . . ," Irma Skinner, "Ye Towne Gossip," clipping, Pontiac, Illinois, *Daily Leader*, n.d.

7. Abby Gunn Baker, "With the Hardings in the White House," *Christian Herald*, August 27, 1921; *Churches of the Presidents*, p. 116; guest list for May 17, 1922, reception, Reel 237, WGHP; Louise Cromwell MacArthur to FKH, August 4, 1923; Catholic group, Philadelphia *Public Ledger*, October 12, 1921; on Sanger, Mrs. George F. Richards, "The Mistress of the White House," *National Magazine* clipping, n.d.

8. Philadelphia *Public Ledger*, n.d. [April 1923]; FKH to Olive Harriman, president of the Camp Fire Girls, *WS*, November 4, 1921; Chapple, p. 170; Roosevelt anecdote, KLM, chapter 1, p. 4; FKH on flappers, article by Minnie Brown, Boston Sunday *Advertiser*, August 19, 1921, and *WP*, December 25, 1921, and August 5, 1923.

9. Joan of Arc, clipping, Harding scrapbooks, Marion Public Library, FKH to Mrs. Brown Meloney, December [?], 1923; on Curie, FKH to Mrs. Minnie Galloway Kirby, February 7, 1922. Although this first Miss America sailed in the air in a Curtiss plane and dipped into the ocean protected by the whole lifeguard force, meeting the Hardings was the "crowning glory," *WH*, September 12, 1921; Sacramento *Union*, July 23, 1923; Barry remark, Philadelphia *Public Ledger*, August 9, 1923; on sugar, FKH draft to Mrs. Louis Welmiller, n.d.

10. Fifty-dollar bond, *NYH*, May 3, 1923; "business woman" quote, *National Magazine* (March 1923); FKH letter to Southern Tariff Convention of Women, *NYT*, January 19, 1920, and editorial reaction, February 20, 1920; *WS*, May 29, 1922; Nathan Miller to FKH, June 4, 1921; FKH to Nathan Miller, June 15, 1921; FKH to Jim Prendergast, December 26, 1921; FKH to Mrs. Minnie Galloway Kirby, February 7, 1922.

11. *NYT*, November 14, 1920, Section VI; Philadelphia *Public Ledger*, November 7, 1920; "very great . . . ," FKH to Alena Lorimar, April 7, 1922; Hattie Jewell Anderson to FKH, January 28, 1922; Edward H. Hamilton, "This Woman Shows Politicians," clipping, n.d., n.p.; Hattie Jewell Anderson to FKH, n.d. Carbons of FKH

responses to Anderson were apparently destroyed; FKH to Mary Lee, typed draft of letter with handwritten additions, May 30, 1921; Lois Marshall to FKH, May 29, 1923; *NYT*, November 8, 1920; WGH to Republican Club banquet, clipping, n.d., n.p., WGHP; FKH to Mrs. Tod, January 25, 1923; FKH to ?, torn letter, n.d, and FKH to Alena Lorimar, April 7, 1922; FKH to Mary Tillinghast, Republican Women of Massachusetts, November 21, 1921.

12. FKH and Lewis of National Woman's party, January 21, 1921, prints and photo collection, LC; *The Capitol: A Pictorial History of the Capitol and of the Congress*, 96th Congress, 2d Session, House Document No. 96–374, p. 128; *NYT*, February 17 and 18, 1921; Sawyer I; Edith Wilson quote, Ishbel Ross, *Sons of Adam, Daughters of Eve: The Role of Women in American History* (New York: Harper & Row, 1969), p. 70; ERA, *NYT*, March 21, 1921; FKH on equal rights fight for women, Boston Sunday *Advertiser*, August 19, 1921; FKH on inviting picketers into tea, New York *Evening Telegraph*, June 18, 1921; ". . . the present is a most inauspicious time," FKH to Alena Lorime, April 7, 1922; her letter on joining the Women's National Republican Club, *NYT*, February 17, 1921.

13. Ruth McCormick, Republican National Committee, to FKH, March 8, 1922; FKH to Mrs. Charles Broomfield, January 26, 1922; Philadelphia *Public Ledger*, January 17, 1922; Batelle visit, clipping, n.d., n.p.; FKH to Agnes Livermore, January 12, 1922; WGH message in "Mrs. Harding Urges Loyalty to Party" clipping, n.p. [New York paper], and *NYT*, January 15, 1922; "If the president's wife and her faithful male and female cohorts had sought to inform themselves, instead of jumping at the opportunity which politicians held out to them, [her] letter," the *Morning Record* continued, "would not have been written," Meridian *Morning Record*, n.d.; Philadelphia *Public Ledger*, August 24, 192?

14. FKH to Mrs. Frank Hays, April 4, 1922, FKH to Mrs. John Vickes, March 2, 1922; FKH: "Your statement that 'the political party in the United States is the only efficient agency through which women citizens can work effectively,' is justified by the country's political history. . . . Certainly the present is a most inauspicious time for experimentation in new methods of political procedure. . . . It should be the particular aim of women to insure that their participation shall prove a real contribution to the right determination of vital questions," FKH to Mrs. Lorimer, April 10, 1922.

15. The canceled National Republican Committee women's event had been scheduled for May 6, 1922 [scribbled note, n.d.]; Ruth McCormick to FKH, n.d.; HD to Ned McLean, June 4, 1923; Ruth McCormick to FKH, n.d.; FKH draft of telegram to Ruth McCormick, n.d.

16. Ishbel Ross, *Ladies of the Press*, p. 312; "I love . . . ," Cuneo, p. 66; scrap handwritten note, Laura Harlan to?, n.d.; syndicated articles by Kate Marcia Forbes, 1921–1922 series carried by 21st Century Press; reporters, *National Magazine* (March 1923), *WS*, August 7, 1923, Louisville *Courier-Journal*, January 15, 1922, KLM, chapter 31, p. 17; "You are . . . ," Boston Sunday *Advertiser*, August 19, 1921; "I feel . . . ," FKH handwritten draft for letter, 1923–1924, on Western Union Telegraph pad, frame 0401. FKH first press conference tea was held on April 4, 1921, *WP*, April 5, 1921; 1922 tea, *WS*, March 26, 1922. FKH's 1922 tea for the women reporters grew to a list of forty-eight from thirty-six the year before. Guest list for March 25, 1922 tea, Reel 237, WGHP; guest list for July 14, 1921, Reel 237, and *NYT*, July 5, 1921; on FKH

discussion of interviews, quoting and public speaking, New York *Evening Telegraph*, June 18, 1921; recorded text of FKH speech, from clipping from Atlanta newspaper [probably *Constitution*], n.p., n.d. [circa September 1921].

17. *Christian Herald*, August 27, 1921; FKH to James Henry, August 1, 1922. Decorator Elsie De Wolfe, for one, supported the idea of a week in April set aside in honor of the wounded vets, *NYT*, March 14, 1921; WGH speech at Walter Reed, *NYT*, March 21, 1921.

18. Through Walter Thacker, the Washington area's American Legion post commander, FKH kept informed on boys at Walter Reed. FKH to Lieutenant W. N. Williams, April 13, 1923; CES to FKH, September 20, 1921; sister's letter, Irene Basford to FKH, September 20, 1921; Roberta Jacobs to the Hardings, September 3, 1921; "No . . . ," "Summer in Washington," clipping, n.d. [circa summer 1921], n.p; reporter's observations, *Marion Star*, November 21, 1924; after-dinner trips to Walter Reed, *WS*, August 7, 1923; Ike Hoover White House guest books for 1921–1923, Ike Hoover P. Cyril Clemens typescript chapter, "The Hardings at Home," Reel 254, WGHP. She told the head gardener to make certain that her weekly order of White House flowers was sent to "my boys. . . ." "If any one . . . ," New York *Evening Telegraph*, June 18, 1921. When she was presented with a fifty-pound peppermint stick, she brought it to Walter Reed for her boys for Halloween, also had candy made at White House for them, *WS*, August 7, 1923; *WP*, December 25, 1921; "I was in . . . ," *NYT*, November 22, 1924, September 8, 1922; ". . . one of my greatest . . . ," Edith C. Dunton article manuscript, p. 3. EWM continued to underwrite recreational extras for the boys, F. W. Doherty to EWM, August 31, 1921, EWMP; "In the promise . . . ," Jane Dixon, "Remember Duty to Heroes, Mrs. Harding's Please to Women," New York *Evening Telegraph*, n.d. [1922]; Women's Press Club of New York City to FKH, June 9, 1921, and FKH to Soldier Boys, June 11, 1921. The vets' storefront shop was at 1223 Connecticut Avenue in Washington, *WS*, November 20, 1921; "She treasured . . . ," *WS*, August 7, 1923; "Will Make Harding Beads," clipping, Kansas City *Star* [?], n.d.; icon, Gary tour I.

19. "President's Wife Gives Wounded Soldier a Lift," clipping, n.d., n.p.; Baltimore *American*, June 15, 1922; *Buck on Leave*, *WS*, March 31, 1922; "Lest We Forget," "Chief of Week's Events for Mrs. Harding," n.d., n.p.; Chamlee performs, "Dinner Party at the White House Last Night for French Visitors One of Unusual Brilliancy," clipping, n.d., "Society" column, n.p.; "I'll just wear . . . ," Cyril Clemens typescript chapter, "The Hardings at Home," Reel 254, WGHP; dancing by Hardings as wounded vet played waltz, Baltimore *American*, September 17, 1922, clipping, n.p., n.d.; *WS*, August 8, 1923, clipping, WGHP.

20. Mark Sullivan said that whenever he mentioned Forbes, Harding "looked pleased," Sullivan, pp. 143–44, 239; Charlie Forbes recollections in New York *World*, December 4, 1927.

21. Rinehart, p. 371; *NYT*, August 13, 1923, Sawyer I; Francis Russell, p. 522; Murray, p. 430; January 20, 1922, social office memo and guest list of reception, clippings of White House social office entertaining for January 1922, Reel 237, WGHP; A. D. Williamson, War Department, to Ellen Lowder, March 22, 1921, Rebecca Mogle, March 22, 1921, Mrs. S. A. Eldridge, March 22, 1921; Elmer Dover to WGH in FKH files, March 18, 1921.

22. FKH was not able to initiate changes in all cases or to stop the closing of a hospital at Fort McHenry in Baltimore, Laura Harlan to CES, April 3, 1922, CES to FKH, April 8, 1922; CES to FKH, May 19, 1922; CES to FKH, March 7, 1922, CES to Heber Votaw, February 23, 1922; CES to FKH, December 16, 1922; Fort McHenry, Ward 31 to FKH, December 10, 1922; dining rations, CES to FKH, January 13, 1922; South Dakota, Mrs. Henry Crutcher to FKH, February 4, 1922, CES to FKH, March 27, 1922; CES to FKH, May 4, 1922; CES to FKH, December 20, 1921; CES to FKH, January 25, 1922; CES to FKH, January 30, 1922; CES to FKH, February 15, 1922; Charlie Forbes to CES, March 4, 1922; CES to FKH, March 7, 1922.

23. Los Angeles vocational training program abuse, "An Old Mother" to WGH, August 21, 1921, Reel 231; pay inequity at Staten Island, War Secretary John Weeks to FKH, January 13, 1922, and Coranella Mattern to Emma Frohman, January 20, 1922; materials on Perryville investigation, Anonymous to Dr. Mullan, January 9, 1921; "Colored Help" to FKH, August 4, Endorsement 1921; CES to Surgeon General H. S. Cumming, August 11, 1921; 1st Endorsement, General Inspection Service, USPHS, August 15, 1921, J. M. Lowrey, 2d Endorsement, August 16, 1921, E. H. Mullan, 3d Endorsement, August 18, 1921, J. M. Lowrey; CES to FKH, August 23, 1921; FKH to CES, August 24, 1921; "the efforts . . . ," torn scrap of letter.

24. CES to FKH, January 13, 1922; CES to FKH, February 23, 1922; CES to FKH, March 4, 1923; CES to FKH, January 25, 1922.

25. Longview, Charles Forbes to CES, February 15, 1922, CES to FKH, February 15, 1922, Disabled American Veterans to WGH, January 19, 1922; second angry letter of Doc, CES to FKH, February 28, 1922; Campbell case, CES to Charles Forbes, March 7, 1922; Charles Forbes to CES, March 14, 1922; CES to FKH, March 22, 1922; Charlie Forbes to CES, March 29, 1922, and CES to FKH, April 7, 1922.

26. First Lady on bonus bill, FKH to Elizabeth Noblett, May 6, 1922. The Bursum bill would have added an estimated $108 million annually to the pensions of Civil War vets and widows. FKH explained: "The President would have gladly signed the Bursum bill had it been limited to the old veterans and widows of veterans who married prior to 1905. He did not feel justified in providing for widows who married later than forty years after the war. He pointed out the injustice to Congress, but no effort was made to modify the bill by eliminating the objectional provisions." FKH handwritten two-page draft letter, n.d.; civil service waived for vets applying for postal positions, Executive Order 3560, Gary I, October 14, 1921, notation, Reel 259, WGHP; clipping and FKH notation "Ha-Ha" on it, n.p., n.d. [transition 1920].

27. *"The Chief Executive and Mr. Harding"*

1. First day, *NYT*, March 5, 1921; Ira Smith, p. 114; KLM, chapter 20, p. 5.

2. One example of the letters FKH sent to newspaper editors is FKH to the editor of the Ocala, Florida, *Star*, April 26, 1923; MJ to FKH, March 18, 1922; FKH to Marie Sullivan, Mark Sullivan P, Container 7; guest list of April 2, 1923, Reel 237; "Whenever . . . ," New York *Evening Telegraph*, June 18, 1921; "I've lived so long . . . ," Vancouver, British Columbia, *Daily Province*, July 25, 1923; McLeans, "Today in Saratoga" clipping, n.d., n.p., and anonymous scrap to Ned McLean, addressed simply

"Editor," n.d. [1921–1923], EWMP; small article San Francisco *Bulletin,* August 4, 1923.

3. Mary Randolph, pp. 231–32; New York *Evening Telegraph,* June 18, 1921; JB memoirs, chapter 17, p. 111, and JBOH, chapter 17, p. 112; HD, pp. 170–71; *WS,* March 4, 1921; *National Magazine* (March 1923).

4. *National Magazine* (March 1923) quote of WGH, to Frederic William Wile, *WS,* November 22, 1924; KLM, chapter 1, p. 1, chapter 2, p. 9; on Assyrians, FKH to Charles Weller, January 28, 1922; Albert Fall quote, Emma Fall to Cyril Clemens, June 19, 1940, and n.d., Reel 254, WGHP; astrology prediction of WGH, January 4, 1922, clipping, n.p.; astrology and scheduling, Gary tour I; WGH on being President, to journalist David Lawrence, *WP,* August 10, 1923; WGH hard work habits, JB to Ray Baker Harris, June 27, 1938, Reel 259, Charles Hard to Cyril Clemens, November 23, 1939, Reel 254, WGHP; *NYT,* March 26, 1972.

5. Parks, pp. 161–63; Cyril Clemens typescript chapter, "The Hardings at Home;" HD to Cyril Clemens, September 8, 1939, Reel 254, WGHP; Ike Hoover, p. 275; Senator Park Trammell to FKH, August 9, 1922; case of "Mr. Nichols," handwritten draft of FKH letter to Albert Lasker, n.d.; R. B. Creager to FKH, August 2, 1922; CES to FKH, February 27, 1923; FKH to Barney De Wolfe, December 16, 1921, Schermer collection; Porter, New York *Evening Mail,* July 15, 1921; FKH to James Woods, August 2, 1922, Schermer collection.

6. Constance Drexel, "Mrs. Harding Wins Nation . . . ," Philadelphia *Public Ledger,* n.d. [circa March 1922]; Dewey Hilles to FKH, July 15, 1922; Nicholas Butler Murray to FKH, June 20, 1922; Charlie Kling to FKH, n.d.; Hiram Johnson to Evalyn McLean and two-page report, July 9, 1922, EWMP.

7. Edith C. Dunton, "The President and I . . . ," p. 4; U.S. Public Health Service cars, CES to FKH, November 3, 1921; Marine Corps uniforms, "Memorandum" scrap, n.d.; FKH to Mrs. W. W. Brink, June 24, 1921.

8. HD to FKH, n.d. [acknowledged February 16, 1923]; Mrs. J. MacColl to FKH, May 24, 1921; "Mrs. Harding Intervenes for Boy Prisoners," clipping, International News Service, n.d., n.p.; J. E. Russell to FKH, n.d.; Albert B. Fall to FKH, March 28, 1921; Edwin Denby to FKH, May 23, 1921; FKH to War Secretary Weeks, April 15, 1922; Laura Harlan to Congressman Allan Moore, June 21, 1922; "it would be . . . ," FKH to Elizabeth Noblett, May 6, 1922; "an impropriety," FKH to E. L. Mather, March 6, 1922; Alabama offender, HD to FKH, July 13, 1922.

9. *Life* magazine cartoon clipping, WGHP; two clippings on "boss" reference, in FKH clipping files, n.d., n.p., WGHP; article on farmer, n.p., n.d.; "Presidential Succession Fixed on Mrs. Harding" clipping, NYH April 8 [n.y.].

10. Heber Votaw to FKH, n.d.; "Better Work for Uncle Sam IS Aim of President's Sister" clipping, n.d., n.p.; CES to WGH, September 1, 1921; CES to WGH, February 16, 1923.

11. WGH to CES, February 16, 1922, and CES to WGH, February 13, 1922; WGH to Zionist Organization of America, May 14, 1922; *American Hebrew,* August 10, 1923; FKH to Alfred M. Cohen, July 2, 1924, in letter of Cohen's to Cyril Clemens, September 19, 1939, Reel 254, WGHP; Harding policies, Downes, p. 561; Baltimore tea, KLM, chapter 4, p. 28; New Orleans lunch, Scanlon, pp. 70–71; clipping, n.d. [circa October 1921], n.p. [Birmingham newspaper]; Katherine Livingston Eagan to

FKH, June 5, 1922; "To the White Republicans of Florida," open letter from W. G. Lawson, [1921], and "Footprints of the Invisible Government," Katherine Livingston Eagan to WGH, April 16, 1923, Laura Harlan to Katherine Livingston Eagan, April 23, 1923.

12. N.p., n.d. [circa 1922]; "It was Mrs. Harding . . . ," Gross, p. 45; HD, pp. 171–72, 174–76; article clipping from FKH to WGH, "League US Not into Temptation," n.d., n.p.

13. *NYT*, November 10, 1921; KLM, chapter 29, no page number; Colman, p. 400. WGH appointed four women as part of the President's Advisory Council; Chapple, *After-War*, p. 209; handwritten notecard, FKH to EWM, n.d. [November 1921], EWMP.

14. Clipping, *Saturday Evening Post* (April 28, 1923), Roll 246, WGHP; manuscript of Edith C. Dunton article, p. 2, EWMP; *WP*, November, 23, 1924; "This coming conference . . . ," "The First Lady," clipping, n.d., n.p., January 15, 1922; Garibaldi, *WP*, December 29, 1921.

15. Clippings of social notices, n.d., n.p. [1921–1922], WGHP; Washington *Times*, November 22, 1921; FKH to Governor Pinkham, December 22, 1921; Chapple *After-War*, p. 181–204;

16. Christmas, *NYH*, December 21, 1921; *WP*, December 22, 1921; New York *Tribune*, December 25, 1921; *NYT*, December 22, 1921; Cyril Clemens typescript chapter, "The Hardings at Home," Reel 254, WGHP; Randolph, p. 229; scrap, n.d.; WGH to Jennings, Sinclair, p. 239; Forbes recollection, Shover, pp. 38–39.

17. George Christian to Ned McLean, December 26, 1921; Jess Smith to Ned McLean, November 25, 1921; EWM manuscript, pp. 359–60; Sparkes-EWM transcript December 11, 1934; New Year's reception, Colman, pp. 385–86, *NYT*, August 8, 1923; *WP*, January 3, 1922; FKH to EWM, February 8, 1922.

18. "Problems of President Harding's First Year," clipping, nd., n.p.; "Mrs. Harding's First Year in Office" clipping, n.p., n.d. [circa March 1922]; Constance "Mrs. Harding Wins Nation . . . ," Drexel, Philadelphia *Public Ledger*, n.d. [circa March 1922]; New York *World*, January 19, 1922; New York *Tribune*, January 19, 1922.

19. Jess Smith letter and Evalyn quotes, EWM manuscript, pp. 378–84; Sparkes-EWM transcript, December 10, 1934, and n.d. [1935], eleventh sitting, pp. 511–15.

20. Rochester, New York, *Democrat and Chronicle*, August 8, 1923; "Mrs. Harding" one-column clipping, n.p., n.y. [circa 1923]; Lukin Johnson, "Glimpses of Late President Harding . . . ," clipping, n.d. [post–August 3, 1923], n.p. [Vancouver, Canada, publication].

28. *The Summer of '22*

1. Three-paragraph social column clipping, n.d. [spring 1922], n.p.; Ray Baker Harris Papers, typed page, Reel 258; New York *World*, Dec. 4, 1927; "Vacation Plans of Official Families Remain Uncertain" clipping, n.p., n.d. [circa June 1922]; FKH remarks from "Dolly Madison" social column clipping, printed May 6, 1922.

2. JB typed diary, May 27, and June 3, 1922; "untrained eye," JB to Ray Baker Harris, June 27, 1938, Reel 259, WGHP; "spies," JB typed diary, June 11, 1922. JB

was condescending about Evalyn: "showy and jewel bedecked," "unattractive," JB typed diary, May 19, 1922; CES speech, JB typed diary, June 21, 1922; JB to Ray Baker Harris, June 27, 1938, Reel 259, WGHP; WGH health, CES to WGH, June 20, 1922; JB on Jess Smith, Boone memoirs, Chapter 17, p. 43; JB typed diary, June 18, 1922.

3. HD, pp. 246–47; Sullivan, p. 447.

4. *WP*, May 30, 1922; Baltimore *American*, June 8, 1922; *WS*, June 8, 1922; *WH* June 8, 1922; *WP*, June 8, 1922; New York *Tribune*, May 28, 1922; Washington *Times*, May 26, 1922; *WS*, May 26, 1922; clover still preserved in FKH jewelry box, WGH home; guest list for June 7, 1922, garden party, Reel 237, WGHP.

5. JB typed diary, May 24, 1922, August 9, 1922; EWM, p. 266; May 12–13, 1922, notation, Reel 259, WGHP; JB typed diary, June 12, 1922; WGH to Ambassador Richard W. Child, July 24, 1922, Reel 231; August 6, 1921, and August 13, 1921, issue of "General Intelligence Bulletin," J. E. Hoover to Ned McLean, August 13, 1921, August 27, 1921, all EWMP. It is hard to believe that the loose-lipped Ned and Evalyn would not have discussed at least some of the FBI activities with the Hardings. William J. Burns to Ned McLean, September 8, 1921. Ned was enmeshed in a multitude of nefarious and harmless complicated plots, schemes, cover-ups, and games with Jess and the Justice Department, Means, Burns, and Daugherty. Some documentation on his activities remains; for most, however, there are only enigmatic, cryptic, and coded scraps, the trail of which is nearly impossible to track. One mysterious twenty-one-page confidential letter to Chief W. H. Moran of the Secret Service was sent by an unnamed Cabinet secretary "at the suggestion of the Attorney General, transmitting a letter from Jess W. Smith with its enclosure from Harry F. Jaeckel, Raymond Street Jail, Brooklyn, New York, handed to Smith by Martin Finn, E. B. McLean's valet," typed description of letter to W. H. Moran, April 24, 1922, Reel 147; WGH to EBM, January 12, 1922, EWMP.

6. GC to Walter F. Lineberger, May 2, 1922, and GC to HD, n.d., enclosed brochure, John O'Dwyer to GC, July 15, 1922, GC to John O'Dwyer, July 15, 1922, WGHP. After examining one of the rare editions of this crudely printed, poorly edited racist work, the careful Professor Alderfer, in his study of Harding, points out that while the book abounds with "typographical errors, repetitions and dogmatic asser-tions," they "cannot hide the knowledge of intimate and personal politics which the author has at his finger tips. Nor can it obscure some rather profound observations . . . it deserves more attention than one would give it after receiving a first impression," Alderfer, p. 373. In pointing out that Warren's family members rarely visited the White House, Chancellor attempted to make the case that the President had a "fear of ex-posure" by his "black" relatives when in fact, Dr. Harding was elderly and rarely left Marion and Charity lived in California, while Carrie Votaw and Deac were actually frequent guests; Chancellor, pp. 42, 62, 80, 88; Francis Russell, pp. 431, 538; Boroson *Fact* magazine, January 1964, p. 58; Sparkes-EWM transcript, January 4, 1935.

7. CES to FKH, July 24, 1922; Sawyer I; *NYT*, July 4, 1922; Marion, Johnson, p. 21; George Christian Sr., to FKH, June 7, 1922, Reel 249, WGHP; KLM, chapter 20, p. 5, chapter 31, p. 20; FKH to Esther Metzger, July 31, 1922; Washington *News*, September 9, 1922; Phillips, Chancellor manuscript notes, Sawyer I; FKH to Carl Sawyer, July 14, 1922; Britton, pp. 216–17, 224; Christian, Sr., manuscript, pp. 206–

07, Reel 249, WGHP; *WP*, July 9, 1922; FKH to Carl Sawyer, July 14, 1922; FKH to Esther Metzger, postmarked July 31, 1922; FKH to EWM, July 28, 1922, EWMP.

8. New York *Tribune*, July 16, 1922, and two-column social article clipping, n.p., n.d. [July 1922]; *WS*, August 29, 1922, and Washington *Times*, August 30, 1922; EWM to FKH, n.d. [July 1922], FKHP; FKH to Esther Meztger, August 24, 1922, postmark; FKH to Laura Harlan, July 31, 1922; FKH to Esther Metzger, August 24, 1922.

9. Charles D. Hilles to FKH, August 1, 1922; Birch Helms to FKH, August 5, 1922; *WH*, n.d. [September 1, 1922], and September 2, 1922; "The days . . . ," FKH to Charles Hilles, July 28, 1922; EWM to FKH, n.d. [August 1922].

10. Hudson Country District Society for the Prevention of Cruelty to Animals to FKH, August 1, 1922; "President's Wife Buys Oldest Horse," clipping, Catawissa, Pennsylvania, August 14, 1922, n.p.; Detroit *Free Press*, October 16, 1921; New York *Call*, August 15, 1922; cartoon of Laddie Boy and Oh Boy, n.d., n.p. There was some praise for her saving of Clover in, for example, the Buffalo *Times*, August 29, 1922.

11. Alderfer, p. 233; *NYT*, October 25, 1922; Sawyer cartoon is from *Life*, frame 0309, Reel 245, WGHP; W. D. Upshaw to CES, August 5, 1922, Reel 245, WGHP; C. Garnet Day and William F. Deegan to CES, August 8, 1922, Reel 245, WGHP; John D. Weing to CES, August 7, 1922; Colonel Ray of the South Dakota American Legion telegram quoted in Department of Interior, Office of Commissioner of Indian Affairs (signature indistinct) to CES, August 23, 1922; John Leach to CES, August 8, 1922; W. P. Miller to CES, August 8, 1922; Reel 245, WGHP; S. Clyde McCarley and Elbert J. Dickert to CES, August 7, 1922; Reel 245, WGHP; bonus bill, Boone typed diary, August 31, 1922; anonymous to CES, Grand Rapids, Michigan, August 19, 1922; Reel 245, WGHP; JB typed diary, August 24, 1922.

12. CES to WGH, March 22, 1922, CES to WGH, May 11, 1922; CES to WGH, May 18, 1922; Rinehart, pp. 249–350; on Carolyn Votaw role, Francis Russell, pp. 523–525; Mee, pp. 149–154; Sawyer I.

13. Stella Marks to FKH, April 5, and August 4, 1922; FKH to Stella Marks, August 11, 1922; also incomplete letter scrap, one paragraph, n.d.

14. Entries for August 22, 1922, White House guest register, Reel 237, WGHP; Kate Forbes quote, *HS*, November 1, 1969.

15. "Watching Legislation, Pulling Wires . . . ," clipping, Washington, August 26, 1922, n.p.; "Report read from Mr. Klein from [indistinct] by Hammerlein, FBI file 62-3441-2a; Hammerlein speech is from "Statement of Mike Sikorski made in the presence of Daniel F. Dyer and John Curtin, special agents, Bureau of Investigation, US Department of Justice," September 15, 1922, Buffalo office of the Bureau, FBI file 62-3441-6; confidential report of Daniel Dwyer and John Updegrove, September 9, 1922, for William J. Burns, FBI file 62-3441-3; Sparkes-EWM transcript December 11, 1934; JB typed diary, August 22, 1922; W. J. Burns to E. J. Brennan, September 7, 1922, FBI file 62-3441.

16. Britton, pp. 173, 174, 175, 177, 183, 187, 198–99, 206, 209, 210, 224, 228, 352; Parks I; JB typed diary, June 15, 1922; Walter Ferguson account from New York Sunday *News*, August 2, 1964; ARL I; Francis Russell, p. 467; Marcia quote, Miller, p. 223; anonymous [Mary Howbert?] to FKH, August 22, 1922.

17. FKH to Esther Metzger, August 24, 1922, quoted in Marion *Newslife*, May

5, 1980; Boone typed diary, August 26 and 27, 1922; FKH to EWM, September 6, 1922, EWMP; JB typed diary, September 8, 1922.

29. *The Valley of Death*

1. *WP*, September 8, 1922; JB typed diary, September 8, 1922; illness background, New York *Tribune*, September 13, 1922; JB typed diary, September 8, 1922; JBOH, p. 17. Powderly was about thirty years old and the niece of Knights of Labor leader Terence Powderly. JB memoirs, chapter 17, p. 56; JB typed diary, September 7, 1922; *WH* September 9, 1922; *NYT*, September 9, 1922; New York *Tribune*, September 9, 1922; Philadelpha *Public Ledger*, September 12, 1922.

2. *WP*, September 9, 1922; *NYT*, September 10, 1922; "Ill as she is, she is interested in everything that pertains to her husband . . . ," New York *Tribune*, September 9, 1922; JB typed diary, September 8 and 9, 1922; San Francisco *Call and Post*, July 31, 1923.

3. JB memoirs, chapter 17, p. 66; Washington *News*, September 11, 1922; *WS*, September 10, 1922; *Marion Star*, *WS*, September 10, 1922; WGH on signing letters, September 8, 1922, notation, Reel 259, WGHP; telegrams to CES from "Autotherapy Duncan," W. A. Guild, Eugene Kuhne, William Burell, Nicolas Motaxas, September 9 and 10, 1922; "Crippled Colored Man Sends Rose to Mrs. Harding," clipping, n.d., n.p., Boone clipping file on Hardings, JBP; the Wilsons, Thomas H. Russell, p. 129; entries for first half of September 1922, White House guest register, Reel 237, WGHP; Chapple, *After-War*, p. 215.

4. *WP*, September 10, 1922; Washington *Daily News*, September 11, 1922; *WH* October 18, 1922; Ike Hoover appointment book entries for September 9 and 10, 1922; White House guest register, Reel 237, WGHP; EWM, pp. 266–67; EWM manuscript, pp. 385–86.

5. JBOH, p. 20; JB memoirs, chapter 17, p. 62; *WS*, September 13, 1922; KLM, chapter 5, p. 5; EWM quote, *WP*, September 11, 1922; HD, *WS*, September 9, 1922; prediction, *WH*, September 10, 1922; WGH during illness, KLM, foreword, p. 2, chapter 4, p. 7; Charles H. Mayo to Ray Baker Harris, June 27, 1933, Reel 259, WGHP.

6. *NYH*, September 10, 1922; *WH*, September 9, 1922; FKH "near-death" experience, from JB typed diary, September 10, 1922, JB memoirs, chapter 17, pp. 63 and 63a, JBOH, p. 22; *National Magazine* (March 1923); Louise Kling, Marion *Newslife*, May 5, 1980; sudden physical change, JB memoirs, chapter 17, p. 63, JBOH, p. 22; reaction to change, JB memoirs, chapter 17, p. 63a.

7. JB memoirs, chapter 17, p. 64; Chapple, *After-War*, p. 215; *NYH*, September 9, 1922; *NYT*, September 12, 1922, *WP*, September 12, 1922. *WP*, September 15, 1922; New York *World*, September 15, 1922; *WH*, November 27, 1922; JB typed diary, September 11–17, 1922; bonus bill, JB typed diary, September 19, 1922; WGH to E. Mont Reilly, September 19, 1922, Reel 259, WGHP; JB typed diary, September 21, and 26, 1922; JBOH, p. 26; WGH to Catherine New, October 12, 1922, Reel 259, WGHP; *WS*, October 1, 1922; *WP*, October 14, 1922. CES to WGH, September 14, 1922; Edythe Tate Thompson to FKH, September 24, 1922; Laura Harlan to CES, October 2, 1922, CES to Laura Harlan, October 24, 1922.

8. JB typed diary, September 21, September 24, September 30, October 9, November 20, 1922, January 8 and 18, 1923; clippings of White House social office entertaining for December 1922, Reel 237, WGHP; San Francisco *Chronicle*, October 22, 1922; election day, JB memoirs, chapter 17, p. 83; Grace Coolidge to "Knight of the Arts," Charles Moore, November 23, 1922, Box 10, Moore P; Philadelphia *Public Ledger*, December 21, 1922; FKH activities, *WH*, October 26, 1922; announcement of recuperation, New York *Tribune*, November 11, 1922; *NYH*, February, 25 1923; John Stephan to FKH, October 28, 1922; *National Magazine* (March 1923); WHG to Joe Mitchell Chapple, March 5, 1923, Chapple, *After-War*, p. 136; *WS*, December 1, 1922; JB memoirs, chapter 21, p. 272.

9. EWM to FKH, November 22, 1922, FKHP; EWM to WGH, December 12, 1921, Reel 229, WHGP; Watson, pp. 228–29; Parks I; February 25, 1923. It is not absolutely clear that the woman in question was Nan Britton. ARL I; Miller, p. 225.

10. JB typed diary, November 22 and 23, 1922; FKH to Ada Denman, January 17, 1923, Reel 241, WGHP; JB typed diary, November 30, 1922; *NYT*, December 1, 1922. At this time, a Congressman Kaller unsuccessfully initiated an effort to impeach the Attorney general. The House in a 204–77 vote so acquiesced against Daugherty's impeachment, Washington *News*, September 11, 1922; CES to WGH, November 29, 1922; U.S. Department of Agriculture to CES, November 28, 1922; WGH to CES, November 29, 1922; CES to WGH, December 21, 1922; WGH to CES, December 28, 1922.

11. Clemenceau, JB typed diary, December 7 and 8, 1922; first handwritten letter, FKH to Esther Metzger, December 19, 1922; Christmas Day, JBOH, p. 24; various clippings on 1923 White House Christmas—"Hardings Enjoy Quiet Xmas Holiday," December 20, 1920, "President's Wife to Join Him in Xmas Dinner," "Quiet Yule for White House," "Mrs. Harding Presides at Christmas Dinner"—*WH*, December 22, 1922; WGH to Esther Metzger, January 1, 1923; FKH to Esther Metzger, January 17, 1923.

12. "Hardings to See Coué" clipping, n.p., n.d. [post January 17, 1923]; "My recovery . . . ," Edith C. Dunton, p. 2; see also FKH to Ada Denman, January 17, 1923, Reel 241, WGHP, ". . . struck anew," FKH to Bertha Wollenweber, February 19, 1923; JBOH, chapter 17, p. 112; *Liberty* (April 9, 1938 and (June 11, 1938), Collier's (May 16, 1925); FKH to Esther Metzger, postmarked February 25, 1923.

13. EWM, pp. 267–69; "When she was sick or not . . ." Sparkes-EWM transcript, December 11, 1934; WGH to Joe Mitchell Chapple, September 14, 1922, Chapple, *After-War*, p. 144; Lillian Rogers Parks, p. 170; "In one way . . . ," Thomas H. Russell, p. 137; Yellowstone, Chapple, *After-War*, p. 137; French Ambassador Jusserand to WGH, February 8, 1923; Christian, Sr., manuscript, pp. 193–94; "You are always . . . ," EWM to FKH, n.d., [1923] "Thursday," Atlantic City; "some days the morale . . . ," FKH to Ada Denman, January 17, 1923, Reel 241, WGHP; "made her preparations . . . ," JB memoirs, chapter 17, pp. 129–30; confidence in CES, Gross, *Vindication*, p. 48; "vindicated her feeling . . . ," *NYT*, November 22, 1924.

30. One Suicide and Two Resignations

1. Chapple, *After-War*, p. 144; JB typed diary, January 18, 1923; *WS*, January 17, 1923; Philadelphia *Public Ledger*, February 13, 1923; Gus Karger, "Sway of the First Lady's Scepter Is Supreme," Cincinnati *Times-Star*, January 30, 1923; FKH to Aunt Nellie, February 13, 1923; Seattle *Times*, January 7, 1923.

2. JB typed diary, January 21 and January 26, 1923; WGH to HD, January 26, 1923, Reel 259, WGHP; CES to WGH, January 29, 1923; meeting with FKH, Burns, and Forbes, JB typed diary, January 22, 1923; Edythe Tate Thompson to FKH, December 29, 1922; incomplete one-page letter from unidentified (Stella Marks) to Laura Harlan, "Confidential Secretary to Mrs. Harding," January 15, 1923; *Good Housekeeping* (February 1932); JB typed diary, January 26, 1923.

3. JB memoirs, chapter 12, p. 18; Sullivan, vol. 6, pp. 240–41; HD to FKH, January 6, 1923. "It was C. E. Sawyer and Mrs. Harding both who came to Harding about the end of Forbes," author interview with Dick West, July 18, 1991; Forbes resignation process, Boone memoirs, chapter 17, p. 120; "never recovered," Russell, p. 558; CES and Blacksten affair, "Why Mrs. Bloestone [*sic*] accompanied Gen'l. Sawyer to Washington [from Pittsburgh], then he got her a ticket and she immediately returned to Columbus?," wondered Boone, JB typed diary, February 26 and March 4, 1923.

4. Bertha Winne Eldred to FKH, February 17, 1923; *Liberty* (April 9 and June 11, 1938); astrological clipping of First Lady, Account Books, Box 790, Folder 1, WGHP, quoted in Murray, p. 429; FKH to EWM, February 5, 1923; Philadelphia *Public Ledger*, February 13, 1923; "Mrs. Harding Well: First Lady Again," clipping, n.p., n.d. [February 1923]; rumors of illness [single social column clipping], n.d., n.p.; rumors of Europe trip, FKH to Mrs. Todd, January 25, 1923; press conference, "This Neighborhood," clipping, n.p., n.d. [February–March 1923]; "Mrs. Harding Again Acts as Hostess," clipping, n.p., n.d. [February 1923]; "Mrs. Harding Now Recovered to Go South with President," New York *Evening World*, February 26, 1923, and clipping, n.d., n.p.; February 24, 1923, Reel 237, WGHP; Colman, pp. 387–88; "Women Writers Glimpse White House Sanctums," clipping, n.p., n.d. [February 1923]; Albertson-Wilson I, p. 4.

5. FKH to EWM, February 2, 1923, EWMP; EWM to FKH, n.d. [January–February 1923], FKH to EWM, January 22, 1923, FKH to EWM, February 17, 1923, EWM to FKH, February 25, 1922, WGHP.

6. Two letters, ARL to FKH, n.d. [February 14–March, 1923]; FKH to ARL, March 4, 1922, and ARL to FKH, n.d. [March 1922]; ARL, Parks Is; she merely gave them popular currency with a devilish twist. Another possible venue to FKH may have been Jess Smith or someone else, through Gaston Means. Gaston knew EWM very well. And he knew a great deal more about her and the Hardings than she suspected because of his association with William O. Duckstein, Ned McLean's private secretary and the husband of Jessie Duckstein, private secretary to Billy Burns. While he worked as a special agent for the bureau, Means became very close to Mrs. Duckstein. Hearings of Special Senate Committee Investigating Conduct of Attorney General, vol. 3, pp. 2415–2559; *NYT*, June 9, 1932. Whoever told her first,

FKH discovered the betrayal by EWM. "She always knew everything, knew about what everybody was doing," FKH's niece recalled. "She had many people in different places looking out for her . . . People always trusted her . . . and [they] told her things," Kling, I.

7. David Lawrence report, *Marion Star*, March 7, 1923; WGH to Ned McLean, EWM, p. 270; HD to FKH, n.d. [February 28, 1923]; Ruth Powderly to FKH, April 17, 1923; dinner and movie, Cleveland *Plain Dealer*, March 4, 1923; Alfred M. Cohen to Cyril Clemens, September 19, 1939, Reel 254, WGHP; FKH to Ethel Jennings, February 21, 1923.

8. Fall resignation, KLM, chapter 27, p. 62, *WP*, March 4, 1923, Washington *Times*, March 1, 1923, Emma Fall to GBC, June 20, 1931, Reel 249, WGHP; *WS*, March 5, 1923; HD to FKH, n.d. [FKH responded on March 4, 1923]; JB memoirs, chapter 18, pp. 8, 12, chapter 17, pp. 1213–14.

9. EWM condition, FKH to Ethel Jennings, April 11, 1923; Harding activities in Florida, New York *World*, March 13, 1923; Tampa *Union*, March 12, 1922; *WP*, March 9, 1923 [returned to D.C. on March 12, 1922]; kimono given to FKH by Senate wife, Mrs. Warren, FKH to Mrs. Warren, February 27, 1923; JB memoirs, chapter 18, pp. 11, 21; FKH in Miami, Miami *Herald*, March 16, 1923.

10. JB memoirs, chapter 18, pp. 13, 17; Marx, pp. 323–26, 332; draft of Edith C. Dunton article, pp. 1–2; Rinehart, p. 372; Sullivan, pp. 241, 363.

11. "President's Vacation Continues Unbroken" clipping, n.d., n.p.; FKH to Elk Ladies, April 4, 1923, and Christine Gillette to Rudolph Forster, WHGP; Harry New to FKH, March 24, 1923; Laura Harlan to Harry New, April 2, 1923; Harry New to Laura Harlan, April 2, 1923; FKH to Esther Metzger, March 27, 1923; JB memoirs, vol. 18, pp. 31, 33, 39, 43.

12. New York *World*, October 16, 1922; Mark Sullivan article, n.p., n.d., Reel 246; FKH to Lucretia Pattern Wright, February 23, 1923; JB typed diary, March 28 and 29, 1923; Chapple, *After-War*, p. 216; JB memoirs, chapter 18, pp. 41–43; "Warren a Candidate, Says Mrs. Harding," n.p., n.d. [March 1923], Frame 1196, Roll 246, WGHP; column by Edward G. Lowry, Philadelphia *Public Ledger*, March 7, 1923.

13. Louise Kling quote, from Marion *Newslife*, May 5, 1980. The garden included "Mrs. Harding Rose," Washington *Times*, March 23, 1923; Kathleen Lawler to FKH, June 13, 1923, FKH to "Ann," June 14, 1923; newspaper clippings, n.p., n.d. [April 1923].

31. *Astral Premonitions*

1. "Mrs. Harding Again Takes Place in Washington Society," clipping, April 22, 1923, n.p.; clippings of White House social office entertaining for April and May, 1923, Reel 237, WGHP; Ruth Dayton, "Mrs. Harding's 'First' Day Is Busy," Cosmopolitan News Service, New York dateline, April 25, 1923, and "Mrs. Harding Glad to 'Do Things' Again," clipping, n.p., April 25, 1923; quote from Patten, KL, chapter 30, p. 7; account of defeated vice presidential mansion bill, from Nicholas Butler Murray, *Across the Busy Years* (New York: Scribner's, 1939), pp. 355–56.

2. Carl Ackerman, "How the President Keeps Well," *Saturday Evening Post* (May 5, 1923); William Wrigley to FKH, April 20, 1923; planned visit to Hollywood, clipping, n.d. [February 1923], n.p.; FKH to Charlie Kling, June 14, 1923, Frank Carpenter to FKH, May 7, 1923.

3. Fall's policy dispute with Agriculture Secretary Wallace, New York *World*, May 12, 1923; Emma Fall to Cyril Clemens, Reel 254, WGHP; Harding liquor use, "Why, Albert!," clipping, n.p., n.d. [March–August 1923]; Harry F. Sinclair to FKH, May 17, 1923; Olive Clapper, *One Lucky Woman*, p. 93.

4. *Liberty* (April 9 and June 11, 1938); Sparkes-EWM transcript, December 10, 1934, *True* magazine, n.d. [late 1950s], clipping, p. 134; Poindexter, New York, *Tribune*, January 30, 1923, *WS*, April 4, 1923.

5. Jess Smith to Ned McLean, May 19, 1923, EWM; JB typed diary, April 19 and 25, 1923; Jess Smith to JB, May 19, 1923, JBP.

6. JBOH, p. 57; Herbert Hoover, p. 49; JB memoirs, chapter 18, p. 6211, b; quoted from passages of testimony of Roxy Stimson; on pp. 504–558 of vols. 1 to 4, U.S. Senate hearings, Investigation of the Attorney General; 1924; the passages are here condensed. *True* magazine, clipping, p. 134, late 1940s.

7. JB typed diary, handwritten entry for May 29, 1923; "J. W. Smith Suicide in Apartment of Attorney General," May 30, 1923, n.p. [Washington newspaper], JB clippings; EWM manuscript, pp. 394–95.

8. "J. W. Smith Suicide in Apartment of Attorney General," May 30, 1923, n.p. [Washington newspaper], JB clippings; police report of Sergeant S. J. Marks, JBP; Coroner Ramsey Nesbitt's statement, Washington *Daily News*, December 21, 1923; Alan Hynd story, *True* magazine, n.d. [late 1950s], clipping, p. 134, JB's version, from his memoirs, chapter 18, pp. 68–76.

9. JB memoirs, chapter 18, pp. 68–76; FBI file 62–7824, note.

10. "J. W. Smith Suicide in Apartment of Attorney General," May 30, 1923, n.p. [Washington newspaper], JB clippings; HD to Ned McLean, June 4, 1923; Sullivan, p. 232; typescript of second of several articles on HD by Edgar Mels, n.d, n.p., Reel 256, WGHP; Burton K. Wheeler, *Yankee from the West* (Garden City, N.Y.: Doubleday, 1962), HD, pp. 248–49.

11. Alan Hynd, *True* magazine, clipping p. 134, late 1940s. Even at the time of Jess's demise, Means told EWM, "I don't know who did it, but it was done . . . his gun on the floor beside him not fired. . . . The darn fools they left their gun and forgot to shoot it off and I took the gun—wrapped a pillow around it and shot it out the window twice. No, he was already done before I got there," Sparkes-EWM transcript, December 10, 1934, May Dixon Thacker, "Gaston B. Means—Master Bad Man," *Liberty* clipping, ([n. week], 1937); EWM, pp. 272–73; EWM manuscript, pp. 394–96.

12. Sparkes-EWM transcript, December 10, 1934, ARL, Sawyer Is; Albertson-Wilson I.

13. Gary I; *True* magazine (September 1966), p. 83; FKH to Ethel Jennings, February 21, 1923; Sullivan, pp. 233–37; JB, May 30 and 31, 1923. Heflin quote, *Congressional Record*, March 18, 1924, p. 4412; the crack about Smith and Cramer's death was made by a British reporter, *You.S.A.* magazine, April 1963, p. 12, and given circulation by ARL; ARL I.

14. HD to FKH, February 14, 1923; FKH to HD, February 16, 1923; FKH to

Esther Metzger, May 27, 1923; Pengiana [? name undecipherable] Todd (secretary to EWM) to FKH, May 6 and 12, 1923; EWM to FKH, May 25, 1923.

15. Speeches in May, clipping, one column, n.p., n.d. [circa May 1923]; HMD to Cyril Clemens, August 15, 1939, Reel 256, WGHP; itinerary and plans, *WP*, June 5, 1923; Cottrill, p. 207, Chapple, *After-War*, p. 220.

16. Birch Helms to FKH, May 8, 1923; WGH to Walter Brown, June 5, 1922; FKH to Esther Metzger, May 25, 1923, FKH to Esther Metzger, May 27, 1923.

17. Philadelphia *Public Ledger*, June 8, 1923; *WP*, June 8 and 9, 1923; *WS*, June 7, 1923; FKH to Esther Metzger, May 27, 1923; WGH's antibigotry speeches were to Shriners and also at the Alexander Hamilton statue dedication at the Treasury Department, New York *Tribune*, June 6 and May 18, 1923. Stetson Kennedy and Elizabeth Gardiner tape-recorded Young's recollections in the 1940s while Young was on his deathbed in a New Jersey hospital, Stetson Kennedy to Wyn Craig Wade, June 5, 1985, in Wade, p. 165; half sheet of paper, n.d., n.a., "Harding in Klan" clipping, n.d., n.p., Reel 37, Coolidge P.

18. WGH to Henry R. Shaffner, June 19, 1923, Reel 237; HD, p. 264; Britton, pp. 235–37, 241; KL to Charles Hard, January 27, 1932, Reel 256, WGHP.

19. KLM, chapter 30, p. 9a; West I; Deac Harding quote, *WP*, August 3, 1923; Carrie Votaw quote, Britton, p. 253; WGH sold the *Star* in witness of George Christian, Charles Hard, George H. Mueller, Louis Brush, and Roy D. Moore, Agreement of Sale of Harding Publishing Company, June 18, 1923, Reel 237, WGHP; John Tebbell and Sarah Miles Watt, *The Press and the Presidency* (New York: Oxford, 1985), p. 40; Emma Fall to Cyril Clemens, Reel 256; George Cortelyou to Cyril Clemens, June 28, 1939, Reel 254, WHGP; E. Mont Reily to Cyril Clemens, October 12, 1939, Reel 254, WGHP; Howard Sutherland to Cyril Clemens, January 12, 1940, Reel 254, WGHP; Starling, pp. 192–93; E. Mont Reily to Cyril Clemens, October 12, 1939, Reel 254, WGHP; June 16, 1923, entry, guest books for 1921–1923, Ike Hoover P.

20. *Liberty* (April 9 and June 11, 1938); Miller, p. 215; Harding to Burke, *WP*, August 5, 1923; CES to JB, April 16, 1923; CES to JB, May 3, 1923; ECG reading, notes of JB on death of WGH, JBP; Carl Sawyer to FKH, May 17, 1923; JBOH, p. 64; JB memoirs, chapter 21, p. 236.

21. EWM, p. 274; ARL I; JBOH, p. 43; FKH to EWM, June 19, 1923, EWMP; *Good Housekeeping* (February 1932); GC to Charles Moore, June 26, 1923, Charles Moore P, LC; JBOH, pp. 30, 54–56; FKH to Esther Metzger, May 27, 1923.

22. "Only death . . . ," *WP*, August 3, 1923; "the stars . . . ," "Alaska Trip 7-Year Dream of Mr. and Mrs. Harding," clipping, n.p., n.d. [April 1923]; Howard Sutherland to Cyril Clemens, January 12, 1940, Reel 254, WGHP; Starling, pp. 195–96; KLM, chapter 30, pp. 3–10; Jaffray, pp. 90–91.

23. JB to Ray Baker Harris, June 27, 1938, Reel 259, WGHP; Ross Bartley quote, Portland *Oregonian*, July 31, 1923; KLM, chapter 30, pp. 3–10; clipping of single column besides "Laddie Boy Hides . . ." clipping, New York *Tribune*, August 8, 1923; JB memoirs, chapter 19, p. 101.

32. *The Duchess of America*

1. Popularity, article on First Ladies traveling, n.d., n.p., clipping; Pocatello *Tribune*, June 28, 1923, Butte, *Daily Pass*, June 29, 1923; "Crew of Pullman Is Proud of Hardings," clipping, n.p., n.d. [probably Tacoma newspaper, July 5, 1923]; crowds, Spokane *Chronicle*, July 2, 1923; Richard Oulahan quote, Juneau *Sunday Capital*, July 15, 1923. There were forty-three reporters and ten cameramen. The Secret Service included Dick Jervis, Barker, Ferguson, and seven others. There were three administrative staffers, four telephone engineers, a telegraph engineer, various Commerce, Agriculture, and Interior department and railroad officials, JBP. Along the trip, the full party would swell in number.

2. "Those . . . ," n.p., n.d. clipping, WGHP; Tut fashions, n.p., July 5, 1923, clipping, JBP, San Francisco *Bulletin*, July 30 and 31, 1923, Denver *Post*, June 23, 1923; ARL I; "It is Mrs. Harding . . . ," Anaconda *Standard*, June 30, 1923.

3. "I want . . . ," New York *World*, August 9, 1923; "back porch . . . ," San Francisco *Call and Post*, July 30, 1923; speaking from morning until night, JB memoirs, chapter 19, p. 40c; "what Mrs. Harding says . . . ," Anaconda *Standard*, June 30, 1923; "little talks . . . ," Christian, Sr., manuscript, p. 205; *WS*, August 8, 1923; Warren Flynn recollection, Pasadena *Star-News*, August 3, 1923.

4. Boy Scout, Kansas City *Journal*, July 8, 1923; Kansas City *Post*, June 22, 1923; blue lips, MacMahon and Curry, pp. 81–82; CES quote, Kansas City *Post*, July 22, 1923; "I'll take your place . . . ," *WP*, August 4, 1923; JB manuscript, chapter 19, pp. 9–10, 40e; quotes on FKH, Kansas City *Post*, June 22, 1923; Emma Fall to GBC, June 20, 1931, Reel 249, WGHP; Emma Fall to JB, July 11, 1939, JB memoirs, chapter 20, p. 195; Emma Fall to Cyril Clemens, n.d., WGHP; E. Mont Reily to Cyril Clemens, October 12, 1939, Reel 254, WGHP; White, pp. 623–24; William Allen White to Ray B. Harris, March 5, 1934, Reel 259, WGHP.

5. "Warren, have you . . . ," Denver *Post*, June 23, 1923; Hutchinson, JB to Ray Baker Harris, June 27, 1938, Reel 259, WGHP; JB memoirs, chapter 19, p. 10; incident at University Club, JB typed diary, June 24, 1923; CES remarks, Denver *Post*, June 25, 1923.

6. FKH getting WGH to stop drinking, *NYT*, November 22, 1924; Martin article in JB memoirs, chapter 19, pp. 13–17; accidents, Denver *Post*, June 25, 1923; Cheyenne cowgirls, New York *World*, August 6, 1923.

7. Francis Russell, pp. 577–78; JB memoirs, chapter 19, pp. 19–24. She gave another speech in Cedar City, Utah, "expressing her pleasure at being in this part of the country," Cedar City, Utah, *Iron County Record*, June 29, 1923; Sacramento *Union*, July 23, 1923.

8. Woman threat, Portland *Journal* article by Carl Smith, July 4, 1923; at the mines, Butte *Daily Pass*, June 29, 1923, and Anaconda *Standard*, June 30, 1923; "congenial, middle-aged . . . ," n.d., n.p., Western trip clipping, WGHP; Yellowstone trip, Horace Albright's recorded reminiscences, Yellowstone National Park, excerpted in Francis Russell, pp. 579–80.

9. Harding incidents at Spokane, *Spokesman Review*, July 3, 1923; Meacham incidents, JB memoirs, chapter 19, pp. 32–33; Dr. Lee C. Johnson to Warren Sawyer,

October 26, 1969, reprinted in *HS*, November 1, 1969; "she is a marvel . . . ," Portland *Oregonian*, August 3, 1923; "savages," Sullivan, p. 247; "never felt better," *Oregon Journal*, July 4, 1923; Meachem incidents, Portland *Oregonian*, July 5, 1923.

10. Portland *Oregonian*, August 3, 1923, and n.p., July 5, 1923; Portland *Oregonian*, July 5, 1923, clipping, JBP; "fanatic" woman, Portland *Journal* story by Carl Smith, July 4, 1923.

11. Portland incidents with FKH, Tacoma *Times*, July 5, 1923; JB memoirs, chapter 19, pp. 40c–e; "That was a wonderful speech . . . ," Portland *Oregonian*, July 5, 1923; Portland veterans' hospital, Portland *Oregonian*, July 5, 1923; Spokane *Chronicle*, July 2, 1923; CES quote Kansas City *Post*, July 22, 1923.

12. Bartley quote, Portland *Oregonian*, July 31, 1923; whitewashed memories, Tacoma *Ledger*, July 5, 1923; "It can be said . . . ," *WP*, August 5, 1923; engineer's death, Vancouver *Sun*, August 3, 1923; FKH taking cards from flowers and "Unless it is . . . ," JB memoirs, chapter 19, p. 38, 40-d.

33. *Poison*

1. Descriptions of *Henderson*, Ficken, (July 1975), p. 107; H. L. Denton report on Alaska to Cliff Kling, May 29, 1924; JBOH, pp. 45, 52, 62; JB memoirs, chapter 19, p. 40b. At thirty-four, Dauser was a native of Anaheim, California, and trained as a nurse in Los Angeles. She had joined the Navy in December 1917 and was ordered to Philadelphia, where she headed a group of nurses being sent to the front. She sailed for Europe in August 1918 on the first medical ship sent. In Scotland she worked in a hospital converted from a home for the elderly, treating soldiers whose uniforms were sometimes still muddy from the battlefields of France, San Diego *Union*, May 13, 1966.

2. Chapple, *After-War*, pp. 227–28, 232; JB memoirs, chapter 19, pp. 41–42, 52–55; "Harding's Lifetime Hope Realized Today When He Stepped on Alaska Soil," clipping, n.p., July 9, 1923; Metlakatla, JB memoirs, chapter 19, p. 50; Juneau, Thomas H. Russell, p. 233; JB memoirs, chapter 19, pp. 56–57; Juneau *Sunday Capital*, July 15, 1923.

3. JB memoirs, chapter 19, pp. 57–60; *HS*, January 1, 1969; Alaska briefing papers, file, JBP; Chapple, *After-War*, p. 236 and all of chapter 29, "The Last Transcontinental Journey"; confrontation, Vancouver, *Daily Province*, July 25, 1923; Americanism in Alaska, Anchorage newspaper, July 14, 1923; editorial, n.p. [Anchorage newspaper], July 17, 1923; FKH, comments on Alaskan industry, Edith Dunton manuscript, p. 4; WGH on Alaska statehood, Seattle *Daily Times*, July 27, 1923.

4. Thomas Russell, photo caption, pp. 225 and 232–33; Anchorage newspaper, n.p. clipping, July 14, 1923; James G. Steese to JB, November 11, 1939, JBP and JB memoirs, chapter 19, pp. 63–67; book, letter to Francis Russell, March 1, 1964, from Jane Schermerhorn of Detroit *News*, Russell P; Fairbanks *Daily News-Miner*, July 16, 1923; Chapple, *After-War*, pp. 244–77; Colonel Steese to Cyril Clemens, April 8, 1939, and December 10, 1938, Reel 254, WGHP; Chickaloon stairs, photos from Ohio Historical Society; Harding's nephew, a physician, stated that the strain on WGH in Alaska helped kill him, Nancy Harvison Hooker, ed., *The Moffat Papers: Selections*

from the Diplomatic Journals of Jay Pierrepont Moffat. 1919–1943 (Cambridge, Mass.: Harvard University Press, 1956), p. 138. Steese was angry when JB later said Steese would have had no control over what was fed WGH. "I did not 'refuse to let the President eat crabs' as implied, but merely ordered his staff not to serve them . . . ," Steese letter to Cyril Clemens, n.d., quoted in Clemens manuscript, "President Harding's Mysterious Death," JBP.

5. Chapple, *After-War*, p. 255–56, JB memoirs, chapter 19, pp. 68, 74, 78, 81, 86–88; JBOH, pp. 61–62; Colonel Steese to Cyril Clemens, July 9, 1939, Reel 254, WHGP; *NYT*, November 22, 1924. The compounds in the sedatives are not known, Marx, p. 332; Steese to Cyril Clemens, July 9, 1939, Reel 254, WHGP; fragment of description of Alaska trip itinerary, n.d., Cyril Clemens Papers, Reel 254, WGHP; Steese to Cyril Clemens, April 8, 1939, Reel 254, WHGP; letters include FKH to E. L. Bedell, Anchorage *Times*, July 21, 1923, to L. B. Shelby, Seward Gateway, July 21, 1923; Vancouver *Daily World*, July 28, 1923; Juneau *Sunday Capital*, July 15, 1923; Sitka *Tribune*, July 27, 1923; H. L. Denton report on Alaskan trip to Clifford Kling, May 29, 1924; Sitka, Seattle paper clipping, n.d., n.p.; Bartley quote, AP story, July 29, 1923; Lukin Johnson, "Glimpses of Late President Harding . . . ," clipping, n.d. [post August 3, 1923], n.p. [Vancouver, Canada, publication].

6. Chapple, *After-War*, pp. 277–79; JB memoirs, chapter 19, p. 90; seaplane message, Vancouver *Sun*, July 26, 1923. The message was transmitted from Minister J. H. King.; Senator Dill's recollections are from 1971 clipping, courtesy of Dick West; Herbert Hoover, p. 49; Sparkes-EWM transcript, December 11, 1934; WGH to Bone, KLM, chapter 30, p. 9a; JB memoirs, chapter 20, pp. 163–64.

7. At a Cordova reception, for example, the meal began with creamed clams. Marguerite Brooks, a *Henderson* dietitian, insisted, "I would swear on anything those oysters were perfect when they left my kitchen." The supply list of the steward's pantry did not list crabmeat as being already on board, and Commander Harold Shaw, the supply officer, was "quite sensitive" to the charge that he approved serving the seafood. Cordova clams, "Meier's Alaskan Presidential Menu," WGHP; Brooks's comment on oysters, from Schruben (March 1966), p. 72; no crab on list, Allen, p. 136; Shaw remark and Boone notation, Randolph Downes to JTB, October 31, 1961, JBP; Nourse quote, Salt Lake *Tribune*, July 29, 1923; *NYT*, July 29, 1923; "the doctors," clipping, Harding P, n.p., August 4, 1923; "gift of fishermen," San Francisco *Examiner*, July 29, 1923. Reddy Baldinger was interviewed by Francis Russell, Russell, pp. 587–88. The Vancouver *Sun* said the poisoning happened at dinner on July 24, the *NYH* said it was the day before, see Vancouver *Sun*, August 3, 1923, and *NYH*, August 1, 1923. The most accurate authority was probably Steese, who remained in Cordova: "A day later, after he passed out of jurisdiction, the steward of the Navy transport picked up some crabs in Sitka, and instead of serving them immediately, waited a day, so the President and a lot of the party had ptomaine poisoning when they reached Vancouver," Steese to Cyril Clemens, December 10, 1938, Reel 254, WHGP, and "President Harding's Mysterious Death," JBP; Bartley, *HS*, July 1, 1969. The most prominent person who much later claimed "careful inquiry among the members of the party showed that others had eaten freely of the crab and had had no digestive disturbance whatsoever . . ." was Ray Wilbur, who was not on the scene but was probably told this by Boone. Wilbur, pp. 379–80. Many newspapers during the days of Harding's

illness listed Lou Hoover and George Christian among those who did suffer from ptomaine poisoning, Salt Lake City *Tribune*, July 29, 1923, and *NYT*, July 29, 1923; symptoms of poisoning for which CES treated WGH, Wilbur, pp. 379–80.

8. GH to Tisdall, San Francisco *Call and Post*, July 31, 1923; "I am only here . . ." and Women's American Club, Vancouver *Daily World*, July 28, 1923; FKH, Vancouver *Daily Province*, July 25, 1923. In Vancouver, WGH had more crab, JB memoirs, chapter 19, pp. 107, 133–34, and Spokane menu and July 26, 1923, Vancouver Hotel menu, JBP; Lukin Johnson, "Glimpses of Late President Harding . . . ," clipping, n.d. [post–August 3, 1923], n.p. [Vancouver, Canada, publication]; departure, Vancouver *Daily World*, July 28, 1923; "exhausted," Wilbur, pp. 379–80. Zeilen hit, San Francisco *Chronicle*, August 3, 1923; Ficken, (1975), p. 105. Brooks quote, EWM manuscript, p. 399, is slightly different version from EWM, p. 276; incident of "attack" and JB not being called by CES, JBOH, pp. 76–77, and JB memoirs, chapter 19, pp. 116–17 and chapter 20, pp. 2–4.

9. JBOH, p. 77, and JB memoirs, chapter 20, pp. 2–4, 29; Brooks quote, EWM manuscript, p. 399, EWM, p. 276; Harry Barker to EWM, Vancouver, July 26, 1923, EWMP; accident to *Henderson*, Vancouver *Sun*, August 3, 1923; "When we were in Seattle . . . ," KL, chapter 30, p. 3.

34. *The Heart of San Francisco*

1. Arrival in Seattle, Seattle *Times*, July 27, 1923, JB memoirs, chapter 20, p. 4; picnic and HD, JB memoirs, chapter 20, p. 4, Herbert Hoover, p. 50; speech, Seattle *Evening Record*, August 2, 1923, *NYT*, August 1, 1923, JB memoirs, chapter 20, p. 29; Hoover, p. 50; physical symptoms of Harding's attack during speech, MacMahon and Curry, p. 84.

2. Seattle *Evening Record*, August 2, 1923; "Warren must . . . ," Paoli, Kansas, *Western Spirit*, August 8, 1923; *NYT*, August 1, 1923; "felt it . . . ," Wilbur, pp. 379–80; JB memoirs, chapter 20, pp. 7, 15, 21–22.

3. WGH health, and purgatives, Wilbur, pp. 379–80, Salt Lake *Tribune*, July 29, 1923, *NYT*, July 29, 1923; Eugene, Portland *Telegram*, August 3, 1923; Roseburg train security problem, FBI file, 62-6216-3; San Francisco *Journal*, August 3, 1923; Salt Lake *Tribune*, July 29, 1923; *NYT*, July 29, 1923.

4. "I wondered . . . ," JB memoirs, chapter 20, pp. 22–23, and "General Sawyer had been . . . ," p. 165; purgatives, Salt Lake City *Tribune*, July 29, 1923; *NYT*, July 29, 1923; "would stay up . . . ," JB memoirs, p. 165; JBOH, p. 80; "absolutely not . . . ," JB memoirs, chapter 20, p. 23.

5. Steve Early emphasized that the trip would have continued "had it not been for Mrs. Harding's standpat opposition." WGH "steadily refused" such an idea but yielded to her. FKH decision to cancel trip, Portland *Oregonian*, July 31, 1923; desire to go back to Washington, San Francisco *Chronicle*, July 31, 1923; FKH also spoke at Ashland, Salt Lake *Tribune*, July 29, 1923; H. L. Denton report on Alaska to Cliff Kling, May 29, 1924; San Francisco *Journal*, July 29, 1923; Dunsmuir, San Francisco *Chronicle*, July 29, 1923.

6. JB memoirs, chapter 20, pp. 23–25; the insert into the previous quote of the

expression ". . . well out beyond . . . one and a half inches to the left, and abnormally moved over . . ." from JBOH, pp. 80–81; JB and CES disagreement, MacMahon and Curry, p. 85, JB going to Hoover, Hoover contacting other doctors, JB memoirs, chapter 20, pp. 24–25, 67, and Hoover, p. 51.

7. Ray Wilbur, introduction to Cyril Clemens biography of WGH, April 25, 1939, Reel 259, WGHP; CES health, JB typed diary, September 23, 1924, August 28, 1922; welcome ceremony Oakland *Tribune*, July 29, 1923; arrival at Palace, JB memoirs, chapter 20, pp. 26–27, and JBOH, p. 84.

8. Configuration and description of rooms, JB typed diary, July 29, 1923, Riverside *Daily Press*, July 30, 1923; clipping, n.d., n.p., and July 31, 1923, article, n.p., JBP; Pomona *Progress*, August 2, 1923, Oakland *Tribune*, July 31, 1923. Harding was given milk, toast, and at least one egg every two hours, San Bernardino *Sun*, August 1, 1923. There is dispute about who prepared WGH's food. Powderly told reporters that she cooked eggs in suite kitchen (Riverside *Daily Press*, August 1, 1923); cook Frederick W. Sandrock told a United Press reporter, "I prepare his meals and I should know. Also I serve them myself, putting the tray on the little swing leaf table by the President's bed." Sandrock pushed his way into WGH suite with reporter, past Secret Service (Sandrock interview with United Press reporter, Pomona *Progress*, August 2, 1923). His story conflicted with a San Francisco *Bulletin* interview and photograph of the Palace's head chef, Phillip Roemer, reporting that "all of the food was prepared personally" by him, and "Sawyer directed just what and in what manner the President should eat," (San Francisco *Bulletin*, July 30, 1923, San Francisco *Call and Post*, July 30, 1923). CES press conference, "visit to . . . ," San Francisco *Chronicle*, July 30, 1923, and San Francisco *Examiner*, July 29, 1923; "the information . . . ," San Bernardino *Telegram*, August 1, 1923, Riverside *Daily Press*, July 30 and July 31, 1923; JB examines WGH alone, JB typed diary, July 29, 1923; Riverside *Daily Press*, July 30, 1923; JB, OH says JB called in consultants because of WGH's condition but planned to publish instead that he did so because he and CES "were not registered physicians in California," JB memoirs, chapter 20, p. 28. A stomach specialist, Wilbur became Stanford's president in 1916. Work had served as Colorado State Board of Medical Examiners president and was one of that state's leading doctors, Oakland *Tribune*, July 31, 1923. Wilbur had been sent for on Sunday at two in the morning, an official car rushing to fetch him in the High Sierras, where he was vacationing. It was the calling of Cooper that tipped off reporters that there seemed to be something more serious than Sawyer's claim of ptomaine, Salt Lake City *Deseret News*, July 30, 1923, and Santa Ana *Daily News*, July 30, 1923; "felt very comforted . . . ," JBOH, p. 86. CES stated to Wilbur that WGH had an "increased blood pressure, attacks of dyspnoea at night . . . indigestion particularly at night with pain and distress, relieved at times by pressure upon the upper abdomen . . . history of pain in the chest, radiating down the arms, particularly the left arm . . . attacks of indigestion suggestive of gallstones . . ." Wilbur observed WGH's "heart rate was about 120 and 130 with extra systoles . . . blood pressure was about 150, the heart was enlarged both to right and left . . . ," Wilbur, pp. 379–81; "I always felt each of them . . . ," JBOH, p. 96; Hoover quote, from MacMahon and Curry, p. 86; "joined together . . . ," JBOH, p. 86, official bulletin, July 30, 1923, 10:30 A.M.; JB memoirs, chapter 20, p. 30.

9. "Keeping . . . ," Pottsville, Pennsylvania, *Journal*, July 31, 1923; "she be-

lieves . . . ," Salt Lake City *Deseret News,* July 30, 1923; press conference, San Francisco *Call and Post,* July 30, 1923, San Francisco *Chronicle,* July 31, 1923, clipping, n.p., n.d, WGHP; activity in business office, AP story, July 31, 1923; editorial Riverside *Enterprise,* August 5, 1923; "cold medical . . . ," n.p., n.d.; "We had . . . ," Wilbur, p. 381; "I did not share . . . ," KLM, chapter 30, p. 3a. FKH quoted as saying she disagreed with the "doctors" who said it was a "slight illness," but it was only CES alone who felt this way; FKH quoted in "Everything will come . . . ," George Christian to Walter Brown, July 30, 1923, Reel 259, WGHP.

10. San Francisco *Chronicle,* July 31, 1923, San Francisco *Call and Post,* July 30, 1923, Santa Ana *Register,* July 30, 1923. WGH worsened his own condition by refusing to use a bedpan and walked himself to the bathroom, defying medical orders for complete bedrest. JB noted, "Found him on toilet. I forceably impressed upon him the necessity for not getting out of bed." JB then "found it necessary to manually reduce his hemorrhoidal protrusion, JB typed diary, July 30, 1923, JB memoirs, chapter 20, p. 35. Lab tests were also taken, on the President's blood count, p. 30; Los Angeles *Times,* July 31, 1923; San Francisco *Call and Post,* July 31, 1923; Godfrey, San Francisco *Bulletin,* July 31, 1923; veterans' hospitals, San Francisco *Call and Post,* July 31, 1923; Riverside *Enterprise,* July 31, 1923; San Francisco *Call and Post,* August 3, 1923; Portland *Oregonian,* July 31, 1923.

11. Anaheim *Plain Dealer,* July 30, 1923; San Francisco *Chronicle,* July 31, 1923; JBOH, p. 87; disagreement among the doctors, Portland *Oregonian,* July 31, 1923. Other papers noted pointedly, "NOTE: None of the daily medical bulletins from the president's sick room mentioned arteriosclerosis." Lawrence Martin wrote with slight cynicism that the serious heart problems developed "with surprising suddenness," clipping, n.p., August 4, 1923, and San Bernardino *Evening Telegram,* July 30, 1923, and Oakland *Tribune,* July 30, 1923; "Great American . . . ," Pottsville *Journal,* July 31, 1923; "Heart Attack . . . ," Los Angeles *Record,* July 31, 1923. The Los Angeles *Herald* printed, "Harding had a heart condition when he left Washington according to one of the many rumors circulated in Los Angeles. . . . It was asserted on the authority of persons who have been in Washington recently . . . from men in the federal service who were in a position to know the facts but whose names must be withheld for obvious reasons. . . . [T]hey gave no information until pressed to state what they knew as to the facts," Los Angeles *Herald,* July 30, 1923; Marion residents claimed WGH had a minor heart attack in 1893, Salt Lake City *Deseret News,* July 30, 1923.

12. "Calling visiting . . ." and "no doctor living . . . ," San Francisco *Call and Post,* July 30, 1923; "declined . . . ," San Francisco *Chronicle,* July 31, 1923. "Perhaps one of the most hopeful conditions," Illinois Medical Board examiner Dr. Gilbert Fitzpatrick spoke of "the great confidence that the distinguished patient has for his physician." Burton Hazeltine, surgery chief of U.S. Hospital 28, said it was "reassuring" that CES was treating WGH, who was thus receiving the same care as that given in veterans' hospitals!, Quotes from Los Angeles *Times,* August 2, 1923; "the practice . . . ," San Francisco *Chronicle,* n.d. [July 30–August 1], 1923; copper poisoning, San Francisco *Chronicle,* July 30, 1923, and George Sloan telegrams to JB, July 30–31, 1923, and letter, August 13, 1923, JBP; JBOH, p. 75. Berries and seafood, Ray Baker Harris to JB, June 4, 1948, JBP; "the most important factor . . . administering of purgatives . . . ," Salt Lake City *Deseret News,* July 30, 1923.

13. "[T]o show . . . ," San Francisco *Chronicle*, July 31, 1923. CES would mention heart troubles only as a possible complication of the whole body strain caused by the poison. "When his heart is beating 50 above normal, it can be readily seen that the situation is serious," Riverside *Enterprise*, July 31, 1923; "specific condition . . . ," San Francisco *Chronicle*, n.d. [July 30–August 1], 1923; "frank statement . . . ," San Francisco *Chronicle*, n.d. [July 30–August 1], 1923; one drink, JB memoirs, chapter 19, p. 17; diet and eggnogs, Los Angeles *Times*, August 1, 1923, San Francisco *Call and Post*, July 31, 1923; heart stimulants, Marx, pp. 333–34; *Journal of the American Institute of Homeopathy* (December 1923); *Marion Star*, July 20, 1991. CES off-shift, Los Angeles *Record*, July 30, 1923 and Anaheim *Plain Dealer*, July 31, 1923; digitalis use, MacMahon and Curry, p. 86. On the single remaining chart kept by JB, for July 30, he left blank the patient's name and diagnosis but recorded that a caffeine "digitalac" was started at 9:00 P.M. It was the time of night when CES had retired, leaving JB on night duty alone, except for night nurse Dauser. JB injected digitalis at hours when CES was off-shift. Through the night WGH continued to have "difficult breathing." Whether JB managed more injections of "6 hours each" as he wrote on the chart is unknown. Also unknown is how much he revealed of the digitalis use to CES. JB also recorded WGH's blood pressure as S. 124 over 92, clinical chart for WGH, JBP; JB memoirs, chapter 20, p. 40; JB on his relationship with CES, JB memoirs, chapter 20, p. 165, chapter 21, pp. 165, 195; "deep seated . . . ," JBOH, p. 75; JB, memoirs, chapter 20, pp. 204–05; "poison had not . . . failed to respond . . . ," Los Angeles *Examiner*, July 31, 1923, and clipping, n.p., July 31, 1923; "Mrs. Harding knows . . . ," Riverside *Enterprise*, July 31, 1923; "Sawyer's voice . . . ," *Marion Star*, August 2, 1923; Glendale *News*, July 31, 1923. CES goes in to see WGH before other doctors gather, Pomona *Progress*, July 31, 1923, and Riverside *Daily Press*, July 31, 1923; "Sawyer felt . . . ," San Francisco *Call and Post*, July 30, 1923.

14. Mayo, "It is both my wish . . . ," clipping, n.p., July 31, 1923; Buchanan, *NYT*, August 1, 1923; laughing, San Francisco *Chronicle*, August 3, 1923; ambassador to Italy, San Bernardino *Sun*, July 30, 1923; blackberry juice, *NYT*, August 1, 1923; "scientific side," Oakland *Tribune*, August 2, 1923; "utmost confidence . . . ," Oakland *Tribune*, July 31, 1923; FKH quote, KLM, chapter 30, p. 4.

15. "The chances are nine . . . ," *NYT*, August 1, 1923; "heart action . . . great strain," Oakland *Tribune*, August 31, 1923; "questions of a technical," Cleveland *Plain Dealer*, August 1, 1923; "So much seemingly irreconcilable . . . ," San Francisco *Call and Post*, August 1, 1923; Levine recollections, Downes, *Northwest Ohio Quarterly*, p. 11; interviews of Madame Marcia, Harry Hunt story, August 8, 1923; "Even though the President . . . ," JB memoirs, chapter 20, p. 44; "we have reached clearer . . . ," n.p., n.d., San Francisco paper, clipping, JBP; "peakload," Tucson *Citizen*, August 1, 1923; CES wired his son, Christian, Sr., manuscript, p. 24; "building up . . . keeping the system," Glendale *Press*, August 2, 1923; "are now a unit in diagnosing . . . ," Los Angeles *Times*, p. 812; "demonstrated his . . . past the crisis . . . 'I will not say . . . ,' " Associated Press story, August 2, 1923, San Francisco dateline; "Physicians doubtless noted that the bulletins were written in two languages—scientific and popular. The medical profession of the world knew with exactness the president's condition," the Stockton *Daily Independent* editorialized. "The exact scientific information was then translated into popular language of much less precision."

16. Incidents between Sawyer and Oulahan, *NYT*, August 2, 1923; FKH "had the President . . . ," San Francisco *Call and Post*, August 1, 1923; FKH working and "several important . . ." and "I know . . . ," Los Angeles *Times*, August 2, 1923, and Riverside *Daily Press*, August 2, 1923; *NYT*, August 2, 1923; Riverside *Daily Press*, August 2, 1923; "inwardly rejected . . . ," Carter Field, "Mrs. Harding Slows Train," *NYT*, August 8, 1923; WGH state of mind and suggestions he knew he might die, JB to Cyril Clemens, July 19, 1939; Wilbur, pp. 380–81, and *Saturday Evening Post* (October 13, 1923), JB memoirs, chapter 20, p. 32; "from the moment . . ." and "memorial," Washington Observations column, n.p., n.d. [circa June 1931], Elbert Remsberg comment, AP story, August 4, 1923; prediction of return to work, *NYT*, August 2, 1923; Harding planned to resign, Hooker, p. 138; Herbert Hoover, p. 51; Schruben (March 1966). Merritt's claim seems partially collaborated by August 2, 1923, Los Angeles *Times* article reporting that Los Angeles and San Francisco would turn over funds for rental of a California property for WGH.

17. Charity Remsberg, JBOH, pp. 88–89; San Francisco paper clipping, August 4, 1923; San Francisco *Call and Post*, August 2, 1923, Charity Remsberg to Cyril Clemens, January 13, 1937, Reel 254, WGHP: Daugherty, clipping, n.p., July 31, 1923, dateline, Wilbur, pp. 380–81, San Francisco *Chronicle*, August 2, 1923, Pomona *Progress*, August 1, 1923, San Francisco *Call and Post*, August 3, 1923, San Francisco *Examiner*, August 3, 1923, HD to Cyril Clemens, August 15, 1939, Reel 256, WGHP; Francis Russell, p. 591; HD, pp. 270–71.

18. "leave him at least . . . ," Vancouver *Daily Province*, August 2, 1923; Oulahan report on indigestion and heart, *NYT*, August 3, 1923; JBOH, p. 89; JB memoirs, chapter 20, p. 47; Starling, p. 198; Work quote, San Francisco *Chronicle*, July 31, 1923; "badly impaired" purgative reference by George Holmes, *Marion Star*, August 2, 1923; further quote of FKH, "death was stamped on Mr. Harding's face, but they tried to reassure me. . . . My husband was dying! I knew he was going . . . ," KLM, chapter 30, p. 4; HD to Cyril Clemens, August 15, 1939, Reel 256, WGHP, and Russell, p. 591; Cooper and Wilbur leaving, JB memoirs, chapter 20, p. 56, and JBOH, p. 97; William Allen White to Ray Baker Harris, March 5, 1934, Reel 259, WGHP; Cyril Clemens typescript of Ray Lyman Wilbur's reminiscences of WGH death, n.d., Reel 254, WGHP; Holman visit, San Francisco *Journal*, August 3, 1923; *WP*, August 3, 1923.

35. Negligent Homicide

1. JBOH, p. 97.

2. JB conflicting accounts of whether he spoke to Pershing, JB memoirs, chapter 20, pp. 50–58, and JBOH, p. 94; Oulahan account, *NYT*, August 3, 1923; De Quoin *Tribune*, August 10, 1928; Ross Bartley account, AP story, August 2, 1923, appears in *WP*, August 3, 1923. Vancouver *Daily Province*, August 3, 1923. The book that Boone did not dispute was Thomas Russell's *Illustrious Life and Work of Warren G. Harding*, and the account of his dinner with Pershing is on p. 252; Starling, p. 199; Christian, JB memoirs, chapter 20, p. 69.

3. Two newspaper photos of JB on roof, one with CES and Powderly, n.p., August 2, in JB handwriting and Philadelphia *Enquirer*, JB memoirs, chapter 20, p. 50;

Philadelphia *Enquirer*, July 31, 1923; Colonel Filmer drive, JB typed diary, August 1, 1923; "I was never away from his bedside except for occasions of a few minutes duration," JB to *American Heritage* (June 12, 1963), JBP, and "I rarely left his bedside for even a few minutes until his death at the Palace . . . ," JB to Ray Baker Harris, June 27, 1938, Reel 259, WGHP; "subconscious feeling . . . ," JBOH, p. 94.

4. San Francisco *Call and Post*, August 3, 1923, San Francisco *Examiner Extra*, August 3, 1923; San Francisco *Chronicle*, August 3, 1923; San Francisco *Journal*, August 3, 1923; "snapped," from JB; Ross Bartley initial account of CES "able to reach the room," from AP story, August 2, 1923, and CES "worked desperately within the room," AP story, August 3, 1923; "later . . . a correction was issued . . . ," San Francisco *Call and Post*, August 3, 1923; Sue Dauser, San Diego *Union*, May 13, 1966, JBOH, p. 98; JB memoirs, chapter 19, pp. 274–75, and chapter 20, p. 77; Powderly, "Doesn't he look fine?," *NYT*, August 3, 1923; "attended to . . . had her back turned . . . ," JBOH, pp. 96, 99; Powderly about to give Harding water for his medicine, Francis Russell, p. 591; CES saying he went for ten-minute walk, *You.S.A.* (April 1963), p. 15; FKH to Dolly Gann, *WS*, April 1933 clipping, JBP.

5. "President Harding's Last Days," Herbert Hoover dictated memorandum, prepresidential papers, Herbert Hoover Library, also "Once Wilbur and then Boone arrived, they too "at once started further methods of stimulation in an attempt to restore respiration"; Wilbur's version was that he got to the sickroom "within a minute after he [WGH] had passed away," Ray Lyman Wilbur, introduction to Clemens biography of WGH, April 25, 1939, Reel 259, WGHP; Wilbur statement of only three in room, CES calm, and FKH not believing WGH dead, Wilbur, pp. 381–82; Wilbur account of scene he found, Clemens typescript of Wilbur's reminiscences of WGH death, n.d., Reel 254, WGHP and Hoover-dictated memo; San Francisco *Chronicle*, August 3, 1923. When HD joined other Cabinet members, they telegraphed Coolidge to take the oath. HD never revealed if he was told CES or JB "reached the President before he actually died," HD to Cyril Clemens, August 15, 1939, Reel 256, WGHP.

6. JBOH, pp. 94–95, 99, 103, and JB memoirs, chapter 20, pp. 50–58; Hoover-dictated memo.

7. San Francisco *Journal*, August 3, 1923. United Press story, n.p., August 2, 1923; *NYT*, August 3, 4, and 5, 1923. Adding credence to the notion that his source was JB, Oulahan said he went out for a walk for air, "became confused, turned into an unfamiliar street" and took "ten minutes or so to arrive in the sickroom."

8. JBOH, pp. 95, 98; WGH death certificate, local register #4520, California State Board of Health, Bureau of Vital Statistics; Starling, p. 200; MacMahon and Curry, pp. 88–89; Clemens typescript of Wilbur's reminiscences of WGH death, n.d., Reel 254, WGHP.

9. Sue Dauser to Mont Reily, January 22, 1932, in Reily's "Years of Confusion," p. 364, quoted in Murray, p. 450.

10. JBOH, p. 95. In another version he said he "put my arm around her and escorted her into her own bedroom"; Wilbur and Hoover quotes, Hoover-dictated memo; San Francisco *Chronicle*, July 3, 1923; "He was . . . ," Oakland *Tribune*, August 4, 1923; "Still . . . ," Glendale *News Bulletin*, August 3, 1923; Charity Remsberg breaks down, San Francisco *Call and Post*, August 3, 1923; "said kind things . . . ," Thomas Russell, p. 253; "She is going to be . . . ," Helen Pryor, *Lou Hoover: Gallant First*

Lady (New York: Dodd, Mead, 1969), p. 132; officials, *NYT*, August 3, 1923; "Let us leave . . . ," San Francisco *Call and Post*, August 3, 1923; Riverside *Daily Press*, August 3, 1923; FKH to Esther De Wolfe Metzger, August 25, 1923.

11. Description of body, San Francisco *Call and Post*, August 3, 1923; prevention of death mask, New York *World*, August 4 and 6, 1923, *NYT*, August 6, 1923. It was "usual custom" to have death masks made of Presidents who died in office; McKinley and Lincoln were known instances; Sawyer I; MacMahon and Curry, p. 88; armed guards, *You.S.A.* (April 1963); San Francisco *Call and Post*, August 3, 1923; Will J. Thorpe of N. Gray and Company morticians, "Details of President Harding's Funeral," *Mortician* (August 1923).

12. San Francisco *Call and Post*, August 3, 1923; EWM to FKH, telegram, August 3, 1923, private collection and McLean manuscript, p. 397; Christian, Sr., manuscript, p. 205; handwritten recollections of James S. West, n.d., Cyril Clemens P, Reel 254, WGHP; HD's account quoting FKH had her in room alone reading when "he threw his right arm over his head. I saw his face twitch. I leaped to my feet, bent over him. He was dead. It all happened in a second. I rushed to the hall and cried: 'Call Dr. Boone—get Dr. Boone—quick, please.' " These quotes seem to be pieced together by HD's ghostwriter from news reports, HD, p. 272; FKH asleep and morning, Thomas Russell, p. 247, Riverside *Daily Press*, August 3 and 4, 1923; plans for body in White House, *NYT*, August 6 and 8, 1923. "Those we probably value as much as any of them—from our old friends in Marion and other parts of Ohio," she said, "might not receive the attention that others coming from the more prominent people would receive," Thomas Russell, p. 140; "She was poised . . . ," Los Angeles *Record*, August 3, 1923; funeral train arrangements, Los Angeles *Times*, August 3, 1923; San Francisco *Call and Post*, August 3, 1923; undertaker arrangements, Thomas Russell, p. 140; *WP*, August 3, 1923; Riverside *Press*, August 3, 1923, Will J. Thorpe of N. Gray and Company morticians, "Details of President Harding's Funeral," *Mortician* (August 1923); Masonic ring, *WH*, August 9, 1923; Ernestine Black article, "Wonderful in Death," San Francisco *Call and Post*, clipping, n.d., n.p., August 4, 1923.

13. "[R]umors began . . . ," Washington newspaper clipping, n.d. [probably August 3, 1923]; Baltimore *Sun*, August 3, 1923; letter and editorial in Fresno *Bee*, August 7, 1923; Pottsville, Pennsylvania, *Journal*, October 12, 1923, also includes Markey diagnosis; "certainly . . . ," A. A. Hoehling to JB, June 27, 1959, JBP, and "I am certain . . . ," A. A. Hoehling to Ray Baker Harris, September 7, 1961, WGHP; draft of JB to A. A. Hoehling, July 28, 1959, JBP; "due to heart attack . . . ," *NYT*, November 22, 1924; George Christian quote, San Francisco *Bulletin*, August 3, 1923. Homeopath Alexander Markey further believed that WGH's "whole system had been completely saturated with acid toxin poisons, which his body tried feverishly to get rid of . . . [that] to feed the body in this state is to court certain death. The only sensible thing to do in such cases, is to put the patient on a complete fast, because every ounce of food taken during this period turns into added poison . . . these distinguished scientists proudly announced again and again that 'nourishment is being taken regularly . . . they were actually, if unwittingly, feeding President Harding to death." Daughter and sister of homeopathic doctors, Charity Remsberg confirmed this fourteen years later: ". . . the food he ate did something to lower his resistance and had these physicians

understood how to feed one in his condition I do believe he might have been living today . . . he should have been fed nothing but liquids or light fruit juices but instead he was stuffed with egg-nogs, heavy proteins . . . it was a fatal thing to do. Purely ignorance on their part . . . people perish due for lack of knowledge and he was at their mercy . . . all good intentions of course," Charity Remsberg to Cyril Clemens, January 13, 1937, Reel 254, WGHP.

14. JB handwritten diary, June 14, 1924; Hubert Work to Ray Lyman Wilbur, October 22, 1923, Wilbur P, Stanford University; Wilbur and Cooper statement, quoted in JB memoirs, chapter 20, p. 61; Charles M. Cooper to CES, August 8, 1923, JBP; Charles Minor Cooper to Ray Wilbur, August 13, 1923, in Wilbur, p. 384, initially agreed with CES solely on the basis of examination some hours before WGH's moment of death; McKenzie reference, Randolph Downes to JTB, October 31, 1961; Ray Lyman Wilbur, "The Last Illness of a Calm Man," *Saturday Evening Post* (October 13, 1923); Ray Wilbur introduction to Clemens biography of WGH, April 25, 1939, Reel 259, WGHP; Wilbur, pp. 383–84; Herbert Hoover, p. 51.

15. JB to Ray Wilbur, April 28, 1947; JB memoirs, chapter 20, pp. 57–58. JB also wrote that there had been no "worse feeling as a physician than [to] stand beside the bed of a patient when out of the clear, life is taken" when, in fact, he was not at the death bedside. "It was a great . . . ," JB to Ray Baker Harris, June 27, 1938, Reel 259, WGHP; Slemp and Forster confrontation, JB memoirs, chapter 21, p. 121; JB to HD, November 28, 1930, HD to JB, December 4, 1930; HD warnings about CES, JB typed diary, December 30, 1923; JB handwritten diary, November 18, 1923; Major Arthur Brooks's heart attack and CES's secretary's illness, JB typed diary, December 31, 1923, and JB handwritten diary, March 8, 1924. A draft of JB's planned memoirs was often whitewashed of facts, his diary notes conflicting with what he planned to publish, JB memoirs, chapter 20, p. 66; draft of letter from JB to Clare Boothe Luce, n.d. [circa early 1960s], JBP; Steese to Clemens, December 10, 1938, and April 8, 1939, Reel 254, WHGP; JB to Clemens, n.d., file copy, JBP; Steese to Clemens in Clemens, "President Harding's Mysterious Death," JBP; "unfortunate remark . . . ," JB to Cyril Clemens, September 24, 1939, WGHP; JB to Ray Baker Harris, June 27, 1938, Reel 259, WGHP; letter printed in JB memoirs, chapter 20, p. 200; "I wish to withhold certain knowledge, I shall be pleased . . . ," JB to Ray Baker Harris, June 27, 1938, Reel 259, WGHP; "the possibility of . . ." and JB note to self, "Gave no medical . . . ," Randolph Downes to JB, July 9, 1960, and "I do not feel . . . ," JB to Randolph Downes, November 10, 1961, JBP; "I wish to withhold certain knowledge . . . ," JB to Cyril Clemens, September 24, 1939, Reel 254, WHGP; Dr. George Tyron Harding III to Ray Baker Harris, August 3, 1950, Reel 259, WGHP; Dr. Warren G. Harding II recollection is from November 25, 1973, clipping, n.p., courtesy of Dick West and also Hooker, p. 138; "to definitely modify . . ." draft of letter, JB to A. A. Hoehling, July 28, 1959, JBP.

16. "There has never been . . . ," from "President to Be Kept at Palace, Not in Hospital," clipping, n.d., n.p., JBP; "Sawyer thinks . . . ," JB handwritten diary, March 8, 1924. The Eddy article continues, "[L]ong study of his patient had shown him Harding is subject, when well, to a variable pulse rate. Normally his pulse beat is 74, but after a game of golf, Sawyer says, it frequently would register 100," "Dr. Sawyer, President's Physician, Describes in Detail, Harding Malady," July 31, 1923, n.p. [San

Francisco paper], Boone clippings; *WS*, August 8, 1923; CES speech to Rotarians manuscript, n.d. [1923–1924], p. 11, Reel 245, WGHP; CES revelation, Christian, Sr., manuscript, p. 203.

17. Hoover cabal theory, Wilbur, p. 384; JB diary, December 1, 1926. Thayer's manuscript was compiled over seven years at the cost of twenty-five thousand dollars. Thayer wanted federal grand jury action. He even enlisted Charity Remsberg's support, and she tried to get Mandy Sawyer interested. His letters were ignored by Hoover, who suggested he was "mentally unbalanced," Walter Thayer to Senator Robert La Follette, October 1, 1936, Walter Thayer to J. Edgar Hoover, October 7, 1936, Walter Thayer to Rush Holland, November 7, 1935, J. Edgar Hoover, November 26, 1935, Lawrence Smith memo to J. Edgar Hoover, June 15, 1940, FBI case file 62-5490. Thayer had first been an agent, then Seattle manager of the Burns Agency, been appointed a special agent of the FBI, then hired as a Secret Service agent three days after the Harding inaugural. He was discharged from the agency after "another Secret Service agent and he had furnished radical elements with certain confidential information from the files of the Secret Service." Thayer made a persistent case that Harding was slowly killed by German spies in compliance with someone close to the President, FBI file 62-6216-9.

18. A former food preparer at Clark Hall at the University of Washington to HD, FBI files, 62-76216-3, 62-6216-3; Catholics and Klan killing WGH, Oscar Winn to Governor Jack Walton of Oklahoma, September 20, 1923, Reel 37, Calvin Coolidge P, LC; Mrs. Hugh O'Neill to Clemens, December 7, 1938, Reel 254, WGHP; page 3 of Clemens typed letter to Samuel Hopkins Adams, n.d. [post 1939], Reel 259, WGHP; Bill Barnett to author, phone call, July 22, 1991; Gary, Sawyer, Napper, Parks Is; Gross, p. 45. The only action of Florence that could even remotely be mistaken for poisoning occurred in fact after Warren convulsed, and she ran her finger in his mouth, thinking he had choked on gum, Murray, p. 450, from Dauser letter in the Mont Reily manuscript, "Years of Confusion." Part of the reason for such lurid theories stemmed from a growing doubt of homeopathy in light of strides being made in the medical profession by 1923. Since it involved the use of some poisons in highly diluted form, it was an obvious cause of suspicion for WGH's demise, and there were poisons that could provoke symptoms as described by the death certificate, MacMahon and Curry; Schruben *Southern California Quarterly*, p. 73. Had WGH been administered lethal dosages of poisonous homeopathic medicine it could be detected only by autopsy. Sometime after WGH's death some "sections" labeled as his allegedly showed up in a Stanford Department of Pathology lab cabinet. Mark Gerstel, then an intern to a Dr. Orfels of the department, recalled being told to "destroy" a "number" of these; still no claim of foul play emerged from these. Since there was no known autopsy, these "sections" are inexplicable, the only possibility being that somehow Wilbur, Stanford's president, had some way managed some limited autopsy. This seems impossible, particularly since Wilbur spent most of his time with FKH after WGH's death, JB typed diary, August 23, 1959; Wilbur, pp. 382–83; hotel service, *WP*, August 4, 1923, and "Simple, but Impressive Service Held," August 4, 1923, n.p., Marion Public Library Clipping Book; recollections of West, Clemens P, n.d., Reel 254, WGHP; *NYT*, November 22, 1924.

19. Clipping, "Simple, but Impressive Service Held," August 4, 1923, n.p. Marion Public Library Clipping Book; San Francisco cortege, *NYT*, August 4, 1923; general information sheet of WGH Estate, Reel 241, WGHP; Christian, Sr., manuscript, p. 210.

36. *The Fires of August*

1. Funeral train, Sullivan, pp. 252–53, *WP*, August 5, 1923; New York *Tribune*, August 6, 1923, *NYT*, August 6, 1923, August 8 and 11, 1923, New York *World*, August 6, 1923, Salt Lake *Tribune*, August 5, 1923, Tucson, Arizona, newspaper clipping, August 5, 1923, Philadelphia *Public Ledger*, August 7, 1923; Chapple, *After-War*, p. 264–65; story by Carter Field, New York *Tribune*, August 8, 1923.

2. Gregg, Napper Is; *NYH*, August 11, 1923; *NYT*, August 3, 1923, pp. 4, c. 7 and 8; pp. 6, c. 5; Downes and Walker, *Northwest Ohio Quarterly* (Winter 1962–1963), p. 14; Babe Ruth, *HS*, November 2, 1969; San Francisco *Chronicle*, August 4, 1923; *NYT*, August 11, 1923; *WP*, August 8, 1923; Seymour quote and Blythe ad, *NYT*, August 17, 1923; JB memoirs, chapter 20, p. 123.

3. JB memoirs, chapter 20, pp. 120–21; HD claimed FKH often sent for him, HD, p. 273; Watson, p. 232; FKH clippings on the train, from papers including Tucson, Arizona, newspaper clipping, August 5, 1923, New York *American*, August 5, 1923; *NYH*, August 5, 1923.

4. Parks I; McLeans at Union Station, *NYT*, August 8, 1923; rose petals, *WP*, August 7, 1923; "His body was lifted . . . ," New York *World*, August 8, 1923; EWM, p. 274; Rinehart, p. 365; EWM manuscript, p. 397 New York *Tribune*, August 9, 1923; *WP*, August 9, 1923; *Marion Star*, August 8, 1923.

5. Christian, Sr., manuscript, p. 208, Reel 249, WGHP; EWM manuscript, p. 399; *WP*, August 9, 1923; *Marion Star*, August 8, 1923; Associated Press story, "Mrs. Harding's Last Gift," August 8, 1923, n.p., clipping, WGHP.

6. Story by Carter Field, New York *Tribune*, August 8, 1923; Kansas City Post, August 5, 1923; AP story, August 3, 1923; Boston *Evening Transcript*, August 3, 1923; New York *Tribune*, August 9, 1923; "The Standard for Wifehood," *Idaho Statesman*, clipping, n.d., WGHP; *NYH*, August 13, 1923; Reverend A. E. Beatley sermon, "What the Mourning over Warren Harding Means," August 5, 1923, clipping, n.p., WGHP; August 6, 1923, *Daily Oklahoman*: "Marriage had its perfect exemplification in the lives of the Hardings because they knew that love must be cultivated—it will not stand neglected. . . . The president was Mrs. Harding's lover and protector. She was his sweetheart. . . . In a time of . . . much divorcing and recurrent home-breaking what a lesson is furnished us in the lives of Warren and Florence Harding. . . ."

7. New York *Tribune*, August 6, 10, and 11, 1923; Marion *Newslife*, September 2, 1979; B. Bartram, Gregg, Elsasser Is; KLM, chapter 30, pp. 20b, 21; Chapple, *After-War*, pp. 278–79; *True* magazine (September 1966), p. 84; *WP*, August 10–11, 1923; Salt Lake City *Tribune*, August 5, 1923; Starling, pp. 202–03; Philadelphia *Public Ledger*, August 11, 1923; Los Angeles *Express*, August 4, 1923.

8. Kansas City *Post*, August 5, 1923; San Francisco *Bulletin*, August 4, 1923; Philadelphia *Public Ledger*, August 10 and 11, 1923. The Coolidges moved into the

White House on August 21, Fuess, p. 153; Grace Coolidge's influence, *NYT*, August 7, 1923.

9. Clipping, n.d., n.p., courtesy of Bartrams; Russell-Duckett, *American Heritage* (February 1965); Marion *Newslife*, May 5, 1981; New York *World*, August 12, 1923; *NYT*, August 13, 1923.

10. Hoes, p. 32; Washington *Times*, September 11, 1923; Laura Harlan to EWM, August 14, 1923, EWMP; FKH to EWM, August 15 and 16, 1923, EWMP.

11. Varying accounts have Grace Coolidge, Harlan, Christian, Powderly, and Jim Haley, the new First Lady's Secret Service agent, also escorting FKH, but in none of EWM's writings or correspondence are they mentioned, *WH*, August 18, 1923; Washington *Times*, August 18, 1923; New York *Tribune*, August 18, 1923; Colman, p. 391; EWM manuscript, p. 400; EWM, p. 276; FKH to EWM, August 25, 1923, EWMP; Grace Coolidge to EWM, n.d. [Friday morning], EWMP; KLM, chapter 27, p. 62; Charles Evan Hughes to Harry New, October 6, 1923, Reel 259, WGHP; FKH to Esther De Wolfe Metzger, August 25, 1923.

12. Laura Harlan to D. Shaffner, August 15, 1923, C. D. Shaffner to FKH, August 15, 1923, Reel 237, WGHP; Russell-Duckett, *American Heritage* (February 1965); FKH to EWM, September 5, 1923. She left her De Laszlo portrait to the McLeans.

13. *WH*, September 6, 1923, and n.p., clipping, September 6, 1923; *Spectacular Rogue*, p. 288; Russell-Duckett, *American Heritage* (February 1965); *Introduction and Provenance to the Warren G. Harding Papers*, Ohio Historical Society, pp. 4–5; Laura Smith to Edward Matlack, October 1, 1923; Laura Bey Smith was a temporary secretary to FKH.

14. Charles Hard to FKH, September 7, 1923, WGHP; FKH notes on letter, W. P. Webster to FKH, October 4, 1923, WGHP; Marion civic memorial, *WP*, September 7, 1923; on Armistice Day address, Reed Smoot to FKH, October 19, 1923, WGHP; Christian, Sr., manuscript, pp. 210–11, Reel 249, WGHP; Schedule H of WGH Estate and General Information Sheet and WGH Will, Reel 241, WGHP; JB typed diary, October 10, 1924; Miller, p. 228; Carl Sferrazza Anthony, *First Ladies*, vol. 1 (New York: Morrow, 1990), p. 303; Kansas City *Post*, August 5, 1923, FBI file 62-7824-1, part I. FKH "decided to take under the will . . . one year's income" ahead of time, as was her option, Hoke Donithen to FKH, December 8, 1923; "Estate of WGH" receipt for government bonds and "Estate of Warren Harding" receipt of interest on government bonds and publishing shares, from C. D. Shaffner to FKH, n.d., Reel 237, WGHP; FKH to Louis Brush, January 1, 1924.

15. MJ to FKH, September 19, 1923, private collection; San Francisco's planned WGH municipal golf course was to be at Merced Lake, *WP*, September 21, 1923; *HS*, October 8, 1966; CES to FKH, October 20, 1923, WGHP; KLM, memorandum, p. 5; Carl Sawyer to JB, September 27, 1923; MJ to James Emery, October 19, 1923; MJ, "A Journey and Its End," September 11, 1923; CES speech text, n.d. [circa 1923– 1924], CESP, WGHP.

16. JB typed diary entries, September 27, October 25, October 30, and December 13, 1924; JB memoirs, chapter XXI, p. 167. Grace Coolidge had become instantly popular by being a radically different First Lady from FKH. Instead of regaling reporters with stories of her life, as FKH had, Grace said, "We always felt that those

things belonged exclusively to us." There were now two teenage boys in the White House. Grace made no public remarks on politics or women's roles and lacked ambition to involve herself in policy. "I shall like going to Washington," she said, when she first came to the capital city, "but I know I shall like returning to Massachusetts again ever so much better," Chapple, *After-War*, pp. 304–05.

17. FKH to Esther Metzger, December 21, 1923, private collection; FKH to EWM, January 26, 1923, EWMP.

37. *Spies and Scandals*

1. HD to FKH, n.d. [fall 1923], FKH to governor of Hawaii, n.d. [fall 1923]; United Press story, August 11, 1923. The suite previously used by Lloyd George, and before that by Senator and Mrs. du Pont. FKH to Esther Metzger, January 11, 1924, Schermer collection.

2. JB typed diary, January 3, 1923, and JB memoirs, chapter 21, pp. 65, 74.

3. MJ to FKH, January 24, 1924; JB typed diary, January 2, 1924; K. S. Robinson to FKH, January 29, 1924; CES to Harry Barker, January 16, 1924; CES to Mr. Hite, January 11, 1924.

4. *HS*, January 1, 1969, New York *Daily News*, February 14, 1924, New York *Daily News*, February 16 1924; FKH to MJ letters, n.d. [February–April, 1924], MJ to FKH, March 11, 1924, private collection.

5. Mosby-Coleman to FKH, January 27, 1924; "It is my intention . . . ," FKH handwritten draft on Western Union Telegraph pad, n.d. [fall 1923]; Russell-Duckett, *American Heritage* (February 1965); FKH to MJ, n.d. [February–April 1924], private collection; KLM, chapter 32, p. 4; *Good Housekeeping* (February 1932); Charles Moore to FKH, October 12, 1923.

6. [Indistinct, Princeton University] to FKH, April 12, 1924, Laura Harlan to Wilson Gill, March 17, 1924; CES to Charles Baumgardner, February 7, 1924; Harry New to FKH, May 15, 1924; KLM, chapter 32, memorandum, pp. 3–6; FKH seemed pleased with MJ's drafts for her: "I liked that 'for more efficient citizenship'—you certainly gave Mayfield College something to think about." FKH to MJ, n.d. [February–April 1924], private collection; FKH support of preservation of George Washington's birth site and Ohio flood, FKH to Charles Moore, July 19, 1924, and n.d. [Summer 1924], Moore P, LC.

7. FKH to Esther De Wolfe Metzger, March 25, 1924; Hoes, p. 32; EBW to FKH, n.d. [February 1924]; EBW to FKH, February 8, 1924, FKHP; Dolly Gann *Dolly Gann's Book* (Garden City, N.Y.: Doubleday, 1933), pp. 63–64.

8. Edith Wilson to FKH [January 27, 1924]; Emma Fall to FKH, December 25, 1923, WGHP; George Shanton memo for J. Edgar Hoover, January 25, 1924, Orville Dewey memo for William J. Burns, January 24, 1924, Albert Fall FBI file 62-3088-1; Sparkes-EWM transcript, April 2, 1935; W. J. Burns to HD, March 1, 1924, Albert Fall FBI File 62-3088; FKH to MJ, n.d. [February–April, 1924], private collection.

9. Stratton, *Southwestern Studies* (1966), p. 9; KLM, chapter 27, pp. 62–63. If not Fall's guilt, than whose? Paranoia reigned supreme among the Harding crowd,

looking for any possible alternative to thinking Fall a crook, anonymous letter to William Burns, February 21, 1924, Fall FBI file 62-3088-22x; MJ to FKH, March 15, 1924, and MJ to Gus Creager, February 18, 1924, private collection; Emma Fall to GC, June 20, 1931, Reel 249, WGHP; MJ scrap of note on Harding Memorial Association board being formed from lists submitted by FKH; Sparkes-EWM transcript, April 2, 1935. When Fall, Doheny, and Sinclair were brought to trial, it was discovered that Burns and his private agents were "subjecting jurors in the Fall-Sinclair case to objectionable and improper surveillance under direction of a 'client,'" Washington *Daily News*, November 3, 1927. Navy Secretary Denby offered FKH use of Navy ship for river cruises as a widow in Washington, and Marion Denby told her "no one who has ever known you can ever forget you or cease to love and admire you as a woman—for yourself," Edwin Denby to FKH, October 9, 1923; FKH draft of letter to Denby, n.d., Marion Denby to FKH, October 1, 1923.

10. Boyden Sparkes-EWM transcript, April 2, 1935, HD to JB, June 22, 1926, HD to JB, September 12, 1926, JBP; JB to HD, July 12, 1926, JBP. Once Wheeler began investigation of HD, Burns put Bureau of Investigation spies on Wheeler, confidential report to Director Burns, March 7, 1924, case file 62-7824, 23x1.

11. All materials on Roxy Stinson, taken from FBI file 62-7824-1, part I; New York *Daily News*, April 16, 1924. Burns had agents spy on Means during his testimony, FBI file 62-7824, part II; Means's FBI files missing, FBI file 62-7824-1, part I: Means's testimony that WGH attended the fight films, New York *Daily News*, March 15, 1924.

12. FKH to MJ, n.d. [February–April 1924], private collection.

13. FBI file 62-7824-1, part II; MJ to FKH, n.d. [March–April 1924], private collection; JB diary, February 8, 1924; Francis Russell, p. 626; Adams, pp. 414–21. Nan was briefly married to a Captain Nielsen in June 1924, Britton, pp. 289–90, 311–17, 353–54.

14. KLM, memorandum, p. 5; Sparkes-EWM transcript, n.d. [February 1935]; FKH to MJ, n.d. [February–April 1924], private collection.

15. MJ to FKH, April 9, 1924; Herbert Hoover, p. 54; JB typed diary, February 7, February 27, February 29, March 12, and March 30, 1924; HD to JB, November 1, 1926, JBP; HD to CC, February 17, 1929, contained in HD to JB, October 5, 1939; Herbert Hoover, p. 54.

16. FKH to MJ, n.d. [April–May 1924]; MJ to FKH, April 25, 1924; FKH to Alex Moore, April 16, 1924; FKH to MJ, n.d. [February–April 1924], private collection; Harris.

17. FKH to Alexander Moore, April 16, 1924; MJ to FKH, March 20, 1924, *NYT*, November 22, 1924; MJ to FKH, March 15, 1924; FKH to MJ, n.d. [February–April 1924], private collection.

18. JB typed diary, February 7 and 27, 1924.

19. FKH to EWM and Ned, April 20, 1924, EWMP; FKH to Tal Kling, Easter Sunday, private collection; MJ to FKH, April 9, 1924.

20. Votaw, New York *Daily News*, April 15, 1924; FBI file 62-7824-1, part II; FKH to MJ n.d. [February–April 1924], private collection; JB typed diary, March 14, 27, and 28, April 1 and 7, and May 22, 1924, and JB handwritten diary, June 14, 1924; JB memoirs, chapter 21, p. 235.

21. FKH to MJ, n.d. [February–April 1924], private collection. The degree was

conferred on May 27, 1924, Genevieve Wheelock to Ray Baker Harris, November 9, 1961; FKH to MJ, n.d. [February–April 1924], private collection. FKH's trip to New York with EWM went unreported in press but was confirmed in two of her undated letters from the late spring of 1924, one, a draft to John Wanamaker, the other to Mr. Kellar; FKH to Alexander Moore, April 16, 1924.

22. FKH to MJ, n.d. [February–April 1924], private collection; George Harding to FKH, November 8, 1923, WGHP; MJ to FKH, n.d., MJ to FKH, February 2, 1924; KL to GC, January 2, 1932, Reel 249, WGHP; vivisection discussion, FKH to MJ, n.d. [February–April 1924], private collection; MJ to FKH, March 15, 1924.

23. JB memoirs, chapter 20, p. 217; JB typed diary, June 24, 25, 27, and 28, 1924; FKH to Carl Sawyer, July 8, 1924, Schermer collection; *You.S.A.* (April 1963), p. 17.

24. KLM, chapter 30, p. 3 and chapter 32, pp. 2–3, 10; FKH to MJ, n.d. [July 5–17, 1924], private collection, Ohio; EWM to FKH, n.d. [June–July 1924], WGHP.

38. *Life at the Sanitarium*

1. KLM, chapter 32, p. 22; Sawyer, Brashares, Stowe Is; White Oaks Farm bill of November 22, 1924, Reel 237, WGHP; *Marion Star*, November 21, 1924.

2. Donithen appointment conflict, KLM, chapter 32, pp. 17–19; Sawyer quote, Marion *Newslife*, May 5, 1980; FKH to JEB, August 9, 1924, JB memoirs, chapter 20, pp. 213–14; poem reprinted in *HS*, August 1, 1969.

3. KLM, chapter 32, pp. 10–15; EWM to FKH, fragment of letter [summer 1924], WGHP; FKH to Charlie Kling, n.d. [about August 15] 1924.

4. Sawyer I; KLM, chapter 32, p. 22; "He worked up until almost the last minute, drove his car home, went into his office, felt a little badly, talked to mother and I, told us after we had taken some measures to assist him, that he felt better and that he wanted to lie down and sleep and never wakened," Dr. Carl further reported to Boone, Carl Sawyer to JB, October 2, 1924; JB typed diary, September 23, 1924; MJ to Gus Creager, December 30, 1924; *Marion Star*, November 21, 1924.

5. Carl Sawyer to Helen Boone, October 2, 1924; FKH to Charlie Kling, n.d. [post–September 6, 1924]; FKH to Albert Lasker, n.d. [late September 1924], private collection; on financial matter, Schermer I, July 18, 1991; Shaffner dutifully wrote her, "[W]ill notify Mr. Hunt and the 'Star' to send rent direct to you after Nov. 1st"; memoirs, *You.S.A.* (April 1963); Nancy Christy to FKH, September 25, 1923, Reel 237, WGHP; Hoes, p. 32.

6. *Marion Star*, November 21, 1924; *NYT*, November 22, 1924 *Marion Star*, October 9, 1988; JB typed diary, October 15 and 25, 1924; voting, *WS*, November 23, 1924.

7. EWM manuscript, p. 400; EWM to FKH, n.d. [circa September 1924]; *HS*, November 1, 1968; FKH final will and testament, Reel 241, WGHP; *NYT*, November 22, 1924; EWM to FKH, incomplete letter, n.d. [November 1924]; *NYT*, November 8, 14, 16, 21, 22, and 24, 1924.

8. The Marion Club fed the soldiers for $60; the Columbus Glee Club was given $100 for traveling expenses; a funeral robe for the corpse was bought for $125.00, Schedule H, Estate of FKH, Reel 241, WGHP; *NYT*, November 22, 23, 24, 25, 1924;

JB typed diary, November 24, 1924; clipping, n.p., November 29, 1924. Secretary Wilbur even postponed the christening of a ZR-3, a new dirigible, KLM, chapter 2, p. 9; United Press, November 28, 1924, story; *Marion Star*, November 21, 1924; *WP*, November 23, 1924. At the time of FKH's death, there was a $600 bill from Dr. Wood and $125 for White Oaks nurse service, $6 owed to the Blake Flower Shop, $3 for dry cleaning, $17.50 to the Letts sisters for the Duchess's last beauty treatments, $40 as the salary balance owed to E. A. Miller, her chauffeur, a $2.40 bill left over from the Willard Hotel, and ironically, a bill for $47.23 from Uhler-Phillips, Schedule I, Estate of FKH, Reel 241, WGHP. Baldinger oversaw the placement of FKH's personal effects in storage. Jewelry included gold, diamond, emerald, sapphire, jade, ivory, pearl, enamel, crystal, garnet and crystal hairpins, hatpins, dress pins, scarf pins, crosses, cameos, combs, chains, brooches, lockets, watches, bracelets, cuff links, mesh bags, neckpieces, and gold cigarette cases that EWM had given her and she had never used. The most valuable piece was her famous diamond and platinum sunburst, given her by WGH but chosen by EWM. It was worth $5,000, a full 25 percent of the total listed miscellaneous property (the Hardings' 1921 car was valued only at $2,000). Her clothing collection of ermine, sealskin, sable, silk, mink, persian lamb, silver fox, and red blush coats, robes, wraps, collars, and scarves all were to be turned over to Jean when she reached twenty-one years old, and it eventually scattered into private hands as the girl matured, became alcoholic, and pawned off her grandmother's items when she needed money, Schedule H, Estate of FKH, Reel 241.

   9. *WP* editorial, "Florence Kling Harding," November 22, 1924.

39. Remembering

   1. KLM, chapter 4, p. 15c; *Collier's* (May 1925); Sparkes-EWM transcript, n.d. [1935].

   2. Francis Russell, p. 624; clipping, n.d., n.p., Reel 259, WGHP; AP story, December 31, 1925; Russell-Duckett, *American Heritage* (February 1965). Carl Sawyer pointed out that FKH had stated in her will that WGH's papers were willed to the association for the public, they were not the property of any Harding family and they had no right to them, their copyright, or any other literary rights, Marion *Newslife*, September 2, 1979. Even HD was troubled by "the embarrassing situation" of Carl Sawyer's refusal to let legitimate historians go through the papers, HD to Ray Baker Harris, July 21, 1939, Reel 259, WGHP. How much Carl Sawyer might have destroyed can't be known, but historians did not put destruction of Harding papers past him. ". . . agitation of the matter at this time would likely be irritating to Dr. Sawyer and might lead to some undesirable result. . . . [He] separated the correspondence of a purely personal or private nature" from the "official" papers, Ray Baker Harris to Kenneth W. Duckett, November 6, 1961; conflict between Harding nephews and Carl Sawyer on papers, HMD to Ray Baker Harris, April 15, 1935, and May 29, 1939, Reel 259, WGHP.

   3. Russell-Duckett, *American Heritage* (February 1965), p. 108; Russell, *Antioch Review*, pp. 66, 70.

   4. Many Marionites who knew and disliked Nan, according to Philamen Gregg,

believed that WGH had fathered her daughter, Gregg I. On how he would manipulate the jury and discredit Nan, Mouser wrote, "I probably won't even mention this Britton girl's name, but the jury will get the point, and do their duty, unless I have lost my touch. Remind me to wear a wrinkled suit, and to have some cigarette ashes spilled on my vest. . . . I have done everything I possibly could to suppress any publication" of the "ugly facts." He feared that "there was a dangerous influence surrounding the jury. . . . Who was back of her? Where are they? Are they present in this court?,'' Grant Mouser, Sr., to GC, October 5, 1931, November 11 and 27 and December 1, 1931; GC to Grant Mouser, Sr., October 9, 1931, November 9, and 30, 1931; transcript of *Britton* v. *Klunk,* 1931, Reel 250, WGH Papers. Also see a slightly different version of transcript of *Britton* v. *Klunk,* 1931, Reel 245, WGHP; results of case Francis Russell, pp. 642–43, Murray, pp. 489–90; later quotes, from Nan Britton and Elizabeth Ann Harding, Chicago *Tribune,* December 4, 1939; Marion *Newslife,* September 2, 1979; Marion *Star,* July 17, 1964; Chicago *Tribune,* July 17, 1964; Blaesing I; HD quote, Adams, p. 428.

5. Gregg I; *HS,* February 1, 1968; Carl Sawyer to JB, June 22, 1931, JBP.

6. *Liberty* (November 7, 1931); Sparkes-EWM transcript, n.d. [February 1935]. tr. As late as 1991, when an unfounded rumor circulated in Marion that Harding would be exhumed, for "publicity" about this book, a Gary Barnhart told a local newspaper, "What if they dig him up and discover that he was poisoned. What will they do next? Dig up her bones and throw them in jail?" Added local Tom Wagner, "I'm 100 percent certain that if they exhume President Harding they will find trace quantities of two or at least three of what we consider poisons today," *Marion Star,* July 18 and 20, 1991. If they were to exhume the Hardings, another Marionite added, they wouldn't find anything. "There was so much water leakage down there. I think old W. G. and the Duchess got pumped out with the water," Gregg, West, Gary Is; on books in libraries, George Bowerman to Ray Harris, November 1, 1932, and C. Vernon Eddy to Ray Harris, November 2, 1932, Reel 259, WGHP; United Press story, November 21, 1924.

7. FKH grandchildren received the bulk of her estate. Property lots ($65,000) stocks, bonds, treasury notes ($187, 364.54), debts ($49,494.90, Heber Votaw owing $500). Gross estate total was $348,676.50, General Information Sheet and Schedules A, B, C, Estate of FKH, Reel 241, WGHP; *NYT,* November 29, 1924; JB typed diary, written notation, November 28, 1924.

8. *HS,* April 1, 1968; Florence's three great-grandsons, several great-great-grandsons and -granddaughters and at least one great-great-great-grandchild, born in 1991, are the surviving Klings. Brashares I.; Vetallis Kling death notice, *Marion Star,* July 1, 1938; Elsasser, Kling, Gary Is. Carolyn Votaw died in October 1951. Charity Remsberg died a month later. Daisy Lewis died on March 22, 1935. Heber Votaw died in 1961. George Harding died in 1934.

9. The Harding Home and tomb was turned over to the state in the 1970s, when the Harding Memorial Association was disbanded. J. and B. Bartram, Neidhart, Gary Is; tomb dedication, *Marion Star,* June 16, 1931; obituary of Reddy Baldinger, *Marion Star,* June 15, 1978.

10. Robert Snow, assistant director, Office of Government Liaison and Public

Affairs, U.S. Secret Service to author, December 20, 1991; story by Robert Barry August 11, 1923; n.p., clipping, Secret Service files; Ira Smith, pp. 114–16.

11. On Forbes, HD to Cyril Clemens, February 12, 1940, Reel 254, WGHP; a "flurry," Emma Fall to GC, June 20, 1931, Reel 249, WGHP; "Greatest desire . . . ," Emma Fall to Cyril Clemens, November 25, 1939, and n.d.; others in Harris papers, Reel 254, WGHP; on political situation, Emma Fall to Cyril Clemens, June 19, 1940, Reel 256, WGHP. When Emma wrote Christian and he responded, his lawyer reprimanded him. "The unwisdom of your writing to Mrs. Fall on any controversial subject," warned Frank Hogan, "is manifest." He drafted a careful response for Christian: ". . . utterly impossible it is for me to contribute anything to controversial subjects. It has been thought wise during the years which have elapsed since 1923 that I should, for the time being, remain unquoted, in respect of these matters which came under my observation as Secretary to the President," Emma Fall to GC, June 19, 1931, GC to Emma Fall, June 20 and July 20, 1931, GC to Frank Hogan, July 14, 1931, Frank Hogan to GC, July 18, 1931, Reel 249, WGHP; Fall's portrait, *WS*, January 14, 1967.

12. During investigations into whether the Hardings ever personally profited, a transcript of FKH's Metropolitan National Bank record was requested for "information . . . of vital importance to an investigation now being conducted . . . ," William Donovan to George White, February 23, 1926, FBI file 62-8878-511; HD to JB, April 5, 1927; HD to Edgar Mels, September 20, 1924, Reel 256, WGHP; Sparkes-EWM transcript, December 10, 1934; HD to Ray Harris, May 29, 1939, Reel 259, WGHP; HD's death, Katherine Carroll to Ray Harris, October 28, 1941, Reel 259, WGHP; Miller, p. 227. KL was unable to obtain enough subscriptions to buy her memoirs and was therefore unable to get it published ("for some reason, Marion takes no interest. . . . I have received rebuffs rather than encouragement"), KL to Charles Hard, January 27, 1932, WGHP.

13. Napper, West, Guthrie Is; Marion *Newslife*, September 2, 1979; Francis Russell, *Antioch Review* (Winter 1978). James Cross was born on March 2, 1911, Joan Cross to author, November 21, 1991; Albertson-Wilson interview, pp. 2–4.

14. Sparkes-EWM transcripts, February 27, 1935, and March 4, 1935.

15. Sparke-EWM transcripts, December 10, 1934, February 27, 1935, and April 2, 1935.

16. *Fact* (January 1964), "The Lindbergh thing—now I never made a move until . . . Lindbergh consented to go ahead, when they raised it [ransom] to $100,000 I couldn't stop. My name was never to be brought out," Sparkes-EWM, transcripts, n.d. and December 10, 1934; Gaston Means file, FBI file 62-2697-816; P. E. Foxworth to E. A. Tamm, memo, December 9, 1938, FBI file 62-26978-868.

17. E. P. Coffey to J. Edgar Hoover, July 1, 1943, EWM FBI file. As she sat for hours and endless days talking to Sparkes in preparing her memoirs, EWM declared, "I hate to hide anything," and thought that she could come out with a published book and a privately printed one "and put everything in it." Sparkes estimated that there was "$10 million worth of libel there," Sparkes-EWM transcript, February 27, 1935, memo for Mr. Tamm, February 16, 1938, Louis Lobel to J. Edgar Hoover, February 13, 1938, Evalyn McLean file; R. D. Brown to J. Edgar Hoover, September 4, 1937, EWM FBI file.

18. Clipping, April 26, 1943, n.p., courtesy Dick West; Beale I; R. B. Hood to J. Edgar Hoover, November 15, 1945, Edward Tamm to J. Edgar Hoover, April 28, 1947, EWM FBI file. In the manuscript of what was anticipated to be her memoir, EWM included a passage that stated: "I never heard a whisper of that scandal until both Harding and his wife were dead. . . . I have no information on that subject. . . . I am satisfied that none of Mrs. Harding's jealousy was fruit of any knowledge that she had of that alleged affair. I say again, and mean it, that I know nothing that convinces me he ever was a father. . . ." In the end EWM left this out of the book; in her private remarks to Sparkes, EWM knew Nan Britton to be WGH's mistress, that Ned had taken love letters from her; EWM was not convinced that Nan's child was WGH's. EWM manuscript, p. 387; *WP*, November 24, 1924; FKH diary.

Index

De Wolfe, Simon Eugene, 22, 23–24, 25, 26, 28, 33, 84
De Wolfe, Susan Busby, 23
De Wolfe, Teddy, 84
De Wolfe family, 4, 5, 22, 23, 32, 33, 34, 68, 86
Dickey, Carl, 114, 304
Dill, C. C., 435
Disabled American Veterans, 333, 371, 378, 383
Dixon, Hattie, 316
Dixon, Jane, 3, 9, 12, 49–50, 53, 54, 73, 79, 80, 94, 115–116, 152–153, 213, 272, 323, 324
Dr. Janes' Vermifuge Almanac, 172
Doheny, Edward L., xix, 357, 402, 493, 496, 500, 502
Doherty, Patrick, 310
Domesday Book, 232
Donithen, Hoke, 96, 202, 492, 519–520, 529
Doubleday, Frank N., 497–498
Dows, Alice, 142
Doyle, Arthur Conan, 479–480, 508–509
Drake, Captain, 14
Draper, Ruth, 274
Dressler, Marie, 172, 280
Drexel, Constance, 214, 260, 289, 352
Duchess Blue, 273
Duckett, Ken, 96
Duckstein, Jessie, 301, 501
Duckstein, William, 501
Dunbar High School, 313
Dwyer, Elmer, 406
Dyson, Henry, 326

Eagan, Katherine, 347
Early, Mary Catherine, 237
Early, Steve, 441, 457
Edison, Thomas, 19
Egypt, 87, 88, 424
"Egyptia," 133
Einstein, Albert, 267
Eldred, Bertha, 391
elections:
    of 1880, 200
    of 1888, 200
    of 1896, 68, 200
    of 1910, 88, 91–92, 94, 101
    of 1912, 101, 104–105, 108–109, 126, 189
    of 1914, 104, 109–112, 126
    of 1916, 128–129
    of 1920, 159–160, 176–178, 184–236, 342
    of 1924, 398–399, 424
Eliot, Charles, 226
Eliot, George, 21, 41
Elizabeth, queen of Belgium, 161
Elizabeth I, queen of England, 8
Elk Hills oil lease, xx, 500, 502
Elks club, 55, 69, 132
Ellington, Duke, 269
Ellis Island, 309
Elsasser, Glen, 56, 59, 71
Emerson, Haven, 330
"End of a Perfect Day" (Bond), 100, 431

England, 7, 8, 100–101, 143
Epworth Methodist Church, 5, 16, 65
Equal Rights Amendment (ERA), 320, 498
Erie Railroad, 39
Evans family, 151

Fairbanks, Charles, 167
Fairbanks, Douglas, 220, 253
Fairbanks *Daily News-Miner*, 434
Fall, Albert Bacon, 127–128, 160, 166, 216, 227, 229, 239, 251, 263, 278, 401, 415, 481, 492, 494
    FH and, 128, 156, 162, 187, 344, 401–402, 487–488, 502–503
    Interior Department post of, xix, 240, 243, 256, 261, 295–296, 304–306, 344
    resignation of, 395
    secret naval oil deal of, xix, 305–306, 357, 401–402, 415, 425, 493, 500–503
    Senate investigation of, 493, 500–503
Fall, Emma Morgan, 127, 128, 216, 261, 263, 357, 395, 415, 425, 481, 488, 500, 503
Farmers' and Mechanics' Bank, 12
Faulkner, James Miller, 232
Fay, Bernard, 347, 473
Federal Board for Vocational Education, 329
Federal Bureau of Investigation (FBI), xix, 259, 304, 371–372
    Burns as chief of, 244, 255–256, 294, 362, 372, 406
    McLean at, xviii, 256, 294–295, 360–361
Federal Hospitalization Board, 329, 330, 367, 368–369, 382, 426
federal penitentiaries, xii, xvii, 345, 350, 392
Federal Reserve Bank, 245
Federal Reserve Board, 294, 341–342
Ferguson, Walter G. "Fergy," 211, 229, 248, 285, 300, 303, 373–374, 491
Fess, Simeon, 188, 192
Field, Carter, 449–450, 478, 482
Finn, Martin, 295
Finn, William, 274
Finney, John, 376, 377, 379, 396, 403, 417
First Church for Animal Rights, 311
First Year, The, 253
Fitzgerald, Zelda, 540
Fitzpatrick, Gilbert, 446
Fling, Arthur R., 61
Fling, Marion Louise Hodder, 61–62, 122, 194, 298
"Flo from Ohio," 363
Florence Harding Campaign Club, 206
Florence Harding Retreat, 370
Flynn, Warren, 424
Food Administration, 189
    Food Conservation Division of, 128
Foraker, Joe, 47, 68, 77, 110, 124
Forbes, Charles R. "Charlie," 113–115, 119, 122, 197, 263, 323, 357, 490, 494
    corruption of, xix, 292, 304, 369–371, 388–391, 398, 414, 430, 473, 492–493, 513